The Literature of PROPAGANDA

VOLUME **2**

The Literature of PROPAGANDA

GROUPS

THOMAS RIGGS, *editor*

ST. JAMES PRESS
A part of Gale, Cengage Learning

GALE
CENGAGE Learning

Detroit • New York • San Francisco • New Haven, Conn • Waterville, Maine • London

GALE
CENGAGE Learning·

The Literature of Propaganda

Thomas Riggs, Editor

Michelle Lee, Project Editor

For product information and technology assistance, contact us at
Gale Customer Support, 1-800-877-4253.
For permission to use material from this text or product,
submit all requests online at **www.cengage.com/permissions.**
Further permissions questions can be emailed to
permissionrequest@cengage.com

LIBRARY OF CONGRESS CATALOGING-IN-PUBLICATION DATA

The literature of propaganda / Thomas Riggs, editor.
    volumes cm
    Summary: Contains 300 entries that explore literary works that deal with propaganda. The set includes a wide variety of genres and has an international scope. It explores the works of authors shaped by a variety of political, social, and economic movements, and places each work in its historical context. Each entry includes an overview of the work, historical context, primary themes and style, and critical discussion -- Provided by publisher.
    Includes bibliographical references and index.
    ISBN 978-1-55862-858-8 (set) -- ISBN 978-1-55862-859-5 (vol. 1) -- ISBN 978-1-55862-860-1 (vol. 2) -- ISBN 978-1-55862-861-8 (vol. 3) -- ISBN 978-1-5586-2878-6 (e-book) -- ISBN 1-5586-2878-9 (e-book)
    1. Literature in propaganda. 2. Persuasion (Psychology) in literature.
3. Persuasion (Rhetoric) in literature. 4. Authors--Political and social views.
I. Riggs, Thomas, 1963- editor.
    PN51.L5744 2013
    809'.93358--dc23

                                                    2013001494

Gale
27500 Drake Rd.
Farmington Hills, MI, 48331-3535

ISBN-13: 978-1-55862-858-8 (set)   ISBN-10: 1-55862-858-4 (set)
ISBN-13: 978-1-55862-859-5 (vol. 1)   ISBN-10: 1-55862-859-2 (vol. 1)
ISBN-13: 978-1-55862-860-1 (vol. 2)   ISBN-10: 1-55862-860-6 (vol. 2)
ISBN-13: 978-1-55862-861-8 (vol. 3)   ISBN-10: 1-55862-861-4 (vol. 3)

This title will also be available as an e-book.
ISBN-13: 978-1-55862-878-6 ISBN-10: 1-55862-878-9
Contact your Gale, a part of Cengage Learning, sales representative for ordering information.

Printed in the United States of America
1 2 3 4 5 6 7 17 16 15 14 13

ADVISORY BOARD

CHAIR

Russ Castronovo
Dorothy Draheim Professor of English and American Studies, University of Wisconsin-Madison. Author of *Beautiful Democracy: Aesthetics and Anarchy in a Global Era* (2007); *Necro Citizenship: Death, Eroticism, and the Public Sphere in the Nineteenth-Century United States* (2001); and *Fathering the Nation: American Genealogies of Slavery and Freedom* (1995). Coeditor, with Jonathan Auerbach, of *The Oxford Handbook of Propaganda Studies* (forthcoming).

ADVISORS

Laura R. Braunstein
Librarian, English Language and Literature, Dartmouth College, Hanover, New Hampshire.

Maria Teresa Micaela Prendergast
Associate Professor of English, College of Wooster, Wooster, Ohio. Author of *Railing, Reviling and Invective in Early Modern Literary Culture, 1588–1617* (2012); and *Renaissance Fantasies: The Gendering of Aesthetics in Early Modern Fiction* (2000). Coauthor, with Thomas Prendergast, of "The Invention of Propaganda: A Translation and Critical Commentary of *Inscrutabili Divinae*," in *The Oxford Handbook of Propaganda Studies,* edited by Jonathan Auerbach and Russ Castronovo (forthcoming).

Thomas Prendergast
Associate Professor of English and Department Chair, College of Wooster, Wooster, Ohio. Author of *Chaucer's Dead Body: From Corpse to Corpus* (2004). Coauthor, with Maria Teresa Micaela Prendergast, of "The Invention of Propaganda: a Translation and Critical Commentary of *Inscrutabili Divinae*," in *The Oxford Handbook of Propaganda Studies*, edited by Jonathan Auerbach and Russ Castronovo (forthcoming). Coeditor, with Barbara Kline, of *Rewriting Chaucer: Culture, Authority and the Idea of the Authentic Text, 1400–1602* (1999).

EDITORIAL AND PRODUCTION STAFF

TABLE OF CONTENTS

PARTIES AND FACTIONS

SOCIAL CLASSES

INTRODUCTION

If in the beginning was the Word, propaganda soon followed. The relationship between discourse and persuasion is intimate and almost always troubling. Our modern notion of propaganda is suffused by pejorative connotations involving falsification and manipulation. The term is often used to discount opponents' views or to invalidate a contrasting perspective. This book encourages an understanding that is at once neutral and explanatory, one that seeks to define propaganda as neither good nor bad and instead promotes a definition that is more pragmatic: Propaganda is publicly disseminated information intended to influence others in belief, action, or both. A reconsideration of the subject in this light can produce corresponding changes in our understandings of literature.

The proper use of rhetoric—oral and written communication or persuasion—was a hotly debated issue in ancient Greece, as any of Plato's interlocutors or Aristotle's students knew. Across the centuries the debate has only intensified. The word "propaganda" first appeared in modern languages as part of Pope Gregory XV's establishment of the Sacra Congregatio de Propaganda Fide (Sacred Congregation for Propagating the Faith) in 1622. The mission of this body was to spread what the Catholic Church considered to be the one true faith during the crisis of the Counter Reformation. The next notable use of the term is associated with the cataclysmic upheavals of the French Revolution. From the perspective of alarmists in England, the revolutionaries in Paris had organized various institutions of propaganda to spread their radical creed across Europe.

Our negative understanding of propaganda emerged during World War I, when the Allies waged an information war accusing Germany of spreading atrocity stories and distorting events; Germany similarly denounced the Allies. Wartime governments also directed biased media persuasion at their own populations in order to mobilize support for the war. Some sixty years earlier, when Harriet Beecher Stowe penned the best-selling novel of the nineteenth century, *Uncle Tom's Cabin* (1852), she did not see herself as peddling false or deceptive information; her aim was to educate readers about the fundamental humanity of the so-called "merchandise" that was legally sold in the antebellum United States. Jumping forward a century and a half, in 2010 Julian Assange uploaded "The WikiLeaks Manifesto" in an equally daring endeavor: to challenge the monopoly on information held by corporations and governments. The German cultural critic Siegfried Kracauer asks in his 1960 book *Theory of Film,* "Is not truth the best propaganda weapon?"[1] Like many of the authors discussed in the following pages, Pope Gregory, Stowe, and Assange would have agreed, approving the spread and circulation of information as both enlightening and persuasive.

From ancient Greek times to the present, propaganda has served many different masters, has appeared across many media, from engraving to film, and has been variously condemned and appreciated. Written propaganda can be sorted according to three overlapping functions. It can be literature that (1) attempts to persuade, manipulate, or even deceive; (2) depicts the use of propaganda and its impact upon people and the society that they inhabit; (3) theorizes about propaganda, examining its techniques and psychological mechanisms, its media, and its modes of dissemination and circulation.

Rarely does a work of literature satisfy only one of these conditions. More often, it bleeds across categories. In a radio address in spring 1941, George Orwell took stock of World War I, the Russian Revolution, and the advance of Hitler and Nazi Germany across Europe. In conclusion, he contended that "propaganda in some form or other lurks in every book."[2] From this perspective, all texts are susceptible to propaganda. Authors often inveigh against propaganda while employing it themselves. Consider Upton Sinclair's muckraking novel of the meatpacking industry, *The Jungle* (1906), which exposes the emptiness of capitalist propaganda by delivering impassioned sermons about the Christian virtues of socialism. Try to determine whether Langston Hughes's six-line poem "Johannesburg Mines" (1928) is an example of or a critique of propaganda. Observe the ways in which Edward Bernays's seemingly definitive book *Propaganda* (1928), while explaining modern techniques of advertising and mass persuasion, becomes a public relations pitch for ad men and other spin artists. These examples support Orwell's conclusion that "literature has been swamped by propaganda."[3]

The ubiquity of propaganda is neither cause for despair nor a reason to give up on literature. In fact, Orwell construed its prevalence as an urgent reminder that "every work of art has a meaning and purpose—a political, social and religious purpose."[4] The surest sign that art is intended to engage the world in these ways is that it seeks to affect our beliefs, attitudes, and actions. Writers labor over manuscripts in the hopes of intervening in the course of human events, whether through straightforward confrontation, by means of gripping or gentle narrative, or in a more elliptical fashion that employs irony, satire, and other tactics. And writing does engage: readers pore over books, debating meanings and wresting interpretations to support their individual view of the work and its applications to life. Looking at literature through the lens of propaganda reminds us that it is not produced simply for its own sake but rather to change history and how people understand it.

An overview of the table of contents for this book reveals that authors have combined imagination, outrage, accusation, and wit with any number of goals: abolishing slavery; reforming slum conditions; creating scapegoats and targeting internal enemies; rallying support for war; fomenting revolution; and many more. Unquestionably, utopian optimism and commitment, cynicism and hatred have been poured into such efforts. What remains debatable, however, is the effectiveness of these appeals. Can a discrete set of social events ever be tied to a specific work of literature? This incalculability generates further questions about propaganda's possibilities of success. Does it risk galvanizing opponents even as it seeks to encourage the most ardent supporters? When it focuses on a specific social ill—for example, squalid tenements and unsafe factory conditions in the early twentieth century—does it miss the need for more thoroughgoing, systemic reform? Why do its utopian dimensions so often seem destined for failure? The huge range of literature examined in these volumes—from the rhetoric of the classical world to the digital spread of information in the twenty-first century—provides readers with plenty of material to ponder in regard to these questions. It also generates new lines of debate and inquiry.

The Literature of Propaganda's three-part structure affords multiple lenses through which to assess plays, novels, poems, exposés, manifestoes, short stories, biographies, memoirs, and essays that circulate as or comment on propaganda and mass persuasion. Divided into Approaches (volume 1), Groups (volume 2), and Effects (volume 3), this work seeks to account for the diversity and richness, the optimism, and the terror that have resulted from efforts to create change through textual means.

Because the definitions and connotations of the term "propaganda" have shifted over time, the first volume, Approaches, registers varied understandings and uses of the concept. It sets out theories of persuasion formulated in ancient Greece, the World War I era, the postcolonial world, and postmodern society. With this foundation in place, the volume then identifies different types of propaganda, including appeals and exhortations, exposés, education and indoctrination, histories, and political declarations. The "Formal Innovations" chapter explores texts that respond to political crises and social exigencies—for example, Theodore Dwight Weld's cut-and-paste method in *American Slavery As It Is* (1839) and Art Spiegelman's illustrated panels in his graphic novel *The Complete Maus* (1991). The selections in this first volume invite readers to consider literature as variously surveying, commenting on, deploring, and utilizing propaganda. Only a fraction of the works represent "pure" propaganda (if such a category could be defined). Instead, such texts as W. E. B. Du Bois's "Criteria of Negro Art" (1926) and Theodor W. Adorno's "Freudian Theory and the Pattern of Fascist Propaganda" (1951) embody earnest attempts to unlock the mechanisms that have given misrepresentation, paranoia, and fear such a hold over modern life.

Volume 2, Groups, studies texts produced by parties and factions, dissidents and rebels, various social classes, and cultural critics. These works suggest that, whereas in its most negative incarnations, propaganda becomes weaponized speech, with its own targets and triggers, literature carries liberating potential as well. The chapter "Social Classes" explores writing that, among other things, advocates for the economically oppressed. Works ranging from Rebecca Harding Davis's "Life in the Iron Mills" (1861) to the "Preamble to the Constitution of the IWW" (1905) have been crafted to rally public opinion in support of human rights. Literature has also been used to promote group cohesion in the form of nationalism. The chapter titled "Nations" features a discussion of one of the most infamous pieces of propaganda in history, Adolf Hitler's *Mein Kampf* (1925). Invidious language that appeals to feelings of superiority or fear is often associated with xenophobic nationalism, but those seeking to redress a problem or call attention to a social movement may also draw on emotion in propagating a message. While this potential may often go unrealized, it is hard to overestimate the poignant force of such a piece (included in the chapter "Dissidents and Rebels") as Rodolfo Walsh's "Open Letter from a Writer to the Military Junta," written the day before his death at the hands of government soldiers. Including such works as Aristophanes's *Lysistrata* (411 BCE), this volume offers readers a literature that allows human actors to comment upon and intervene in political and social affairs.

Because the impact of such interventions can be difficult to gauge, the final volume, Effects, considers literary works that have been tied to legislative reform, religious conversion, changes in economic policy, and other aspects of historical significance. The chapter "Myths and Martyrs" explores the ways in which real-world results often ensue from mythic representations, such as those that render a figure such as George Washington larger than life or depict Joan of Arc as a martyr. Embellishment can play an instrumental role in making national heroes of ordinary men and women. As the chapter "Distortions and Delusions" reveals, people can eagerly gobble up these fictive portraits; we consume fanciful versions of history as readily as the characters in Aldous Huxley's *Brave New World* (1932) consume drugs to adjust to a deluded view of reality. The chapters "Dystopias and Utopias," "Legislation and Reform," "Predictions and Prescriptions," and "Suppression and Scapegoating" round out the volume. Analyzing perspectives on such reactionary texts as Ayn Rand's *Atlas Shrugged* (1957) and William Luther Pierce's *Turner Diaries* (1978) alongside those on progressive documents such as Elizabeth Cady Stanton's "Declaration of Sentiments" (1848) and Charlotte Perkins Gilman's *Herland* (1915), the chapters span the political spectrum. The settings evoked by this literature are just as diverse, ranging from the jail cell of American Indian activist Leonard Peltier evoked in his *Prison Writings: My Life Is My Sun Dance* (1999) to the repressive landscapes of Margaret Atwood's *The Handmaid's Tale* (1985) and Suzanne Collins's *The Hunger Games* (2008). The fact that Collins's novel depicting teenage gladiatorial combat, like many of the works discussed in these pages, also achieved blockbuster status as a Hollywood film evidences the popularity of the literature of propaganda and its capacity to inspire and generate other creative media projects.

Many believe that the value of literature rests on its enduring artistic merit (determined by assessing style, tone, and other formal features) rather than on its political and social impacts. By implicitly fusing it with propaganda, these volumes confirm literature not only as a zone of aesthetic contemplation but also as an impetus for action, so that our ideas about the social and political force of words are reinvigorated. The 300 individual essays that comprise *The Literature of Propaganda* add nuance and complexity to the concept of mass persuasion—through literature—that leads to action. The essays do not coalesce into a single viewpoint; there is no unity to be found among the revolutionary writings of Edmund Burke, Bertolt Brecht, and Ho Chi Minh—and the same might be said of any cohort of authors represented in the pages that follow. This diversity makes the collection, above all else, an arena for debate and continued investigation.

Russ Castronovo,
Advisory Board Chair

---

[1] Siegfried Kracauer. *Theory of Film: The Redemption of Physical Reality* (New York: Oxford University Press, 1960) 161.

[2] Orwell, George. "The Frontiers of Art and Propaganda." BBC Overseas Service. 30 Apr. 1941.

[3] Orwell 30 Apr. 1941.

[4] Orwell 30 Apr. 1941.

EDITOR'S NOTE

The Literature of Propaganda, a three-volume reference guide, provides critical introductions to 300 texts from around the world. Some of these texts function as propaganda, while others discuss propaganda or use propaganda as a theme or setting. For this guide the term propaganda is defined as information spread publicly in order to influence others in belief, action, or both, regardless of whether the intent is seen as honorable or evil-minded.

An early text covered in this guide is the *History of the Kings of Britain,* written by English bishop Geoffrey of Monmouth around 1136. Purportedly a complete history of the British monarchy, it includes inaccuracies, heroic legends presented as truth, and supernatural content. The book helped popularize King Arthur as a national hero and create a British historical and cultural identity. A much different example of propaganda discussed in the guide is the "Battle Hymn of the Republic," a pro-Union poem published during the Civil War by American abolitionist Julia Ward Howe and set to the popular tune of "John Brown's Body." A well-known propaganda text from India is *Hind Swaraj,* written in 1909 by Mohandas Gandhi, who urged his country to reject materialist Western culture in favor a homegrown, spiritually based movement and to use satyagraha, or nonviolent resistance, against British authority. Among more recent propaganda works covered in the guide is *The Coming Insurrection,* written in 2007 by the Invisible Committee, an anonymous French group, which called for an end to capitalism.

The structure and content of *The Literature of Propaganda* was planned with the help of the project's advisory board, chaired by Russ Castronovo, Dorothy Draheim Professor of English and American Studies, University of Wisconsin-Madison. His introduction to this guide provides an overview of the literature of propaganda.

ORGANIZATION
All entries share a common structure, providing consistent coverage of the works and a simple way of comparing basic elements of one text with another. Each entry has six parts: overview, historical and literary context, themes and style, critical discussion, sources, and further reading. Entries also have either an excerpt from the original text or a sidebar discussing a related topic, such as the life of the author.

The Literature of Propaganda is divided into three volumes, each with 100 entries. Volume 1, Approaches, has seven sections—appeals and exhortations, education and indoctrination, exposés, formal innovations, histories, political action, and theories. The works covered in this volume are examples of how propaganda is used. *The Feminine Mystique,* for example, an exposé published in 1963 by American feminist Betty Friedan, exposes and critiques the social pressure on women to become mothers and housewives. Volume 2, Groups, has five sections—cultural critics, dissidents and rebels, nations, parties and factions, and social classes. These entries provide examples of how propaganda works for or against groups of people. Volume 3, Effects, has six sections—distortions and delusions, dystopias and utopias, legislation and reform, myths and martyrs, predictions and prescriptions, and suppression and scapegoating. The texts covered in this volume illustrate common results of propaganda.

Among the criteria for selecting entry topics were the importance of the work in university curricula, the genre, the region and country of the author and text, and the time period. Entries can be looked up in the author and title indexes, as well as in the subject index.

ACKNOWLEDGMENTS

Many people contributed time, effort, and ideas to *The Literature of Propaganda*. At Gale, Philip Virta, manager of new products, developed the original plan for the book, and Michelle Lee, senior editor, served as the in-house manager for the project. *The Literature of Propaganda* owes its existence to their ideas and involvement.

We would like to express our appreciation to the advisors, who, in addition to creating the organization of *The Literature of Propaganda* and choosing the entry topics, identified other scholars to work on the project and answered many questions, both big and small. We would also like to thank the contributors for their accessible essays, often on difficult topics, as well as the scholars who reviewed the text for accuracy and coverage.

I am grateful to Erin Brown, senior project editor, especially for her work with the advisors and on the entry list; Greta Gard, project editor, who managed the writers; Mary Beth Curran, associate editor, who oversaw the editing process; David Hayes, associate editor, whose many contributions included organizing the workflow; and Hannah Soukup, assistant editor, who identified and corresponded with the academic reviewers. Other important assistance came from Mariko Fujinaka, managing editor; Anne Healey, senior editor; and Janet Moredock and Lee Esbenshade, associate editors. The line editors were Heather Campbell, Cheryl Collins, Tony Craine, Holli Fort, Laura Gabler, Harrabeth Haidusek, Ellen Henderson, Joan Hibler, Constance Israel, Jane Kupersmith, Dehlia McCobb, Kathy Peacock, Donna Polydoros, Natalie Ruppert, Mary Russell, Lisa Trow, Will Wagner, and Whitney Ward.

Thomas Riggs

CONTRIBUTORS

DAVID AITCHISON

Aitchison is a PhD candidate in literary studies and a university instructor.

GREG BACH

Bach holds an MA in classics and is a freelance writer.

CRAIG BARNES

Barnes holds an MFA in creative writing and has been a university instructor and a freelance writer.

MARIE BECKER

Becker holds an MA in humanities.

KAREN BENDER

Bender holds an MFA in creative writing and an MPhil in Anglo-Irish literature. She has taught high school English.

KATHERINE BISHOP

Bishop is a PhD student in English literature and has been a university instructor.

ALLISON BLECKER

Blecker is a PhD candidate in Near Eastern languages.

ELIZABETH BOEHEIM

Boeheim holds an MA in English literature and has been a university instructor.

WESLEY BORUCKI

Borucki holds a PhD in American history and is a university professor.

GERALD CARPENTER

Carpenter holds an MA in U.S. intellectual history and a PhD in early modern French history. He is a freelance writer.

ADAM CARSON

Carson is a PhD student in history and a university instructor.

MARK CASELLO

Casello is a PhD candidate in American literature and a university professor.

CURT CLONINGER

Cloninger holds an MFA in studio arts and is a university professor.

KEVIN COONEY

Cooney holds a PhD in English literature and is a university professor.

ALEX COVALCIUC

Covalciuc is a PhD candidate in English literature. He has been a university instructor and a freelance writer.

GIANO CROMLEY

Cromley holds an MFA in creative writing and is a university instructor.

COLBY CUPPERNULL

Cuppernull holds an MA in writing and has been a university instructor and a freelance writer.

ANNA DEEM

Deem holds an MA in education and is a freelance writer.

CHAD DUNDAS

Dundas holds an MFA in creative writing and has been a university instructor and a freelance writer.

RICHARD ESBENSHADE

Esbenshade holds a PhD in history and has been a university professor and a freelance writer.

TAYLOR EVANS

Evans is a PhD student in English literature and has been a university instructor.

DAISY GARD

Gard is a freelance writer with a background in English literature.

GRETA GARD

Gard is a PhD candidate in English literature and has been a university instructor and a freelance writer.

SARAH GARDAM

Gardam is a PhD candidate in English literature and has been a university instructor.

CLINT GARNER

Garner holds an MFA in creative writing and is a freelance writer.

TINA GIANOULIS

Gianoulis is a freelance writer with a background in English literature.

CYNTHIA GILES

Giles holds an MA in English literature and a PhD in interdisciplinary humanities. She has been a university instructor and a freelance writer.

QUAN MANH HA

Ha holds a PhD in American literature and is a university professor.

HARRABETH HAIDUSEK

Haidusek holds an MA in English literature and is a university instructor.

GREG HALABY

Halaby is a PhD candidate in Arabic and Islamic studies and a teaching fellow.

RODNEY HARRIS

Harris is pursuing a PhD in history and has been a university instructor.

MICHAEL HARTWELL

Hartwell holds an MFA in creative writing. He has been a university instructor and a freelance writer.

RON HORTON

Horton holds an MFA in creative writing and has been a high school English instructor and a freelance writer.

FRANKLYN HYDE

Hyde holds a PhD in English literature and is a university instructor.

LAURA JOHNSON

Johnson holds a PhD in English literature and is a university professor.

EMILY JONES

Jones holds an MFA in creative writing and has been a university instructor.

ALICIA KENT

Kent holds a PhD in English literature and is a university professor.

ROBERT KIBLER

Kibler holds a PhD in English literature and is a university professor.

DENNIS KLEIN

Klein holds a PhD in history and is a university professor.

LISA KROGER

Kroger holds a PhD in English literature and has been a university instructor.

HANA LAYSON

Layson holds a PhD in English literature and has been a university instructor and a freelance writer.

GREGORY LUTHER

Luther holds an MFA in creative writing and has been a university instructor and freelance writer.

THEODORE MCDERMOTT

McDermott holds an MFA in creative writing and has been a university instructor and a freelance writer.

MAGGIE MAGNO

Magno has an MA in education. She has been a high school English teacher and a freelance writer.

PHILLIP MAHONEY

Mahoney is a PhD candidate in English literature and has been a university instructor.

ABIGAIL MANN

Mann holds a PhD in English literature and is a university professor.

RACHEL MINDELL

Mindell holds an MFA in creative writing and has been a freelance writer.

JIM MLADENOVIC

Mladenovic holds an MS in clinical psychology and is pursuing an MA in library science.

KATHRYN MOLINARO

Molinaro holds an MA in English literature and has been a university instructor and a freelance writer.

CAITIE MOORE

Moore holds an MFA in creative writing and has been a university instructor.

JANET MOREDOCK

Moredock is an editor and has been a university instructor and a freelance writer.

ROBIN MORRIS

Morris holds a PhD in English literature and has been a university instructor.

AARON MOULTON

Moulton holds an MA in Latin American studies. He is a PhD candidate in history and a university instructor.

JANET MULLANE

Mullane is a freelance writer and has been a high school English teacher.

ELLIOTT NIBLOCK

Niblock holds an MTS in the philosophy of religion.

ELIZABETH ORVIS

Orvis is a freelance writer with a background in English literature.

JAMES OVERHOLTZER

Overholtzer holds an MA in English literature and has been a university instructor.

MARC OXOBY

Oxoby holds a PhD in English literature and has been a university instructor.

MEGAN PEABODY

Peabody is a PhD candidate in English literature and a university instructor.

EVELYN REYNOLDS

Reynolds is pursuing an MA in English literature and an MFA in creative writing and has been a freelance writer.

CHRIS ROUTLEDGE

Routledge holds a PhD in English literature and is a university lecturer and a freelance writer.

REBECCA RUSTIN

Rustin holds an MA in English literature and is a freelance writer.

CATHERINE E. SAUNDERS

Saunders holds a PhD in English literature and is a university professor.

CARINA SAXON

Saxon is a PhD candidate in English literature and has been a university instructor and a freelance editor.

JACOB SCHMITT

Schmitt holds an MA in English literature and has been a freelance writer.

GINA SHERRIFF

Sherriff holds a PhD in Spanish and is a university professor.

KIRKLEY SILVERMAN

Silverman is pursuing her PhD in English literature and has been a university instructor.

NANCY SIMPSON-YOUNGER

Simpson-Younger is a PhD candidate in literary studies and a university instructor.

CLAIRE SKINNER

Skinner holds an MFA in creative writing and is a university instructor.

ROGER SMITH

Smith holds an MA in media ecology and has been a university instructor and a freelance writer.

HANNAH SOUKUP

Soukup holds an MFA in creative writing.

NICHOLAS SNEAD

Snead is a PhD candidate in French language and literature and has been a university instructor.

SCOTT STABLER

Stabler holds a PhD in history and is a university professor.

SARAH STOECKL

Stoeckl holds a PhD in English literature and is a university instructor and a freelance writer.

SARA TAYLOR

Taylor holds an MA in theater history, theory, and literature and is pursuing her PhD in the same field.

PAMELA TOLER

Toler has a PhD in history and is a freelance writer and former university instructor.

ELIZABETH VITANZA

Vitanza holds a PhD in French and Francophone studies and has been a university and a high school instructor.

JOHN WALTERS

Walters is pursuing a PhD in English literature and has been a university instructor.

KATRINA WHITE

White is a PhD candidate in Spanish language and literature and a university instructor.

ACADEMIC REVIEWERS

RAJA ADAL
Assistant Professor of History, University of Cincinnati, Ohio.

KHALED AL-MASRI
Assistant Professor of Arabic, Swarthmore College, Pennsylvania.

JOHN ALVIS
Professor of English and Director, American Studies Program, University of Dallas, Irving, Texas.

ARLENE AVAKIAN
Emeritus Professor and former Department Chair of Women, Gender, Sexuality Studies, University of Massachusetts-Amherst.

ROBERT BANNISTER
Professor Emeritus of History, Swarthmore College, Pennsylvania.

IAN BARNARD
Associate Professor of English, California State University-Northridge.

CONSTANTIN BEHLER
Associate Professor of German Studies, University of Washington, Bothell.

STEPHEN BEHRENDT
George Holmes Distinguished Professor of English, University of Nebraska, Lincoln.

WILLIAM BELDING
Professorial Lecturer, School of International Service, American University, Washington, D.C.

DORON BEN-ATAR
Professor of History, Fordham University, New York.

JILL BERGMAN
Professor of English and Chair, Department of English, University of Montana, Missoula, Montana.

STEPHEN BLACKWELL
Professor of Russian, University of Tennessee, Knoxville.

FLORENCE BOOS
Professor of English, University of Iowa, Iowa City.

MOULAY-ALI BOUÂNANI
Professor of Africana Studies, Binghamton University, Vestal, New York.

MICHAEL BREEN
Associate Professor of History and Humanities, Reed College, Portland, Oregon.

PAUL BRIANS
Professor Emeritus of English, Washington State University, Pullman.

STEPHEN BRONNER
Distinguished Professor of Political Science, Rutgers University, New Brunswick, New Jersey.

JAMES BROWN
Assistant Professor of English, University of Wisconsin-Madison.

ALISON BRUEY
Assistant Professor of History, University of North Florida, Jacksonville.

PETER BUTTON
Assistant Professor of East Asian Studies, New York University.

VERA CAMDEN
Professor of English, Kent State University, Ohio; Clinical Assistant Professor of Psychiatry, Case Western Reserve University, Cleveland, Ohio; Clinical Professor of Social Work, Rutgers University, New Brunswick, New Jersey.

RUSS CASTRONOVO
Dorothy Draheim Professor of English and American Studies, University of Wisconsin-Madison.

SARAH E. CHINN
Associate Professor of English, Hunter College, New York.

ANN CIASULLO
Assistant Professor of English and Women's and Gender Studies, Gonzaga University, Spokane, Washington.

PAULA CIZMAR
Adjunct Assistant Professor of Playwriting, University of Southern California, Los Angeles.

NATHAN CLARKE
Assistant Professor of History, Minnesota State University-Moorhead.

WILLIAM CLEMENTE
Professor of Literature, Peru State College, Nebraska.

MARC CONNER
Jo M. and James Ballengee Professor of English, Washington and Lee University, Lexington, Virginia.

JANE CRAWFORD
Faculty, History and Political Science Department, Mount St. Mary's College, Los Angeles, California.

LAWRENCE J. CUSHNIE

PhD candidate in Political Science, University of Washington, Seattle.

JOHN T. DALTON

Assistant Professor of Economics, Wake Forest University, Winston-Salem, North Carolina.

ALISTAIR DAVIES

Senior Lecturer in English, University of Sussex, Brighton, United Kingdom.

KIRK DENTON

Professor of East Asian Languages and Literatures, Ohio State University, Columbus.

MUSTAFAH DHADA

Professor of African, Middle Eastern, and World History, California State University-Bakersfield.

GABRIELE DILLMANN

Associate Professor of German, Denison University, Granville, Ohio.

JANE DOWSON

Reader in Twentieth-Century Literature, De Montfort University, Leicester, United Kingdom.

JEANNE DUBINO

Professor of English and Global Studies, Global Studies Faculty Member, Appalachian State University, Boone, North Carolina.

JILLIAN DUQUAINE-WATSON

Senior Lecturer I, School of Interdisciplinary Studies, University of Texas-Dallas.

ELIZABETH DUQUETTE

Associate Professor of English, Gettysburg College, Pennsylvania.

MICHAEL J. DUVALL

Associate Professor of English, College of Charleston, South Carolina.

TAYLOR EASUM

Assistant Professor of Global Histories, Faculty Fellow of Draper Program, New York University.

SIÂN ECHARD

Professor of English, University of British Columbia, Vancouver.

JAMES ENGLISH

John Welsh Centennial Professor of English, Director of the Penn Humanities Forum, University of Pennsylvania, Philadelphia.

MICHAEL FALETRA

Associate Professor of English and Humanities, Reed College, Portland, Oregon.

DANINE FARQUHARSON

Associate Professor of English, Memorial University of Newfoundland, St. John's.

CHARLES FORD

Professor of History and Chair, History Department, Norfolk State University, Virginia.

LUANNE FRANK

Associate Professor of English, University of Texas-Arlington.

JOANNE E. GATES

Professor of English, Jacksonville State University, Alabama.

JAMES GIGANTINO

Assistant Professor of History, University of Arkansas, Fayetteville.

ROBERT W. GLOVER

CLAS Honors Preceptor of Political Science, University of Maine, Orono.

SHARON GORMAN

Walton Professor of Music, University of the Ozarks, Clarksville, Arkansas.

QUAN MANH HA

Assistant Professor of American Literature and Ethnic Studies, University of Montana, Missoula.

RAFEY HABIB

Professor of English, Rutgers University, New Brunswick, New Jersey.

ANDREW HALEY

Associate Professor of American Cultural History, University of Southern Mississippi, Hattiesburg.

EIRIK LANG HARRIS

Assistant Professor of Philosophy, City University of Hong Kong, Kowloon.

BRUCE HARVEY

Associate Professor of English, Associate Director of SEAS, and Director of Liberal Studies, Florida International University, Miami.

ROBERT HEGEL

Professor of Chinese and Comparative Literature, Washington University, St. Louis, Missouri.

MARGUERITE HELMERS

Professor of English, University of Wisconsin-Oshkosh.

RICHARD HIGGINS

Lecturer of English, Franklin College, Indiana.

WALTER HÖLBLING

Professor of American Studies, Karl-Franzens-Universität, Graz, Austria.

PIPPA HOLLOWAY

Professor of History and Program Director, Graduate Studies, Middle Tennessee State University, Murfreesboro.

TED HUMPHREY

President's Professor, Barrett Professor, Lincoln Professor of Ethics and Latin American Intellectual History, and Professor of Philosophy at the School of Historical, Philosophical and Religious Studies, Arizona State University, Tempe.

FRANKLYN HYDE

Adjunct Professor of English, University of Manitoba, Winnipeg.

WILLIAM IRWIN

Professor of Philosophy, Kings College, Wilkes-Barre, Pennsylvania.

STEVEN JACOBS

Associate Professor of Religious Studies and Aaron Aronov Endowed Chair in Judaic Studies, University of Alabama, Tuscaloosa.

JAKE JAKAITIS

Associate Professor of English and Director, Undergraduate Studies in English, Indiana State University, Terre Haute.

JENNIFER JAY

Professor of History and Chinese, University of Alberta, Edmonton.

KELLY JEONG

Assistant Professor of Comparative Literature and of Korean Studies, University of California, Riverside.

JAMES JONES

Professor of History, West Chester University, Pennsylvania.

ISAAC KAMOLA

American Council for Learned Societies (ACLS) New Faculty Fellow, Department of Political Science, Johns Hopkins University, Baltimore, Maryland.

AHMED KANNA

Assistant Professor of Anthropology, University of the Pacific, Stockton, California.

WARD KEELER

Associate Professor of Anthropology, University of Texas-Austin.

STEVEN G. KELLMAN

Professor of Comparative Literature, University of Texas-San Antonio.

DAVID KENLEY

Associate Professor of History, Elizabethtown College, Pennsylvania.

ALICIA A. KENT

Associate Professor of English, University of Michigan-Flint.

ROBERT KIBLER

Professor of English Literature and Humanities, as well as Coordinator, English Program, Minot State University, North Dakota.

RICHARD KING

Professor of Chinese Studies, University of Victoria, British Columbia.

HIROSHI KITAMURA

Associate Professor of History, College of William and Mary, Williamsburg, Virginia.

CHRISTOPHER KNIGHT

Professor of English, University of Montana, Missoula.

KRISTIN KOPTIUCH

Associate Professor of Anthropology, Arizona State University at the West campus, Phoenix.

JOSÉ LANTERS

Professor of English, University of Wisconsin-Milwaukee.

MURRAY LEAF

Professor of Anthropology and Political Economy, University of Texas-Dallas.

MARY LEDERER

Independent Scholar of African Literature, Botswana.

MICHAEL LEVY

Professor of English, University of Wisconsin-Stout, Menomonie.

HUA LI

Assistant Professor of Chinese, Coordinator of Chinese, Montana State University, Bozeman.

GRANT LILFORD

Lecturer in English, University of Zululand, South Africa.

RUTH LOOPER

Professor of English, Dean of the Division of Humanities, Young Harris College, Georgia.

DAVID MCCANN

Korea Foundation Professor of Korean Literature, Harvard University-Korea Institute, Cambridge, Massachusetts.

DEREK MAUS

Associate Professor of English and Communication, State University of New York-Potsdam.

RICHARD J. MOLL

Associate Professor of English Literature, University of Western Ontario, London, Canada.

JOHN MORILLO

Associate Professor of English Literature, North Carolina State University, Raleigh.

MICHAEL MUNGER

Professor of Political Science, Economics, and Public Policy, as well as Director, PPE Program, Duke University, Durham, North Carolina.

BRIAN MURDOCH

Professor Emeritus of Languages, Cultures, and Religions, University of Stirling, Scotland, United Kingdom.

SARA MURPHY

Clinical Assistant Professor, New York University-Gallatin.

EVAN MWANGI

Associate Professor of English, Northwestern University, Evanston, Illinois.

MICHAEL NIMAN

Professor of Journalism and Media Studies, SUNY Buffalo State, New York.

STACEY OLSTER

Professor of English, Stony Brook University, New York.

FEMI OSOFISAN

Professor of Drama, University of Ibadan, Nigeria.

ANDREW PARKER

Professor of French and Comparative Literature, Rutgers University, New Brunswick, New Jersey.

MICHEL PHARAND

Director, Disraeli Project, Queen's University, Kingston, Ontario.

ADAM PIETTE

Professor of English Literature, University of Sheffield, United Kingdom.

ELIZABETH PIKE

Undergraduate Advisor and Instructor, Department of Geography, University of Colorado-Boulder.

MARIA POLSKI

Associate Professor of English and Communications, East-West University, Chicago, Illinois.

JANET POWERS

Professor Emerita of Interdisciplinary Studies and Women, Gender, and Sexuality Studies, Gettysburg College, Pennsylvania.

H. L. T. QUAN

Assistant Professor of Justice and Social Inquiry, Arizona State University, Tempe.

PATRICK QUINN

Professor of English Literature, Chapman University, Orange, California.

KENNETH REEDS

Assistant Professor of Spanish, Salem State University, Massachusetts.

PATRICIO RIZZO-VAST

Instructor of Spanish and Portuguese, Northeastern Illinois University, Chicago.

PHILLIP ROTHWELL

Professor of Portuguese, Rutgers University, New Brunswick, New Jersey.

ELI RUBIN

Associate Professor of History, Western Michigan University, Kalamazoo.

ELIZABETH RUSS

Associate Professor of Spanish, Southern Methodist University, Dallas, Texas.

BURTON ST. JOHN III

Associate Professor of Communication, Old Dominion University, Norfolk, Virginia.

BRETT SCHMOLL

Lecturer of History, California State University-Bakersfield.

ROBERT SCHUHMANN

Associate Professor of Political Science and Head, Criminal Justice Department, University of Wyoming, Laramie.

DANIEL SCHWARTZ

Assistant Professor of History, George Washington University, Washington, D.C.

BEDE SCOTT

Assistant Professor of World Literature, Nanyang Technological University, Singapore.

KEN SEIGNEURIE

Associate Professor of Literature and Director, World Literature Program, Simon Fraser University, Surrey, British Columbia.

HORACIO SIERRA

Assistant Professor of English, Bowie State University, Maryland.

MICHAEL SIZER

Assistant Professor of History and Intellectual History, Maryland Institute College of Art, Baltimore.

MAREK STEEDMAN

Associate Professor of Political Science and Director, American Studies, University of Southern Mississippi, Hattiesburg.

ALAN STEWART

Professor of English and Comparative Literature, Columbia University, New York.

NANCY STOCKDALE

Associate Professor of History, University of North Texas, Denton.

GARY TAYLOR

Distinguished Research Professor, Florida State University, Tallahassee. General Editor of the Oxford editions of Shakespeare's Complete Works *and* Middleton's Collected Works.

LARRY THORNTON

Professor of History, Hanover College, Indiana.

JOHN TONE

Professor of History, Technology, and Society, as well as Associate Dean, Ivan Allen College of Liberal Art, Georgia Institute of Technology, Atlanta.

THOMAS UNDERWOOD

Senior Lecturer (Master Level), College of Arts and Sciences Writing Program, Boston University, Massachusetts.

RUJIE WANG

Associate Professor of Chinese and Chair, Chinese Department, College of Wooster, Ohio.

ANNETTE WANNAMAKER

Associate Professor of Children's Literature and Coordinator of the Children's Literature Program, Eastern Michigan University, Ypsilanti. North American Editor-in-Chief of Children's Literature in Education: An International Quarterly.

ALLYNA WARD

Assistant Professor of English, Booth University College, Winnipeg, Manitoba.

JEFF WEINTRAUB

Lecturer, Philosophy, Politics and Economics Program, University of Pennsylvania, Philadelphia.

JOLEE WEST

Director of Academic Computing and Digital Library Projects, Wesleyan University, Middletown, Connecticut.

CRAIG WHITE

Professor of Literature, University of Houston-Clear Lake, Texas.

KENNETH WILBURN

Assistant Professor of History, East Carolina University, Greenville, North Carolina.

PHILIP WILLIAMS

Visiting Professor of Chinese, Montana State University, Bozeman, and Professor Emeritus of Chinese, Arizona State University, Tempe.

DONALD WOLFF

Professor of English, Eastern Oregon University, La Grande.

SIMONA WRIGHT

Professor of Italian, College of New Jersey, Ewing.

RALPH YOUNG

Professor of History, Temple University, Philadelphia, Pennsylvania.

YU ZHANSUI

Assistant Professor of Chinese, Nazareth College, Rochester, New York.

PETER ZINOMAN

Professor of History, University of California-Berkeley.

CULTURAL CRITICS

ARABESQUES

Anton Shammas

OVERVIEW

Published in Hebrew in 1986 and translated into English in 1988 during a period of increased political tension between Jewish Israelis and Palestinians, *Arabesques* by Anton Shammas is a semiautobiographical account of an Arab Israeli family divided into two distinct but interwoven sections, "The Tale" and "The Teller." The former, ostensibly narrated by the character Anton, relates the history of the Shammas family, beginning in the early nineteenth century with their relocation from Syria to Fassuta, a village in Galilee. "The Teller," set in the 1980s, narrates Anton's residency at the International Writer's Program at the University of Iowa. By writing *Arabesques* in Hebrew, Shammas, a Christian Palestinian with Israeli citizenship, provoked outrage and challenged conceptions of Israeli national identity and Hebrew literature as essentially Jewish, while emphasizing the presence of a significant non-Jewish Arab Israeli minority within Israel and the necessity for a truly secular Israeli state.

Arabesques was published amid an emerging tradition of Arab Israeli authors writing in Arabic and Hebrew. Its linguistic sophistication and reappropriation of Hebrew and Israeli sources immediately located it at the center of intense debate. Scholars praised its literary style even as they questioned the author's decision to write in the Hebrew language. The novel contributes to a broader conversation about Israeli identity and has been examined within the frameworks of postcolonial studies, postmodernism, and minority literature. Today it is available in eight languages—although it has never appeared in Arabic—and it remains the subject of scholarly debate and study for its resistance to ethno-religious conceptions of national identity and disputation of Israeli origin and ownership narratives that seek to possess both the land and the Hebrew language.

HISTORICAL AND LITERARY CONTEXT

The 1936–39 Arab Revolt comprised a popular uprising against Jewish immigration to Palestine and against British control of the area, which had been legalized by a 1922 British mandate. Widespread violence resulted in massive casualties, a weakened economy, and a scattered Arab leadership, undermining later resistance efforts. Although many Christians shared the nationalist aspirations of the mostly Muslim Arab leadership,

they were often suspected of British or Zionist collaboration, leading to persecution or compulsory participation. Following the end of British rule in 1948, the state of Israel was established, provoking the Arab-Israeli War. A Jewish-majority state was engineered through the expulsion of the native Arab population from within its borders, a crisis known as the *nakba,* or catastrophe. In addition to creating a massive refugee problem, the emergence of the Jewish state isolated the Christian and Muslim Arab population that remained within the nation, estimated at 160,000. Only the Palestinian Israelis who could prove their uninterrupted residence in the state were granted citizenship; however, they were denied true equality.

Political Zionism required a Jewish homeland, and the state of Israel was founded to fulfill this role. Because Hebrew was not the native tongue of the majority of the Jewish population, a monolingual community had to be created. Although Hebrew and Arabic are both official languages of Israel, an Israeli Palestinian could not receive an education or get a job without learning Hebrew. However, since Hebrew is historically the language of an ethno-religious community, not all Israeli citizens have equal ownership of it. The Hebrew language is a key element of Israeli national identity, and its borders are policed as carefully as the state's physical territory, especially since the presence of a significant non-Jewish minority threatens the vision of a Jewish state. During the 1980s the Israeli government was controlled by the Likud, a conservative political party that aggressively persecuted the Palestinian population within Israel, particularly in the occupied territories that the party hoped to annex. Nearly a decade of oppressive policies culminated in the 1987 Palestinian intifada, or uprising. The publication of *Arabesques,* a novel written by a Christian Arab Israeli, challenges Jewish Israeli dominance by consciously locating itself within the Hebrew canon.

Arabesques emerged as part of a larger body of literature concerned with depicting the experiences of the Palestinian Israeli population. Novels by Arab Israeli authors published in Hebrew, such as Atallah Mansour's *In a New Light* (1966), and in Arabic, such as Emile Habiby's *The Secret Life of Saeed: The Pessoptimist* (1974), explored the complexities of a hybrid identity. Prominent Jewish Israeli authors also treated the subject of the Arab Israeli minority in Hebrew

Key Facts

Time Period:
Late 20th Century

Genre:
Novel

Events:
Israeli government controlled by conservative Likud party; Israeli persecution of Palestinians in Israel and the occupied territories leading to Palestinian intifada

Nationality:
Arab Israeli

ARAB ISRAELI POET MAHMOUD DARWISH

Palestinian poet Mahmoud Darwish was born in the Upper Galilee village of Birweh within the borders of the modern-day State of Israel. He and his family fled their home in 1948, and Birweh—along with hundreds of other Arab villages—was destroyed by Jewish forces. Although Darwish returned to Israel in 1949, he was denied citizenship because he had not been present for the census. In 1971 he finally left Israel, becoming part of a massive population of Palestinian refugees. By the time he died in 2008, he was internationally renowned for his poetry.

Although he wrote in Arabic and his poetry was centrally concerned with Palestine, Darwish, like Anton Shammas, refused to relinquish his claim to the Hebrew language. During his time in Israel, Hebrew was the language of everyday life and poetry; through Hebrew he discovered the work of Hebrew and European poets. In a 1996 interview in *Chadarim* he states, "Hebrew does not signify for me the language of the occupier because it is my language of love and friendship … the language of my childhood memories." In 2000 the Israeli Ministry of Education suggested that some of his poetry be added to the national curriculum, provoking outrage among the Israeli right wing. The resistance to incorporating a Palestinian voice into Israeli consciousness demonstrates the rigidity with which national identity is policed in Israel, as well as the fragility of that identity.

fiction prior to the publication of *Arabesques,* albeit as outsiders and often through the use of stereotypes. The most famous example is A. B. Yehoshua's *The Lover* (1977).

Upon its publication, *Arabesques* sparked a fierce debate among Israeli writers and literary critics about its classification and the proper categorization of its author, raising questions about what constitutes Hebrew/Israeli literature and who has the right to produce it. In 2002 Palestinian Israeli novelist Sayed Kashua's *Dancing Arabs,* also written in Hebrew, received an enthusiastic reception from critics and the Israeli public. *Arabesques,* which portrays the deep historical roots of the Arab Israeli population, also played a role in Shammas's advocacy for a fully secular state. In his weekly newspaper column, he opposed a two-state solution that would grant him equal citizenship in a Palestinian state, pushing instead for recognition of all Arab Israelis as citizens. Because of its groundbreaking role, *Arabesques* continues to intrigue scholars and critics, as evidenced by a 2010 colloquium on the novel and its multiple translations held at the University of Michigan at Ann Arbor.

THEMES AND STYLE

Drawing on personal and communal memory, Shammas writes Arab Israelis back into the literary narrative and locates them within the historical geography of modern-day Israel. One of Anton's contemporaries in the novel, Yehoshua Bar-On, an Israeli writer, recognizes the necessity of such a project, stating, "There has to be an Arab this time, as some sort of solution to some sort of silence. An Arab who speaks the language of Grace, as Dante once called it." The evocation of common themes in traditional Jewish literature, such as homelessness and wandering, and Bar-On's references to Anton as "my Jew" link the former subjugation of the European Jews to the contemporary inequality of the Palestinian Israelis. The liminal position of the Arab Israeli narrator complicates the simplistic division between Palestinian and Jewish Israelis that allows each to define itself against the other, as when Bar-On abandons his character study of Anton in favor of Paco, a "pure Palestinian" who "forces [Bar-On] to respond and take a stand toward him." Together, Bar-On and Anton "constitute a schizophrenia, two faces of a single person," that undermines both Israeli and Palestinian nationalist narratives that seek to excise the other half without damaging the whole.

Rhetorically, the seamless weaving of written records, biblical and literary allusions, oral history, legend, and memories, in combination with the text's parallel narratives, calls into question the nature of authorship and ownership over narrative. "The Tale" mimics the wandering orality of the stories of Anton's Uncle Yusef, which "were plaited into one another, embracing and parting, twisting and twining in the infinite arabesque of memory." Personal and collective memory blurs into myth as allusions to American, European, Jewish, and Hebrew texts—rather than to Arabic texts—introduce an intertextuality that is self-consciously Israeli, even as Shammas alters these references. However, "The Teller" obscures whether the narrative is Anton's autobiography or a fictionalization produced by Bar-On. Thus, the infiltration of imagination, the corruption of memory, and the confusion of authorship reveal the impossibility of producing an "authentic" narrative.

Shammas locates the Palestinian narrative of dispossession and inequality within modern Hebrew literature but preserves the novel's Arab identity through traditional storytelling structures and magical realism. He utilizes the story-within-a-story technique popularized by the *Arabian Nights,* a collection of Middle Eastern folktales dating to the ninth century, and echoes the language of legend. The figure of Ar-rasad, the rooster that guards the village caves full of Crusader gold, appears throughout: "But the feather that Ar-rasad leaves behind once every seventy years has never been seen by a mortal, for who is wise enough to know the secret of how the *djinnis* [genies] calculate and who is wise enough to know the *djinnis'* calendar?" Shammas's self-conscious adoption of the language of folklore and the structure of the arabesque confronts Jewish Israeli authors' reliance on stereotypes for the representation of Arabs in their fiction.

CRITICAL DISCUSSION

Although critics commend *Arabesques*'s structure and style, Shammas's decision to write in Hebrew has been challenged by scholars working in Arabic, Hebrew, and English. The novel provoked a heated debate in the Israeli press after A. B. Yehoshua, possibly the inspiration for the character of Bar-On, suggested in 1986 in *Qol ha-ir* that Shammas "pick up his belongings and move a 100 meters east, to the becoming Palestinian nation where he could realize his Palestinian identity fully." Stressing the impossibility of this kind of solution, Shammas responds in 1987 in *Iton*: "What [Yehoshua] does not realize is that his own left hand is *already* an integral part of my own Israeli identity just as *at least* one finger of his right hand is my own." Yumna al-'Id criticizes Shammas's choice to write in Hebrew, echoing the disapproval of other critics writing in Arabic who tend to view the novel as a betrayal. In an essay in *al-Karmel* (1990), al-'Id asserts that by writing in Hebrew, Shammas grants the language "the authority to write the reality of the land and shape the biography of [his] Arab-Christian family." Following the novel's translation into English, the *New York Times Book Review* named it one of the seven best works of fiction for 1988.

The public conversation surrounding *Arabesques* has been nearly as important as the novel itself. Shammas's mastery of the Hebrew language and Jewish literary sources challenges notions of what it means to be Arab, Israeli, or even Jewish. In a 1987 review in *Journal of Palestine Studies,* French-Israeli filmmaker Simone Bitton writes that Shammas plays a major role in the revival of the Hebrew language: "Thanks to him, the Israeli literary buff finally reads phrases in which the objects, actions, and sentiments all have Hebrew names, wrested from the obscurity of texts, forgotten by a public cut off from the true sources of a culture it nevertheless claims to perpetuate." Hillel Halkin similarly praises the novel's "Jewishness" in a 1988 essay in the *New Republic,* while John Updike lauds Shammas's layered prose. Updike writes in a 1988 review for *New Yorker,* "In a world whose political trend is always toward strident simplification and brute loyalty, this almost stiflingly complex confession of complexity is a brave attempt."

Many scholars study *Arabesques* within the framework of Gilles Deleuze and Félix Guattari's conception of a minor literature, identifying Hebrew as a hegemonic language and focusing on the text's deterritorialization of that language. In a 1999 essay for *PMLA,* Yael S. Feldman emphasizes Shammas's Christian identity, arguing that the central trauma of *Arabesques* is not 1948, the year of the nakba, but 1936, the beginning of the Arab Revolt. She contends, "Hebrew is his only language that allows him to speak the memory of a minority, to work through the unnameables of his other majority language, Arabic." Gil Z. Hochberg describes in his book *In Spite of Partition: Jews, Arabs, and the Limits of Separatist*

Imagination (2007) the real-life political implications of linguistic deterritorialization. Through an examination of the "dual status" of Hebrew as both an Israeli and a Jewish language, Hochberg addresses "the Israeli-Palestinian and the challenges this figure introduces to the logic of partition and the prospect of resolving the Israeli-Palestinian conflict by means of ethno-national separation."

BIBLIOGRAPHY

Sources

Al-'Id, Yumna. Rev. of *Arabesques,* by Anton Shammas. *al-Karmel* 35 (1990): 83–84. Print.

Bitton, Simone. "Changing Guises." Rev. of *Arabesques,* by Anton Shammas. *Journal of Palestine Studies* 17.1 (1987): 165–67. Print.

Darwish, Mahmoud. Interview with Hilit Yeshurun. *Chadarim* 12 (1996): 194–95. Print.

A play organized by Palestinians for the 60th anniversary of the nakba, the creation of the State of Israel in 1948. Anton Shammas's 1986 novel *Arabesques* weaves a family's history with the history of Palestine and Israel. © IDEALINK PHOTOGRAPHY/ALAMY.

Feldman, Yael S. "Postcolonial Memory, Postmodern Intertextuality: Anton Shammas's *Arabesques* Revisited." *PMLA* 114.3 (1999): 373–89. Print.

Halkin, Hillel. "One Hundred Years of Multitude." Rev. of *Arabesques,* by Anton Shammas. *New Republic* 189 (1988): 28–32. Print.

Hochberg, Gil Z. *In Spite of Partition: Jews, Arabs, and the Limits of Separatist Imagination.* Princeton: Princeton UP, 2007. Print.

Shammas, Anton. "Kitsch 22; or, the Limits of Culture." *Iton* 77 (1987): 24–26. Print.

Updike, John. "Satan's Work and Silted Cisterns." Rev. of *Arabesques,* by Anton Shammas. *New Yorker* 17 Oct. 1988: 117–21. Print.

Yehoshua, A. B. "If You Stay You Are a Minority." *Qol ha-ir* 31 Jan. 1986: 42–43. Print.

Further Reading

Caspi, Mishael, and Jerome David Weltsch. *From Slumber to Awakening: Culture and Identity of Arab Israeli Literati.* Lanham: UP of America, 1998. Print.

Habiby, Emile. *The Secret Life of Saeed: The Pessoptimist.* Trans. Salma Khadra Jayyusi and Trevor Le Gassick. Northampton: Interlink, 2003. Print.

Mansour, Atallah. *In a New Light.* Trans. Abraham Birman. London: Vallentine, 1969. Print.

Pappe, Ilan. *The Forgotten Palestinians: A History of the Palestinians in Israel.* New Haven: Yale UP, 2011. Print.

Yehoshua, A. B. *The Lover.* Trans. Philip Simpson. Garden City: Doubleday, 1978. Print.

Allison Blecker

"Bangladesh I," "Bangladesh II," and "Bangladesh III"

Faiz Ahmed Faiz

OVERVIEW

Written during the 1971 civil war in Pakistan and after the secession of Bangladesh, the poems "Bangladesh I" ("Stay Away from Me"), "Bangladesh II," and "Bangladesh III" by Faiz Ahmed Faiz capture through visceral images the passion and anguish many Bangladeshis experienced under the Pakistani military dictatorship. Collectively, the poems serve as a warning, implying that the speaker is dangerous, dissatisfied, and unforgiving. The first two poems detail the author's horror regarding the war, while the third, written in 1973 upon the poet's return from exile in Beirut, elaborates on feelings of acute estrangement. The latter is especially notable in that it ostensibly recounts a heartbreak while remaining overtly political in tone. Written in colloquial Urdu, the poems are easily grasped, memorized, and recited by the literate and illiterate alike and function as a testament to the enduring effects of political upheaval, especially in Bangladesh.

After the publication of the poems, Faiz was credited with expanding the subject matter of Urdu poetry beyond themes of romantic love and nature to themes of social justice and oppression. He is widely regarded in the Middle East as the greatest contemporary Urdu poet, and his poems are still sung by pop singers in the region. In particular, his "Bangladesh" poems express a universal humanism while maintaining fidelity to specific historical events. In spite of the fact that the government of Pakistan has historically denied accusations of malfeasance and has neglected to issue a formal apology to Bangladesh, the poems affirm the lasting effects of war and the lived experiences of the Bangladeshi people.

HISTORICAL AND LITERARY CONTEXT

After the partition of India in 1947, which ended British rule and broke the colony into new countries based on religion, Pakistan became a sovereign state. A rapid succession of rulers in the 1950s bred instability and corruption, resulting in violent tensions. When the first general elections were held in 1970, the party based in East Pakistan won a majority of votes, but power was never relinquished to the party. During the demonstrations that followed, the Pakistani army massacred roughly 300,000 people in Bangladesh, specifically targeting intellectuals and students.

The years leading up to the independence of Bangladesh in 1971 were a time of civil unrest across the world, reflected in the work of many Western poets, from Denise Levertov to Ernesto Cardenal. Of the political poets writing at the time, Faiz is most often compared with Pablo Neruda because both composed deceptively simple poems using objects from daily life. In addition, both had political aspirations and are as still revered as when they were alive for articulating the struggle of the underclasses. Moreover, Faiz and Neruda were persecuted by their governments and, while in exile, wrote deft love poems that continue to inform readings of their political poetry. Faiz was quite famous in his lifetime, in part due to his Marxist politics, for which he was arrested in 1951 and was incarcerated for four years, concurrent with the period that McCarthyism dominated the social and literary environment in the United States. Like his fellow political poets Cesar Vallejo and Nazim Hikmet, Faiz continued to write poetry while in jail, criticizing the power structure that had placed him there.

Before the partitioning of India, Faiz was affiliated with the Progressive Writers' Movement, an organization of authors that denounced colonialism and encouraged rebellion and social revolution. Members opposed conservative ideals and authored manifestos that encouraged writers to become politically engaged and to produce work that was critical of oppression. The group's first publication, released in 1932, was a collection of short stories titled *Angare* (*Burning Coal*). Through the movement, Faiz found his first supporters and developed his belief that personal and social progress, as well as literature and liberation, are inextricably linked.

The "Bangladesh" poems are part of a body of postcolonial literature, specifically the literature of postpartition India. Faiz's work has influenced contemporary poets writing in this context, particularly Mahmoud Darwish and Agha Shahid Ali, the latter of whom has been a respected translator of Faiz's writing. Ali in a 1990 essay for *Grand Street* notes that Faiz was a "poet who drew as many as fifty thousand people to

+ *Key Facts*

Time Period:
Late 20th Century

Genre:
Poetry

Events:
Pakistani Civil War

Nationality:
Pakistani

THE PRISON NOTEBOOKS

In 1951 Faiz Ahmed Faiz was jailed for his alleged involvement in what came to be known as the Rawalpindi conspiracy, a plotted coup that involved various military officials. Faiz's wife, Alys, notes in her memoirs that when she was granted visitation, his body showed evidence of torture. However, his wife and friends commented that he seemed in good spirits, even though the charges of conspiracy carried the death penalty. Initially, he was denied paper and pens, leading him to compose verses in his head to be written down later. When writing implements were at last available to him, he was forced to use coded imagery to ensure that the political content would remain undetected by government censors.

Despite these restrictions, Faiz wrote two books while in prison, *Dast-e-Saba* (*The Wind Writes*) and *Zindam Naza* (*Prison Journal*), which some critics have hailed as his best works. He resisted the misery that afflicts many political prisoners and ultimately viewed his time while incarcerated as positive. Historians have credited the experience with turning him into a self-avowed political poet.

his readings" even though he remained little known in the West. Darwish, Ali, and Faiz shared various states of forced exile, lending their poems an outsider's perspective tinged with a longing for return. Faiz once stated that his poetry was aided by his political commitments and vice versa. In fact, he saw little difference between his various roles as a labor organizer, a teacher, and a poet; in each situation his aim was to understand and expose the reality of workers' lives. His use of the romantic as a political metaphor was subsequently adopted by Ali, whose "Ghazal" from *The Country without a Post Office* (1998) reads much like "Bangladesh III" in its rhythmic couplets: "I beg for haven: Prisons, let open your gates / A refugee from Belief seeks a cell tonight. / Executioners near the woman at the window. / Damn you, Elijah, I'll bless Jezebel tonight."

THEMES AND STYLE

The "Bangladesh" poems hinge on images of the mutilated body and psyche of the speaker, whose "emaciated body [is] nearly drained of blood." The first poem describes how the speaker's "heart is thirsting for blood," a warning to enemies. The second poem echoes this sentiment of retribution in the opening and closing lines as a "healer" advises the speaker that the only cure for the "dust of bitterness" is more blood until "now my blood-filled eyes see blood." By contrast "Bangladesh III" is much more subdued in its imagery and syntax. The speaker is no longer exclaiming but questioning and reminiscing. Form and content combine to evoke a cold, formal tone through rigid couplets. Whether addressed to a friend, a beloved, or—as

Ali sees it—the revolution that has not returned, the third poem reiterates that the speaker's "reconciling word remained unspoken."

In the poems, Faiz creates an intimate setting by using objects that signal familiar poetic subjects. However, the "moons," "suns," "flowers," and "goblets" that usually adorn love poems have been changed by the events and by the speaker's perception of the landscape. The first two poems are written in the style of the nazm, a form that is more open to colloquial language than the ghazal, which is the form of the third poem. The lack of restriction in form gives space for the poet to vent his rage. However, Faiz avoids syntactical fragmentation; instead his verses are focused and overflowing. His is not a speaker who has lost connection with language, as with the modernist poets of Europe after World War I; rather his verses are replete "with the brilliant crimson of anger, / of suffering, of the passion of martyrdom."

Additionally, the poems employ modes of prayer and direct address to involve the reader in the dramatic situation. Lines such as "don't let this happen, my healer," point the reader toward action and imply the audience's direct involvement with political outcomes. Whereas many poets of the late twentieth century used several voices or a range of diction to create universal works, Faiz creates a unified voice to express collective grief: "Merciless, merciless was the moment when love ended, / cruel, cruel were the mornings, after the nights of tenderness."

CRITICAL DISCUSSION

Despite having received the Lenin Prize for his writing in 1963, Faiz became most widely recognized in the West after his death in 1984. His relative obscurity until the early 1990s may be due to the dearth of media attention on Bangladesh, which lacked the notoriety of other countries in the region. Critics have noted that the sentiments and rhythm of Urdu are notoriously difficult to reproduce; however, authors of similarly "difficult" languages, such as Yehuda Amichai (who wrote in Hebrew) and Nazim Hikmet (who wrote in Turkish), have garnered a fair amount of praise. Nevertheless, Faiz has become more visible in the last few decades owing to early translations by V. G. Kiernan and Naomi Lazard and is now considered among the most famous modern poets of Bangladesh and Pakistan.

Recently, Ali and Caroline Kizer have been instrumental in reopening the conversation about Faiz's work and its relevance. Both have translated the "Bangladesh" poems in ways that attend less to Faiz's original rhyme and meter but still adhere to the rules of the ghazal or the nazm, which differ in many ways. For example, the ghazal's couplets are meant to stand alone and their order should be nonlinear, whereas the nazm should have a cohesive subject and aim throughout.

In *The True Subject: Selected Poems of Faiz Ahmed Faiz* (1988), Lazard notes the cultural differences she encountered when translating and corresponding with Faiz, remarking that "what was crystal-clear to an Urdu-speaking reader meant nothing at all to an American." Added to these obstacles for Western readers is Faiz's blurring of traditional Western boundaries between writing and activism and the personal and the social. Ali notes that it is common in Urdu for "beloved" to mean "friend, woman, God. Faiz not only tapped into these meanings, but extended them to include the Revolution." Recent scholarship by Aamir R. Mufti and Christi Ann Merrill has examined this holistic perspective, further elucidating how the political elements in Faiz's work must be read in terms of the social.

BIBLIOGRAPHY

Sources

Ali, Agha Shahid. *The Country without a Post Office.* New York: Norton, 1998. Print.

———. "The True Subject: The Poetry of Faiz Ahmed Faiz." *Grand Street* 9.2 (1990): 129–38. *JSTOR.* Web. 11 Sept. 2012.

Faiz, Faiz Ahmed. *The True Subject: Selected Poems of Faiz Ahmed Faiz.* Trans. Naomi Lazard. Princeton: Princeton UP, 1988. Print.

———. *The Rebel's Silhouette: Selected Poems.* Rev. ed. Trans. Agha Shahid Ali. Salt Lake City: Peregrine Smith, 1995. Print.

———. *Cool, Calm & Collected: Poems 1960–2000.* Trans. Carolyn Kizer. Port Townsend: Copper Canyon, 2001. 427–29. *LitFinder for Schools.* Web. 11 Sept. 2012.

Genoways, Ted. "Let Them Snuff Out the Moon." *Annual of Urdu Studies* 19 (2004): 94–119. Web. 11 Sept. 2012.

Further Reading

Ali, Ahmed, and N. M. Rashed. "The Progressive Writers' Movement in Its Historical Perspective." *Journal of South Asian Literature* 13.1 (1977): 91–97. *JSTOR.* Web. 11 Sept. 2012.

Aslan, Reza, ed. *Tablet and Pen: Literary Landscapes from the Middle East.* New York: Norton, 2011. Print.

Faiz, Faiz Ahmed. *Poems.* Trans. V. G. Keirnan. Allen & Unwin, 1971. Print.

Habib, M. A. R., ed. *An Anthology of Modern Urdu Poetry in Translation.* New York: Modern Language Association, 2003. Print.

Jamal, Mahmood, ed. *The Penguin Book of Modern Urdu Poetry.* New York: Penguin, 1986. Print.

Jones, Allen. "Interviews with Faiz Ahmed Faiz." *Journal of South Asian Literature* 10.1 (1974): 141–44. *JSTOR.* Web. 11 Sept. 2012.

Merrill, Christi Ann. "The Lyricism of Violence: Translating Faith in Revolution." *boundary 2* 38.3 (2011): 119–45. Print.

Mufti, Aamir R. "Towards a Lyric History of India." *boundary 2* 31.2 (2004): 245–74. Print.

Caitie Moore

After the Bangladesh Liberation War, a Bengali boy runs through a field of dead bodies near Dhaka, 1971. Poet Faiz Ahmed Faiz's "Bangladesh I," "Bangladesh II," and "Bangladesh III" address the atrocities perpetuated against the people of Bangladesh during the war. © PENNY TWEEDIE/ ALAMY.

"THE BETTER PART"

Booker T. Washington

✧ *Key Facts*

Time Period:
Late 19th Century

Genre:
Speech

Events:
Spanish-American War;
implementation of Jim
Crow laws

Nationality:
American

OVERVIEW

"The Better Part," a speech delivered by Booker T. Washington at the National Jubilee Conference in Chicago in 1898, argues that African Americans have earned an opportunity for greater advancement and equality due to their consistent record of valor and fidelity to the United States. It marked a critical departure from Washington's famous "Atlanta Compromise" speech three years earlier, in which many thought he conceded too much to segregationist white southerners. Washington delivered "The Better Part" at a celebration of the United States' quick victory in the Spanish-American War. As the title suggests, the speech posits that African Americans have repeatedly chosen "the better part" of their nature to serve their country despite their unjust treatment based on skin color. The speech recognizes the brave actions of black troops throughout history, and particularly in the Spanish-American War, in order to push listeners to question discrimination and afford blacks more chances to prove themselves.

"The Better Part" points directly to the South as the source of racism in the United States, and the southern press excoriated him for this, arguing that he had broken the pledge he had made in Atlanta. As southern whites had begun the process of implementing Jim Crow laws, Washington had tried compromising with them to avoid a direct confrontation. His Atlanta speech supported this philosophy and is his most recognized piece of propaganda. However, "The Better Part" moved Washington away from the spirit of compromise and toward a declaration of black rights. Though the speech is significant, it has been largely lost to history.

HISTORICAL AND LITERARY CONTEXT

When the Confederacy surrendered and the Civil War ended in 1865, the institution of slavery effectively ended in the United States. African Americans expected this to mean the inauguration of true freedom and equality, but their struggles with racism, disenfranchisement, and oppression continued in the late nineteenth century. In the 1880s southern states began to pass laws that institutionalized the segregation of races. These so-called Jim Crow laws, which were upheld in the 1896 Supreme Court case *Plessy v. Ferguson,* eroded many of the gains blacks had made during Reconstruction, the period immediately following the Civil War. Though not as ingrained or severe, racism also persisted in the North.

When "The Better Part" was delivered in 1898, the United States had just earned a quick victory in the Spanish-American War and Washington was the most prominent advocate for African American rights in the country. Though he had garnered broad support for his cause, Washington had also conceded an important point to powerful southern whites, who would support him as long as he did not question segregationist Jim Crow laws. Washington agreed to this, arguing that African Americans had to evolve economically in order to obtain white-collar jobs and, in turn, gain equal footing with whites. That so many African Americans had fought so bravely in the Spanish-American War presented Washington with an opportunity to argue that blacks had indeed demonstrated their virtue and earned the right to further prove themselves.

In 1895, three years before delivering "The Better Part," Washington introduced his accommodationist philosophy toward white southerners in a speech at the Atlanta Cotton States and International Exposition. The speech, which most term today as the "Atlanta Compromise," created a bargain between white southerners and African Americans. In exchange for not agitating against segregation, disfranchisement, and the lack of basic civil rights, southern blacks would be allowed to obtain an education and continue to receive largesse funding from northerners. The famous statement "cast down your buckets where you are" served as the guide for blacks to take a "slow go" approach and reach equality through the accumulation of wealth. Washington's speech at the Atlanta Exposition brought him renown as well as criticism, and "The Better Part" can be viewed as an elaboration and response to the position he outlined in it.

In the early twentieth century, historian and activist W. E. B. Du Bois, among others, voiced serious opposition to the position Washington outlined in "The Better Part" and elsewhere. Du Bois dubbed Washington the "great accommodator" for the belief that confrontation would result in disaster for minorities and that economic mobility would lead to equality in the long run. Du Bois felt that civil rights had to be gained before African Americans could garner economic equity. In works such as *The Souls of Black Folk* (1903), Du Bois argues that race is the preeminent American problem and that it can only be solved through the achievement of full civil equality for blacks.

THEMES AND STYLE

The central theme of "The Better Part" is that African Americans have demonstrated their fidelity to the country and, therefore, are owed equality. Delivered just three years after the "Atlanta Compromise" speech that had drawn praise from southern whites, "The Better Part" more directly confronts racism: "We have succeeded in every conflict except in the effort to conquer ourselves in the blotting out of racial prejudices." He goes on to declare: "I make no empty statement when I say that we shall have, especially in the southern part of our country a cancer gnawing at the heart of this Republic that shall one day prove as dangerous as an attack from an army from without or within." In this speech, the person many came to call an accommodationist directly exhorts southern whites to extend to blacks the opportunities they deserve.

Washington makes his case by illustrating African Americans' long history of sacrifice for the greater good of their nation. At the speech's start, Washington evokes the Christian criteria for virtue: choosing "the better part" when faced with "two courses of action." He then seeks to "apply this test to the American Negro," beginning with the initial arrival of Africans as slaves in America and proceeding through the recently concluded Spanish-American War. Citing African Americans' repeated selfless deeds for their country, Washington asks his audience to "decide within yourselves whether a race that is thus willing to die for its country, should not be given the highest opportunity to live for its country." Rather than make strident demands for equality, he declares that blacks will continue to earn the trust and goodwill of their countrymen: "We shall make the task easier for you by acquiring property, habits of thrift, economy, intelligence and character, by making himself of individual worth in his own community."

Stylistically, the speech is distinguished by a syntactic repetition that drives home Washington's point about the long-standing patriotism of African Americans. In a number of sequential paragraphs, he invokes times, places, and situations in which blacks chose their "better part." This series begins, "When in the childhood of this nation the Negro was asked to submit to slavery or choose death and extinction, as did the aborigines, he chose the better part, that which perpetuated the race." In this way, Washington establishes a historical record that "proves" his case. Significant, too, is his tone of gratitude, which further

BOOKER T WASHINGTON, THE APOSTLE OF LEARNING.
'In all thy getting, get wisdom.'

Booker T. Washington in a detail of the print "Afro-American Monument," c. 1897. COURTESY EVERETT COLLECTION.

bolsters the notion that African Americans wish to participate in the long-established national dynamic rather than overturn it.

CRITICAL DISCUSSION

"The Better Part" garnered much attention after Washington delivered it, as almost all the major newspapers in the country ran the text of the speech. It sparked controversy among southerners, who felt that Washington had broken from his "Atlanta Compromise" by specifically mentioning the South in conjunction with racism. Washington responded in the Birmingham, Alabama, *Age-Herald* newspaper, writing:

> I said that I made the same plea that I had made in my address at Atlanta, for the blotting out of race prejudice in 'commercial and civil relations.' I said that what is termed social recognition was a question which I never discussed, and then I quoted from my Atlanta address what I had said there in regard to that subject.

This response seems to dismiss the thought that, in contrast to his Atlanta speech, "The Better Part" offers a cathartic message. Thus, while "The Better Part" represented a shift away from compromise, Washington's response served as a retreat from this new position.

Washington's accommodationist position began to be widely criticized in the early twentieth century, when those in the black community saw increased lynching in all parts of the country and the lack of progress in the civil rights movement became apparent. Du Bois, for example, originally praised the Atlanta speech before strongly criticizing Washington in 1903 in *The Souls of Black Folks*. Such critiques of Washington only increased as the

PRIMARY SOURCE

EXCERPT FROM "THE BETTER PART"

In the life of our Republic, when he has had the opportunity to choose, has it been the better or worse part? When in the childhood of this nation the Negro was asked to submit to slavery or choose death and extinction, as did the aborigines, he chose the better part, that which perpetuated the race.

When in 1776 the Negro was asked to decide between British oppression and American independence, we find him choosing the better part, and Crispus Attucks, a Negro, was the first to shed his blood on State street, Boston, that the white American might enjoy liberty forever, though his race remained in slavery.

When in 1814 at New Orleans, the test of patriotism came again, we find the Negro choosing the better part; Gen. Andrew Jackson himself testifying that no heart was more loyal and no arm more strong and useful in defense of righteousness.

When the long and memorable struggle came between union and separation, when he knew that victory on the one hand meant freedom, and defeat on the other his continued enslavement, with a full knowledge of the portentous meaning of it all, when the suggestion and the temptation came to burn the home and massacre wife and children during the absence of the master in battle, and thus insure his liberty, we find him choosing the better part, and for four long years protecting and supporting the helpless, defenseless ones entrusted to his care.

When in 1863 the cause of the Union seemed to quiver in the balance, and there was doubt and distrust, the Negro was asked to come to the rescue in arms, and the valor displayed at Fort Wagner and Port Hudson and Fort Pillow, testify most eloquently: again that the Negro chose the better part.

When a few months ago, the safety and honor of the Republic were threatened by a foreign foe, when the wail and anguish of the oppressed from a distant isle reached his ears, we find the Negro forgetting his own wrongs, forgetting the laws and customs that discriminate against him in his own country, and again we find our black citizen choosing the better part. And if you would know how he deported himself in the field at Santiago, apply for answer to Shafter and Roosevelt and Wheeler. Let them tell how the Negro faced death and laid down his life in defense of honor and humanity, and when

THE TUSKEGEE INSTITUTE

Booker T. Washington is one of the most famous African Americans in U.S. history. Born during the final decade of slavery and raised by his mother, he benefited from the reforms initiated during Reconstruction and had the opportunity to attend college at Virginia's Hampton Institute, where he became a major proponent of education. He later taught at his alma mater, and in 1881, at age twenty-five, he became the first president of Alabama's Tuskegee Normal and Industrial Institute for African Americans, which he led for decades.

At the Tuskegee Institute (now Tuskegee University), he promoted the notion that the acquisition of practical trade skills offered the most viable means of educating young blacks in the wake of emancipation. Though criticized by some, Washington made a gentleman's agreement with southern whites that he would not question blacks' lack of civil rights if his educational endeavors were allowed to continue. This truce permitted the Tuskegee Institute to thrive, largely due to Washington's fund-raising and advocacy efforts. By the time of his death in 1915, he had built the institute from nothing into a 1,500-student school with more than 100 buildings and a $2 million endowment. The Tuskegee Institute still serves the black population of the South.

twentieth century proceeded and the civil rights struggle continued. Many came to see Washington as a "sellout" who set back civil rights. When Martin Luther King Jr. at last led the movement to success in the 1960s, it was largely due to African Americans' confrontation and rejection of the segregation that Washington had encouraged them to tolerate and circumvent. Scholars have approached Washington's position, as stated in "The Better Part" and elsewhere, in shifting ways as the civil rights movement has proceeded.

The work of scholar Louis Harlan (1922–2010) has been the most influential in furthering the notion of Washington as an accommodator. However, Harlan's conception of Washington has been challenged in more recent criticism. The question of where Washington should stand is investigated in Pero Gaglo Debovie's 2007 article "Exploring a Century of Historical Scholarship of Booker T. Washington." Robert J. Norrell's *Up from History: The Life of Booker T. Washington,* published in 2009, places Washington's actions within a historical context. Norrell provides a framework of Washington's youthful experiences as a slave and then a freedman during Reconstruction, which adds to the understanding of his actions.

you have gotten the full story of the heroic conduct of the Negro in the Spanish-American war—heard it from the lips of Northern soldiers and Southern soldiers, from ex-abolitionist and ex-master, then decide within yourselves whether a race that is thus willing to die for its country, should not be given the highest opportunity to live for its country.

In the midst of all the complaints of suffering in the camp and field, suffering from fever and hunger, where is the official or citizen that has heard a word of complaint from the lips of a black soldier? The only request that has come from the Negro soldier has been that he might be permitted to replace the white soldier when heat and malaria began to decimate the ranks of the white regiment, and to occupy at the same time the post of greatest danger.

This country has been most fortunate in her victories. She has twice measured arms with England and has won. She has met the spirit of a rebellion within her borders and was victorious. She has met the proud Spaniard and he lays prostrate at her feet! All this is well, it is magnificent. But there remains one other victory for Americans to win—a victory as far-reaching and important as any that has occupied our army and navy. We have succeeded in every conflict, except the effort to conquer ourselves in the blotting out of racial prejudices. We can celebrate the era of peace in no more effectual way than by a firm resolve on the part of the Northern men and Southern men, black men and white men, that the trench which we together dug around Santiago, shall be the eternal burial place of all that which separates us in our business and civil relations. Let us be as generous in peace as we have been brave in battle. Until we thus conquer ourselves, I make no empty statement when I say that we shall have, especially in the Southern part of our country, a cancer gnawing at the heart of the Republic, that shall one day prove as dangerous as an attack from an army without or within. …

You know us; you are not afraid of us. When the crucial test comes, you are not ashamed of us. We have never betrayed or deceived you. You know that as it has been, so it will be. Whether in war or in peace, whether in slavery or in freedom, we have always been loyal to the Stars and Stripes.

SOURCE: *The Booker T. Washington Papers 1895–98*, pp. 490–492.

BIBLIOGRAPHY

Sources

Debovie, Pero Gaglo. "Exploring a Century of Historical Scholarship of Booker T. Washington." *Journal of African American History* 92.2 (2007): 239–64. Print.

Norrell, Robert J. "Understanding the Wizard of Tuskegee." *Journal of Blacks in Higher Education* 42 (2003–04): 96–109. Print.

———. *Up from History: The Life of Booker T. Washington.* Cambridge: Belknap P of Harvard UP, 2009. Print.

Smock, Raymond. *Booker T. Washington in Perspective: Essays of Louis R. Harlan.* Oxford: U of Mississippi P, 2006. Print.

Washington, Booker T. *Up from Slavery: An Autobiography.* New York: Doubleday, 1901. Print.

Further Reading

Bieze, Michael Scott, and Marybeth Gasman, eds. *Booker T. Washington Rediscovered.* Baltimore: Johns Hopkins UP, 2012. Print.

Harlan, Louis R. *Booker T. Washington: The Making of a Black Leader, 1856–1901.* New York: Oxford UP, 1972. Print.

———. *Booker T. Washington: The Wizard of Tuskegee, 1901–1915.* New York: Oxford UP, 1983. Print.

Washington, Booker T., and W. E. B. Du Bois. *The Negro in the South: His Economic Progress in Relation to His Moral and Religious Development.* Philadelphia: G. W. Jacobs, 1907. Print.

Scott Stabler

THE BONE PEOPLE

Keri Hulme

✥ *Key Facts*

Time Period:
Late 20th Century

Genre:
Novel

Events:
Economic crisis in New Zealand; rise of Maori land rights and cultural nationalist movements

Nationality:
New Zealander

OVERVIEW

Written over a twelve-year period encompassing much of the Maori protest movement, *The Bone People* (1984) is author Keri Hulme's exploration of the blended cultures of contemporary New Zealand. During the 1970s the protest movement called attention to the situation of the Maori people, who faced land rights violations and racism at the hands of the Pākehā, or people of European descent. In the novel Hulme follows the intersecting lives of three damaged people—a Maori laborer, his adopted Pākehā son, and a bicultural hermit painter—depicting the spiritual crisis facing the Maori people in the face of a deracinated cultural identity. Peppered with Maori phrases and appended with a Maori-to-English glossary of terms, the novel reflects Hulme's bicultural heritage and her interest in giving a voice to both the Maori and Pākehā people in the dialogue over land rights and race relations.

After it was published by the feminist Spiral Collective, *The Bone People* enjoyed popular and critical success in New Zealand. Its popularity has been attributed, at least in part, to growing nationalism shaped by loosening ties with the British crown and a conscious desire by Maori and Pākehā New Zealanders to understand and preserve their heritage. Internationally, the book did not fare as well, garnering some positive reviews but also sparking controversy over its merit as a Booker Prize recipient. Some commentators have deemed the work, with its dreamlike passages and use of Maori phrases, unintelligible and pretentious. Although opinions remain mixed about the novel's literary value, *The Bone People* is noteworthy as a serious attempt to grapple with New Zealand's complex ethnic cultural history and as an exemplary text in postcolonial university literature review courses.

HISTORICAL AND LITERARY CONTEXT

The position of Maori people in the broader culture of New Zealand reflects a complex history of interaction with the Pākehā. Descended from Polynesian islanders who settled in New Zealand around 1250–1300 BCE, the Maori witnessed the arrival of Europeans beginning in the seventeenth century. Significant colonization did not occur until William Hobson, under orders of Great Britain's Queen Victoria, arrived on the island in 1840 and signed the Treaty of Waitangi

with various Maori chieftains. In the years following the signing of the treaty, governance shifted from the Crown to a locally established parliament, which represented settlers' interests—particularly the need for land—over Maori land rights. In addition, two competing versions of the document—the English treaty and the Maori te Tiriti—raised serious conflicts over land rights. The British interpretation of the treaty emphasized England's sovereignty over New Zealand, with provisions for protection of Maori lands against encroachment by European settlers. The Maori understanding of Great Britain's intentions focused more on partnership, with a central British government functioning as support for chieftains in governing their own territories.

More than a century after the Treaty of Waitangi was signed, the Maori relationship to the Pākehā remained contentious. Influenced by global protest against war, discrimination, and marginalization of minority cultures, Maori activists became more organized and strident in the late 1960s and 1970s, with protests centered on New Zealand Day, which honors the contested Waitangi treaty. In addition to the loss of Maori land, activists, writers, and critics raised the issue of loss of classical Maori culture, which was based on rural, tribal ways of life and which had virtually disappeared.

Hulme, who claims Pākehā and Maori ancestry, has written several works about the consequences of the two cultures intermingling, particularly as biculturalism affects modern Maori families. In her 1981 essay "Mauri: An Introduction to Bicultural Poetry in New Zealand," she writes of the disconnectedness of the Maori people: "in the cities, you are cut off from the land, the sea, your family marae, your ancestral roots." Without a true foundation, she asserts, many Maori struggle with alcoholism and with their ethnic identity, sometimes preferring to live life as "a brown Pākehā." Hulme notes a number of "mongrel" writers like herself who have dealt with similar themes, among them Apirana Taylor, whose poetry, including "Te Kooti," is quoted in Hulme's essay and centers on the loss of Maori tradition and identity.

The Bone People, which won the 1985 Booker Prize for fiction, generated considerable controversy about the judging process and the book's merit. The novel was the first from New Zealand to be nominated for the prize, breaking ground for works by other nativist authors, including Patricia Grace, whose *Dogside Story* was under consideration for the prize in 2001, and Lloyd Jones, whose *Master Pip* was short listed in 2007. The novel may have also laid the groundwork for the success of Alan Duff's 1990 novel *Once Were Warriors* and the acclaimed film based on the book. Like Hulme's novel, the book and film paint a harrowing portrait of violence and alcoholism in contemporary Maori families.

THEMES AND STYLE

The central theme of *The Bone People* is one of isolation, as the three main characters are adrift, each cut off from their home or their origins, trapped in patterns of self-destructive behavior. Kerewin Holmes, who is part Maori, lives in self-imposed isolation in a tower she has built, which has stripped her of the ability to paint. However, her solitude is broken by the arrival of Simon Gillayley, a white child who was orphaned by a boating accident and who was adopted by Joe, a Maori laborer with a drinking problem. Kerewin describes her spiritual impoverishment: "estranged from my family, bereft of my art, hollow of soul, I am a rock in the desert. Pointing nowhere, doing nothing, of no benefit to anyone or anything." This description corresponds to Hulme's depiction, in her earlier essay, of the "heart-rending" experience of sitting perched on the fence of "cross cultural contact." Each character, in his or her isolation, shares this perch.

Rhetorically, Hulme depicts the ravages of cultural disconnection by separating her characters from their surroundings. Kerewin is physically cut off from others in her hermitage. Simon, who cannot or will not speak, is also apart from others, particularly in the ways in which his asocial, violent behavior alienates him from caretaking adults. Joe, while quick to speak and socialize, is unable to form positive, emotionally meaningful attachments to others, and his alcohol dependence reinforces his propensity to use violence as a means of communication. Even the love he feels for Simon is marred by the beatings he dishes out to his adopted son.

The novel's shifting tone, as well as Hulme's extensive use of Maori words and disorienting flashes of gory violence, results in an unsettling narrative that recreates the fragmenting forces at work in postcolonial New Zealand. Although told primarily from Kerewin's point of view, the novel permits each of the three main characters to narrate. Their voices are introduced as the novel opens, and they each briefly describe walking along a road. Simon's passages reflect a poignant desire to bask in the "light" of attention, although he cannot directly communicate this desire. Joe, who thinks of "creation and change, destruction and change," represents a force of violent protest, later beating Simon until "the blood pours from everywhere … his mouth, his ears, his eyes, his nose." Kerewin, whose passages are often lyrical and introspective and

 ## *MARAE* IN MAORI CULTURE

In Maori culture *marae* refers to cleared space, often a meeting ground for celebrations, ceremonies, and other community activities, many of which are centered on the whare rūnanga, or meeting house. The marae is considered a sort of spiritual home for Maori communities, a place of shared language and custom. However, despite the signing of the Treaty of Waitangi, much Maori land, including the marae, was lost following colonization by European settlers. Starting in the early twentieth century, the Maori Land Court, which ruled on land disputes, began to have real power over the marae, culminating in the 1993 Te Ture Whenua Māori Act. This act granted the court authority to hear all claims on land and disputes over the purpose of the land.

Under the act, the marae is given special status as a reserve, which is governed by a board of trustees. The use of individual marae is governed by *tangata whenua,* the local "people of the land," who are also responsible for maintaining the property and the buildings on it. Pākehā may visit marae if granted permission from Maori elders but must strictly adhere to customs, treating the marae with the reverence it demands as the spiritual center of the Maori people.

who seems at times to be a potential savior for Simon, is implicated in the beating, telling Simon she "hopes his father knocks him sillier than he is now."

CRITICAL DISCUSSION

Published during a period of strong nationalist sentiment, *The Bone People* enjoyed both popular and critical success in its home country, garnering the New Zealand Book Award for Fiction. However, international reaction was mixed. While the novel won the Pegasus Prize in 1984 and the Booker Award in 1985, critics remained skeptical. Writing in 1985 for the *New York Times,* Michiko Kakutani praises Hulme's ability to convey "the coexistence of two contrary emotions … through both action and extended monologues," while also suggesting that the novel could have benefited from some "judicious pruning." Others criticized the novel's depiction of child abuse as disturbing and overly graphic, a charge famously reported as the reason for Booker judge Joanna Lumley's vehement objection to the novel's win.

The Bone People has been regarded as one of the first works in English to describe the contemporary Maori experience and the ways in which the loss of traditional cultural identity affects communities, families, and individuals. Robert Ross, in a 1986 review for *World Literature Today,* writes that Hulme "dramatically" introduces postcolonial themes, long present in African and other developing literatures, "into the New Zealand tradition." The novel also sparked an ongoing debate about what constitutes "Maori" literature, with critics such as C. K. Stead questioning the degree to which Hulme's novel, and Hulme herself, can be fairly classified as Maori.

Maori bone pendant from New Zealand. Keri Hulme's novel *The Bone People* incorporates the mythology of the Maori, people native to New Zealand. WERNER FORMAN/ART RESOURCE, NY.

as a supernormal Christ figure." For Fox, Hulme's project is not merely to talk about postcolonial problems of dispossession and the destruction of families; she also "extend[s] her themes into a more general healing of humanity at large. She is not interested simply in reviving the glory of her tribal patrimony. She wants to unite us all."

BIBLIOGRAPHY

Sources

Fox, Stephen D. "Keri Hulme's *The Bone People*: The Problem of Beneficial Child Abuse." *Journal of Evolutionary Psychology* (2003): 40–54. *Literature Resource Center.* Web. 30 Sep. 2012.

Hulme, Keri. *The Bone People.* Baton Rouge: Louisiana State UP, 1985. Print.

———. "Mauri: An Introduction to Bicultural Poetry in New Zealand." *Only Connect: Literary Perspectives East and West.* Ed. Guy Amirthanayagam and S. C. Harrex. Adelaide: Centre for Research in the New Literatures in English, 1981. 290–310. Print.

Kakutani, Michiko. Rev. of *The Bone People,* by Keri Hulme. *New York Times.* The New York Times Company, 13 Nov. 1985. Web. 30 Sept. 2012.

Mercer, Erin. "'Frae Ghosties an Ghoulies Deliver Us': Keri Hulme's *The Bone People* and the Bicultural Gothic." *JNZL* 27 (2009): 111–30. *Literature Resource Center.* Web. 30 Sept. 2012.

Ross, Robert L. Rev. of *The Bone People,* by Keri Hulme. *World Literature Today* 60.2 (1986): 363. *Literature Resource Center.* Web. 30 Sept. 2012.

Further Reading

Barker, Clare. "From Narrative Prosthesis to Disability Counternarrative: Reading the Politics of Difference in *Potiki* and *The Bone People*." *JNZL* 24.1 (2006): 130. *Literature Resource Center.* Web. 1 Oct. 2012.

Covi, Giovanna. "Keri Hulme's *The Bone People*: A Critique of Gender." *Imagination and the Creative Impulse in the New Literatures in English.* Ed. M-.T. Bindella and G. V. Davis. Rodopi, 1993. 219–31. *Literature Resource Center.* Web. 1 Oct. 2012.

Duff, Alan. *Once Were Warriors.* Auckland Tandem, 1990. Print.

Stachurski, Christine. *Reading Pakeha?: Fiction and Identity in Aotearoa New Zealand.* Amsterdam: Rodopi, 2009. Print.

Stead, C. K. "Keri Hulme's *The Bone People,* and the Pegasus Award for Literature." *Ariel* 16.4 (1985): 102. Print.

Daisy Gard

Questions about the cultural point of view from which Hulme operates have provided a way to approach the text, and scholars have taken up genre tropes and bicultural allusions to examine the unique ways these function in *The Bone People*. In a 2009 essay for *JNZL,* Erin Mercer explores the novel as a "bicultural gothic" text that "advances an understanding of how the mode operates in a postcolonial society by moving beyond such categories as 'settler Gothic' or 'indigenous' … identifying potential disharmony and disjuncture within a bicultural framework." Similarly, Stephen Fox, in a 2003 essay for *Journal of Evolutionary Psychology,* elucidates the manner in which Simon Gillayley as an abused child "displays the forces of the Maori life principle 'mauri'" and "functions just as easily

CRY, THE BELOVED COUNTRY

Alan Paton

OVERVIEW

Published in 1948, the novel *Cry, the Beloved Country* by Alan Paton details the trials of a black family struggling against the social system of South Africa. Written in simple, concise language, the novel tells the story of Stephen Kumalo, a small-town black preacher who goes to Johannesburg to care for his ailing sister. While there, he finds that his sister has fallen into a life of prostitution and his son has been accused of killing a white man, Arthur Jarvis. Contrasting the experiences of the Kumalo family with those of the Jarvises, Paton's novel calls into question a society that treats blacks and whites so differently, serving as a bleak reminder of the problematic political structure that would produce apartheid in 1948.

Cry, the Beloved Country enjoyed immense success upon its publication, making Paton a best-selling author worldwide. The success of the novel made him the voice of antiapartheid literature, as the novel details the important historical moment when apartheid was becoming law in South Africa. During apartheid, blacks faced increased racial tensions and cultural disintegration, especially as many left life in rural villages to move to the city. For some, Paton's identity as a white author complicated his ability to accurately portray the plight of blacks during this tumultuous period. Nevertheless, the novel continues to be noteworthy as a simple, honest portrayal of one man's attempt to help his family—and his culture—to survive in the rapidly changing environment of South Africa on the cusp of apartheid.

HISTORICAL AND LITERARY CONTEXT

Cry, the Beloved Country addresses the black experience of South African society in the 1940s. At that time, white South Africans were less than sympathetic to the troubles of the black population. Most supporters of segregation, such as South African statesman and prime minister Jan Smuts, believed that separation by race not only preserved the white Afrikaner culture but also benefited the black population, which was believed to be an inferior race and therefore in need of guidance and policing by white government.

In 1948, when *Cry, the Beloved Country* was first published, the National Party introduced the policy of apartheid, or forced segregation based upon race. Although segregation was not new to the country, the institution of segregation laws exacerbated the

separation of the races. South African citizens were given racial designations (native, white, colored, or Asian/ Indian), and strict lines of segregation were drawn in order to separate neighborhoods. Black South Africans were sometimes removed from their homes and forced into black-designated areas. They were given passbooks, which they were required to show in order to enter into white neighborhoods, usually for work-related reasons.

Before the implementation of apartheid, South African literature mainly reflected the colonial experience of white Afrikaners. Depictions of black characters were often unsympathetic and even hostile. *The Story of an African Farm* (1883) by Olive Schreiner, which is considered the genesis of white South African literature, focuses on the rural life of white farmers but ignores the presence of black South Africans. Increasingly, white writers began to question this depiction— or lack thereof—of race relations. *Mine Boy* (1946) by Peter Abrahams, a mixed-race author, deals with the black struggle in a white urban environment, and his next book, *The Path of Thunder* (1948), broaches the subject of interracial romance. White writer Herman Charles Bosman addresses the complex preapartheid social structure from the Afrikaner point of view, often infusing his brutal honesty with irony, satire, and wit. The simple style of his prose and his treatment of Afrikaner culture, particularly in his 1947 collection of stories *Mafeking Road*, may have influenced Paton's novel.

Cry, the Beloved Country was met with mixed reviews in Paton's home country for its strong criticism of Afrikaners and the South African ruling party. However, following its success in the United States, the novel quickly became a worldwide best seller. The legacy of the novel is evident in the works of African writers who followed Paton's example. Authors such as Nadine Gordimer and J. M. Coetzee have shed light on the complex political environment of South Africa in works such as Gordimer's *July's People* (1981) and Coetzee's *Boyhood: Scenes from Provincial Life* (1997). In addition, popular culture has embraced Paton's novel, which was adapted into two movies (in 1951 and 1995) and was selected for Oprah Winfrey's book club.

THEMES AND STYLE

The primary theme of *Cry, the Beloved Country* is the cycle of injustice faced by the black population in segregated South Africa. Forced from their lands for

+ *Key Facts*

Time Period:
Mid-20th Century

Genre:
Novel

Events:
Introduction of apartheid; institutionalization of racism in South Africa

Nationality:
South African

ALAN PATON: SOUTH AFRICAN AUTHOR

Alan Paton, author of more than a dozen novels, often wrote about the problematic race relations and turbulent political climate of South Africa. His novel *Too Late the Phalarope* (1953) revisits themes familiar to readers of *Cry, the Beloved Country.* The novel's plot focuses on a white Afrikaner who faces tragedy after he breaks the law by having an affair with a black girl. Through the story, Paton questions the morality of racial segregation and the legality of apartheid in a civilized and largely Christian country.

In 1989, one year following Paton's death, a collection of his essays, mainly short newspaper pieces, was published in a book called *Save the Beloved Country.* The text offers Paton's opinions of the current political landscape of his home country. He writes of major political figures from Jan Smuts to Nelson Mandela to Desmond Tutu, often criticizing the kind of nationalism and activism that has been prevalent in South Africa. The book, which followed a lifetime of political writing for Paton, was well received, though most critics agreed that it was more useful to read it as a work by an important South African writer than as a political treatise.

economic reasons and separated from their native culture, they find the once-attractive urban lifestyle to be unwelcoming and harsh, with rampant crime and racial injustice. In the opening of the book, the narrator implores South Africans to care for the land and warns, "destroy it and man is destroyed." The words prove to be prophetic as the young blacks who leave to make a new life in the city ultimately become "children [who] break the law" because "the white man has broken the tribe." Kumalo, too, finds his family disintegrating as a result of the new social order, as his sister and son both become involved in crime. Through Kumalo's family's experiences, Paton suggests that South Africa is not the civilized Christian country it pretends to be; rather the country's divisive politics are destroying the fabric of the nation.

Rhetorically, Paton communicates this message by contrasting South Africa's natural beauty with the violent and crime-filled narrative. He describes a countryside that is "lovely" with "grass-covered and rolling" hills and "rich and matted" grass. By contrast, Claremont, a black township, is a "garbage-heap" with "liquor running in the streets." Such descriptions are repeated throughout the book to emphasize the difference between the conditions in which whites and blacks live. Although both groups share the same land, the black land, Kumalo's home, is "desolate" with "the earth torn away like flesh"; it produces little, forcing the youth to move to the cities to make a living. The Jarvis farm, indicative of the white way of life, is "well tended" and "one of the finest farms." As the narrative

shifts between white and black characters, the novel suggests that although the two groups share a homeland, they are deeply divided by the conditions in which they live.

Paton's novel is marked by its simple, unpretentious prose, which is appropriate for a man like Kumalo from a rural area. At the same time, Paton incorporates the language of the King James Bible and Christian imagery in order to depict the incongruity of a Christian society that tolerates injustice. In addition, South African slang, both in Zulu and Afrikaans, appears throughout the text. For example, Kumalo is called *umfundisi,* instead of preacher or pastor, and the grasslands are referred to using the Afrikaans word *veld.* Paton uses this dialect to achieve more than just local color: the language, which is of mixed origin, suggests that blacks' and whites' contributions to South African culture are equally important and cannot be separated.

CRITICAL DISCUSSION

Cry, the Beloved Country received mixed reviews in South Africa for its bold criticism of Afrikaners and South African political leadership. Nevertheless, the novel made Paton an international literary celebrity. In the United States, the book was declared an instant classic. In a 1949 review for *International Review of Mission,* Elsie Fox calls it "a book which everyone should read for his own enlightenment." In 1951 *Cry, the Beloved Country* was adapted into a film starring Canada Lee and Sidney Poitier, catapulting the book to further international renown. A 1951 review of the film in *Ebony* calls the book "an astringent commentary on South Africa's smouldering racial situation," noting that South Africa's black population would most likely not be permitted to see the film. The review also discusses the "basically Christian message" of Paton's book, commenting that it would "arouse both praise and fury."

Paton's novel has come to be regarded as the premier preapartheid text to emerge from South Africa. It stands as a warning of what civilized cultures are capable of if the subject of race relations is neglected. Readers have sympathized with the trials Kumalo faces in an unjust and segregated society and have connected with his struggle and his hopes to keep his family intact. Even so, critics have questioned Paton's ability as a white writer to accurately detail the struggles of a black man during apartheid. African literary critic Ezekiel Mphahlele, in a 1964 essay published in the *Proceedings of the First International Congress of Africanists,* examines the relationship between Paton's race and his ability to identify with his black characters. Mphahlele concludes that white writers, though they may sympathize with their black characters, "are on the white side of the colour line."

Cry, the Beloved Country is Paton's most discussed work among literary critics, particularly with respect to its status as an antiapartheid text. Not surprisingly,

Film still from the 1995 adaptation of *Cry, the Beloved Country*, starring Richard Harris (left) and James Earl Jones. VIDEOVISION/MIRAMAX/DISTANT HORIZONS/THE KOBAL COLLECTION/ART RESOURCE, NY.

modern critics have read the novel as a study in race relations in preapartheid South Africa. Gordimer, as a white South African author, notes that white authors have a unique way of writing about their country, especially when describing the land. According to Gordimer, Paton fills his novel with descriptions of the countryside of South Africa because "whites are always having to assert their claim on the land" while "blacks take the land for granted, it's simply there." Thus, the language of Paton's novel, as well as the plot, reveals an ongoing struggle for ownership of South Africa.

BIBLIOGRAPHY

Sources

Bazin, Nancy Topping, and Marilyn Dallman Seymour, eds. *Conversations with Nadine Gordimer*. Jackson: UP of Mississippi, 1990. Print.

Rev. of *Cry, the Beloved Country*, dir. Zoltan Korda. *Ebony* 6.9 (1951): 57. *MasterFILE Premier*. Web. 15 Aug. 2012.

Fox, Elsie. "*Cry, the Beloved Country*: A Story of Comfort in Desolation." Rev. of *Cry, the Beloved Country*, by Alan Paton. *International Review of Mission* 38.149 (1949): 130–31. *ATLA Religion Database*. Web. 15 Aug. 2012.

Mphahlele, Ezekiel. "African Literature." *The Proceedings of the First International Congress of Africanists*. Ed. Lalage Bown and Michael Crowder. London: Longmans, 1964. 220–32. Print.

Paton, Alan. *Cry, the Beloved Country*. New York: Scribner's, 1948. Print.

———. *Save the Beloved Country*. New York: Scribner's, 1989. Print.

Further Reading

Bloom, Harold, ed. *Alan Paton's* Cry, the Beloved Country. Philadelphia: Chelsea, 2004. Print.

Bryfonski, Dedria. *Race Relations in Alan Paton's* Cry, the Beloved Country. Detroit, MI: Greenhaven, 2009. Print.

Callan, Edward. *Cry, the Beloved Country: A Novel of South Africa*. Boston: Twayne, 1991. Print.

Chiwengo, Ngwarsungu. *Understanding* Cry, the Beloved Country: *A Student Casebook to Issues, Sources, and Historical Documents*. Westport, CT: Greenwood, 2007. Print.

Coetzee, J. M. "South African Liberals: Alan Paton, Helen Suzman." *Stranger Shores: Literary Essays, 1986–1999*. New York: Viking, 2001. 261–71. Print.

Van der Vlies, A. "'Local' Writing, 'Global' Reading, and the Demands of the 'Canon': The Case of Alan Paton's *Cry, the Beloved Country*." *South African Historical Journal* 55.1 (2006): 20–32. *Arts & Humanities Citation Index*. Web. 15 Aug. 2012.

Media Adaptations

Cry, the Beloved Country. Dir. Zoltan Korda. Perf. Canada Lee, Sidney Poitier, and Charles Carson. London Film Productions, 1951. Film.

Cry, the Beloved Country. Dir. Darrell Roodt. Perf. Richard Harris, James Earl Jones, and Tsholofelo Wechoemang. Mirimax Films. 1995. Film.

Lisa Kroger

THE GREAT SCOURGE AND HOW TO END IT

Christabel Pankhurst

✣ *Key Facts*

Time Period:
Early 20th Century

Genre:
Pamphlet

Events:
Women's suffrage
movement in England;
foundation of the
National Union of
Woman Suffrage
Societies (NUWSS),
followed by the more
radical Women's Social
and Political Union
(WSPU); formation of the
1912 Royal Commission
to investigate venereal
disease

Nationality:
English

OVERVIEW

The Great Scourge and How to End It, a pamphlet written by militant suffragist Christabel Pankhurst and published in 1913, is an exposé on venereal disease in Britain. Presenting venereal disease, the "great scourge," as the harbinger of society's destruction, Pankhurst declares that the rampant spread of sexually transmitted maladies is caused by men who refuse to curb their sexual appetites. Using contemporary medical data as empirical proof, she contends that the vast majority of the male population is infected with venereal disease due to frequent contact with prostitutes, and these men are subsequently transmitting the diseases to their wives. Pankhurst argues that until women have the right to vote, they will continue to be subjected to sexual exploitation by men and the scourge will rage on. Denouncing male sexual behavior, she proposes a simple but radical solution: "Votes for women and chastity for men."

Initially published as a series of articles in the weekly newsletter the *Suffragette, The Great Scourge* received mixed reviews. Pankhurst's treatment of the controversial subject prompted discussion among British and international audiences. Believing women to be morally superior to men, Pankhurst, who earned a law degree in 1906 but was not allowed to practice because she was a woman, stresses sexual purity as a means of securing emancipation, which was the dominant view held by most educated women of the time. Other radical freethinkers challenged Pankhurst's sexual puritanism, arguing instead for sexual freedom. The diverse reactions to *The Great Scourge* reveal the heated debates about sexuality that were occurring among women in the late stages of the suffragist movement. Pankhurst's polemic remains a subject of feminist discourse, although it is occasionally misunderstood as a medical text by uninformed readers.

HISTORICAL AND LITERARY CONTEXT

The feminist movement in Great Britain began with Mary Wollstonecraft's pioneering work *A Vindication of the Rights of Woman* (1792). During the 1830s and 1840s, the Chartists, unsuccessful champions of human rights, significantly aided and encouraged suffragism. In subsequent years, a string of male liberal legislators kept the suffrage issue before the British public. In 1865 philosopher, economist, and political theorist John Stuart Mill cofounded the first British suffrage association. Despite strong opposition from Queen Victoria and prime ministers William Gladstone and Benjamin Disraeli, the suffrage movement acquired momentum when several feminist groups formed the National Union of Woman Suffrage Societies (NUWSS) in 1897. Pankhurst later joined the NUWSS and the Independent Labour Party in 1901.

By the time Pankhurst wrote *The Great Scourge,* she had earned a reputation for militancy in the fight for women's suffrage and was in exile in Paris. In 1910 she fled to France to avoid arrest for engaging in increasingly violent actions with the Women's Social and Political Union (WSPU). However, she continued to direct the radical activities of the WSPU from Paris and to write a stream of suffragist propaganda that was published in the WSPU's newsletter, the *Suffragette.* She composed the series of articles that eventually became *The Great Scourge* shortly after the formation of the 1912 Royal Commission, which was created to investigate the subject of venereal disease. At the time, the militant campaign against the sexual double standard found renewed energy when the feminist intent behind the Criminal Law Amendment Bill of 1912 was purposefully corrupted by lawmakers and enforcers.

The Great Scourge is similar to other publications of the time. The polemic is akin to Louisa Martindale's pamphlet, *Under the Surface* (1908), the first feminist text devoted solely to venereal disease. Commissioned by the NUWSS, Martindale's tract quotes eminent physicians on the harmlessness of male celibacy, describes the various effects of venereal disease, links prostitution with the spread of venereal disease, and argues for women's right to vote in order to rid the world of prostitution. In *The Real Facts of Life* (1994), author Margaret Jackson writes that *The Great Scourge* "shared many features of the emerging feminist model of sexuality articulated by [feminists Elizabeth] Blackwell, [Elizabeth] Wolstenholme Elmy, [Frances] Swiney, and many of the contributors to the debates in [the journal] *The Freewoman.*"

The Great Scourge is one of the most well known and controversial tracts produced during the prewar suffrage movement. With the outbreak of World War I in 1914, Pankhurst ceased her militant activities and returned to England in order to concentrate her energies on supporting the war effort. In October 1915 the WSPU changed its newsletter's name from the *Suffragette* to *Britannia*, reflecting the group's patriotic shift in focus. When the war ended in 1918, women over the age of thirty who met certain requirements received the right to vote in Britain. In 1928 voting rights became equal for men and women. Today *The Great Scourge* and Pankhurst's radical voice reverberating within the feminist movement are credited with helping British women receive the right to vote, an achievement that echoes throughout modern feminism.

THEMES AND STYLE

Central to *The Great Scourge* is the argument against the double standard of sexual morality. Seeing women as morally superior to men, Pankhurst is convinced that "there can be no mating between the spiritually developed women of this new day and men who in thought and conduct with regard to sex matters are their inferiors." Cautioning wives about the danger of contracting venereal disease from their unfaithful husbands, she insists on the need to control male sexual behavior: "Self control for men who can exert it! Medical aid for those who cannot!" However, she warns against a "reliance upon remedies as a substitute for clean living," insisting that "the way of purity" is the only true cure for gonorrhea and syphilis. She states that the elimination of prostitution is essential to ending the scourge but can only be achieved when women have the right to vote. She argues that men want to limit the vote because of their innate promiscuity: "The opponents of votes for women know that women, when they are politically free and economically strong, will not be purchasable for the base uses of vice. Those who want to have women as slaves, obviously do not want women to become voters."

Pankhurst's carefully crafted tract achieves its rhetorical effect by inverting the medical discourse that dominated many antisuffrage arguments appearing in newspapers at the time. Although the medical profession recognized men as the cause of venereal disease within the home, it still chiefly placed blame on women, believing that the diseases originated with prostitutes and were passed on by mothers to their offspring. Pankhurst declares, "Doctors [are at last] breaking through the secrecies and traditions of long years and sounding the note of alarm." Quoting extensively from American and British physicians to support her argument about rampant male sexual immorality, she claims that 75 to 80 percent of men are infected with gonorrhea and "a considerable percentage" carry syphilis. With the authority of the male-dominated medical community behind her, she argues that men are destroying the nation: "Men whose will-power fails them are constantly infecting and reinfecting the race with vile disease, and so bringing about the downfall of a nation!"

The Great Scourge is simultaneously rational and sensational in tone. Steering clear of melodramatic narratives and a romanticized discussion of sexuality, Pankhurst draws on various medical statistics to bolster her arguments. The careful citation of scientific data gives the text a tone of objectivity. Although Pankhurst was criticized for allegedly exaggerating scientific data, the sensational nature of the text is best attributed to her bold and unflinching treatment of sexuality. For example, she frankly discusses the topic of nocturnal emissions and claims semen may "be easily gotten rid of by an involuntary emission during sleep once or twice a month, a state of things which is perfectly natural." She describes operations in which "the sex organs have to be removed by the surgeon's knife" and refers to "the secretion of the testicles … as the poisonous fangs of venomous reptiles." By boldly discussing the taboo subject of sexuality, she endeavors to shock her readers.

CRITICAL DISCUSSION

The Great Scourge received both enthusiastic and negative reactions from readers. In letters published in the *Suffragette* in 1914, several doctors praise Pankhurst for her open discussion of venereal disease. According to Janet Lyon in *Manifestoes: Provocations of the Modern* (1999), Jean Finot reviewed Pankhurst's pamphlet in *La Revue de Paris*, describing it as "an exceedingly passionate and unusual book, despite a surfeit of feminist propaganda." Some feminists described the book as courageous but found Pankhurst's claims to be misleading, disliking the implication that all men are bad and all women are good. According to Les Garner in *Stepping Stones to Women's Liberty* (1984), feminist Dora Marsden questions the accuracy of Pankhurst's venereal disease statistics in an article in the *Egoist* on February 2, 1914. She reasons that if the figures are accurate, then "the number of those who are free from it neither means nor matters—we are all tainted and presumably inoculated in fact." She adds, "If Miss Pankhurst desires to exploit human boredom and the ravages of dirt she will require to call in the aid of more subtle intelligence than she appears to possess." Author Lucy Bland notes in *Banishing the Beast* (2001) that feminist Rebecca West argues that Pankhurst's remarks on sex are "utterly valueless and likely to discredit the cause in which we believe."

Although *The Great Scourge* provoked significant discourse at the time of its publication, it was soon forgotten because of World War I. Garner contends, "the interests of women were submerged beneath the interests of the nation." After women over the age of thirty were enfranchised, Pankhurst ran for office in the 1918 general election as a Women's Party candidate and was narrowly defeated by the Labor party candidate. Eschewing politics, she moved to the United States in 1921 and became a prominent member of the Second Adventist movement. Many scholars are confused by this period of her life and regard her dedication to evangelizing as a rejection of her earlier feminism. However, author Timothy Larsen argues in *Christabel*

PRIMARY SOURCE

EXCERPT FROM *THE GREAT SCOURGE AND HOW TO END IT*

It did not need the doctors' manifesto to warn the more instructed amongst women that prostitution and the diseases caused by it are a menace to themselves and their children. But vast numbers of women are still without this knowledge. Innocent wives are infected by their husbands. They suffer torments; their health is ruined; their power to become mothers is destroyed, or else they become the mothers of diseased, crippled, blind, or insane children. But they are not told the reason of all this. Their doctor and their husband keep them in ignorance, so that they cannot even protect themselves from future danger.

Healthy girls enter into marriage without the smallest idea of the risk they are incurring. Nobody tells them, as Dr. John W. Barrett tells us in his article in the *Bedrock,* the scientific review, that 'we know, from very careful insurance medical records, that the great majority of men put themselves in the way of infection before marriage.'

Those who read this statement will have their minds prepared to receive the further appalling statement, widely accepted by medical authorities, that 75 per cent to 80 per cent of men have before marriage been infected with one form of venereal disease. Some of these men may seem to be cured, but we have seen how little cure in this connection means. Very sad cases are on record of men who marry when apparently cured, and yet infect their wife. It is therefore hardly too much to say that out of every four men there is only one who can marry without risk to his bride.

Such facts are terrible indeed, and the sooner they are grasped the better for the individual and for the race.

Even after marriage, danger arises over and over again unless the husband abstains from immoral acts. In future chapters we shall show more fully what venereal disease means to a woman.

We may point out in passing that prostitution and its evils are largely a medical question, and must be dealt with by medical men. Prison doctors administer medicine which keeps under control the 'human nature' of men prisoners who have no natural self-control. Apart from that, to instruct men in sex hygiene is the doctors' primary duty.

It would indeed be an extraordinary thing if the medical profession, which has discovered means of regulating every other bodily function, should be unable to tell men how to regulate the sex function, and to prevent that excessive sex activity which, as they themselves admit, is fatal to the health of the race. …

The belief that women are naturally weak is the greatest of all delusions. It is true that many women's strength is now, owing to artificial causes, less than it ought naturally to be, but these artificial causes must be done away with. One of them is, as we have already shown, the great prevalence of sexual disease, which directly attacks the sexual health and vitality of women. Want of exercise, unhygienic dress, and other such circumstances contribute to make a great many women weaker than they are by nature.

Yet, even as things are today, we find women, in addition to bringing children into the world, doing some of the hardest and most unremitting toil. It is only when the question of wage-earning arises,

Pankhurst: Fundamentalism and Feminism in Coalition (2002) that Pankhurst did not disavow her feminism but maintained it by becoming enormously successful in the male-dominated Christian fundamentalist movement. He also contends that many of the purity arguments she employs in *The Great Scourge* prove that she already had Christian beliefs before she moved to the United States.

Modern scholars regard *The Great Scourge* as a window into later years of suffragism. The text provides perspective on the militant contingency of the feminist movement and debates about sexuality. Lyon writes, "*The Great Scourge* offered one blueprint of the reconfiguration of gender and sexuality within the pre-war avant-garde." Jackson contends that the polemic

is a critique of human nature "and the notion that men's sexual needs were natural … Pankhurst poured scorn on the theory that prostitution was necessary and inevitable." In *The Militant Suffrage Movement* (2003), Laura E. Nym Mayhall notes that Pankhurst's articles "defined women's political disabilities in sexual terms … Pankhurst narrated *The Great Scourge* through the metaphor of slavery, making a sensationalist and separatist argument about the consequences of sexual slavery for women." Garner suggests Pankhurst wrote the sensational polemic to revive the flagging WSPU: "*The Great Scourge,* and the 'Moral Crusade' of which it was a part, perhaps reflected the political bankruptcy of Christabel Pankhurst and the militant campaign."

or when women claim the right to be active in the higher fields of human activity, that it is argued that maternity unfits them for equality with men.

We repeat, then, that for women to establish their freedom and equality with men, apart from any question of maternity and sex, is a necessary step towards the abolition of prostitution. It is largely because men have been too much persuaded of women's unlikeness to themselves, that they have wanted to put and keep them in subjection and exploit them for purposes of vice. For the abolition of prostitution, it is necessary that men shall hold women in honour, not only as mothers, but as human beings, who are like and equal unto themselves.

Another aspect of the problem is economic. More and more women are becoming persuaded of the fact that, both in marriage and out of it, they must be economically independent, and that there must be no question of living by the sale of sex. For sex is degraded by any hint of sale or barter. …

In the opinion of the Suffragettes sex is too big and too sacred thing to be treated lightly. Moreover, both the physical and spiritual consequences of a sex union are so important, so far-reaching, and so lasting, that intelligent and independent women will enter into such union only after deep consideration, and only when a great love and a great confidence are present.

And here we may, perhaps, deal with the statement made by some men, that women suffer who are not mated with men, and that what they are pleased to term 'the unsatisfied desires' of women are a problem. Now, in the old days when marriage was the only career open to women, those who did not marry

regarded themselves, and were regarded, as failures—just as a lawyer might who never got a brief, as a doctor might who never got a customer. But nowadays the unmarried women have a life full of joy and interest. They are not mothers of children of their flesh, but they can serve humanity, they can do work that is useful or beautiful. Therefore their life is complete. If they find a man worthy of them, a man fit physically and morally to be their husband, then they are ready to marry, but they will not let desire, apart from love and reason, dominate their life or dictate their action.

It is very often said to women that their ideas of chastity are the result of past subjection. Supposing that were so, then women have the satisfaction of knowing that their subjection has brought them at least one great gain—a gain they will not surrender when the days of their subjection are over. The mastery of self and sex, which either by nature or by training women have, they will not yield up.

Warned by the evils which the tyranny of sex has produced where men are concerned, women have no intention of letting matter triumph over mind, and the body triumph over the spirit, in their case.

This being the point of view of the Suffragettes, the most modern of all modern women, it will be seen that out of the present impasse in sex matters, there is only one way—chastity for men, guaranteed and confirmed by the greater independence which the Vote will give to women.

SOURCE: *The Sexuality Debates,* edited by Sheila Jeffreys, pp. 337–38. Copyright © 1987. Reproduced by permission of Taylor & Francis Group, LLC. (http://www.tandfonline.com).

BIBLIOGRAPHY

Sources

Bland, Lucy. *Banishing the Beast: Feminism, Sex and Morality.* London: Tauris Parke, 2001. Print.

Garner, Les. *Stepping Stones to Women's Liberty: Feminist Ideas in the Women's Suffrage Movement 1900–1918.* Cranbury: Associated UP, 1984. Print.

Jackson, Margaret. *The Real Facts of Life: Feminism and the Politics of Sexuality c1850–1940.* London: Taylor & Francis, 1994. Print.

Lyon, Janet. *Manifestoes: Provocations of the Modern.* Ithaca: Cornell UP, 1999. Print.

Mayhall, Laura E. Nym. *The Militant Suffrage Movement: Citizenship and Resistance in Britain, 1860–1930.* Oxford: Oxford UP, 2003. Print.

Pankhurst, Christabel. "The Great Scourge and How to End It." *Suffrage and the Pankhursts.* Vol. 8. Ed. Jane Marcus. Women's Source Library. London: Routledge & Kegan Paul, 1987. 187–240. Print.

Segal, Lynn. *Straight Sex: Rethinking the Politics of Pleasure.* Berkeley: U of California P, 1994. Print.

Further Reading

Comentale, Edward P. "Thesmophoria: Suffragettes, Sympathetic Magic, and H. D.'s Ritual Poetics." *Twentieth-Century Literary Criticism.* Vol. 214. Ed. Thomas J. Schoenburg. Detroit: Gale, 2009. *Literature Resource Center.* Web. 23 Sept. 2012.

Larsen, Timothy. *Christabel Pankhurst: Fundamentalism and Feminism in Coalition.* Woodbridge: Boydell, 2002. Print.

Suffragettes Edith New and Mary Leigh following their release from prison in an 1908 illustration from *Le Petit Journal*. Fellow suffragette Christabel Pankhurst wrote of women's vulnerability to sexually transmitted diseases in *The Great Scourge* (1913). GIANNI DAGLI ORTI/THE ART ARCHIVE AT ART RESOURCE, NY.

Mitchell, David J. *Queen Christabel: A Biography of Christabel Pankhurst.* London: Macdonald and Jane, 1977. Print.

Mort, Frank. *Dangerous Sexualities: Medico-Moral Politics in England Since 1830.* London: Routledge & Kegan Paul, 1987. Print.

Pal-Lapinski, Piya. *The Exotic Woman in Nineteenth-Century British Fiction and Culture: A Reconsideration.* Lebanon: UP of New England, 2005. Print.

Pugh, Martin. *The Pankhursts: The History of One Radical Family.* London: Vintage, 2008. Print.

Rappaport, Helen. *Encyclopedia of Women Social Reformers.* Vol. 1. Santa Barbara: ABC-CLIO, 2001. Print.

Thom, Deborah. "A Lop-Sided View: Feminist History or the History of Women?" *The European Women's History Reader.* Ed. F. Montgomery. London: Routledge, 2002. 27–43. Print.

Maggie Magno

THE IMAGE, THE ICON, AND THE COVENANT

Sahar Khalifeh

OVERVIEW

Originally published in Arabic in 2002 and translated into English in 2007, *The Image, the Icon, and the Covenant* is a novel by Palestinian female author Sahar Khalifeh about the romantic relationship between a Muslim Palestinian man and a Christian woman. Written in a lyrical style with dream-like narration, the novel is set in Jerusalem and the West Bank in the mid-1960s. Palestinian Muslim schoolteacher Ibrahim falls in love with Christian Mariam while he is working in Ramallah, a small village in rural Jordan. After discovering that Mariam is pregnant, however, he flees the village, allowing himself to be seduced by the revolutionary fervor of the West Bank, rather than face the complications presented by his relationship with Mariam. Upon his return thirty years later, he is forced to face the reality of the growing Palestinian-Israeli conflict. Against the backdrop of the male-dominated Middle East, Khalifeh achieves a powerful portrayal of the unequal gender roles in Palestine and brings to light the complex nature of religious tolerance and politics in the context of the Palestinian-Israeli conflict.

First published during the period known as the second intifada (2000–2005), or the Al-Aqsa intifada in Palestine, the novel received an overall positive response from journalists in the region who recognized Khalifeh's significant literary contribution to defending women's rights in Palestine. However, the text received little international acclaim. *The Image* speaks to the continued oppression of Palestinian women, whose rights have been overshadowed by the urgency of war and the idealism of the male-led revolutionary movement. Steeped in biblical symbolism, *The Image* reads as a national allegory for Palestine that historicizes the people's struggle as one filled with loss and tragedy. The significance of Khalifeh's novel is in its contribution to a growing body of feminist work about Palestine that attempts to bring the struggles of Palestinian women to the attention of a more widespread audience.

HISTORICAL AND LITERARY CONTEXT

Khalifeh wrote *The Image* after the first intifada, a Palestinian uprising against the Israeli occupation of formerly Palestinian-controlled territory that lasted from 1987 to 1993. Although the presence of Palestinian women in the struggle was not largely publicized, Khalifeh has emphasized their active participation. She writes in a 2002 essay published in *Aljadid* that during the first intifada, "Woman proved to the whole world that she was not a nonentity, but the heart, the mind, the feeling, and the living conscience of the revolution." The uprisings—as well as other regional events such as the Gulf War—helped lead to the Madrid Conference in 1991, although attempts at peace negotiations were largely unsuccessful. The ensuing 1993 Oslo Peace Accords bestowed Palestinians with limited self-rule in some parts of the territories through the establishment of the Palestinian Authority. However, as Khalifeh has explained, Palestinians felt that the Oslo negotiations were a hoax and that the peace accord ultimately contributed to continued unrest and bloodshed in the region.

The second intifada, a period of increased Palestinian-Israeli violence, was underway when *The Image* was published in Arabic in 2002. Khalifeh and other women's rights activists in the region grew increasingly disillusioned with a revolutionary movement that was unwilling to address its own internal issues, especially the continued oppression and subordination of women in Palestinian society. Prior to this time, after completing her graduate studies in the United States, Khalifeh returned to Palestine in 1988, where she continued to witness the Palestinian struggle firsthand. Since then, she has dedicated her career to defending Palestinian women's rights, helping to found the Women's Affairs Center in Nablus in the West Bank to defend women's rights in Palestine. *The Image* evinces the author's dedication to bringing international attention to the reality of Palestinian women's pivotal roles in the Palestinian-Israeli conflict and their contributions to Palestinian society, which have often been overlooked or ignored.

The work of Khalifeh has been largely influenced by that of earlier Palestinian and Arab women writers, whose writing echoes the author's own anger at the oppression of women in the Middle East. Palestinian author Raymonda Tawil had a strong impact on Khalifeh; Tawil's autobiography *My House My Prison* (1979) about her experience of house arrest in the West Bank was a source of inspiration for Khalifeh in its critical representation of the Palestinian-Israeli conflict and women's role in Middle Eastern society. The work of other outspoken women Arab writers

✢ *Key Facts*

Time Period:
Early 21st Century

Genre:
Novel

Events:
Second intifada in Palestine

Nationality:
Palestinian

PALESTINIAN WOMEN'S LITERATURE

Most literature written by Palestinian women has been published only recently because of the group's historically oppressed position in the region, where their role has been limited to the private sphere of the family and the home. Raymonda Tawil and Sahar Khalifeh are among the earliest female Palestinian writers and were neighbors in the West Bank in the late 1960s when Tawil was under house arrest. The two founded a local women's society to respond to the economic needs of displaced villagers after the invasion of 1967. Another early Palestinian female author, Soraya Antonius, born in Jerusalem before 1948, wrote two historical novels, *The Lord* (1986) and *Where the Jinn Consult* (1987), which present the events that led to the destruction of Palestine during the early twentieth century.

Critic Suha Sabbagh has identified as a common theme in Palestinian women's writing that gender conditions the individual experience of the occupation. For example, Palestinian author Samira Azzam wrote several collections of short stories after fleeing Palestine in 1948, including *Small Things* (1954) and *The Big Shadow* (1956), in which she describes the anguish of a mother and daughter who are separated by the new borders formed by the creation of the State of Israel in 1948. Recently, a younger generation of female authors has emerged in Palestine, including Samah al-Shaykh and Basima Takrouri, who bring a fresh perspective to the experience of women.

also influenced Khalifeh, including Egyptian feminist writer Nawal El Saadawi's *The Fall of the Imam* (1987), a novel that reveals the hypocrisy engrained in a patriarchal religious state. The daring nature of Lebanese writer Hanan al-Shaykh's novels, including *Women of Sand and Myrrh* (1989), which tells the story of four women coping with life under an oppressive, insular society, also inspired Khalifeh's writing.

The work of Khalifeh—who is one of the most widely read Arab women writers in the Middle East and is regarded as the first feminist Palestinian writer—has strongly influenced a new generation of Palestinian women writers who champion women's rights and gender equality within Palestine. Most notable among these are Adania Shibli, who has twice won the Young Writer's Award from the A. M. Qattan Foundation and published her first novel, *Touch*, in 2010. Khalifeh's influence spans the Middle East and is evident in the work of female Syrian writer Maha Hassan, who has been banned from publishing in Syria since 2000 and fled to France in 2004 because of threats against her life. Hassan's novel *Umbilical Cord* (2011) narrates the experiences of a young Syrian woman who finds a freedom in France that she was denied in her own country. Khalifeh has become an increasingly prominent figure in the Middle Eastern literary field because of *The Image*, which earned her a coveted Naguib Mahfouz Medal for Literature in 2006.

THEMES AND STYLE

Khalifeh's novel addresses multiple aspects of the corrupt period in Palestine between the Arab-Israeli war of 1967 (also called the Six-Day War) and the second intifada. Central to the narrative is an underlying theme of women's oppression and lack of options in contemporary Palestinian society, embodied by the experiences of Mariam, whose repressive life—dictated by Roman Catholicism and the overwhelming vigilance of her brothers—provokes her to rebel in ways that bring about her stigmatization within Palestinian society. Ibrahim recounts, "She told me her story, the story of her exile. She was a stranger in her homeland … an only girl among seven brothers, lonely amid strangers. She felt at ease only in Jerusalem, in a dark convent where she hid from the world and her family's supervision." This particular theme of repression, and the resulting desperation of Palestinian women deprived of their identity, draws the reader's attention to the plight of women in Palestine, seeking to inform a wider public of their struggle.

In *The Image*, Khalifeh combines political and religious symbolism into a story of a doomed love and tragic loss. Narrated in the first person by protagonist Ibrahim, the novel does not give Mariam her own voice; she is always in the shadow of a man, whether her lover, her father, or her brothers. Khalifeh recasts the story of the Holy Family, aligning Mariam at once with the figures of the Virgin Mary and Mary Magdalene. Mariam recalls her earlier love affair with a Brazilian priest: "I knocked at his door and confronted him, saying that Christ had Mary and I was Mary. He was surprised by my presence and what I said to him … I repeated what I had said, 'Mary Magdalene was his.'" The author portrays Mariam as a fallen woman, whose later pregnancy out of wedlock further alienates her from society. With the agency afforded a man, Ibrahim flees his life in Ramallah, while Mariam is trapped within an oppressive, patriarchal society with no alternatives.

The Image is written in lyrical prose, with Ibrahim's narration reading as if he were in a dream-like state. In the opening of the novel, the narrator states, "Jerusalem is a different city now, a city that belongs to history. But Jerusalem to me was Mariam. It was my memory, my first love, and a part of history. Today I am a man without a present, without Mariam, and without history." The countless, tragic losses that Ibrahim, Mariam, and all Palestinians have endured come through in the protagonist's melancholy tone. Thus, the novel conveys Palestine's experience of helplessness and loss while simultaneously bringing to the forefront the subordination of Palestinian women.

CRITICAL DISCUSSION

Upon its initial publication in Arabic in 2002, *The Image* received a generally positive reception from critics, who praised it as a layered and well-developed allegory of the Palestinian nation. Early Arabic reviews are unavailable in English, but according to scholar Miriam

Cooke in a 2007 article for *Contemporary Islam,* members of the Mahfouz Award Committee, which supports contemporary Arabic literature, praised the novel as a "narrative of loss *par excellence. ...* Woman's agency is deliberately obscured by the male revolutionary who seeks to liberate the plundered homeland with no success." Reviewers of the 2007 English translation, such as Hala Halim, praised the original text but criticized the translation as too literal. Halim writes in the *Journal of Palestine Studies* (2008), "In the case of *Image ...* 'fidelity' appears to have been construed as closeness to the denotative signification of the words ... the specificity of Arabic diglossia has not received much attention in the translation."

The Image, as part of Khalifeh's larger body of work, has been praised for its contribution to Palestinian and Muslim women's literature. Cooke notes, "Muslim women writers are articulating new ways of being strong religious and gendered persons. They want their readers, like the men in their stories, to come to terms with newly empowered women who live their sexuality, their sex and their religion in sometimes unexpected ways." Cooke lists Khalifeh's novel as an example of this trend, noting that "journalists deplored the lateness of this recognition [in the form of the Naguib Mahfouz Medal] for her 40-year defense of women's rights in Palestine."

Because of the novel's relatively recent publication in English, *The Image* has yet to receive much scholarly attention in the West. One issue addressed by the few extant English-language reviews is the lack of character development and the vague and confusing nature sections. A 2007 review in *Kirkus Reviews* comments that Khalifeh "skips over more than three decades, during which Ibrahim roams the world and has three failed, childless marriages, but prospers as a businessman. ... A novel about character and identity needs sharper, stronger protagonists than the blurry Ibrahim and Mariam." In a discussion of Khalifeh's general narrative approach, professor Philip Metres writes in a 2010 article for *College Literature,* "Khalifeh dispels Orientalist ... views of Palestinian society, while dramatizing the struggles for individual Palestinians to come to terms with their own existential and personal location vis-à-vis the larger Arab-Israeli conflict."

BIBLIOGRAPHY

Sources

Cooke, Miriam. "The Muslimwoman." *Contemporary Islam* 1.2 (2007): 139–54. Print.

Halim, Hala. Rev. of *The Image, the Icon, and the Covenant,* by Sahar Khalifeh. *Journal of Palestine Studies* 37.4 (2008): 85. Print.

Khalifeh, Sahar. *The Image, the Icon, and the Covenant.* Northampton: Interlink, 2008. Print.

———. "My Life, Myself, and the World." *Aljadid* 8.39 (2002): 1. Web. 1 Oct. 2012.

Rev. of *The Image, the Icon, and the Covenant,* by Sahar Khalifeh. *Kirkus Reviews* 15 Dec. 2007. Web. 3 Oct. 2012.

Metres, Philip. "Vexing Resistance, Complicating Occupation: A Contrapuntal Reading of Sahar Khalifeh's *Wild Thorns* and David Grossman's *The Smile of the Lamb.*" *College Literature* 37.1 (2010): 81–109. Print.

Further Reading

Al-Mallah, Majd Yaser, and Coeli Fitzpatrick, eds. "Sahar Khalifeh." *Twentieth-Century Arab Writers.* Detroit: Gale Cengage Learning, 2009. 131–36. Print.

Ashour, Radwa. "Palestine and Jordan." *Arab Women Writers: A Critical Reference Guide, 1873–1999.* Ed. F. Ghazoul, H. Reda-Mekdashi, and R. Ashour. Cairo: American U in Cairo P, 2008. 204–34. Print.

Bamia, Aida A. "Sahar Khalifeh: Novelist and Feminist." *Banipal* 15/16 (2002): 26. Print.

Harlow, Barbara. "Partitions and Precedents: Sahar Khalifeh and Palestinian Political Geography." *Intersections: Gender, Nation, and Community in Arab Women's Novels.* Syracuse: Syracuse UP, 2002. 113–31. Print.

Nazareth, Peter. "An Interview with Sahar Khalifeh." *Iowa Review* 11.1 (1980): 67–86. Print.

Nidal, Nazih Abu. "The Novels of Sahar Khalifeh." *Palestine-Israel Journal of Politics, Economics and Culture* 10.2 (2003): 113. Web. 1 Oct. 2012.

"Renowned Palestinian Writer Sahar Khalifeh: Men Are Not Used to Taking a Brave Look at Things That Might Hurt Their Soul." *Jordan Star* 26 Nov. 1998: n. pag. Web. 1 Oct. 2012.

Sabbagh, Suha. "An Interview with Sahar Khalifeh, Feminist Novelist." *Palestinian Women of Gaza and the West Bank.* Ed. Suha Sabbagh. Bloomington: Indiana UP, 1998. 136–44. Print.

———. "Palestinian Women Writers and the Intifada." *Social Text* 22 (1989): 62–78. Print.

Katrina White

Palestinian Christian women attend an Easter service in Gaza City, Gaza Strip, Palestinian Territory. © ZUMA PRESS, INC./ALAMY.

INFANTS OF THE SPRING

Wallace Thurman

✥ Key Facts

Time Period:
Mid-20th Century

Genre:
Novel

Events:
Harlem Renaissance

Nationality:
American

OVERVIEW

Infants of the Spring, published in 1932, is a satirical novel written by a radical figure of the Harlem Renaissance, Wallace Thurman. Thurman portrays Harlem Renaissance artists and writers as dependent on white privilege for recognition and living under the searing lights of the "white spotlight," a motif that signifies the gaze of whites, which he conflates with the public gaze. It is the blinding light of publicity that brings about the downfall of the characters residing in Niggerati Manor, the Harlem house in which Raymond, an African American writer and in many ways a stand-in for Thurman himself, lives with a group of black artists, all of whom are expected to represent their race through their art. Thus, this art is racial propaganda that, in Thurman's eyes, contaminates the purity of aestheticism. Paradoxically, it is the only avenue by which blacks of the Harlem Renaissance world of *Infants* can gain recognition for their work.

Infants of the Spring was published two years before Thurman died of tuberculosis at the age of thirty-two, by which time he was penniless and had become a somewhat marginalized figure. *Infants* did not gain the recognition of his 1929 novel *The Blacker the Berry: A Novel of Negro Life.* In a review of *Infants* written by the author himself in 1932, Thurman calls the harshly critical public reception of his work as "prejudiced" and "myopic." Through the character of Raymond, Thurman eschews propaganda, although the work itself is an act of propaganda calling for the New Negro Movement's forward march. Today, critics and scholars recognize *Infants* as a satire that mocks the conventions of the Harlem Renaissance and rails for an end to racism from within and outside of the African American community.

HISTORICAL AND LITERARY CONTEXT

The Harlem Renaissance flourished between World War I and II, from about 1919 until 1940. The movement was a fertile time for African Americans within the realms of literature and the arts, beginning with W. E. B. Du Bois's First Pan-African Congress in 1919 and fading in 1940 with the publication of Langston Hughes's *The Big Sea* and Claude McKay's *Harlem: Negro Metropolis.* Much of the world in this period was witnessing "anticolonial and cultural nationalist movements" in full swing, according to Harlem Renaissance expert George Hutchinson in *The Cambridge Companion to the Harlem Renaissance* (2007): "Seen from an international perspective the Harlem Renaissance was part of a global phenomenon in which cultural nationalisms … were mobilized against imperialisms." It was a variegated movement, with occasionally conflicting agendas from its divergent voices, that cannot be summarized with a single statement, other than calling for an end to segregation laws. Major writers of the movement included Zora Neale Hurston, James Weldon Johnson, and Countee Cullen.

Despite the Great Depression that had settled over the United States, by 1932 African American artists and writers centered in the vibrant Harlem neighborhood of New York City had reached a critical mass in which their works reached a wide audience that was newly educated and self-aware of their position in the fast-changing cultural landscape of the United States. Among Thurman's influences were Jean Toomer, a writer of a mixed-race background and the author of the classic *Cane* (1923), and H. L. Mencken, a white satirical journalist and cultural critic. By the time he wrote *Infants,* Thurman had launched two literary journals, *Harlem* and *Fire!!;* the latter was influenced greatly by Thurman's friend Hughes, who also contributed to it. Other contributors to *Fire!!* were Thurman's friends Hurston, author of *Their Eyes Were Watching God* (1937), and Arna Bontemps, writer of *God Sends Sunday* (1931).

Thurman, publishing his work as both a gay man and an African American who faced discrimination within his own community due to his dark skin tone, exhorted African American rights. But beyond that, *Infants* is a work of propaganda that demands an end to discrimination within the black community while at the same time calling for reforms within the Harlem Renaissance. According to J. Martin Favor in his essay in *The Cambridge Companion to the Harlem Renaissance,* Thurman disliked the "dangerously faddish, superficial, and intellectually suspect [character] of the Harlem Renaissance and its leaders" and sought greater authenticity and radicalism within the movement.

Infants is a work of propaganda because it serves both an artistic and a political purpose; its satiric narrative calls on African Americans to use the agency they already possess to lessen their dependence on the white community for acknowledgement, patronage, and praise of their work. Hughes, a literary giant of the time known for his activism, plays, novels, and poems, always supported Thurman's work and was one of the only Harlem Renaissance figures to comment on *Infants* positively.

THEMES AND STYLE

Thurman portrays the Harlem Renaissance in *Infants of the Spring* as a failed attempt on the part of black artists to create quality art for art's sake—or "pure" art divorced from propaganda. This is evinced most saliently and thematically in Paul—one of the inhabitants of Niggerati Manor and an openly gay, African American artist who refuses to create art as propaganda and who commits suicide at the close of the novel. As a work of propaganda, *Infants* calls for pure art divorced from propaganda. In Thurman's purview, the African American artists in his novel are doomed to failure. Furthermore, they lack the ability to manage their own lives in the process of their half-hearted artistic efforts.

In this roman à clef, the characters are thinly veiled caricatures of real members of the Harlem Renaissance. Dr. Parkes is a stand-in for Alain Locke, an intellectual leader of what he called "the New Negro" movement. Real-life Harlem YMCA art instructor Rex Goreleigh appears as Pelham Gaylord, both of whom are accused of rape; William Service Bell, described by critic Eleonore van Notten as "a black vocalist with a revulsion for black music" becomes Eustace Savoy; and the character of Lucille is modeled on Thurman's wife, Louise Thompson. The novel's meandering episodes of raucous parties shows that little work gets done in the manor. Finally, Paul's tragic and bizarre suicide, foreshadowed in a conversation between Raymond and his friend Lucille, is Thurman's comment on the Harlem Renaissance's wasted opportunity to make good on the promise of socially responsible, politically active art.

Much of the novel consists of dialogue among the residents and visitors of Niggerati Manor, which illuminates the conflicts of African American artists both within and outside the Harlem community. The actions of many of the characters are desperate and wanton, from Paul's suicide to Pelham's desperate sexual desire for a minor living upstairs. Dr. Parkes—the stand-in for Locke—functions as something of an antagonist in the lives of these artists when he exhorts the members of Niggerati Manor to start a social movement of African Americans. He tells them to go "back to your racial roots, and [cultivate] a healthy paganism based on African traditions." In response, Raymond can barely "suppress a snort," as he imagines "Keats, fingers on a typewriter, mind frantically conjuring African scenes." Raymond finds the idea of Africanist propaganda melded with art to be absurd and inauthentic.

CRITICAL DISCUSSION

Infants did not receive much praise upon its publication. Martha Gruening wrote one of the few positive reviews of *Infants* in the *Saturday Review of Literature,*

WALLACE THURMAN: A DYNAMIC LIFE

Wallace Thurman was born in Salt Lake City, Utah, in 1902. Despite being an avid reader, his education was sporadic in his younger years due to poor health, and half-hearted in his later years, when he attended the University of Utah as a premed student. He transferred to the University of Southern California to study journalism, but he never earned a college degree. He wrote for numerous papers and worked as an editor, a writer, and a publisher for the duration of his short career. Thurman was an alcoholic, and his death at age thirty-two in 1934 from tuberculosis was exacerbated by his drinking.

His purported homosexuality manifests strongly in the character of Paul in *Infants of the Spring*, as well as in the social dynamics among several of the novel's male characters. Thurman himself was a target of discrimination not only because of his dark skin color but also because of his homosexuality. *The Blacker the Berry* explores discrimination among African Americans based on skin color; he never acknowledged his homosexuality. According to Harlem Renaissance expert Kevin Mumford, "Thurman [was] probably the most gifted writer of the Harlem Renaissance." From 1926 to 1928 Thurman's social circle was ensconced in what he called "Niggerati Manor," a large house in Harlem, New York, where many artists and writers, whom he called the "Niggerati" congregated.

lauding it for "unflinchingly [telling] the truth about color snobbery within the color line." Friend Hughes, writes van Notten, was kind, but his public comments were geared "more [toward] the author of the novel than the text itself." At least one other critic, according to van Notten, cited Thurman's "modest" ability to write fiction. But multiple critiques of *Infants* lambasted the work. The *New York Times Book Review* referred to *Infants of the Spring* as "pretty inept," "clumsily written," and "incredibly bad." Lois Taylor, in a review for *Opportunity* magazine, called the novel "monotonous" and "boring," with theses that were "left at loose ends." An anonymous reviewer in *Abbott's Monthly Review,* quoted by van Notten, called *Infants of the Spring* Thurman's attempt "to mix a fantastical plot with a criticism of literature, an analysis of the race problem, and a satire of the social and scholastic leaders of the Race into a hodgepodge of punk literature."

Today, critics paint Thurman as a prescient outside figure of the Harlem Renaissance who knowingly depicted caricatures for the purpose of satire. Unappreciated in his time, his purpose in the satirical *Infants* was to bring attention to social themes that more prominent members of the Harlem Renaissance neglected to address and to address racism within the African American community. Thurman's legacy, according to Hutchinson, was to react against the "dangerously faddish, superficial, and intellectually suspect" character of the Harlem Renaissance and

its predominant figures. In his assessment of the work in *Hollins Critic,* Allen Sawyer-Long appreciates the novel as a deft portrayal of race relations during the 1920s, in which black women try to pass for white and blacks of both sexes vie for the attentions of white suitors. Despite its "undeveloped characters" and "long speeches," Sawyer-Long states that Thurman "uncovers a number of truths."

Scholarship of Thurman's *Infants* has focused on the novel's status as satire and as a reaction against movements within the Harlem Renaissance. Later criticism has overlooked the technical shortcomings of Thurman's work and focused on its "humor" and "attacks on convention," according to Favor. In his piece for the *African American Review,* Terrell Scott Herring notes that the book's "characters do function as ciphers in order to illuminate the various clashing problematics of the New Negro Movement." Amritjit Singh and Daniel M. Scott III point out in *The Collected Writings of Wallace Thurman* that Thurman "challenged the provincialism of all Americans, the double standards and patronizing attitudes with which most whites approached African American art, and the black bourgeoisie's obsessions with respectability."

BIBLIOGRAPHY

Sources

Favor, J. Martin. "George Schuyler and Wallace Thurman: Two Satirists of the Harlem Renaissance." *The Cambridge Companion to the Harlem Renaissance.* Ed. George Hutchinson. Cambridge: Cambridge UP, 2007. 198–212. Print.

Gruening, Martha. "Two Ways to Heaven." Rev. of *Infants of the Spring,* by Wallace Thurman. *Saturday Review of Literature* 12 Mar. 1932. Print.

Herring, Terrell S. "The Negro Artist and the Racial Manor: *Infants of the Spring* and the Conundrum of Publicity." *African American Review* 35.4 (2001): 581–97. Web. *Literature Resource Center.* 13 Nov. 2012.

Hutchinson, George. *The Cambridge Companion to the Harlem Renaissance.* Cambridge: Cambridge UP, 2007. Print.

Mumford, Kevin J. "Homosex Changes: Race, Cultural Geography, and the Emergence of the Gay." *American Quarterly* 48.3 (1996): 395–414. Print.

Sawyer-Long, Allen. "*Infants of the Spring.*" *Hollins Critic* 17.3 (1980): 20. *Literature Resource Center.* Web. 13 Nov. 2012.

Taylor, Lois. Rev. of *Infants of the Spring,* by Wallace Thurman. *Opportunity* Mar. 1932: 89. Print.

Thurman, Wallace. *Infants of the Spring.* New York: AMS, 1975. Print.

———. Rev. of *Infants of the Spring,* by Wallace Thurman. *Abbott's Monthly Review* Apr. 1932: 51, 63. Print.

Thurman, Wallace, Amritjit Singh, and Daniel M. Scott III. *The Collected Writings of Wallace Thurman: A Harlem Renaissance Reader.* Ed. Amritjit Singh and Daniel M. Scott III. New Brunswick: Rutgers UP, 2003. Print.

Van Notten, Eleonore. "*Infants of the Spring.*" *African American Review* 27.4 (1993): 693. *Literature Resource Center.* Web. 13 Nov. 2012.

———. *Wallace Thurman's Harlem Renaissance.* Amsterdam: Rodopi, 1994. Print.

Further Reading

Anderson, Jervis. *This Was Harlem: A Cultural Portrait, 1900–1950.* New York: Farrar, 1987. Print.

Bell, Bernard W. *The Afro-American Novel and Its Tradition.* Amherst: U of Massachusetts P, 1987. Print.

Bronz, Stephen. *Roots of Negro Racial Consciousness. The 1920s: Three Harlem Renaissance Authors.* New York: Libra, 1964. Print.

Ganter, Granville. "Decadence, Sexuality, and the Bohemian Vision of Wallace Thurman." *MELUS* 28.2 (2003): 83. *Literature Resource Center.* Web. 13 Nov. 2012.

Gaither, Renoir W. "The Moment of Revision: A Reappraisal of Wallace Thurman's Aesthetic in *The Blacker the Berry* and *Infants of the Spring*." *College Language Association Journal* 37.1 (1993): 81–93. Print.

Haslam, Gerald. "Wallace Thurman: A Western Renaissance Man." *Western American Literature* 6 (1971): 53–59. Print.

Silberman, Seth Clark. "Looking for Richard Bruce Nugent and Wallace Henry Thurman: Reclaiming Black Male Same-Sexualities in the New Negro Movement." *In Process* 1 (1996): 53–73. Print.

Thurman, Wallace. *The Blacker the Berry …* 1929. New York: Scribner's, 1996. Print.

Kirkley Silverman

THE LONE RANGER AND TONTO FISTFIGHT IN HEAVEN

Sherman Alexie

✧ *Key Facts*

Time Period:
Late 20th Century

Genre:
Short Story

Events:
Rise of multiculturalism;
growth of Native
American identity

Nationality:
American

OVERVIEW

The Lone Ranger and Tonto Fistfight in Heaven (1993) is Sherman Alexie's first collection of short stories. The original publication included twenty-two short stories; the work was reissued in 2005 with two additional short stories and an introduction by Alexie. The collection focuses on Thomas Builds-the-Fire, Victor Joseph, Junior Polatkin, and other characters living on the Spokane Indian Reservation in Washington, the reservation where Alexie grew up. The interconnected short stories do not shy away from the poverty of reservation life and the lasting effects of colonial oppression on Native Americans, but they also depict individual creativity, tribal autonomy, resiliency, and resistance to oppression, all with a mix of compassion, imagination, and humor. In juxtaposing hope and despair, the collection serves to reveal conditions on reservations while challenging long-held stereotypes of Native Americans. Alexie's use of satire fits in with a rhetorical tradition in Native American letters that uses humor to build community and combat stereotypes and builds on a long cultural tradition that precedes European contact.

Alexie, a Spokane and Coeur d'Alene Indian who was born in 1966, has been called a new, inventive voice in Native American literature. *The Lone Ranger and Tonto* has won many awards and was a finalist for the 1994 PEN/Hemingway Foundation Award for Best First Book of Fiction, which Alexie has said means he "tied for second place." Alexie later won the PEN/Faulkner Award for Fiction in 2010 for *War Dances,* a collection of stories and poems. A prolific novelist, poet, children's writer, and screenwriter, Alexie adapted stories from *The Lone Ranger and Tonto* in the screenplay for *Smoke Signals* (1998), a feature film produced, directed, and acted by Native Americans. The film won many awards, including the 1998 Sundance Film Festival's Audience Award.

HISTORICAL AND LITERARY CONTEXT

Historically, Americans have based their perceptions of Native Americans on portrayals by non-Indians. The earliest English-language publications by Native Americans date back to the 1770s, and the first novel written by a Native American was published in 1854.

With an increased emphasis on multiculturalism following the civil rights movement in the 1960s and 1970s, literature by Native American writers has attracted greater attention. After Kiowa Indian N. Scott Momaday was awarded a Pulitzer Prize for his novel *House Made of Dawn* in 1968, interest in Native American literatures began to increase, as did the number of publications by Native Americans. Despite the growing popularity of Native American-authored texts and a steady increase in the number of Native Americans, most mainstream portrayals have continued to mourn the disappearance of Native Americans as a casualty of the modern era, while others have idealized Native American cultures as an antidote to problems of the modern world.

There are 565 federally recognized Indian tribes and about 200 Native American languages in the United States. Some scholars thus argue that the umbrella term "Native American" is imprecise and ineffectual and does not emphasize the distinct histories and literary traditions of each tribe. For his part, Alexie dispenses with the term altogether, calling it a meaningless product of liberal white guilt, and chooses "Indian" instead. Many other scholars, while recognizing cultural and historical differences among tribes, argue that there is a shared history based on native people's experience as an indigenous group and their categorization as Native American. Native American literary texts "enact a Native aesthetic of literature and culture" that differs from that of non-Indian literatures, argues literary scholar and poet Kimberly M. Blaeser, an enrolled member of the Minnesota Chippewa tribe. *The Lone Ranger and Tonto* confronts misrepresentations of Indians by deploying and reconfiguring those misrepresentations. Alexie portrays characters who survive and persist despite centuries of loss caused by European American colonialism.

The Lone Ranger and Tonto is part of a larger trend among Native American writers—including Louise Erdrich, Linda Hogan, Adrian C. Louis, Louis Owens, and Leslie Marmon Silko—who have developed various strategies to counter depictions of Native Americans as primitive and doomed. As James Cox notes, "Native American authors write new narratives of self-representation that critically question and often radically revise and subvert the dominant culture's conquest narrative and the mass-produced misrepresentations of Native Americans." *The Lone Ranger and Tonto* refuses to romanticize the daily lives of Indians. Instead it offers a brutally painful but ultimately honest portrayal of reservation life, including the negative realities of poverty, dysfunction, and alcoholism alongside camaraderie, endurance, and love.

Whether *The Lone Ranger and Tonto* has altered the popular image of Native Americans is difficult to measure, but this provocative collection has transformed perceptions of what Native American literatures are and can be. Alexie is one of the most prominent Native American writers of his generation. His work has been celebrated as perceptive and denounced as combative by Native American and non-Native American audiences. *The Lone Ranger and Tonto* was one of several books the Tucson Unified School District in Arizona banned in January 2012. In contrast, the collection has been embraced in some public school curricula in the Northwest, and individual stories from the collection have been reprinted in anthologies used widely in high school and college courses. *The Lone Ranger and Tonto* has helped Alexie gain national prominence: in addition to publishing more than twenty books, the author is increasingly sought out for interviews, political commentary, lectures, and graduation speeches.

THEMES AND STYLE

Alexie writes, "The sons in this book really love and hate their fathers," but the collection also explores many themes beyond father-son relationships, including modern Indian identity, cultural alienation, the legacy of historical injustices, American popular culture, and the rage and shame of those whose cultures have been misunderstood and denied. Characters struggle with efforts to maintain Spokane autonomy, adapt to American ways, and resist cultural commodification. The collection depicts a reservation distinct from mainstream America (with pow wows, Department of Housing and Urban Development housing, government cheese and other commodity foods, and fry bread) yet immersed in popular American culture: images of the rock stars Jimi Hendrix and Elvis Presley and the corporate emblems of Pepsi and 7-Eleven appear alongside those of Jesus Christ, Crazy Horse, Christopher Columbus, and astronaut Neil Armstrong. Most of the stories include characters in various stages of inebriation. Alexie portrays alcohol as a tool to exploit Native Americans. Basketball is just as prominent a symbol as alcohol, however. In the story "The Only Traffic Signal on the Reservation Doesn't Flash Red Anymore," Victor explains, "Indians kind of see ballplayers as saviors. I mean, if basketball would have been around, I'm sure Jesus would've been the best point guard in Nazareth."

With a diverse cast of characters and a variety of narrators, the collection offers a more nuanced portrait than the one-dimensional mainstream representations

NATIVE AMERICAN HUMOR: A MILLENNIA-OLD TRADITION

Sherman Alexie's use of humor is one of the most celebrated and criticized elements of his writing. His humor continues a long tradition in Native American cultures. Scholar Kenneth Lincoln argues in his study *Indi'n Humor* that Native Americans have used humor to survive more than 500 years of colonial subjugation. From one-liners to anecdotes, humor is used to persuade, organize, motivate action, celebrate accomplishment, cope with grave problems, and expose hypocrisies. Alexie similarly views humor as a survival mechanism. In a 2004 radio interview he said that "the best defense against colonization is irony. And Indians are very good at it. If you look at the history of comedy, you'll find the two funniest groups in the world are Indians and Jewish people. So I guess that says something about the inherent humor of genocide."

Historian Vine Deloria Jr., a member of the Standing Rock Sioux, shares a variety of Indian jokes in his essay "Indian Humor." In this chapter of his groundbreaking manifesto, *Custer Died for Your Sins*, Deloria suggests that Indian humor is a rhetorical tool used to create unity and build community, establish individual humility, maintain tribal norms, foster pan-tribal connections, manage intertribal conflict, make sense of Euro-American ways, and enlighten inquisitive whites. Deloria notes that Christopher Columbus, George Armstrong Custer, missionaries, and the Bureau of Indian Affairs are all fair game, as are differences among Indians and the misunderstandings of non-Indians.

that have served to mythologize and homogenize Native American cultures. Each story can be read as a separate entity, but added together, these vignettes create a novel-like collection, with recurrent characters demonstrating the interlocking fates of the people in the stories and, by extension, of Native Americans. Alexie offers an insider's view of reservation life but is careful to warn against reading these stories as representative of other Indians' experiences: "They are the vision of one individual looking at the lives of his family and his entire tribe, so these stories are necessarily biased, incomplete, exaggerated, deluded, and often just plain wrong." Alexie, who left the reservation while in high school, is also an outsider to the Spokane tribe he fictionalizes, just as his main character Thomas is set apart by his storytelling.

Alexie's language is candid, and his description is plain, minimal, and blunt. A decade after the collection was first published, Alexie called the stories "reservation realism." More than half of the stories have upbeat endings, but as a whole it is not an uplifting collection. Alongside the desolation, however, is Alexie's satiric humor. At times polemic and even strident, this humor is edgy, sometimes unsettling, and often irreverent. Alexie's wit takes aim at both liberals and conservatives, as well as white racists and Native Americans. In "A Drug Called Tradition," Victor says, "We

Sherman Alexie at the 58th National Book Awards in New York in 2007. The occasionally surreal narratives in Alexie's *The Lone Ranger and Tonto Fistfight in Heaven* depict life on the Spokane Indian Reservation. AP PHOTO/ SETH WENIG.

never can tell whether they're laughing at the Indians or the whites. I think they're laughing at pretty much everybody." Alexie is laughing at everyone, laying bare the hypocrisy of white paternalism and federal policies while also highlighting the self-destructive dependencies of Native Americans. His use of irony, parody, and satire attempts to expose oppression, combat injustices, create alliances, and heal historical wrongs.

CRITICAL DISCUSSION

The Lone Ranger and Tonto has been celebrated by many audiences, academic and popular, and Native American and non-Native American. While mainstream media first emphasized its bleak portrayal of reservation life, reviewers also noted its artistry. The *Chicago Tribune* described it as "poetic and unremittingly honest" and called it "a shout of anger, pain, bitterness, loss, self-hate and despair." Literary scholars have praised it as lyric, humorous, politically incisive, and frank, and it has won numerous awards. In an early review in *American Indian Quarterly*, Denise Low focuses on the collection's use of irony in its political critique but also notes the collection's "tone of compassion that takes away the emotional distancing of irony." The collection has also been criticized by Native American and non-Native American readers for its anger and for its depiction of drunken Indians and other stereotypes.

Alexie's prose fiction debut, *The Lone Ranger and Tonto* is regarded by many as an important intervention in the portrayal of Native Americans. Similarly, Alexie has been increasingly praised as a new and original voice. After publishing *The Lone Ranger and Tonto*, Alexie continued to develop characters and themes from the collection. His first novel, *Reservation Blues* (1995), focuses on Thomas and Victor from *The Lone Ranger and Tonto*—as

does his screenplay for *Smoke Signals*, which he adapted from the story "This Is What It Means to Say Phoenix, Arizona"—and other elements in the collection. In recent years, Alexie has expanded his focus on reservation life to include urban Indians and has added to his many genres by writing novels for young adults. His recent work has also more explicitly explored themes of gender, gay and lesbian issues, and cross-cultural mixing. Notably, his works have continued his legacy of political commentary, references to popular culture, challenging of stereotypes, and brash humor.

While some recent scholarship connects Alexie's collection to Native American oral, performance, and ceremonial traditions, much has focused on its portrayal of Native Americans and Alexie's use of humor, debating whether its satiric portrayal of reservation life does more harm than good. Native American writer and literary critic Louis Owens writes that Alexie's fiction "too often simply reinforces all of the stereotypes desired by white readers: his bleakly absurd and aimless Indians are imploding in a passion of self-destructiveness and self-loathing … and in the process of self-destruction the Indians provide Euramerican readers with pleasurable moments of dark humor or the titillation of bloodthirsty savagery." In contrast, many critics argue that Alexie's humor is incisive and even redemptive. Literary critic Steven F. Evans counters that Alexie's deployment of stereotypes is part of a new, ethical form of satire that functions as a survival mechanism. Philip Heldrich similarly suggests that Alexie provokes interracial dialogue and engenders social change by "providing a means of survival amid often-bewildering and absurd conditions."

BIBLIOGRAPHY

Sources

Alexie, Sherman. *The Lone Ranger and Tonto Fistfight in Heaven.* New York: Grove, 2005. Print.

———. "Museums, Tribes, Lonewolf." *Studio 360.* National Public Radio, 18 Sept. 2004. Web. 4 May 2006.

Blaeser, Kimberly M. "Like 'Reeds through the Ribs of a Basket': Native Women Weaving Stories." *American Indian Quarterly* 21.4 (1997): 555–65. JSTOR. Web. 4 Aug. 2012.

Cox, James. "Muting White Noise: The Subversion of Popular Culture Narratives of Conquest in Sherman Alexie's Fiction." *Studies in American Indian Literatures* 9.4 (1997): 52–70. Web. 4 Aug. 2012.

Deloria, Vine, Jr. *Custer Died for Your Sins: An Indian Manifesto.* 1969. Norman: U of Oklahoma P, 1988. 146–67. Print.

Evans, Steven F. "Sherman Alexie's Drunken Indians." *American Indian Quarterly* 25.1 (2001): 46–72. JSTOR. Web. 4 Aug. 2012.

Heldrich, Philip. "'Survival = Anger x Imagination': Sherman Alexie's Dark Humor." *Sherman Alexie: A Collection of Critical Essays.* Ed. Jeff Berglund and Jan Roush. Salt Lake City: U of Utah P, 2010. 25–43. Print.

Lincoln, Kenneth. *Indi'n Humor: Bicultural Play in Native America.* New York: Oxford UP, 1993. Print.

Low, Denise. Rev. of *The Lone Ranger and Tonto Fistfight in Heaven,* by Sherman Alexie. *American Indian Quarterly* 20.1 (1996): 123–25. *JSTOR.* Web. 31 July 2012.

Owens, Louis. "Through an Amber Glass: Chief Doom and the Native American Novel Today." *Mixedblood Messages: Literature, Film, Family, Place.* Norman: U of Oklahoma P, 1998. Print.

Reardon, Patrick T. "Life on The Reservation Yields Never-ending Losses." Rev. of *The Lone Ranger and Tonto Fistfight in Heaven,* by Sherman Alexie. *Chicago Tribune.* Tribune Newspapers, 27 Sept. 1993. Web. 6 Aug. 2012.

Further Reading

Berglund, Jeff, and Jan Roush, eds. *Sherman Alexie: A Collection of Critical Essays.* Salt Lake City: U of Utah P, 2010. Print.

Coulombe, Joseph L. "The Approximate Size of His Favorite Humor: Sherman Alexie's Comic Connections and Disconnections in *The Lone Ranger and Tonto Fistfight in Heaven.*" *American Indian Quarterly* 26.1 (2002): 94–115. *JSTOR.* Web. 5 Aug. 2012.

Grassian, Daniel. *Understanding Sherman Alexie.* Columbia: U of South Carolina P, 2005. Print.

Herman, Matthew. "Sherman Alexie and the Politics of Literary Value." *Politics and Aesthetics in Contemporary Native American Literature: Across Every Border.* New York: Routledge, 2009. 67–101. Print.

Krstovic, Jelena, ed. "Sherman Alexie." *Short Story Criticism.* Vol. 107. Ed. Jelena Krstovic. Detroit: Gale, 2008. *Literature Criticism Online.* Web. 31 July 2012.

Lewis, Leon. *Sherman Alexie, Volume 1.* Pasadena: Salem, 2011. Print.

McGrath, Jacqueline L. "'The Same Damn Stories': Exploring a Variation on Tradition in Sherman Alexie's *The Lone Ranger and Tonto Fistfight in Heaven.*" *Southern Folklore* 57.2 (2000): 94–105. Print.

Moore, David L. "Sherman Alexie: Irony, Intimacy, and Agency." *The Cambridge Companion to Native American Literature.* Ed. Joy Porter and Kenneth M. Roemer. Cambridge: Cambridge UP, 2005. 297–310. Print.

Peterson, Nancy J., ed. *Conversations with Sherman Alexie.* Jackson: UP of Mississippi, 2009. Print.

Umphrey, Christabel. "*The Lone Ranger and Tonto Fistfight in Heaven*: Alexie and History." Ed. Heather E. Bruce, Anna E. Baldwin, and Christabel Umphrey. *Sherman Alexie in the Classroom: "This is not a silent movie. Our voices will save our lives."* Urbana: National Council of Teachers of English, 2008. 38–60. Print.

Media Adaptation

Smoke Signals. Dir. Chris Eyre. Perf. Adam Beach, Evan Adams, and Irene Bedard. ShadowCatcher Entertainment, 1998. Film.

Alicia Kent

THE LYING DAYS

Nadine Gordimer

✥ *Key Facts*

Time Period:
Mid-20th Century

Genre:
Novel

Events:
Introduction
of apartheid;
institutionalization of
racism in South Africa

Nationality:
South African

OVERVIEW

Published in 1953, South African writer Nadine Gordimer's autobiographical novel *The Lying Days* tells the story of a young woman growing up with white privilege under the racist South African system of apartheid. Helen Shaw, Gordimer's protagonist, first becomes aware of the contradictions within her community and her country while living in a small mining town near Johannesburg, where black miners live in a mysterious separateness and whites are tightly wrapped in superiority and fear. Helen escapes this claustrophobic atmosphere when she enters the university in Johannesburg and becomes part of the more politically conscious world of the progressive intellectual community. There she begins to understand the complex effects of the racist system and discovers both the power and the limitations of friendship and love. She finally leaves the increasing tensions of apartheid to go to Europe, but she rejects the idea of running away from her responsibility as a white South African and declares her determination to return.

Gordimer's story of the alienating effects, even for whites, of life under racism was written when the apartheid system of South Africa was in the early stages of development. As the world watched the harsh new measures warily, critics and readers were riveted by the deeply personal nature of her narrative and moved by Helen's struggle to find a place for herself within the narrowly defined limits of her society. Although the novel's white perspective was viewed as a limitation by some, to others it helped white readers identify the network of blame, accountability, and grief that formed the complex barrier between the races in South Africa.

HISTORICAL AND LITERARY CONTEXT

Beginning in the mid-seventeenth century, the native people of southern Africa were subjugated and enslaved, first by the Dutch and then by the British. Both sets of colonizers exploited the area's resources and introduced slaves from Asia who intermixed with the native population to form a mixed-race subgroup that became known as "coloured." The British and the Dutch struggled for control of the area, resulting in the founding of the British-controlled Union of South Africa in 1910. To repress native African resistance, colonizers imposed a rigid social order with economic and political power resting entirely in the hands of a small white minority while the lives of the black majority and the coloured were severely limited.

The early 1950s, when Gordimer wrote and published *The Lying Days,* marked the change in South Africa from an informal system of racial segregation to an official policy of apartheid ("apartness," in the Dutch-derived language Afrikaans). In 1948 the ultraconservative Nationalist party took power, and in 1950 a number of repressive laws were enacted to cement the power of the white minority. The Population Registration Act required black South Africans to carry identity papers and restricted their movements. The Group Areas Act established separate residential and business areas for different races, resulting in the appropriation of even more land by the white minority and the relocation of many blacks to remote primitive townships. As opposition to racist policies increased, the government passed the Suppression of Communism Act, banning virtually any group promoting social change. Resistance continued, however, and in 1952 the Defiance Campaign mobilized antiapartheid activists of all races in an opposition movement. *The Lying Days* documents the uncomfortable place of socially conscious whites in a state dominated by white racist ideology.

Even if the increasing deprivations of apartheid were discouraging to the human spirit, they inspired a vibrant literature of resistance. In 1946 mixed-race author Peter Abrahams explored the lives of black laborers in *Mine Boy,* followed by an examination of mixed marriage in *The Path of Thunder* in 1948. Es'kia Mphahlele gave voice to the black South African experience in *Man Must Live and Other Stories* in 1946, and in 1948 Alan Paton articulated the white conscience in *Cry, the Beloved Country.* The literary journal *Drum,* founded as *African Drum* in 1951, provided a forum for a number of black writers. Influenced by influential social criticism such as Upton Sinclair's 1906 novel *The Jungle,* Gordimer voiced her own political awareness in her earliest writings, publishing her first book of short stories, *Face to Face,* in 1949.

The Lying Days joined these early works of social analysis and critique to become one of the earliest articulations of a powerful antiapartheid campaign. As human rights activists around the world began to protest the injustice of South Africa's racist system, other white South African writers—such as dramatist Athol Fugard, poet Breyten Breytenbach, and novelists André Brink and J. M. Coetzee—added their voices to Gordimer's in opposing apartheid. Gordimer's own work became increasingly outspoken, and two of her novels, *World of Strangers* (1958) and *The Late Bourgeois World* (1966), were banned by the government for several years.

THEMES AND STYLE

Reflecting Gordimer's own complex reactions to growing up in a society founded upon deep injustice, *The Lying Days* explores the ethical contradictions of living under apartheid in the 1950s. Primarily a coming-of-age novel built around a child's growth from innocence through disillusionment to understanding, *The Lying Days* is also a deep examination of the ways in which political reality intrudes into personal life and relationships. The racism that surrounds Helen is "an unwritten law so sternly upheld and generally accepted that it would occur to no child to ask why." Another deep resonance, recurrent in colonial literature, is the theme of displacement and belonging. Helen is raised in an atmosphere of colonialism, "This rickety thing, everybody's makeshift Europe." She mourns, "Sometimes the things we want most are impossible for us. You may long to come home, yet wander forever." She grows to understanding, partly through her relationship with Paul, a welfare worker, but her whole self seems to fit nowhere. She finally accepts "disillusionment as a beginning rather than an end" and leaves her homeland to go to Europe, affirming, "I'm not practicing any sort of self-deception any longer. ... Whatever it was I was running away from—the risk of love? the guilt of being white? the danger of putting ideals into practice?—I'm not running away from now because I know I'm coming back here."

Gordimer takes the title of her novel from Irish author William Butler Yeats's 1916 poem "The Coming of Wisdom with Time," and her characterization of Yeats's "lying days of my youth" gives the novel much of its power. The first-person narrative demonstrates a developing vision of stultifying injustice through the eyes of a child, watchful and naive, as she learns both the limitations and the possibilities of her world: "A little girl must not be left alone because there were native boys about. That was all." The mine becomes a symbol of the depths of knowledge unavailable to her about the lives and experience of her black countrymen: "The Mine houses had their fences and hedges around them … inside Mine houses it was always dark."

Gordimer's writing in *The Lying Days* is detailed and nuanced. She describes Helen's early life in the mining town with the nonjudgmental sensuality of a child's discovery: "There were people there, shadowy, strange to me as the black men with the soft red inside their mouths showing as they opened in the

SUCCESS OF A MOVEMENT: THE FIGHT TO END APARTHEID

Black Africans and other people of color in South Africa resisted racial discrimination and the institution of official apartheid, but their resistance was met with harsh reprisals. In 1960 sixty-nine antiapartheid demonstrators were shot in the township of Sharpeville, and in 1976 more than one thousand police officers arrived with military force to put down an uprising in the township of Soweto, killing hundreds of protesters. Some movement leaders, such as Nelson Mandela, were jailed. Others, such as Stephen Biko, were killed. Activists within South Africa continued to organize pickets, rent strikes, and boycotts, but they soon began to understand that they needed help.

In the 1980s Anglican archbishop Desmond Tutu risked charges of treason to issue an appeal to the nations of the world, calling for "punitive sanctions against this government to help us establish a new South Africa." Human rights activists around the world responded, launching campaigns to persuade their governments, universities, athletic teams, and other institutions to boycott South African products and events and divest from South African businesses. Even many celebrities joined the protest, forming Artists United Against Apartheid and refusing to perform in the nation's famous resort Sun City. Continued repression of antiapartheid activists within South Africa only won more support for the campaign of sanctions. By the end of the 1980s, the South African government began negotiations for the end of apartheid. In 1990 activist Nelson Mandela was released from prison, and in 1994 he was elected president of the new Republic of South Africa.

concentration of spending money." As Helen's world expands from the limitations of the mining town to the more expansive society of Johannesburg, this sensuality matures as love opens Helen to a new awareness and she marvels at her "sense of wonder at the pin speck of myself in a swirling universe, a creature perpetually surrounded by a perpetual growth, stars and earthworm, wind and diamond."

CRITICAL DISCUSSION

The Lying Days was received by reviewers as a crucial early document of the South African experience. In an article for *English in Africa,* critic Ileana Dimitriu (2002) quotes a reviewer, identified as A. O. D., who writes, "Read this book; it is a memorable experience and it is the yardstick by which future South African novels will be judged." *New York Times* reviewer James Stern (1953) agrees, commenting, "I can think of no modern first 'novel' superior to Miss Gordimer's." He acknowledges the persuasive power of the text by noting, "We have been made to feel the sense of doom that pervades it." Many mid-twentieth-century critics, including Richard Hayes in *Commonweal,* believed that art should remain separate from political messaging. Hayes (1953) said of Gordimer's writing in *The Lying Days,* "She cannot dominate her

South African writer and political activist Nadine Gordimer at the Hay Festival of Literature and Arts in Wales, 2010. © JEFF MORGAN 15/ALAMY.

In the years following the publication of *The Lying Days*, critics and scholars have continued to reexamine Gordimer's book. In the 1980s, English professor Stephen Clingman echoes Hayes's earlier criticism that the novel was limited by its focus on social issues, while John Cooke in *The Novels of Nadine Gordimer: Private Lives / Public Landscapes* (1985) calls it "one of her bleakest, Gordimer's only novel in which private and public responsibilities are avoided and nothing learned." Scholar Judie Newman in *Nadine Gordimer* (1988) interprets the text in light of feminist analysis, asserting that the protagonist is patronized and trivialized by the males in her life: "Helen is marginalized, her experience appropriated and narrated by the male."

BIBLIOGRAPHY

Sources

Clingman, Stephen. *The Novels of Nadine Gordimer: History from the Inside.* Johannesburg: Ravan, 1986. Print.

Cooke, John. *The Novels of Nadine Gordimer: Private Lives / Public Landscapes.* Baton Rouge: Louisiana State U, 1985. Print.

Dimitriu, Ileana. "The Civil Imaginary in Gordimer's First Novels." *English in Africa* 29.1 (2002): 27. *Literature Resource Center.* Web. 11 Sept. 2012.

Hayes, Richard. "A Coming of Age in South Africa." *Commonweal* 59.3 (1953): 66. *Literature Resource Center.* Web. 11 Sept. 2012.

Newman, Judie. *Nadine Gordimer.* London: Routledge, 1988. Print.

Stern, James. Rev. of *The Lying Days,* by Nadine Gordimer. *New York Times* 4 Oct. 1953: n. pag. Web. 10 Sept. 2012.

Further Reading

Bazin, Nancy Topping, and Marilyn Dallman Seymour, eds. *Conversations with Nadine Gordimer.* Jackson: Mississippi UP, 1990. Print.

Clark, Nancy L., and William H. Worger. *South Africa: The Rise and Fall of Apartheid.* New York: Longman, 2011. Print.

Gordimer, Nadine. *None to Accompany Me.* New York: Penguin, 1994. Print.

———. *No Time Like the Present.* New York: Farrar, 2012. Print.

Smith, Rowland. "Nadine Gordimer." *South African Writers.* Ed. Paul A. Scanlon. Vol. 225. Dictionary of Literary Biography. Detroit: Gale Group, 2000. *Literature Resource Center.* Web. 11 Sept. 2012.

Temple-Thurston, Barbara. *Nadine Gordimer Revisited.* New York: Twayne, 1999. Print.

Tina Gianoulis

experience … because she does not exist at a sufficient distance from it; the page is still freshly dusted with the heat and squalor of battle." However, he praises her "impeccable clarity of focus and a poetic texture of range and intensity."

The Lying Days is a pioneering work in the struggle against apartheid and the first of many Gordimer works that brought this issue to the center of the world stage. Her writing, along with the work of many other artists and activists, helped to initiate an international outcry against the white South African government. Apartheid was dismantled in 1994, but Gordimer continued to write perceptive explorations of the intersection between the political and the personal. Her novel *None to Accompany Me* (1994) describes the complex historical moment of the end of apartheid, and *No Time Like the Present* (2012) explores the ongoing political passions of antiapartheid activists almost two decades after the struggle. Even years after the end of apartheid, *The Lying Days* remains relevant as an articulation of the roots of racism and its deep and enduring costs.

MARIA; OR, THE WRONGS OF WOMAN

Mary Wollstonecraft

OVERVIEW

Maria; or, The Wrongs of Woman, a novel by Mary Wollstonecraft that was unfinished at the time of her death in 1797, continues the feminist arguments that the author had begun in *A Vindication of the Rights of Woman (with Strictures on Political and Moral Subjects)* (1792). The fragmentary text was edited and published in 1798 by William Godwin, a political writer and Wollstonecraft's husband. In the novel, an omniscient narrator introduces the protagonist, Maria, who is chained in a madhouse. A love affair with Darnford, a fellow inmate, begins through an exchange of books containing margin notes, highlighting the role of romantic novels in shaping Maria's sensibility and thereby her misfortunes. The narrator gives way to Jemima, a guard who, despite her lower-class origins, speaks eloquently. Jemima tells her appalling life story, which demonstrates how women of all classes are victimized by their lack of legal autonomy. The relentless depiction of oppression, combined with impassioned speeches and documents, conveys Wollstonecraft's criticism of British laws pertaining to marriage and inheritance (which held that women were the property of fathers or husbands) and indicts for-profit mental institutions.

The novel was published along with Godwin's *Memoirs of Mary Wollstonecraft* (1798), in which Godwin offers considerable detail about his unconventional marriage to Wollstonecraft and discusses such controversial topics as the child born out of wedlock to Wollstonecraft and a former lover. Critical reception of *Maria* was clouded by the scandal that accompanied Godwin's disclosures. The revelation about Wollstonecraft's child, combined with the novel's defense of adultery, led both radical and conservative readers to condemn her work. The anti-Jacobins believed her immorality proved the error of her ideas, as presented in both the novel and the better-known *A Vindication of the Rights of Woman*. Without mentioning Wollstonecraft directly, later authors, such as Maria Edgeworth and Jane Austen, dramatized and satirized the patriarchal legal system, which slowly began to institute reforms, including an 1839 act that gave mothers the right of custody of their children (provided the Lord Chancellor approved of the mother's character). Further nineteenth-century legislation granted women control of the wages they earned and instituted supervision of private mental asylums.

HISTORICAL AND LITERARY CONTEXT

Earlier in the eighteenth century, the Americans and the French had rejected tyranny and created constitutions establishing rights for men who owned substantial property; women, the poor, people of color, and others were largely excluded. Great Britain outlawed slavery, but only within its geographic borders. Abolition in the colonies was a heated topic among Enlightenment thinkers, including Wollstonecraft, who connected the plight of slaves with the status of women. In Great Britain, only men possessing substantial property had the vote, and when a woman married, her personal possessions (including any monetary wealth) became her husband's property under the laws of coverture. As a result, many women felt trapped by marriage. If a women left her marriage, she would lose her children. In *A Vindication of the Rights of Woman,* Wollstonecraft argued that women needed an education equal to that afforded men in order to become independent and to raise children in a manner commensurate with a free society, as well as to become more "companionate" partners for their husbands.

In Wollstonecraft's view, marriage and inheritance laws and the dependence they enforced made women little better than slaves or prostitutes. The events of *Maria* show the "wrongs of woman" resulting from marriages that were essentially financial arrangements privileging men. Wollstonecraft drew on her life experiences for many of the novel's illustrations of injustice. Like Maria's father, for example, Wollstonecraft's father was a spendthrift who mistreated her mother. To escape him, Wollstonecraft had worked as a governess, one of the few options open to a single woman. In the novel this kind of work experience leads to a more dramatic outcome for Maria's sister, who "declines" and dies as a result of her lonely isolation.

Wollstonecraft's novel bears the influence of and reacts to a number of literary trends of the period, including the sentimental novel, gothic literature, and social conduct literature. The sentimental novel had become popular in the mid-eighteenth century. Wollstonecraft disapproved of this form of literature and of the way in which it encouraged sensibility rather than reason in its female readership. In her novel, Maria, although confined to an asylum, reads a novel by Jean-Jacques Rousseau, an author against whom

❖ *Key Facts*

Time Period:
Late 18th Century

Genre:
Novel

Events:
Birth of feminism; fight for women's rights

Nationality:
English

PRIMARY SOURCE

EXCERPT FROM *MARIA; OR, THE WRONGS OF WOMAN*

She approached the small grated window of her chamber, and for a considerable time only regarded the blue expanse; though it commanded a view of a desolate garden, and of part of a huge pile of buildings, that, after having been suffered, for half a century, to fall to decay, had undergone some clumsy repairs, merely to render it habitable. The ivy had been torn off the turrets, and the stones not wanted to patch up the breaches of time, and exclude the warring elements, left in heaps in the disordered court. Maria contemplated this scene she knew not how long; or rather gazed on the walls, and pondered on her situation. To the master of this most horrid of prisons, she had, soon after her entrance, raved of injustice, in accents that would have justified his treatment, had not a malignant smile, when she appealed to his judgment, with a dreadful conviction stifled her remonstrating complaints. By force, or openly, what could be done? But surely some expedient might occur to an active mind, without any other employment, and possessed of sufficient resolution to put the risk of life into the balance with the chance of freedom.

A woman entered in the midst of these reflections, with a firm, deliberate step, strongly marked features, and large black eyes, which she fixed steadily on Maria's, as if she designed to intimidate her, saying at the same time "You had better sit down and eat your dinner, than look at the clouds."

"I have no appetite," replied Maria, who had previously determined to speak mildly; "why then should I eat?"

"But, in spite of that, you must and shall eat something. I have had many ladies under my care, who have resolved to starve themselves; but, soon or late, they gave up their intent, as they recovered their senses."

"Do you really think me mad?" asked Maria, meeting the searching glance of her eye.

"Not just now. But what does that prove?— Only that you must be the more carefully watched, for appearing at times so reasonable. You have not touched a morsel since you entered the house."— Maria sighed intelligibly.—"Could any thing but madness produce such a disgust for food?"

Wollstonecraft argues in *A Vindication*. Maria's reading clouds her perception of Darnford, who ultimately lets her down. Writers in the cult of sensibility were drawn to medievalism, producing such gothic novels as *The Castle of Otranto* (1764), by Horace Walpole, and *The Mysteries of Udolpho* (1794), by Ann Radcliffe. Wollstonecraft begins *Maria* by evoking that genre: "Abodes of horror have frequently been described.... But, formed of such stuff as dreams are made of, what were they to the mansion of despair, in one corner of which Maria sat, endeavoring to recall her scattered thoughts!" The reality of the oppression her protagonist must face, Wollstonecraft declares, is worse than the sufferings of gothic heroines. In addition to the gothic influence, conduct books such as Lady Pennington's "Unfortunate Mother's Advice to her Absent Daughters" (1761) were also significant predecessors to Wollstonecraft's novel: a substantial portion of *Maria* takes the form of a letter from Maria to her absent daughter.

Despite the disapproval occasioned by the publication of *Maria* and Godwin's memoirs, a number of writers began to follow Wollstonecraft's lead. Edgeworth, in her 1798 edition of *Letters for Literary Ladies*, dramatizes an exchange between a woman of sense and a woman of sensibility, offering the same critique of sensibility as that put forward by Wollstonecraft. In her novels, Austen uses irony to deal with similar situations: women who cannot inherit, in their desperation to marry and subject to the folly of sensibility, often make serious errors of judgment.

THEMES AND STYLE

The position of women as subject to the whims of their fathers, husbands, or brothers is shown in the lives of middle-class Maria and working-class Jemima and explained by the omniscient narrator. Although Jemima is a guard, she is essentially a prisoner in the madhouse, but at first she cannot sympathize with Maria. The narrator explains that "she had felt the crushing hand of power, hardened by the exercise of injustice, and ceased to wonder at the perversions of the understanding, which systematize oppression." Jemima's self-reliance is both a fault and her salvation. Maria is educated enough to read sentimental literature, leaving her prey to the deceptions of men. As she reads the notes that Darnford has made in the books he lends her, "fancy, treacherous fancy, began to sketch a character, congenial with her own, from these shadowy outlines." Developing fancy, rather than reason, keeps Maria reliant on untrustworthy men.

The novel consists of stories within stories. Readers must wait to learn how Maria has come to be captive in a solitary cell, as Darnford narrates his story first. Even the male is subject to the injustice of incarceration in a privately run madhouse, an abused

"Yes, grief; you would not ask the question if you knew what it was." The attendant shook her head; and a ghastly smile of desperate fortitude served as a forcible reply, and made Maria pause, before she added—"Yet I will take some refreshment: I mean not to die.—No; I will preserve my senses; and convince even you, sooner than you are aware of, that my intellects have never been disturbed, though the exertion of them may have been suspended by some infernal drug." …

Had her master trusted her, it is probable that neither pity nor curiosity would have made her swerve from the straight line of her interest; for she had suffered too much in her intercourse with mankind, not to determine to look for support, rather to humouring their passions, than courting their approbation by the integrity of her conduct. A deadly blight had met her at the very threshold of existence; and the wretchedness of her mother seemed a heavy weight fastened on her innocent neck, to drag her down to perdition. She could not heroically determine to succour an unfortunate; but, offended at the bare supposition that she could be deceived with the same ease as a common servant, she no longer curbed her curiosity; and, though she never seriously fathomed her own intentions, she would sit, every moment she could steal from observation, listening to the tale, which Maria was eager to relate with all the persuasive eloquence of grief.

It is so cheering to see a human face, even if little of the divinity of virtue beam in it, that Maria anxiously expected the return of the attendant, as of a gleam of light to break the gloom of idleness. Indulged sorrow, she perceived, must blunt or sharpen the faculties to the two opposite extremes; producing stupidity, the moping melancholy of indolence; or the restless activity of a disturbed imagination. She sunk into one state, after being fatigued by the other: till the want of occupation became even more painful than the actual pressure or apprehension of sorrow; and the confinement that froze her into a nook of existence, with an unvaried prospect before her, the most insupportable of evils. The lamp of life seemed to be spending itself to chase the vapours of a dungeon which no art could dissipate.—And to what purpose did she rally all her energy?—Was not the world a vast prison, and women born slaves?

loophole in the legal system and a symbol of the social structure. In the following chapter, Jemima tells her woeful tale, and because of her lower economic status, it is far worse than anything that has befallen Maria or Darnford. The narrative that Maria has written to her infant daughter is not presented until Maria is told that the child is dead and is thus an incomplete act of communication. Darnford comments that her account demonstrates "the absurdity of the laws respecting matrimony, which, till divorces could be more easily obtained, was … the most insufferable bondage." Nevertheless, the male interpretation does not necessarily reflect Maria's, or Wollstonecraft's, intent. Wollstonecraft wanted women to be treated equally under the law.

The fragmentary, "choose your own ending" style of the novel is the result of both Wollstonecraft's untimely death and her struggle to write in the relatively new genre of the novel. Given Wollstonecraft's critique of sentimental fiction, it is appropriate that *Maria* remains unfinished, its ending present only in note form and contradicted by a fragment in which the dead daughter is found to be alive. Wollstonecraft's ambivalence is evident in chapter 4, when the narrator begins, "We mean not to trace the progress of this passion, or recount how often Darnford and Maria were obliged to part in the midst of an interesting conversation." However, a few sentences later, Wollstonecraft cannot resist describing, in language to rival any romantic fiction, how "a magic lamp now seemed to be suspended in Maria's prison, and fairy landscapes flitted round the gloomy walls, late so blank. Rushing from the depth of despair, on the seraph wing of hope, she found herself happy.— She was beloved, and every emotion was rapturous." The novel's inchoate state and internal contradictions suggest Wollstonecraft's own ambivalence toward the genre, interwoven as it is with the sentimental.

CRITICAL DISCUSSION

Maria; or, The Wrongs of Woman, unfinished at the time of Wollstonecraft's death and published by her widower, met with disapproval for its apparent support of adultery. The fact that it was printed with Godwin's memoir of Wollstonecraft, in which her unorthodox life choices were revealed, compounded the condemnation. In July 1798 the *Anti-Jacobin Review* included an index listing for "Prostitution" with the note to "See Mary Wollstonecraft." The *Monthly Review* excoriated Wollstonecraft's morals as well. Few feminists dared to refer to her directly, though they continued to draw upon her ideas.

Female British novelists of the nineteenth century followed Wollstonecraft's lead in creating fiction that revealed the suffering caused by women's legal status. Austen's novels ironically depict women who must marry or face homelessness because of inheritance

Scene from Bedlam, an insane asylum in Britain. SCENE IN BEDLAM, PLATE VIII, FROM *A RAKE'S PROGRESS*, ILLUSTRATION FROM 'HOGARTH RESTORED: THE WHOLE WORKS OF THE CELEBRATED WILLIAM HOGARTH, RE-ENGRAVED BY THOMAS COOK,' PUB. 1812 (HAND-COLOURED ENGRAVING), HOGARTH, WILLIAM (1697–1764)/ PRIVATE COLLECTION/THE STAPLETON COLLECTION/ THE BRIDGEMAN ART LIBRARY.

laws. Charlotte Brontë's protagonist Jane Eyre faces poverty and other hardships of life as a governess, and, in the gothic tradition, a madwoman in an attic. George Eliot's middle-class protagonist Dorothea (in *Middlemarch*, 1874) thirsts for a better education and conceives of ways to alleviate the impoverished conditions of the tenants on the estate where she lives. In the twentieth century, the novelist Virginia Woolf wrote a meditation on Wollstonecraft, and in her modernist novels, such as *To the Lighthouse* (1927), Woolf illuminates the subjugation of women to the whims of dominant males.

Feminist literary scholars began to pay attention to Wollstonecraft's final novel in the 1970s. Ellen Moers situates *Maria* within what she terms the female gothic, a subgenre that also attracted Wollstonecraft's daughter, Mary Shelley, author of *Frankenstein*. Susan Gubar, in a 1994 essay, criticizes Wollstonecraft's "feminist misogyny" and suggests that "the odd juxtapositions between *A Vindication of the Rights of Woman* and the novels imply that the misogynist portrait of the feminine penned by the feminist … represents Wollstonecraft's efforts to negotiate the distance between desire and dread, what she thought she should have been and what she feared herself to be." Later critics, such as Tilottama Rajan, have tried to disentangle the fragmentary text of *Maria* from the

editing and consolidation Godwin performed. Daniel O'Quinn notes that Godwin's desire for narrative detracts from the story's critique of the influence of sentimental fiction on Maria. O'Quinn argues that Godwin's "interventions, perhaps unwittingly, tend to minimize the characters' delusive projections, and give them the status of narrative events." More recent interpretations contextualize Wollstonecraft's novel and argue that the author was creating something new from the common materials of sensibility and motherhood.

BIBLIOGRAPHY
Sources

Godwin, William. *Memoirs of Mary Wollstonecraft*. Ed. W. Clark Durant. New York: Gordon, 1972. Print.

Gubar, Susan. "Feminist Misogyny: Mary Wollstonecraft and the Paradox of 'It Takes One to Know One.'" *Feminist Studies* 20.3 (1994): 452–73. *ProQuest Central*. Web. 31 Aug. 2012.

Moers, Ellen. *Literary Women: The Great Writers*. New York: Anchor, 1977. Print.

O'Quinn, Daniel. "Trembling: Wollstonecraft, Godwin and the Resistance to Literature." *ELH* 64.3 (1997): 761–88. *JSTOR*. Web. 31 Aug. 2012.

Wollstonecraft, Mary. *Maria; or, The Wrongs of Woman*. Ed. Moira Ferguson. New York: Norton, 1975. Print.

Further Reading

DeLucia, JoEllen. "From the Female Gothic to a Feminist Theory of History: Ann Radcliffe and the Scottish Enlightenment." *Eighteenth Century* 50.1 (2009): 101+. *Proquest Central.* Web. 31 Aug. 2012.

Ford, Thomas H. "Mary Wollstonecraft and the Motherhood of Feminism." *Women's Studies Quarterly* 37. 3–4 (2009): 189–205. *Project Muse.* Web. 31 Aug. 2012.

Gordon, Lyndall. *Vindication: A Life of Mary Wollstonecraft.* London: Little, Brown, 2005. Print.

Jones, Vivien. "Mary Wollstonecraft and the Literature of Advice and Instruction." *Cambridge Companion to Mary Wollstonecraft.* Ed. Claudia L. Johnson. New York: Cambridge UP, 2002. 119–40. Print.

Myers, Mitzi. "Unfinished Business: Wollstonecraft's *Maria.*" *Wordsworth Circle* 11.2 (1980): 107–14. *Proquest.* Web. 31 Aug. 2012.

Poovey, Mary. "Mary Wollstonecraft: The Gender of Genres in Late Eighteenth-Century England." *Novel* 15.2 (1982): 111–26. *JSTOR.* Web. 31 Aug. 2012.

St. Clair, William. *The Godwins and the Shelleys: The Biography of a Family.* London: Faber, 1989. Print.

Robin Morris

"THE NEW YEAR'S SACRIFICE"

Lu Xun

✧ *Key Facts*

Time Period:
Early 20th Century

Genre:
Short Story

Events:
Republic Revolution
of 1911; Opium
Wars; Warlord Era;
modernization of China

Nationality:
Chinese

OVERVIEW

"The New Year's Sacrifice," a realist short story written by Lu Xun in 1924, exposes the inherent cruelty of conventional Confucian traditions and the problematic gap that existed between modern Chinese intellectuals of his day and the "masses" they wished to uplift. The story begins with a disappointed reformer who returns for a visit to his hometown, where he encounters a woman he once knew, "Xianglin's Wife," who now begs for a living. She asks him questions about the afterlife that he fails to answer satisfactorily, and her death the following day prompts him to recall, in what comprises the story's longer, second narrative, what he can of the repeated victimization that characterizes the woman's life. This segment includes a brief third tale of her son's violent death, an event she narrates so repetitively and so frequently that the townspeople eventually mock and shun her. This nameless woman's tragedy testifies to the cruelty and hypocrisy inherent in hierarchical Confucian traditions. Lu Xun considered the blind obedience to tradition the central "disease" of Chinese culture that modernity would hopefully remedy.

Truly devastating in its portrayal of the power of poverty, patriarchy, and ignorance to snuff out a poor woman's life, the story was an appropriate fit for its initial publication in *Xinqingnian* (New youth) magazine, the primary vehicle for the leftist New Culture Movement that attempted to identify China's problems within the culture rather than blaming Japan and other foreign influences. This movement opposed traditional Chinese thought, behavior, and literary style in favor of new gender ideas and outside cultural elements that might be beneficial to the cause of modernizing China. Eventually published in the short story collection *Wandering* in 1960, Lu Xun's "The New Year's Sacrifice" and his other stories of the era are often cited as the first examples of revolutionary, modernist literature in China.

HISTORICAL AND LITERARY CONTEXT

The years leading up to the story's publication were politically tumultuous ones in China. The 1911 Republic Revolution, which had overthrown the Manchu Dynasty, had failed to improve conditions for the poor. In the fifteen years following the revolution, warlords, old gentry, and mercenaries fought with one another for control of China and preyed upon the weak. Lu Xun was one of the first to notice that the revolution had failed, and he made frequent satirical attacks on the warlord government in his writing of the 1920s. His work was also influenced by the cultural fragmentation that had resulted from the Opium Wars of the nineteenth century, when English merchants and American missionaries infiltrated China.

"The New Year's Sacrifice" appeared during the Warlord Era of 1916–27, when politics were in shambles and Western influences had begun to make an impression on intellectuals such as Lu Xun, who sought to modernize China. Originally planning to devote his life to the modernization of Chinese medicine, Lu Xun eventually forsook that pursuit, deciding that China's illnesses of spirit were more crippling to its advance into modernity. This insight prompted his turn to a literary life that would challenge the ruling ideologies of his day, eventually leading to his posthumous appropriation as the literary figurehead of the Communist Party.

Despite his later lionization as the greatest proletarian writer of China, Lu Xun was ever dubious of the grandiose utopian schemes of his younger contemporaries in the 1920s and 1930s. He had been deeply discouraged by the failure of earlier revolutions and of his own literary magazine, *Xin sheng* (New life), which he had tried to begin while in Tokyo. He only reluctantly agreed to begin writing political short stories, beginning with his famous "Diary of a Madman" in 1919, at the urging of younger writers Hu Shi and Jin Xinyi. Lu Xun's writings became extremely influential in the revitalization of Chinese literature through the New Culture Movement and the related May Fourth Movement of the same period. He often used positive closures to otherwise tragic stories, inserting them in an attempt to overcome the determinism of realism. He admitted to doing this in his preface to his short story collection *Outcry* (1923), acknowledging that many of the stories were "written to order."

"The New Year's Sacrifice" and other stories also made a significant political and artistic impact on later writers of the 1930s and 1940s. The New Culture Movement sought to extend the quest for social reform and revolution to the arena of literature by embracing literary experimentation and use of vernacular language over adherence to the revered classical styles that had ruled unchallenged for so long. Lu Xun's approach raised the literary standard of the sometimes clumsy and often precious proletarian fiction so common during that era. His deep understanding of the challenges that accompany efforts to change traditional culture contributed to his almost immediate (and permanent) national celebrity.

THEMES AND STYLE

"The New Year's Sacrifice" differs from much of the revolutionary propaganda of its day in that it conveys a more cautious and skeptical attitude toward the possibilities of true revolution and change in China. The failed communication between the scholar narrator of the story and the beggar woman he encounters emphasizes the long-standing social gap that Lu Xun saw as an inhibiting factor to the modernization and democratization of China. The narrator's intense discomfort at being "accosted" by the poor woman speaks volumes in itself, as he confesses that his "flesh crept" and that "a shiver r[a]n down [his] spine" when the woman asks him if there is such a thing as ghosts. He attempts to placate her by giving her the answer he thinks she wants but quickly realizes that he has guessed wrong and, further, that he does not know how to answer these direct and basic questions about the afterlife. He escapes with an "I'm not sure," so as "to avoid being pressed by any further questions." His desire to escape her presence suggests that those who possess the tools of education, those who most aspire to "give voice to 'Silent China,'" are often the least capable of doing so.

While Lu Xun appears pessimistic when compared to other propagandists of his day, his realism gave his writing considerable social power. The formal and thematic innovations of "The New Year's Sacrifice" reflect the influence of short story realist writers such as Nikolai Gogol and Anton Chekhov, who had used this form—with its poor, nonheroic protagonists; its omniscient narration; and its exposure of false, hypocritical ideologies—as a political weapon against traditional hierarchies in their own culture. The beggar's repeated story of her child's death, and the mocking it incurs by the villagers, is particularly effective in facilitating Lu Xun's most consistent message: that traditional ethical codes are mere justifications of an inherently cruel hierarchy that devours many lives, particularly those of women, who become "sacrifices" to a bogus value system enforcing female chastity and subordination to men.

The political import of "The New Year's Sacrifice" is enabled by its stark style. In his piece on the author in *Chinese Fiction Writers, 1900–1949,* Jon Eugene von Kowallis writes that Lu Xun values "brevity, subtle suggestions, and irony" and tends to spare all but the most directly significant details, prompting critical comparisons between his fiction and the sparse, expressive outlines of a woodblock print. According to Wang Tso-Liang, Lu Xun tends to use older forms of Chinese words in new, colloquial ways, sometimes borrowing Western syntactical structures. As a result,

LU XUN'S ETHICAL DILEMMA

When Lu Xun's friend Jin Xingyi first entreated him to write his own fiction rather than working on translations of the writings of others, Lu Xun resisted, worried that he would "infect" these young dreamers with the bitter loneliness and disillusionment that he had experienced. He offered the following metaphor to explain his ethical dilemma:

> Imagine an iron house without windows, absolutely indestructible, with many people fast asleep inside who will soon die of suffocation. But you know since they will die in their sleep, they will not feel the pain of death. Now if you cry aloud to wake a few of the lighter sleepers, making those unfortunate few suffer the agony of irrevocable death, do you think you are doing them a good turn?

Lu Xun's friend replied, "But if a few awake, you can't say there is no hope of destroying the iron house." This reply induced Lu Xun to write because, as he explains, "in spite of my own conviction, I could not blot out hope, for hope lies in the future. I could not use my own evidence to refute his assertion that it might exist. So I agreed to write.... From that time onwards, I could not stop writing."

Drew Kalasky writes in *Short Story Criticism,* "the old coinages from the classics not only shine with a rich antique glow, but have a keen new edge that cuts deep into the marrows." Even in translation, his lean sentences often suggest feelings that lie too deep to be elaborated fully: "I listened quietly to the hissing of the snow outside, until little by little I felt more relaxed. But the fragments of her life that I had seen or heard about before combined now to form a whole."

CRITICAL DISCUSSION

"The New Year's Sacrifice" earned instant popularity with revolutionary democrats, mainly for its political import. The primary critical approach to his story at the time of its reception was to evaluate its potential as a social satire that might contribute to revolution. However, Lu Xun's lifelong refusal to consistently and neatly toe the party line did provoke attacks by revolutionaries Guo Moruo and Cheng Fangwu, who called Lu Xun a "feudal element" and an "outsider to the proletariat." These accusations were distorted by the jealousy of these less-talented writers. Furthermore, the youthfulness of his critics allowed them a more fanatical and optimistic utopianism than anything that the experienced and reflective Lu Xun—who was in his late thirties at the time he began writing short fiction in earnest—could ever produce or fully endorse.

The popular view in China, according to Kalasky, is that Lu Xun "has been admired, imitated, but not equaled," although critics such as C. T. Hsia have challenged this view, claiming that Lu Xun's popularity over several other talented writers may be due more to

Portrait of Chinese writer Lu Xun, author of "The New Year's Sacrifice." LU XUN (1881–1936) (COLOUR LITHO), CHINESE SCHOOL, (20TH CENTURY)/ PRIVATE COLLECTION/ ARCHIVES CHARMET/THE BRIDGEMAN ART LIBRARY.

his politics than his superior craftsmanship. Although Lu Xun himself was often ambivalent about expressing hope in his fiction, he allowed room enough for hope to enable the Communist Party to ally itself with his legacy shortly after his death, championing him as a father of the revolution. Lu Xun's first story, "The Diary of a Madman," is now considered by many to be the first piece of revolutionary writing in China, and Chairman Mao himself touted Lu Xun's writing as major force in inspiring the Cultural Revolution.

Lu Xun scholarship written in English tends to stray away from the stridently political. In his essay in *Lu Xun and His Legacy* (1985), Marston Anderson discusses "The New Year's Sacrifice" and other tales in terms of Lu Xun's "lifelong commitment to the introduction of foreign literary forms," praising the author's skill at naturalizing such forms for Chinese culture, while other scholars have investigated his relationship to classical Chinese styles and language. Recent criticism also turns toward Lu Xun's existential tendencies and his treatments of solitude, with Alexander Huang and Yin Xiaoling examining Lu Xun's stories as tragic and Aili Zheng and Cheung Chiu-yee discussing a nihilistic tendency in his work. Other academics have studied his use of irony, particularly in "The New Year's Sacrifice," in which the celebratory ending stands in what might be read as an ironic contrast to the tales just narrated.

BIBLIOGRAPHY

Sources

Anderson, Marston. "The Morality of Form: Lu Xun and the Modern Chinese Short Story." *Lu Xun and His Legacy.* Ed. Leo Ou-Fan Lee. 32–53. Berkeley: U of California P, 1985. Print.

Huang, Alexander. "Tropes of Solitude and LuXun's Tragic Characters." *Neohelicon: Acta Comparation is Litterarum Universarum (Neohelicon)* 37.2 (2010): 349–57. Print.

Huters, Theodore. "The Stories of Lu Xun." *Masterworks of Asian Literature in Comparative Perspective: A Guide for Teaching.* Ed. Barbara Stoler Miller. *Literature Resource Center.* Web. 25 July 2012.

Kalasky, Drew, ed. "Lu Hsün (1881–1936)." *Short Story Criticism.* Vol. 20. Detroit: Gale Research, 1995. Print.

Kowallis, Jon Eugene von. "Lu Xun." *Chinese Fiction Writers, 1900–1949.* Ed. Thomas Moran. *Literature Resources from Gale.* Web. 25 July 2012.

Xiaoling, Yin. "Lu Xun's Parallel to Walter Benjamin: The Consciousness of the Tragicin 'The Loner.'" *Tamkang Review* 26.3 (1996): 53–68. *Literature Resource Center.* Web. 25 July 2012.

Xun, Lu. *Selected Stories of Lu Hsun.* 1960. Trans. Yang Xianyi and Gladys Yang. Bloomington: Indiana UP, 1981. Print.

Zheng, Aili. "The Image of the Outsider: Nietzsche's 'Der tolle Mensch' and LuXun's 'Kuang Ren Ri Ji.'" *The Image of the Outsider II in Literature, Media, and Society: Proceedings of the 2008 Conference of the Society for the Interdisciplinary Study of Social Imagery.* Ed. Will Wright and Steven Kaplan. Pueblo: Colorado State University-Pueblo, 2008. Print.

Further Reading

Chiu-yee, Cheung. *Lu Xun: The Chinese "Gentle" Nietzsche.* Frankfurt am Main: Peter Lang, 2001. Print.

Jameson, Frederic. "Third World Literature in the Era of Multinational Capitalism." *Social Text* 15 (1986): 65–80. Print.

Jenner, W. J. F. "Lu Xun's Disturbing Greatness." *East Asian History* 16 (2000): 1–26. Print.

Lee, Leo Ou-fan. *Voices from the Iron House: A Study of Lu Xun.* Bloomington: Indiana UP, 1987. Print.

Sabin, Margery. "On LuXun." *Raritan* IX.1 (1989): 41–67. Print.

Xun, Lu. "A Preface to *Cheering from the Sidelines.*" *Lu Xun: Diary of a Madman and Other Stories.* Trans. William A. Lyell. Honolulu: U of Hawaii P, 1990. Print.

Yu'an, Zhang. "If Lu Xun Were Still Alive." *Seeds of Fire: Chinese Voices of Conscience.* Ed. and trans. Geremie Barmé and John Minford. New York: Hill & Wang, 1988. Print.

Media Adaptations

Zhu Fu. Dir. Hu Sang. Perf. Yang Bai, Li Di, and Zongxiang Guan. Beijing Film Studio, 1956. Film.

Chu Fu. Written by Xia Yan. Dir. Hu Sang. Cinematography by Qian Jiang. Perf. Bai Yang and Wei Heling. [San Francisco?]: Solid Video; San Francisco, CA: Sole distributor of North America, China Video Movies Distributing Co., © 1983. VHS.

Sarah Gardam

NINE PARTS OF DESIRE

Heather Raffo

OVERVIEW

Nine Parts of Desire (2003), a play by Iraqi-American Heather Raffo, offers nine portraits of Iraqi women, focusing on their lives during the period from the 1991 Gulf War to the 2003 invasion of Iraq. The play, structured as a series of monologues, premiered at the Edinburgh Fringe Festival with Raffo playing all nine parts. The nine characters are Mullaya, a woman hired to lead mourning at funerals; Layal, an artist who survives by collaborating with the Iraqi regime; Amal, a thirty-eight-year-old Bedouin; Huda, an Iraqi living in London; the Doctor, who was educated in Britain but has returned to Iraq to work; Iraqi Girl, a nine-year-old child; Umm Ghada, which means "mother of Ghada," whose children were killed at the Amiriyah air raid shelter during a U.S. strike; the American; and Nanna, a poor, elderly woman. Although some characters condemn Saddam Hussein, others rely on his regime for their livelihood, and *Nine Parts of Desire* does not seek to provide a simplistic reading of current events. Through its nuanced presentation of nine different, complex female characters, the play counters generalizations and stereotypes about Arab, Muslim, and Iraqi women and humanizes the faceless "other."

Raffo's play has been praised by critics, who recognize that its central concern with the lives of ordinary Iraqi women fills an important gap in theater inspired by the Iraq War. *Nine Parts of Desire* received the Susan Smith Blackburn Prize Special Commendation and the Marian Seldes-Garson Kanin Award and has been produced in Brazil, Greece, Sweden, Turkey, Malta, France, Iraq, Egypt, Israel, and Canada. Although some critics speculated that *Nine Parts of Desire* would become less influential as new historical and political realities emerged, the play continues to attract scholarly attention.

HISTORICAL AND LITERARY CONTEXT

Although the United States supported Hussein and the ruling Ba'th Party throughout the 1980s, the 1991 Gulf War and increased U.S. dependence on Iraqi oil led to a shift in policy. Ba'th rule saw the development of Iraq's educational system and infrastructure, and during the 1980s Iraqi women made educational and professional advances. However, Hussein's regime silenced political dissent through arrests, torture, mass executions, and ethnic cleansing. The U.S. call for regime change was justified through the publication of atrocities and human rights abuses committed under Hussein's rule and later through the exploitation of a post-9/11 atmosphere of fear fed by the false claim that Iraq was hiding weapons of mass destruction.

Nine Parts of Desire draws from interviews conducted during and after Raffo's 1993 visit to Iraq, and although the play was written in 1998 as her master's thesis, the 2003 edition focuses on the period between the Gulf War and the Iraq War. The cost of the Gulf War was high for Iraq and included the death of 408 civilians at the Amiriyah air raid shelter in Baghdad when U.S. forces mistook it for a military command center. In the succeeding years, economic sanctions, limited military actions, and a policy of containment failed to significantly weaken Hussein. The 2001 terrorist attacks on New York and Washington, D.C., prompted U.S. President George W. Bush to declare a "war on terror" that soon led him to Iraq. The Iraq War began with the U.S.-led invasion in March 2003, and *Nine Parts of Desire* premiered in August of that year.

In the years leading up to the publication of *Nine Parts of Desire,* a number of English-language texts drew from the lives of Arab Muslim women, including Jean Sasson's *Princess: A True Story of Life behind the Veil in Saudi Arabia* (1992) and Azar Nafisi's *Reading Lolita in Tehran* (2003). These testimonials were presented as "authentic" accounts and revealed narrators who were resilient but oppressed, victims of their social, political, and religious reality who looked to the West for salvation. Raffo's effort can be seen as part of a larger movement by Arab, Middle Eastern, and Muslim American dramatists to humanize their communities and challenge common stereotypes. This trend is exemplified by the work of theater collectives such as Nibras in New York, Silk Road Theatre Project in Chicago, and Golden Thread in San Francisco.

Nine Parts of Desire was well received by critics and scholars, and Raffo has since contributed to other projects related to the Iraq War, including penning the libretto for *Fallujah: The First Opera about the Iraq War. Nine Parts of Desire* was followed by other documentary plays, such as Victoria Brittain and Gillian Slovo's *Guantanamo* (2004), which was based on accounts of detainees at the U.S. prison camp. Additional English-language productions inspired by the Iraq War include

⁘ *Key Facts*

Time Period:
Early 21st Century

Genre:
Play

Events:
Gulf War; Iraq War

Nationality:
Iraqi-American

WHAT ARE THE NINE PARTS OF DESIRE?

Ali ibn Abu Taleb, the cousin and son-in-law of the prophet Mohammad and the fourth caliph, or leader, of the Islamic world, said, "God created sexual desire in ten parts; then he gave nine parts to women and one to men." This saying has alternately been interpreted as an indication that women's sexual desires need to be fulfilled and a warning against the dangers of female sexuality. The title of Geraldine Brooks's 1994 *Nine Parts of Desire: The Hidden World of Islamic Women* is taken from this saying, and Raffo credits both Taleb and Brooks for her own title.

Brooks draws on her experiences as a *Wall Street Journal* foreign correspondent covering the Middle East, portraying the world she inhabits as "a window … open only to me." She intersperses her narrative with historical glosses, quotations from and commentary on the Qur'an, and tales of early Muslim women. Like Raffo, Brooks is intent on undoing monolithic understandings about women in the Arab and Muslim worlds. However, while Raffo's focus is on Iraqi women, and she is careful not to erase their historic, geographic, and temporal contexts, Brooks's efforts concentrate on Muslim women, ultimately focusing on Islam as the defining aspect of identity for all of the women with whom she interacts.

Tim Robbins's *Embedded,* David Hare's *Stuff Happens,* and George Packer's *Betrayed. Nine Parts of Desire* continues to be the subject of scholarship, and in 2009 Raffo helped create a "concert version" of the play, *Sounds of Desire.*

THEMES AND STYLE

All of the play's monologues center on desire, and although it is at times sexual, the characters also yearn for political and artistic freedom, health, justice, friendship, and peace. Despite their differences, their shared desire is that their voices be heard and that they be recognized as distinct individuals worthy of attention. Amal, after she relates to Layal the tale of her failed relationships, explains, "I have never talked this before / nobody here knows this thing about me," elaborating, "This is the most free moment of my life." Umm Ghada similarly calls her trailer by the Amiriyah air raid shelter her "witness stand" and explains that all those who come to see "what really happen here / not what they read in papers / or see in the CNN" sign a guestbook. She invites her audience to sign as well: "your name will be witness too." The American, frustrated at her helplessness and distance from her relatives and the conflict overseas, asks, "Why don't we count the number of Iraqi dead?" This central question demands that the play's audience really see the unique, complex lives of Iraqis, rejecting oversimplifications and generalizations that dehumanize the conflict's non-Western victims. At the same time, however, *Nine Parts of Desire* resists the victimization of its

characters. Layal, for example, turns the microscope on Western women who justify their own oppression by comparing their situation with that of the women in Iraq: "Your western culture, sister, will not free me / from being called a whore / not my sex. / Women are not free."

The individuality of each of Raffo's nine characters is communicated in the text of the play through careful variations in language and tone and monologues that reveal complex—and at times contradictory—identities. Huda, for example, who resides in London, has always been against war but cannot bring herself to protest a war that will remove Hussein. Each woman possesses a distinct vocabulary, even though all of the characters but the American speak English with an Iraqi accent. The Iraqi Arabic words for "yes" and "no"—*aa* and *la*—pepper the English monologues. During the one-woman stage productions, the manipulation of a black *abaya,* or cloak, serves to further distinguish and develop each personality. At the end of the play, the disintegration of Layal's monologue into the fragmented repetition of other characters' lines signals her psychological meltdown.

Nine Parts of Desire utilizes dark humor that resists the transformation of its characters into victims of oppression with no agency. Layal talks about a girl whom Uday, Hussein's son, covers with honey and feeds to a pack of Doberman pinschers. She hints at her horror and a subtle subversion by painting the girl as "the branch's blossom / leaning over the barking dogs / they cannot reach / no matter how hungry they are." However, as a collaborator, she will not speak out and jokes that "Iraqis know they don't open their mouth, not even for the dentist."

CRITICAL DISCUSSION

Nine Parts of Desire was warmly received by critics following its August 2003 debut at the Traverse Theater Edinburgh and its performance at the Bush Theater in London's off-West End, and it garnered more praise during its off-Broadway run at the Manhattan Ensemble Theatre. Writing in the *Wall Street Journal* in 2005, Terry Teachout praises the three-dimensionality of the nine women characters: "We believe in their reality because Ms. Raffo inhabits each one so fully, both as actor and as author, and because we never feel, not even for a moment, that she is making them tell us what we—or she—want to hear." In a 2006 review in *Theatre Journal,* Maria Beach similarly notes that *Nine Parts of Desire* "never simplifies politics," adding that "the intensity of Raffo's concern for the people of Iraq is palpable, and she is such an engaging performer that spectators may leave the theatre feeling as if they also share a connection with the women whose stories inspired this compelling play."

Although some critics have questioned the continued relevance of *Nine Parts of Desire* given its historical specificity and dated frame of reference, the play can be viewed as part of a broader post-9/11 movement in the United States spotlighting the multifaceted nature and diversity of Arab and Muslim identities, particularly female identities, both at home and abroad. Precisely because of the play's grounding within a specific geographical region and historical sequence of events, it continues to stand out as an expression of the complex voices of ordinary Iraqis.

Scholars have focused on the text's documentary qualities. In her 2009 article "Not Yet beyond the Veil: Muslim Women in American Popular Literature," Dohra Ahmad condemns the "ethnographic reading practice" that leads audiences to read "'third-world' and 'minority' writing as exclusively mimetic." She cites *Nine Parts of Desire* as an example of a text whose heteroglossia resists this "literary tourism." Magda Romanska's 2010 article, "Trauma and Testimony: Heather Raffo's *Nine Parts of Desire*," studies the play's characters through the lens of psychology, attempting to understand the psyche of those traumatized by the war. Romanska "analyzes the relationship between trauma, testimony, and performance, as constructed, represented, and performed in Raffo's play, with particular attention to the interface between the survivors, the performer, and the audience."

Heather Raffo, author of *Nine Parts of Desire*, in 2005. AP PHOTO/JOE TABACCA.

BIBLIOGRAPHY

Sources

Ahmad, Dohra. "Not Yet beyond the Veil: Muslim Women in American Popular Literature." *Social Text* 27.2.99 (2009): 105–31. Print.

Beach, Maria. Rev. of *Nine Parts of Desire,* by Heather Raffo. *Theatre Journal* 58.1 (2006): 102–03. Print.

Romanska, Magda. "Trauma and Testimony: Heather Raffo's *Nine Parts of Desire*." *Alif: Journal of Comparative Poetics* 30 (2010): 211–39. Print.

Teachout, Terry. "Invisible Women." Rev. of *Nine Parts of Desire,* by Heather Raffo. *Wall Street Journal.* Dow Jones and Company, 14 Jan. 2005. Web. 4 Nov. 2012.

Further Reading

Afzal-Khan, ed. *Shattering the Stereotypes: Muslim Women Speak Out.* Northampton: Olive Branch, 2005. Print.

Brooks, Geraldine. *Nine Parts of Desire: The Hidden World of Islamic Women.* New York: Anchor Books, 1996. Print.

Hare, David. *Stuff Happens.* London: Faber, 2004. Print.

Kachachi, Inaam. *The American Granddaughter.* Trans. Nariman Youssef. Doha: Bloomsbury, 2010. Print.

Mikhail, Dunya. *The War Works Hard.* Trans. Elizabeth Winslow. New York: New Directions, 2005. Print.

Tripp, Charles. *A History of Iraq.* 2nd ed. Cambridge: Cambridge UP, 2002. Print.

Media Adaptation

Raffo, Heather. *Nine Parts of Desire.* Dir. Joanna Settle. Washington Area Performing Arts Video Archive, 2006. DVD.

Gerald Carpenter

THE OUTSIDER

Richard Wright

❖ *Key Facts*

Time Period:
Mid-20th Century

Genre:
Novel

Events:
Cold War; McCarthyism;
rise of the civil rights
movement

Nationality:
American

OVERVIEW

Published in 1953, Richard Wright's second novel, *The Outsider*, explores the tensions surrounding racial liberalism at the height of McCarthyism and at the dawn of the civil rights movement. The work expands and complicates the dynamics examined in Wright's renowned first novel, *Native Son* (1940). Evoking the violence and melodrama of popular noir fiction, *The Outsider* tells the story of Cross Damon, an African American intellectual who is presumed dead after he narrowly escapes a major accident. When he tries to create a new identity for himself, as a black man he is still denied access to most intellectual communities. He becomes entangled in the Communist Party and turns to violence, fighting often and killing four men during his involvement with the party. By comparing Americans' distorted perceptions of the black community with the hysterical demonizing of communists, Wright demonstrates how mainstream society vilifies outsiders despite the fact that outsiders, through their alienation, can clearly perceive the ills of mainstream society.

The Outsider was released less than a year before the landmark *Brown v. Board of Education* (1954) decision banned segregation in public schools, at a time when U.S. racial tensions were reaching new heights. The early 1950s also marked the apex of the Second Red Scare, a period of government-sanctioned manhunts for suspected communists and communist sympathizers. Wright, who in his earlier writing had chronicled identity struggles from an exclusively African American perspective, saw an opportunity to address outsider dynamics from a new point of view. However, the novel's wanton violence alienated white critics, while its use of existential theory alienated black readers who thought Wright had lost touch with his roots. Today the novel is read as a fiercely individualistic work that consciously departs from the literary tradition of W. E. B. Du Bois, informed by Wright's interaction with communist and existentialist intellectuals of the period.

HISTORICAL AND LITERARY CONTEXT

During and after World War II, the contrast between seemingly noble U.S. efforts overseas and inhumane racial practices at home placed increasing political pressure on the U.S. government. Many intellectuals decried the duplicitous nature of a nation that claimed to spread democracy and freedom yet refused to grant African Americans basic equalities. The country's hypocrisy became even more apparent as the Cold War dawned, producing a new domestic cultural norm characterized by anticommunist paranoia that often turned violent. As the United States sought to recreate the world in its own image, international critics pointed out the glaring inconsistencies between U.S. foreign policy and domestic practices.

By the time *The Outsider* was published in 1953, McCarthyist paranoia dominated the American political and social landscapes. Between 1940 and 1950, a series of federal laws was passed to criminalize communism. Most notably, the Internal Security Act of 1950 restricted civil liberties in the name of security and provided legislative grounds for the investigative practices of the House Un-American Activities Committee and the FBI. Wright, an African American and a former member of the Communist Party, pounced on the opportunity to explore the parallel narratives of segregationist and anticommunist hostilities, illuminating the global politics of race during the Cold War era.

Before Wright published *The Outsider*, twentieth-century African American literature under the guidance of Du Bois had often focused on identity struggles as a way to uplift the black community's cultural status. Works written in this tradition avoided violent narratives in order to showcase African Americans' education and civility, qualities commonly thought exclusive to the privileged white population. However, some writers felt that such portrayals of the black experience, though uplifting, were dishonest. Following the model of Harlem Renaissance writers, Wright's novel *Native Son* and his autobiography *Black Boy* (1945) rejected the tenets of Du Bois's racial uplift program in favor of representations of racial injustice that were more realistic and often violent.

Through the parallel narratives of racism and anticommunism, Wright created a new approach to literary racial discourse and inspired a new generation of black authors. James Baldwin, an African American writer who early in his career idolized Wright, cited *The Outsider* as a direct model for his writing, which examines the experience of being black and homosexual at a time when neither was acceptable in American culture. Later black authors, such as Toni Morrison, Ralph Ellison, and Gwendolyn Brooks, also have cited Wright as a major influence, and the parallel narrative structure used in *The Outsider* has become a staple in the continued development of racial discourse in American letters.

THEMES AND STYLE

The major theme of *The Outsider* is that anticommunism, as a corollary to racism, breeds systematic degradation and dehumanization. At times Wright directly aligns the two marginalized communities. For example, toward the middle of the novel, he describes the struggle of an individual who claims both identities: "He was black and, in the baleful eyes of the men who were coming, he had no right to be here … as a Negro, he was not even free to choose his own allies." In the social dynamic Wright presents, no level of civilization can save an individual from the totalitarian practices of segregation and McCarthyism. This dynamic is complicated by Wright's, and by the end of the novel Damon's, rejection of communist ideology.

Wright empowers his arguments against discriminatory public policy by situating them within the framework of existentialist study. Instead of presenting acts of discrimination for the reader to independently assess, he engages his characters in conversations about the social psychology of oppression. For example, a communist affiliate tells Damon, "Men who cannot manage their sexual appetite launch crusades against vice…. Here are the psychological origins of tyranny." In addition, Wright depicts his communist characters exactly as the public perceives them: power hungry, brainwashed, without humanity. One declares, "I've no life except that of the Party … no wish, no dream, no will except that of the Party." Through this type of melodramatic portraiture, Wright shows how public paranoia can become extreme, even absurd, in its effort to vilify and how crude stereotypes can easily lead to violence.

By adhering to the constraints of noir fiction, *The Outsider* takes a detached, philosophical approach to its subject matter. Rather than appealing to the reader's sense of sympathy, Wright engages the reader's intelligence, peppering each scene with existentialist philosophy to inform the story through narration and dialogue. In an early exchange, district attorney and Communist Party member Ely Houston tells Damon that African Americans "are going to inherit the problems [white people] have, but with a difference. They are outsiders and they are going to know that they have these problems." Through his dispassionate, ruminative tone, Wright models the objectivity he attributes to blacks and other outsiders. Houston later tells Damon to "imagine a man inclined to think, to probe, to ask questions. Why, he'd be in a wonderful position to do so, would he not, if he were black and lived in America? A dreadful objectivity would be forced upon him." By making an indirect, intellectual appeal instead of a confrontational, emotional one, Wright

WRIGHT'S EXILE TO PARIS

Richard Wright became affiliated with the Communist Party in 1933 through his participation in Chicago's John Reed Club, a predominantly communist organization. However, Wright's insistence that the party give young communist writers space to cultivate their talents, as well as his working relationship with a black nationalist communist, led to a public falling out with the party. Threatened at knifepoint by fellow travelers and denounced as a Trotskyite by labor strikers, he was physically assaulted by his former comrades when he tried to join them during the 1936 May Day March.

Although he developed a more positive relationship with the Communist Party in New York, Wright eventually grew weary and left the party altogether in 1944; he publicly denounced the party in an *Atlantic Monthly* essay in 1944 titled "I Tried to Be a Communist," which detailed his entire history with the organization. Under surveillance by the CIA since 1943, Wright expatriated to France in 1946 and was blacklisted by the House Un-American Activities Committee. In Paris he befriended existentialist philosophers Jean-Paul Sartre and Albert Camus, whose friendship and guidance informed the philosophies behind *The Outsider* and many of Wright's later novels. The philosophers' influence also led Wright to engage in anti-Communist Party activism, which is most clearly seen in his decision to republish the controversial *Atlantic* essay in the 1949 anthology *The God That Failed*.

demonstrates African Americans' unique ability as outsiders to perceive mainstream society's failings.

CRITICAL DISCUSSION

Upon the novel's publication, critics' reactions were tepid at best and derisive at worst. Orville Prescott wrote in the *New York Times* that Wright's avoidance of emotional honesty in favor of philosophical examination caused the novel to lack "the persuasive impact that only fully individualized characters can give to fiction." Wright's intellectual approach also attracted criticism from African American critics. Lorraine Hansberry in an essay for *Freedom* stated that the existentialist structure of *The Outsiders* indicates that Wright has lost touch with the black community: "He has forgotten which of the streets of the Southside [of Chicago] lie south of others, an insignificant error, except that it points up how much he has forgotten."

In view of Wright's larger body of work, *The Outsiders'* use of parallel narratives and double consciousness (or recognition of one's identity as simultaneously self and other) can be seen as a progression from the description of racial identity in *Native Son*. Whereas in *Native Son*, society directly reinforces racial subservience, racial subordination is less overt in *The Outsider*. The shift demonstrates Wright's increasing concern with the psychological dimension of double consciousness in the formation of African American identity. Paul Gilroy notes that in Wright's work, "the

Richard Wright at his desk in his home. © BETTMANN/CORBIS.

process of internal conflict that Du Bois described as the joining of 'two warring souls in one black body' is taken further," such that unconscious elements, such as self-loathing in *Native Son,* become part of the social psychology of oppression in *The Outsider.* The latter novel conflates the predicaments of the black intellectual and black underclass, reflecting a cynical view of the future for African Americans.

Contemporary criticism draws from scholarship of the 1960s and 1970s, when critics began to see the merits of *The Outsider* as an existential thesis on the psychological underpinnings of American culture. Scholars such as Yoshinobu Hakutani perceive the self-loathing and hyperbolic violence, which early critics derided, as key elements of the principle of self-creation that guided the later stages of the civil rights movement. In *The World of Richard Wright* (2009), Michel Fabre writes that the novel is "undoubtedly clumsier and psychologically less convincing" than the works of existentialist writers Albert Camus or Jean-Paul Sartre, with whom Wright associated in

Paris, though it remains "a fascinating piece of writing, and one that still speaks to our present needs." Sarah Relyea declares that through his characterization of Cross Damon, Wright transcends "all ethical laws to become a vanguard of modern consciousness," defying "both the moral institutions and the revolutionary movements of the West" and becoming a pivotal figure in critical approaches to African American literature.

BIBLIOGRAPHY

Sources

Butler, Robert. *The Critical Response to Richard Wright.* Westport: Greenwood, 1995. Print.

Fabre, Michel. *The World of Richard Wright.* Jackson: U of Mississippi P, 2009. Print.

Gilroy, Paul. *The Black Atlantic: Modernity and Double Consciousness.* Cambridge: Harvard UP, 1993. Print.

Hakutani, Yoshinobu. *Richard Wright and Racial Discourse.* Columbia: U of Missouri P, 1996. Print.

Relyea, Sarah. "The Vanguard of Modernity: Richard Wright's *The Outsider.*" *Texas Studies in Literature and Language* 48.3 (2006): 187–219. *Academic OneFile.* Web. 25 June 2012.

Wright, Richard. *The Outsider.* New York: Harper & Row, 1969. Print.

Further Reading

Abdurrahman, Umar. "Quest for Identity in Richard Wright's *The Outsider*: An Existentialist Approach." *Western Journal of Black Studies* 30.1 (2006): 25–34. *Academic OneFile.* Web. 25 June 2012.

Bloom, Harold, and Blake Hobby. *Alienation.* New York: Bloom's Literary Criticism, 2009. Print.

Demirturk, Lale. "The Politics of Racelessness in Richard Wright's *The Outsider.*" *CLA Journal* 50.3 (2007): 279–97. *Academic OneFile.* Web. 25 June 2012.

Felgar, Robert. *Student Companion to Richard Wright.* Westport: Greenwood, 2000. Print.

Keith, Joseph. "Richard Wright, *The Outsider* and the Empire of Liberal Pluralism: Race and American Expansion after World War II." *Black Scholar* 39.1–2 (2009): 51–58. *Academic Search Complete.* Web. 25 June 2012.

Lynch, Michael F. "Haunted by Innocence: The Debate with Dostoevsky in Wright's 'Other Novel,' *The Outsider.*" *African American Review* 30.2 (1996): 255–66. *Academic OneFile.* Web. 27 June 2012.

Macksey, Richard, and Frank E. Moorer. *Richard Wright, a Collection of Critical Essays.* Englewood Cliffs: Prentice-Hall, 1984. Print.

McMahon, Frank. "Rereading *The Outsider*: Double-Consciousness and the Divided Self." *Mississippi Quarterly* 50.2 (1997): 289–305. *Academic OneFile.* Web. 27 June 2012.

Thompson, Carlyle V. *Black Outlaws: Race, Law, and Male Subjectivity in African American Literature and Culture.* New York: Peter Lang, 2010. Print.

Wald, Alan. "The Cry Was Unity: Communists and African Americans, 1917–1936." *African American Review* 34.4 (2000): 716. *Academic OneFile.* Web. 27 June 2012.

Clint Garner

RACHEL

A Play in Three Acts

Angelina Weld Grimké

OVERVIEW

First performed in 1916, *Rachel: A Play in Three Acts,* written by Angelina Weld Grimké and published in 1920, examines the profound psychological repercussions of racism and racial violence on an upstanding African American family. Intended as an appeal to white mothers to end antiblack violence, *Rachel* focuses on a young, sensitive, altruistic African American woman who learns of her father and half brother's murder at the hands of a white mob and ultimately vows not to have children because they could become victims of a racist society. Deliberately written as literary propaganda, *Rachel* calls on the moral conscience of white Americans to remedy their treatment of African Americans. It is considered the first use of the American stage for race propaganda aimed at shedding light on the deplorable treatment of African Americans in the early twentieth century.

Rachel is considered to be a foundational work in twentieth-century African American drama: it is the first serious drama written, produced, and performed by African Americans and the first known play by an African American that was written for staging. In its day *Rachel* was seen as the first play to portray African Americans in a positive light. It won a contest held by the National Association for the Advancement of Colored People (NAACP) for playwrights in 1916, and Harlem Renaissance leaders celebrated it for its use of the stage to advance a political agenda for the good of African Americans. Yet others criticized it as fatalistic and feared it advocated race suicide, a claim that Grimké publicly denied. Largely forgotten for decades, *Rachel* enjoyed renewed interest for its compelling portrait of racial and gender injustices in the early twentieth century.

HISTORICAL AND LITERARY CONTEXT

In the early twentieth century, African Americans were still treated as less than full citizens of the United States, a condition they actively resisted. Slave-like conditions persisted in the South, legalized job and housing discrimination flourished in the North, and the nation saw a significant increase in antiblack violence, including lynchings, sexual violence, and massacres. African Americans responded by leaving these oppressive conditions, and millions migrated to northern and western cities in search of a better life. The Harlem Renaissance, the first collective movement of African Americans in the arts, grew out of this significant demographic shift, as African Americans sought opportunities for political change and self-expression in poetry, fiction, visual arts, drama, music, dance, and other arts.

Some scholars date the start of the Harlem Renaissance to the 1916 production of *Rachel*. With its focus on cultured, educated African Americans, *Rachel* participates in the discourse of racial uplift espoused by Harlem Renaissance leader W. E. B. Du Bois. Billed as a protest play and sponsored by the NAACP as part of its national antilynching campaign, *Rachel* anticipates Du Bois's argument in the essay "Criteria of Negro Art" (1926) that art should be used to improve the situation of African Americans. *Rachel* thus functions as a literary form of resistance to lynching, part of a larger political effort spearheaded by African American women to secure federal antilynching legislation.

Rachel also marks a significant departure from the one-dimensional blackface portrayals and inauthentic dialect used to portray African Americans on the American minstrel stage and in early film. Grimké instead endows her refined characters with complex psychology and depicts their emotional responses to racism. The biblically resonant Rachel, with her eloquence and passion, challenges widespread perceptions of African American women as lacking femininity, respectability, and virtue. The play avoids dialect, and the characters use formal language, placing the play in a vibrant tradition in the African American arts that relies on elegant language to demonstrate the humanity and intelligence of African Americans. *Rachel*'s emotional appeal also builds on the slave narrative tradition in which African Americans wrote of their enslavement with extreme emotion and drama to appeal to northern white readers' sense of morality, as well as abolitionist writing, such as Harriet Beecher Stowe's *Uncle Tom's Cabin* (1852), which like *Rachel* uses the theme of motherhood to evoke sympathy.

Rachel opened up new possibilities for African Americans in the theater. Grimké's play transcends musical and comic genres that had long been the only realms in which African Americans could write and

❖ *Key Facts*

Time Period:
Early 20th Century

Genre:
Play

Events:
Pervasive racial discrimination and violence against blacks in the United States; advent of Harlem Renaissance

Nationality:
American

PRIMARY SOURCE

EXCERPT FROM *RACHEL: A PLAY IN THREE ACTS*

(Through the open window comes the laughter of little children at play. Rachel, shuddering, covers her ears.) And once I said, centuries ago, it must have been: "How can life be so terrible, when there are little children in the world?" Terrible! Terrible! *(In a whisper, slowly)* That's the reason it is so terrible. *(The laughter reaches her again; this time she listens)*. And, suddenly, some day, from out of the black, the blight shall descend, and shall still forever the laughter on those little lips, and in those little hearts. …

TOM *(Slowly; as though thinking aloud)* I hear people talk about God's justice and I wonder. There, are you, Ma. There isn't a sacrifice that you haven't made. You're still working your fingers to the bone sewing just so all of us may keep on living. Rachel is a graduate in Domestic Science; she was high in her class; most of the girls below her in rank have positions in the schools. I'm an electrical engineer and I've tried steadily for several months to practice my profession. It seems our educations aren't of much use to us: we aren't allowed to make good because our skins are dark. (Pauses) And, in the South today, there are white men (Controls himself). They have everything; they're well-dressed, well-fed, well-housed; they're prosperous in business; they're important politically; they're pillars in the church. I know all this is true I've inquired. Their children (our ages, some of them) are growing up around them; and they are having a square deal handed out to them college, position, wealth, and best of all, freedom, without galling restrictions, to work out their own salvations. With ability, they

may become anything; and all this will be true of their children's children after them. (A pause). Look at us and look at them. We are destined to failure they, to success. Their children shall grow up in hope; ours, in despair. Our hands are clean; theirs are red with blood red with the blood of a noble man and a boy. They're nothing but low, cowardly, bestial murderers. The scum of the earth shall succeed. God's justice, I suppose.

MRS. LOVING *(Rising and going to Tom; brokenly)* Tom, promise me one thing.

TOM *(Rises gently)* What is it, Ma?

MRS. LOVING That you'll try not to lose faith in God. I've been where you are now and it's black. Tom, we don't understand God's ways. My son, I know, now He is beautiful. Tom, won't you try to believe, again?

TOM *(Slowly, but not convincingly)* I'll try, Ma.

MRS. LOVING *(Sighs)* Each one, I suppose, has to work out his own salvation.

TOM Today, we colored men and women, everywhere are up against it. Every year, we are having a harder time of it. In the South, they make it as impossible as they can for us to get an education. We're hemmed in on all sides. Our one safeguard the ballot in most states, is taken away already, or is being taken away. Economically, in a few lines, we have a slight show but at what a cost! In the North, they make a pretence of liberality: they give us the ballot and a good education, and then snuff us out. Each year, the problem just to live, gets more difficult to solve. How about these children, if we're fools enough to have any?

---

perform for the stage. Lorraine Hansberry's widely performed play *A Raisin in the Sun* (1959) is considered a descendant of *Rachel,* as is the black arts movement of the 1950s and 1960s, which sought to unite art and politics. Thematically *Rachel* also pioneers the exploration of the interlocking oppressions of race and gender. Grimké later took up themes from *Rachel* of racial prejudice, lynching, motherhood, the lives of African American women, and the fragile psyches of young women in several short stories and in her only other play, *Mara*, which was never published.

THEMES AND STYLE

Rachel is a sentimental drama aimed at pulling on the heartstrings of its audience in order to expose the inhumane treatment of African Americans. While lynching is not directly portrayed onstage, its reverberations are

the immediate focus of Grimké's political critique. She characterizes her young protagonist Rachel as caring and devoted in order to appeal to the maternal instincts of white women and to evoke their sympathy for African Americans. Early in the play Rachel declares, "I think the loveliest thing of all the lovely things in this world is just *(almost in a whisper)* being a mother!" and later, "I pray God every night to give me, when I grow up, little black and brown babies—to protect—and guard." By the end of the play, however, she avers she will never have children, hoping to spare them from the horrors she fears they will inevitably face as African Americans. She states, "It would be more merciful—to strangle the little things at birth." The play ends with the sounds of weeping, suggesting the inability of language to articulate the horrors of racism.

A march in Washington, D.C., in 1922 protesting the lynching of blacks. The NAACP (National Association for the Advancement of Colored People) sponsored Angelina Grimké's anti-lynching play *Rachel* in 1916. © BETTMANN/ CORBIS.

Structured as an initiation story in which Rachel undergoes a life-changing realization about the depth of American racism, *Rachel* follows its titular character's metaphorical journey from childhood to adulthood. At the start of the play, the stage directions describe her as bringing "the spirit of abounding life, health, joy, youth." Her expulsion from her Eden-like world occurs after she learns of her father and half brother's murders ten years earlier, watches her brother Tom's struggles to find a decent job despite his education as an electrical engineer, and hears about the trauma her adopted son faces when white children call him racial epithets and throw stones at him. Her loss of innocence results in her announcement that she will not marry or have children. The play's depressing conclusion frustrates the happy ending of the racial uplift dramas of the period.

Grimké uses the tools of melodrama to advance her agenda. The play relies on excessive sobbing, and little other action occurs on stage. Instead, the characters engage in long speeches and verbal wit. Some critics describe Grimké's style as heavy-handed, overwrought, and dated, with sentimental verbiage and excessive characterization. Gloria T. Hull, for example, argues in her book, *Color, Sex and Poetry* (1987) that Rachel comes across as "too sensitive, too good, too sweet—almost saccharine." Despite its journey to the depths of human sorrow, *Rachel* is typically categorized in the realist tradition for bearing witness to the very real threat of lynching African Americans faced, and Grimké was heavily influenced by her study of early realist playwrights Anton Chekhov and Henrik Ibsen.

CRITICAL DISCUSSION

Rachel did not receive much attention when it first premiered at the Myrtilla Miner Normal School in Washington, D.C. in 1916, although audiences were sympathetic to its message. When published in 1920, however, it gained more notice, receiving nearly fifty reviews. According to Hull, the *Courier,* a newspaper in Buffalo, New York, noted, "There is a terrible tragic note throughout the three acts of this little play, which compels one to think, and if possible, to lend aid to try and remove the prejudice against the colored race." Leaders of the Harlem Renaissance praised the play as precisely the kind of marriage of art and propaganda that African Americans needed, but others criticized *Rachel* as too dogmatic, arguing that it sacrificed artistry for politics. In a 1921 review for *Journal of Negro History,* critic Lillie Buffum Chace Wyman praises the play as "a beautiful and poetic creation" and includes information about recent lynchings to demonstrate its realism. Other early reviews, however, criticize the play's sense of futility. According to Hull, the *Post-Express* newspaper in Rochester, New York, describes it as "morbid and overstrained."

Rachel is considered the earliest full-length play in the antilynching tradition in American drama.

WOMEN WRITERS OF THE HARLEM RENAISSANCE

Well into the twentieth century, scholarship on the Harlem Renaissance focused on male writers. However, as scholar Cheryl A. Wall asserts in *Women of the Harlem Renaissance* (1995), "the Harlem Renaissance was not a male phenomenon." Beginning in the late twentieth century, feminist literary scholars sought to recover the works of women writers of the Harlem Renaissance who, according to Venetria K. Patton and Maureen Honey in their introduction to *Double-Take: A Revisionist Renaissance Anthology* (2001), "participated in all of the period's artistic venues." Angelina Weld Grimké's poetry, for example, was published in every major Harlem Renaissance anthology of the 1920s. Other famous women writers of the Harlem Renaissance include fiction writer Zora Neale Hurston; novelist and literary editor Jessie Redmon Fauset; novelist Nella Larsen; poet, short-story writer, and playwright Georgia Douglas Johnson; poet Alice Dunbar-Nelson; short-story writer and poet Gwendolyn B. Bennett; and fiction writer Dorothy West.

While their works were largely forgotten or ignored for many decades, these women writers were central to the Harlem Renaissance in the 1910s through the 1930s. Fauset's *There Is Confusion* (1924) is considered the first significant novel of the Harlem Renaissance, and Johnson published in every major journal and anthology—and produced three poetry collections—during the Harlem Renaissance. Hurston, author of *Their Eyes Were Watching God* (1937), is now arguably the most well-known novelist of the Harlem Renaissance. Women's rights and gender issues were also important themes of the era, as were metaphors of motherhood, fertility, birth, and domesticity.

Although the play does not directly depict a lynching, *Rachel* examines the profound, devastating impact of violence on African American families to bolster the efforts of the antilynching movement. However, as a propaganda play, *Rachel* has long been dismissed by scholars for its lack of literary quality, and Grimké was largely forgotten after the Harlem Renaissance, with only a few of her poems appearing in anthologies. In recent years, recovery efforts have emerged, led by the groundbreaking work of scholars Gloria T. Hull and Claudia Tate. In their reexamination of *Rachel*, they argue for its importance as a landmark play of African American drama and admire its artistic achievement, although it is rarely performed publicly.

As a play written by an African American woman at the start of the Harlem Renaissance, *Rachel* is claimed by scholars in a wide range of fields, including African American, Harlem Renaissance, literary, theater, and women's studies. Offering a psychoanalytic reading of the play, William Storm argues in a 1993 essay for *African American Review*, "Rachel is a figure of considerable psychological intricacy and emotional volatility." In a 1992 essay for *African American Review*, Judith L. Stephens argues that

Rachel challenges the status quo "by unmasking the racist and gendered assumptions of white-male dominance." While initial focus was almost solely on race issues in the play, an important later effort examines gender issues in *Rachel* and highlights Grimké's feminist project. In *Women of Color* (1996), Elizabeth Brown-Guillory examines the tensions between mothers and daughters, and in a 2007 article in the *Journal of American Drama and Theatre*, Robin Bernstein focuses on the play's portrayal of children. Koritha A. Mitchell argues in *Post-Bellum, Pre-Harlem* (2006) that *Rachel* emphasizes the violence to the African American family that lynching wreaks, placing the home as the primary victim of racial violence. In the area of biographical literary criticism, several scholars have speculated about how Grimké's life shaped *Rachel*, including Grimké's decision not to marry or have children, her repressed lesbian desire, and her mother's abandonment at a young age.

BIBLIOGRAPHY

Sources

Grimké, Angelina Weld. "Rachel." *Double-Take: A Revisionist Renaissance Anthology.* Ed. Venetria K. Patton and Maureen Honey. New Brunswick: Rutgers UP, 2001. 189–226. Print.

Hull, Gloria T. *Color, Sex and Poetry: Three Women Writers of the Harlem Renaissance.* Bloomington: Indiana UP, 1987. 97–112. Print.

Patton, Venetria K., and Maureen Honey. Introduction. *Double-Take: A Revisionist Renaissance Anthology.* Ed. Venetria K. Patton and Maureen Honey. New Brunswick: Rutgers UP, 2001. Print.

Stephens, Judith L. "Anti-Lynch Plays by African American Women: Race, Gender, and Social Protest in American Drama." *African American Review* 26 (1992): 329–40. JSTOR. Web. 18 Aug. 2012.

Storm, William. "Reactions of a 'Highly-Strung Girl': Psychology and Dramatic Representation in Angelina W. Grimké's *Rachel*." *African American Review* 27.3 (1993): 461–71. JSTOR. Web. 18 Aug. 2012.

Wall, Cheryl A. *Women of the Harlem Renaissance.* Bloomington: Indiana UP, 1995. Print.

Wyman, Lillie Buffum Chace. Rev. of *Rachel,* by Angelina Weld Grimké. *Journal of Negro History* 6.2 (1921): 248–54. JSTOR. Web. 22 Aug. 2012.

Further Reading

"Angelina Weld Grimké." *Drama Criticism.* Vol. 38. Ed. Lawrence J. Trudeau. Detroit: Gale, 2010. 87–142. *Literature Criticism Online.* Web. 18 Aug. 2012.

Bernstein, Robin. "'Never Born': Angelina Weld Grimké's *Rachel* as Ironic Response to Topsy." *Journal of American Drama and Theatre* 19.2 (2007): 61, 75. Print.

Brown-Guillory, Elizabeth. "Disrupted Motherlines: Mothers and Daughters in a Genderized, Sexualized, and Racialized World." *Women of Color: Mother-Daughter Relationships in 20th-Century Literature.* Ed. Elizabeth Brown-Guillory. Austin: U of Texas P, 1996. 188–207. Print.

Du Bois. W. E. B. "Criteria of Negro Art." *Double-Take: A Revisionist Renaissance Anthology.* Ed. Venetria K. Patton and Maureen Honey. New Brunswick: Rutgers UP, 2001. 47–51. Print.

Mitchell, Koritha A. "Antilynching Plays: Angelina Weld Grimké, Alice Dunbar-Nelson, and the Evolution of African American Drama." *Post-Bellum, Pre-Harlem: African American Literature and Culture.* Ed. Barbara McCaskill and Caroline Gebhard. New York: New York UP, 2006. 210–30. Print.

Miller, Ericka M. *The Other Reconstruction: Where Violence and Womanhood Meet in the Writings of Ida B. Wells-Barnett, Angelina Weld Grimké, and Nella Larsen.* New York: Routledge, 1999. Print.

Perkins, Kathy A. "Angelina Weld Grimké." *Strange Fruit: Plays on Lynching by American Women.* Ed. Kathy A. Perkins. Bloomington: Indiana UP, 1998. 23–26. Print.

Rice, Anne P. *Witnessing Lynching: American Writers Respond.* Rutgers UP, 2003. Print.

Tate, Claudia. *Domestic Allegories of Political Desire: The Black Heroine's Text at the Turn of the Century.* New York: Oxford UP, 1992. Print.

Young, Patricia. "Shackled: Angelina Weld Grimké." *Women and Language* 15.2 (1992): 25–31. *Proquest.* Web. 20 Aug. 2012.

Alicia Kent

SECOND-CLASS CITIZEN

Buchi Emecheta

✣ *Key Facts*

Time Period:
Late 20th Century

Genre:
Novel

Events:
Advent of Nigerian
independence; rise
of Western feminist
movements

Nationality:
Nigerian

OVERVIEW

Buchi Emecheta's novel *Second-Class Citizen* (1974) fictionalizes the author's real-life struggle against sexual and racial oppression in the story of its protagonist, Adah. A young Igbo woman from Lagos, Nigeria, Adah follows her student husband to London in the early 1960s only to have her dreams of economic opportunity and sexual equality undone by the racist attitudes of the British people and an African immigrant community that exaggerates the patriarchal customs of her tribal upbringing. Despite mounting hardships—an abusive marriage, multiple and difficult pregnancies, the loss of her job, and the humiliations of accepting welfare—Adah returns to school and becomes a successful writer able to support her five children on her own. Janet J. Montelaro observes that one of "the primary concerns that [Emecheta's] fiction addresses is the status of women in Nigeria and Western Africa, as well as African women who live abroad. Emecheta firmly believes that writing about women's problems and the contradictions of African women's social status will draw attention to the many inequities they face, which, in effect, becomes the first step toward social change."

Published in the decade following the liberation of many African countries from European colonial rule and influenced by the emerging women's liberation movement, *Second-Class Citizen* was immediately recognized as a significant contribution to the identity politics of the times. The success of *Second-Class Citizen* and its predecessor volume, the autobiographical essays collected as *In the Ditch* (1972), made Emecheta one of the first internationally famous African women writers. She went on to produce a large body of work, including over a dozen novels taking up themes of gender politics and imperial oppression, which has earned her a reputation as the most sustained presence in black Africa's literary tradition of female protest.

HISTORICAL AND LITERARY CONTEXT

Emecheta is highly critical of the British colonial presence in Nigeria for aggravating the sexist assumptions of the Igbo, a traditionally male-dominated culture that limited the identity of women to their value as domestic property: subservience in marriage, ability to bear children—preferably male, and willingness to remain confined to the home. During the colonial occupation, which extended from the late nineteenth century to Nigeria's declaration of independence in 1960, the British government imposed its own patriarchal social, political, and economic policies on an Igbo society already overdetermined by gender. Because women were valued among the Igbo solely for faithful compliance to domestic routine, typically only male children were granted access to the missionary schools that had been established by the British. The restrictions on schooling were a particularly effective method of subjugating Igbo women, since a Western education was considered vital to having a voice in changing Africa.

Emecheta's interest in women's rights was strengthened by her exposure to Western liberal values in England. As a sociology student at the University of London, she was deeply influenced by her reading of *Sexual Politics,* American Kate Millet's groundbreaking 1970 study of the position of women in patriarchal capitalist society. In the opinion of Lloyd Brown, Emecheta's vision for reform connects her "more closely to the militant temper and rhetoric of contemporary feminism in Europe and the United States than any other female writer in Black Africa."

Yet Emecheta has objected to being too closely aligned with Western feminists, whom she feels tend to selectively appropriate her message to circumstances to which it does not apply. She writes in the essay "Feminism with a Small 'f'!": "Being a woman, and African born, I see things through an African woman's eyes. I chronicle the little happenings in the lives of African women I know. I did not know that by doing so I was going to be called a feminist. But if I am now a feminist then I am an African feminist with a small f." Emecheta claims as her foremost models the "literary sisterhood" that preceded her: Bessie Head, of Botswana; Grace Ogot, of Kenya; Ama Ata Aidoo and Efua Sutherland, both of Ghana; and, especially, fellow Igbo writer Flora Nwapa. Following Nwapa's lead, Emecheta drew on the example of Igbo women's grassroots protest organizations, whose power was severely curtailed by the British colonial administration.

According to Florence Stratton, "Emecheta's awareness of her membership in a literary sisterhood marks the emergence of a self-conscious female literary tradition." The writings of this group are seminal for their addition of themes of female subjugation and liberation to the paradigm of anticolonial African literature established by Chinua Achebe's *Things Fall Apart* (1958). Along with her forerunners, Emecheta was hailed as an important female voice in the male-dominated canon of postcolonial African literature.

THEMES AND STYLE

The main themes of *Second-Class Citizen* are sexual and racial exploitation, women's freedom, and motherhood. *Second-Class Citizen,* like *In the Ditch,* describes the alienation and culture shock of Adah's first years in her adopted country, but *Second-Class Citizen* supplies greater context for Adah's hard fight for liberation by tracing the origins of many of her problems back to their roots in colonial Nigeria. Adah is a victim of color prejudice in England, where the government is in negotiations to halt the flow of immigration from its former colonies. The influx of immigrants is resented by the British people as unfair competition for the short supply of jobs, housing, and welfare. Adah is also discriminated against by the Nigerian diasporic community for transgressing gender roles by seeking to better herself through education. However, Adah's miseries are mostly caused by her husband, Francis, an irresponsible and domineering brute discouraged by the high expectations placed upon him in European society and his failure to pass his exams. Utterly demoralized, Francis wallows in his second-class citizenship. He subjects Adah to conflicting and unreasonable demands. He refuses to work, which makes Adah the sole breadwinner, but he also refuses her birth control. Threatened by her professional aspirations, he is physically abusive and sexually voracious. Adah finally determines to strike out on her own with her children after Francis destroys the manuscript of her first novel. When she leaves, she is twenty-two years old and pregnant with her fifth child in an alien country that disapproves of the high rates of procreation so valued by Igbo men.

Critic Nancy Topping Bazin describes a strategy of dual perspectives operating in all of Emecheta's novels: "The first perspective evolves from personal experience. It requires personal growth on the part of the individual to extract herself from an oppressive environment. Personal growth leads into a second perspective that is social or communal. It demands an analysis of the causes of oppression within the social mores and the patriarchal power structure." Marilyn Richardson also identifies complementary perspectives in her discussion of *In the Ditch* and *Second-Class Citizen*: "Insider and outsider, client and social scientist simultaneously, Emecheta writes of being a black welfare mother. As she describes the pain, the camaraderie, and at times even the humor of life 'in the ditch,' she can nail the system's stupidities, blind

EDUCATION FIRST

Born to Igbo parents in Yaba, a small village outside Lagos, Nigeria, Buchi Emecheta had to compete with her younger brother Adolphus for the limited funds the family could allot to schooling. Her parents kept her home from school because she was a girl, but she repeatedly escaped to join Adolphus in the local classroom. The teachers finally convinced Emecheta's parents, Jeremy and Alice, that a Western education would increase her bride price when she reached marriageable age. When Emecheta was nine years old, Jeremy died, and her mother became the property of Jeremy's brother. Emecheta was then sent to live with her mother's brother in Lagos. The second chapter of *Second-Class Citizen* documents Emecheta's struggle to gain admission to the prestigious Methodist Girls' High School in Lagos. When Adah is given two shillings to buy a pound of steak for the family, she appropriates the money to pay for her entrance examinations. For this offense, she is whipped with a cane: "After a hundred and three strokes … Adah did not mind. She was, in fact, very happy. She had earned the two shillings." Adah scores so well on the exam she is awarded a four-year scholarship.

spots, and cruelties as only a woman could who has not only studied the system, but, at risk of life and sanity, survived it."

The language of *Second-Class Citizen,* though straightforward and simple, is carefully constructed to incorporate Emecheta's reverence for the Igbo oral culture, known as *Ifo.* She makes use of Igbo riddles, proverbs, and songs in a process Susan Arndt describes as "writing back" to *Ifo* to challenge the imperialist domination that replaced tribal dialects with the English language. Arndt adds that Emecheta's "igboization of English" is also achieved through the integration of Igbo syntax, metaphors and similes, and place and character names. In a different interpretation of language in *Second-Class Citizen,* Obododimma Oha argues that Adah's vilification of her husband is a type of conflict rhetoric common to propaganda, as articulated by Sam Keen in his *Faces of the Enemy: Reflections of the Hostile Imagination*: "In all propaganda, the face of the enemy is designed to provide a focus for our hatred. He is the other. The outsider, the alien. He is not human."

CRITICAL DISCUSSION

Upon the first appearance of *Second-Class Citizen,* its portrait of sexual inequality was widely praised as realistic, even documentary, in its scope and supporting detail. Roger Ballard, for example, placed *Second-Class Citizen* within the tradition of the "informant's account" of cultural change made fashionable by anthropologists Oscar Lewis and Ursula Sharma. However, some critics—most of them male—considered *Second-Class Citizen* ineffective as a public

Nigerian writer Buchi
Emecheta, author of
Second-Class Citizen.
© ART DIRECTORS & TRIP/
ALAMY.

are African society and family; the historical, social, and political life in Africa as seen by a woman through events. I always try to show that the African male is oppressed and he too oppresses the African woman…. I have not committed myself to the cause of African women only. I write about Africa as a whole." The influence of Western culture on the Igbo, both male and female, is viewed as essential to Emecheta's understanding of the liberated Nigerian national identity. Stratton concludes, "Buchi Emecheta is, then, both a disruptive and cohesive force within the contemporary African literary tradition. She situates herself quite firmly within a specifically female tradition which she celebrates, and from the position of which she launches an attack on the male tradition. But she also displays some affinities with the male tradition, sharing, for example, similar views on colonialism."

BIBLIOGRAPHY

Sources

Arndt, Susan. "Buchi Emecheta and the Tradition of *Ifo*: Continuation and 'Writing Back.'" *Emerging Perspectives on Buchi Emecheta.* Ed. Marie Umeh. Trenton, NJ: Africa World, 1996. 28–56. Print.

Ballard, Roger. Rev. of *Second-Class Citizen,* by Buchi Emecheta. *RAIN* 10 (1975): 17. *JSTOR.* Web. 24 Sept. 2012.

Bazin, Nancy Topping. "Feminist Perspectives in African Fiction: Bessie Head and Buchi Emecheta." *The Black Scholar* 17.2 (1986): 34–40. *JSTOR.* Web. 9 Aug. 2012.

Bruner, Charlotte, and David Bruner. "Buchi Emecheta and Maryse Condé: Contemporary Writing from Africa and the Caribbean." *World Literature Today* 59.1 (1985): 9–13. *JSTOR.* Web. 24 Sept. 2012.

Emecheta, Buchi. "Feminism with a Small 'f'!" *Criticism and Ideology: Second African Writers' Conference.* Ed. Kirsten Holst Petersen. Uppsala, Sweden: Scandinavian Institute of African Studies, 1988. 173–85. *Literature Resource Center.* Web. 25 Sept. 2012.

Montelaro, Janet J. "Buchi Emecheta: Overview." *Feminist Writers.* Ed. Pamela Kester-Shelton. Detroit: St. James, 1996. *Gale Biography in Context.* Web. 8 Sept. 2012.

Oha, Obododimma. "Language and Gender Conflict in Buchi Emecheta's *Second-Class Citizen.*" *Emerging Perspectives on Buchi Emecheta.* Ed. Marie Umeh. Trenton, NJ: Africa World, 1996. 289–308. Print.

Richardson, Marilyn. "A Daughter of Nigeria." *The Women's Review of Books* 2.8 (1985): 6–7. *JSTOR.* Web. 9 Aug. 2012.

Stratton, Florence. "Their New Sister: Buchi Emecheta and the Contemporary African Literary Tradition." *Contemporary African Literature and the Politics of Gender.* London: Routledge, 1994. Print.

Umeh, Marie. "Buchi Emecheta." *Post-Colonial African Writers: A Bio-Bibliographical Critical Sourcebook.* Ed. Pushpa Naidu Parekh and Sigma Fatima Jagne. Westport, CT: Greenwood, 1998. 148–63. Print.

crusade because of the very personal nature of the problems it recorded.

Emecheta's early literary celebrity has been largely attributed to the attentions of Western feminist critics, who embraced her militant stance on such issues as education, employment, and marriage. Later critics—and Emecheta herself in the essay "Feminism with a Small 'f'!"—objected to the distortions caused by this early scholarship, which has been faulted as racist for privileging the Western feminist perspective. By thus reinforcing the African woman's position of powerlessness, it is argued, Western feminist critics encouraged the production of paternalistic readings of *Second-Class Citizen* that denied the African female agency.

Revisionist interpretations of Emecheta's works have tended to emphasize the centrality of her critique of imperialism to her understanding of the African consciousness, another feature of her writing generally ignored by Western feminists. Stratton notes that Western feminist scholarship appropriated the ideas of Emecheta and other African women to their own specific concerns, many of them dealing with sexual mores. Stratton writes, "Such a reading demands the suppression of the anti-colonial discourse of Emecheta's texts." Other critics have similarly argued that gender discrimination, while constituting the locus of Emecheta's protest, is not her sole concern. Remarks that Emecheta made in a 1979 interview with Inny Tioye are cited in support of this view: "[The] main themes of my novels

Further Reading

Emecheta, Buchi. *In the Ditch*. London: Barrie and Jenkins, 1972. Print.

———. *Second-Class Citizen*. London: Allison & Busby, 1974. Print.

Mekgwe, Pinkie. "Post Africa(n) Feminism?" *Third Text* 24.2 (2010): 189–94. Print.

Mikell, Gwendolyn, ed. *African Feminism: The Politics of Survival in Sub-Saharan Africa*. Philadelphia: U of Pennsylvania, 1997. Print.

Porter, Abioseh Michael. "*Second-Class Citizen*: The Point of Departure for Understanding Buchi Emecheta's Major Fiction." *Emerging Perspectives on Buchi Emecheta*. Ed. Marie Umeh. Trenton, NJ: Africa World, 1996. 267–88. Print.

Solberg, Rolg. "The Woman of Black Africa, Buchi Emecheta: The Woman's Voice in the New Nigerian Novel." *English Studies* 64.3 (1983): 247–62. *Literature Resource Center*. Web. 18 Sept. 2012.

Sougou, Omar. "Autobiography and Self-Definition: *In the Ditch* and *Second-Class Citizen*." *Writing Across Cultures: Gender Politics and Difference in the Fiction of Buchi Emecheta*. Amsterdam: Rodopi, 2002. 29–55. Print.

Walker, Alice. "Watered with Blood." *Alice Walker: A Life*. Ed. Evelyn C. White. New York: Norton, 2004. 180–84. Print.

Janet Mullane

THE SECRET LIFE OF SAEED
The Pessoptimist
Emile Habiby

✥ *Key Facts*

Time Period:
Late 20th Century

Genre:
Novel

Events:
Arab-Israeli War and its aftermath

Nationality:
Palestinian Israeli

OVERVIEW

The Secret Life of Saeed: The Pessoptimist, an epistolary novel first published by Emile Habiby in serialized form between 1972 and 1974, contrasts the Israeli conception of itself as a liberal democracy with the Palestinian Israeli experience of exclusion and oppression. Published as a book in 1974, the novel has been noted for Habiby's straightforward prose and dark humor. Born into an ill-fated family of cowards, informers, and collaborators, the narrator, Saeed, is last in a long line of Pessoptimists; even when a dreadful misfortune befalls them, the Pessoptimists "thank Him that it was no worse." Elements of the fantastic enter the story when Saeed encounters a being from outer space, who later rescues him from a high stake from which he has been suspended. By tracing the tragicomic episodes of Saeed's life from the 1948 creation of the State of Israel to the aftermath of the 1967 Arab-Israeli War, *The Secret Life of Saeed* demonstrates that the Israeli myth of equality conceals the suffering of a significant Palestinian minority.

Although a distinct Palestinian literature had begun to emerge after 1948, Habiby was one of the first Palestinian Israelis to produce a narrative about life inside the new nation. In the years following its publication, the novel was well received by critics and became a best seller in the Arabic-speaking world. Both Yasser Arafat, head of the Palestine Liberation Organization, and Prime Minister Itzhak Shamir of Israel awarded Habiby for his work. In 1990 he received the al-Quds Prize, which recognized his contributions as a Palestinian author, and in 1992 he garnered the Israel Prize, which celebrated him as an Israeli author. With his acceptance of the Israel Prize, Habiby officially acknowledged his status as an Israeli citizen, even though the perceived betrayal provoked outrage among Arab intellectuals. As a fictionalized eyewitness account of real historical inequality and oppression, the novel has continued to attract scholarly attention since its publication.

HISTORICAL AND LITERARY CONTEXT

In 1948 the State of Israel was established as the answer to the Zionist call for a Jewish homeland. Israeli historical discourse characterized the struggle that culminated in the birth of the new nation as a war for independence, but the widespread persecution and displacement of the native Arab population became known in Arabic as the *nakba,* or catastrophe. Hundreds of Arab villages were destroyed, and Arabic place names were Hebraized in an effort to remap the geography and erase the public memory of the Palestinian claim to the land. Despite these efforts, the presence of a significant non-Jewish Arab minority within Israel's borders contested the ethno-religious foundation of national identity. Christian and Muslim Palestinian Israelis were granted nominal equality but in actuality suffered as second-class citizens subject to discrimination and disempowered by the state.

Habiby, a Palestinian Christian and a minority in Israel, wrote *The Secret Life of Saeed* just a few years after the 1967 Arab-Israeli War, which had led to another devastating Arab defeat, known in Arabic as the *naksa,* or setback. A new wave of refugees was created, Palestine remained occupied, and Israel succeeded in expanding its territory, which led to a mobilization of the Palestinian resistance movement. Hostilities intensified in the early 1970s, and the Palestinian nationalist movement expected full support from Palestinian Israelis, while Israel tolerated nothing short of complete loyalty to the state. The need to consolidate control over the territories occupied during the 1967 war officially ended military rule within Israel. The mainstream assertion that a "liberal democracy" then emerged has been disputed by such scholars as Ilan Pappe, who argue that what actually occurred was a "normalization" of oppression, enforced by laws rather than by force. Palestinians remained second-class citizens, segregated from the rest of the population at home and at school and largely limited to work as unskilled laborers. Exceptions were usually obtained through collaboration, and the state relied on a large network of informers. By the mid-1970s, 13 percent of the Israeli population was Palestinian, constituting a threat to the Jewish character of the state. *The Secret Life of Saeed* undermines the image of post-1967 Israel as a liberal democracy, exposing the institutionalized inequality of the state by holding up a mirror to Israeli society.

After 1948 Palestinian literature began to constitute a distinct corpus, in conversation with broader Arabic literary trends but differentiated by its historical and political concern with the *nakba* and later the *naksa.* Its authors were split into those writing outside Israel, such as Ghassan Kanafani and Mahmoud Darwish, and those writing within its borders. The latter group was further divided into those who wrote in Hebrew, such as Atallah Mansour, and those who wrote in Arabic, as Habiby did. In 1968 Habiby published *The Sextet of the Six Day War,* a collection of six linked short stories that similarly use humor and irony to deal with the 1967 Arab-Israeli War.

The Secret Life of Saeed received critical acclaim from scholars writing in Arabic, Hebrew, and English and quickly became a best seller, going through three Arabic printings in the first three years after its publication. The Palestinian Israeli writer Anton Shammas translated the text into Hebrew in 1984, two years before his own Hebrew novel, *Arabesques,* appeared. Habiby was one of the first Arab authors to write about life inside Israel, and through the translation of his novel into Hebrew, he forcefully added a Palestinian voice to the Israeli conversation. The novel's deft use of irony and humor influenced the satirical tone of later Palestinian fiction, and *The Secret Life of Saeed* continues to be the subject of scholarly work and debate.

THEMES AND STYLE

At the heart of the novel is a contrast between the Israeli public discourse on equality and democracy and the lived reality of the Palestinian population residing within the state. The reality for this population, along with the land, was of having "become government property." Palestinian Israelis remain second-class citizens who are persecuted, discriminated against, and consistently denied justice. They have been exploited to build the very Israeli state that now disempowers them: "Yes, who erected the buildings, paved the roads, dug and planted the earth of Israel, other than the Arabs who remained there?" Saeed nevertheless chooses to stay in Israel after it is created in 1948. When Saeed is imprisoned, he meets a resistance fighter, also named Saeed, who mistakes him for a fellow nationalist. Although the narrator Saeed's cowardice prevents him from engaging in any act of outright rebellion, his pride in this false identity leads him to abandon his work as an informer and become a fruit and vegetable seller. However, it is not easy to escape his family history of collaboration, as informers are "inherited by the state from [their] own fathers." Saeed begins "to see the jail's iron gate as a door connecting the two yards of one prison." An official confirms this perception when he tells Saeed, "Our democracy is just not right for you people," meaning the Palestinians. Habiby does not overlook the role Saeed's weakness and cowardice play in determining his fate, but the narrator's hapless bumbling simultaneously undermines the national myth of democracy.

The novel takes the form of a long letter that Saeed has composed while in the safety of outer space to describe the fate of the Palestinians in Israel to those below. It is a satirical response to the Palestinian poet

Samih al-Qasim's call to action, which forms the novel's epigraph: "Don't wait still more, don't wait! / Now, off with your sleep-clothes / And to yourselves compose / Those letters you so anticipate!" In the epilogue, the recipient searches for Saeed in a nearby mental institution but fails to determine whether the letter writer was ever a patient. The novel thus resists the easy resolution of its fantastical elements, even while its historical and cultural emplacement anchors the narrative in reality. Saeed reminds his readers that "the moon is closer to us now than are the fig trees of our departed village. You accept all these wonders—why not mine too?" *The Secret Life of Saeed* is divided into three sections, each organized around a woman. Their names—creations of the author—are suggestive of particular historical periods. Saeed's first love, Yuaad (a name that means "will return" or "again"), was driven out in 1948 and has become a refugee. Saeed then marries Baqiyya, "the one who remains," who has escaped the fate of forced expulsion. In the final book, Saeed meets the second Yuaad, the first Yuaad's daughter. It is post-1967, and she lives in the Diaspora although she still harbors hope of return. While the presence of supernatural elements detaches Saeed from his suffering, the novel's structure and historical focus reaffirm it as a concrete critique of contemporary Palestinian reality.

Literary and historical allusions, jokes, and elements of the absurd are interwoven with episodic accounts of Saeed's various mishaps, creating a disjointed narrative related in straightforward prose and short, quick chapters. Together these brief sketches of Saeed's misadventures produce a sardonic social commentary that is further emphasized by the narrator's unintentional interrogation of Israeli society, as well as the Israeli characters' inadvertent revelation of its inherent contradictions. This fact is evident in Yuaad's description of the fall of Nazareth. After detaining the men in a vacant lot exposed to the sun, denying them water, and imprisoning those Palestinians identified by an informer, the military governor tells

A Palestinian man hands his identification card to an Israeli soldier at a Jerusalem checkpoint. *The Secret Life of Saeed* is about a Palestinian who becomes a citizen of Israel. © DAVID H. WELLS/ CORBIS.

PRIMARY SOURCE

EXCERPT FROM *THE SECRET LIFE OF SAEED: THE PESSOPTIMIST*

I met Yu'ad where meetings in Israel often occur—in prison. Actually, I was on my way out of prison at the time. I got there in the first place when I overdid my loyalty bit, so that the authorities saw it as disloyalty.

It all came about on one of those devil-ridden nights of the June War. I was tuned in, to be on the safe side, to the Arabic-language broadcast of Radio Israel. I heard the announcer calling upon the "defeated Arabs" to raise white flags on the roofs of their homes so that the Israeli servicemen, flashing about arrow-quick all over the place, would leave them alone, sleeping safe and sound inside.

This order somewhat confused me: to which "defeated Arabs" was the announcer referring? Those defeated in this war or those defeated by the treaty of Rhodes? I thought it would be safe to regard myself as one of those "defeated" and convinced myself that if I was making a mistake, they would interpret it as an innocent one. So I made a white flag from a sheet, attached it to a broomstick, and raised it above the roof of my house in Jabal Street in Haifa, an extravagant symbol of my loyalty to the state.

But who, one might ask, was I trying to impress? As soon as my flag was flying for all to see, my master Jacob honored me by bursting in on me, without so much as a "How are you?" So I did not greet him either.

He yelled, "Lower it, you mule!"

I lowered my head until it touched his very feet and asked, "Did they appoint you King of the West Bank, Your Majesty?"

Jacob seized me by the lapels of my pajamas and began pushing me up the stairs towards the roof, repeating, "The sheet, the sheet!" When we reached the broomstick, he grabbed it, and I thought he wanted to beat me with it. So we fought over it, as if doing the stick dance together, until finally he collapsed at the edge of the roof.

He began to weep, saying, "You're finished, old friend of a lifetime; you're finished and so am I along with you."

I tried to explain: "But I raised the sheet on the broomstick in response to the Radio Israel announcer."

"Ass! Ass!" he responded.

"How is it my fault if he's an ass?" I asked. "And why do you employ only asses as announcers?"

the Palestinians, "You have become citizens, precisely like us." Throughout the novel, Habiby's dark humor channeled through Saeed's guileless simplicity effectively undermines the Israeli myth of egalitarianism.

CRITICAL DISCUSSION

In the decade following the 1967 Arab-Israeli War, *The Secret Life of Saeed* was welcomed by readers and critics in the Arab world. Its Hebrew and English translations received a similarly warm reception. In a 1980 review, Trevor Le Gassick describes the novel as "the snarl of a tiger in chains," while Roger Allen, in his 1983 review, calls it "one of the most remarkable recent contributions to the tradition of the Arabic novel." *The Secret Life of Saeed* has been repeatedly anthologized and excerpted and has evoked comparisons with *Good Soldier Schweik* (1923) by Jaroslav Hašek as well as *Slaughterhouse Five* (1969) by Kurt Vonnegut. In *After the Last Sky* (1986), Edward Said names *The Secret Life of Saeed* "the best work of Palestinian writing yet produced, precisely because the most seemingly disorganized and ironic."

In combination with the debate surrounding Habiby's controversial acceptance of the Israel Prize, critical reactions and reader responses to *The Secret Life of Saeed* have often pointed to broader ideological

trends. Rachel Feldhay Brenner, in "Hidden Transcripts Made Public" (1999), studies the reception of the novel, as well as its theatrical adaptation, in Israel. She suggests that "Israeli Jewish liberals interpret Habiby's writing as a benevolent satiric representation of human folly," universalizing his critiques of war and society. This view allows them to escape the concrete criticism of Israel that confronts them in the story, revealing "an unfamiliar derogatory version of their own history, which shatters the idealized version that they had taken for granted." In her article "Reading Inside and Out" (2000–2001), Nancy Coffin is similarly concerned with reader response. She observes that although Palestinians living within Israel after 1967 generally held different political views from those living outside its borders, there was an "amiable camaraderie of readers of *The Pessoptimist*." Coffin concludes that each group of readers focused on those aspects of the novel that seemed to support their political views, revealing more about their own political perspectives than the text itself.

The novel has been the subject of numerous investigations into its "palimpsestic" intertextuality, with particular focus on its use of Voltaire's *Candide* and the stories of the *Arabian Nights*. Ahmad Harb, for example, argues in "Invisibility, Impossibility: The Reuse of Voltaire's *Candide* in Emile Habiby's *Sa'eed*

He then made it clear that I was the ass to whom he had referred. He also pointed out that all Radio Israel's announcers are Arabs; they must have worded the request badly, he commented, but I must still be a fool to have misunderstood it.

In defense of my own people, the Arabs who worked at the radio station, I said, "The duty of a messenger is to deliver the message. They say only what is dictated to them. If raising the white flag on a broomstick is an insult to the dignity of surrender, it's only because broomsticks are the only weapons you permit us.

"However," I continued, "if, since the outbreak of this war, they too have become some kind of deadly white weapon we are not permitted to carry without a permit, like the shotguns only village chiefs and old men who've spent all their lives serving the state are permitted to carry, then I'm with you as always, all the way. You know full well, old friend of a lifetime, of my extravagant loyalty to the state, its security and its laws, whether promulgated or still to be so."

My friend Jacob, standing there with his mouth open and listening to my gabbling, was unable to stop either the tears pouring down his cheeks or my raving.

Finally he regained his composure and explained how my "misunderstanding" had been considered something quite different by the Big Man, nothing less than a case of rebellion against the state.

"But it's only a broomstick," I objected.

"That announcer," he emphasized, "was telling the West Bank Arabs to raise white flags in surrender to Israeli occupation. What did you think you were up to, doing that in the very heart of the state of Israel, in Haifa, which no one regards as a city under occupation?"

"But you can't have too much of a good thing," I pointed out.

"No," he insisted, "it's an indication that you do regard Haifa as an occupied city and are therefore advocating its separation from the state."

"That interpretation never crossed my mind."

"We don't punish you for what crosses your mind but for what crosses the Big Man's mind…"

SOURCE: *Modern Arabic Fiction: An Anthology,* edited by Salma Khadra Jayyusi. Copyright © 2005 Columbia University Press. Reprinted with permission of the publisher.

the Pessoptimist" (2010) that Habiby's reappropriation of *Candide* is a form of "writing back" and that his "aesthetics of narrative and form … are best understood a deliberate reshaping, reworking, and reclamation of Western and Arabic literary traditions."

BIBLIOGRAPHY

Sources

Allen, Roger. Rev. of *The Secret Life of Saeed: The Pessoptimist,* by Emile Habiby. *World Literature Today* 57.3 (1983): 506. Print.

Brenner, Rachel Feldhay. "'Hidden Transcripts' Made Public: Israeli Arab Fiction and Its Reception." *Critical Inquiry* 26.1 (1999): 85–108. Print.

Coffin, Nancy. "Reading Inside and Out: A Look at Habibi's 'Pessoptimist.'" *Arab Studies Journal* 8.2/9.1 (2000/2001): 25–46. Print.

Habiby, Emile. *The Secret Life of Saeed: The Pessoptimist.* Brooklyn, NY: Interlink, 2002. Print.

Harb, Ahmad. "Invisibility, Impossibility: The Reuse of Voltaire's *Candide* in Emile Habiby's *Sa'eed the Pessoptimist.*" *Arab Studies Quarterly* 32.2 (2010): 92–106. Print.

Le Gassick, Trevor. "The Luckless Palestinian." Rev. of *The Secret Life of Saeed: The Pessoptimist,* by Emile Habiby. *Middle East Journal* 34.2 (1980): 215–23. Print.

Said, Edward W. *After the Last Sky: Palestinian Lives.* New York: Pantheon, 1986. Print.

Further Reading

Boullata, Issa J. "Symbol and Reality in the Writings of Emile Habibi." *Islamic Culture* 62.2–3 (1988): 9–22. Print.

Heath, Peter. "Creativity in the Novels of Emile Habiby, with Special Reference to *Sa'id the Pessoptimist.*" *Tradition, Modernity, and Postmodernity in Arabic Literature.* Ed. Kamal Abdel-Malek and Wael Hallaq. Boston: Brill, 2000. 158–72. Print.

Pappe, Ilan. *The Forgotten Palestinians: A History of the Palestinians in Israel.* New Haven, CT: Yale UP, 2011. Print.

Shammas, Anton. *Arabesques.* Trans. Vivian Eden. New York: Harper, 1988. Print.

Allison Blecker

TAXI

Khaled al-Khamissi

✛ **Key Facts**

Time Period:
Early 21st Century

Genre:
Novel

Events:
Growing unrest under
President Hosni
Mubarak due to political
repression and economic
inequality

Nationality:
Egyptian

OVERVIEW

Taxi, the first novel by Egyptian writer and journalist Khaled al-Khamissi, was published in Arabic in 2007 and translated into English in 2008. It brings together the fictional stories of fifty-eight taxi drivers in the city of Cairo. Al-Khamissi's novel has been categorized as ethnography, urban sociology, and oral history, among other genres, and is recognized for its use of colloquial Egyptian language as well as its sharp political irony. Each chapter reads as the monologue of a single cabbie, who tells his story to the narrator. The central theme running through every narrative is the incredible difficulty of making a living in Cairo as a taxi driver. Collectively these individual stories, which are woven together by the perspective of a single narrator, amount to a meta-critique of the pre-revolutionary Egyptian government, drawing attention specifically to its corrupt and unjust nature.

Al-Khamissi's first novel became an instant best seller in the region, gaining international acclaim as soon as it could be translated into other languages. *Taxi* emerged at a politically charged moment in Egypt's history, when popular dissent became focused on issues other than Israel and the United States for the first time in decades. An increasingly incensed Egyptian public began to turn against the state, initiating a series of political activities that took center stage on the streets of Cairo beginning in the early 2000s. The novel functions as a platform for representatives of the Egyptian working class—the taxi driver—to voice their dissatisfaction with the increasingly corrupt and unjust tactics of the Egyptian government, a sentiment that led to the Egyptian revolution of 2011 and the overthrow of President Hosni Mubarak.

HISTORICAL AND LITERARY CONTEXT

Upon the publication of *Taxi* in 2007, Egypt was already in a state of growing unrest as a result of increasing political repression and the growth in recent decades of social inequalities. Mubarak's seemingly endless presidency, which began in 1981, ushered in a period of neo-authoritarian rule and governmental restructuring that led to greater restrictions on free speech and the press, widespread government corruption, and increased police brutality enabled by a decades-old state of emergency law that suspended constitutional rights. In her essay in *Transition to What:*

Egypt's Uncertain Departure from Neo-Authoritarianism (2011), Daniela Pioppi explains that restructuring "did grant the country political stability but at the cost of a general decline in the country's economic and political influence in the region, and domestically, in an increase in social inequalities." By 2007 Egyptians had begun to express their grievances in public displays of dissent.

Al-Khamissi, a Cairo native and former political scientist, witnessed these public protests and sought to better understand the political attitudes of the average Egyptian through discussions with taxi drivers. As Omayma Abdel-Latif explains, "[Taxi drivers] have the privilege of mingling with people from across the social spectrum…. Their views often reflect the thinking of … the lower strata of society who live on the periphery of politics and yet are so affected by it." Al-Khamissi wrote *Taxi* after a year of conducting interviews with cabbies on the streets of Cairo. He writes that taxi drivers "really are one of the barometers of the unruly Egyptian street…. These taxi drivers have a broad knowledge of society…. Through the conversations they hold they reflect an amalgam of points of view, which are most representative of the poor in Egyptian society." With its international distribution beginning in 2008, *Taxi* thus played a pivotal role in publicizing Egypt's social unrest and growing political tensions to the rest of the world.

The work of many Egyptian authors during the last century has become increasingly committed to social and political issues—a trend that has increased with the rise of online magazines and blogs, which generally do not face the same censorship as written publications do in many Arab countries. The theme of urban Egyptian life presented by al-Khamissi in *Taxi* is also present in many earlier narratives penned by Egyptians. The most notable of these is *The Yacoubian Building* (2002) by Alaa al-Aswany, which is one of the most popular pieces of modern Egyptian literature, presenting a bleak but powerful portrait of contemporary Cairo and Egypt. Al-Aswany's incorporation of political commentary into his fiction is echoed in the work of al-Khamissi. Earlier Egyptian authors such as Naguib Mahfouz, whose 1966 *Chatter on the Nile* criticized the decadence of Nasser-era Egyptian society, also had an impact on al-Khamissi's work. *Whatever Happened to the Egyptians* by Galal Amin, though not fiction, also serves as an important predecessor as it highlighted contemporary injustices.

The political conviction displayed by al-Khamissi in *Taxi* and in much of his journalism and online blogging has influenced a younger generation of Egyptian writers whose work, especially following the 2011 revolution, reflects a renewed investment in political and social issues. Much of this writing appears almost exclusively online due to its more radical nature and is embodied in the blogging of Maikel Nabil Sanad, Alaa Abd El-Fattah, and Aliaa Magda Elmahdy—a women's rights activist whose posting of a nude "revolutionary" photo of herself in 2011 earned her both praise and criticism. Reporter and author Youssef Rakha's 2011 novel *Book of the Sultan's Seal* evidences a similar attention as al-Khamissi to the decay of Cairo, also reading as a call to arms for the Egyptian people. Interest in *Taxi* grew even greater in the aftermath of the 2011 revolution, and it was recently republished by Bloomsbury Qatar Foundation Publishing with a post-revolution note by the author.

THEMES AND STYLE

Each of the fifty-eight chapters in *Taxi* describes the individual experiences of one taxi driver, oftentimes sharing their hopes, concerns, and political views. A main theme in many of the narratives is a sentiment of outrage and weariness at the injustice and abuses carried out by the Egyptian government. In chapter 3, the cabbie discusses a demonstration going on that day as "not much of a demonstration in the first place. In the old days we used to go out on the streets with 50,000 people, with 100,000. But now there's nothing that matters. How many people are going to step out of their front door for something no one understands?" The driver describes a frustration with the current state of affairs and conveys an intimate knowledge of Egyptian politics and history, referencing the Egyptian Bread Riots of 1977 as the root of revolution in the country.

Al-Khamissi mitigates the raw, occasionally crude nature of the cabbie's monologues with the first-person narration of the male passenger—a fictional representation of the author himself—to contextualize the drivers' narratives and reflect on their larger significance. In chapter 29, the narrator introduces the issue of education, stating, "With a driver who has children of school age, you only have to push the education button for him to set off like a rocket and no one can stop him, not even NASA engineers in person…. As soon as I sat down in the taxi … I pressed the start button and off the driver went." The narrator's voice frames each story and functions as the narrative thread that weaves the stories together. Al-Khamissi also employs humor throughout to further engage the reader.

An important and revolutionary aspect of *Taxi* is its reproduction of the colloquial Egyptian dialect spoken on the streets of Cairo, which conveys the mood of the public in a candid and faithful manner. Its use

KHALED AL-KHAMISSI: FROM AUTHOR TO POLITICAL ACTIVIST

Khaled al-Khamissi is an Egyptian writer, producer, blogger, and political activist who was born in Cairo in 1962. He received a bachelor's degree in political science from Cairo University in 1984 and a master's degree in foreign policy from the Sorbonne in Paris in 1987. Early in his career, al-Khamissi worked as a journalist for several Egyptian newspapers, during which time he gained prominence in the field for his perceptive reporting on social conditions within Egypt. He also has been involved in documentary and feature films as a director, producer, and scriptwriter. The success of al-Khamissi's first novel, *Taxi*, which became an immediate international best seller, shot the author to international fame. He is now regarded as one of Egypt's foremost writers.

Al-Khamissi's second novel, *Noah's Arc* (2009), speaks for Egyptian migrants who have fled the nation in search of a better life abroad. His books have been translated into at least nine languages, including English, French, Malaysian, Korean, and Greek. Because *Taxi*'s scathing criticism of the Egyptian state emerged shortly before the Egyptian revolution broke out in early 2011, al-Khamissi has been hailed as the man who "predicted the uprising." The author was an outspoken proponent of the 2011 revolution and has now added the titles of blogger and political activist to his diverse public roles in Egyptian society.

of language challenged the canon and is also part of a broader trend of texts being published at least partially in Egyptian colloquial Arabic. This flies in the face of a literary tradition that elevated Modern Standard Arabic and formal prose. It also gives the illusion that al-Khamissi was speaking in the voice of the people, even though the text was his own recreation of reality. For example, the cabbie in chapter 33 conveys his anger at the constant police abuse he is forced to endure on the streets. Recounting his encounter with a policeman the previous day, he states, "He didn't think for a moment that I might be telling the truth. The truth! How could [we] tell the truth when we're all liars and we're bastards and we have to be beaten like old shoes. I really feel that we aren't human beings, we're old shoes." The taxi driver's frank tone and use of colloquial phrases such as "old shoes" emphasizes his indignation and enables the reader to more easily identify with his feeling of injustice.

CRITICAL DISCUSSION

Taxi received overwhelmingly positive reviews upon its publication, quickly becoming a best seller. Omayma Abdel-Latif wrote in 2007, "*Taxi*'s brilliance is that it captures the point at which cabs cease to be just a means of transportation and instead become a space for debate and exchange … Khamissi's conversations yield several great insights into the schizophrenic relationship between the Egyptian and the state." Many early critics had similar comments, recognizing

Khaled al-Khamissi, author of *Taxi*, in 2012. MAHMUD HAMS/AFP/GETTYIMAGES.

al-Khamissi's success at conveying the actual mood of the public on the streets of Cairo. Writing for the *Sydney Morning Herald Review,* Dorothy Johnston commented, "No doubt it's partly Khamissi's humour that has made *Taxi* a bestseller in Egypt," adding that "the relentless long hours and back-breaking tedium of the job gives the drivers' jokes and stories a dignity and authenticity that transcends any individual tale."

Since the events of early 2011 that led to the overthrow of President Mubarak, *Taxi* has quickly become associated with the revolution and the popular dissent of the Egyptian people that led to the uprising. As a result of the connection to the Egyptian people demonstrated by al-Khamissi in *Taxi,* he has become an outspoken advocate for the Egyptian working class since 2011, communicating the reality of the revolution's aftermath. In an October 2011 interview with CNN, al-Khamissi said, "My taxi drivers are among the 55 percent of the population living under the poverty line of $2 a day.... Those 55 percent were not on the streets during the revolution and are without a real voice now.... Life has changed for them in the wrong direction." *Taxi* continues to receive widespread critical attention on an international scale.

Another area of interest to scholars is *Taxi*'s relevance to human rights issues. According to Rebecca Wright in her essay in *BEYOND THE LAW,* "The personal stories told by taxi drivers [in *Taxi*] are a far cry from the neat, polished stories of human rights abuses that are generally told in legal briefs challenging human rights abuses.... Emotional stories of starving families, of sons who have been locked away without a charge.... As they are circulated, identified with and acknowledged throughout a society, they can slowly drive citizens to demand change." Other critics have expressed interested in the socially ethnographic nature of al-Khamissi's novel. In her piece in

the *National Review,* Alice Johnson comments, "Its 58 narratives weave a story of despair, poverty and hopelessness through the voices of Cairo's taxi drivers.... *Taxi* serves as a microcosm of Egyptian society and its problems."

BIBLIOGRAPHY

Sources

Abdel-Latif, Omayma. "Taxicab Confessions in Cairo." Review of *Taxi,* by Khaled al-Khamissi. *Foreign Policy* Sept.-Oct. 2007: 80, 82, 84. Print.

Al-Khamissi, Khaled. "Intro: Words That Need to Be Said." *PBS: Frontline World.* WGBH Educational Foundation, March 2006. Web. 3 Oct. 2012.

———. Excerpt from *Taxi*: Chapter 29 and Chapter 33. *PBS: Frontline World.* WGBH Educational Foundation, March 2006. Web. 3 Oct. 2012.

———. Excerpt from *Taxi*: Chapter 3 and Chapter 42. *African Writing Online* 6 (n.d.). Web. 3 Oct. 2012.

———. *Taxi.* Laverstock: Aflame, 2008. Print.

Davies, Catriona. "Hard Life of Cairo's 80,000 Taxi Drivers." *CNN.* Cable News Network, 21 Oct. 2011. Web. 5 Oct. 2012.

Johnson, Alice. "Egyptian Author Gives Fuel for Thought." *National Review.* National Review, 20 Nov. 2011. Web. 3 Oct. 2012.

Johnston, Dorothy. "Khaled Al Khamissi's Drivers Remain Prisoners of Their City." Review of *Taxi,* by Khaled al-Khamissi. *Sydney Morning Herald Review.* Fairfax Media, 9 May 2008. Web. 3 Oct. 2012.

Pioppi, Daniela. "Transition to What: Egypt's Uncertain Departure from Neo-Authoritarianism." Washington, DC: The German Marshall Fund of the U.S., 2011. Web. 6 Oct. 2012.

Wright, Rebecca. "The Role of Personal Narratives in Egypt's 2011 Spring Revolution." *BEYOND THE LAW: Multi-disciplinary Perspectives on Human Rights.* Ed. F. Vijoen and J. Njaus. Pretoria: Pretoria U Law P (PULP), 2012. 189–208. Print.

Further Reading

Abdoh, Salar. "On the Way to the Wind: Contemporary Writing from the Middle East and North Africa." *Callalloo* 32.4 (2009): 1082–85. Print.

Amin, Galal. *Whatever Happened to the Egyptians? Changes in Egyptian Society from 1950 to the Present.* Cairo: American U in Cairo P, 2000. Print.

"Books for the People: Populist Concerns in Contemporary Egyptian Literature." *Hydra Magazine.* Hydra Magazine, 30 Jan. 2011. Web. 5 Oct. 2012.

Noueihed, Lin, and Alex Warren. *The Battle for the Arab Spring: Revolution, Counter-Revolution and the Making of a New Era.* New Haven: Yale UP, 2012. Print.

Sabry, Tarik. *Cultural Encounters in the Arab World: On Media, the Modern and the Everyday.* New York: I. B. Tauris, 2010. Print.

Yeva, Ando. Rev. of *Taxi,* by Khaled al-Khamissi. *African Writing Online* 6. (n.d.). Web. 3 Oct. 2012.

Katrina White

THREE GUINEAS

Virginia Woolf

OVERVIEW

Virginia Woolf's book-length essay *Three Guineas* (1938) expands on ideas introduced in her earlier works to create a feminist, pacifist, and antifascist polemic. The work responds to a letter from an organization advocating pacifism and the preservation of culture and intellectual liberty. The letter asks, "How in your opinion are we to prevent war?" and requests a one-guinea (just over a pound) donation. Woolf's response examines this and two similar correspondences, one from a women's college building fund and the other from a society promoting professional advancement for women. Each donation request triggers an epistolary investigation into the social dynamics that have left these organizations underfunded to begin with. Written in a predominantly academic register, the essay criticizes the policies and practices of Western nations and calls for a shift among British citizens from blind faith and patriotism to informed critical thinking.

The work was originally devised as a "novel-essay," alternating between fiction and epistolary nonfiction passages. Unable to make the formulation work to her satisfaction, Woolf separated the two, with the fiction passages becoming *The Years* (1937), the most popular of her novels during her lifetime. Although *Three Guineas* was met with resistance from Woolf's academic peers, it built on the novel's favorable public reception and was embraced and praised by working-class men and women, many of whom wrote to her to express their pleasure and gratitude. Among the essay's most lauded attributes was its openness, finally pronouncing outright the ideologies that had so long informed her writing. It expands most noticeably on the socioeconomic trends outlined by Woolf in *A Room of One's Own* (1929), and the two works would later be adopted almost as founding charters by the second wave of the feminist movement of the 1970s.

HISTORICAL AND LITERARY CONTEXT

The material for *Three Guineas* was written between 1932 and 1937, a period of escalating social crisis in Europe. In the two decades since World War I, the European political landscape had become dominated by fascism, a nationalist ethos that radicalized existing patriarchal tendencies toward misogyny and violent patriotism. The atrocities being committed by fascist regimes in Spain, Italy, and especially Germany were increasingly hard to ignore, and the imminent threat of yet another global conflict loomed large. Woolf and her nephew, Julian Bell, argued about foreign and domestic policy before he left to fight in the Spanish Civil War as a volunteer ambulance driver on the Republican side. He was killed in 1937 at the age of twenty-nine. Their discussions later served as a basis for the "dialogue" in *Three Guineas*.

By the time Woolf's tract was released in 1938, Germany had annexed Austria and the British government had begun an extensive campaign of nonliterary propaganda (including posters, war bond advertisements, and film reels) to foster support for a war they would not officially enter for another year. With tensions mounting, the question of how to prevent war acquired a heightened sense of urgency. Woolf's response to the donation letters she received distinguished itself from other propaganda by refusing to work within a failing patriarchal system. She believed that war could only be avoided by first addressing the despotism of the male-dominated British family structure and then conducting policy change in an entirely new discourse that included outsiders such as the poor, minorities, and women. Tyrannized at home—denied education, the right to hold property, and any voice in political decisions—marginalized groups were nevertheless asked to support their country's efforts against tyranny overseas.

Woolf was not alone in identifying feminist consciousness as paramount in the understanding of public violence. In fact, her career is often seen as being paralleled by that of English author, journalist, and literary critic Rebecca West. Both responded to World War I with fictive narratives: Woolf's *Jacob's Room* (1922) and West's *The Return of the Soldier* (1918). The two works detect the same problems in patriarchal culture—that it glorifies martial and capitalist models of masculinity and that it renders women complicit in male violence. Both women then addressed World War II through nonfiction works: Woolf's *Three Guineas* (1938) and West's hybrid travelogue *Black Lamb and Grey Falcon* (1941). With a conscious self-referentiality, the two later works propose women's writing as the only antidote to the incessant public violence of men and to the continued private disengagement of women.

Key Facts

Time Period:
Mid-20th Century

Genre:
Essay

Events:
Rise of fascism in Europe; Spanish Civil War; German annexation of Austria

Nationality:
English

BLOOMSBURY AND WOOLF'S INFLUENCE ON GENDER STUDIES

After the death of their father and Woolf's second nervous break-down, Virginia and her siblings Vanessa and Adrian sold their home at 22 Hyde Park Gate and bought a house at 46 Gordon Square in Bloomsbury. There, and through her attendance at Cambridge, Woolf became acquainted with Lytton Strachey, Clive Bell, Rupert Brooke, Saxon Sydney-Turner, Duncan Grant, Leonard Woolf (whom Virginia would later marry), John Maynard Keynes, and Roger Fry. Together, they formed the core constituency of the intellectual circle known as the Bloomsbury Group. Politically, Bloomsbury espoused predominantly left-liberal stances (pacifism and socialism, for example), but its associations and gatherings were not activist.

The romantic profile of the group's members is noteworthy, demonstrating a sexual freedom that was progressive for their time. Beginning in 1925, Virginia Woolf engaged in a passionate affair with Vita Sackville-West. Overwhelmed by her affection for Vita, Woolf wrote what has become a seminal work of gay fiction, the experimental fantasy *Orlando* (1927). A semibiographical novel based loosely on the life of Sackville-West, the novel has become increasingly influential, particularly in the spheres of women's and gender studies.

The last of Woolf's nonfiction works published before her death in 1941, *Three Guineas* stands as a final protestation against the inequities of patriarchal society. Her disquisition not only fostered (sometimes heated) debate over the state of British policy, but by sheer force of quality helped secure Woolf's literary legacy. Her willingness to question the status quo informed the somber poetics of Sylvia Plath, as well as the patriarchal dystopias of Doris Lessing and Margaret Atwood.

THEMES AND STYLE

Three Guineas responds to what Woolf posits as three interrelated questions from separate correspondents: "How should war be prevented?"; "Why does the government not support education for women?"; and "Why are women not allowed to engage in professional work?" For Woolf, all three can be traced to the continued dominance of patriarchal political and family structures, which located both misogyny and martial patriotism in the fragility of the masculine ego. She reinforces this belief by including with the essay a series of photographs of prominent British figures in lavish uniforms, underlining the masculine need for prideful display. Rather than providing a monetary donation, as each correspondent requests, Woolf instead provides suggestions for how to subvert and subsequently change the societal norms that have left their organizations underfunded in the first place.

By including the text of each letter and addressing each in turn, Woolf creates a sense of dialogue, allowing her to evade categorization of the essay as mere polemical diatribe. Further, the epistolary mode informs the rhetorical strategy of the essay. For Woolf, letter writing was a process that moved both writer and reader alike, fundamentally altering the consciousness of both. In expository political writing Woolf saw the potential for the writer to dehumanize the reader and become detached, whereas in letters both writer and reader cannot help but visualize "someone warm and breathing on the other side of the page." Thus, by engaging the questions posed in the epistolary mode, Woolf enacts the paradigm shift she seeks: relocating the power of political discourse from abstraction and naming to interactive process.

Departing from her famously lyrical prose, but not from her trademark satirical bite—employed here to disparage male thought processes—Woolf adopts a distinctly academic voice for most of the essay, relying more on rhetorical prowess than emotional poignancy to lend credence to her claims. Predicting the scrutiny with which the essay would be met, particularly from male academes eager to dismiss feminine antifascist writing as sentimental and irrational, Woolf also substantiates her arguments by including extensive statistical and contextual endnotes, appending 51 pages of notes to a 171-page essay. Fearful, however, that her academic approach would alienate her growing base of working-class readers, Woolf also interjects moments of colloquial address and self-deprecation, as when in the opening passage she admits to her first correspondent that she "had hoped that [the letter] would answer itself, or that other people would answer it" for her. This attention to all demographics within the essay's intended readership shows an acute awareness of audience missing from nonliterary propaganda of the era.

CRITICAL DISCUSSION

When Virginia Woolf's *Three Guineas* was published in 1938, it was met with opposition within both the academic and political spheres. Even loyal friends such as E. M. Forster felt affronted by her insistence that "fascist" thinking was not only possible but pervasive in Britain's outdated political systems and indeed within the typical British family. A desire to maintain clear and definitive boundaries in relation to fascism was common among antifascist writers of the 1930s and 1940s, who often identified the ethos as entirely "other" or "perverse," a stance reinforced by nearly all official British propaganda from World War I onward. Woolf's postulation that fascism was present in and ought to be eradicated from Britain before Britain focused on the Continent, was, at the very least, inflammatory. In his 1941 Rede Lecture following Woolf's death, Forster expressed a common view among Woolf's male contemporaries when he called her feminism a "disease that breaks out in spots all over her work."

Not until the second-wave feminist movement of the 1970s did *Three Guineas* enjoy widespread positive reception. Such feminist critics and theorists as Christine Froula praised Woolf's essay for aspiring "to abolish the sacrificial foundations of the gender-marked division between private house and public world." Victoria Middleton offers that in *Three Guineas* Woolf "gives us a model of the revisionary process" that will lead to progress, "demonstrating how written texts and signs have different meanings for their readers … who listen and speak differently—but together." Following Woolf's vision, second-wave feminism has sought to alter not only public discourse but also the language with which individuals speak to each other in their private lives.

Although some scholars still disparage the essay— Theodore Dalrymple contends that the book is "a locus classicus of self-pity and victimhood as a genre in itself" and that "the book might be better titled: How to Be Privileged and Yet Feel Extremely Aggrieved"— it is now widely considered a seminal feminist work. Jane Marcus, in her introduction to the 2006 reissue of the essay, hails it as the moment Woolf transitioned from a notable public voice to "an important European theorist of feminism, pacifism, and socialism." This shift is perhaps most directly attributable to what Brenda R. Silver identifies as the essay's, and indeed Woolf's, greatest strength: the ability "to overcome [a] deep fear of anger and ridicule" from male colleagues.

Virginia Woolf, author of *Three Guineas*. PORTRAIT OF VIRGINIA WOOLF (1882–1941), PUBLISHED BY EDITIONS STOCK (B/W PHOTO), FRENCH PHOTOGRAPHER, (20TH CENTURY)/ PRIVATE COLLECTION/ ARCHIVES CHARMET/THE BRIDGEMAN ART LIBRARY.

BIBLIOGRAPHY

Sources

Dalrymple, Theodore. *Our Culture, What's Left of It: The Mandarins and the Masses.* Chicago: Dee, 2005. Print.

Froula, Christine. "St. Virginia's Epistle to an English Gentleman: Sex, Violence, and the Public Sphere in *Three Guineas.*" *Virginia Woolf and the Bloomsbury Avant-Garde.* New York: Columbia UP, 2005. 259–84. Print.

Mackay, Marina. "The Lunacy of Men, the Idiocy of Women: Woolf, West, and War." *NWSA Journal* 15.3 (2003): 124–44. *Academic Search Complete.* Web. 18 June 2012.

Marcus, Jane. Introduction. *Three Guineas.* Orlando: Harcourt, 2006. xxxv–lxxii. Print.

Middleton, Victoria. "Three Guineas: Subversion and Survival in the Professions." *Twentieth Century Literature* 28.4 (1982): 405. *Academic Search Complete.* Web. 19 June 2012.

Wollaeger, Mark A. *Modernism, Media, and Propaganda: British Narrative from 1900 to 1945.* Princeton: Princeton UP, 2006. Print.

Woolf, Virginia, Jane Marcus, and Mark Hussey. *Three Guineas.* Orlando: Harcourt, 2006. Print.

Further Reading

Barker, Jennifer. "Indifference, Identification, and Desire in Virginia Woolf's *Three Guineas,* Leni Riefenstahl's *The Blue Light and Triumph of the Will,* and Leontine Sagan's *Maedchen in Uniform.*" *Women in German Yearbook* 26 (2010): 73–96. *Academic Search Complete.* Web. 19 June 2012.

Deane Patrick. *History in Our Hands: A Critical Anthology of Writings on Literature, Culture, and Politics from the 1930s.* London: Leicester UP, 1998. Print.

Forster, E. M. *Virginia Woolf.* Cambridge: Cambridge UP, 1942. Print.

Gualtieri, Elena. "*Three Guineas* and the Photograph: The Art of Propaganda." *Women Writers of the 1930s: Gender, Politics and History.* Ed. Maroula Joannou. Edinburgh: Edinburgh UP, 1999. Print.

Hsieh, Lili. "The Other Side of the Picture: The Politics of Affect in Virginia Woolf's *Three Guineas.*" *JNT: Journal of Narrative Theory* 36.1 (2006): 20–52. Print.

Pawlowski, Merry M. "Reassessing Modernism: Virginia Woolf, *Three Guineas,* and Fascist Ideology." *Woolf Studies Annual* 1 (1995): 47–67. Print.

Schaefer, Josephine O'Brien. "*Three Guineas.*" *New Republic* 170.1/2 (1974): 21–24. *Academic Search Complete.* Web. 18 June 2012.

Silver, Brenda. "*Three Guineas* Before and After: Further Answers to Correspondents." *Virginia Woolf: A Feminist Slant.* Ed. Jane Marcus. Lincoln: U of Nebraska P, 1983. Print.

Solomon, Julie Robin. "Staking Ground: The Politics of Space in Virginia Woolf's *A Room of One's Own* and *Three Guineas.*" *Women's Studies* 16.3/4 (1989): 331. *Academic Search Complete.* Web. 19 June 2012.

Winterhalter, Teresa. "'What Else Can I Do But Write?' Discursive Disruption and the Ethics of Style in Virginia Woolf's *Three Guineas.*" *Hypatia* 18.4 (2003): 236–57. *Academic Search Complete.* Web. 19 June 2012.

Woolf, Virginia. *A Room of One's Own.* San Diego: Harcourt, 1989. Print.

———. *The Years.* New York: Harcourt, 1937. Print.

Clint Garner

"TOBA TEK SINGH"

Sa'adat Hasan Manto

✥ *Key Facts*

Time Period:
Mid-20th Century

Genre:
Short Story

Events:
Partition of the Indian subcontinent

Nationality:
Indian

OVERVIEW

"Toba Tek Singh" (1953) is a short story by Sa'adat Hasan Manto that satirizes the relationship between India and Pakistan following the 1947 Partition of the Indian subcontinent. A time of intense violence and political instability, the post-Partition period was marked by the migration of millions of Muslims, Sikhs, and Hindus across new national boundaries and by the assault and murder of religious minorities on both sides. Manto's story is a satire of this movement, using the exchange of insane asylum inmates as an allegory for the sense of disillusionment felt by Pakistanis and Indians alike, as well as for the perceived absurdity of the political process that gave rise to Partition and engendered hundreds of thousands of deaths in its aftermath. Without making an overt political statement, Manto's confused protagonist, Bishan Singh, exemplified what many Pakistani and Indian readers felt during this era.

"Toba Tek Singh," a work beloved by many, has become the most famous Partition text. Based on a real agreement between Pakistan and India, Manto's story is a fictional account of the exchange of Pakistani and Indian asylum inmates. The story focuses on Bishan Singh, known by his fellow inmates as Toba Tek Singh, the name of his hometown. After Partition, Singh obsesses over determining in which nation his hometown is now located until the inmate exchange, when he collapses in a no-man's-land, unwilling to abandon his home nation and confused about where he is headed and why. "Toba Tek Singh," one among many of Manto's short stories about Partition, stands out for its poignancy and sympathetic main character. Described in Leslie Flemming's "Riots and Refugees" as "the most powerful and most moving of these stories expressing the human pain of partition," the work's legacy endures into the twenty-first century.

HISTORICAL AND LITERARY CONTEXT

"Toba Tek Singh" responds both to the loss of identity felt by more than 12 million Muslims, Sikhs, and Hindus displaced following Partition—which has divided the Indian subcontinent into India and East and West Pakistan—and to the poor execution of this division. A contentious decision, Partition forced millions to migrate from their homelands to ill-equipped, alien nations and was seen by many as a political failure. Negative sentiment continued after the division, as both countries faced unprepared governments, communal violence, and uncertain national identity. Moreover, many emigrants struggled to give up attachments to the land in favor of an identity primarily founded on religious affiliation. Manto's story subtly indicts the politics of Partition, depicting it as an irrational event, and compassionately illustrates the sense of displacement and disillusionment shared by many.

By the time "Toba Tek Singh" was published, Pakistan and India had been independent countries for eight years. The 1947 Indian Independence Act declared the end of British India and the creation of two sovereign nations: Pakistan (which would be home to most of the region's Muslims) and India (which would be home to most of the subcontinent's Sikh and Hindu populations). Partition, demarcated by the controversial Radcliffe line, was mired in controversy years after its enactment. Extreme violence plagued both countries, resulting in nearly a million deaths and an estimated 100,000 abducted women. Manto's story takes place a few years after Partition in Lahore and Wagah, both located in the Punjab province, where the majority of population transfers occurred. A Muslim himself, Manto was forced to relocate from Bombay to Lahore, Pakistan, and so felt the deep wounds of dislocation that characterize "Toba Tek Singh."

A defining moment in developing a sense of identity for subcontinent writers, Partition has generated an entire genre of literature devoted to representing and understanding its effects. "Toba Tek Singh" keeps company with a large body of work by both Pakistani and Indian writers. Many authors have dealt with the event's immediate violence, pursuant land wars, and the rebuilding aftermath. Sa'adat Hasan Manto is perhaps the best known Partition writer; many of his more than 200 short stories treat the subject. His narratives are recognized for their impartiality and for exploring the depths of humanity that enabled such destruction and despair. Among his most famous Partition stories are "The Assignment," "The Return" (which condemns Muslims for inciting violence), "Losing Bargain," and "The Dog of Titwal."

Among Partition literature, "Toba Tek Singh" is often regarded as one of the most humanized and generous of the many works on the subject and has been

Indian soldiers in 2012 participating in the daily border-closing ceremony at the international border between Attari, India, and Wagah, Pakistan. The short story "Toba Tek Singh" by Sa'adat Hasan Manto also addresses relations between the two countries. © JENS BENNINGHOFEN/ALAMY.

looked to for its eloquent articulation of confusion and loss. Published at the time of Manto's death, the story went on to be adapted for the stage and screen. Urdu poet Gulzar wrote the poem "Toba Tek Singh," in which the speaker visits Bishan Singh at Wagah to describe Partition's continued madness into the late twentieth century. Several postcolonial works, including the nonfiction text *Freedom at Midnight* (1975) and Salman Rushdie's novel *Midnight's Children* (1980), have tackled the topic in a variety of ways. In the twenty-first century, Partition continues to be a significant and weighty subject for writers, as its effects remain a part of Pakistani and Indian national consciousnesses.

THEMES AND STYLE

The central themes of "Toba Tek Singh" are madness and identity. The story is an allegory that uses life in an asylum as a metaphor for the experience of the Partition period. Manto employs the trope of madness to depict confusion and helplessness among the Indian and Pakistani inhabitants and to deride bureaucratic decisions, depicting those in charge as lacking rationality. Translator Frances Pritchett calls the story a "bitter indictment of the political processes and behavior patterns that produced Partition." Manto explores identity through the main character, Bishan Singh, who is known by others in the asylum by the name of his hometown, Toba Tek Singh. He so deeply identifies with the land that he is disoriented by the remapped subcontinent, to which many sane inhabitants could relate. Singh's demise, fallen between his place of birth and the land of his religious affiliation, is symbolic of post-Partition identity conflict.

As an allegory, "Toba Tek Singh" achieves its rhetorical effect through satire and irreverence. Originally written in Urdu, Manto's audience would be intimately familiar with the circumstances of Partition and would immediately recognize Manto's dark humor. This sense of irreverence is achieved through the repetition of nonsense phrases and witticisms that convey an apparent ignorance of the actual location of the place called Toba Tek Singh. Single-mindedly concerned with determining which country his hometown is in, Bishan Singh asks everyone he encounters. A visitor from Toba Tek Singh responds, "Where is it? ... Why ... right where it was!" Manto plays with geographical location to highlight the arbitrariness of the Radcliffe line. Although "Toba Tek Singh" avoids the intense violence and drama of the post-Partition era, Manto definitively communicates disdain for the seemingly illogical machinations that put Partition into effect.

Stylistically, "Toba Tek Singh" is typical of a short story: the language is succinct and straightforward with few embellishments. Despite being a "bitter indictment" of Partition, Frances Pritchett says, "There's not a single word in the story that tells us so. The story presents itself as a deadpan, factual, non-judgmental chronicle" inviting comparison to Jonathan Swift's scathing "Modest Proposal." The story is told with subtlety and restraint, and humorous sections are dark without being overtly comical: "A Muslim inmate who had read *Zamindar* regularly every day for twelve years was asked by a friend, 'Maulvi Sahib, what is this Pakistan?' After full reflection he replied, 'It is a place in India where they make razor blades.' His friend was satisfied with that answer." Couching his critique in the symbol of an insane asylum enables Manto to denigrate the entire Partition enterprise but also helps to mitigate the critique by putting words of condemnation into the mouths of the insane.

CRITICAL DISCUSSION

When "Toba Tek Singh" was first published in the short story collection *Phundne* (1955), many of Manto's critics were silenced. Put on trial for obscenity six times, Manto was primarily associated with taboo themes and scandalizing imagery. Alternately, "Toba Tek Singh" was more surprising for its lack of overt controversy. Praising the poignancy of the story's ending, one critic emphasized such contrast: "Although the brutally shocking ending … became Manto's stock-in-trade, here … he has used a delicately ambiguous ending." The work stands out for its humanity and its thoughtful treatment of the post-Partition era. The initial English translation by Mohammad Iqbal in 1956 exposed millions of new readers to Manto's masterpiece.

In the decades that followed "Toba Tek Singh," Manto became a central figure, for both Pakistanis and Indians, in understanding Partition, and the story has been widely recognized as being among the best Partition stories. Deftly able to communicate the feeling of alienation, loss of identity, and confusion of the era, "Toba Tek Singh" continues to be a source of inspiration for readers and is often called on to illustrate the formation of national identity after Partition. The story has been celebrated through readings and productions of a stage adaptation, performed to commemorate the anniversary of Partition and Manto's birth. These performances, as well as television and film adaptations, ensure that ever-broader audiences are exposed to the story and Manto's message. Despite his controversial legacy, Manto is best remembered for "Toba Tek Singh."

Scholarship of "Toba Tek Singh" has predominantly focused on the historical account of Partition, its impact on the politics and culture of the Indian subcontinent, and theories of borderlands. Because of the breadth of texts written about Partition, a subgenre of critical studies has emerged to consider this interdisciplinary body of work that includes literature, official documents, historical accounts, and other documents. Ian Talbot compares the representation of Partition in a variety of texts, while both Jennifer Yusin and Bede Scott invoke the concept of borderland in discussing "Toba Tek Singh." In the essay "Beyond Nationalism," Yusin asserts that "the history of the Partition is a history of borders in which the border became and continues to be the central site of trauma for that history." In the article "Of Territorial Borders and Test Cricket," Scott argues that, for Manto, the border is representative of "nationalist ideologies of divergence." Both scholars see the story's closing scene, which takes place between nations, as representative of the border's significance as a site that at once defines and requires definition. As "Toba Tek Singh" continues to be instrumental to understanding the Indian subcontinent after Partition, scholarship will continue to focus on this much-lauded work.

BIBLIOGRAPHY

Sources

Flemming, Leslie A. "Riots and Refugees: The Post-Partition Stories of Sa'adat Hasan Manto." *Journal of South Asian Literature* 13.1/4 (1977–78): 99–109. Print.

Ispahani, Mahnaz. "Sa'adat Hasan Manto." *Grand Street* 7.4 (1988): 183–93. Print.

Manto, Sa'adat Hassan. "Toba Tek Singh." *Fires in an Autumn Garden: Short Stories from Urdu and the Regional Languages of Pakistan.* Trans. Robert B. Haldane. Ed. Asif Farrukhi. Karachi: Oxford UP, 1997. 45–52. Print.

Pritchett, Frances. "Toba Tek Singh: About the Story." *South Asia Study Resources.* Columbia University. N.d. Web. 29 Aug. 2012.

Scott, Bede. "Of Territorial Borders and Test Cricket: Exploring the Boundaries of the Postcolonial State." *Journal of Commonwealth Literature* 44.1 (2009): 23–34. Print.

Yusin, Jennifer. "Beyond Nationalism: The Border, Trauma, and Partition Fiction." *Thesis Eleven* 105.1 (2011): 23–34. Print.

Further Reading

Chanin, Clifford. *Blooming through the Ashes: An International Anthology on Violence and the Human Spirit.* New Brunswick: Rutgers UP, 2008. Print.

Chatterjee, Partha. "Democracy and the Violence of the State: A Political Negotiation of Death." *Inter-Asia Cultural Studies* 2.1 (2001): 7–21. Print.

Grewal, Harjeet. "Uncomfortable Residues of Dislocation: Migration and Modern Panjabi Short Stories." *Sikh Formations: Religion, Culture, Theory* 4.2 (2008): 97–113. Print.

Jalal, Ayesha. "Secularists, Subalterns and the Stigma of 'Communalism': Partition Historiography Revisited." *Modern Asian Studies* 30.3 (1996): 681–89. Print.

Kumar, Amitava. "Splitting the Difference." *Transition* 89 (2001): 44–55. Print.

Nagappan, Ramu. *Speaking Havoc: Social Suffering and South Asian Narratives.* Seattle: U of Washington P, 2005. Print.

Smita, Das. "Space of the Crazy in Sa'adat Hasan Manto's 'Toba Tek Singh.'" *South Asian Review* 26.2 (2005): 202+. Print.

Talbot, Ian. "Literature and the Human Drama of the 1947 Partition." Spec. issue of *South Asia: Journal of South Asian Studies* 18 (1995): 37–56. Print.

Vadhavan, Jagdish Candar. *Manto Naama: The Life of Sa'adat Hasan Manto.* New Delhi: Roli, 1998. Print.

Media Adaptations

Partition. Dir. Ken McMullen. Perf. Bhasker Patel, Saeed Jaffrey, and Shaheen Khan. Bandung Productions, 1987. Film.

Toba Tek Singh. Dir. Afia Nathaniel. Perf. Midhat Kazim, Omair Rana, and Imran Siddiqui. 2005. Film.

Elizabeth Boeheim

THE WORMING OF A MAD DOG

Or, A Sop for Cerberus the Jailer of Hell

Constantia Munda

OVERVIEW

The pamphlet *The Worming of a Mad Dog: Or, A Sop for Cerberus the Jailer of Hell* (1617), the one and only work ever published by the pseudonymous author Constantia Munda, was an entry in the brief pamphlet war that arose in response to Joseph Swetnam's *The Arraignment of Lewd, Idle, Froward, and Unconstant Women* (1615). Though the author claims to be a woman, the gender of "Constantia Munda" has never been confirmed. The pseudonym is Latin for "pure constancy," and "munda" is similar to the Latin word for a woman's dress, *mundum*—possibly a nod to the common complaint that women dressed provocatively in order to entrap men. The work is dedicated to "her Most Dear Mother, the Lady Prudentia Munda," a declaration of aristocracy (Swetnam, by contrast, was a self-declared commoner) and superiority, as *prudentia* is Latin for foresight, wisdom, and discretion. Munda uses many learned references to counter Swetnam's casually hostile arguments against women, catching him in several errors of scholarship, while demonstrating her familiarity with legal terminology, the Bible, and classical works. Taken together, the two works reiterate an attack-and-defense scenario that had already been played out multiple times in literature with regard to the question of women's worth. Munda's work is significant in that it advanced the notion that women could participate directly in their own defense, even if, given the status of women with regard to voting rights, property, and education—most had none—the fight remained purely rhetorical.

The Worming of a Mad Dog was only issued once, while Swetnam's *Arraignment* enjoyed multiple reprintings. Munda wrote that Swetnam appealed to "the itching eares of silly swains, and rude / Truth-not-discerning rusticke multitude," and in his own epistle "to the Reader" in 1615, which he originally signed Thomas Tell-Troth, Swetnam addresses "the ordinary sort of giddy young men." In light of other pamphlet wars surrounding politics of church and state, which turned into actual, bloody wars in seventeenth-century England and Scotland, the so-called *querelle des femmes*—the fight over women—proved an entertaining spectacle for the reading public. Munda's contribution challenged received ideas of women as ignorant and powerless.

HISTORICAL AND LITERARY CONTEXT

Medieval universities used the formal debate about women to instruct students (all of them male) in rhetoric, and it was a popular topic in medieval courts; by the sixteenth century, publishers found in the growing middle class a profitable audience for published works on the matter. William Heale, author of a 1608 text countering another writer's argument in favor of violence against women, observed that "detraction was the vogue from courtier to cobbler," as jokes that denigrated rather than praised women were the norm in popular ballads and various types of literature. John Lyly's best-selling novel *Euphues* (1578) includes a condemnation of women by a spurned lover that begins with the exact phrase Swetnam opens with: "Musing with myself being idle"; this is reminiscent of popular Roman orator Marcus Fabius Quintilianus's preface to *Institutio Oratoria,* which begins: "Having at length, after twenty years devoted to the training of the young, obtained leisure for study…."

As the *Worming* suggests, seventeenth-century European views of women were mired in a tendency to exaggerate either their goodness and worth or lack thereof. Daniel Tuvil's pamphlet *Asylum Veneris* (1616) praises the usual virtues of modesty and chastity, advising women to exercise caution in choosing a husband. The first explicit response to Swetnam came from Rachel Speght, a nineteen-year-old unmarried clergyman's daughter, whose pamphlet *A Mouzell for Melastomus* (1617) ("a muzzle for Melastomus"; the melastomus a type of shark) is addressed to "our pestiferous enemy" and his "illiterate pamphlet (titled *The Arraignment of Women*)" but turns into a fairly pious defense of women as modest handmaidens to men. The pseudonymous Ester Sowernam contributed a second response to Swetnam, *Ester Hath Hang'd Haman* (1617). "Sowernam" (sour-nam) is thought to play on "Swetnam" (sweet-nam); "Ester" refers to the biblical heroine who saved the Jewish people from Haman, a murderous villain. In 1619 an anonymously written play appeared—*Swetnam the Woman-Hater, Arraigned by Women*—that incorporated elements of Speght, Sowernam, and Munda's tracts, along with the popular fifteenth-century story *Grisel y Mirabella.* In the play, Swetnam's alias is "Misogenos."

❖ *Key Facts*

Time Period:
Early 17th Century

Genre:
Pamphlet

Events:
Rise of the middle class; invention of the printing press; beginning of the women's rights movement

Nationality:
English

BIRDS OF QUARREL, BIRDS OF PRAISE

Adapted from Old French poems featuring "parliaments" of birds that debated romance, springtime, and whether a clerk or knight would make a better lover, Middle English bird debates provided literary context for exploring a range of ideas. An early example is *The Owl and the Nightingale* (1189–1216?), in which the two female birds argue bitterly over which one of them is superior; English church politics also come up more than once. Like Ovid's doom-heralding owl in *Metamorphoses* (5.550), owls in medieval folklore were associated with cunning and gloom.

The Thrush and the Nightingale (c. 1275), in which both birds are male, pits a woman-hating thrush against a defending nightingale: "I cannot praise women at all, / Since they are treacherous and false-minded," says the thrush. "The greatest happiness that man has on earth / Is when a woman becomes his mate," counters the nightingale. *The Cuckoo and the Nightingale* (1390?–1410?) is attributed to Thomas Clanvowe, and Robert Vaughan's *A Dyalogue Defensyue for Women, against Malycyous Detractours* (1542) has a "fawcon [falcon] most gentyll" telling a magpie not "to judge all unparfyte, thoughe one lack perfection." And Geoffrey Chaucer's *Parliament of Fowls* (early 1380s?) features a cast of birds embodying various states of romantic love.

Early seventeenth-century writing by women was exceptionally rare. Most women could neither read nor write, although there is some evidence that some who could not write could read. Munda's portrait of a proudly educated woman was therefore remarkable. Some women did publish; Amelia Lanyer's 1611 book of verse *Salve Deus Rex Judaeorum* includes a section called "Eve's Apologie in Defense of Women" that defends the biblical Eve against the charge, repeated by Swetnam, that she instigated sin. Lady Elizabeth Cary's play *The Tragedy of Mariam* (1613) won critical praise, as did her other works, including a controversial translation, *The Reply of the Illustrious Cardinal Perron* (1630), that endeared her to her fellow Catholics but ostracized her from her own family. A sixteen-year-old Bathshua Makin published *Musea Virginea* (1616), verses in seven languages presented to King James I (who reportedly responded, "But can she spin?"). Lady Mary Wroth, née Sidney, published a chivalric romance, *Urania,* in 1621. Her aunt Mary Sidney, sister to Sir Philip, was also a noted editor, poet, and translator.

The extent to which Munda's pamphlet encouraged women writers is unknown. Wroth wrote a Petrarchan sonnet sequence, *Pamphilia to Amphilanthus* (1621); although it sounds like the word "pamphlet," *pamphilia* means "all-loving." Speght refers to Munda and the Swetnam controversy in her poem "The Dream" (1621), about women's troubled relationship with knowledge. In 1639–40 a male author, John Taylor, assumed both the male and female roles

in a self-generated pamphlet war, writing two tracts that denounced women and one that defended them. The question of women's worth and place in society has been examined by Virginia Woolf, whose essays about women's education and work helped form the foundation of contemporary feminism.

THEMES AND STYLE

The *Worming* presents a female speaker exasperated by the continuous misrepresentation of women in print by men who are often intellectually insipid. There is a touch of Shylock's "hath not a Jew eyes" speech from William Shakespeare's *The Merchant of Venice* (1597–98) in Munda's lament for the practice of heaping insults on women. Munda hints at familiarity with the pamphlet wars of the 1580s and 1590s involving the Martin Marprelate tracts, a series of anti-episcopal attacks by a pseudonymous Presbyterian, who scolds the powerful Anglican bishops, "how can you escape the danger of a premunire" (*The Epistle,* 1588)—an act against royal authority—when she taunts Swetnam, "your pamphlet hath brought you within the compass of a *praemunire.*" Munda's message is clear: women were capable of sophisticated intellectual discourse and ought to be spared Swetnam's criticism.

Munda wastes no time in establishing a stance of outrage in the verse epistle "To Joseph Swetnam," all but cursing him; his "barren, idle, dunghill brain"; and his "vile untutored muse." This tone is maintained throughout, though Munda soon shifts to prose, the better to include sections of the *Arraignment* she finds particularly offensive, and she frequently digresses into Latin, Greek, and occasionally Italian. A verse from Juvenal's *Satire* is quoted in full. Having established Swetnam as being "of that brood which Homer calls, *tanuglossoi*" (always lolling out the tongue), Munda returns to verse: "let all thy labours be / Condemned by upright judgements," closing with a Latin couplet from Martial's *Epigrams.* The pose is one of triumph over stupidity.

Stylistically, the *Worming* is skillful in its wordplay, affecting a learned grandiosity and an energized, righteous spirit. It evokes an earlier work attributed to Jane Anger, the pamphlet *Her Protection for Women* (1589). Weary of woman-haters, Anger writes: "If we hide our breasts, it must be with leather, for no cloth can keep their long nails out of our bosoms." Munda demonstrates familiarity with Aristotelian logic: "A man that is accounted a scold hath great discredit; / Joseph Swetnam is accounted a scold; / *Ergo,* Joseph hath great discredit." Munda compares Swetnam to the Bible's foul-mouthed Assyrian vizier—"to be a profane railing Rabsheka, 'tis odious"—and gives Speght a sisterly nod, taunting Swetnam: "your black grinning mouth hath been muzzled by a modest and powerful hand." Munda also ridicules Swetnam's writing, "the crabbedness of your style, the unsavoury periods of your broken-winded sentences." As polemic, the *Worming* is thorough and forceful, less restrained than Speght and more trenchant than Sowernam. It succeeds in making Swetnam appear foolish; in its first edition, *The Arraignment* describes Cerberus as "two-headed"; after Munda's mockery—"you bit off one of his heads"—it was amended.

CRITICAL DISCUSSION

Swetnam's *Arraignment* continued to be reprinted well into the eighteenth century, with a final edition issued in 1807 alongside Sowernam's 1617 response, but Munda's response remained unique in the literature of gender controversy. The early 1620s saw a debate over women's cross-dressing, with King James I exhorting clergymen to preach against "the insolency of our women," and two anonymously penned works, *Hic Mulier* and *Haec Vir* (both 1620) combining the old literary definitions of gender with a theatrical form of satire. Conduct books for women continued to be written by men and women well into the eighteenth century. *An Essay to Revive the Ancient Education of Gentlewomen* (1673), by the educator Bathshua Makin, argued in favor of keeping the pathways to knowledge open for women, anticipating objections that "the end of learning is public business, which women are not capable of" with "it is private instruction I plead for, not public employment." In his 1880 edition of the play *Swetnam the Woman-hater*, A. B. Grosart writes of Munda and the other responses to Swetnam: "Unfortunately not one of these 'Answers' rises above the level of a theological-Biblical 'defence' of Woman. Now and again there is a swift, dexterous making of a point against Swetnam from his own ungrammatical and illogical *laches* [mistakes]; but sooth to say, they are somewhat dreary reading."

In the twentieth century, as universal suffrage spread throughout the Western world, tracts such as Swetnam's became anathema—replaced by the subtler misogynies of the new media—and feminist scholars sought harbingers of a feminist mentality in *The Worming of a Mad Dog*. Louis B. Wright, writing in 1958, has more praise for Sowernam but also mentions Munda, "apparently also a woman…. The beginning of the pamphlet, which is merely an exposure of the ignorance and malice of Swetnam, throws further light on the abundance of anti-feminist literature." Suzanne W. Hull's 1982 study of early modern books for women omitted Munda from her discussion of the Swetnam controversy. In 1985 Simon Shepherd anthologized Munda alongside Anger, Speght, and Sowernam, and Mary Tattle-well and Joan Hit-him-home (both of whom Shepherd reveals to be John Taylor). Of the *Worming* Shepherd writes: "if it is a man who has written it (which I half suspect)" the work is "learned and astute, if sometimes plagiarising."

Later twentieth-century feminist scholars tended to see Munda as female. In *Women and the English Renaissance* (1984), Linda Woodbridge enjoys the spectacle of a nascent feminism: "Munda presents herself as a street scrapper, her confrontation with

Swetnam as an open brawl…. This is no debate: it is a mugging." In his 1994 essay in *Attending to Women in Early Modern England*, David Cressy questions "the success of William Gouge's *Of Domesticall Duties* and its ilk," religious conduct books, and "male utterance in a ritualized and conventionalized setting." Betty S. Travitsky wrote in 1996, perhaps in response to Shepherd's remark that Munda's "mind seems almost too learned for a woman": "To doubt that this caustic work could have emerged from a woman's pen is to disparage female ability unnecessarily."

BIBLIOGRAPHY

Sources

Crandall, Coryl. *Swetnam the Woman-hater: The Controversy and the Play.* Lafayette: Purdue University Studies, 1969. Print.

Cressy, David. "Response: Private Lives, Public Performances, and Rites of Passage." *Attending to Women in Early Modern England.* Ed. Betty S. Travitsky and Adele F. Seeff. Newark: U of Delaware P, 1994. Print.

Grosart, Rev. A. B., ed. *Swetnam the Woman-Hater Arraigned by Women [A Play, in Reply to The Arraignment of Lewd Women].* Manchester: Charles E. Simms, 1880. *Google Play.* Web. 10 Aug. 2012.

Sir Francis Bacon, pictured here in a portrait attributed to William Larkin, served as attorney general during the pamphlet wars of which *The Worming of a Mad Dog* was an essential component. Bacon ruled in favor of laws of equality over common law in 1615. PORTRAIT OF FRANCIS BACON (1561–1626) 1ST BARON OF VERULAM AND VISCOUNT OF ST. ALBANS (OIL ON CANVAS), LARKIN, WILLIAM (FL.1608–19) (ATTR. TO)/ PRIVATE COLLECTION/THE BRIDGEMAN ART LIBRARY.

Shepherd, Simon. *The Women's Sharp Revenge*. London: Fourth Estate, 1985. Print.

Swetnam, Joseph. *The Arraignment of Lewd, Idle, Froward and Unconstant Women*. London: F. Grove, 1667. *Early English Books Online*. Web. 10 Aug. 2012.

Travitsky, Betty S. "The Possibilities of Prose." *Women and Literature in Britain, 1500–1700*. Ed. Helen Wilcox. Cambridge: Cambridge UP, 1996. Print.

Woodbridge, Linda. *Women and the English Renaissance: Literature and the Nature of Womankind, 1540–1600*. Urbana: U of Illinois P, 1984. Print.

Further Reading

Agrippa, Cornelius. *De nobilitate et praecellentia foeminei sexus declamatio/Female Pre-eminence. 1529. Esoteric Archives*. University of Texas at Austin/Joseph H. Peterson. Web. 10 Aug. 2012.

Boleyn, Deirdre. "Because Women Are Not Women, Rather Might Be a Fit Subject of an Ingenious Satyrist: Constantia Munda's *The Worming of a Mad Dogge* (1617)." *Prose Studies* Apr. 2010. *Literature Online*. Web. 10 Aug. 2012.

De Pizan, Christine. *The Book of the City of Ladies*. Rev. ed. Trans. Earl Jeffrey Richards. New York: Persea, 1998. Print.

Hull, Suzanne W. *Chaste, Silent & Obedient: English Books for Women, 1475–1640*. San Marino: Huntingdon Library, 1982. Print.

———. *Women According to Men*. London: AltaMira, 1996. Print.

Kelso, Ruth. *Doctrine for the Lady of the Renaissance*. Urbana: U of Illinois P, 1956. Print.

Lewalski, Barbara K. *The Polemics and Poems of Rachel Speght*. New York: Oxford UP, 1996. Print.

Magnusson, A. Lynne. "'His Pen with My Hande': Jane Anger's Revisionary Rhetoric." *English Studies in Canada* Sept. 1991. *ProQuest*. Web. 10 Aug. 2012.

Utley, Francis Lee. *The Crooked Rib*. New York: Octagon, 1970. Print.

Rebecca Rustin

DISSIDENTS AND REBELS

AN ADDRESS TO THE PEOPLE ON THE DEATH OF THE PRINCESS CHARLOTTE

Percy Bysshe Shelley

OVERVIEW

Quietly published following the untimely death of Princess Charlotte of Wales in November 1817, Percy Bysshe Shelley's *An Address to the People on the Death of the Princess Charlotte* is a vigorous denunciation of England's political system and popular values. The essay, distributed in propagandistic pamphlet form, urges citizens to grieve losses of liberty, parliamentary and monarchical mismanagement, and the everyday tragic deaths of common citizens—not just the unfortunate yet, to Shelley's mind, meaningless death of a young royal with "amiable manners." Ultimately, *An Address* has little to do with Princess Charlotte herself; rather, Shelley uses her death as an opportunity to awaken English men and women to the nation's rampant social inequalities and moral corruptions. In particular, he urges readers to reconsider the role of the death penalty in nineteenth-century life, arguing that the reckless use of violence and capital punishment as a method for controlling the masses is detrimental to the human spirit.

As England mourned a beloved daughter, Shelley questioned such an outpouring of sadness, arguing that grief should be reserved for authentic tragedy, such as the grisly imprisonment and killing of political activists Jeremiah Brandreth, Isaac Ludlam, and William Turner by the government's hand. The pamphlet attempted to counter the government's efforts to eclipse conversation about the activists' deaths by bereavement for Princess Charlotte. The Princess, however, was widely popular with the English people (far more so than her father, the Prince Regent George IV, or estranged mother, Princess Caroline). The author's revolutionary call to action, therefore, was heard by few. *An Address,* along with Shelley's other wide-ranging writings on sociopolitical reform, nonetheless have had a lasting influence on subsequent essayists, philosophers, and poets interested in the relationship of the radical individual to dominant culture.

HISTORICAL AND LITERARY CONTEXT

An Address was published nineteen years after William Wordsworth and Samuel Taylor Coleridge's *Lyrical Ballads,* a groundbreaking text that jump-started English Romanticism. Born out of disillusionment with Enlightenment ideals as well as an interest in revolutionary fervor in France and elsewhere, the Romantic movement placed primacy on direct experience, human imagination, and emotions. A troupe of Romantic poets emerged in the wake of *Lyrical Ballads,* including Lord Byron, John Keats, and Shelley. To varying degrees, these writers were interested in social reform, and many used their personal lives as laboratories for progressive Romantic values: Byron is still remembered for his amorous pursuits, Keats for sacrificing physical love for the sake of art, and Shelley for experiments with vegetarianism and atheism.

Throughout the Romantic period, England was ruled by a series of conservative monarchs. Unable to remain in office due to mental illness and physical deterioration, King George III ceded power to his son George IV in 1811. By all accounts, the new prince regent was unprepared for the position. Indeed, many lost respect for the monarchy, especially after the implementation of authoritarian actions, including spying on citizens, after the conclusion of the Napoleonic Wars in 1815. Although most were not fond of the current prince, they reserved affection for his headstrong daughter, Charlotte, the presumptive future queen. The country attentively followed her rocky courtships, engagements, eventual marriage, and pregnancy. Shelley was frustrated by the flood of grief for Charlotte, a lofty sovereign—while daily injustices against everyday citizens went unnoticed—and he used the pamphlet as propaganda to open others' eyes to this incongruity.

In Shelley's day, political pamphlets had the power to sway opinion and foment civic change. Thomas Paine's widely circulated pamphlet *Common Sense,* for instance, inspired the American Revolution. Along with his poetic and aesthetic interests, Shelley was devoted to sociopolitical reform. He published a handful of pamphlets over the course of his short, but intense, writing career. Influenced by political philosophers such as William Godwin and Mary Wollstonecraft, Shelley composed *A Philosophical Review of Reform* in which he further expanded the ideas found in *An Address,* calling for parliamentary reform and civic equality. Firm in his belief that the arts are equipped to discuss political concerns and shape meaningful social change, Shelley notes in *A Defence of Poetry* that poets are "the unacknowledged legislators of the world."

✧ *Key Facts*

Time Period:
Early 19th Century

Genre:
Pamphlet

Events:
Romanticism; death of Princess Charlotte of Wales; public execution of political dissidents Jeremiah Brandreth, Isaac Ludlam, and William Turner

Nationality:
English

PAMPHLET: A MEDIUM OF PERSUASION

Smaller than a book and larger than a newspaper article, pamphlets—often unbound and printed on cheap paper, with a paper cover or no cover at all—occupied a crucial place in public life in England, France, and Germany from the sixteenth century until the close of the nineteenth. Percy Bysshe Shelley's *An Address to the People on the Death of the Princess Charlotte* represents a typical pamphlet: propagandistic, argumentative, and concerned with pressing political or religious issues. Perhaps the most well-known pamphleteer is Thomas Paine, an eighteenth-century revolutionary, famous for his pamphlets *Common Sense* and *The Rights of Man*, among others.

Beyond the usual topics of politics and religion, pamphlets often concerned everyday subjects such as fashion, courtship and marriage, etiquette rules, and horoscopes. The word "pamphlet" hails from the Latin *pamphilus*, or brief love poem; by the fourteenth century, the word had evolved into *pamflet*—any text smaller than a book. In the twentieth century, pamphlets fell out of favor, replaced by new technologies such as radio, television, and cable news. Today, blogs, online forums, and social media sites have made the pamphlet virtually obsolete.

An Address, while an important piece in Shelley's body of work and an informative picture of English political life in 1817, was not widely influential. It is unknown how many copies of the pamphlet were printed and distributed; the inflammatory subject matter (the princess's death as a platform from which to discuss social reform) was at odds with the national sentiments of the time. Shelley understood that his views would most likely be controversial, noting in a letter to his publisher that "the subject tho' treated boldly is treated delicately." Other prose works by Shelley—*A Defence of Poetry* especially—have had greater impacts on subsequent literature and received more critical attention.

THEMES AND STYLE

Shelley's aim in *An Address* is a hefty one: namely, to convince readers to reform government not just in one arena but across the board. Not only that, Shelley advocates that his countrymen cease frittering away their energy weeping for a figurehead when they could be "worship[ing]" liberty and equality. Shelley's specific causes for concern are the national debt generated by an "idle" class of royalty and government ministers, described as "petty and creeping weeds"; the government's practice of spying on its citizens interested in reform as well as disturbing peaceable protests; and the unfair working conditions of the lower and middle classes. He pits the

English "everyman" against the villains or "remorseless blood-conspirators" of the state and declares that the only paths forward for England are "despotism, revolution, or reform."

In *An Address*, Shelley steadily bolsters his argument through a series of numbered contrasts. While he acknowledges that many mourn the death of the Princess Charlotte and her stillborn child, Shelley asserts that such grief is, in fact, misplaced, noting that "there were thousands of others equally distinguished as she, for private excellencies, who have been cut off in youth and hope," yet little attention is paid to them. He contrasts the princess's relatively quick death in childbirth to the prolonged and distressing imprisonment and brutal executions of Brandreth, Ludlam, and Turner. By placing the death of a royal heir and the deaths of three citizens in opposition to each other, Shelley begs the question: who, or what, should the English people really mourn? A princess who, according to Shelley, "had accomplished nothing, and aspired to nothing," or a culture in which brutal punishments of citizens and activists is a normal activity? The essay is addressed directly to the people of England and, as such, is full of vehement exhortations and commands for citizens to bewail not only the dead princess but also England's untenable and unjust political and social realities.

Throughout the essay Shelley employs persuasive, journalistic language coupled with disturbing descriptions of the punishment of Brandreth, Ludlam, and Turner. Like many propagandists, the author intrinsically understood that the quickest way to readers' hearts is through their emotional faculties. The author describes the reactions of the sentenced men's families at the public execution: "How fearful must have been their agony, sitting in solitude on that day when the tempestuous voice of horror from the crowd, told them that the head so dear to them was severed from the body!" In order to build his case, Shelley also relies on frequent rhetorical questions, syntactical repetitions, and emotional pleading. Figurative language—the entrance of liberty as "Queen" for instance—appears in the last paragraph, in which politics is elevated to the level of philosophy and spirituality.

CRITICAL DISCUSSION

The political impact of *An Address* in 1817 is not known. In fact, Shelley's voice was largely drowned out by the public mourning for Princess Charlotte. According to historian Kate Williams, the entire nation wore black and businesses shut down for days. The *Times* of London reported that never before had there been "so strong and general an expression and indication of sorrow," while other newspapers ignored Shelley's pamphlet at the time. Forty-odd years after *An Address*, Harriet Martineau and Charles Knight, in *History of the Peace* (1858), write that Shelley's "age and he were not on the best terms" and that the radical poet was "persecuted for his opinions." Determined to have his voice heard regardless, Shelley published some political writings, including *An Address,* under the pseudonym the Hermit of Marlow.

An Address itself has not enjoyed a significant social or political influence since its publication. However, taken with Shelley's other political pamphlets, newspaper writings, and philosophical texts, the document paints a portrait of a perspicacious and compassionate mind, dedicated to myriad reform movements in England and across Europe. Shelley's wife, acclaimed writer Mary Shelley, noted that her husband's "warmest sympathies were with the people." According to Michael Rossington in his 2007 essay in *Romanticism,* Shelley contributed to political discussion because he believed that his writing had the power to "identify and re-present events that encapsulated civic division with the aim of instilling debate and shifting public opinion." Whether or not Shelley's pamphlets truly made a tangible difference on the ground is unclear; however, scholars still delve into his political works for insights into nineteenth-century political life, as well as for an understanding of Romantic philosophy.

An Address currently receives little critical attention on its own, in part because Shelley's considerable corpus of poetry, essays, and other writings attract the most scholarly interest. Certainly, he is most remembered for his Romantic poetry. His popular lyric poems "Ode to the West Wind" and "Ozymandias" are found in most anthologies of great English poetry. While not widely known, Shelley's 1817 pamphlet, however, is far from forgotten: in 2002 Mark Canuel, in an essay for *Wordsworth Circle,* focused considerable critical attention on how Shelley and other Romantic writers questioned capital punishment and "used their works to address the issue of punishment and saw punishment, curiously, as an opportunity for the imagination to meditate on its own powers." Shelley's numerous writings on reform of all sorts—from penal to personal—provide current scholars with a dynamic snapshot of Romantic philosophy and ethics.

BIBLIOGRAPHY

Sources

Canuel, Mark. "Coleridge, Shelley and the Aesthetics of Correction." *Wordsworth Circle* 33.1 (2002): 7. *Gale Literature Resource Center.* Web. 10 July 2012.

Findlay, L. M. "Percy Bysshe Shelley." *British Reform Writers, 1789–1832.* Ed. Gary Kelly and Edd Applegate. Detroit: Gale Research, 1996. *Dictionary of Literary Biography.* Vol. 158. *Gale Literature Resource Center.* Web. 6 July 2012.

Martineau, Harriet, and Charles Knight. *History of the Peace: Pictorial History of England during the Thirty Years' Peace, 1816–1846.* Edinburgh: W. & R. Chambers, 1858. Print.

Rossington, Michael. "'The Destinies of the World': Shelley's Reception and Transmission of European News in 1820–21." *Romanticism* 13.3 (2007). *Project Muse.* Web. 30 July 2012.

Shelley, Percy Bysshe. "An Address to the People on the Death of the Princess Charlotte." *The Works of Percy Bysshe Shelley in Verse and Prose.* Ed. H. Buxton Forman. London: Reeves and Turner, 1880. *The Percy Bysshe Shelley Resource Page.* Web. 6 July 2012.

Williams, Kate. *Becoming Queen Victoria: The Tragic Death of Princess Charlotte and the Unexpected Rise of Britain's Greatest Monarch.* New York: Random House Digital, 2010. *Google Books.* Web. 12 July 2012.

Further Reading

Clark, Timothy. *Embodying Revolution: The Figure of the Poet in Shelley.* Oxford: Clarendon Press, 1989. Print.

Duffy, Cian. *Shelley and the Revolutionary Sublime.* Cambridge: Cambridge UP, 2005. Print.

Franta, Andrew. "Shelley and the Politics of Political Indirection." *Poetics Today* Winter 2001: 765. *Project Muse.* Web. 30 July 2012.

A portrait of Princess Charlotte of Wales, painted by James Lonsdale. PRINCESS CHARLOTTE (1796–1817) BEFORE 1817 (OIL ON CANVAS), LONSDALE, JAMES (1777–1839)/© GUILDHALL ART GALLERY, CITY OF LONDON/THE BRIDGEMAN ART LIBRARY.

Frosch, Thomas. "Passive Resistance in Shelley: A Psychological View." *Journal of English and Germanic Philology* 98.3 (1999). *JSTOR.* Web. 12 July 2012.

Hoagwood, Terence Allan. *Skepticism and Ideology: Shelley's Political Prose and Its Philosophical Context from Bacon to Marx.* Iowa City: U of Iowa P, 1988. Print.

Jones, Steven E. *Shelley's Satire: Violence, Exhortation, and Authority.* DeKalb: Northern Illinois UP, 1994. Print.

Shelley, Percy Bysshe. *Shelley's Poetry and Prose.* Ed. Donald Reiman and Sharon Powers. New York: Norton, 1977. Print.

———. *The Letters of Percy Bysshe Shelley,* 2 vols. Ed. Frederick L. Jones. Oxford: Oxford UP, 1964. Print.

Webb, Timothy, and Alan M. Weinberg. *The Unfamiliar Shelley.* Farnham: Ashgate, 2009. Print.

Claire Skinner

APPEAL, IN FOUR ARTICLES

David Walker

OVERVIEW

Appeal, in Four Articles, a pamphlet written by David Walker in 1829, is a powerful indictment of slavery that served as a rallying cry for subjugated African Americans and instilled fear in their white oppressors, particularly in the South. Published as *Walker's Appeal, in Four Articles; together with a Preamble, to the Coloured Citizens of the World, but in Particular, and Very Expressly, to Those of the United States of America,* the pamphlet made the first major American call for immediate abolition without financial compensation to slave owners. In the text, Walker, an African American, frames the issue of slavery in terms of Christian morality, arguing that the fight to free slaves from bondage is a Godly mission to overcome evil. He works to expose racist ideology, indict whites for the injustice of slaveholding, and press for black liberation and equality. In so doing, he encourages education for African Americans as a way for them to learn their rights, take responsibility for their own lives, rise up against their masters (with violence if necessary), and achieve their independence.

An immediate success with sympathetic northern audiences, Walker's *Appeal* appeared in three editions within the first year of its appearance. With help from existing black communication and abolitionist networks, Walker was also able to smuggle copies of the pamphlet into the South, often by sewing them into the lining of clothing he sold at his Boston consignment store to sailors bound for southern ports. This caused a firestorm among southern leaders working to keep the pamphlet out of the hands of slaves and free blacks. In response to the *Appeal's* appearance, Georgia even passed a law that barred free blacks from leaving ships while in port and imposed fines for possession of abolitionist propaganda such as Walker's pamphlet. The *Appeal* not only moved enslaved African Americans in the South to take action, but it also helped to catalyze the nascent abolition movement in the North.

HISTORICAL AND LITERARY CONTEXT

Though all northern states had begun to gradually abolish slavery by 1804, it was a deeply ingrained and defended aspect of southern culture, economics, and politics. A movement to abolish slavery throughout the United States had long existed but remained limited until 1816, when the American Colonization Society (ACS) was organized in New Jersey. Founded by African American pastor Robert Finley, the ACS sought to send black Americans to Africa. Members of the ACS saw this proposal as a means of ending slavery that would also quell southern fears of reprisal by freed blacks. While the idea of sending blacks to Africa drew the support of many prominent American abolitionists, others in the movement criticized the plan as being both impractical and cruel.

When *Appeal, in Four Articles* appeared in 1829, some American abolitionists were beginning to look for ways other than the ACS plan to end slavery. The ACS had established a colony called Liberia for former slaves in 1820, but it was not the large-scale solution that organizers and supporters had envisioned. In 1822 a slave rebellion organized by free black man Denmark Vesey in Charleston, South Carolina, was uncovered before it could be implemented. Though it was not a success, the plot was indicative of increasingly well-organized attempts to overthrow the oppression of slavery in the South. In the North, meanwhile, free blacks began to organize and seek strategies for achieving black equality and the abolishment of slavery. Walker's *Appeal* provided a powerful argument that helped to show the abolition movement a path other than that of the ACS.

In tone and rhetorical strategy, *Appeal, in Four Articles* draws from contemporary abolitionist journalism as well as a long tradition of Christian writing about social justice. Throughout the text, Walker makes numerous biblical references. When he implores his audience to "be not afraid or dismayed," for example, he makes reference to 2 Chronicles 20:15. Moreover, he continually cites the story of Moses leading the Israelites from bondage in Egypt as evidence of slavery's injustice and the potential for liberation. In making his case for abolition, Walker also draws from African American newspapers of the early nineteenth century, such as *Freedom's Journal.*

After its publication in 1829, the *Appeal* helped to inspire writings on abolition and racial injustice by both whites and blacks. White abolitionists were inspired by Walker's radical appeal to rid the nation of the sin of slavery. For example, Massachusetts journalist and reformer William Lloyd Garrison founded the abolitionist newspaper the *Liberator* as a means of carrying on the *Appeal's* argument after Walker's death

❖ *Key Facts*

Time Period:
Early 19th Century

Genre:
Pamphlet

Events:
Failure of American recolonization movement; rise of abolitionism

Nationality:
American

THE LIFE OF DAVID WALKER

David Walker was born in Wilmington, North Carolina, in 1785, the son of a slave and a free black woman. Under North Carolina law, he was born a free man due to his mother's status. In 1825, Walker settled in Boston and became involved in the free-black community that thrived there. He had first been exposed to a free-black community while living in Charleston, South Carolina, and again while briefly residing in Philadelphia. He operated his own business in Boston and had some standing in the community. An outspoken critic of slavery and a member of the Massachusetts General Colored Association, he was often called on to speak at abolitionist events.

Following the publication of the *Appeal, in Four Articles* in 1829, Walker's notoriety grew, in part because of the tactics he used to smuggle the pamphlet into the South. Southern states passed special laws aimed at keeping the pamphlet out of the hands of southern slaves, and Georgia even offered a bounty for Walker. He also helped to found the first abolitionist newspaper, *Freedom's Journal.* In the summer of 1830, Walker died unexpectedly in Boston. Many of his contemporaries speculated that he had been poisoned by southern agents, though most historians believe he died from tuberculosis.

in 1830. While Garrison did not embrace the violence that Walker condoned, he did endorse the concept of slave owners being punished by God for owning another human. Black abolitionists such as Frederick Douglass also elaborated upon Walker's argument as the United States moved toward emancipation later in the nineteenth century.

THEMES AND STYLE

The central theme of the *Appeal* is that African Americans must act to achieve their liberation from oppression rather than wait for white Americans to do it for them. Walker writes that the American brand of slavery is the most oppressive form of bondage in history, producing unprecedented suffering among African Americans. The source of this oppression and suffering is described in detail, in the four articles of the text's title. The first of these articles counters white claims that the supposed racial inferiority of blacks justifies their enslavement; the second advocates education as a means of emancipation; the third indicts white Christians for allowing slavery to continue; and the fourth combats the notion that deporting free blacks to a colony in Africa is a just means of abolition. Walker urges blacks to think of the United States as their own country, one in which they have as much of a share as whites do: "America is more our country, than it is the whites—we have enriched it with our *blood* and *tears*."

Walker appeals to foundational tenets of Christianity as a means of illustrating slavery's moral reprehensibility. With repeated references to God and the Bible, he invokes an authority that transcends the whims of man. In ending slavery, writes Walker, whites would not be "giving blacks a gift but rather returning what they had stolen from them and God." He rejects the notion that blacks must appeal to whites to validate their fight for emancipation: "To pay respect to whites as the source of freedom was thus to blaspheme God by denying that he was the source of all virtues and the only one with whom one was justified having a relationship of obligation and debt." According to Walker, only God deserves such adoration. Man's role, he argues, is to implement God's will, which is not "to be slave to dust and ashes like ourselves."

Stylistically, the *Appeal* is distinguished by its urgent tone. Walker calls on slaves to "arise" and take an active role in ending slavery. He writes in language that is meant to incite an emotional response. Appealing to his audience's sense of both outrage and hope, Walker urges blacks to "never make an attempt to gain freedom or natural right, from under our cruel oppressors and murderers, until you see your way clear; when that hour arrives and you move, be not afraid or dismayed." Through his appeals to morality and his invocations of Christian teaching, Walker is able to temper his overarching call for action with an underlying sense of justice and validity. He also employs the first-person point of view in recounting his own experience as a black man who has lived in the South. This adds credence and power to his argument.

CRITICAL DISCUSSION

When *Appeal, in Four Articles* appeared, it inspired abolitionists to take action and, in turn, drew a strong rebuke from proslavery forces. In Boston and other northern cities, the pamphlet circulated through free-black communities and led to the growth of the radical abolition movement. White abolitionists, too, were drawn to Walker's message and were moved to increase their involvement in the effort to end slavery. In publications such as the *Liberator* and the *Boston Daily Evening Transcript,* the work was noticed, discussed, and admired. When *Appeal, in Four Articles* was smuggled into southern states, it alarmed slaveholders who already lived in fear of slave rebellion and considered the pamphlet to be a dangerous piece of propaganda. As the first widely distributed radical abolitionist work in the South, the *Appeal* was met with a series of laws meant to suppress it and similar literature. The state legislature of Louisiana, for example, not only outlawed the document but also made reading it punishable by life imprisonment or death. Georgia, Virginia, and other states followed suit.

Though Walker died within a year of the pamphlet's appearance, the *Appeal* lived on as a source of abolitionist inspiration. When Garrison began publishing the *Liberator* in 1831, he devoted the first editions to Walker's pamphlet. The *Appeal* also provided much of the language that Garrison would use in his *Manifesto of the American Anti-Slavery Society,* which he issued in 1833. Indeed, Walker's *Appeal* called the nation to action, identifying slavery and slave holding as a sin. That message spread gradually, but it eventually helped change the nation forever.

Today the *Appeal* is widely discussed in scholarly works on abolition, slavery, and antebellum social reform. Historians and other scholars tend to credit Walker with raising white awareness concerning slavery. For example, in his book *Bearing Witness against Sin: The Evangelical Birth of the American Social Movement,* sociologist Michael Young credits Walker with pushing Garrison to a more radical form of abolitionism and away from the ACS. Historian Steven Hahn views Walker's *Appeal* as part of a larger set of political currents running though the Atlantic world. Hahn also links the teachings of Walker to later ideas advanced by Marcus Garvey and other black nationalists. In *Closer to Freedom: Enslaved Women & Everyday Resistance in the Plantation South,* Stephanie Camp argues that Walker's *Appeal* "was an impassioned call to slaves to emancipate themselves from mental slavery to their 'natural enemies,' to act like 'MEN' who had 'souls in our bodies.'" Historian Peter P. Hinks issued both a biography of Walker, *To Awaken My Afflicted Brethren,* and an extensively annotated edition of the *Appeal.* These volumes are indicative of the enduring critical interest in Walker and his groundbreaking call for an end to American slavery.

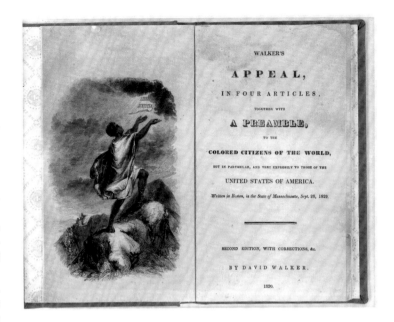

BIBLIOGRAPHY

Sources

Camp, Stephanie M. H. *Closer to Freedom: Enslaved Women & Everyday Resistance in the Plantation South.* Chapel Hill: U of North Carolina P, 2004. Print.

Hahn, Steven. *A Nation Under Our Feet: Black Political Struggles in the Rural South from Slavery to the Great Migration.* Cambridge: Harvard UP, 2003. Print.

Hinks, Peter P. *To Awaken My Afflicted Brethren: David Walker and the Problem of Antebellum Slave Resistance.* University Park: Pennsylvania State UP, 1997. Print.

Rugemer, Edward Bartlett. *The Problem of Emancipation: The Caribbean Roots of the American Civil War.* Baton Rouge: Louisiana State UP, 2008. Print.

Walker, David. *David Walker's Appeal to the Coloured Citizens of the World.* Ed. Peter P. Hinks. University Park: Pennsylvania State UP, 2000. Print.

Young, Michael. *Bearing Witness against Sin: The Evangelical Birth of the American Social Movement.* Chicago: U of Chicago P, 2006. Print.

Further Reading

Alford, Terry. *Prince among Slaves.* New York: Harcourt Brace Jovanovich, 1977. Print.

Berlin, Ira. *Generations of Captivity: A History of African-American Slaves.* Cambridge: Belknap of Harvard UP, 2003. Print.

Cornelius, Janet Duitsman. *When I Can Read My Title Clear: Literacy, Slavery, and Religion in the Antebellum South.* Columbia: U of South Carolina P, 1991. Print.

Crockett, Hasan. "The Incendiary Pamphlet: David Walker's Appeal in Georgia." *The Journal of Negro History* 86.3 (Summer 2001): 305–318. Print.

Genovese, Eugene D. *Roll, Jordan, Roll: The World the Slaves Made.* New York: Vintage Books, 1976. Print.

Jacobs, Donald M. "David Walker and William Lloyd Garrison: Racial Cooperation and the Shaping of Boston Abolition." *Courage and Conscience: Black and White Abolitionists in Boston.* Ed. Donald M. Jacobs. Bloomington: Indiana UP, 1993. 9–17. Print.

O'Donovan, Susan Eva. *Becoming Free in the Cotton South.* Cambridge: Harvard UP, 2007. Print.

Title page and frontispiece of the second edition of Walker's *Appeal.* F&A ARCHIVE/THE ART ARCHIVE AT ART RESOURCE, NY.

Rodney Harris

"BLACK PANTHER PARTY PLATFORM AND PROGRAM"

Huey P. Newton, Bobby Seale

❖ *Key Facts*

Time Period:
Mid-20th Century

Genre:
Manifesto

Events:
Increase of racial
tensions; Watts riots in
Los Angeles; anti-
Vietnam War movement

Nationality:
American

OVERVIEW

The "Black Panther Party Platform and Program," drafted by Huey P. Newton and Bobby Seale in October 1966, was the founding manifesto of the Black Panther Party. This revolutionary African American organization shook up American culture and politics in the late 1960s with its militant stance against black oppression. The document, also known as the "Ten-Point Plan" and subtitled "What We Want, What We Believe," speaks on behalf of the urban black community to make ten forceful demands: self-determination, decent housing, education, full employment, an end to exploitation, exemption from military service, an end to police brutality, freedom for prisoners, the right to trial by peers, and an all-black vote to determine black national destiny. The analysis supporting each demand adds up to an unforgiving critique of white America as a colonialist force brutalizing its black subjects. Concluding with a quotation from the *Declaration of Independence,* the manifesto invokes revolutionary America's insistence on the right to revolt against tyranny to justify its own call for revolution in the name of black equality.

The document gained widespread distribution in the party newspaper, the *Black Panther,* a landmark publication in the history of the black independent press. Originally sold mostly in urban ghettos, the paper at its peak went through several hundred thousand copies a week, including international distribution. Especially appealing to black youths was the manifesto's Article 7, which demanded an end to police brutality. It was while enforcing this point that the Panthers gained enduring notoriety as urban guerrillas, famously in black berets, who dared to confront and monitor white police patrols in poor black neighborhoods. Although the sensational publicity of the Panthers' militancy often distracted from the more nuanced points of the manifesto, Newton and Seale's politics of self-determination proved deeply influential for other activist groups such as the Women's Liberation Movement and the American Indian Movement.

HISTORICAL AND LITERARY CONTEXT

Although the Civil War (1861–65) brought an official end to black slavery in the United States, segregation and racial violence carried far into the twentieth century. Continuing the struggle for equality, early civil rights groups relied on public education, litigation, and lobbying. However, because even those governmental powers that supported racial integration typically opted for incremental rather than sweeping reforms, to many African Americans it seemed that genuine equality was only ever deferred. By the 1950s growing impatience compelled civil rights leaders such as Martin Luther King Jr. to nonviolent acts of civil disobedience: public marches, sit-ins, and boycotts designed to force authorities to confront and resolve racial discrimination. Though King and others like him achieved much, a generation of protestors emerged—among them the Freedom Riders and, later, Malcolm X and Stokely Carmichael—who rejected the tenets of nonviolence and integration in favor of a new militant "Black Power." The Panthers' Ten-Point Plan responds to Black Power's call for armed self-defense—as Malcolm X put it, seeking freedom "by any means necessary"—as well as to the centuries-old struggle for black liberation in the United States.

Newton, assisted by Seale, drafted the Black Panther Party's manifesto in October 1966 in the antipoverty center where they worked in Oakland, California. At that time, the passing of the Civil Rights Act of 1964, which outlawed discrimination based on "race, color, religion, sex, or national origin," seemed to mark a genuine step toward racial equality. Yet disturbances such as the Watts riot of 1965 made it clear that many African Americans continued to live in deprivation due to discrimination—from housing, education, employment, and police authorities. The Panthers' manifesto takes up these concerns in its call for a radical restructuring of American society to liberate the black community.

While the document situates itself in the same tradition as the *Declaration of Independence,* Newton and Seale's communistic and anticolonialist appeals also drew on Marxism as well as more contemporary theories of revolution: Frantz Fanon's *The Wretched of the Earth,* Che Guevera's *Guerrilla Warfare,* Robert F. Williams's *Negroes with Guns,* and Mao Zedong's *Quotations from Chairman Mao.* What these works share is an insistence on popular armed uprising as a legitimate and effective response to exploitation and oppression. All make a case for the capacity of the oppressed masses to find strength enough to throw off exploiters; all acknowledge, as did Malcolm X and

Carmichael, the strategic merits of justified violence in liberation struggles. It is important to note, however, that the Panthers sought a legally sanctioned, rather than a guerrilla, militancy.

Though the Black Panther Party would not officially disband until 1982, it was a vexed enterprise almost from the outset, owing in large part to tactical infiltration and disruption by the FBI's counterintelligence program, COINTELPRO. Arrests and fatal shoot-outs with police were also regular occurrences. Nevertheless, the Ten-Point Plan has remained an inspirational force for the African American imagination as well as other revolutionary movements, providing some of the most memorable expressions of Black Power. To this day it remains a widely circulated document, influential not only in activist circles but also in the realm of popular culture. The spirit of the manifesto, for instance, informs a whole subgenre of radical novels exploring black militancy, evident in the fictions of John A. Williams, Julian Moreau, Sam Greenlee, Melvin Van Peebles, and Kekla Magoon, and a hip-hop tradition including Public Enemy and Talib Kweli.

THEMES AND STYLE

In the "Platform and Program," Newton and Seale describe the black community as a racially subjugated and economically exploited American "black colony." They blame black impoverishment on a "decadent American society" overseen by "a racist government" along with "white American businessmen," "white landlords," "racist police," and "racist military." They invoke a history of oppression to offer a basic proposition: if white America fails to recognize its black citizens' rights, then those citizens should rise up in revolution. Making this claim, it calls for communist solutions that would give the means of production to the community and turn housing and land into cooperatives. To justify such radical politics, it suggests its demands are one and the same with those of the *Declaration of Independence,* a document similarly declaring revolution a legitimate course of action in the pursuit of democratic freedoms. Indeed, for its style and structure as well as its argument, the manifesto relies heavily on America's founding documents.

The Ten-Point Plan ranges widely in its rhetorical appeals, speaking—as "we"—on behalf of the black community against the failings of the white. It offsets bold demands (the "what we want" claims) with rationalizations (the "what we believe" claims). Thus Article 4 reads: "We want decent housing, fit for shelter of human beings. We believe that if the white landlords will not give decent housing to our black community, then the housing and the land should be made into cooperatives so that our community, with government aid, can build and make decent housing for its people." Notable here is the strategic use of "if" to establish a political logic: if *that* problem goes unresolved, expect *this* particular response. Moving from

THE BLACK PANTHER NEWSPAPER: THE PANTHERS REACH OUT

The first issue of the *Black Panther* newspaper—variously known as the *Black Panther Community News Service* and the *Black Panther Intercommunal News Service*—hit the streets of Oakland, California, on April 25, 1967. Its lead story, "Why Was Denzil Dowell Killed," probed the recent fatal shooting by a police officer of a twenty-two-year-old African American in the Richmond neighborhood.

The paper bluntly described the shooting as a racist killing. Casting doubt on the official investigation, the paper then quoted Article 7 of the "Black Panther Party Platform and Program": "We believe we can end police brutality in our black community by organizing black self-defense groups that are dedicated to defending our black community from racist police oppression and brutality. The second amendment of the *Constitution of the United States* gives a right to bear arms. We therefore believe that all black people should arm themselves for self defense." In this manner the party reached out, grounding revolutionary America's call to arms in the very real concerns and problems of the urban black community. Though the *Black Panther* ceased publication two years before the party disbanded in 1982, it continues to symbolize an enduring legacy of radical politics, power, and creativity for American history and culture.

the "will not" to the "should be … so that," this kind of "if" clause primes the reader to think revolutionary action logical and obligatory. The rhetorical work accomplished here epitomizes that of the document as a whole, whose task is to disclose present factual conditions (the black community is exploited by a racist government) and gesture toward a future course of action (the black community should throw off that government).

Charged with urgency, the language of the manifesto insists that the endangered black community must assert and defend itself. Yet the text is never hotheaded. Rather, it consistently opts for measured, if blunt, statements: "We want freedom"; "We want an immediate end to police brutality and murder of black people"; "We want land, bread, housing, education, clothing, justice and peace." The deliberate tone is especially evident in the legalistic appeals to the U.S. Constitution and the *Declaration of Independence,* with which Newton and Seale go to work on the American reader's political feelings. By citing the *Declaration*—which had insisted "that all men are created equal; that they are endowed by their Creator with certain unalienable rights" and "that, whenever any form of government becomes destructive of these ends, it is the right of the people to alter or to abolish it, and to institute a new government"—Newton and Seale invoke the nation's founding documents to indict the United States for failing to live up to its democratic promises.

The Black Panthers marching in the streets of New York City. © PHOTOS 12/ALAMY.

CRITICAL DISCUSSION

Many of the early responses to the Black Panthers were overtly polemical. On the left, groups such as Students for a Democratic Society championed the message of the manifesto and hailed the Panthers—as the vanguard of the black liberation movement—for having "a correct analysis of society." Yet the rhetoric that consolidated their cause for the Left only damned them on the right, who demonized the party as a threat to law and order. For the mainstream mass white audience, meanwhile, the fearful portrayal of the Panthers as violent, racist, and criminal crowded out the progressive and egalitarian concerns of the "Platform and Program."

Bearing in mind that the manifesto has rarely been discussed in its own right, it was not until the 1990s that scholars began to seriously explore the significance of the document beyond its overt politics. In this decade, as Joe Street claims in his 2010 essay in *Journal of American Studies,* Panther historiography "matured" in that it grew less partisan and more nuanced in the ways it tried to make sense of the legacy. Studies in this era ranged widely: from tracing the manifesto's legacy in contemporary hip-hop culture and understanding the ideological work of its legalistic narrative strategies to contextualizing its publication history in the *Black Panther* newspaper.

Works of history and criticism on the Black Panther Party routinely attribute a foundational role to the Ten-Point Plan, deeming it essential reading—whether for understanding the party, the Black Power movement, or the enduring legacy of both. Yet the document, as noted, is rarely discussed in its own right. Rather, it figures as a key to unlocking larger concerns, such as the complexities of Panther ideology, the militant turn away from the civil rights movement, or the political underpinnings of African American art and culture. Several recent studies by Regina Jennings, Jane Rhodes, and Davi Johnson, however, have paid particular attention to the rhetorical, literary, and print contexts surrounding the document. As Rhodes makes clear in her 2001 piece in *Media History,* the *Black Panther* newspaper, each issue of which carried the manifesto, "became an essential part of the Black Panthers' revolutionary culture" and played a "pivotal role in cementing the radical community." Reminding us that the newspaper, after folding in 1980, was relaunched toward the end of the millennium, Rhodes makes a case for the lasting rhetorical and symbolic significance of Newton and Seale's manifesto.

BIBLIOGRAPHY

Sources

Decker, Jeffrey Louis. "The State of Rap: Time and Place in Hip Hop Nationalism." *Social Text* 34 (1993): 53–84. Print.

Foner, Philip S., ed. *The Black Panthers Speak*. New York: Da Capo, 1995. Print.

Jennings, Regina. "Poetry of the Black Panther Party: Metaphors of Militancy." *Journal of Black Studies* 29.1 (1998): 106–29. Print.

Papke, David Ray. "The Black Panther Party's Narratives of Resistance." *Vermont Law Review* 18 (1994): 645–80. Print.

Rhodes, Jane. "*The Black Panther* Newspaper: Standard-bearer for Modern Black Nationalism." *Media History* 7.2 (2001): 151–58. Print.

Street, Joe. "The Historiography of the Black Panther Party." *Journal of American Studies* 44.2 (2010): 351–75. Print.

Further Reading

Anderson, Joshua. "A Tension in the Thought of Huey P. Newton." *Journal of African American Studies* 16 (2012): 249–67. Print.

Hughey, Matthew W. "Black Aesthetics and Panther Rhetoric: A Critical Decoding of Black Masculinity in *The Black Panther,* 1967–80." *Critical Sociology* 35.1 (2009): 29–56. Print.

Johnson, Davi. "The Rhetoric of Huey P. Newton." *Southern Communication Journal* 70.1 (2004): 15–30. Print.

Monaghan, Peter. "New Views of the Black Panthers Paint Shades of Gray." *Chronicle of Higher Education* 53.26 (2007): A12–17. Print.

Self, Robert. "'To Plan Our Liberation': Black Power and the Politics of Place in Oakland, California, 1965–1977." *Journal of Urban History* 26.6 (2000): 759–92. Print.

Media Adaptation

Black Panther. Huey P. Newton, Eldridge Cleaver, and Bobby Seale. United States: [s.n.], 1968. Film.

David C. Aitchison

BLAKE, OR THE HUTS OF AMERICA

Martin Delany

✥ *Key Facts*

Time Period:
Mid-19th Century

Genre:
Novel

Events:
Growth of abolitionism;
passage of the Fugitive
Slave Law

Nationality:
American

OVERVIEW

Though written in the antebellum United States, Martin Delany's novel *Blake, or The Huts of America* served as a foundational text for twentieth-century black nationalism. Published during the buildup to the Civil War, as debates over the ethics and legality of slavery gripped the nation, *Blake* tells the story of a highly intelligent African American named Henry Blake who, after his wife is sold to Cuban slave owners, escapes slavery and organizes insurrections and armed revolts throughout the busiest slave trading areas, including the United States, Cuba, and Africa. The novel was published in serial form between 1859 and 1861 and eventually pushed Delany, one of the earliest African American novelists, to the symbolic forefront of the Black Power movement near the end of the 1960s on the strength of its separatist themes.

Twenty-three of the novel's estimated eighty chapters were released to a limited audience in the *Anglo-African Magazine* in 1859, and the *Weekly Anglo-African* printed the complete text in 1861 and 1862, though the volumes containing the last six chapters have never been found, thus leaving the story without a conclusion to this day. Historian Floyd J. Miller compiled the seventy-four extant chapters into book form in 1970, during the height of the Black Power movement, and *Blake* proved most popular in the twentieth century as African Americans and civil rights activists found inspiration and solidarity in its example of an individual standing up strongly and at times violently to racism.

At the time of its writing, Delany's novel served as a response to Harriet Beecher Stowe's immensely popular 1852 novel, *Uncle Tom's Cabin,* whose title character was perceived by Delany as overly docile and accepting of the slaveholder ideology. In a sense, Henry Blake is the antithesis of Uncle Tom. He escapes a master who heartlessly and illegally sells his wife to Cuba and travels throughout the South, fomenting forceful, sometimes violent, rebellion. He eventually delivers a group of escapees to Canada before journeying to Cuba, where he rescues his wife and seeks to throw off the chains of bondage for the enslaved by working on a slave ship and subverting the system from within.

HISTORICAL AND LITERARY CONTEXT

Delany himself had a long and storied life. Besides perhaps Frederick Douglass, Delany was arguably the most famous black man of the Civil War era. And although the authorship of *Blake* was what ultimately defined his legacy, his many accomplishments included spending time as a physician, a politician, an abolitionist, and an army officer. Delany grew up primarily in Pittsburgh and southern Pennsylvania. He was one of the first African American students admitted to Harvard Medical School, where he studied until white students drove him out. He befriended abolitionists Douglass and William Lloyd Garrison. Delany aided Douglass with the abolitionist newspaper the *North Star* and promoted black emigration to Africa in the book *The Condition, Elevation, Emigration, and Destiny of the Colored People of the United States, Politically Considered,* which was published in 1852, the same year as *Uncle Tom's Cabin.* He traveled to Africa and spent time touring the Niger River Valley in hopes of facilitating black emigration to the continent. In 1874 he ran unsuccessfully for lieutenant governor of South Carolina.

The notion of collective black emigration and the critique of Uncle Tom as weak in the face of white oppression define Delany's place in history, leading those in the Black Power movement of the twentieth century to view him as a radical Pan-Africanist, a supporter of the notion that peoples of African descent around the world form a single and separate nation. However, after Delany served as the first African American officer with field command in the Civil War, he became concerned with the corruption surrounding Republican management of Reconstruction and endorsed southern Democrat Wade Hampton III—the son of a plantation owner and a former Confederate lieutenant general—for governor of South Carolina, much to the dismay of his abolitionist friends and fans. That he worked with southern white racists trying to find a middle ground to allay Reconstruction violence demonstrates that the novel *Blake* offers only a partial view of Delany's experiences and influence.

Prior to 1850 slavery had garnered little attention on the national stage. Though northerners made up about 75 percent of the entire country's white population, they generally did not concern themselves much with slavery until 1850 and the passage of the Fugitive Slave Law, which created special courts and greatly increased the U.S. Marshals Service to aid the return of fugitive slaves to the South. The law had several quirks, but what upset the mainstream northern population was the U.S. Marshals' new ability to deputize northerners to aid in the capture of runaway slaves and its potential to devastate northern farmers that already had to compete with southern farmers and the free labor they received through slavery. The repercussions for not helping were six months in jail or a thousand-dollar fine. A farmer in the middle of his planting season in Minnesota could potentially be interrupted to serve in a posse to chase escaped slaves. The law also infuriated abolitionists—who made up around 10 percent of the population in the 1850s—like Stowe, who wrote *Uncle Tom's Cabin* in order to shed a light on the perils faced by fugitive slaves.

Blake was published at a time of rising tensions between the North and South. Much had happened during the seven years since the publication of *Uncle Tom's Cabin*: a mini civil war broke out over slavery in Kansas; the Supreme Court had ruled Dred Scott to be property; and John Brown's attempt at a violent slave insurrection peaked anxieties. Though never finished and not widely circulated, *Blake* was radical in its calls for blacks to escape and retaliate. The fear of slave insurrection never left the minds of white southerners. The country's bifurcation over John Brown's actions in Kansas demonstrated how fearful white southerners were of another Nat Turner-style slave revolt. As a result, President Andrew Jackson banned abolitionist literature from being sent through the U.S. Postal Service to the South, where works like Douglass's 1845 autobiography, *Uncle Tom's Cabin,* and *Blake* were seen as dangerous propaganda. Nevertheless, abolitionist newspapers such as Garrison's *Liberator* and Douglass's short-lived *North Star* gained wide circulation throughout the country, especially the former after the passage of the Fugitive Slave Law.

THEMES AND STYLE

Blake's primary themes are the perceived docility of slaves and the hypocrisy of a slaveholder's proclaimed Christian faith and the widespread adoption of it by slaves. The docile slave stereotype is dismissed through Henry's eloquence, his willingness to use violence, and his ability to avoid capture through decisive action. The Christian faith conundrum is demonstrated in the author's excoriation of Christianity as a tool that teaches slaves to passively endure their suffering and allows slaveholders to feel magnanimous while simultaneously depriving fellow humans of their basic rights. "Don't tell me about religion! What's religion to me? My wife is sold away from me by a man who is one of the leading members of the very church to which both she and I belong!" proclaims Blake, who later adds, "If I ever were a Christian, slavery has made me a sinner; if I had been an angel, it would have made me a devil. I feel more like cursing than praying—may God forgive me! Pray for me brethren."

Delany's rhetorical strategies include drawing on history to lend credence to Blake's odyssey and validate the potential threat it poses to the institution of slavery. Although not overtly propagandistic, the message of the text is underscored by the many mentions of actual slave

THE EVOLVING POLITICS OF MARTIN DELANY

In his novel *Blake, or The Huts of America,* Martin Delany advocates for an early form of Pan-Africanism and black nationalism, envisioning a separate, free society for Africans and people of African descent. Far from a simple fantasy or naive daydream, Delany's vision inspired him to travel in 1859 to Liberia and Niger in West Africa, where he spoke with leaders in the Abeokuta region and arranged a treaty to repatriate a number of former slaves to their African homelands. Though his plans eventually dissolved under the chaos of the Civil War, records of his exploration were published under the title *Report of the Niger Valley Exploring Party: A Treaty Made, Granted, and Assigned at Abbeokuta, Nigeria,* in 1861.

After the Civil War, however, Delany began to think that an organized, educated, and financially sound African American community in the United States could affect greater change around the world. He sought and held various governmental positions and proposed a "Triple Alliance" between northern financiers, southern landowners, and black laborers that would benefit the entire country by reconstructing the devastated southern states and creating an African American middle class that would spur the nation's economy. Just as Henry Blake sought in Delany's novel to undermine the slave trade by obtaining a job on a slave ship, Delany worked to end racism in the United States by working within its governmental and economic system. Toward the end of his life Delany grew disenchanted with the notion of African American assimilation. In 1877 he founded the Liberian Joint Stock Steamship Line, with the goal of transporting all willing African Americans to a colony in Liberia. The ship only made one voyage, carrying 274 passengers to Liberia in 1878 before Delany lost interest in the endeavor due to financial pressures.

uprisings, like the revolts of Turner and Gabriel Prosser in Virginia and Denmark Vesey's insurrection in South Carolina. Delany also uses slave dialect for most blacks in the book except Henry, whose use of formal English distinguishes him as a formidable and erudite leader in opposition to the dialect used by Tom in *Uncle Tom's Cabin* and other slaves in *Blake.* The slave Rachel, for example, speaks in dialect to Master Franks, "Wh waun dah w'en we go, but she soon come," whereas Henry's call to arms is formal, if not also poetic: "From plantation to plantation did we go, sowing the seeds of future devastation and ruin to the master and redemption to the slave, an antecedent more terrible in its anticipation than the warning voice of the destroying Angel in commanding the slaughter of the firstborn of Egypt."

As a piece of writing *Blake* is unique; it simultaneously demonstrates the plight and division of slave families while showing that both violent and nonviolent resistance could be effective. It attacked the Uncle Tom archetype, whose Christian principles helped racist slaveholders attain salvation even at the slave's own expense. Through Blake's attitude, acceptance

An illustration of a scene from Harriet Beecher Stowe's novel *Uncle Tom's Cabin*. In *Blake, or The Huts of America* (1859–1861), author, activist, and physician Martin Delany criticizes the treatment of slavery in Stowe's novel. UNCLE TOM AND EVA, ENGLISH SCHOOL, (20TH CENTURY)/ PRIVATE COLLECTION/© LOOK AND LEARN/THE BRIDGEMAN ART LIBRARY.

of violence, and overt law breaking, Delany offers a forceful alternative to Uncle Tom's perceived docility.

CRITICAL DISCUSSION

At the time of its initial publication, *Blake* had minimal impact or circulation. In terms of its literary impact, most critics have found the incomplete book to be poorly written, uneven, and too polemical. The historical impact came more than a century after the work's publication when *Blake,* along with other of Delany's writings, served as the backbone of the Black Power movement's connection to the nineteenth century. Delany's promotion of emigration to Africa and violence to overthrow oppression served the movement's motives.

When *Blake* was published in 1970, it sparked renewed interest in Delany's life and works, and a number of biographies and critical studies followed, including Victor Ullman's *Martin R. Delany: The Beginnings of Black Nationalism* (1971), Dorothy Sterling's *The Making of an Afro-American: Martin Robison Delany, 1812–1885* (1971), and Cyril E. Griffith's *The African Dream: Martin R. Delany and the Emergence of Pan African Thought* (1975). Still, perhaps due to its incomplete form or its poor critical reputation, *Blake* was largely regarded as significant only inasmuch as it represented a bridge between nineteenth-century antislavery movements and the Black Power movement of the twentieth century.

Increased interest in African American history and literature in the twenty-first century has made the book more popular with scholars, but the demise of the Black Power movement has lessened its impact

with nonacademics. Delany surfaces regularly in any discussion of African American history; his changing views have created frank discussion about the role of slaves in their own emancipation and in Reconstruction politics. Some make Delany out to be accommodationist with whites, while others see him as a practical political mover in a tough situation, a shrewd opportunist, or a visionary racial theorist. Above all, he remains relevant in an era of increased racial and ethnic pluralism in the United States and around the world. As Katy Chiles writes in "Within and without Raced Nations: Intratextuality, Martin Delany, and *Blake; or the Huts of America,*" "Rather than cleanly supplanting a national perspective with a transnational one, Delany presents a nation-state in which local, regional, national, and transnational figurations overlap and permeate each other." Though *Blake* does not present a complete view of Delany's varied and nuanced beliefs, it exemplifies propaganda of the period in its support of emancipation and is unique in its mantra of freedom by any means necessary.

BIBLIOGRAPHY

Sources

Adelke, Tunde. *Without Regard to Race: The Other Martin Robison Delany.* Oxford: U of Mississippi P, 2003. Print.

Chiles, Katy L. "Within and without Raced Nations: Intratextuality, Martin Delany, and *Blake; or the Huts of America.*" *American Literature* 80.2 (2008): 323–52. Print.

———. "*Blake; or the Huts of America* (1859–1861)." *Encyclopedia Virginia.* Ed. Brendan Wolfe. 2012. Virginia Foundation for the Humanities. Web. 28 Sept. 2012.

Delany, Martin R. *The Condition, Elevation, and Destiny of the Colored People of the United States, Politically Considered.* New York: Arno, 1968. Print.

Further Reading

Biggio, Rebecca Skidmore. "The Specter of Conspiracy in Martin Delany's *Blake.*" *African American Review* 42. 3–4 (2008): 439–54. Print

Clymer, Jeffory. "Martin Delany's *Blake* and the Transnational Politics of Property." *American Literary History* 15.4 (2003): 709–31. Print.

Doolen, Andy. "Be Cautious of the Word 'Rebel'": Race, Revolution, and Transnational History in Martin Delany's *Blake; or, The Huts of America.*" *American Literature* 81.1 (2009): 153–79. Print.

Levine, Robert S. *Martin Delany, Frederick Douglass, and the Politics of Representative Identity.* Chapel Hill: U of North Carolina P, 1997. Print.

———, ed. *Martin R. Delany: A Documentary Reader.* Chapel Hill: U of North Carolina P, 2003. Print.

Shelby, Tommie. "Two Conceptions of Black Nationalism: Martin Delany on the Meaning of Black Political Solidarity." *Political Theory* 31.5 (2003): 664–92. Print.

Scott Stabler

DYKE MANIFESTO

Lesbian Avengers

OVERVIEW

Written by the activist group Lesbian Avengers, the *Dyke Manifesto* (1992) disseminates the Avengers' mission and agenda—in short, to demand social and legal equality for lesbians. Written in a call-to-arms style, the four-page photocopied missive starts off in all capital letters, attempting to recruit lesbians to "get out of the beds, out of the bars and into the streets" and instead "to organize and ignite" and "get together and fight." The remainder of the manifesto is structured in a frequently-asked-questions (FAQ) format with different section headings, including "Who are the Lesbian Avengers?" and "What is direct action?" The manifesto influences its audience by being selective in the information it presents and making the broad implication that in order for lesbians to lead happy, productive lives, they must be out in the streets mobilizing and communicating with one another.

The *Dyke Manifesto* was often the first point of contact that outsiders had with the radical Lesbian Avengers, and its powerful message connected with many lesbians, so much so that dozens of chapters formed across the country to focus on "issues vital to lesbian survival and visibility." Although they gained popularity quickly in the early 1990s, the Lesbian Avengers were mostly ignored by the mainstream media and were often criticized for their overwrought attempts to attract media attention to their cause. Still, the group's message, underscored by the *Dyke Manifesto,* continues to spread awareness across the United States—a feat perhaps best evidenced by the annual Dyke March, an event that typically occurs in major metropolitan areas on the day before pride parades organized by the LGBT (lesbian, gay, bisexual, and transgender) community.

HISTORICAL AND LITERARY CONTEXT

The *Dyke Manifesto* is a reflection of the social and political change surrounding gay rights, which gained impetus in the 1990s. The decade ushered in a period of economic prosperity in the United States, and a new generation was determined to break out of the conservative mold of the 1980s. Members of Generation X—born between the 1960s and the early 1980s—emphasized individuality and acceptance of "alternative" lifestyles. This changed perception was not limited to youth culture: In 1990, homosexuality was removed from the World Health Organization's list of diseases.

The United States was in the throes of the 1992 presidential election season when the Lesbian Avengers published the *Dyke Manifesto.* With the start of third-wave feminism and a record number of women holding elected office, 1992 was the "Year of the Woman," making it a prime time for the Lesbian Avengers' movement to get under way. Founded by six lesbian activists—Anne-Christine D'Adesky, Marie Honan, Anne Maguire, Sarah Schulman, Ana Maria Simo, and Maxine Wolfe—the Avengers relished the politically charged climate. As Avenger Ann Northrop put it, "We're not going to be invisible anymore … we are going to be prominent and have power and be part of all decision making." Instead of recognizing the great strides that had already been made within the LGBT movement, the Avengers acted as if they were starting from square one, recruiting as many lesbians as possible by distributing the *Dyke Manifesto.*

Other important pieces of third-wave feminist literature emerged in the 1990s, touching on such topics as gender violence, reproductive rights, and reclaiming derogatory terms, all in response to the perceived failures of second-wave feminism. Although the third wave began in the 1990s, its roots stem from the early 1980s, with several key texts paving the way for discourse such as the *Dyke Manifesto.* Cherríe Moraga and Gloria E. Anzaldúa's anthology *This Bridge Called My Back* (1981), along with their book *All the Women Are White, All the Blacks Are Men, But Some of Us Are Brave: Black Women's Studies* (1982), criticized second-wave feminism's focus on white women, excluding women of other racial, social, and ethnic backgrounds. The more inclusive nature of third-wave feminism inspired the Lesbian Avengers to give a voice to the LGBT community.

The *Dyke Manifesto* had a profound impact on the LGBT community, most notably in the independent music scene. The feminist punk-rock movement Riot Grrrl got its start in Olympia, Washington, and Washington DC—two cities that had active chapters of the Lesbian Avengers. The groups Bikini Kill, Huggy Bear, and Bratmobile wove the values of third-wave feminism into their songs, writing about sexuality, domestic abuse, and female empowerment. Although most of the groups disbanded at the end of the 1990s,

✤ *Key Facts*

Time Period:
Late 20th Century

Genre:
Manifesto

Events:
American economic prosperity; increasing prominence of women in elected office

Nationality:
American

THE STONEWALL RIOTS AND THE POWER OF PRIDE

Organized pride parades—like the annual Dyke March—have been held in most major metropolitan cities in the United States for more than forty years. The parades are held mainly to celebrate pride in the LGBT community, but their origin dates to violent demonstrations that took place in 1969. The demonstrations occurred in Greenwich Village in New York City on June 28 in response to a police raid at the Stonewall Inn. Although the bar was owned by Mafia members, they allowed openly gay patrons and other marginalized individuals—drag queens, hustlers, and the homeless—to carouse inside the Stonewall. After a police raid that grew more violent than usual, Greenwich Village residents and bar regulars reacted by protesting and eventually inciting a riot against police. Within months of the Stonewall Riots, gay rights organizations were founded to focus on discrimination in the LGBT community. Exactly a year after the riots, on June 28, 1970, the first gay pride parade was held to commemorate the violent attacks. The tradition moved on to other cities, and most contemporary pride parades are held at the end of June to honor those who participated in the Stonewall Riots.

several recent books about the movement—Marisa Meltzer's *Girl Power: The Nineties Revolution in Music* (2010) and Sara Marcus's *Girls to the Front: The True Story of the Riot Grrrl Revolution* (2010)—carry the legacy into the twenty-first century.

THEMES AND STYLE

The *Dyke Manifesto* focuses on themes of awareness, positivity, and empowerment to push the notion that lesbians need to band together in order to be successful within a community. Written as a recruiting guide to be handed out to new members, the *Dyke Manifesto* is very self-aware, discussing at length the issues of discrimination that the LGBT community faces. The manifesto exhorts its recruits to "Wake up!" and to "seize the power of dyke love, dyke vision, dyke anger, dyke intelligence, and dyke strategy." Despite its immediacy, the manifesto's message is one of positivity and lesbian empowerment: "The Avengers is a place where ideas are realized, where lesbians can have an impact." In addition, the manifesto includes an appeal for funds in which the Avengers ask "closeted lesbians, queer boys, and sympathetic straights" to send them money.

When detailing their agenda in the *Dyke Manifesto,* the Avengers use several different rhetorical strategies to capture the attention of new recruits. The first page of the manifesto is written in all capital letters and takes a dramatic tone, declaring, for example, "We're not waiting for the rapture. We are the apocalypse. We'll be your dream and their nightmare." The

Avengers detail their demands—food, shelter, and universal health care—and conclude with an intent to "target homophobes of every stripe and infiltrate the Christian right." The aggressive approach commands attention for the Avengers' mission while its seriousness lends it substance. The remainder of the *Dyke Manifesto* is divided into sections formatted in a question-and-answer style. The organized presentation contrasts with the imperatives of the first page and helps the Avengers' recruits become more informed about the impassioned group.

Both the zealous appeal and the rational questions and answers are detailed with persuasive language and the Avengers' flair for melodrama. With its capitalized letters and declarative statements, the first section of the manifesto is infused with a heightened sense of urgency, as if recruits need to act as soon as possible or face apocalyptic fallout. On the first page, the Avengers remind recruits, "We're invisible and it's not safe—not at home, on the job, in the streets, or in the courts." While the discrimination alluded to here was a real issue, the Avengers frame it as though lesbians cannot walk around in public without encountering the wrath of a straight person. The persuasive and exaggerated language is used to convince recruits of the pressing importance of the organization's mission.

CRITICAL DISCUSSION

When the Lesbian Avengers formed and published the *Dyke Manifesto* in 1992, it was largely disregarded by the public at large. Although the Avengers were a direct-action group that preferred spray-painting their slogans on billboards to picketing and signing petitions, the mainstream media ignored them. Journalist Amy C. Brenner notes in a piece about the 1994 International Dyke March that "Nothing was mentioned in the *Washington Post,* or the *Chicago Tribune,* or the *Los Angeles Times,*" despite the fact that several thousand lesbians attended the march.

Nevertheless, the Avengers and the *Dyke Manifesto* left a lasting effect on the social and political efforts of the LGBT and third-wave feminist communities. The annual Dyke March is ongoing, and local Avengers chapters still mobilize and speak out against issues that threaten the equality of the LGBT community, such as Proposition 8 in California, which called for the elimination of marriage rights for same-sex couples. The *Dyke Manifesto's* role in third-wave feminism also led to the modern era of postfeminism, with television shows such as *30 Rock, Girls,* and *Sex and the City* showcasing a forward-thinking, female point of view.

The Lesbian Avengers evolved into a far less radical group than they were in the early 1990s, and the *Dyke Manifesto* is a relic of their heyday, when photocopying was used to relay its message. A former Avenger named Vikki wrote a guest blog post on the LGBT-friendly website *AutoStraddle* in 2009 in which she noted how technology has changed the group.

The activist group Lesbian Avengers protesting the visit of Pope John Paul II to Colorado in 1993. The following year, the Lesbian Avengers issued the call to action in the *Dyke Manifesto*. © STEVEN RUBIN/THE IMAGE WORKS.

"The distractions might have changed with time but the call for action remains. Now, however, the Avengers think it's time to get off of the blogs and into the streets," she writes, even acknowledging that different Avengers chapters use Twitter and Facebook to mobilize their members instead of passing out flyers. The means of disseminating their message may have changed, and mainstream society may be slightly more tolerant of the LGBT community—gay marriage is now legal in more than half-a-dozen states—but there is still a need for texts such as the *Dyke Manifesto* and direct-actions groups such as the Lesbian Avengers to preside over them.

BIBLIOGRAPHY

Sources

"Her Story: The Lesbian Avengers—Time to Seize the Power & Be the Bomb You Throw!" *AutoStraddle*. AutoStraddle, 24 July 2009. Web. 03 Aug. 2012.

"An Incomplete History." The *Lesbian Avengers*. The Lesbian Avenger Documentary Project. Web. 03 Aug. 2012.

Lesbian Avengers. *Dyke Manifesto: Calling All Lesbians!: Wake Up!* New York: Lesbian Avengers, 1993. Print.

Schulman, Sarah. "What Became of 'Freedom Summer'?" *The Gay & Lesbian Review Worldwide* 11.1 (2004): 20. *Literature Resource Center*. Web. 2 Aug. 2012.

Salholz, Eloise. "The Power and the Pride." *Newsweek* 20 June 1993. Web. 2 Aug. 2012.

Further Reading

Ensler, Eve. *The Vagina Monologues*. New York: Villard, 2001. Print.

Marcus, Sara. *Girls to the Front: The True Story of the Riot Grrrl Revolution*. New York: HarperPerennial, 2010. Print.

Meltzer, Marisa. *Girl Power: The Nineties Revolution in Music*. New York: Faber and Faber, 2010. Print.

Moraga, Cherríe, and Gloria Anzaldúa. *This Bridge Called My Back: Writings by Radical Women of Color*. Watertown, MA: Persephone, 1981. Print.

Schulman, Sarah. *My American History: Lesbian and Gay Life during the Reagan/Bush Years*. New York: Routledge, 1994. Print.

Stein, Marc. *Rethinking the Gay and Lesbian Movement*. New York: Routledge, 2012. Print.

Walker, Rebecca. *To Be Real: Telling the Truth and Changing the Face of Feminism*. New York: Anchor, 1995. Print.

Anna Deem

FIRE FROM THE MOUNTAIN
The Making of a Sandinista
Omar Cabezas

❖ *Key Facts*

Time Period:
Late 20th Century

Genre:
Testimonio

Events:
Nicaraguan Revolution;
victory of the Sandinista
National Liberation Front

Nationality:
Nicaraguan

OVERVIEW

Fire from the Mountain: The Making of a Sandinista (1985; trans. Kathleen Weaver) is Omar Cabezas's account of his time as an organizer and guerrilla for the Sandinista National Liberation Front (FSLN) during the Nicaraguan Revolution. The *testimonio,* or personal account, describes Cabezas's actions, first as part of a 1960s student movement to spread Marxist ideology and raise awareness of the plight of laborers and later in efforts in the 1970s to persuade Nicaraguans to embrace the revolutionary cause and fight against the National Guard of dictator Anastasio Somoza Debayle (1925–1980). Originally titled *La montaña es algo más que una immensa estepa verde* (1982), the work gave voice to those who had lived and fought in the mountains, behind the revolutionary lines, humanizing them and explaining their political aims in a persuasive and influential manner. It also garnered understanding and support for the Sandinista government from people in the United States, where Reagan-era propaganda of the time had painted Sandinistas as left-wing terrorists.

Cabezas's narrative was published three years after the 1979 triumph of the Sandinistas, in the midst of the FSLN socialist government's attempts to rebuild and reform the Nicaraguan economy and social structure. Aimed at fortifying the revolutionaries in their values and at clarifying their motivations and aspirations to compatriots who did not fully understand or support their work, the book was an immediate popular success. It remains the best-selling book ever published in Nicaragua. Finding himself in the international political spotlight, Cabezas earned widespread recognition and increased influence in national politics. Although other works had been published on the same topic, Cabezas's account struck a chord with audiences because of its refreshingly honest, humble, colloquial tone and its reflection of the optimism and revolutionary fervor of a pivotal moment in Nicaraguan history.

HISTORICAL AND LITERARY CONTEXT

The Nicaraguan (or Sandinista) Revolution has roots in the 1927 to 1933 peasant revolts led by Augusto César Sandino against U.S. Marines stationed in Nicaragua. The United States had occupied the country since 1912 in an attempt to control the Panama Canal and keep communism at bay. The armed rebels fought for improvements in the living conditions of the rural poor, and rebellion abated with the 1933 withdrawal of the United States. The United States subsequently forced the appointment of Anastasio Somoza Garcia (1896–1956) as head of the U.S.-trained National Guard. In 1936 Somoza overthrew the elected liberal government of Juan Bautista Sacasa. Somoza and his family and supporters established a dictatorship, taking control of public institutions and brutally repressing the population. While protecting U.S. economic interests, Somoza made himself rich through land and business deals. By directing 90 percent of Nicaraguan exports and much of his people's food resources to the United States, he also rendered his country almost completely economically dependent. His sons, Luis and Anastasio, who ran the country after their father's assassination in 1956, persisted in the same exploitive policies.

Cabezas's *testimonio* in particular concerns the time when the revolution was in full swing: 1975 to 1979. Popular support of the FSLN was bolstered by the Somozas' blatant misappropriation of international aid after the 1972 Managuan earthquake. Anastasio Somoza Debayle's fraudulent reelection as president in 1974 sparked widespread armed resistance, but his National Guard ferociously protected his power. The tide turned in 1978, when U.S. president Jimmy Carter withdrew significant military backing because of Somoza's appalling human rights record. By summer 1979 the FSLN controlled 80 percent of the country. Somoza officially submitted his resignation on July 16, and a five-member Junta de Reconstrucción Nacional (Council of National Reconstruction), established in exile a month earlier, arrived in Managua on July 18 to rebuild a country in physical and economic ruins. In 1980, however, guerrilla counterrevolutionaries (including the Fuerza Democrática Nicaragüense, created and funded by the United States) violently challenged the Sandinistas' power. Immediately after taking office in 1981, U.S. president Ronald Reagan suspended aid to the Nicaraguan government and instituted a propaganda campaign to spread misinformation and unsubstantiated allegations of serious human rights violations in the country. Cabezas's work formed part of the direct opposition to the strong antisocialist discourse of the period, helping to convey the true ideals of the Sandinistas to international audiences. The FSLN overcame these crises and several internal factional rifts to govern throughout the 1980s. By the mid- to late 1980s, however, many revolutionaries had become disillusioned with their government's failure to create peace and realize many of the changes for which they had fought so hard.

Fire from the Mountain participates in two major literary traditions within Latin America: the coming-of-age story, or *novela de formación,* and the political *testimonio.* Following in the footsteps of earlier *novelas de formación,* including Mario Vargas Llosa's *La ciudad y los perros* (1962) and José Lezama Lima's *Paradiso* (1967), Cabezas narrates his transformation from a naive youth into a full-fledged *guerrillero.* The work also draws on the time-honored *testimonio* format as a mode of social and political protest. In his 1989 essay "The Margin at the Center," Latin America scholar John Beverley explains that the *testimonio,* usually written from the perspective of a first-person narrator who witnesses or participates in the events it describes, emerged from "an urgency to communicate a problem of repression, poverty, subalternity, imprisonment, struggle for survival." Many prior *testimonios,* including Che Guevara's *Reminiscences of the Cuban Revolutionary War* (1968); *Miguel Marmol; los sucesos de 1932 en El Salvador* (1972; a revolutionary's story as recorded by poet and journalist Roque Dalton); and Domitila Barrios de Chungara's 1977 *"Si me permiten hablar ...": testimonio de Domitila, una mujer de las minas de Bolivia* (*Let Me Speak!: Testimony of Domatila, a Woman of the Bolivian Mines,* 1978), directly inspired Cabezas's composition of his own work.

Fire from the Mountain influenced a series of later *testimonios,* memoirs, and autobiographies treating the Nicaraguan Revolution, including *Blood of Brothers: Life and War in Nicaragua* (1991), by American author and journalist Stephen Kinzer; *Country under My Skin: A Memoir of Love and War* (2002), by Nicaraguan poet and novelist Gioconda Belli; and *Adiós muchachos: una memoria de la revolución sandinista* (2012), by revolutionary and former Sandinista vice president Sergio Ramirez. Kinzer's and Ramirez's works are notable for their reflection not only on the years of revolution but also on the period of Sandinista governance from 1979 to 1990. During his own political career, Cabezas held the offices of deputy interior minister and human rights ombudsman from 1979 to 1987 and was elected in 1990 to the National Assembly. His renowned *Fire from the Mountain* helped shape the world's perception of the Nicaraguan Revolution, the Somoza regime, and some of the participants in the Sandinista government with whom he lived in the mountains.

THEMES AND STYLE

Fire from the Mountain expresses the humanist and egalitarian spirit of early Sandinismo—including the struggle to unite all the revolutionary factions—and

THE HIGH TIMES AND HARD TIMES OF THE LEFT IN LATIN AMERICA

The Cuban Revolution of 1959 inspired leftist revolutionary movements across Latin America. Omar Cabezas's account of his own radicalization in *Fire from the Mountain* is representative of the experience of many guerrillas in the second half of the twentieth century who were stirred by the then-legendary feats of Che Guevara, Fidel Castro, and the other Cuban insurgents. The success of the Cuban Revolution contributed to prosocialist propaganda throughout the region that very likely inspired the Sandinistas. Cabezas himself engages in the persuasive tactic of connecting his experience to that of both Che and Fidel in his *testimonio,* thus wedding his own cause to the celebrated tradition of Marxist revolution.

Fire from the Mountain reflects an idealistic period when many viewed Marxism as a viable political system for Latin America. Once the Sandinistas were officially in power, however, their pursuit of ideals was frustrated by ongoing attacks from C.I.A.-funded paramilitary groups and by economic sanctions that plunged Nicaragua into a financial crisis. The FSLN's electoral defeat in 1990 finally forced the struggling leftist government out of office and brought in a pro-American administration. In 2006, however, Sandinista and former Nicaraguan president Daniel Ortega was returned to office and, a year later, seemed to have made strides toward creating jobs and eliminating illiteracy and hunger. He petitioned to change the constitution to allow consecutive reelection and was voted president again in 2011.

the physical, psychological, and emotional hardships the rebels faced during the war. Countering romanticized notions about guerrilla warfare, Cabezas reveals the reality of his experience in all its passionate commitment and emotional rawness. "For the first time, I felt really alone, deeply alone ... And in time—unforgiving, unrelenting time that flows on, unchanging—you lose everything, even your mind. You are losing your self." Despite the mental exhaustion of long-term isolation and several serious illnesses that he contracted in the mountains, Cabezas's motivation to fight for sustenance and justice for his people does not falter. He correlates the gradual toughening of his body and mind with the strengthened consciousness of his people as a whole, demonstrating humanitarian success where few expected or acknowledged it.

Rhetorically, Cabezas appeals to his audience's sense of empathy and justice, rendering the Sandinistas as real people in order to commemorate their profound humanity and, where necessary, garner support. He incorporates extensive dialogue and intimate personal anecdotes, including sexual encounters, illness, constant terror, and even bowel movements, to convey the humble yet heroic role he and his comrades played. Through accessible language, he aspires to connect with and inspire common Nicaraguans. By occasionally

A Sandinista soldier in the Nicaraguan jungle in 1986. Former Sandinista Party member Omar Cabezas wrote *Fire from the Mountain*. AP PHOTO/ ANDREW SELSKY.

switching from his first-person narrative to the collective voice, he lends the text an air of authenticity that expresses the shared experience of life in a guerrilla movement. "We transformed our loneliness into a brotherhood among us; we treated each other gruffly, but actually we loved each other with a deep love, with a great male tenderness." This technique emphasizes the group's unity against all antagonistic forces, natural and human, as a source of strength.

Cabezas originally dictated his *testimonio* into a recording device; this may be why *Fire from the Mountain* reads like an oral history. The work's informal, conversational tone, colloquial phrasing, and vivid description draw in his main intended audience—his people—while still appealing to readers all over the world. Cabezas's language is sometimes comical and coarse, as in his narration of an encounter with a drunken guest at a party for wealthy Sandinista supporters: "Manuel and I didn't dare make a sound, and we were pelted with at least four arcs of piss—I'm not exaggerating. Plus two blasts of vomit." At other times he uses an almost poetic rhythm: "It was as if the mountain, too, felt fear. The wind dropped and the trees stopped swaying. There was a quiet, an overwhelming calm. Maybe it was just my own enormous fear, but I remember the trees drew apart, not a leaf stirred." The work's candid mood differentiates it from the more serious, hypermasculine guerrilla accounts of many of his predecessors.

CRITICAL DISCUSSION

On its publication *La montaña es algo más que una immensa estepa verde* was readily praised for its engaging writing style, and it won the 1982 Casa de las Americas Prize for the *testimonio* genre. In his 1985 book review of the English version, Jonathan Steele states, "Omar Cabezas's vigorous, funny and self-deprecating account of his four-year odyssey in the mountains of northern Nicaragua as a young guerrilla volunteer expresses the spirit of Sandinismo more fully than any other available work in English." Other English-language commentators lauded the work for its demythologized depiction of the guerrilla lifestyle; for example, in a 1987 review for *Contemporary Sociology*, Stephen Legeay notes that "Cabezas cuts through much of the fable often accompanying revolutionary literature. What he shows us are the more tender, painful, sensuous, humorous, and poignant moments in the course of his development as a revolutionary. In short, we can see the full human being behind the cloak of 'revolutionary.'"

While Cabezas could not anticipate the turn that the Sandinista government would take during the 1980s, with its increasingly repressive policies directed at those who challenged or opposed its power, the text is considered by some scholars today as being somewhat idealistic about the Sandinista movement and its objectives. Nevertheless, many deem it one of the most important works on the Nicaraguan Revolution. It is often examined for its contributions to the Latin American genre of literary witnessing and has been compared with other Central American civil war *testimonios*, including *I, Rigoberta Menchú: An Indian Woman in Guatemala* (1984). Several scholarly analyses have focused on the literary and stylistic differences between these two very different *testimonies*—one told through an intermediary by an undereducated, indigenous female activist and the other written by an educated, middle-class male guerrilla. Cabezas wrote a sequel, *Canción de amor para los hombres* (1988), that is not as highly acclaimed as his first book and was never translated into English. Documentary filmmaker Deborah Shaffer adapted *Fire from the Mountain* in 1987, producing a film that won awards from the Latin American Studies Association and the American Film Festival, received an Emmy nomination, and aired on the PBS series *POV.*

Fire from the Mountain is widely studied in the fields of Latin American studies, literature, and history. Recent scholarship has paid particular attention to the gender aspect of the text. In her 2003 article "House, Street, Collective: Revolutionary Geographies and Gender Transformation in Nicaragua, 1979–99," Rosario Montoya discusses the "new man" concept that Cabezas adopted from Guevara: a revolutionary identity that "village men invoked to describe the ideological transformations they underwent through their participation in the revolutionary process," which would lead to the formation of a man driven by self-sacrifice and morality rather than material ambitions. Other scholars, such as B. V. Olguin ("Of Truth, Secrets, and Ski Masks: Counterrevolutionary Appropriations and Zapatista Revisions of Testimonio," 2002), have noted the conventional *novela de formación* aspect of the text within the *testimonio* tradition, citing its "trajectory of privations, endurance, and revolutionary transformation that informs what we might now call the 'conventional' guerrilla testimonio."

BIBLIOGRAPHY

Sources

Beverley, John. "The Margin at the Center." *MFS Modern Fiction Studies* 35.1 (1989): 11–28. Print.

———. *Testimonio: On the Politics of Truth.* Minneapolis: U of Minnesota P, 2004. Print.

Cabezas, Omar. *Fire from the Mountain: The Making of a Sandinista.* Trans. Kathleen Weaver. New York: Crown, 1985. Print.

Legeay, Stephen. Rev. of *Fire from the Mountain,* by Omar Cabezas. *Contemporary Sociology* 16.3 (1987): 352–54. Print.

Montoya, Rosario. "House, Street, Collective: Revolutionary Geographies and Gender Transformation in Nicaragua, 1979–99." *Latin American Research Review* 38.2 (2003): 61–93. Print.

Olguin, B. V. "Of Truth, Secrets, and Ski Masks: Counterrevolutionary Appropriations and Zapatista Revisions of Testimonio." *Nepantla: Views from South* 3.1 (2002): 145–78. Print.

Steele, Jonathan. "Sandinismo." Rev. of *Fire from the Mountain,* by Omar Cabezas. *London Review of Books* 19 Dec. 1985: 7–9. Web. 9 Sept. 2012.

Further Reading

Beverley, John, and Marc Zimmerman. *Literature and Politics in the Central American Revolutions.* Austin: U of Texas P, 1990. Print.

Kinzer, Stephen. "In Sandinista Wall, Cracks Revealed." *New York Times* 21 Jan. 1988. Web. 9 Sept. 2012.

———. "Organizing the Revolution." Rev. of *Fire from the Mountain,* by Omar Cabezas. *New York Times.* New York Times, 30 June 1985. Web. 9 Sept. 2012.

Kokotovic, Misha. "Theory at the Margins." *Socialist Review* 27. 3–4 (1999): 29–63. Print.

Millay, Amy Nauss. *Voices from the Fuente Viva: The Effect of Orality in Twentieth-Century Spanish American Narrative.* Lewisburg: Bucknell UP, 2005. Print.

Walton, John. "Structures, Saviors and Saboteurs." Rev. of *Fire from the Mountain,* by Omar Cabezas. *Sociological Forum* 1.4 (1986): 740–46. Print.

Wickham-Crowley, Timothy. *Guerrillas and Revolution in Latin America: A Comparative Study of Insurgents and Regimes since 1956.* Princeton: Princeton UP, 1991. Print.

Media Adaptation

Fire from the Mountain. Dir. Deborah Shaffer. Perf. Omar Cabezas. 1987. Documentary Film.

Katrina White

GENOCIDE IN NIGERIA

Ken Saro-Wiwa

✦ **Key Facts**

Time Period:
Late 20th Century

Genre:
Nonfiction

Events:
Environmental
damage due to Shell
oil extraction; rise of
Movement for the
Survival of the Ogoni
People (MOSOP)

Nationality:
Nigerian

OVERVIEW

Ken Saro-Wiwa's *Genocide in Nigeria* (1992) is an account of the economic and environmental crisis facing the Ogoni ethnic minority in Nigeria during the second half of the twentieth century. Saro-Wiwa introduces the Ogoni as fiercely independent farmers and conservators of some of the most fertile land in Africa, then describes the changes that began under British colonial rule—changes that laid the groundwork for the devastation of the Ogoni at the hands of the corrupt Nigerian government and Shell Oil. Arguing that the deliberate impoverishment of the people and poisoning of the land constitute genocide, Saro-Wiwa makes an outraged plea for the international community to intervene on behalf of the Ogoni because "it will be a disgrace to humanity" for the situation to remain unaddressed "for even one more day."

Genocide in Nigeria was well received in the world community but garnered a negative reaction from the Nigerian military regime of Ibrahim "IBB" Babangida and later from the regime of general Sani Abacha. The work represents a shift that occurred over the course of Saro-Wiwa's writing career, as he turned his attention from fiction and television productions to activism in the struggle for Ogoni rights, writing political columns and drafting the Ogoni Bill of Rights (1990). The accusations of collusion between Shell and the Nigerian government contained in *Genocide in Nigeria* made Saro-Wiwa—by then an internationally visible figure—a target. He was arrested under authority of the Abacha regime, and despite international outcry was executed along with eight other Ogoni activists in 1995. Two decades after its publication, *Genocide in Nigeria* remains a powerful account of the suffering of Saro-Wiwa's native people and a touchstone in debates about corporate responsibility and the rights of indigenous minorities in developing countries.

HISTORICAL AND LITERARY CONTEXT

In 1960, when Nigeria secured independence from the British government—under which it had been a colony and protectorate since 1914—civil war broke out as a number of different indigenous peoples sought to carve out their own states. During the war, many Ogoni were forced to flee their villages only to starve in refugee camps. The civil war was devastating to the Ogoni people and their homeland, and was compounded by the environmental impact of petroleum mining, which began in earnest in the region in the 1970s.

By the time *Genocide in Nigeria* was published, oil extraction in Ogoniland, which was largely conducted by Shell in conjunction with the Nigerian National Petroleum Corporation, had caused contamination of water used for drinking and agriculture, leading to illness, economic devastation, and starvation. Further, the Ogoni people saw little compensation for the use of their land, as a series of legislative decrees by the Nigerian government, including the Land Use Decree and the Petroleum Act, gave corrupt officials control over oil profits. Acting as head of the Movement for the Survival of the Ogoni People (MOSOP), a group formed in 1990, Saro-Wiwa conducted a program of nonviolent protest against Shell and the federal government. His campaign began with the issuance of the Ogoni Bill of Rights and included lobbying for acknowledgment of rights and compensation for land seizures and environmental devastation.

In the late 1980s and early 1990s, Saro-Wiwa, who had made his literary name writing fiction, published a series of columns in the *Lagos Sunday Times*, which were later collected in the books *Similia: Essays on Anomie Nigeria* (1991) and *Nigeria: Brink of Disaster* (1991). These pieces treat a multitude of problems plaguing Nigeria but like the autobiographical *On a Darkling Plain: An Account of the Nigerian Civil War* (1989), published during the same period, continually return to what Saro-Wiwa viewed as the overarching problem—the inequality of peoples and the exploitation of the mineral wealth of ethnic minorities' land.

The publication of *Genocide in Nigeria,* which openly accuses the Nigerian government of collusion with Shell in the genocide of the Ogoni, drew harsh reprisals from the Babangida regime, and Saro-Wiwa was arrested in 1993 and charged with treason. He was released but was arrested again in 1994, accused of involvement in the deaths of four Ogoni chiefs who were murdered by a crowd. Despite pleas from the international community, Saro-Wiwa, along with eight other MOSOP activists, was executed by Abacha's order on November 10, 1995. *A Month and a Day: A Detention Diary,* Saro-Wiwa's account of his 1993 arrest, was published posthumously. As quoted by Rob Nixon in *Slow Violence* (2011), an incarcerated Saro-Wiwa wrote to friend William Boyd, "I've used my talents as a writer to allow the Ogoni people to confront their tormentors. I think I have the moral victory." Indeed, *Genocide in Nigeria* remains a lasting testament to Saro-Wiwa's skills as a writer and the courage of his convictions.

THEMES AND STYLE

Testifying as an eyewitness, Saro-Wiwa describes how the Ogoni, inheritors and thoughtful stewards of "the food basket of the eastern Niger delta," have "gradually been ground to dust" by the boot of Shell and the Nigerian government. Accusing Western oil-consuming countries of playing a supporting but significant role in the devastation, he pleads with the international community to "do something to mitigate the Ogoni tragedy," which he asserts conforms to the United Nation's definition of genocide. *Genocide in Nigeria* makes this case through argument, reprinted correspondence, and photographs of land and water fouled with crude oil.

At the heart of the book, and of Saro-Wiwa's rhetorical strategy, is the contrast between the evidence of the catastrophic impact of civil war and oil extraction on the Ogoni and the callous, disingenuous responses from government officials and representatives of Shell when presented with this evidence. Saro-Wiwa reprints an account by Port Harcourt lawyer Peter Akere of an exchange between Ogoni refugees in Alba province and provincial administrator M. N. Onwuma. The refugees, having fled Ogoniland into Ibos territory, though destitute and starving, were subjected to midnight raids and pilfering by their host villagers. The response by the administrator to the refugees' appeal for help begins, "I am in receipt of your very pathetic letter." After dismissing the refugees' claims, he urges the Ogoni to "cheer up." Likewise, letters to Shell following an oil blowout in Dere, which describe "an ocean of crude oil … moving swiftly like a great river in flood," elicited, according to Saro-Wiwa, no response.

Genocide in Nigeria is marked by a pleading tone of urgency and anger as Saro-Wiwa contemplates the imminent dangers facing the Ogoni and their desperate need for immediate aid. Starting with his choice of the word *genocide* to describe the Ogoni plight, Saro-Wiwa uses language calculated to emphasize the gravity of the situation and to provoke outrage. He claims, for example, that the Nigerian government planned the "gradual despoliation and eventual extermination" of the Ogoni, while Shell inflicted "deep and mortal wounds," such as those caused by the blowout at the oilfield in Dere. Saro-Wiwa artfully reprints letters sent by Dere youth to Shell in the wake of the explosion, accusing Shell of pitching the people into a "a darkened and bleak horizon of despondency, abject poverty, extinction of our lives

OGONI BILL OF RIGHTS

Two years before Ken Saro-Wiwa published *Genocide in Nigeria* (1992), the Movement for the Survival of the Ogoni People (MOSOP) issued the Ogoni Bill of Rights. As a member of and spokesman for MOSOP, Saro-Wiwa helped drive the struggle for self-determination and was one of the document's lead authors. The bill was initially presented to and signed by the Ogoni people and leadership in August 1990. After listing twenty enumerated facts about the history of the Ogoni and their persecution at the hands of the British colonial system, the Nigerian government, and the oil industry, the bill demands "that the Ogoni people be granted POLITICAL AUTONOMY to participate in the affairs of the Republic as a distinct and separate unit."

In August 1991, after receiving no response from the Nigerian government, MOSOP issued an addendum to their bill of rights. In it, they address a global rather than a domestic audience and recommend that the international community take ten urgent actions. The first of these is: "Prevail on the American Government to stop buying Nigerian oil. It is stolen property." Although MOSOP has not achieved autonomy for the Ogoni, the organization remains committed to the nonviolent campaign that Saro-Wiwa was so central in catalyzing.

and destruction of our crops." One letter is signed poignantly "yours in distress."

CRITICAL DISCUSSION

In the author's note at the beginning of the book, Saro-Wiwa writes, "I expect the ethnic majority of Nigeria to turn the heat of their well-known vindictiveness on me for writing this book." His prediction was quickly borne out by the government's response. Indeed, most early reviews of *Genocide in Nigeria* were responses to the book's political meaning and the validity of its charges rather than treatments of the work's literary merits. Critics have noted the power of Saro-Wiwa's prose but have tended to echo Ezenwa-Ohaeto's point in *Twentieth-Century Caribbean and Black African Writers, Third Series* (1996) that "much of what he has to say about Nigeria is interesting and important, but sometimes he lets his anger get the better of his argument."

As part of Saro-Wiwa's body of writing on the Ogoni, *Genocide in Nigeria* has been regarded as a protest on behalf of all minority indigenous peoples who have been denied their basic human rights. Saro-Wiwa's activism drew international attention to issues of corporate responsibility in developing countries, although debate continues about the magnitude of the improvement of conditions in Nigeria. Nixon credits Saro-Wiwa's writing with "lay[ing] the ground for a broader estimation of the global cost … of the ongoing romance between unanswerable corporations and unspeakable regimes."

Poster commemorating Ogoni activist and writer Ken Saro-Wiwa, author of *Genocide in Nigeria.* In 1995 the Nigerian government executed Saro-Wiwa for his activities. © JOHNNY GREIG TRAVEL PHOTOGRAPHY/ALAMY.

Saro-Wiwa's nonfiction, including *Genocide in Nigeria,* is discussed little outside the context of his activism and its consequences, although some scholars have explored the interrelation between his literary and political commitments. Frank Schulze-Engler, in a 1998 study of Saro-Wiwa's early satirical novels, published in *Ogoni's Agonies: Ken Saro-Wiwa and the Crisis in Nigeria,* discusses the social critique of Nigerian society evident even in Saro-Wiwa's work on the popular television series *Basi and Company,* a satire that depicts a society of cheats and criminals that would presage the more explicit critiques of his later nonfiction. Quoting from *A Month and a Day,* Schulze-Engler also suggests that it was Saro-Wiwa's immersion in the Ogoni struggles that occasioned a shift to the view of "the political role of writers in terms of direct political involvement in mass organizations rather than in terms of critical writings," a shift that is reflected in Saro-Wiwa's turn away from the business of entertainment to more direct attempts to use his writing to persuade others to join him in taking up the cause of his people.

BIBLIOGRAPHY

Sources

Ezenwa-Ohaeto. "Ken Saro-Wiwa." *Twentieth-Century Caribbean and Black African Writers.* 3rd ed. Ed. Bernth Lindfors and Reinhard Sander. Detroit: Gale Research, 1996. 331–39. *Dictionary of Literary Biography Complete Online.* Web. 20 Oct. 2012.

Garuba, Harry. "Ken Saro-Wiwa's *Sozaboy* and the Logic of Minority Discourse." *Before I Am Hanged: Ken Saro-Wiwa, Literature, Politics, and Dissent.* Ed. Onookome Okome. Trenton, NJ: Africa World Press, 2000. 25–36. Print.

Movement for the Survival of the Ogoni People. "Ogoni Bill of Rights." *MOSOP.* MOSOP, Oct. 1990. Web. 3 Dec. 2012.

Nixon, Rob. *Slow Violence and the Environmentalism of the Poor.* Cambridge: Harvard UP, 2011. Print.

Saro-Wiwa, Ken. *Genocide in Nigeria.* Port Harcourt: Saros, 1992. Print.

Schulze-Engler, Frank. "Civil Critiques: Satire and the Politics of Democratic Transition in Ken Saro-Wiwa's Novels." *Ogoni's Agonies: Ken Saro-Wiwa and the Crisis in Nigeria.* Ed. Abdul-Rasheed Na' Allah. Trenton, NJ: Africa World Press, 1998. 285–306. Print.

Further Reading

Falola, Toyin, and Matthew Heaton. *A History of Nigeria.* Cambridge: Cambridge UP, 2008. Print.

Johansen, Bruce. *Indigenous Peoples and Environmental Issues: An Encyclopedia.* Westport: Greenwood, 2003. Print.

Khan, Sarah Ahmad. *Nigeria: The Political Economy of Oil.* Oxford: Oxford UP, 1994. Print.

Peel, Michael. *A Swamp Full of Dollars: Pipelines and Paramilitaries at Nigeria's Oil Frontier.* Chicago: Lawrence Hill, 2010. Print.

Rowell, Andrew. *Green Backlash.* London: Routledge, 1996. Print.

Saro-Wiwa, Ken. *A Month and a Day: A Detention Diary.* London: Penguin, 1995. Print.

Daisy Gard

I WRITE WHAT I LIKE

Steve Biko

OVERVIEW

I Write What I Like (1978) is a collection of speeches and essays by South African activist Steve Biko (1946–77) that addresses issues of oppression and exploitation in apartheid South Africa. The work reflects the period from 1969 until 1972 when Biko was active in the black consciousness movement, which sought to bestow upon the next generation of black Africans a sense of pride in their heritage and cultivate an active engagement with the political situation around them. Utilizing an accessible style that captures the rhythms of everyday speech, Biko delves into deep political, social, and philosophical problems. His aim is to develop an independent black consciousness in order to free individuals from the mental and physical oppression inherent in the institutionalized racism of South African apartheid.

Most of the essays originally appeared in the South African Students' Organization (SASO) newsletter as a recurrent column under the pen name Frank Talk. In 1973 the apartheid regime banned Biko from traveling, speaking in public, or writing for publication. Four years later he was stopped at a police roadblock seventy miles from his home and arrested for breaking his ban. He died in police custody, allegedly from wounds sustained from severe and unnecessary police force. Though Biko's writings were enormously influential among South African intellectuals and activists throughout the late 1960s and early 1970s, it wasn't until they were collectively published the year after his death that he became an internationally known symbol of the black consciousness movement. His death incited a wave of student riots and rebellion in South Africa that led the government to declare a state of emergency and ultimately contributed to the downfall of the apartheid system in 1994.

HISTORICAL AND LITERARY CONTEXT

Racial segregation existed in South Africa from the time of colonial rule by Dutch and British governments in the seventeenth century. After the National Party victory in the 1948 election, this segregation was introduced as an official policy known as apartheid and enforced through legislation. The Population Registration Act of 1950 required that residents be classified into one of three categories: white, black ("African," "native," "Bantu"), or colored (mixed descent). The Bantu Authorities Act of 1951 established a basis for ethnic government in African reserves, called "homelands," but all political rights, including voting, held by an African were restricted to these homelands. In other words, Africans were no longer granted citizenship in South Africa or any kind of involvement with South African Parliament, which held complete hegemony over the homelands. Anticolonial nationalist organizations such as the Pan-African Congress and the African National Congress organized a series of protests against these laws beginning in early 1960. On March 21, 1960, an initially peaceful protest in the township of Sharpeville escalated into the police firing into the crowd of about 5,000 to 7,000 protestors, killing sixty-nine. The Sharpeville massacre sparked uproar throughout South Africa's black population, which responded with demonstrations and riots that prompted the government to incarcerate prominent antiapartheid activists and declare a state of emergency.

In an attempt to fight the forced segregation, Biko initially joined the National Union of South African Students (NUSAS), a multiracial group that stood up for nonracialism and nonsexism. However, after working with NUSAS, Biko became convinced that black and colored students needed an independent organization for themselves that fought for fostered self-empowerment rather than assimilation. He helped form the South African Students' Organization, which was inaugurated in 1969 with Biko as president. The group sought to unify black students through appreciation of their shared cultural and ethnic identity and a rejection of the white social structure that labeled them as inferior. Biko's writings appeared in the SASO newsletter, and he gave many speeches elucidating the ideals that would become the core of the black consciousness movement in the 1970s.

Biko's writing concerns itself with concrete and existential struggles that shape black existence. Black consciousness as a movement can be traced to Martin Delany, a nineteenth-century African American who maintained that pride in black culture and identity was a necessary step toward freedom. The ideas engendered in this argument influenced notable black intellectuals such as philosopher and critic Alain Locke, who wrote during the Harlem Renaissance in the United States, and poets Aimé Césaire and Léopold

❖ *Key Facts*

Time Period:
Late 20th Century

Genre:
Essay

Events:
Rise of the antiapartheid movement; growth of the black consciousness movement

Nationality:
South African

THE INFLUENCE OF *DRUM* MAGAZINE

In the 1950s *Drum* magazine emerged as an important means of expressing South Africa's black culture and identity. Launched in 1951 in Johannesburg, it portrayed everyday black life through short stories, poems, investigative journalism, and photography. *Drum* provided a forum for fresh, new voices of the generation influenced by the black consciousness movement and the leadership of Steve Biko. The material in the magazine balanced exposition of hardships with celebration in a way that captivated readers and translated to steady circulation.

Drum broke new ground in black South African investigative journalism by offering feature reports on gangs, crime, and slave-like working conditions on farms. These articles were enhanced by striking photographs. In addition to exposing social grievances, *Drum* reported regularly on the introduction and implementation of apartheid laws, black political movements and organizations, and political events important to the black community. In this respect, it existed as an organ of the black consciousness movement.

Senghor, who brought about the négritude movement in France. Malcolm X, Charles Hamilton, and Stokely Carmichael—who, in 1960s America, attempted to portray black identity in terms of power and beauty—were also informed by Delaney.

Biko's contribution to racial discourse continues to be relevant for its attempt to embrace the paradox of simultaneously acknowledging cultural and ethnic differences while also expressing cohesive national identity. His work has had an impact on fellow African writers such as Chinua Achebe, Ngũgĩ wa Thiong'o, and Nadine Gordimer. In addition, the Steve Biko Foundation, which was launched in 1998, works to facilitate increased dialogue through seminars, workshops, and an annual lecture, and it promotes leadership training and community involvement.

THEMES AND STYLE

One of the key ideas espoused in *I Write What I Like* is psychological emancipation for black Africans. Biko aims to free blacks from self-pity and feelings of inadequacy, a form of mental oppression that had to be overcome before any political liberation could take place. He writes that "the first step … is to infuse him with pride and dignity; to remind him of his complicity in the crime of allowing himself to be misused and therefore letting evil reign supreme in the country of his birth." Biko also wants to help whites see themselves as ordinary citizens in a diverse society rather than in a patronizing role to their black brothers. In the essay "Black Souls in White Skins," for example, Biko denounces "white liberals" who hold "the false belief that we are faced with a black problem." Instead,

they must realize that "there is nothing the matter with blacks. The problem is WHITE RACISM and it rests squarely on the laps of white society."

In order to promote self-acceptance among black individuals and provide a powerful critique of the political structures around him, Biko roots his writing in Western philosophy and makes frequent appeals to emotion. He utilizes German philosopher Georg Wilhelm Friedrich Hegel's theory of dialectical materialism as a way to understand the racism of apartheid. In this dialectic, power is ostensibly held and represented by whiteness, while the perceived lack of power is with those of color. Using Hegel's structure of thesis/antithesis/synthesis, Biko examines white racism (thesis), black solidarity (antithesis), and balance (synthesis) to ascertain the most effective way of bringing about liberation for the black individual and concludes, like Hegel, that true power rests in the hands of the oppressed since the oppressor's false sense of superiority can be taken away should the oppressed finally realize their self-worth. For Biko, this reversal of power necessarily entails a psychological element that recasts blackness in a positive light. This includes understanding and appreciating the common African history that existed before white colonial exploration and eventual domination. He exhorts members of the black community to understand one another in relation to this shared history rather than "be fooled by white society who have made white standards the yardstick by which even black people judge each other."

Biko's writing affects an authoritative tone intended to call the passive and disengaged into action. His language is at times inflammatory and even hostile, although his anger is backed up with strong, well-reasoned arguments. The writing carries with it an urgency that relates the struggle for liberation, as he urges a "re-awakening of the sleeping masses" and proclaims that "now is the time." Many of his essays and speeches adopt an easy tone of camaraderie bolstered by frequent use of the pronoun "we," which is meant to forge solidarity among the readers/listeners. Imperatives are common; he speaks of what "must" be done in order to create a world more receptive to different identities.

CRITICAL DISCUSSION

Biko's untimely death left a gaping hole for his friends and followers and prompted publishers to revisit his life's work and release his writings as a collection. The immediate reaction was largely favorable, compelling Gail M. Gerhert in a review from 1979 to comment on the "lucidity of Biko's thinking," as well as the author's "forcefulness as an articulator of black demands" that richly inform the "humaneness of his political values." In a review from 1981, Femi Ojo-Ade describes Biko's language as "tough" and "aggressive" and the position he takes as a "soul-shattering" but necessary step in the process of liberation.

Biko has become an international symbol of the injustices suffered by black people during the apartheid system in South Africa. *I Write What I Like* was republished in 1987, as the apartheid regime was embroiled in massive uprisings that brought it to the brink of collapse, and again in 2002, the twenty-fifth anniversary of Biko's death. In addition, the story of Biko's friendship with Donald Woods, a reporter who risked his life to expose the circumstances of Biko's death, was the focus of the Oscar-nominated film *Cry Freedom* (1987), starring Denzel Washington as Biko. Along with Franz Fanon's *The Wretched of the Earth* (1961), Biko's words are an indispensable source for understanding white domination and black resistance in African history.

The black solidarity Biko promotes in his writing continues to be relevant in South Africa, where problems of disempowerment and disproportionate wealth distribution did not disappear with the dismantling of the apartheid system in 1994. In "Remembering Biko for the Here and Now," Ahmed Veriava and Prishani Naidoo contend that Biko's greatest legacy is that his message is not static but part of the ongoing evolution of psychological development that is applicable to a variety of situations. His message, they write, "allows for the changing, lived experiences of people to shape its use and evolution." They point to "the potential for revolution" that is within "each of the oppressed and the oppressed as a group" for which Biko's words can at any time act as a catalyst for change.

A demonstrator holds a photo of antiapartheid activist Steve Biko outside the Palace of Justice in Pretoria, South Africa, on November 17, 1977, as a judicial inquest is opened into the death of Biko while in police custody. © SELWYN TAIT/SYGMA/CORBIS.

BIBLIOGRAPHY

Sources

Biko, Steve. *I Write What I Like.* Ed. Aelred Stubbs. New York: Harper & Row, 1979. Print.

Gerhert, Gail. "Three Portraits of a Revolutionary." Rev. of *Steve Biko: Black Consciousness in South Africa,* by Millard Arnold; *I Write What I Like: A Selection of His Writings Edited with a Personal Memoir by Aelred Stubbs C. R.,* by Steve Biko and Aelred Stubbs C. R.; and *Biko,* by Donald Woods. *Africa Today* 26.2 (1979): 59–62. *JSTOR.* Web. 6 Sept. 2012.

Mngxitama, Andila, Amanda Alexander, and Nigel Gibson, eds. *Biko Lives! Contesting the Legacies of Steve Biko.* New York: Palgrave Macmillan, 2008. Print.

Ojo-Ade, Femi. "Stephen Biko: Black Consciousness, Black Struggle, Black Survival." Rev. of *Steve Biko,* by Hilda Bernstein; *Steve Biko—I Write What I Like,* by Aelred Stubbs; and *Biko,* by Donald Woods. *Journal of Modern African Studies* 19.3 (1981): 539–46. *JSTOR.* Web. 6 Sept. 2012.

South African Democracy Education Trust. *The Road to Democracy in South Africa, 1970–1980.* Pretoria: Unisa, 2006. Print.

Further Reading

Arnold, Millard W., ed. *Steve Biko: Black Consciousness in South Africa.* New York: Random House, 1978. Print.

Formigari, Lia. *The Muzzled Muse: Literature and Censorship in South Africa.* Trans. Gabriel Poole. Philadelphia: John Benjamins, 1997. Print.

Lalu, P. "Incomplete Histories: Steve Biko, the Politics of Self-Writing and the Apparatus of Reading." *Current Writing: Text and Reception in Southern Africa* (2010). Taylor Francis Online. Web. 16 Aug. 2012.

Magaziner, Daniel R. *The Law and the Prophets: Black Consciousness in South Africa, 1968–1977.* Athens: Ohio UP, 2010. Print.

Matteau, Rachel. "The Circulation and Consumption of Banned Literature in Apartheid South Africa: Readership, Audience, Censorship with Reference to *I Write What I Like.*" MA thesis U of the Witwatersrand, 2005. Print.

Switzer, Les. *South Africa's Resistance Press: Alternative Voices in the Last Generation under Apartheid.* Athens: Ohio UP, 2000. Print.

Media Adaptation

Cry Freedom. Dir. Richard Attenborough. Perf. Denzel Washington, Kevin Kline, Josette Simon. Universal Pictures, 1987. Film.

Elizabeth Orvis

LYSISTRATA

Aristophanes

✦ **Key Facts**

Time Period:
5th Century BCE

Genre:
Play

Events:
Athenian decline;
replacement of
democracy with
oligarchy

Nationality:
Greek

OVERVIEW

Lysistrata, a bawdy antiwar comedy by classic Greek playwright Aristophanes, was first performed in 411 BCE in the city-state of Athens. Extremely topical, the play is set in an Athens embroiled in devastating war and tells the story of the Athenian woman Lysistrata, whose name translates as "dismisser of armies." Angered by the damage and death caused by the war and disgusted by men's ongoing unwillingness to end the fighting, Lysistrata calls a secret meeting of the women affected by the war. Female representatives of Athens, Sparta, Corinth, and Thebes gather to hear Lysistrata's devilishly simple plan: to withhold sex from all the warring men until they agree to make peace. The young women quickly agree, and aided by the old women, who take possession of the sacred Acropolis and seize the treasury to prevent the financing of further combat, they ultimately convince their sex-starved men to reconcile. Using the mask of farce, the playwright is able to speak out frankly against self-serving politicians and the ruinous consequences of war without fear of serious accusations of treason or sedition.

Introduced in the midst of the Peloponnesian War (431–404 BCE), *Lysistrata* was first viewed by war-weary Athenians seeking escape from bad news about the bloody conflict. Though little evidence survives of ancient audiences' reaction to the play, the author's sharply satiric view of war and his lively depiction of the battle between the sexes have remained fresh and vibrant to generations of scholars and activists. Inspired by Aristophanes' ribald use of the ridiculous to make a persuasive argument against war, authors and theatrical producers have adapted the play repeatedly in efforts to sway public opinion on other political issues, from women's suffrage to fascism.

HISTORICAL AND LITERARY CONTEXT

The fifth century BCE ushered in a Golden Age in Greece, especially in the cultured city-state of Athens, where the study of science and philosophy flourished. The late sixth century had seen the introduction of the Athenian democracy, which, though limited to propertied men, gave an unprecedented number of citizens a voice in their own governance. Territorial disputes and ambitions of conquest, however, led to constantly shifting alliances and frequent outbreaks of regional warfare among the various Greek city-states and with such outside forces as the Persians. By 431, Athens' relations with its most powerful competitor, the city-state of Sparta, had degenerated into all-out war. Between 430 and 426 BCE, a devastating epidemic struck the walled city of Athens, weakening the city by wiping out almost a quarter of its population.

Athens experienced a series of severe setbacks in the period immediately preceding the debut of *Lysistrata.* A 413 BCE expedition to support Athenian allies on the island of Sicily ended in disastrous defeat and the complete destruction of the expeditionary forces. Sparta continued to win territory in the Aegean as Athens frantically attempted to rebuild its navy in order to reclaim captured lands. Military losses and a depleted treasury led to political unrest, and in 411 the democracy was overthrown when the oligarchy known as the Council of Four Hundred took power. Aristophanes's *Lysistrata,* with its clear message of scorn for leaders who waste money and lives in pointless war, must have resonated deeply with Athenians disheartened and frightened by the disintegration of their way of life.

Though Greek tragedy had been evolving since the seventh century BCE, comedic theater achieved its first widespread popularity during the grim years of the Peloponnesian War, when it provided an escapist form of entertainment. The earliest comedies were likely slapstick caricatures of local figures, and later playwrights such as Aristophanes and Cratinus continued this tradition, using the classical conventions of actors and chorus to lampoon political and military leaders and policies, as well as human foibles in general. The plays of Aristophanes make up most of what has survived of this ancient body of work, generally called Old Comedy, but his comedies clearly represent the sentiments of a society tired of conflict and mistrustful of its leaders. The playwright had previously hammered home the same message of opposition to war, corruption, and venality in *Acharnians* (425 BCE) and *Peace* (419 BCE). Though Greek drama was written by men and performed by men (even the female roles) for male audiences, Aristophanes had also employed female characters as subversives in *Thesmophoriazusai* (*Women Celebrating the*

Festival, 411 BCE) and *Ekkleszusai* (*Assemblywomen,* 391 BCE).

Lysistrata, with its comic role reversal and ribald sexual overtones, is perhaps the best known of Aristophanes' plays today. As both war and the status of women have remained significant social issues, *Lysistrata* has continued to inspire modern authors, and various translations of the play have emphasized different aspects of its commentary. Though the staid Victorians recoiled from the open sexuality in the play, the influence of *Lysistrata* can be seen in Percy Shelley's 1820 satire *Oedipus Tyrannus.* The twentieth century saw several reworkings of the play, with some highlighting its feminist implications, as in The Little Theater's 1910 production, and others its antiwar message. The Theatre Workshop's 1938 staging protested the Spanish Civil War, and its 1947 production, titled *Operation Olive Branch,* premiered shortly after the end of World War II.

THEMES AND STYLE

The overriding focus of *Lysistrata* is the horror of war and the longing for peace: "How are we to cure these folk of their warlike frenzy?" Ancient Greek society was so completely male-dominated that it is unlikely Aristophanes intended his play as a demand for women's rights. Rather, he probably used women as he might have used animals or visitors from another planet, as a voice so separate from the power structure that it can speak directly and freely on controversial subjects. Still, his women are so eloquent about their restricted lives that the play has since become a strong feminist statement: "You never allowed us to utter a sound, But you needn't imagine, for that, / That our thoughts were content. We watched what you did / From the quiet rooms where we sat." Another subtext woven into the narrative is the power of unity and common humanity. The success of Lysistrata's plot to end the war depends on the unification of women from all sides: "if the Boeotian and Peloponnesian women join us, then Greece is saved."

To deliver his antiwar message with maximum effect, Aristophanes employs a number of comedic devices, primary of which is the paradox of the women who, though generally considered powerless and ignorant of public matters, see the problem more clearly than the men and take control, "We saw it was up to the women, at last, / To muster their forces and cope / With the plague that was ruining Hellas." Like most comic writers of the time, Aristophanes makes broad use of sexual innuendo ("Let's probe into this shocking affair," the men shout) and overt obscenity ("If Dickus might dockus between your thighs again," a husband pleads), in which are couched more serious themes ("You wrack Hellenic cities, bloody Hellas / With deaths of her own sons, while yonder clangs / The gathering menace of barbarians"). Typically, *Lysistrata* employs a chorus to interpret events and propel the action. In this case, Aristophanes makes innovative

THE LYSISTRATA PROJECT

In 2003, as the U.S. government and its allies seemed resolved to invade Iraq, a broad-based international peace movement sought ways to voice its opposition to the war. New York actors and peace activists Kathryn Blume and Sharon Bower conceived the idea of using Aristophanes's ancient antiwar comedy to protest current military aggression. In coordination with the organization Theaters Against War, they began to publicize the Lysistrata Project, a worldwide endeavor to encourage women to call attention to the approaching war by staging readings of the play on the same day.

Organizers chose a version of *Lysistrata* translated by a woman, Drue Robinson, and established a website that made free copies of the script available. Women responded eagerly to the creative project, and on March 3, 2003, at least 1,000 readings were staged in 59 countries and in each of the United States. Several readings were performed in New York alone, including one six-minute version for children. In areas where women were afraid to speak out against war publicly, many held readings in their homes.

Though the Lysistrata Project did not prevent war in Iraq, it allowed pacifist women to make a powerful statement of opposition. The project continues to maintain its website as "an educational resources portal dedicated to peace and the transformation of consciousness necessary to create it."

use of dueling choruses, one of old women and one of old male war veterans who joust verbally while representing the long-term results of a culture of war. At the end, the quarreling choruses unite, reinforcing the theme of unity by saying, "A hell it is to live with you; to live without, a hell ... So let's join ranks and seal our bargain with a choric song."

Though Aristophanes makes his moralizing palatable with a tone of rollicking lewdness throughout, there is a seriousness, even sadness, that underlies *Lysistrata.* Even as the old women and men of the choruses banter, moments of earnestness emerge: "Oh these dreadful old men / And their dark laws of hate," the old women lament. Later, they chide the men: "You are fool enough, it seems, to dare to war with me, / When for your faithful ally you might win me easily." When the magistrate praises Lysistrata's husband for refusing to discuss the war with her, she replies with poignant simplicity, "Is it sensible, never to take / The advice of a friend, and never confess / When you know you have made a mistake?"

CRITICAL DISCUSSION

There is no record of *Lysistrata* winning public recognition in its era, though as translator and scholar Jeffrey Henderson observes, "the popularity of (Aristophanes's) plays would seem to indicate that the sentiments they express were broadly shared among the be familiar with its themes and plot devices through such modern versions as Meg Wolitzer's novel *The Uncoupling* (2011) and the musical *Lysistrata Jones* (2011), by Douglas Carter Beane and Lewis Flinn, which replaces the Peloponnesian War with a college basketball rivalry.

Students of classical theater and political science continue to examine *Lysistrata* to better understand its author's original intent and the script's lasting effect on modern culture. Although Michael Rex views the play as, "much more about sex and its politics than … power and peace," Sheri Metzger questions the playwright's feminist intent: "There is little in *Lysistrata* that tells the audience of women's lives." Alan Sommerstein argues that those who read the play as a pacifist statement have misunderstood the playwright's intention, pointing out that neither Aristophanes nor his heroine espouse nonviolence or advocate the end to all war.

BIBLIOGRAPHY

Sources

Henderson, Jeffrey. Introduction. *Acharnians, Lysistrata, Clouds*. By Aristophanes. Newburyport: Focus, 1997. Print.

Hugill, William Meredith. "Panhellenism in Aristophanes." *Panhellenism in Aristophanes*. The U of Chicago P, 1936. Rpt. in *Classical and Medieval Literature Criticism*. Vol. 4. Ed. Jelena O. Krstovic. Detroit: Gale, 1990. *Literature Resource Center*. Web. 23 July 2012.

Metzger, Sheri E. "Overview of 'Lysistrata.'" *Drama for Students*. Vol. 10. Ed. Michael L. LaBlanc. Detroit: Gale, 2001. *Literature Resource Center*. Web. 19 July 2012.

Rex, Michael. "Overview of 'Lysistrata.'" *Drama for Students*. Vol. 10. Ed. Michael L. LaBlanc. Detroit: Gale, 2001. *Literature Resource Center*. Web. 19 July 2012.

Sommerstein, Alan H. *Talking about Laughter: And Other Studies in Greek Comedy*. Oxford: Oxford UP, 2009. Print.

Tylee, Claire. "'A Better World for Both': Men, Cultural Transformation, and the Suffragettes." *The Women's Suffrage Movement: New Feminist Perspectives*. Ed. Maroula Joannou. Manchester: Manchester UP, 1998. Print.

Further Reading

Corrigan, Robert Willoughby. *Classical Comedy: Greek and Roman*. New York: Applause Theater and Cinema, 1987. Print.

Faraone, Christopher A. "Priestess and Courtesan: The Ambivalence of Female Leadership in Aristophanes' *Lysistrata*." *Prostitutes and Courtesans in the Ancient World*. Ed. Christopher A. Faraone and Laura K. McClure. Madison: U of Wisconsin P, 2006. 207–23. Print.

Kitano, Masahiro. "Aristotle's Theory of Comedy." *Bulletin of Gunma Prefectural Women's University* 22 (2001): 193–201. Print.

Romy Schneider (Myrrhine) and Barbara Ruetting (Lysistrata) in the 1961 television movie *Die Sendung der Lysistrata*, directed by Fritz Kortner. © INTERFOTO/ALAMY.

theatrical public." This echoes the judgment of William Hugill, who wrote of *Lysistrata* in 1936, "Aristophanes felt the full force of the submerged popular longing for peace, and he alone had the courage to give it public expression at this time." Perhaps the most meaningful contemporary tribute to the playwright is found in Plato's mid-fourth century *Symposium*, where he places Aristophanes at the side of Socrates, carousing with the philosopher and holding forth with comic pathos about the nature of sexuality and gender.

However *Lysistrata* was received by its initial audience, its poignant ridicule of sexual politics and war has remained an effective vehicle for propaganda through the centuries. Primarily viewed as a classic argument against war, the play was adapted in 1910 by Laurence Housman, who used it to highlight a pro-suffrage message, calling it, "a play of feminist propaganda which offered lurid possibilities." During the mid-1930s a U.S. production with an all-black cast added racism to the social ills lampooned onstage, but the production was shut down after its premiere, ostensibly for indecency, though many blamed racial prejudice. By the twenty-first century, *Lysistrata* was firmly established in popular culture, and those who have never seen or read the original play may

Kotini, Vassiliki. "Aristophanes' Response to the Peloponnesian War and the Defeat of the Comic Hero." *Alif* 30 (2010): 134+. *Literature Resource Center.* Web. 23 July 2012.

Robson, James. *Humour, Obscenity and Aristophanes.* Tübingen: Narr, 2006. Print.

Van Steen, Gonda A. H. *Venom in Verse: Aristophanes in Modern Greece.* Princeton: Princeton UP, 2000. Print.

Media Adaptations

Lysistrata, or Triumph of Love. Dir. Kaspar Loser. Perf. Judith Helzmeister, O. W. Fischer, and Marie Kramer. Distinguished Films, 1947. Film.

Die Sendung der Lysistrata. Dir. Fritz Kortner. Perf. Romy Schneider, Barbara Ruetting, and Karin Kernke. Norddeutscher Rundfunk (NDR), 1961. TV Movie.

Lysistrata. Dir. Ludo Mich. Perf. Jacques Ambach, Annie Cré, and Armand De Heselle. Varia Films, 1976. Film.

Lysistrata: Female Power and Democracy. Dir. James Thomas. Perf. Jane Fonda and Katrina Vanden Heuvel. MacMillan Films for Public Broadcasting Service, 2009. DVD.

Tina Gianoulis

MANIFESTO OF UMKHONTO WE SIZWE

Nelson Mandela

✤ *Key Facts*

Time Period:
Mid-20th Century

Genre:
Manifesto

Events:
Sharpeville massacre;
ban of the African
National Congress
(ANC); Umkhonto we
Sizwe, or "Spear of
the Nation," begins
coordinated attacks on
government-related
facilities

Nationality:
South African

OVERVIEW

Published anonymously, but credited to South African politician Nelson Mandela, the *Manifesto of Umkhonto we Sizwe* (1961) proposes the taking up of arms in the struggle against the South African government's policy of apartheid. Setting forth the goals and methods of the militant group Umkhonto we Sizwe ("Spear of the Nation," abbreviated MK), the manifesto describes a kinship with preceding liberation movements and indicates a shift toward violence as a means of combating government militarization and ultimately achieving peace and justice for the people of South Africa. Arguing that the National Party government's tactics have necessitated the rise of MK, the manifesto appeals to the support of the people in this new phase of struggle.

The manifesto appeared immediately after MK began a series of coordinated acts of sabotage against apartheid-related facilities, starting with an electricity substation. The attacks were a response to the South African regime's increasing use of force, which culminated in the deaths of sixty-nine protestors at Sharpeville in 1960. The government condemned MK and its leaders and began arresting prominent members, including Mandela, who was imprisoned on unrelated charges in 1962. He subsequently received a life sentence for sabotage, which later sparked international outrage. Largely defunct since the early 1990s, MK has a controversial legacy, particularly as its history intertwines with the influential African National Congress (ANC) and the South African Communist Party (SACP). As an illustration of the change in framing and fighting the battle against apartheid, the *Manifesto of Umkhonto we Sizwe* remains a significant historical document.

HISTORICAL AND LITERARY CONTEXT

While apartheid was rooted in racial segregation practiced in the European colonies, it was not officially instituted as law in South Africa until D. F. Malan's National Party came to power in 1948. Starting with the Prohibition of Mixed Marriages Act in 1949, the government enacted multiple bills ensuring segregation of the races. The Population Registration Act of 1950 required that each person be classed as white, black, or colored, with minority whites receiving preferential treatment in housing, education, and political representation. Blacks were relegated to the least-desirable areas and were provided inferior facilities and services. Moreover, laws were put in place to suppress the growing resistance to apartheid: The Suppression of Communism Act (1950) outlawed the Communist Party of South Africa (later the SACP) and used language broad enough to be applied to most organized resistance activities, regardless of whether they were based in communist ideology.

The ANC, formed in 1912 as the South African Native National Congress to promote the views of black South Africans, gained strength under the oppression of apartheid. After party activities were banned, many communists sought refuge in the ANC as a political outlet, and the ANC benefited from its experience with mass organization, which was applied through the 1950s defiance campaigns of noncooperation and other protests. Increasingly violent crackdowns on protestors culminated in the 1960 Sharpeville massacre. The same year, the ANC was banned, with much of its active leadership living in exile. With political means closed, a contingent of those left on the ground asserted the right to avail themselves of illegal means, including violence, to continue the fight. Following its formation, MK began sabotaging strategic installations around the country, issuing the *Manifesto of Umkhonto we Sizwe* immediately afterward to define its aims and justify its methods.

The antiapartheid movement in South Africa sparked a number of documents claiming equal rights for people of all races. The most important of these, the Freedom Charter of 1955, was created by the Congress of the People using demands collected from individuals around the country. The charter was endorsed by all members of the South African Congress Alliance, including the ANC, the South African Indian Congress, the South African Congress of Democrats, and the Coloured People's Congress. With its iconic opening salvo—"The People shall govern!"—the charter calls for democracy, declaring: "These freedoms we will fight for side by side, throughout our lives, until we have won our liberty." Indeed, the *Manifesto of Umkhonto we Sizwe* states an intention to "carry on the struggle for freedom and democracy" but adds that the struggle will be conducted by "new methods."

These new methods would be elaborated more directly in publications to follow. In 1963 the ANC published a pamphlet titled *The ANC Spearheads Revolution*, which declares emphatically that "organized violence will smash apartheid." Similar in structure to the *Manifesto of Umkhonto we Sizwe*, the pamphlet declares the civil war that the manifesto sought to forestall. Another publication, *We Are at War!*, alludes to the demands of the Freedom Charter by urging South Africans to "mobilise and prepare!…. Let your courage rise with your anger!" The ANC continues to produce manifestos as a means of disseminating organizational objectives, although those produced in recent years take a much less militant tone, reflecting the group's altered political status.

THEMES AND STYLE

The *Manifesto of Umkhonto we Sizwe* asserts the right of MK to meet the violence of the Nationalist government with violent resistance of its own, as earlier liberation movements had exhausted all peaceable methods of resistance. The manifesto claims a philosophical continuity with these groups, states its goal to seek "liberation without bloodshed or civil clash," and casts the acts of sabotage and the new policy of violence as a "choice made by the Nationalist government." The government, according to the authors, has "beat down peaceful, non-violent strike action of the people in support of their rights." Further, the manifesto warns that the government is preparing to take "full-scale military actions against the people," building an army and "drawing the white civilian population into commandos and pistol clubs." Within this framework, the authors argue, the attacks of MK constitute defense.

The manifesto's attempts to legitimize violence are predicated on the characterization of the South African government as an oppressive regime that has taken advantage of the liberation movement's policy of nonviolence, choosing "the course of force and massacre, now, deliberately, as it did in Sharpeville." Appealing to the need of black South Africans for justice and for protection from increasing amounts of protest-related violence by the police, the authors describe MK as "the front line of the people's defense." Indeed, MK's tactics are further legitimized through its portrayal as "the fighting arm of the people" with the noble project of seeking "liberty, democracy and full national rights and equality for all people of this country."

Both a declaration and an appeal, the manifesto exhibits a tone of steely determination augmented by a plaintive note of warning as the authors ask for understanding and support in the face of the looming threat of "civil war and military rule." Opening with a bold announcement of executed attacks, the manifesto introduces MK and its new methods as "necessary." Developing the argument for violent resistance, the authors punctuate the text with exclamations, emphasizing that while a peaceful resolution is desired "even at this late hour," it is important to

SHARPEVILLE MASSACRE

Among the many burdens apartheid placed on black South Africans, pass laws were one of the heaviest. Designed to regulate movement and enforce segregation, these laws required blacks to carry passbooks authorizing them to traverse white areas when they traveled outside their home neighborhoods. Any white could ask any black to produce a pass, and failure to deliver could lead to arrest.

In December 1959, as black frustration mounted, the African National Congress (ANC) announced a series of marches to protest the laws. A newly formed antiapartheid group called the Pan Africanist Congress (PAC) preempted the planned marches, however, issuing its own call for protest: on March 21, 1960, supporters would deliberately fail to carry their passes and present themselves at police stations for arrest. That morning approximately 5,000 residents of Sharpeville Township, near Johannesburg, arrived at the local police station. A lengthy standoff during which the police refused to arrest protesters ensued. It ended when police panicked and opened fire on the crowd. Widely disputed official figures state that sixty-nine people were killed and 180 were injured. The evidence that a nonviolent demonstration could lead to such violence helped catalyze the ANC and other groups to take up arms against the oppression of apartheid.

strike before the government's militarization can be fully realized. The manifesto closes with "an appeal for the support and encouragement of all those South Africans who seek the happiness and freedom of the people of this country," a sentiment echoed by the final exhortation "Afrika Mayibuye!" This phrase, a rallying cry performed at many apartheid-era protests, roughly translates to "let it return, the Africa we have lost, let it return."

CRITICAL DISCUSSION

Following MK's explosive entrance into the struggle against apartheid, the South African government and its allies denounced the organization and its manifesto advocating violence. Arrests, and in some cases executions, of MK members soon followed. Mandela was arrested in 1962, with much of the rest of the MK leadership rounded up the following year in a raid on a farm at Rivonia. Internationally, the United States and most other major Western powers continued their Cold War alliance with the South African government, ignoring several UN resolutions denouncing apartheid. Dissent existed among antiapartheid activists as well. Prominent figures such as attorney Bram Fischer, while generally supportive of MK's objectives during the early 1960s, later admitted the childish grandiosity of MK's rhetoric.

Contemporary accountings appraise the aims and methods enshrined in the manifesto as important in the struggle against apartheid, though less in a

Black South African being beaten by a white police officer on August 21, 1985. The *Manifesto of Umkhonto we Sizwe* was a cry of war against the apartheid policies of the South African government. © LOUISE GUBB/ CORBIS SABA.

military sense and more as symbol. While connecting the end of apartheid to factors such as international isolation and economic collapse, South African journalist Mondli Makhanya, writing for *Times Live* in 2011 on the fiftieth anniversary of the first MK bombings, credits the organization as "a force that kept the hope of freedom alive and inspired thousands to risk life, limb and a lot more in pursuit of a democratic South Africa." Now defunct, MK is largely treated in historical analyses of twentieth-century South African politics and remains a potent symbol of the resistance movement.

The *Manifesto of Umkhonto we Sizwe* receives little attention as a stand-alone work. Nonetheless, it contains a broad statement of MK's program of armed resistance, which is of interest to scholars attempting to separate fact from myth in defining the meaning of the group in South African history. In a number of articles, such as Stephen Ellis's 1991 essay for *African Affairs,* scholars discuss the evolution of the group, which was complicated by the sometimes overlapping, sometimes conflicting influence of the SACP and the exiled ANC. Noting the combined history of human rights violations of the ANC and MK, which runs counter to the notion of the groups as liberators, Ellis argues the importance of "the extent to which [the ANC's] armed struggle against a ruthless opponent, which had itself been profoundly militarized, has affected its political nature."

BIBLIOGRAPHY

Sources

African National Congress. *The ANC Spearheads Revolution.* Johannesburg: African National Congress, 1963. Web. 23 Sept. 2012.

———. *Manifesto of Umkhonto we Sizwe.* Johannesburg: African National Congress, 1960. Web. 23 Sept. 2012.

———. *We Are at War!* Johannesburg: African National Congress, 1968. Web. 23 Sept. 2012.

Ellis, Stephen. "The ANC in Africa." *African Affairs* 90.360 (1991): 439–47. Print.

Makhanya, Mondli. "Flawed It May Have Been, But MK Helped Liberate South Africa." *Johannesburg Times* 18 Dec. 2011. Web. 24 Sept 2012.

Further Reading

Ellis, Stephen. "The Genesis of the ANC's Armed Struggle in South Africa 1948–1961." *Journal of Southern African Studies* 37.4 (2011): 657–76. Print.

Johnson, R. W. *South Africa's Brave New World: The Beloved Country Since the End of Apartheid.* New York: Overlook, 2009. Print.

Lodge, Tom. *Black Politics in South African Since 1945.* New York: Longman, 1983. Print.

Russell, Alec. *Bring Me My Machine Gun: The Battle for the Soul of South Africa from Mandela to Zuma.* New York: PublicAffairs, 2009. Print.

Worden, Nigel. *The Making of Modern South Africa.* 5th ed. Malden: Wiley-Blackwell, 2012. Print.

Daisy Gard

MAYOMBE

A Novel of the Angolan Struggle

Pepetela

OVERVIEW

Mayombe: A Novel of the Angolan Struggle (1980) is a book about the Angolan War of Independence written by Artur Carlos Maurício Pestana dos Santos, a white Angolan who fought in the war as a member of the Popular Movement for the Liberation of Angola (MPLA) and wrote under the name Pepetela. The novel focuses on an isolated group of MPLA rebels in Mayombe—a rainforest in the Cabinda enclave of northeastern Angola—and their attempts to overcome ideological and cultural differences in pursuit of a unified and independent Angola. Written in 1971 while Pepetela was serving as a commander on the eastern front, *Mayombe* treats a major issue facing postcolonial societies, namely the challenge of integrating a diverse group of people, forced for decades to coexist within arbitrary borders set by European powers, under a single national identity without merely substituting the oppression of colonialism with the stifling conformity of nationalism.

Because of its skeptical treatment of the war's aims and potential outcomes, *Mayombe* was suppressed by the MPLA leadership for nearly a decade, even after Angola achieved independence in 1975. Pepetela's concerns in the novel proved to be well founded, however, as the country immediately fell into a twenty-six-year civil war between rival political and ethnic factions. Although the book remained controversial after its publication, it was praised by Angola's first president, António Agostinho Neto, and received the Angolan National Prize for Literature in 1980. It has since been recognized as an earnest and prescient analysis of the hardships inherent in national liberation and of the larger problem of forming a collective identity out of a highly fragmentary African society.

HISTORICAL AND LITERARY CONTEXT

Arriving in the area of present-day northern Angola in the late 1400s, the Portuguese were primarily traders whose disputes with the occupying peoples led them to encourage and exploit rivalries between the various kingdoms to gain a strong foothold in western and central Angola. In the twentieth century, the fascist New State (Estado Novo) government came to power in Portugal, drastically increasing exports of coffee,

sugar, and other natural resources from Angola and introducing a large military presence in the region to suppress native groups that had begun to complain about forced labor and poor working conditions. In response, a number of anticolonial nationalist groups arose in the 1950s and 1960s, loosely organized along ethnic lines: the Mbundu people, concentrated in the capital city of Luanda, formed the Marxist-leaning MPLA; the rural Bakongo from the north formed the National Front for the Liberation of Angola (FNLA); and the southern Ovimbundu formed the National Union for the Total Independence of Angola (UNITA). The people of Cabinda, despite their ties to the Bakongo and the FNLA, viewed themselves as culturally and geographically separate from Angolans and formed a separatist movement known as the Front for the Liberation of Cabinda (FLEC). Each of these groups not only engaged in guerrilla warfare against the Portuguese but also viewed each other with suspicion. The rural fighters, for example, accused the urbanized MPLA, with its large population of intellectuals and mixed-race mestizos, of harboring sympathies for the Portuguese, while others labeled the people of Cabinda as traitors for refusing aid to the rebel groups.

Pepetela, whose mother's family had resided in Angola for generations, was a student in Portugal when the first guerrilla attacks were staged in 1961. Identifying more with his upbringing in the Angolan town of Benguela than with his Portuguese ancestry, Pepetela refused to serve in the Portuguese army when called upon in 1962 and fled to France and later Algeria, where he was approached by representatives of the MPLA and helped to create the Center for Angolan Studies. He returned to Africa in 1969, advocating the MPLA cause in neighboring Congo before joining the MPLA fighters stationed in Cabinda. It was there that Pepetela learned firsthand the true depth of the divisions and infighting that plagued the liberation effort. Although he had touched upon such problems in other novels, including *As Aventuras de Ngunga* (1972) and *Muana Puó* (1978), *Mayombe* was the first of his works, and perhaps the first work of Angolan literature, to provide a space for all the competing voices within the struggle to engage in discourse over the future of the nation.

⁘ *Key Facts*

Time Period:
Late 20th Century

Genre:
Novel

Events:
Angolan War of Independence

Nationality:
Angolan

WARRIOR POETS OF ANGOLA

Pepetela was not the only writer and intellectual to contribute to the Angolan independence effort on both the battlefield and the printed page. Several other members of the MPLA gave voice to their political beliefs in poetry and prose before or during their service. Some of the most influential of these warrior poets include António Jacinto, Viriato da Cruz, and António Agostinho Neto.

Jacinto, a white Angolan, served an eleven-year prison sentence for speaking out against Portuguese rule before joining the MPLA guerrillas in 1973 and later holding several positions in the Angolan government. His first poetry collection, *Colectânea de Poemas* (1961), featured several poems that were later turned into patriotic songs celebrating Angola's independence. Cruz, who served as president of the Angolan Communist Party before joining forces with Neto's Party of the United Struggle for Africans in Angola and becoming secretary general of the MPLA in 1956, published a collection of poems in 1961 that is said to have ignited the nationalist fervor that eventually led to an independent Angola. Neto, the country's first president, published a number of highly regarded poetry collections, including the celebrated *Sagrada Esperança* (1974; *Sacred Hope*), which helped to form the Angolan national identity. Neto also established a National Literacy Campaign in 1979, highlighting the important role that literature played in shaping and sustaining his country's long march toward independence.

Angola's war for independence occurred in the midst of a wider push for autonomy and an end to colonialism in Africa and around the world. For example, neighboring Congo—along with fifteen other African countries—achieved independence in 1960, inspired in part by the nationalist victories of many European countries in the wake of World War II. The psychoanalyst and philosopher Frantz Fanon wrote what is considered the seminal text on African independence efforts, *Les damnés de la terre* (1961; *The Wretched of the Earth*, 1963), while participating in the Algerian revolution of 1954–62. In the study, he describes the violent overthrow of colonial rulers as a "cleansing force" that "frees the native from his inferiority complex" and "restores his self respect." Critics suggest that *Mayombe* can be read in relation to Fanon's work as a critique of the notion that violent revolution can serve as a panacea for the historical divisions that prevent the formation of a unified national identity.

While Pepetela had already become something of a literary celebrity in Angola with the publication of *As Aventuras de Ngunga*, the release of *Mayombe* propelled him to international recognition, leading to the translation of both works into English in 1980. His later novels expanded upon the Utopian optimism and eventual disillusionment described in *Mayombe*

and earned him the Camões Prize, the most prestigious award in Lusophone literature, in 1997. He was also a major influence in the formation of the Angolan Writer's Union, which is credited with fostering a diverse Angolan literary scene.

THEMES AND STYLE

One of the central concerns of *Mayombe* is the challenge that the guerrillas—and by extension all Angola—face in balancing the need for political unity against their desire to retain a sense of individualism and respect for the various mindsets and histories of the Angolan people. Pepetela depicts the issue as a kind of mythical confluence of abstract social and political ideas, naming his characters after the various dispositions they embody: Fearless, the group's commander, is either seen as the individualist of the novel, who castigates his soldiers for holding "absolute and ready-made" ideas about their role in Angolan society, or as the idealist who knows his Utopia is doomed; New World, the Marxist ideologue, insists that "man as an individual is nothing"; Theory, a mestizo who exemplifies the often conflicted loyalties that many of the guerrillas hold, complains of those who "insist on purity and reject compounds"; Struggle, a Cabindan, joins the effort to prove that his people are not the traitors they are often accused of being; the Political Commissar, who at the end of the novel takes over Fearless's command, gradually transforms from a rigid dogmatist to a person who believes in compromise and the need to find an alternative to the false choice between absolute good and absolute evil, to locate "the frontier between truth and lies."

Pepetela underscores the need for Angolans to abandon their preconceived notions about what makes a "true" Angolan and inhabit this frontier in a number of ways. He begins the novel with an epigraph evoking Ogun, the African god of iron, war, and politics:

> To the guerillas of Mayombe
>
> who dared to defy the gods
>
> opening a path in the dark forest
>
> I will tell the story of Ogun
>
> the African Prometheus

As Sandra T. Barnes explains in the introduction to *Africa's Ogun: Old World and New* (1997), "As a consequence of his harmful or beneficial acts, he is viewed either as a lonely, isolated figure—the quintessential marginal man—or, in almost complete contrast, as a central force whose revolutionary and creative acts give birth to new social forms." By likening the guerrillas to Ogun, who inhabits the place between good and evil and reshapes the world through acts both constructive and destructive, Pepetela underscores the ambiguous morality of the guerrillas' fight against the Portuguese, calling into question the use of extreme tactics such as attacks on civilians while simultaneously celebrating the country's move toward independence. The geographic setting of the novel, a remote jungle area isolated from the rest of Angola by territory belonging to the Democratic Republic of the Congo, further underscores the guerrillas' liminal state and associates them with the "isolated" and "marginal" Ogun.

Pepetela makes the case for a future Angola characterized by inclusiveness and thoughtful discourse rather than dogmatism and distrust by offering a number of internal monologues throughout the text that neither privilege nor denigrate any single viewpoint. Since the narrative features relatively few scenes of combat, the author seems to suggest that the guerrillas do far more to shape the future of the country by sharing and evaluating ideas than they do by killing the opposition. Pepetela's avoidance of the kind of myopic nationalist cheerleading that characterizes many works of war literature written by participants signals his own ability to subsume personal bias in favor of a more nuanced approach to the work inherent in postindependence life. Ana Maria Mão-de-Ferro Martinho touches upon this subject in "Utopian Eyes and Dystopian Writings in Angolan Literature" (2007), writing, "The various narrators show different perspectives and allow an understanding of how the author is willing to hide his presence in favor of an idea that is to result from a polyphonic and at the same time multipolar reality."

CRITICAL DISCUSSION

When Pepetela presented his manuscript to MPLA leadership in 1971, it was viewed as potentially subversive to the war effort and suppressed. Only after a personal request by Angola's first president, Neto—who himself published several popular literary works— was *Mayombe* approved for publication. Although its themes made the novel a target of those who sought to project the image of an infallible MPLA, *Mayombe*'s honest portrayal of the war and consideration of the potential pitfalls of independence made it the object of study in universities across Africa.

In the years after the novel's publication, Angola's political situation devolved into a bloody civil war between MPLA and UNITA factions that displaced millions of Angolans and only dissipated in 2002 with the death of UNITA leader Jonas Savimbi. During this time, *Mayombe* came to be seen as a remarkably perceptive analysis of the way in which ideologically charged revolutions tend to re-create the worst offenses of their opponents in the aftermath of independence. Writing in 2006, critic Sean Rogers notes in "Imagining Revenge: The Adoption of Violence by *Mayombe*'s Fighters" that "it would seem that Pepetela understands that colonialism and its violence will live on in Angola for many years to come as a result of the damage that both it and the resistance to it have done to the citizens of the land."

Contemporary critics take a number of approaches to the novel, focusing on its appropriation and reinvention of African mythology, the rela-

tionship between Pepetela's concerns and those of postcolonial theorists such as Fanon or Edward Said, the use of competing narrative voices in the text, or its depiction of women and sexuality as a representation of evolving social values. These varied interpretations, mirroring the competing interpretations of experience voiced by the novel's characters, confirm that Pepetela succeeded in surpassing the mundane realities of protracted warfare and touched upon the multifaceted significance of independence and nation building.

BIBLIOGRAPHY

Sources

Barnes, Sandra T. *Africa's Ogun: Old World and New.* 2nd ed. Bloomington: Indiana UP, 1997. Print.

Fanon, Frantz. *The Wretched of the Earth.* Trans. Constance Farrington. New York: Grove, 1965. Print.

After Angola's war for independence from Portugal ended in 1975, the country descended into civil war, primarily between the UNITA and the communist MPLA. The conflict lasted more than two decades and destroyed many towns and cities, along with untold numbers of human lives. TRAVEL INK/GALLO IMAGES/GETTY IMAGES.

Martinho, Ana Maria Mão-de-Ferro. "Utopian Eyes and Dystopian Writings in Angolan Literature." *Research in African Literatures* 38.1 (2007): 46–53. Print.

Pepetela [Artur Carlos Maurício Pestana dos Santos]. *Mayombe: A Novel of the Angolan Struggle.* Trans. Michael Wolfers. London: Heinemann, 1983. Print.

Rogers, Sean. "Imagining Revenge: The Adoption of Violence by *Mayombe*'s Fighters." *Transformation: Critical Perspectives on Southern Africa* 62 (2006): 118–29. Print.

Further Reading

Cusack, Igor. "Janus or Hydra? Pepetela, the New Man and the Construction of Angolan Masculinities." *Sexual/Textual Empires: Gender and Marginality in Lusophone African Literature.* Ed. Hilary Owen and Phillip Rothwell. Bristol: Dept. of Hispanic, Portuguese and Latin American Studies, U of Bristol, 2004. 99–116. Print.

Henighan, Stephen. "*Muana Puó* and *Mayombe*: Colonial Pasts and Utopian Futures in Two Early Works by Pepetela." *Romance Quarterly* 54.2 (2007): 164–77. Print.

Munatamba, P. M. *The Profane and the Sacred Refuge in War Literature: The Case of Pepetela's* Mayombe. Lusaka: Dept. of Literature and Languages, University of Zambia, 1992. Print.

Peres, Phyllis. "Traversing PostColoniality: Pepetela and the Narrations of Nation." *Luso-Brazilian Review* 40.2 (2003): 111–17. Print.

Rothwell, Phillip. "Unmasking Structures: The Dynamics of Power in Pepetela's *Mayombe*." *Luso-Brazilian Review* 39.1 (2002): 121–28. Print.

Willis, Clive. "*Mayombe* and the Liberation of the Angolan." *Portuguese Studies* 3 (1987): 205–14. Print.

Jacob Schmitt

"OPEN LETTER FROM A WRITER TO THE MILITARY JUNTA"

Rodolfo Walsh

OVERVIEW

"Open Letter from a Writer to the Military Junta," written by Argentine journalist, novelist, and activist Rodolfo Walsh on March 24, 1977, accuses the Argentine military government of misrule and violation of human rights. In the direct and unadorned style of investigative journalism, Walsh compiles a list of the government's crimes against its own people, such as press censorship, denying the writ of *habeus corpus,* corrupt economic policies, and the kidnapping and murder of innocent civilians. Disheartened by the need for militants and activists to work in secret, Walsh opted to write an open letter, printing his name and national identification number at the end of the text. Well aware of the immense risks he took in writing and disseminating this information, Walsh believed that by exposing the atrocities of the government to the world he could serve his country better than any form of military combat.

It was not the first time that Walsh had stirred up controversy with his political writing. Since the late 1940s, he had published novels, short stories, news articles, and political missives exposing the corruption and criminal actions of the Argentine government. Although his 1977 letter was not published in Argentina, it was widely read throughout Latin America and beyond, passed along from one reader to another, or placed directly in mailboxes in order to avoid censorship from the postal system. The greatest indicator of the impact of Walsh's work, however, was the swift and brutal response from the military junta itself: on March 25, 1977, only a day after he finished writing his letter, government officials decided to silence the writer once and for all. Walsh was shot by military police in Buenos Aires and went missing, thereby joining the thousands of other *desaparecidos* ("the disappeared") who were victims of the government. His fate was confirmed by two political prisoners who were released in 1979 and testified to having seen the dead body of the writer.

HISTORICAL AND LITERARY CONTEXT

In 1974 the death of president Juan Perón left Argentina in political disarray and prompted internecine conflicts for government control. A coup d'état in 1976 brought to power a military junta that ran the country until 1983 through a combination of intimidation, manipulation of domestic and international media, and violent repression of dissidents. This period, known as the *Guerra Sucia,* or Dirty War, resulted in the death or disappearance of anywhere from 10,000 to 30,000 persons. Celeste Frasier Delgado describes the Argentine military government as "a death-dealing machine" during the Dirty War.

Among the many accusations in his "Open Letter," Walsh challenges the legitimacy of the military regime, alleging that the junta seized power through illegal means, put an end to the democratic process in Argentina, and denied the political wishes of its citizens. Written only a year after the junta came to power, Walsh's letter anticipated the international media's eventual discovery of the crimes of the Argentine government. Within Argentina, writers and intellectuals who were openly critical of the government put themselves at risk: Jacobo Timmerman, head of the Buenos Aires newspaper *La Opinión,* was imprisoned in 1977 as a result of his paper's unfavorable views on Argentine politics.

Argentina has a long history of dictatorial rule as well as literature that responds to and is critical of dictatorship. Domingo Faustino Sarmiento's 1845 *Facundo: Civilization and Barbarism* and Esteban Echevarría's 1840 short story "The Slaughterhouse" both denounce the dictatorship of Juan Manuel de Rosas, a military *caudillo* who rose to power in the mid-nineteenth century through violent coercion and intimidation. Walsh's 1957 novel *Operation Massacre* exposes a civilian massacre committed by the military junta that deposed Perón in a 1955 coup. Yet none of these works projects the sense of urgency and anger toward the government of Walsh's "Open Letter."

At the end of his "Open Letter" Walsh acknowledges that he composed it "without hope of being listened to" by the government; indeed, his letter had little impact on the actions of the military junta, but it did help to bring their injustices to the attention of the international media. Walsh's disappearance prompted an international group of writers that

❖ *Key Facts*

Time Period:
Late 20th Century

Genre:
Letter

Events:
Dirty War of Argentina's military government

Nationality:
Argentinian

OPERATION MASSACRE

The nonfiction novel *Operation Massacre* is widely considered Rodolfo Walsh's literary masterpiece and the beginning of his career as a political resistance writer. Published in 1957, the novel tells the story of a massacre committed by the military junta that ruled Argentina from 1955 to 1958. On a June night in 1956 eleven men were arrested on suspicion of participating in an attempted coup d'état against the government. They were detained for hours without being charged and then transported to a nearby garbage dump and shot. Six of the eleven survived to tell their story, which would become *Operation Massacre*.

Finding no evidence that any of the men had participated in the coup, Walsh argues that the military police were acting unlawfully, and he demands justice for the survivors and the families of the murdered men. He published the results of his investigation in the Buenos Aires newspaper *Mayoría*, which resulted in numerous threats by the government and even a failed attempt on Walsh's life. Although Walsh was unable to bring about justice for the survivors, his novel became wildly popular throughout Latin America and is often compared favorably to Truman Capote's novel *In Cold Blood*, published in 1966.

included Roland Barthes, Michel Foucault, and Italo Calvino to compose their own letter to the Argentine government on the writer's behalf. Nearly three decades after the fall of the dictatorship Argentine schoolchildren read the "Open Letter" every year on the anniversary of the 1976 coup in order to realize Walsh's dream, to bear witness to the atrocities of the Dirty War.

THEMES AND STYLE

Walsh structured his "Open Letter" as a succinct and highly detailed exposé of the Argentine government's offenses against its people during the first year of military rule. As a whole, Walsh characterizes the first year of the military junta as a catastrophe, despite the government's claims to the contrary: "what you call successes are failures, the failures you recognize are crimes and the disasters you have committed are omitted altogether." The letter is separated into six numbered sections, each corresponding to a different type of injustice. Walsh begins by discussing the junta's illegitimate seizure of power and suspension of democracy in the first section, moves on to provide specific examples of their violent criminal acts in sections two through four, and finishes in sections five and six with a critical analysis of their mismanagement of the nation's economy.

Walsh's background as a journalist is evident in the strategic writing style he employs in this letter. He presents himself as a concerned citizen, mentioning the ways in which the government has invaded his home life, including "a recent police raid on my house, the murder of dear friends and the loss of a daughter who died fighting the dictatorship." Walsh's writing is passionate but not overly emotional, focusing on a litany of well-researched facts. He uses three sections to support his claims of murder of "genocidal magnitude" by the government, juxtaposing large-scale numbers with individual details that illustrate the regime's brutality. "Between 1,500 and 3,000" people were murdered during the first year of military reign, including "the 15-year-old youth, Floreal Avellaneda, hands and feet bound, 'with wounds in the anal region and visible fractures,' according to his autopsy." Readers are meant to try to imagine the suffering of this individual victim and then multiply it by the thousands in order to comprehend the enormity of the harm inflicted by the military government.

The overall tone of the "Open Letter" is confrontational, as Walsh openly challenges the government's actions and the steps it has taken to conceal any wrongdoing. He addresses the military junta directly, stating that "you overthrew a government" and "you suppressed the right to publish information." He discusses the "violation of human rights which you have committed," and he takes on an ironic tone when addressing the issues of censorship and pro-government propaganda, which he describes as "a twisted reflection of half-truths … claiming that the junta is trying to bring peace." He points out the transparency of government propaganda in order to remind the regime that its citizens know and fully comprehend what is really happening in Argentina. The confrontational and ironic tones reach a fever pitch toward the end of the letter as Walsh poses a rhetorical question to the regime: "Taking all these facts into account you have to ask yourself who are the real traitors of the official communiqués … and what is the ideology which threatens our national identity."

CRITICAL DISCUSSION

It is likely that Walsh's disappearance, originally designed to silence him, actually helped bring greater international attention to his cause and to his "Open Letter." On May 2, 1977, when Walsh's whereabouts were still unknown, the *Times* (London) published a report on his disappearance. In July of that same year the Committee to Save Rodolfo Walsh published a small pamphlet with an English-language version of the "Open Letter" in order to shed light on the dictatorship in Argentina. The pamphlet likens the experience of writers and intellectuals who oppose the dictatorship to "that of the Resistance in countries occupied by the Nazis" and urges readers to take action by writing letters to express concern for the safety of Walsh and other political prisoners. Nobel Prize-winning Colombian novelist Gabriel García Márquez profiled Walsh in the Peruvian magazine *Marka*, calling

On December 12, 2011, in Argentina's northern province of Tucumán, forensic anthropologists work on a common grave allegedly containing the remains of at least fifteen people apparently slain during the country's 1976–1983 dictatorship. Thousands of Argentine civilians were victims of the regime, including writer Rodolfo Walsh, who was murdered one day after finishing his "Open Letter from a Writer to the Military Junta." AP PHOTO/ARGENTINE JUDICIAL OFFICES.

his "Open Letter" a "masterwork of journalism" and reminding readers of the dangers of investigative journalism in Argentina.

However, some critics tend to overlook the "Open Letter" in favor of Walsh's more literary work, or they consider him a novelist first and a journalist second. Uruguayan author Eduardo Galeano, for example, presents the rhetorical question of how to explain "that the best Argentine narrator of his generation was essentially a journalist." Walsh is now best known for the works in which he combines investigative journalism with the language of hard-boiled detective fiction, such as his novels *Operation Massacre* (1957), *Caso Satanowsky* (1958), and *Who Killed Rosendo?* (1969), which critics such as David William Foster consider masterpieces of the genre. Foster argues that *Operation Massacre* "demands to be read as a sociohistorical document" as well as a work of literature.

Galeano and García Márquez now consider Walsh a forerunner of the region's literary "boom" of the late 1970s. Foster reads his work alongside Latin American dictator novels such as Augusto Roa Bastos's 1975 novel *I, The Supreme* as well as testimonial narratives such as Miguel Barnet's 1966 *Autobiography of a Runaway Slave*. David Viñas, in contrast, focuses more specifically on the political content of Walsh's work, comparing it to the writings of Ernesto "Che" Guevara for its unwavering critique of injustice in Latin America. Whether seen as journalism or literature, it is clear that Walsh's "Open Letter from a Writer to the Military Junta"

introduces readers to the power of the written word as resistance against tyranny and as testimony for future generations.

BIBLIOGRAPHY

Sources

Foster, David William. "Latin American Documentary Narrative." *PMLA* 99.1 (1984): 41–55. Print.

Fraser Delgado, Celeste. "Private Eyes in Argentina: The Novel and the Police State." *Latin American Literary Review* 22.44 (1994): 49–73. Print.

Galeano, Eduardo. "Un historiador de su propio tiempo." *Rodolfo Walsh, vivo.* Ed. Roberto Baschetti. Buenos Aires: Ediciones de la Flor, 1994. 324–25. Print.

García Márquez, Gabriel. "Rodolfo Walsh: El escritor que se adelantó a la CIA." *Rodolfo Walsh, vivo.* Ed. Roberto Baschetti. Buenos Aires: Ediciones de la Flor, 1994. 313–15. Print.

McCaughan, Michael. *True Crimes: Rodolfo Walsh: The Life and Times of a Radical Intellectual.* London: Latin American Bureau, 2002. Print.

Viñas, David. "Déjenmehablar de Walsh." *Rodolfo Walsh, vivo.* Ed. Roberto Baschetti. Buenos Aires: Ediciones de la Flor, 1994. 337–41. Print.

Walsh, Rodolfo J. *A Year of Dictatorship in Argentina: March 1976–March 1977. An Open Letter to the Military Junta from Rodolfo Walsh.* London: Committee to Save Rodolfo Walsh, 1977. Print.

Further Reading

Anderson, Martin Edwin. *Dossier secreto: Argentina's Desaparecidos and the Myth of the "Dirty War."* Boulder: Westview, 1993. Print.

Feitlowitz, Marguerite. *A Lexicon of Terror: Argentina and the Legacies of Torture.* Oxford: Oxford UP, 2011. Print.

Guevara, Ernesto. *The Motorcycle Diaries: Notes on a Latin American Journey.* New York: Ocean, 2004. Print.

Lewis, Paul H. *Guerillas and Generals: The Dirty War in Argentina.* Santa Barbara: Praeger, 2001. Print.

Mohlenhoff, Jennifer Joan. *Reading for Bodies: Literature from Argentina's Dirty War (1976–83).* Ithaca: Cornell UP, 1997. Print.

Verbitsky, Horacio. *Confessions of an Argentine Dirty Warrior: A Firsthand Account of Atrocity.* New York: New, 2005. Print.

Media Adaptations

Las AAA son las tres armas. Dir. Jorge Denti. Cine de la Base, 1979. Film.

Walsh, Rodolfo. *Las A.A.A. son las tres armas: Fragmentos de la carta abierta a la junta militar argentina del escritor Rodolfo Walsh.* Dir. Raymundo Gleyzer. Argentina: Cine de la Base Argentina, 1978. Film.

Letter to the Military Junta. Grupo Alavío, 1996. DVD.

Gina Sheriff

"A PLEA FOR CAPTAIN JOHN BROWN"

Henry David Thoreau

OVERVIEW

A powerfully persuasive and impassioned lecture, "A Plea for Captain John Brown" was written by Henry David Thoreau in 1859 and presented to audiences several times, the first on October 30 of that year. Inspired by the trial of abolitionist John Brown after the defeat of his insurrection in Virginia, Thoreau's "Plea" is filled with fiery eloquence and elevated imagery, as he seeks not only to lionize Brown but also to express his own evolving beliefs and influence his audience to intensify the fight to end slavery. Thoreau's image of Brown as an ardent reformer and deeply spiritual and courageous man did much to establish the public view of the militant abolitionist as a martyred hero rather than a violent fanatic.

Thoreau's speech, which was delivered in Concord, Boston, and Worcester, Massachusetts, as Brown was being tried and condemned to death in the South, was composed during a period of passionate public debate on the subject of slavery. An important voice in this debate was that of the Transcendentalists, a group of highly educated New England writers and artists who espoused the romantic ideals of intuitive knowledge, social reform, and the perfection of human beings in their natural state. Though morally opposed to slavery, many who respected the Transcendentalist philosophy were reluctant to interfere in politics, preferring to believe that appeals to conscience and humanity would convince slaveholders to end the institution of their own accord. With "A Plea for Captain John Brown," Thoreau articulated a growing conviction that slavery would not end without the direct intervention of committed abolitionists. By speaking out in defense of Brown's militancy, Thoreau risked accusations of inconsistency with his previous nonviolent stance, but he convinced many that stronger measures were required to uproot the institution of slavery.

HISTORICAL AND LITERARY CONTEXT

Thomas Jefferson sought unsuccessfully to include wording in the Declaration of Independence that indicted King George III for imposing the slave trade on the colonies, and slavery became enshrined in the United States with the ratification of the U.S. Constitution in 1789. By the mid-1800s, the country was polarized around the issue of slavery. Continuing westward, expansion intensified the debate as each new territory required new decisions and compromises in order to keep a tenuous balance between proslavery and antislavery factions. In 1820 the Missouri Compromise had seemed to solve the problem by establishing 36° 30′ latitude as the North-South border for slavery. In 1854, however, Congress passed the Kansas-Nebraska Act, which repealed the 1820 compromise and allowed residents to decide the legality of slavery in newly forming states, satisfying the demands of slave owners and infuriating abolitionists.

One of these abolitionists was an Ohio tanner named John Brown, a deeply religious and uncompromising frontiersman who, while still a teenager, began helping runaway slaves escape through the Underground Railroad. Brown's violent resistance to slavery began in Kansas, where he participated in the May 1856 massacre of proslavery leaders in the town of Pottawatomie. On October 16, 1859, he and his followers, hoping to arm a slave rebellion, attempted the takeover of a military arsenal at Harper's Ferry, Virginia. Brown was captured by U.S. Marines on October 18. His trial on charges of murder, conspiracy, and treason began in Charles Town, Virginia, on October 27; a week later, he was found guilty on all three counts and sentenced to death. He was executed in a public hanging on December 2.

Brown's attack and defeat at Harper's Ferry sparked a nationwide reevaluation of armed resistance as a route to ending slavery, and Thoreau's "Plea" was one of the earliest analyses of the event. Delivered to audiences in 1859 and published in the anthology *Echoes of Harper's Ferry* in 1860, it was influential in changing public opinion about Brown and formed the basis for many of Thoreau's later writings about slavery.

Thoreau's portrait of Brown as a Christlike hero was prompted by scathing contemporary depictions in the press. In the North, the *New York Times* called him "mad John Brown," though they sympathized with his hatred of slavery. In the South, the *Richmond Enquirer* and the *Charleston Mercury* raged that Brown's actions justified separation from the Union. Thoreau's voice was one of the first to counter these images, and other abolitionists, such as Henry Ward Beecher, Wendell Phillips, and Samuel Longfellow, followed in characterizing Brown as a visionary and a martyr. Walt Whit-

✛ *Key Facts*

Time Period:
Mid-19th Century

Genre:
Speech

Events:
Passage of the Kansas-Nebraska Act; abolitionist agitation; John Brown's thwarted rebellion

Nationality:
American

ENSLAVED AFRICANS WORKING TOGETHER FOR FREEDOM: THE CONVENTION MOVEMENT

Often the American abolitionist movement is viewed in terms of eminent white liberals, such as Henry David Thoreau and other Transcendentalists, but enslaved and free people of color themselves worked tirelessly for freedom and racial equality, though such resistance was often illegal and always dangerous. One of the more successful efforts in this work was the Convention movement, which began in 1830 with the September 15 National Negro Convention in Philadelphia.

Organized by a number of prominent free blacks and led by Bishop Richard Allen, the founder of the African Methodist Episcopal Church, the convention hosted more than forty delegates for several days of discussions about the situation of African American people. The convention established the American Society of Free People of Colour for Improving Their Condition in the United States, for Purchasing Lands, and for the Establishment of a Settlement in the Province of Canada, to pursue the study of options and to organize annual national conventions. Delegates also set up the American Society of Free Persons of Labor to organize local Negro conventions around the country. The Convention movement remained active until the Civil War and was the inspiration for the Chatham (Ontario) Convention, called by John Brown in May 1858, which adopted a new Constitution (written by Brown) based on racial equality and set up a command structure for a war on slavery.

man's 1865 Civil War collection, *Drum Taps,* contains "Year of Meteors" about Brown's trial, and Julia Ward Howe's rousing "Battle Hymn of the Republic" was set to the tune of the popular song "John Brown's Body." Though this admiration for militant action represented a clear shift in the Transcendentalists' heretofore nonviolent approach, Thoreau himself had long advocated challenging unjust laws. His 1849 essay, "Resistance to Civil Government" (later retitled "Civil Disobedience"), advanced a seminal argument for following one's conscience, and "Slavery in Massachusetts," a speech Thoreau delivered in Framingham, Massachusetts, on July 4, 1854, in response to the conviction of a fugitive slave in Boston, signaled the author's increasingly radical antislavery stance.

Thoreau's speech exerted a significant influence on the way Brown was viewed by the growing ranks of abolitionists. Historians such as David S. Reynolds theorize that Brown's violent tactics and maniacal public image, along with the failure of his mission at Harper's Ferry, might have resulted in his being dismissed as a fanatic and forgotten by history. Thoreau's "Plea," along with other Transcendentalist writings, however, transformed Brown into an powerful inspiration for the antislavery movement.

THEMES AND STYLE

Thoreau's speech is both a defense of Brown's actions, past and present, and an indictment of slavery, the horrors of which provided the primary justification for Brown's subversive activities. Knowing he is speaking to a hardheaded New England audience, Thoreau begins by appealing to their sense of justice: "It costs us nothing to be just." He calls on them to do nothing less than revise their idea of what it is to be American, contrasting Brown's passionate commitment to justice with those who "ask, Yankee-like, 'What will he gain by it?'" He devotes much of his speech to the condemnation of slavery, and he charges his audience with responsibility for its continuation: "The slave-ship is on her way ... a small crew of slaveholders, countenanced by a large body of passengers, is smothering four millions under the hatches."

Though Thoreau's speech was given as John Brown stood trial in Virginia, he makes clear that his purpose is "to plead not for his life, but his character." Even the title, which gives Brown his military rank, legitimizes the captured insurrectionist and predisposes his listeners toward respect. The plea is, above all, the portrait of a hero, and in describing Brown's larger-than-life qualities, Thoreau employs emotionally laden comparisons with Oliver Cromwell, the gallant Light Brigade that fell at Balaclava during the Crimean War, and, primarily, Jesus Christ. Appealing to his audience's deep Puritan roots, Thoreau develops his picture of Brown as a Christlike figure, with "as many at least as twelve disciples," and compares proslavery forces to Pontius Pilate and the Inquisition. Like Jesus, Brown is the "saviour of four millions," who possesses a "superior nature" and the "spark of divinity." In contrast, he censures "a government that pretends to be Christian and crucifies a million Christs every day!" and says, "When a government puts forth its strength on the side of injustice ... it reveals itself a ... demoniacal force."

The impassioned tone of Thoreau's speech is driven by the fact that his own politics are transforming as he works to change the minds of his audience. With language that is sometimes high-flown and sometimes scathing, he compares Brown, "A man of rare common sense and directness of speech, as of action," to those who, like Thoreau himself, "proceed to live their sane, and wise, and altogether admirable lives, reading their Plutarch," claiming that "our foe is the all but universal woodenness of both head and heart, the want of vitality." Brown embodies this vitality, and it is through this glorification of Brown that Thoreau hopes to revitalize the abolitionist movement. Throughout the speech, he exhorts his listeners to action, saying, "Take a step forward and invent a new style of out-houses. Invent a salt that will save you, and defend our nostrils," and, "Do your work, and finish it. If you know how to begin, you will know when to end."

CRITICAL DISCUSSION

Thoreau first delivered his speech to an audience predisposed by temperament and an unfriendly press to view John Brown as a misguided and dangerous lunatic. Though the writer's growing antislavery sentiments had been expressed with increasing ferocity in his journals, he carefully crafted his "Plea" to arouse his audience without alienating those who abhorred Brown's violent methods. Many listeners responded to the plea with enthusiasm, including New Hampshire abolitionist Mary Jennie Tappan, who called it, "Just *the* words I so longed to have some living voice speak." Newspapers such as the *New York Herald* quoted Thoreau's speech as part of their coverage of Brown's trial for the Harper's Ferry conspiracy. Thoreau had included abolitionist editor William Lloyd Garrison among those who vilified Brown, and Garrison responded by reminding readers that papers such as his *Liberator* had laid the political groundwork for the success of Thoreau's "Plea." William Dean Howells wrote a profile of the author for *Harper's Magazine,* stating that Thoreau had created "a John Brown ideal … to cherish and to nurture ourselves upon."

If "A Plea for Captain John Brown" provides an overly glorified picture of John Brown, it offers a clearer view of the Northern abolitionist movement, with its romantic ideals of social justice, equality, and dedication to a cause. Thoreau's writings on confronting governmental wrongs by actions of civil disobedience inspired generations of social activists, from Mahatma Gandhi and Martin Luther King Jr. to the anti-Vietnam War movement of the 1960s and early 1970s and the Occupy movement of the 2010s. His argument in the plea that violence may be a necessary tactic in the struggle for justice presaged an ongoing debate among social activists about the legitimacy of militant protest. It has also sparked lively discussion among scholars about the development of Thoreau's principles and actions regarding the abolition of slavery.

The nineteenth and twentieth centuries encompassed a number of powerful social movements, and the writings of Thoreau inspired the ideas and the tactics of many of the leaders of these movements, from abolition to gay liberation. Social analysts and academics have studied Thoreau's writings in order to better understand his influence on modern ideas of social responsibility and political reform. Though most Thoreau analysts have focused on essays such as "Civil Disobedience" as most representative of the author's true convictions, the beginning of the twenty-first century saw a revival of interest in "A Plea for Captain John Brown," which began to appear in anthologies of the author's work. Though some scholars have decried the plea's support of violent tactics as atypical of Thoreau, Sandra Petrulionis calls it "the next iteration of the reformist sensibility that produced 'Civil Disobedience.'"

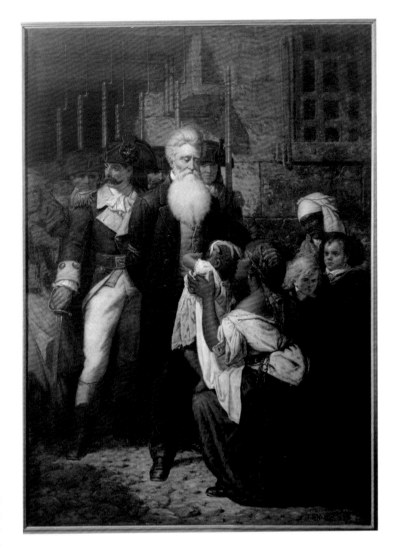

BIBLIOGRAPHY

Sources

Fuller, David G. "Correcting the Newspapers: Thoreau and 'A Plea for Captain John Brown.'" *Concord Saunterer* 5 (1997): 165–75. Print.

"John Brown's Raid on Harper's Ferry." Secession Era Editorials Project. *Furman University Department of History.* Web. 2 July 2012.

"John Brown's Work." *New York Times.* 27 Oct. 1859: 4. *ProQuest Historical Newspapers: The New York Times (1851–2008).* Web. 1 July 2012.

Petrulionis, Sandra Harbert. *To Set This World Right: The Antislavery Movement in Thoreau's Concord.* Ithaca: Cornell UP, 2006. Print.

"Reminiscence of Thoreau." *New York Times.* 29 July 1894: 22. *ProQuest Historical Newspapers: The New York Times (1851–2008).* Web. 7 July 2012.

Reynolds, David S. *Waking Giant: America in the Age of Jackson.* New York: HarperCollins, 2008. Print.

"Thoreau, Civil Disobedience and the Underground Railroad." *Henry David Thoreau.* Calliope Film Resources, 2001. Web. 5 July 2012.

John Brown's Blessing, painting by Thomas Satterwhite Noble, 1867. *JOHN BROWN'S BLESSING,* 1867 (OIL ON CANVAS), NOBLE, THOMAS SATTERWHITE (1835–1907)/© COLLECTION OF THE NEW-YORK HISTORICAL SOCIETY, USA/THE BRIDGEMAN ART LIBRARY.

Further Reading

Albrecht, Robert C. "Thoreau and His Audience: 'A Plea for Captain John Brown.'" *American Literature*. 32.4 (1961): 393–402. Print.

Donahue, James J. "'Hardly the Voice of the Same Man': 'Civil Disobedience' and Thoreau's Response to John Brown." *Midwest Quarterly* 48.2 (2007): 247–65. *Literature Resource Center*. Web. 1 July 2012.

Erlich, Michael Glenn. *Henry David Thoreau's "Plea for Captain John Brown": A Rhetorical Analysis.* Columbus: Ohio State U, 1967. Print.

Linder, Douglas O., ed. "The Trial of John Brown, 1859." *Famous Trials*. Douglas O. Linder, 2005- . Web. 25 July 2012.

Myerson, Joel, ed. *Emerson and Thoreau: The Contemporary Reviews.* Cambridge: Cambridge UP, 1992. Print.

Rosenblum, Nancy. "Thoreau's Militant Conscience." *Political Theory* 9 (1981): 81–110. Print.

Rowe, John Carlos. *At Emerson's Tomb: The Politics of Classic American Literature.* New York: Columbia UP, 1996. Print.

Schwieger, Florian. "Thoreau, John Brown, and the Sublime Spectacle of History." *Nineteenth-Century Prose* 36.2 (2009): 113–24. *Literature Resource Center*. Web. 5 July 2012.

Tina Gianoulis

THE RED MAN'S REBUKE

Simon Pokagon

OVERVIEW

The Red Man's Rebuke is an 1893 essay written by Potawatomi orator Simon Pokagon condemning the United States for having corrupted the American Indians and the natural environment in the course of developing as a nation. Originally produced as a sixteen-page booklet made from white birch tree bark, the essay was distributed by Pokagon and his publisher, C. H. Engle, at the World's Columbian Exposition in Chicago (popularly known as the Chicago World's Fair)—a six-month-long exhibition marking the four hundredth anniversary of Christopher Columbus's arrival in the New World. Mixing Christian and traditional Indian motifs, Pokagon imagines a Great Spirit who readjusts the balance of power between whites and American Indians, and curbs the hellish, iniquitous tendencies of American progress.

Raised in the Midwest at a time when removal of American Indians from their traditional lands was at its peak, Pokagon was billed on his late-nineteenth-century speaking tours as an exemplary orator and the most educated American Indian of his day. Meanwhile, his poetry and essays gained him the titles of the "red-skin bard" and the "Longfellow of his race." When the Chicago World's Fair opened, however, he was dismayed to see that the American Indians were not among the many nations given serious recognition in the exhibits. In response, he wrote his essay, which he then distributed at the fair. Also published as *Red Man's Greeting,* the document is not to be confused with his speech at the fair (also called "Red Man's Greeting") made on October 10, Chicago Day, before a huge crowd. Although the essay and the speech ultimately make a case for Indian assimilation to American life, the essay—much more than the speech—retains the brand of anger at white America that would become characteristic of American Indian literature in the late twentieth century.

HISTORICAL AND LITERARY CONTEXT

The colonization of North America caused a clash of European and indigenous peoples and cultures. By the early 1900s, the U.S. government's solution to what it called "the Indian problem" was twofold: it compelled some Indians in the eastern states to assimilate to American life and to become economically dependent on trade relations with white Americans while also removing others to the western territories. In time these removals became more aggressive. In the course of westward expansion, the United States continued to displace Indian tribes, some multiple times. Eventually, most American Indians were corralled in reservations administered by the federal government in the hopes that American influences would undermine traditional American Indian ways. Pokagon invokes this long history when he indicts the "pale faces" for killing off and corrupting the American Indians.

By the 1890s, the traditional Indian had become something of a nostalgic figure in popular culture as depicted in dime novels, Wild West shows, and museum exhibits. At the edge of the Chicago World's Fair in 1893, Buffalo Bill Cody set up his famous Wild West show, which included real American Indians who reenacted historic raids and wars. The myth of the "vanishing Indian"—that the American Indians were a dying race and their way of life was doomed to extinction in the face of American progress—predominated. Even Pokagon reiterates this myth, though he hardly deems the loss of traditional American Indian culture as a reasonable price for America's success.

Polemically, *The Red Man's Rebuke* works both with and against the emerging ideology of American exceptionalism. In *The Idea of America: Reflections on the Birth of the United States* (2011), historian Gordon Wood describes exceptionalism as the belief that "we Americans are a special people with a special destiny to lead the world toward liberty and democracy." The essay draws on the language of Christian missionaries and temperance movements in its open disgust toward drinking, smoking, and other vices that were corrupting American Indians. Meanwhile, as an aesthetic work, it taps the spirit and language of English poet John Milton's *Paradise Lost* (1667), whose themes of sin, punishment, and redemption Pokagon borrows to describe the American Indian crisis as a battle with "bad" whites. In spite of an obvious debt to the English literary canon, however, Pokagon repeatedly returns to what native "tradition says," attributing to American Indians their own discerning and critical culture.

Pokagon occupies a significant place in American and American Indian literary history. His essay influenced Chicago's mayor to invite him to the World's Fair as a "guest of the city" to speak publicly. Billed as the son of the Potawatomi chief who once owned the site on

Time Period:
Late 19th Century

Genre:
Essay

Events:
End of Indian Wars; establishment of land reservations; Chicago World's Fair

Nationality:
Native American (Potawatomi)

SIMON POKAGON'S BIRCH-BARK BOOK

In his preface to *The Red Man's Rebuke,* Simon Pokagon explains why he printed his book—which measured approximately three-and-a-half by five inches—on the bark of the white birch tree. He describes it as an act of "loyalty to my people, and gratitude to the Great Spirit, who in his wisdom provided for our use for untold generations, this most remarkable tree with manifold bark used by us instead of paper." He details the extensive use his people made of the bark, producing a range of materials from clothing, domestic wares, and fuel for lighting tribal council meetings and sacred dances, to wigwams and canoes.

The tree and its bark, for Pokagon, sustain the practical, political, and spiritual life of the tribe. The problem, however, is that "like the red man, the tree is vanishing from our forests." So the book's birch, in addition to its utility and aesthetic appeal, takes on a sentimental function, commemorating the passing of a people along with their natural environment. This sentimentality in turn has a political function because it raises the question, if subtly, why such a life in harmony with nature should become so endangered.

which Chicago was built, Pokagon drew a huge crowd. Critics speculate that the appearance helped change white perceptions of American Indians. Pokagon also wrote for magazines such as *Harper's, The Forum,* and *The Arena,* sharing his concerns about the future of American Indians with a national audience. Notably, his *Queen of the Woods,* published posthumously in 1899, is now regarded as the second American Indian novel to be written by an American Indian author.

THEMES AND STYLE

Taking Christianity's account of the fall of humankind and the promise of redemption by God's grace as its main theme, *The Red Man's Rebuke* transposes Eden onto the North American continent. Pokagon describes the naive first Americans, who like Adam and Eve fell prey to the temptations of "treacherous" enemies. Reimagining the fruit with which Satan tempted Eve, he foregrounds the corrupting role of alcohol introduced by the Europeans. He explains, "Now as we have been taught to believe that our first parents ate of the forbidden fruit, and fell, so we as fully believe that this fire-water is the hard cider of the white man's devil, made from the fruit of that tree that brought death into the world, and all our woes." Skillfully shifting from an American Indian expression ("fire-water") to Miltonic phrasing ("the fruit of the forbidden tree"), Pokagon brings the Old Testament story of original temptation into the nineteenth century. Although he admits that the modern American Indian is dissipated, he lays the blame at the feet of sinful colonials.

Rhetorically, the text moves through a series of appeals, drawing the reader to Pokagon's side. It begins

in a context of racial division, setting up two opposing parties: "I in behalf of my people" and "you, the pale-faced race that has usurped our lands and homes." Pokagon then reimagines "you" as someone who might just regret America's treatment of the Indians. "Reader, pause here," he urges, "close your eyes, shut out from your heart all prejudice against our race, and honestly consider ... was there ever a people without the slightest reason of offense, more treacherously imprisoned and scourged than we have been?" After hailing the reader, he addresses the "Almighty Spirit of humanity" with the plea to "let thy arms of compassion embrace and shield us ... and save us from further oppression." Here, the essay shifts from a question of race to one of morality—from a problem of red versus white to one of compassion versus cruelty—distinguishing in effect between good and bad Americans. Pokagon closes with a monologue in the voice of God, addressing those "pale-faces" who have broken treaties: "You shall not tread upon the heels of my people, nor tyrannize over them any more.... And if any attempt is made on your part to break these commandments, I shall forthwith grant these red men of America great power, and delegate them to cast you out of Paradise."

Pokagon strikes a register somewhere between Milton's religiosity and poet Percy Bysshe Shelley's romanticism. For example, he invokes the moment in *Paradise Lost* when God casts the rebel angels into Hell. Such allusions prevent him from establishing a colloquial Indian voice but allow him to indict the colonial forces that corrupted the first Americans. Whereas Milton is useful for channeling anger at the most treacherous whites, shades of Shelley (with debt to Homer) serve the more sentimental purpose of lamenting the plight of the Indians. When describing how the natives succumbed to European diseases, he writes, "[O]ur people fell as fall the leaves before the autumn's blast." Of course, he does more than merely parrot English classics; he makes the texts speak anew to struggles for American Indian justice.

CRITICAL DISCUSSION

Some early readers of *The Red Man's Rebuke* were so sympathetic to Pokagon's critique of the relative exclusion of American Indians from representation at the World's Fair that they invited him to speak publicly. Already an accomplished lecturer, he was well received at the event and lauded in the press. His birch-bark book, however, fell out of circulation and for several decades remained, as Cheryl Walker in *Indian Nation: Native American Literature and Nineteenth-Century Nationalisms* (1997) writes, a "difficult-to-find piece of Native American literature" though one "certainly worth resuscitating." Not until 1997, in the appendix to *Indian Nation,* was the text reprinted in its entirety.

The Red Man's Rebuke appeared at a critical moment, the same year in which Frederick Jackson Turner presented his famous thesis on the closing of the American frontier—a frontier, he insisted, that had

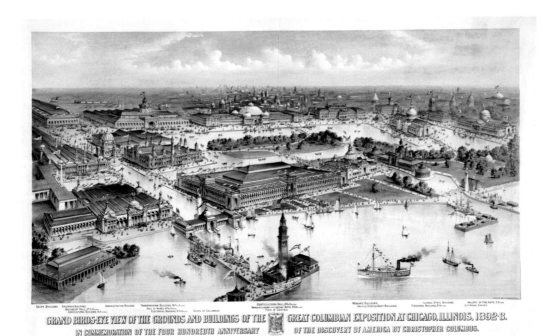

formed the American character and defined national progress. As Nancy Bentley notes in *Frantic Panoramas: American Literature and Mass Culture, 1870–1920* (2009), Pokagon refused to sweep under the carpet the "defacement" underwriting national "improvement" in the course of U.S. expansion. Indeed, Bentley and other scholars, including David Treuer, have expertly shown Pokagon's critical role as a "civilized Indian" who called national destiny into question.

Early scholars such as James Clifton treated Pokagon with much skepticism, revealing many of his biographical claims—such as being a Potawatomi chief—to have been fabrications. When they were not suggesting that Pokagon was but a semiliterate showpiece for his publisher, Clifton and others tended to write him off as more or less a dupe of white culture. Subsequent scholars have made the opposite case, describing Pokagon as a sophisticated thinker with lasting significance for the study of American history and literature. Recently, scholars including Jonathan Berliner and Alex Corey have given special attention to Pokagon's essay, contextualizing it as an artifact with a complex mission of negotiating the different worldviews of traditional American Indians and urban Americans.

BIBLIOGRAPHY

Sources

Bentley, Nancy. *Frantic Panoramas: American Literature and Mass Culture, 1870–1920*. Philadelphia: U of Pennsylvania P. 2009. Print.

Berliner, Jonathan. "Written in Birch Bark: The Linguistic-Material Worldmaking of Simon Pokagon." *PMLA* 125.1 (2010): 73–91. Print.

Clifton, James. *The Pokagons, 1683–1983: Catholic Potawatomi Indians of the St. Joseph River Valley*. Lanham: UP of America. 1984. Print.

Corey, Alex. "Fair Material: Birch-Bark, Politics, and the Market in Simon Pokagon's *The Red Man's Rebuke* and 'Red Man's Greeting.'" *MALS Quarterly* Spring 2010: 5–21. Print.

Treuer, David. *A New Literary History of America*. Cambridge, MA: Belknap P of Harvard UP. 2009. Print.

Walker, Cheryl. *Indian Nation: Native American Literature and Nineteenth-Century Nationalisms*. Durham: Duke UP. 1997. Print.

Wood, Gordon S. *The Idea of America: Reflections on the Birth of the United States*. New York: Penguin, 2011. Print.

Further Reading

Dippie, Brian W. *The Vanishing American: White Attitudes and U.S. Indian Policy*. Middletown: Wesleyan UP. 1982. Print.

Hoxie, Frederick E., ed. *Talking Back to Civilization: Indian Voices from the Progressive Era*. Boston: Bedford / St. Martin's. 2001. Print.

Jaskoski, Helen, ed. *Early Native American Writing: New Critical Essays*. New York: Cambridge UP. 1996. Print.

Murray, David. *Forked Tongues: Speech, Writing, and Representation in American Indian Texts*. Bloomington: Indiana UP. 1990. Print.

Peyer, Bernard C., ed. *American Indian Nonfiction: An Anthology of Writings, 1760–1930s*. Norman: U of Oklahoma P. 2007. Print.

Rydell, Robert. *All the World's a Fair*. Chicago: U of Chicago P. 1984. Print.

David Aitchison

NATIONS

AENEID

Virgil

OVERVIEW

The *Aeneid,* an epic poem written in Latin by the Roman poet Virgil, was composed over a period of ten years early in the reign of Augustus Caesar (ca. 31 BCE-14 CE). It was published only after the author's death in 19 BCE. Its ten thousand lines recount the story of Aeneas, a Trojan survivor of the great conflict between Troy and Greece. Aeneas undergoes a series of personal trials, eventually reaching the Italian peninsula and defeating indigenous tribes in order to found the city of Rome. Although Virgil's work on the poem ended abruptly with his unexpected death, the *Aeneid* is thought to be for the most part complete. The epic was commissioned by Augustus, whose goals were to establish a founding myth for the Roman Empire and to legitimize his own rule. He was in the process of dissolving the centuries-old Roman Republic and replacing it with a militaristic monarchy, and he needed the *Aeneid* to help engender public support.

Augustus was also eager to portray himself as a patron of the arts who would restore the glory of Rome. Virgil's reputation as a skilled, thoughtful poet made him the ideal candidate to construct an Augustan epic. Many scholars, however, believe that Virgil was uncomfortable with his role as a propagandist and that he introduced ironies, ambiguities, and other voices to complicate the poem's apparent support of Augustus. In its own time, the *Aeneid* was widely praised even before it was published, and it has been recognized for many centuries as a literary masterpiece. Debate continues, however, about whether Virgil meant for the poem to paint a positive picture of Roman martial values or a tragic vision of the human condition.

HISTORICAL AND LITERARY CONTEXT

The *Aeneid* was written during the early years of the Roman Empire, a time of political and social change in Rome. The overthrow of the monarchy in around 509 BCE led to the Roman Republic, which in turn fell in 44 BCE as a result of internal strife. The government was formally reconstituted in 27 BCE under the rule of Augustus Caesar. Instructed to portray Augustus as the predestined leader of a new epoch in Roman history, Virgil began his account with the Trojan War, a conflict that was believed to have taken place about a thousand years earlier. Although the story of a great battle between Troy and Greece was largely a myth, it was viewed by the Romans not only as an historical event but also as one of history's great turning points.

Augustus's rise to power involved a long and complicated series of events that included shifting alliances, civil wars, and political manipulations. Many Romans suspected that Augustus was consolidating too much authority and that he planned to institute a hereditary monarchy in place of the republican form of government, which had traditionally included two elected consuls and a senate. In order to create a more favorable political climate for his ambitions, Augustus sought to link himself personally to the foundations of Roman society and to encourage a spirit of national unity. The early Greeks had produced several widely admired epic poems, and Augustus determined that a similar work glorifying the origins of Rome would gain support for his goals.

Augustus chose Publius Vergilius Maro (Virgil), the highly esteemed poet and author of the *Eclogues* (a collection of pastoral poems, ca. 39 BCE) and the *Georgics* (a lengthy, thematically complex poem about agriculture, ca. 29 BCE) to write his new epic. During the Age of Augustus, as it came to be called, Latin literature flourished, producing such outstanding works as Horace's *Satires* (ca. 35 BCE) and *Odes* (ca. 23 BCE), Ovid's *Metamorphoses* (ca. 8 BCE), and Livy's great prose history of the Roman people, *History of Rome* (25 BCE). None of these works equaled the *Aeneid* in ambition or execution, however; nor did any of the other authors set out to inspire or persuade the public on such a grand scale. Rather than taking the works of Roman writers as his model, Virgil looked to Homer's *Iliad* and *Odyssey,* which were considered the pinnacle of achievement in poetic narrative. Virgil's challenge was to incorporate Roman themes into an essentially Greek form and to match the eloquence of Homer.

The *Aeneid* created a new model of epic poetry that has been emulated by writers ever since. For centuries it was the most widely known work of classical literature in the Western world, in large part because it was required reading in Latin classes, which were often compulsory in European and early American schools. By the Middle Ages, Virgil was so admired that he was given a key role in the great epic of that period, Dante's *Divine Comedy* (1472), and until the nineteenth century he was generally thought of as the

Key Facts

Time Period:
1st Century BCE

Genre:
Poetry

Events:
Reign of Augustus Caesar; fall of the Roman Republic

Nationality:
Roman

AN EPIC THROUGH THE AGES

Widely admired in the ancient world, the *Aeneid* was so revered during medieval times that a popular form of divination involved interpreting a randomly selected passage from the poem. Beginning in the Renaissance, however, and especially as the *Aeneid* became available in English translation, views of Virgil's epic were increasingly shaped by the dominant cultural attitudes of various periods. In the seventeenth century, often referred to by literary historians as the English Augustan Age, the *Aeneid* was highly esteemed for its classical restraint and conservative sensibility. The eminent poet and literary critic John Dryden produced a popular translation of the work in 1697.

The great Romantics of the eighteenth century, including Byron and Shelley, however, preferred Homer's passionate heroes to the pious Aeneas, and critics faulted Virgil as a flatterer who sacrificed artistic integrity in the service of imperial propaganda. The tide turned yet again in the following century, when a combination of Victorian seriousness and British empire-building brought the *Aeneid* back into favor. The poem was considered a model for teaching not only the virtue of duty but also the importance of patriotism, and that view prevailed well into the twentieth century. In fact, the influential modernist poet T. S. Eliot was one of Virgil's most eloquent supporters. As the century closed, however, the complexities of contemporary culture began to overtake the *Aeneid,* calling into question not only the values of the poem but also the traditional understanding of Western civilization. The work's popularity was reenergized in 2006, however, when Robert Fagles (who had translated both of Homer's epics) produced a translation that jettisons meter for a more modern cadence, reminding readers of current militaristic bids for empire.

greatest of all classical authors. At that time new discoveries in archaeology and literary history generated great enthusiasm for Homer, while Virgil began to be viewed as merely a propagandist hired by Augustus. In the twentieth century the *Aeneid* resurfaced as a favored work among conservative political thinkers and cultural commentators.

THEMES AND STYLE

The twelve books of the *Aeneid* are divided into two parts, each of which has a predominant theme. The first part stresses the Roman concept of *pietas,* meaning duty or devotion to family, country, and gods, while the second part focuses on experiences of war—battle, loss, wrath, and revenge. For that reason books one through six are often referred to as Virgil's *Odyssey.* Like the Greek war hero Odysseus, the Trojan Aeneas survives the war and undertakes a sea voyage. Both men are looking for "home," although Odysseus is trying to get back to his old home, while Aeneas—with Troy destroyed—is looking for a new home. Both encounter women who endanger their mission, and both travel to the underworld. Books seven through

Opposite page:
Mercury appears to Aeneas to remind him of his destiny in this 1757 fresco by Giambattista Tiepolo. GIANNI DAGLI ORTI/THE ART ARCHIVE AT ART RESOURCE, NY.

twelve of the *Aeneid* place Aeneas in a situation similar to that which confronts the protagonist of the *Iliad,* the Greek Trojan War hero Achilles. Each man is consumed with wrath after a close friend is killed, and each seeks vengeance through personal combat. A major difference is that Aeneas is a reluctant hero. His main motivation is not heroism but piety; this difference, along with the bloody ending of the poem, raises questions about Virgil's support for Augustus and his empire-building.

Virgil employed both direct and indirect narrative strategies to fulfill his patron's desire to associate himself with Rome's historic foundations. An unmistakable connection is made during Aeneas's journey in the underworld when he is shown a pageant representing the future of Rome. Within the spectacle Augustus is depicted among Rome's greatest heroes. Aeneas receives a shield from his mother, Venus, goddess of love and victory; her gift illustrates not only Aeneas's suffering and sacrifices but also the struggles that lie ahead of him when he returns to the real world. The story prefigures the momentous event in 31 BCE that would seal Augustus's rise to power—his triumph at the Battle of Actium. Less directly, Virgil provides inspiration for national pride and unity by linking Aeneas's ancient journey to the Roman triumph over Carthage during the Punic Wars (264–146 BCE). The *Aeneid* constructs a fatal love story between Aeneas and Queen Dido of Carthage that mythically accounts for the wars.

The emotional tone of parts one and two differs considerably. The first half of the poem focuses on the virtue of pietas—for example, through the poignant image of Aeneas physically carrying his aged father, along with the statues of their household gods. The noble tone of the scene serves to remind Roman readers of the importance of duty. Aeneas's difficult decision to follow the destiny laid out for him, even though it means leaving Carthage and breaking Queen Dido's heart, sends a similar message. In part two Virgil must show Aeneas as a more conventionally heroic figure: a powerful warrior. The poem shifts toward the rhetoric of warfare and increasingly reflects the emotional conditions of the combatants, who are driven by the gods to a state of *furor* (frenzy or madness) and *ira* (anger). Throughout the poem Virgil uses rich imagery and persuasive language to engage the reader's sympathy and admiration for Aeneas.

CRITICAL DISCUSSION

As a commissioned work, written in the service of a powerful ruler, the *Aeneid* was bound to be well received in its own time. In fact, the poem was declared a masterpiece even before it was completed, based on a few chapters Virgil read to Augustus at the sovereign's behest. On his deathbed Virgil requested that the unrevised manuscript be destroyed, but Augustus insisted that the poem be preserved in its unedited state and published. Although few would have dared

to criticize Virgil's epic, most scholars and writers of the time were undoubtedly sincere in their praise for the *Aeneid,* which despite its flaws, represents an extraordinary achievement. By the following century, however, literary tastes had already begun to change, and such Roman writers as Seneca and Lucan could acknowledge problems within the *Aeneid,* even while treating it as a model expression of Augustan ideology.

In the centuries since it was written, the *Aeneid* has often been viewed in one way by scholars and in another by the many generations of students who have derived their ideas of ancient Rome from Virgil's poem. As R. J. Tarrant points out in an essay in *The Cambridge Companion to Virgil* (1997), the poet is unique among Roman poets because of "the pervasive quality of his influence, which is visible both at the level of popular culture and of official ideology." The poem has generally been taken at face value, as an ode to the glory of Rome and a validation of imperialism. Yet a literary view of the *Aeneid* reveals many ambiguities and unanswered questions. From early times to the modern era, for example, debate has swirled around the poem's abrupt ending, in which Aeneas's wrathful denial of mercy to his enemy seems to be at odds with his piety. While some contend that Virgil—who had planned to spend another three years on the poem—would have integrated these aspects of Aeneas's character more effectively, others believe the violent conclusion was designed to legitimize Augustus's own violent conduct.

In the later twentieth century, critical attitudes toward the *Aeneid* were largely divided into two well-defined camps. Traditionalists, or the "optimists," contended that the poem conveys a positive vision of Roman (and by association, Western) civilization, embodying such ideals as progress and order. The pessimists, on the other hand, maintained that Virgil purposefully and subtly undercut the Augustan message in order to suggest a darker, more critical vision of the imperial ideology. Since the 1990s new approaches to the poem have expanded the critical discussion. Several scholars in particular—among them, Richard F. Thomas (*Virgil and the Augustan Reception,* 2001) and Craig Kallendorf (*The Other Virgil,* 2007)—have called attention to the poem's "other voices," which provide a counterpoint to the focus on Aeneas and add greater complexity to the poem's message. Despite these contemporary trends, however, Ronald Syme's 1939 reading of the *Aeneid* as propaganda, *The Roman Revolution,* which has been regularly reprinted since its initial publication, is still considered by many to be the essential analysis.

BIBLIOGRAPHY

Sources

Evans, Jane D. R. *The Art of Persuasion: Political Propaganda from Aeneas to Brutus.* Ann Arbor: U of Michigan P, 1992. Print.

Kallendorf, Craig. *The Other Virgil: "Pessimistic" Readings of the* Aeneid *in Early Modern Culture.* Oxford: Oxford UP, 2007. Print.

Syme, Ronald. *The Roman Revolution.* Oxford: Oxford UP, 2009. Print.

Tarrant, R. J. "Aspects of Virgil's Reception in Antiquity." *The Cambridge Companion to Virgil.* Ed. Charles Martindale. Cambridge: Cambridge UP, 1997. 56–72. Print.

Thomas, Richard F. *Virgil and the Augustan Reception.* Cambridge: Cambridge UP, 2001. Print.

Further Reading

Adler, Eve. *Vergil's Empire: Political Thought in the* Aeneid. Lanham: Rowman, 2003. Print.

Farrell, Joseph, and Michael C. J. Putnam. *A Companion to Vergil's* Aeneid *and Its Tradition.* Chichester: Wiley, 2010. Print.

Foley, John M. *A Companion to Ancient Epic.* Malden: Blackwell, 2005. Print.

Galinsky, Karl. *Augustan Culture: An Interpretive Introduction.* Princeton: Princeton UP, 1998. Print.

Hardie, Philip R. *Virgil: Critical Assessments of Classical Authors.* London: Routledge, 1999. Print.

Nappa, Christopher. *Reading after Actium: Vergil's* Georgics, *Octavian, and Rome.* Ann Arbor: U of Michigan P, 2005. Print.

Putnam, Michael C. J. *Virgil's* Aeneid: *Interpretation and Influence.* Chapel Hill: U of North Carolina P, 1995. Print.

Quint, David. *Epic and Empire: Politics and Generic Form from Virgil to Milton.* Princeton: Princeton UP, 1992. Print.

Stahl, Hans-Peter. *Vergil's* Aeneid: *Augustan Epic and Political Context.* Swansea: Classical P of Wales, 2009. Print.

Virgil. *The Aeneid.* Trans. Robert Fagles. New York: Viking, 2006. Print.

Media Adaptation

Aeneas and the Aeneid. Prod. Vogelsberg Film. Irwindale: Barr Films, 1990. VHS.

Cynthia Giles

"Battle Hymn of the Republic"

Julia Ward Howe

OVERVIEW

Published on the front page of the *Atlantic Monthly* in 1862, Julia Ward Howe's propagandist poem "Battle Hymn of the Republic," sung to the popular tune of "John Brown's Body," became the definitive anthem of the American Civil War (1861–65). Upon its initial publication (for which Howe earned four dollars), the nationalistic poem became immediately popular, in part because it captured the fierce idealism and determination of the Union at the outset of the Civil War. Unsurprisingly, "Battle Hymn" blends the language style found in a Christian hymnal with the robust fighting language of a marching song. The poet, a staunch abolitionist, asserted that the fight to rid America of slavery was supported by God. Howe's notion that holy powers supported righteous military action is an idea prevalent throughout the history of Christianity, from Bible narratives to the medieval crusades to the settling and conquest of the New World. Howe, like many Christian writers and artists before her, dexterously transformed war into a spiritual campaign—not just against the Confederacy but also against forces of moral corruption, religious abnegation, and racial inequality.

In early 1862, not long after the war had begun, "Battle Hymn" captured the hope and optimistic fervor that Union supporters felt at that heady time. Stirring and inspirational, the poem was widely circulated and sung throughout the war. Howe, a devoted women's rights activist, abolitionist, and artist, often found herself at odds with either her socially conservative husband or society at large for a good deal of her life, but she gained renown for her patriotic poem-turned-song. While Howe's other poetry is no longer widely read, the words and tune of "Battle Hymn" are still known by heart and treasured by many Americans.

HISTORICAL AND LITERARY CONTEXT

Rising tensions in relations between the American North and South bubbled over into formal military conflict in 1861. Numerous causes exist for the outbreak of the Civil War, but the primary issue that divided the nation was slavery. After the invention of the cotton gin, Southern plantations grew increasingly dependent upon slave labor to work their profitable fields. As the United States expanded west, Northern interests vied for new states to be "free," while

Southern interests pushed for just the opposite. Abraham Lincoln warned in 1858 that "a house divided against itself cannot stand … this government cannot endure permanently half slave and half free." South Carolina was the first Southern state to secede, in 1860, followed shortly thereafter by other slaveholding states.

In early 1862 no one could foresee how long, gory, and collectively devastating the "war between the states" would become. Massachusetts residents Howe and her husband, Dr. Samuel Howe, were Union supporters and passionate abolitionists: Samuel Howe went so far as to donate directly to radical abolitionist John Brown's efforts to instigate a slave uprising at Harper's Ferry. In 1862 the couple traveled to Virginia, where Samuel Howe provided medical assistance to Union troops. A variety of tales surround the composition of "Battle Hymn." What is known for certain is that one morning of their trip, Mrs. Howe awoke with new lyrics to the tune of "John Brown's Body" "arranging themselves in [her] brain," as she put it later. Howe's words transformed the coarse marching song into a polished hymn, laden with Christian references.

Like many folk songs, "Battle Hymn" has a rich and winding history. The melody and its original lyrics may have been composed by South Carolinian William Steffe in the late 1850s; the song became popular in the South, particularly within black churches and camp meetings. After the failed Harper's Ferry rebellion, the song acquired new words and an apt title: "John Brown's Body." This version found further popularity among abolitionists and, eventually, Union soldiers. Howe's "Battle Hymn," the last reinvention of the song, was not the writer's first foray into political, emotionally fraught poetry: her earliest volumes of poems, *Passion Flowers* (1854) and *Words for the Hour* (1857), also explore the nexus between current events and personal life.

"Battle Hymn" is by far Howe's most recognized and celebrated poem. Howe's other poetic efforts received mixed reviews during her lifetime and, save inclusion in a Civil War anthology or discussion in a scholarly paper, have faded into obscurity. "Battle Hymn," on the other hand, rapidly became a rallying cry for the Union, in part because the song insists that heavenly forces support the Northern cause. The poem remains an integral part of the American military music

Key Facts

Time Period:
Mid-20th Century

Genre:
Song

Events:
Outbreak of the American Civil War; John Brown's failed rebellion; growth of abolitionism

Nationality:
American

THE PLACE OF POETRY IN THE AMERICAN CIVIL WAR

"Battle Hymn of the Republic," the best-known poem to emerge from the American Civil War, was certainly not the only celebrated one. From Walt Whitman to John Greenleaf Whittier to hundreds of lesser-known versifiers, the war produced a wide range of candid, poignant poems that were, most importantly, actually read by the general public. Although Edmund Wilson dismissed the majority of Civil War poetry as "versified journalism," the ubiquity and significance of Civil War poetry must not be discounted.

According to Faith Barnett and Christine Miller, authors of *"Words for the Hour": A New Anthology of American Civil War Poetry,* poetry—its recitation, creation, and appreciation—was a regular part of mid-nineteenth-century daily existence. They note that "with the rise of public education in the 1830s and 1840s, the centrality of poetry to American public life was effectively codified." The explosion of newspapers and magazines that frequently featured poems also contributed to the widespread popularity of poetry in America. Revered by his nineteenth-century American contemporaries, Henry Wadsworth Longfellow transformed American histories and stories into moving, accessible poetry. Today, although mostly overshadowed by nineteenth-century writers Whitman and Emily Dickinson, Longfellow is remembered for his poems "The Song of Hiawatha" and "Paul Revere's Ride," among others.

repertoire and was notably sung at the National Cathedral memorial service, attended by President George W. Bush and other political leaders, after the September 11, 2001, terrorist attacks. The enduring relevancy of "Battle Hymn" stems from its ability to speak directly to any American conflict, not just the Civil War.

THEMES AND STYLE

In "Battle Hymn," Howe elegantly mixes biblical allusions and martial language to create a rousing call to arms. The dirgelike "John Brown's Body," fastened intently on the rebel leader's death and the hoped-for death of Confederate president Jefferson Davis, is neatly altered into a stirring marching song that celebrates the idea of rebirth. The poem boldly asserts that Christian powers (namely, God and Jesus Christ) support the Union and invites readers to see God's glory in all aspects of warfare, including "watch fires" and "dim and flaring lamps." In fact, the poem suggests that just as Christ "died to make men holy," Union soldiers should sacrifice their lives to the abolitionist cause in order to "make men free." Howe insists that Jesus supports the Union and is ready to "[sift] out the hearts of men before His judgment seat" and, presumably, find Confederates and apathetic Union citizens wanting.

Howe employs obvious rhyme and repetition, coupled with regular meter, throughout "Battle Hymn." While each line is a seemingly ponderous fifteen beats, the faster pace given the tune keeps the poem's mood optimistic and hearty. Howe affirms that she "reads" God's "righteous sentence" and "fiery Gospel" in wartime activities; such diction suggests that the writer's job is to interpret the everyday world as if it were a text for symptoms and signs of the Lord's presence. Although the author roots the poem in personal observation, "Battle Hymn" is not particularly concerned with Howe's personal life or specific experiences: inclusion of the pronoun "I" is a style modeled on the diction of gospel music and on traditional biblical rhetoric. In "Battle Hymn," "I" is used in its most encompassing sense, grouping together all Union supporters and soldiers into one united and passionate unit.

"Battle Hymn" does not acknowledge grim or darker aspects of war. Howe focuses instead on powerful images of Jesus and of Union soldiers fighting heroically, and effortlessly winning battles. In this poem victory is as quick and defiant as Jesus "crush[ing] a serpent with His heel" or "trampling out the vintage where the grapes of wrath are stored." Howe paints the Civil War as both exciting and absolutely necessary, elevating the bloody clash into a noble, even holy, endeavor. Overt biblical diction and imagery, coupled with the poem's valiant determination and positive outlook, work to create a joyous hymn, one that aims to inspire Union citizens as well as bolster their frightened or, potentially, war-weary spirits. The fourth line of each stanza (variations of "God is marching on") indicates that Americans should follow God's lead: tirelessly striding forward toward ultimate military triumph.

CRITICAL DISCUSSION

In 1862 most reviewers and Union supporters wholeheartedly embraced "Battle Hymn." In fact, many considered "Battle Hymn" to be the most influential poem to emerge from the Civil War period. The *New York Times* responded to "Battle Hymn" favorably, highlighting the poem's potential for "warming and nerving the soldier's soul like the notes of a trumpet." Likewise, the *Chicago Tribune* averred that the poem was a "choice addition" to war poetry in general. A *North American Review* critic, conversely, argued that what strengths "Battle Hymn" does have were marred by too much "recondite fancy or transcendental allusion." Nevertheless, beyond certain corners of the literary world, "Battle Hymn" was dearly loved by Northerners: Union soldiers sang "Battle Hymn" throughout the duration of conflict.

After the Civil War, "Battle Hymn" remained an essential part of American culture and a necessary piece in any retrospective of Civil War literature. The editors of *"Words for the Hour": A New Anthology of American Civil War Poetry* note that the work "catapulted Howe to national attention, bringing her a kind of celebrity enjoyed by few nineteenth-century women." The thematic content of "Battle Hymn"—"God's vengeance" and "redemptive blood," according to the editors—was not dissimilar from other war poetry of the day; yet Howe's adroit choice to yoke uplifting religious verses with the music of a gritty marching dirge makes her a unique literary figure. Today Howe is best remembered for "Battle Hymn" and her volumes of poetry, but she was also a reviewer and memoirist, admired lecturer, and political activist devoted to issues of reform.

Historians and literary scholars continue to turn to Howe's "Battle Hymn" and her other varied writings for a nuanced understanding of women's life and literature throughout the Civil War era. Recently feminist thinkers have taken an interest in Howe's work as well as her turbulent personal life. In a feminist rereading of "Battle Hymn," Jeffrey Polizzotto, for instance, claims that Howe, not Christ, is the subject or, as he puts it, the "Alpha and Omega of her own poem." While Howe's poetry has been derided by some for its overt "sentimentality," Wendy Dasler Johnson notes that Howe's poetry betrays an "artful, playful, consummate variation on poetic craft of the day." Indeed, an examination of "Battle Hymn" and Howe's other writing provides a vibrant illustration of a politically progressive and emotionally unguarded American woman in the mid-nineteenth century.

BIBLIOGRAPHY

Sources

"Atlantic for February." *Chicago Tribune* 21 Jan. 1862. *ProQuest Historical Newspapers: Chicago Tribune (1849–1988)*. Web. 26 July 2012.

Barrett, Faith, and Christine Miller. *"Words for the Hour": A New Anthology of American Civil War Poetry.* Amherst: U of Massachusetts P, 2005. Print.

Gollin, Rita K. "Hungry Heart: The Literary Emergence of Julia Ward Howe." *Resources for American Literary Study* June 2000: 234. *Project Muse.* Web. 13 July 2012.

Howard, Lori N. "Julia Ward Howe (1819–1910)." *Writers of the American Renaissance: An A-to-Z Guide.* Ed. Denise D. Knight. Westport: Greenwood Press, 2003. *Literature Resource Center.* Web. 13 July 2012.

Rev. of *Later Lyrics,* by Julia Ward Howe; *Poems,* by Elizabeth Akers; *Poems,* by Amanda T. Jones; *The Women of the Gospels: The Three Wakings, and Other Poems. North American Review* April 1867: 644. *JSTOR.* Web. 26 July 2012.

"The Magazines." *New York Times* 27 Jan. 1862. *ProQuest Historical Newspapers: The New York Times (1851–2008).* Web. 26 July 2012.

Polizzotto, Jeffrey J. "Julia Ward Howe, John Brown's Body, and the Coming of the Lord." *Worldmaking.* Ed. William Pencak. New York: Peter Lang, 1996. 185–191. *Literature Resource Center.* Web. 25 July 2012.

Stossel, Sage. "Flashbacks." *Atlantic Monthly.* 18 Sept. 2001. Web. 25 July 2012.

Further Reading

Clifford, Deborah Pickman. *Mine Eyes Have Seen the Glory: A Biography of Julia Ward Howe.* Boston: Little, Brown, 1979. Print.

Grant, Mary. *Private Woman, Public Person: An Account of the Life of Julia Ward Howe from 1819 to 1868.* Brooklyn: Carlson, 1994. Print.

Howe, Julia. *Reminiscences.* New York: New American Library, 1969. Print.

Johnson, Wendy Dasler. "Male Sentimentalists through the "I-s" of Julie Ward Howe's Poetry." *South Atlantic Review* Autumn 1999: 16–35. *Literature Resource Center.* Web.

Williams, Gary. *Hungry Heart: The Literary Emergence of Julia Ward Howe.* Amherst: U of Massachusetts P, 1999. Print.

Wilson, Edmund. *Patriotic Gore: Studies in the Literature of the American Civil War.* New York: Oxford UP, 1962. Print.

Media Adaptation

The Battle Hymn of the Republic. Dir. J. Stuart Blackton and Laurence Trimble. Perf. Ralph Ince, Maurice Costello, and Julia Swayne Gordon. Vitagraph Company of America, 1911. Film.

Claire Skinner

THE UNION VOLUNTEER.

Our Sumters walls OUR FLAG again well wave, | OUR UNION and OUR LAWS maintain we must;
And give to traitors all a bloody grave. | And treason's banner trample in the dust.

NEW YORK PUBLISHED BY CURRIER & IVES.152 NASSAU ST.

The Union Volunteer, a color lithograph published by Currier & Ives in 1861, the same year Julia Ward Howe, a Union supporter, wrote "The Battle Hymn of the Republic." THE UNION VOLUNTEER, PUB. BY CURRIER & IVES, 1861 (COLOUR LITHO), AMERICAN SCHOOL, (19TH CENTURY)/ AMERICAN ANTIQUARIAN SOCIETY, WORCESTER, MASSACHUSETTS, USA/ THE BRIDGEMAN ART LIBRARY.

A BELL FOR ADANO

John Hersey

✤ *Key Facts*

Time Period:
Mid-20th Century

Genre:
Novel

Events:
World War II; U.S.
occupation of Italy

Nationality:
American

OVERVIEW

Published in 1944, John Hersey's *A Bell for Adano* is a fictionalized account of the author's experiences as a *Time* correspondent embedded with U.S. troops in Licato, Sicily (renamed Adano in the novel), during World War II. With the exception of *Hiroshima* (1946), *A Bell for Adano* is Hersey's most widely read book, valued mostly for its insistence that the average American is good-hearted, sentimental, and uncompromisingly fair. Often categorized as a nonfiction novel, the book employs unapologetically pro-American rhetoric, fostering support for the ongoing war effort by reminding the reader that the war is a struggle against tyranny, that government is only as good as the people who govern, and that American democracy is inherently and emphatically better than fascism.

A Bell for Adano was released just six months after the last of the Sicilian war campaigns on which the novel is based, and the political climate impacted the book's reception. The work was an immediate success, selling extremely well and receiving predominantly favorable reviews. Not all critics, however, praised Hersey's first novel; some suggested that *A Bell for Adano* should be read as a tract and should not be expected to meet the criteria for a novel as well. Such criticisms as Malcolm Cowley's, though not entirely unjustified, did not diminish Hersey's instant reputation as an important novelist.

HISTORICAL AND LITERARY CONTEXT

On July 10, 1943, British, Canadian, and American forces invaded Sicily. American occupation policy in Italy contrasted sharply with the initial tenor of U.S. occupations of both Germany and Japan. American policymakers viewed Italian fascism as a philosophy imposed upon an impressionable populace, whereas Nazism and militarism were seen as reflections of the natural character of the German and Japanese peoples. Although Allied commanders expected little resistance on the Italian front, the campaign became the most costly in the Western European theater, with roughly 320,000 casualties between September 1943 and April 1945.

The almost self-righteous mindset that both informed and justified American occupation policies in Italy, though reported and commented on by such writers as John Steinbeck, was popularized most effectively in Hersey's *A Bell for Adano*. The central characters of the novel, Major Joppolo and General Marvin, are commonly thought to represent Major Frank E. Toscani and General George S. Patton, respectively. The story of a small town's bell being melted by the Italian dictator Benito Mussolini for ammunition—the bell being symbolic, as it was the only truly communal item in the town—is also reportedly true, though in the novel the town's name and inhabitants are fictionalized. Additionally, in an effort to portray American armed forces as the friendly occupiers the federal government insisted they were, Hersey left the novel devoid of any armed combat whatsoever, focusing instead on acts of diplomacy. Viewed as helping soldiers understand what they were fighting for and against, and how they should conduct themselves as occupiers, the novel was deemed "free of political taint" by military censors and approved for distribution to troops in theater.

The format of the nonfiction war novel was not unique to *A Bell for Adano* or to Hersey. Ernest Hemingway had already had great success with two such novels—*A Farewell to Arms* (1929), which deals with Hemingway's experiences during the Italian campaigns of World War I, and *For Whom the Bell Tolls* (1940), the story of a young American troop fighting with republican guerillas during the Spanish Civil War. The propagandist slant of *A Bell for Adano* was also not altogether new for Hersey. In 1942 he had published a nonfiction account of General Douglas MacArthur's Pacific campaign titled *Men on Bataan*. The text served primarily as a morale booster for the U.S. military, which had suffered setbacks at Pearl Harbor and in the Philippines. Hersey's first novel is distinct in the marriage of the two formats.

A Bell for Adano was published at the height of American propaganda during World War II. Myriad posters, pamphlets, movies, and songs were aimed at promoting American ideals of democracy and equality by attacking the national socialism and prejudice of the German, Italian, and Japanese regimes. Hersey's novel stood as a rare example of pro-American propaganda that did not attack opposing views. The novel was so intently focused on bolstering public support for both the war and the U.S. vision of spreading its particular brand of democracy that it received criticism for oversimplifying its subject matter. In some ways, more dismal nonfiction war novels, such as Norman Mailer's acclaimed *The Naked and the Dead* (1948), can be seen as revisionist responses to Hersey's war narratives. Whether approached as an iconic chronicle or an oversimplified tract, *A Bell for Adano* continues to inform and shape discussions of American war literature.

THEMES AND STYLE

The primary concern of *A Bell for Adano* is to promote American ideals and efforts in World War II, most notably the virtues of democracy over fascism. The novel frequently highlights this notion of American superiority, such as early on when a U.S. sergeant is tasked with "weed[ing] out the bad Italians" so that his leadership can "make use of the good ones." In the novel the "good" Italians almost literally sing the praises of American democracy; a town crier, for example, openly values "friendliness" over "Fascist punishments." In addition, the American soldiers and officers of the novel are often shown acting in a benevolent, almost biblically virtuous manner. Early in the book, Major Joppolo urges a group of fishers on strike to start fishing again; they hesitate because they are accustomed to fascist corruption and think that the Americans want to take all the profit. Joppolo assures them that he wants only to "line the stomachs of the people of Adano." To make his point, he yells at an old man, saying, "the people of Adano are hungry. They must have fish!"

The real persuasive power of the novel lies in its insistence that American forces are doing the Italians a favor by introducing them to democracy. Major Joppolo's negotiation with the fishermen, for instance, serves primarily as a canvas on which Hersey can paint a bleak portrait of corruption and tyranny, exposing the financial oppression and heavy taxation implemented by the fascist Italian government. Hersey's characters also market American home life to the Italian nationals they encounter. At one point Major Joppolo (an American officer with Italian roots) tells a young Adanan woman named Tina that in Italy his parents "were just poor peasants," but in America both are gainfully employed, noting that "Mother has a washing machine. Father has a car. It is very beautiful for them."

In their exchanges in the novel, both Italians and Americans affect a sentimental and reverent tone, underscoring the author's pro-American agenda. The Italian men are constantly either thanking the American troops or gradually learning to trust them; meanwhile, the Italian women swoon over them, such as when Tina and Major Joppolo dance "until they [are] both sweating in the midsummer heat." Interspersed throughout the dialogue are caricatures of the Italian accent ("I'm a can't a do nothing, a boss"; "Giuseppe's a fix for you") and

JOHN HERSEY: EMBEDDED JOURNALIST

John Hersey was born on June 17, 1914, in Tianjin, China, and initially knew of the United States only from secondhand accounts and from magazines and newspapers. After attending private schools in New York and later studying at Yale and Cambridge, Hersey set his sights on becoming a reporter for *Time* magazine. He was a natural choice to cover the Sino-Japanese War, and he served as a staff writer for *Time* from the fall of 1937 until he was assigned to the Chungking bureau in 1939. There, he began the nomadic life he would lead throughout the war.

An enthusiastic, courageous reporter, Hersey often found his life at risk as he covered the South Pacific campaigns in 1942, the Sicilian occupation in 1943, and the Eastern Front in Russia between 1944 and 1945. Twice he was on a plane that went down; once he crashed into the Pacific, nearly losing the notes he had taken on Guadalcanal. Among the stories he covered was the first account of the torpedo boat *PT-109* and its young lieutenant John F. Kennedy, a report that Kennedy would later use in his campaign for the U.S. Congress.

orations on American ideals: "Democracy is this: democracy is that the men of the government are no longer the masters of the people. They are the servants of the people."

CRITICAL DISCUSSION

When the novel first appeared, it received mixed reviews. On one hand Edward Weeks, writing in *Atlantic Monthly,* describes it as "a morality tale with oversimplified characters to make points about the battle between good and evil," ostensibly represented by democracy and fascism, respectively. However, in a review for the *New York Herald Tribune,* Virginia Sapieha praises the novel for its ability to "underscor[e] the traditional good will toward men which characterizes American occupation forces at their best." Diana Trilling, writing for *Nation,* attributes the book's success to its "folk-idealisms and popular assumptions" but feels that the speed of its composition shows, seeing "very little writing talent" in the novel. Despite critical ambivalence, *A Bell for Adano* was wildly popular and earned Hersey a Pulitzer Prize for Fiction in 1945.

Though his second novel, *Hiroshima,* is more realistic in its depictions of war and is generally more critically acclaimed, Hersey secured his legacy with the popular success of *A Bell for Adano.* In addition to being approved for distribution among troops in World War II, the book has since become required reading for staff sergeants in the U.S. Marine Corps, as the leadership styles and

occupational conduct depicted in the novel still form the basis of military leadership training models. The novel's popularity also opened doors for later propagandist war literature, most notably *To Hell and Back* (1949), the patriotic autobiography of America's most decorated World War II soldier, Audie Murphy.

Critics generally agree that Hersey's greatest strengths as a novelist come from two sources: the observational skills he developed as a journalist and his belief in the significance of individual human beings in difficult situations. For that reason Andrew Buchanan, in a 2008 article for the *Journal of Contemporary History,* calls the novel "and the Henry King movie (1945) that derived from it … the most significant cultural product related to the war in Italy." Additionally, Hersey's "nonfiction novel" format is generally thought to have heralded the rise of New Journalism, as typified early in its development by the books of Norman Mailer and Truman Capote.

BIBLIOGRAPHY

Sources

Buchanan, Andrew. "'Good Morning, Pupil!' American Representations of Italianness and the Occupation of Italy, 1943–1945." *Journal of Contemporary History* 43.2 (2008): 217–40. *Academic Search Complete.* Web. 28 June 2012.

Hersey, John. *A Bell for Adano.* New York: Modern Library, 1946. Print.

Sapieha, Virginia. "With the Americans in a Sicilian Village." Rev. of *A Bell for Adano,* by John Hersey. *New York Herald Tribune* 6 Feb. 1944: 1. Print.

Trilling, Diana. "Fiction in Review." *Nation* 158.7 (1944): 194–95. *Academic Search Complete.* Web. 24 July 2012.

Weeks, Edward. Rev. of *A Bell for Adano,* by John Hersey. *Atlantic* Apr. 1944: 127. Print.

Further Reading

Adamson, Lynda G. *Thematic Guide to the American Novel.* Westport: Greenwood, 2002. Print.

Hersey, John. *Into the Valley: A Skirmish of the Marines.* New York: Schocken Books, 1989. Print.

Geismar, Maxwell D. *American Moderns, from Rebellion to Conformity.* New York: Hill and Wang, 1958. Print.

Gemme, Francis R. *John Hersey's* A Bell for Adano, Hiroshima, *and Other Works: A Critical Commentary.* New York: Monarch, 1966. Print.

Gourse, Leslie. A Bell for Adano: *A Critical Commentary.* New York: American R. D. M., 1966. Print.

Jost, Nancy R. *A Study of the Novel* A Bell for Adano: *Tutorial Course in Comparative Literature under the Direction of Dr. Stout.* Hattiesburg: U of Southern Mississippi, 1951. Print.

Magill, Frank N. *Critical Survey of Long Fiction: English Language Series.* Englewood Cliffs: Salem, 1983. Print.

Sanders, David. *John Hersey.* New York: Twayne, 1967. Print.

Media Adaptation

A Bell for Adano. Dir. Henry King. Perf. Gene Tierney, John Hodiak, and William Bendix. Twentieth Century Fox Film Corporation, 1945. Film.

Clint Garner

THE BLINKARDS
A Comedy
Kobina Sekyi

❖ *Key Facts*

Time Period:
Early 20th Century

Genre:
Play

Events:
Growth of anticolonial effort in Africa; rise of Ghanaian independence movement

Nationality:
Ghanaian

OVERVIEW

The Blinkards: A Comedy is the only published dramatic work of Ghanaian author, philosopher, lawyer, and political theorist Kobina Sekyi. Written and first performed in 1915, the four-act play satirizes the widespread adoption of English language and customs by West Africans in the late nineteenth and early twentieth century—the height of British administration of the Gold Coast crown colony. Sekyi became critical of what he termed "Anglomania" while studying philosophy at University College, London, from 1910 to 1913, and he became an influential leader in the Ghanaian nationalist movement, penning anticolonial works of fiction and nonfiction, and joining political organizations including the Aborigines' Rights Protection Society (ARPS). *The Blinkards* is representative of Sekyi's general critique of colonialism and more importantly the African response to it.

Although *The Blinkards,* along with the rest of Sekyi's literary output, largely fell into obscurity after the author's death in 1956, the explosion of nationalist movements across the African continent in the 1960s and 1970s led to increased interest in political commentaries by African writers. *The Blinkards* was first published in England in 1974 and has since come to be recognized as an important forerunner to the patriotic African literature of the mid-1900s. As George Lang notes in *European-Language Writing in Sub-Saharan Africa* (1986), the play "introduces characters and situations that were to be intensively exploited in African drama after World War II." Furthermore, the sharp criticism of West African society offered in *The Blinkards* provides a revealing, if highly exaggerated, snapshot of the Gold Coast colony's social milieu from an insider's perspective.

HISTORICAL AND LITERARY CONTEXT

The area currently known as Ghana has been occupied by the Akan people since the eleventh century. The first European colonists arrived from Portugal in the fifteenth century, and news of the area's abundant natural resources led over the next several centuries to an influx of Dutch, French, Spanish, and British settlers, who nicknamed the region the Gold Coast. Having subdued several uprisings by the inland Akan-Asante

people, the British claimed administrative rights over the region and its resources with the Crown Lands Bill of 1896 and the Lands Bill of 1897. These bills were met with widespread outrage among the Akan people, and a group of leading intellectuals formed the Aborigines' Rights Protection Society to lobby the British government to return administrative rights to the African people. In later years, the ARPS would be extremely influential in the Ghanaian independence movement.

Sekyi, a Fante, had a number of ties to the ARPS: his maternal grandfather and his uncle both served as president of the organization, a position Sekyi himself would later hold. But he was inundated with English and Christian culture as a child, and he cultivated a love for English literature as a student at Mfantsipim Boys' School. It wasn't until a fellow student at the University of London convinced him to change his major to philosophy that Sekyi became critical of his so-called Anglomania and embraced his African heritage. When he returned to Cape Coast in 1913, Sekyi was disheartened to find that many West Africans had so fervently embraced English language and customs. In response, he set about writing a play that pilloried characters who represent the worst assimilationist tendencies.

Although such dismay at the disintegration of Akan culture in the Gold Coast colony had previously been voiced in the writings of prominent nationalist activists such as Casely Hayford and Mensah Sarbah, Sekyi's humorous and dramatized approach to the subject matter was unique. As Catherine M. Cole writes in *Africa* in 1997, "Gold Coast Africans wrote no other major scripted dramas until J. B. Danquah's *The Third Woman* (1943) and F. Kwasi Fiwaoo's *The Fifth Landing Stage* (1943)." Ironically, then, Sekyi's play falls more in line with nineteenth-century European drawing room comedies. According to critic Keir Elam, "the model seems to be [Irish playwright George Bernard] Shaw's *Pygmalion,* where hegemonic 'proper' English assimilates and corrects dialectical deviations." Indeed, Sekyi was commonly referred to as the Bernard Shaw of West Africa in the literary circles of his day.

The Blinkards appears to have had little immediate impact outside of Cape Coast. No contemporary review of the play has yet been discovered, and Sekyi remained absent from every major anthology of African literature from the era save for one, *Negro* (1934), which included an excerpt from his short story "The Anglo-Fanti." Only after the play was published in 1974 and issued as part of the Heinemann African Writers Series did it gain any critical recognition, with Asiedu Yerenkyi labeling Sekyi "the founding father of the Ghanaian theater" in an article from 1977. Today *The Blinkards* is generally regarded as Sekyi's most important work and is a telling summation of the anticolonial nationalist sentiment that would lead to Ghanaian independence in 1957, just one year after Sekyi's death.

THEMES AND STYLE

Although *The Blinkards* certainly attacks the uncritical acceptance of British religious, governmental, and social values by West Africans, it does not propose a wholesale rejection of Western culture. Cole notes that Sekyi "advocated modernization with a critical, African-centered difference: a deliberate consideration of what was useful and detrimental about ideas and practices adopted from abroad, and a circumspect integration of those ideas with local Fante culture." This distinction is embodied in the play by the character of Mr. Onyimdzi, a European-educated Fante lawyer who has an appreciation for some aspects of British culture (he wears European clothing while in court, speaks fluent English, and drinks European whisky) but also retains a significant amount of pride in his African heritage (he wears traditional African clothing when not working, cites Akan proverbs from memory, and prefers West African foods). In the end, Mr. Onyimdzi, by winning a legal battle to keep a young woman from being incarcerated under the Marriage Ordinance of 1884, shows how a selective appropriation of the colonizers' ways can lead to the destruction of the colonial system from within.

This hybrid approach to nationalism is apparent in the published form of *The Blinkards* as well. The even-numbered pages feature an English-language version of the play, whereas the odd-numbered pages feature the same text in Fante. However, the English version is not exclusively in English, and the Fante side is not exclusively in Fante; both versions contain untranslated phrases that underscore how English ideology pervades Fante society and how Fante culture can survive—and even thrive—under such an influx of outside ideas. Ayo Langley in the introduction to the 1974 edition comments on this technique in his introduction to the play, noting that "the telling Fante proverbs and allusions do much to enrich and enliven the play, as well as drive home the author's moral point of view."

The tone of the play is somewhat over the top, exhibiting what Stephanie Newell in *Literary Culture in Colonial Ghana: "How to Play the Game of Life"* (2002) calls Sekyi's "excessive style," wherein each character

THE ABORIGINES' RIGHTS PROTECTION SOCIETY AND GHANAIAN INDEPENDENCE

Formed in 1897, the Aborigines' Rights Protection Society (ARPS) was an organization of highly educated West African intellectuals, lawyers, and businessmen that sought, like Mr. Onyimdzi in *The Blinkards,* to foster Ghanaian nationalism from within the colonial structure. Rather than advocating for violent revolution, the ARPS petitioned the British government for reforms, often using British law as the framework for its arguments. A prominent example of this technique occurred in 1898 when a delegation including the first ARPS president, J. W. Sey, and founding members T. F. E. Jones and George Hughes, traveled to London and successfully argued for the dismissal of the 1897 Lands Bill, which would have severely limited access to public lands and resources.

Sekyi became a strong supporter of the ARPS and its methods in the 1910s, and was admitted to its executive council in 1921. He was an influential leader in the ultimately unsuccessful fight against tax measures proposed in the early 1930s and was named president of the ARPS in 1946. By this time, however, the ARPS was beginning to give way to the more radical National Congress of British West Africa. Sekyi would prove to be the last president of the ARPS. However, as one of the first nationalist groups in Africa, the importance of the ARPS cannot be understated.

(except perhaps for the exemplary Mr. Onyimdzi) becomes an absurd caricature of the anglicized African. Mrs. Borofosem, for example, makes ridiculous claims such as, "We have gone to England: so we must do English things." Her husband is pummeled into accepting a European lifestyle first by his parents who, he says, "would have bleached my skin, if they could," and now by his relentless wife. He laments the fact that "I, a Fanti, should be able to express my thoughts better in English," and eventually dismisses the charade as "all this showy tomfoolery." Even members of the Cosmopolitan Club, an elite social and literary group, endorse such "showiness" in their agreement that "without tailors and hatters and shoemakers, gentlemen, we are nothing." This statement highlights the overarching concern of Sekyi's literary and political writings that, according to Langley, "what [West Africans] exalted as hallmarks of civilization were merely refinements of the superficial and the artificial."

CRITICAL DISCUSSION

Because there is little record of the play having been performed or of its reception in the early twentieth century, it is difficult to gauge the immediate impact of *The Blinkards.* Sekyi went on to have a lengthy and influential career as a journalist, poet, and political theorist, but most of his manuscripts went undiscovered

by readers outside of Ghana until the 1970s, when historicists began to catalog Ghana's National Archives. Upon the publication of *The Blinkards,* critic Robert L. Berner in a 1975 review for *Books Abroad* called it "a basic document for the student of African nationalism," and critics around the world began to take interest in Sekyi's literary catalog. The play also entered into the repertoire of dramatic groups around West Africa during this period.

The first major survey of Sekyi's works appeared in 1991 with Kofi Baku's *Kobina Sekyi of Ghana: An Annotated Bibliography of His Writings.* Since then, *The Blinkards* has been included in most studies of West African colonial literature, with the prevailing conclusions aligning with Cole's assessment of the play as "an astonishingly prescient analysis of what modernization and civilization could mean for Africa." The play seems to have provided a road map for the integration of certain beneficial elements of British culture into the national character while foreshadowing the renaissance of Akan language and culture in Ghana, which has led to its recognition as Sekyi's most significant work.

Critical approaches to *The Blinkards* are varied. Some scholars focus on Sekyi's use of language in the play, particularly the way in which he manipulates English words to underscore the way they alter and are altered by the experience of West Africans under colonial rule. Others focus on the depiction of social issues,

discussing Sekyi's treatment of women, his suggestions for the future of education in Ghana, or the importance of clothing and appearance as signifiers of social status. By far, though, the most prevalent approach to *The Blinkards* is to read it as a nascent indication of the nationalism that would spur the various liberation movements that radically altered the political landscape in Africa in the mid-twentieth century, lending credence to those who argue for Sekyi's inclusion among the heroes of Ghanaian independence.

BIBLIOGRAPHY

Sources

Berner, Robert L. Rev of *The Blinkards,* by Kobina Sekyi. *Books Abroad* 49.2 (1975): 380. Print.

Cole, Catherine M. "'This Is Actually a Good Interpretation of Modern Civilisation': Popular Theatre and the Social Imaginary in Ghana, 1946–66." *Africa* 67.3 (1997): 363–88. Print.

Elam, Keir. "Tempo's Sickle: Rapping, Zapping, Toasting, and Trekking through History in Black British Drama." *Yearbook of English Studies* 25 (1995): 173–98. Print.

Lang, George. "Ghana and Nigeria." *European-Language Writing in Sub-Saharan Africa.* Vol. 1. Ed. Albert S. Gerard. Budapest: Akadémiai Kiadó, 1986. Print. 108–15. Print

Langley, Ayo J. Introduction. *The Blinkards: A Comedy and The Anglo-Fanti,* by Kobina Sekyi. London: Heinemann Educational, 1974. xiii–xxix. Print.

Newell, Stephanie. "'Been Tos' and 'Never-Beens': Kobina Sekyi's Satires of Fante Society." *Literary Culture in Colonial Ghana: "How to Play the Game of Life."* Bloomington: Indiana UP, 2002. 157–82. Print.

Further Reading

Asante, S. K. B. "The Politics of Confrontation: The Case of Kobina Sekyi and the Colonial System in Ghana." *Universitas* 6.2 (1977): 15–38. Print.

Baku, Kofi. *Kobina Sekyi of Ghana: An Annotated Bibliography of His Writings.* Boston: African Studies Center, Boston U, 1991. Print.

Banham, Martin, James Gibbs, and Femi Osofisan. *African Theatre 9: Histories 1850–1950.* Woodbridge: Boydell & Brewer, 2010. Web. 12 Nov. 2012.

Okonkwo, Rina. "Proposals for the Preservation of African Culture: The Philosophy of Kobina Sekyi."

Agbada to Khaki: Reporting a Change of Government in Nigeria. Ed. Lindsay Barrett. Enugu: Fourth Dimension, 1985. 258–65. Print.

Osei-Nyame, Kwadwo. "Pan-Africanist Ideology and the African Historical Novel of Self-Discovery: The Examples of Kobina Sekyi and J. E. Casely Hayford." *Journal of African Cultural Studies* 12.2 (1999): 137–53. Print.

Saint-André Utudjian, Eliane. "Uses and Misuses of English in *The Blinkards* by Kobina Sekyi." *Commonwealth Essays and Studies* 20.1 (1997): 23–31. Print.

Yerenkyi, Asiedu. "Kobina Sekyi: The Founding Father of the Ghanaian Theatre." *Legacy* 3.2 (1977): 39–47. Print.

Jacob Schmitt

"THE BRITISH PRISON SHIP"

Philip Morin Freneau

✥ *Key Facts*

Time Period:
Late 18th Century

Genre:
Poetry

Events:
Revolutionary War;
British capture of the U.S.
ship *Aurora*

Nationality:
American

OVERVIEW

First published as a pamphlet in 1781, Philip Morin Freneau's "The British Prison Ship" is a polemical poem that denounces the British for their treatment of American prisoners. In heroic couplets, the poem narrates the capture of the *Aurora,* an American privateer bound for St. Eustacia in May 1780, and the subsequent imprisonment of its crew aboard British prison ships off the coast of New York. Describing the wretched conditions aboard the prison ships, the poem portrays the British as cruel and inhumane. Freneau published four different versions of the poem (in 1781, 1786, 1795, and 1809), but the 1786 version has been the most commonly anthologized. In three cantos, the 1786 version narrates the *Aurora*'s defeat in battle, the crew's confinement aboard the *Scorpion,* and the poet's transfer to the hospital ship, the *Hunter.* Freneau's poem "The British Prison Ship" served as propaganda for the American Revolution through its denunciation of British tyranny and demand for revenge.

Although Freneau had written poems in support of the American Revolution since 1774, he felt little personal stake in the war until enduring two months of captivity in 1780. For this reason, "The British Prison Ship" is unique among Freneau's political poems in both the depth of its rage and the intensely personal nature of its denunciation of the British. Originally published as a broadside, the poem was reportedly popular among American soldiers. Later it was published in *The Poems of Philip Freneau* (1786), which attracted the support of hundreds of subscribers. Today "The British Prison Ship" is known for reinforcing Freneau's literary reputation as an important poet of the Revolutionary War.

HISTORICAL AND LITERARY CONTEXT

When the Revolutionary War began, the American colonies had very few military ships with which to confront the vastly superior British navy. To disrupt British supply lines, the Continental Congress authorized private American ship owners, or privateers, to harass and plunder ships engaged in trade with Britain. Risking capture by British warships for the chance to gain immense profits, privateers served as the de facto American navy and succeeded in disrupting British shipping. On May 25, 1780, Freneau sailed from Philadelphia aboard one of these privateers, the *Aurora.* While the primary purpose of its voyage was to sell a cargo of tobacco in St. Eustacia, the *Aurora* also took advantage of opportunities to seize commercial British ships. In fact, the *Aurora*'s capture of a small ship in the Delaware Bay and confiscation of its cargo of corn probably led to its own capture by the British the following day.

During the Revolutionary War, prisoners of war faced an uncertain fate. As "The British Prison Ship" reveals, many American prisoners of war sickened and died onboard British prison ships as a result of filthy living conditions, inadequate or rotten food, and scant medical care. In contrast, most British prisoners were treated relatively well by their American captors, although some were held in city jails or abandoned mine shafts. Freneau's poem works as propaganda not only by dramatizing the suffering of American prisoners but also by attributing the British soldiers' high-handed treatment of prisoners to their support for a monarch's unlimited authority.

American poetry during the Revolutionary War was written in a neoclassical style that emphasized reason, civic virtue, and order. With its heroic couplets and classical allusions, Freneau's "The British Prison Ships" closely follows this neoclassical model. In its style, Freneau's poetry bears comparison with the work of poet Jonathan Odell, a fellow Princeton University alumnus who supported the British cause. Although on opposite sides of the conflict, the revolutionary Freneau and the loyalist Odell tended to employ a similar range of allusion and penchant for satire.

"The British Prison Ship" and similar poems endowed Freneau with his ephemeral fame as "the Poet of the American Revolution" and granted him opportunities as a newspaper editor. However, after his newspapers failed, he quickly fell into obscurity and was largely forgotten at the time of his death in 1832. As a result, his poetry had little subsequent literary influence. Nevertheless, his nature poems seem to anticipate the early poetry of William Cullen Bryant, although Bryant was unaware of Freneau's poetry when composing "Thanatopsis." Although Freneau's influence on other poets has been minimal, scholars continue to study his poetry and journalism for what it reveals about the art, politics, and culture of the Revolutionary era.

PRIMARY SOURCE

EXCERPT FROM "THE BRITISH PRISON SHIP," CANTO II

The various horrors of these hulks to tell,

These Prison Ships where pain and penance dwell,

Where death in tenfold vengeance holds his reign,

And injur'd ghosts, yet unaveng'd, complain;

This be my task—ungenerous Britons, you

Conspire to murder whom you can't subdue.—

That Britain's rage should dye our plains with gore,

And desolation spread through every shore,

None e'er could doubt, that her ambition
knew,—

This was to rage and disappointment due;

But that those legions whom our soil maintain'd,

Who first drew breath in this devoted land,

Like famish'd wolves, should on their country prey,

Assist its foes, and wrest our lives away,

This shocks belief—and bids our soil disown

Such knaves, subservient to a bankrupt throne.

By them the widow mourns her partner dead,

Her mangled sons to darksome prisons led,

By them—and hence my keenest sorrows rise,

My friend—companion—my *Orestes* dies

Still for that loss must wretched I complain,

And sad *Ophelia* mourn her loss—in vain!

Ah! come the day when from this bleeding
shore

Fate shall remove them, to return no more—

To scorch'd Bahama shall the traitors go

With grief, and rage, and unremitting woe,

On burning sands to walk their painful round,

And sigh through all the solitary ground,

Where no gay flower their haggard eyes
shall see,

And find no shade—but from the cypress tree.

So much we suffer'd from the tribe I hate,

So near they shov'd us to the brink of fate,

When two long months in these dark hulks we lay

Barr'd down by night, and fainting all the day

In the fierce fervours of the solar beam,

Cool'd by no breeze on Hudson's
mountain-stream;

That not unsung these threescore days shall fall

To black oblivion that would cover all!—

No masts or sails these crowded ships adorn,

Dismal to view, neglected and forlorn;

Here, mighty ills oppress'd the imprison'd
throng,

Dull were our slumbers, and our nights were
long—

From morn to eve along the decks we lay

Scorch'd into fevers by the solar ray;

No friendly *awning* cast a welcome shade,

Once was it promis'd, and was never made;

No favours could these sons of death bestow,

'Twas endless vengeance, and unceasing woe:

Immortal hatred does their breasts engage,

And this lost empire swells their souls with rage.

Two hulks on Hudson's stormy bosom lie,

Two, on the east, alarm the pitying eye—

There, the black SCORPION at her mooring
rides,

There, STROMBOLO swings, yielding to
the tides;

Here, bulky JERSEY fills a larger space,

And HUNTER, to all hospitals disgrace—

Thou, SCORPION, fatal to thy crowded throng,

Dire theme of horror and Plutonian song,

Requir'st my lay—thy sultry decks I know,

And all the torments that exist below!

The briny wave that Hudson's bosom fills

Drain'd through her bottom in a thousand rills:

Rotten and old, replete with sighs and groans,

Scarce on the waters she sustain'd her bones;

Here, doom'd to toil, or founder in the tide,

At the moist pumps incessantly we ply'd,

Here, doom'd to starve, like famish'd dogs, we tore

The scant allowance, that our tyrants bore.

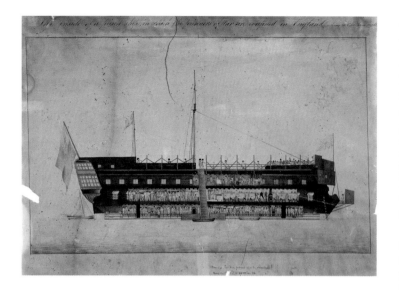

THEMES AND STYLE

The main theme of "The British Prison Ship" is British cruelty to American captives. Recounting the voyage of the *Aurora*, its capture off the coast of New Jersey, and the American crew's imprisonment on British prison ships, Freneau catalogs the prisoners' suffering and characterizes the British as heartless and tyrannical. Aboard the *Scorpion*, the American captives endure "[h]unger and thirst … / And mouldy bread, and flesh of rotten swine, / The mangled carcase, and the batter'd brain, / The doctor's poison, and the captain's cane, / The soldier's musket, and the steward's debt, / The evening shackle, and the noon-day threat." As the catalog makes clear, the British crew only compounds the prisoners' suffering. Freneau declares of the British guards, "On their dark souls compassion has no claim." Similarly, in portraits of the first mate and captain of the hospital ship, the *Hunter*, Freneau emphasizes their violent contempt for Americans. For example, the mate curses those "who dar'd his king disown, / And swore mankind were made for *George* alone." Equally tyrannical in his hatred of the American revolutionary cause, the captain addresses the captives as "rebel dogs" and asserts that they do not deserve better treatment. By tracing the British crew's inhumane treatment of American prisoners to their belief in monarchy, Freneau creates effective propaganda for the evils of British rule.

Throughout "The British Prison Ship," Freneau's main rhetorical strategy is to portray the British as evil through imagery of hell and damnation. For example, the *Iris*, the British frigate that captures the *Aurora*, is described as "[w]ing'd on by hell." The British aboard the *Scorpion* have been "[l]ed on by hell to take the royal side," and the captain of the *Hunter* resembles "Satan in a brimstone blast." As these examples suggest, the poem's imagery of hell intensifies with each successive canto. Each British ship condemns the American crew to a deeper level of hellish experience.

Although the *Iris* inflicts destruction and death, the *Aurora*'s crew quickly learns that "[d]eath was better than the prisoner's fate." Crammed below deck on the *Scorpion* to "pass the infernal night" in stifling heat and filthy conditions, the captives experience a form of hell on earth. Yet, when transferred to the *Hunter*, where malnourished and diseased American prisoners die through abuse and neglect, Freneau discovers a deeper level of suffering: "If [the *Scorpion*] was purgatory, this is hell." The poem's imagery of hell works as propaganda because it suggests that the British crew's treatment of American prisoners is not caused by ignorance or incompetence but by pure malevolence.

The language of "The British Prison Ship" is strident; its emotional outlook is violent and impassioned. Repeatedly, Freneau accuses the British of murdering thousands of Americans and of hoping to murder more: "[U]ngenerous Britons, you / Conspire to murder those you can't subdue." "Flush'd with the blood of thousands," the British "pant to stain the world with gore, / And millions murder'd, still would murder more." In similarly violent language, Freneau urges Americans to "glut revenge on this detested foe" by ridding themselves of all British soldiers and sympathizers: "Defeat, destroy, and sweep them from the land."

CRITICAL DISCUSSION

As the principal poem that established Freneau's reputation as "the Poet of the American Revolution," "The British Prison Ship" gained a measure of popularity with American audiences as a 1781 broadside and as part of a volume of poems in 1786. Described by modern critics as one of the greatest indictments of England of the time, the poem became popular for its unremitting bitterness and contempt for the British—common sentiments after the war's devastation. However, as hostility toward the British faded over the next two decades, Freneau's poem was gradually forgotten. He later revised the poem (in 1795 and in 1809) to tone down its hostile treatment of the British. But despite these changes, the work continued to fade from the public mind. His final volume of poetry was virtually ignored by readers and critics, and after his death in 1832, according to Lawrence J. Trudeau in *Nineteenth-Century Literature Criticism* (2012), his poems "remained relatively obscure for almost a century."

"The British Prison Ship" has been regarded as an expression of Freneau's resistance to tyranny and his commitment to human liberty. The poem's openly partisan allegiance and denunciatory style has been linked not only to Freneau's other poems of the Revolutionary War, but also to his anti-Federalist newspaper articles in the following decade. In other respects, "The British Prison Ship" is an uncharacteristic poem for Freneau. For example, his poems written in Santa Cruz, West Indies, during the early years of the revolution (from 1776 to 1778) are marked by a focus on nature and introspection rather than on public, didactic, or political themes. Critical interest in Freneau's poetry has focused on this divided legacy, which renders him a preeminent example of the conflicting tendencies in early American poetry.

Rediscovered by Fred Lewis Pattee and Henry Hayden Clark, Freneau enjoyed a resurgence of scholarship in the early twentieth century. Beginning in the 1930s, biographies and critical studies of Freneau's literary influences appeared. These studies examined the poet's literary style and revolutionary politics. However, since the 1960s, studies of Freneau have tended to focus less on his Revolutionary War poetry than on his poems dealing with themes of nature and religion. Scholars continue to debate whether his poems are Romantic or neoclassical. In the past half century, scholars of military history and American culture have written on Freneau's "The British Prison Ship," but few literary studies of the poem have appeared.

BIBLIOGRAPHY

Sources

Axelrad, Jacob. *Philip Freneau: Champion of Democracy.* Austin: U of Texas P, 1967. Print.

Bercovitch, Sacvan, and Cyrus R. K. Patell, eds. *The Cambridge History of American Literature.* Vol. 1. Cambridge: Cambridge UP, 1994. Print.

Clark, Henry Hayden. Introduction. *Poems of Freneau.* New York: Hafner, 1929. Print.

Marsh, Philip M. *Philip Freneau: Poet and Journalist.* Minneapolis: Dillon, 1967. Print.

Patton, Robert H. *Patriot Pirates: The Privateer War for Freedom and Fortune in the American Revolution.* New York: Pantheon Books, 2008. Print.

Springer, Paul J. *America's Captives: Treatment of POWs from the Revolutionary War to the War on Terror.* Lawrence: UP of Kansas, 2010. Print.

Trudeau, Lawrence J., ed. "Philip Morin Freneau." *Nineteenth-Century Literature Criticism.* Detroit: Gale, 2012. 1–100. *Dictionary of Literary Biography.* Web. 12 Oct. 2012.

Further Reading

Bowden, Mary Weatherspoon. "In Search of Freneau's Prison Ships." *Early American Literature* 14.2 (1979): 174–92. Web. 12 Oct. 2012.

Cray, Robert E., Jr. "The 'Horrors of these Hulks.'" *Naval History* 20.1 (2006): 42–47. Web. 12 Oct. 2012.

Freneau, Philip. *Poems Written and Published during the American Revolutionary War: A Facsimile Reproduction.* Ed. Lewis Leary. Delmar: Scholars' Facsimiles & Reprints, 1976. Print.

Leary, Lewis. *That Rascal Freneau: A Study in Literary Failure.* New Brunswick: Rutgers UP, 1941. Print.

Ranlet, Philip. "In the Hands of the British: The Treatment of American POWs during the War of Independence." *Historian* 62.4 (2000): 731–58. Web. 12 Oct. 2012.

Vitzthum, Richard C. *Land and Sea: The Lyric Poetry of Philip Freneau.* Minneapolis: U of Minnesota P, 1978. Print.

Kevin Cooney

CARTA DE JAMAICA

Simón Bolívar

+ *Key Facts*

Time Period:
Early 19th Century

Genre:
Letter

Events:
Latin American
independence movement

Nationality:
Venezuelan

OVERVIEW

Venezuelan leader Simón Bolívar wrote the *Carta de Jamaica* (Jamaica Letter) during his exile in Kingston, Jamaica, on September 6, 1815, in response to a letter from Henry Cullen, a British resident of the island. In it Bolívar expounds on the history of the Latin American struggle for independence from Spain and provides a justification for the colonists' desire for autonomy. Written in a formal and deferential yet passionate tone, the *Carta de Jamaica* analyzes the past experiences, present situation, and future prospects of Latin America and looks to Europe for support and collaboration in the Latin American struggle for independence. Bolívar achieves a strong and well-reasoned condemnation of Spain's historic subordination and mistreatment of the peoples of Latin America, which contributes to a persuasive document that publicized the cause of Latin American independence.

The *Carta de Jamaica* was initially published in English, appearing in the July 1818 *Jamaica Quarterly Journal and Literary Gazette* under the title "Letter to a Friend, on the Subject of South American Independence." It was received favorably by a large sector of the British colonial population, to whom it was clearly directed, and initiated a political and intellectual dialogue between Bolívar and the British colonists and authorities, although the relationship did not emerge overnight. The letter reflects Bolívar's reformulation of his original approach to Latin American independence; no longer confident in the ability of the Latin American masses to make what he considered the correct decisions for themselves, he advocated for the creation of an independent government without relying on an electorally democratic system. The *Carta de Jamaica* is now considered a foundational document in Latin American politics.

HISTORICAL AND LITERARY CONTEXT

In 1813 aspiring Venezuelan political and military leader Simón Bolívar initiated what became known as the Admirable Campaign, an attempt to reestablish the independent Venezuelan republic overthrown by Spain in 1811. The campaign was ultimately a failure, with Bolívar's troops falling to the Spanish military under José Tomás Boves in 1814. In 1815 Spain sent an army to subdue its most rebellious Latin American

colonies, and by 1816 Spain had resumed control over both Venezuela and New Granada.

Bolívar went into exile in Kingston, Jamaica, in May of 1815 hoping to obtain British support for Latin America's cause. He was only 32 when he arrived in Jamaica, still a relatively young and inexperienced leader who had been at the forefront of the independence struggle since the 1812 publication of his *Cartagena Manifesto*. Although he lived on the British island only from May to December 1815, his stay was pivotal in the evolution of his political ideology and understanding of world politics. With the power of the Spanish monarchy renewed, Bolívar saw that any new form of opposition would have to take a different approach in order to gain the support of the creole majority, who feared being linked to treasonous activities. Leaders of the Latin American radical minority, including Bolívar and José de San Martín, turned away from outright republicanism, favoring a more conservative path to independence that would appeal to the primarily upper-class creole population.

The *Carta de Jamaica* reflects the ideology of the early nineteenth-century Latin American independence movement and follows Bolívar's 1812 *Cartagena Manifesto,* which calls for the liberation of all Latin American countries from Spanish rule. His 1815 letter was an effort to establish a literary alliance between Britain and Latin America, in the tradition of publications such as *El Español, Variedades,* and the *New Monthly Magazine.* Bolívar's writing also draws on the work of earlier anticolonial thinkers, including Abbe Guillaume Thomas Raynal's *Philosophical and Political History of the Settlements and Trade of the Europeans in the East and West Indies* (1770) and Montesquieu's "On the Spirit of Laws" (1748).

Bolívar's 1815 letter influenced his own later writings, including his well-known Angostura Address (1819), and had a lasting impact on the literature of Latin American independence. Bolívar's increasingly totalitarian approach to political leadership was particularly prevalent in the Bolivian constitution, which he wrote in 1826. His work had a significant impact on the political writing that emerged during the nineteenth-century struggle for Latin American independence, notably the *Declaration of Independence of the United Provinces of South America* (1816) and the 1833 Chilean constitution. Cuban revolutionary José

Martí's *Manifiesto de Montecristi* (1895) and his essay *Nuestra América* (1891), a call for Pan-Latin American unity, both reflect the influence of Bolívar's *Carta de Jamaica*. Today it is regarded as a foundational work reflective of Bolívar's thinking, and it is regularly taught and studied in the sphere of Latin American history, literature, and culture.

THEMES AND STYLE

Bolívar's *Carta de Jamaica* presents a narrative of colonial oppression in the form of a reply to a letter he received from Henry Cullen, a local businessman. By giving voice to the injustices suffered by the Latin American peoples under Spanish rule, Bolívar appeals to the British population for support and understanding. He proclaims, "At present … we are threatened with the fear of death, dishonor, and every harm; there is nothing we have not suffered at the hands of that unnatural stepmother—Spain," emphasizing the immediate threat the colonists feel from Spain to communicate the urgency of their struggle and exploit the political tensions between Spain and Britain.

As Joselyn Almeida notes in "London-Kingston-Caracas: The Transatlantic Self-Fashioning of Simón Bolívar," in *Carta de Jamaica* Bolívar "uses the language of abolition as a critique of empire to gain sympathy for the Latin American cause." Bolívar directly associates the situation of Latin American colonists with the condition of slaves, writing from a first-person perspective that personalizes his message: "We are still in a position lower than slavery, and therefore it is more difficult for us to rise to the enjoyment of freedom … [A people is] enslaved when the government, by its nature or its vices, infringes on and usurps the rights of the citizen or subject." Bolívar, however, is also careful to address the seemingly contradictory British anxiety about slave uprisings in Venezuela, as he was well aware that his British audiences in Kingston shared these concerns: "The soul of a serf can seldom really appreciate true freedom. Either he loses his head in uprisings or his self-respect in chains." British financiers who profited from slavery would have appreciated the antiabolitionist perspective the author presented in the *Carta de Jamaica*.

Bolívar's letter is formulated as a dialogue, restating the questions posed to him by Cullen and then answering them. This approach allows Bolívar to present himself as Cullen's ally and is reinforced by the friendly and humble tone Bolívar adopts and the respectful formality of his letter. He begins deferentially: "I find myself in conflict between the desire to reciprocate your confidence, which honors me, and the difficulty of rewarding it, for lack of documents and books and because of my own limited knowledge of a land so vast, so varied, and so little known as the New World." Bolívar goes on, however, to cite numerous contemporary thinkers, legitimizing Bolívar's knowledge and understanding of world politics in the eyes of his British audience. "It is harder, Montesquieu has written, to release a nation

SIMÓN BOLÍVAR: THE DEMISE OF THE LIBERATOR OF LATIN AMERICA

Simón José Antonio de la Santísima Trinidad Bolívar y Palacios, commonly known as Simón Bolívar, was a Venezuelan military and political leader who is generally regarded as a hero by Latin Americans. In his later political career, however, his political vision transformed dramatically and shifted from advocating for civic rights to a more conservative, totalitarian stance on governing. Bolívar played a pivotal role in the independence of New Granada from Spain, which was achieved under his military command in 1819. Bolívar was also central in the establishment of Gran Colombia in 1821, which was the first union of independent nations in the region. Nevertheless, by the time he published the *Carta de Jamaica* in 1815 during his exile in Jamaica, Bolívar's political leanings had already taken a turn toward authoritarianism.

Bolivar served as president of Gran Colombia beginning in 1819 but his policies and governance became progressively more repressive. By 1828 Bolívar was ruling the region as a full-fledged dictator until he resigned in early 1830. Bolívar died on December 17, 1830, and while the official cause of death was tuberculosis, conspiracy theories have long circulated asserting that the leader was murdered. In recent years, Venezuelan president Hugo Chávez renewed this debate by exhuming Bolívar's body and attempting to prove that he was actually poisoned with arsenic. Chávez's decision to support and publicize this theory can be interpreted as the contemporary politician's attempt to further align himself with Bolívar and his anticolonial, anti-U.S. politics.

from servitude than to enslave a free nation. … South Americans have made efforts to obtain liberal, even perfect, institutions, doubtless out of that instinct to aspire to the greatest possible happiness."

CRITICAL DISCUSSION

The *Carta de Jamaica* did not win Bolívar the immediate support of the British colonists in Kingston as he had hoped, and by the time he received signs of British support from Jamaica he had already moved on to make an appeal to Haiti. The *Carta de Jamaica* was not widely read until its publication in the *Jamaica Quarterly Journal and Literary Gazette* in July 1818 and there was little contemporary literary reaction. However, certain political debates related to Bolívar and his Latin American cause did emerge in the Kingston *Royal Gazette* during his stay on the island, and British colonists did ultimately support Bolívar during his wars for independence, with nearly seven thousand British volunteers, known as the British Legion, fighting with his army beginning in 1819. By the end of the 1820s Bolívar was widely regarded as the liberator of Latin America, and his *Carta de Jamaica* became one of his best-known writings.

Popular imagery from Venezuela extolling Simón Bolívar, c. 1840. *POPULAR IMAGERY EXTOLLING BOLIVAR, C.1840 (COLOUR LITHO), VENEZUELAN SCHOOL (19TH CENTURY)/ BIBLIOTHEQUE NATIONALE, PARIS, FRANCE/ ARCHIVES CHARMET/THE BRIDGEMAN ART LIBRARY.*

The *Carta de Jamaica* directly influenced the writing of later revolutionaries and political leaders including José Martí, Che Guevara, Fidel Castro, and more recently, Hugo Chávez. During Bolívar's lifetime the letter influenced the thinking of such Latin American revolutionaries as Argentinian José de San Martín and Chilean Bernardo O'Higgins. Bolívar's influence is also apparent in scholarly dialogues published throughout the independence era in periodicals such as *New Monthly Magazine* and *Variedades*. By 1833 Bolívar's achievements had inspired Francisco Javier Yanes and Cristóbal Mendoza's publication of the *Colección de documentos relativos a la vida publica del Libertador,* reprinting documents by and about Bolívar that included the first publication in Spanish of the *Carta de Jamaica.*

The *Carta de Jamaica* has frequently been discussed by scholars in relation to Bolívar's engagement with Enlightenment thinking. As John Lynch notes in

his 2006 *Simón Bolívar: A Life,* "In the *Jamaica Letter* [Bolívar] used Montesquieu's concept of oriental despotism to define the Spanish empire, and his entire political thought was imbued with the conviction that theory should follow reality.... But even Montesquieu did not go all the way that Bolívar wanted." Other scholars, including Joselyn Almeida, have examined the transatlantic nature of the *Carta de Jamaica.* In her 2006 "London-Kingston-Caracas: The Transatlantic Self-Fashioning of Simón Bolívar," Almeida states, "A transatlantic reading of Simón Bolívar's 'Carta de Jamaica' ('Jamaica Letter') … shows that he draws on the discursive connection between abolition and independence that Mill and others had made familiar to the British public in order to make his case for continued British support of the Latin American enterprise."

BIBLIOGRAPHY

Sources

Almeida, Joselyn M. "London-Kingston-Caracas: The Transatlantic Self-Fashioning of Simón Bolívar." *Sullen Fires across the Atlantic: Essays in Transatlantic Romanticism.* Eds. Lance Newman, Chris Koenig-Woodyard, and Joel Pace. College Park: U. of Maryland, 2006. Web. 12 Aug. 2012.

Bolívar, Simón. "Reply of a South American to a Gentleman of This Island." Trans. Lewis Bertrand. *Selected Writings of Bolívar.* New York: Colonial, 1951.

Langley, Lester D. *Simón Bolívar: Venezuelan Rebel, American Revolutionary.* Lanham: Rowman & Littlefield, 2009. Print.

Lynch, John. *Simón Bolívar: A Life.* New Haven: Yale UP, 2006. Print.

Further Reading

Bushnell, David. *Simón Bolívar: Liberation and Disappointment.* New York: Pearson Longman, 2004. Print.

Costeloe, Michael P. *Response to Revolution: Imperial Spain and the Spanish American Revolutions, 1810–1840.* New York: Cambridge UP, 1986. Print.

Cussen, Antonio. *Bello and Bolívar: Poetry and Politics in the Spanish American Revolution.* New York: Cambridge UP, 1992. Print.

Davies, Catherine. "Colonial Dependence and Sexual Difference: Reading for Gender in the Writings of Simón Bolívar (1783–1830). *Feminist Review* 79 (2005): 5–19. Print.

Lynch, John. "Bolívar and the Caudillos." *Hispanic American Historical Review* 63.1 (1983): 3–35. Print.

———. *Simón Bolívar and the Age of Revolution.* London: U. of London Institute of Latin American Studies, 1983. Print.

Katrina White

THE CHRYSANTHEMUM AND THE SWORD
Patterns of Japanese Culture
Ruth Benedict

OVERVIEW

The Chrysanthemum and the Sword: Patterns of Japanese Culture, a book by Ruth Benedict published in 1946, is an anthropological study of Japanese society. The text is an adaptation of a study Benedict wrote while working for a government intelligence and propaganda unit during World War II. Through a psychological lens, Benedict examines the central themes in Japanese culture, the duality of the Japanese personality, and the hierarchy imbedded in the society. Scholars often emphasize the author's distinction between the Japanese shame culture and the Western guilt culture. Benedict wrote *Chrysanthemum,* which was published during the occupation and reconstruction of Japan, to persuade American readers and policymakers to think of the Japanese as having a different culture, not as racially different. She hoped for a world in which the United States could "be American to the hilt without threatening the peace of the world.... France may be France, and Japan may be Japan on the same conditions."

Upon its publication, *The Chrysanthemum and the Sword* was widely read and initially well received. Although the book has been frequently criticized since then, many scholars regard the work as Benedict's crowning achievement in her study of national cultures. *Chrysanthemum* continues to be referenced in works concerning Japan and has become the standard against which other studies of national cultures are measured. Not only did the book help popularize anthropology in the public sphere, but it also influenced American public opinion about the Japanese during the occupation of Japan and helped shape U.S. policies concerning postwar Japan. Translated into Japanese in 1947, *The Chrysanthemum and the Sword* was admirably received in Japan and sparked a debate regarding the manner in which the Japanese viewed themselves; the work continues to be discussed in modern Japanese universities and textbooks.

HISTORICAL AND LITERARY CONTEXT

More than two years into World War II, the United States joined the conflict when the Imperial Japanese Navy bombed the naval base at Pearl Harbor, Hawaii, on December 7, 1941. Intended to prevent the United States from interfering with Japanese expansionist plans in the Pacific, the two-hour surprise attack killed or wounded more than 3,500 American citizens, damaged eighteen warships, and destroyed at least 180 aircraft. Not only did the assault motivate millions of people to join the U.S. armed forces, but it also inspired great anger toward the Japanese and aroused suspicion about Japanese Americans, which ultimately led to the relocation of 120,000 Japanese Americans to internment camps. Propaganda based on the attack on Pearl Harbor and other anti-Japanese rhetoric was produced via posters, newspapers, books, radio, and films to spur national pride and keep U.S. citizens in favor of the war against Japan, as well as the internment camps. The Japanese were portrayed as vicious subhuman savages and were referred to as the "yellow peril" and "yellow monkeys" poised to kill themselves or others whenever the need arose.

Benedict contributed to the war effort in an anthropological context after the Japanese attack on Pearl Harbor. Her experience with pattern analysis led to work at the Office of War Information (OWI), a government intelligence agency tasked with analyzing foreign news reports and creating domestic and foreign propaganda. Under the auspices of OWI, she wrote a series of culture and personality profiles of various countries; each study contained suggestions for psychological warfare based on the country's particular pattern of culture. In June 1944 Benedict was commissioned to write a cultural analysis of the Japanese to predict their end-of-war behavior and beyond. The most significant portion of her study focused on the role of the emperor in the Japanese culture and his profound importance to the Japanese people.

Because Benedict could not visit Japan, she had to rely on analytical reports, ethnographies, historical texts, and Japanese novels and films. She also conducted a series of interviews with Japanese Americans. Benedict's study was most significantly influenced by U.S. anthropologist John Embree's ethnographic writings and Japanese educator Inazo Nitobe's philosophical writings. Embree's *Suye Mura: A Japanese Village* (1939) was a product of his ethnographic fieldwork in rural Japan, where he studied relationships between villages and the Japanese state. This work provided Benedict with a feel for contemporary daily life and

Key Facts

Time Period:
Mid-20th Century

Genre:
Anthropological Study

Events:
World War II; bombing of Pearl Harbor; American internment of Japanese citizens

Nationality:
American

RUTH BENEDICT

Ruth Fulton Benedict was born on June 5, 1887, in New York City. Her father died when she was a child, which forced her mother to take a series of teaching and librarian jobs throughout the United States. As a result of a bout of childhood measles, she suffered from profound deafness, which led her to writing as a means of expressing herself. In 1909 she graduated from Vassar College in New York with a bachelor's degree in English literature. Benedict studied philosophy at New York's Columbia University and the New School for Social Research beginning in 1919. She turned to courses in ethnology to address the broad question of identity. During this time, she studied under sociologist and ethnologist Elise Clews Parsons and met Franz Boas, the director of Columbia University's anthropology program.

In 1921 Benedict officially enrolled as a graduate student at Columbia, where she took a course with Robert Lowie, a cultural anthropologist and ethnographer of the Crow and Shoshone tribes. The next year she published her first anthropological paper, "The Vision in Plains Culture." Benedict also undertook fieldwork among the Serrano tribe in California, but her deafness presented great difficulties. Because of this disability, her final dissertation, "The Concept of the Guardian Spirit in North America," was based on previously published works. Benedict received her doctorate in 1923 and eventually became a professor at Columbia.

culture in Japan. She also examined Nitobe's *Bushido: The Soul of Japan* (1900) for its revelation of Japanese nationalistic character. In *Kamikaze, Cherry Blossoms, and Nationalism* (2002), Emiko Ohnuki-Tierney suggests that *Bushido* led Benedict "to her famous, or infamous, thesis distinguishing the cultures of guilt and shame." Benedict also acknowledges the influences of other works, such as journalist Upton Close's *Behind the Face of Japan* (1942) and Yoshisaburō Okakura's *The Life and Thought of Japan* (1913).

After the war, Benedict expanded and adapted her OWI analysis titled "Japanese Behavior Patterns" (1945) for the public and published it as *The Chrysanthemum and the Sword* in 1946, a year after Japan surrendered. Her text helped the U.S. government and citizens to understand the important role of the emperor in Japanese culture, which ultimately contributed to President Franklin D. Roosevelt's recommendation that the emperor be allowed to maintain his reign during the Allied occupation of Japan. Benedict's study directly contradicts the wartime propaganda that was rampantly distributed in the United States. Instead of caricatures of the subhuman "yellow monkeys," she portrays the Japanese as an austere, self-disciplined, and extremely loyal people who adhere to a complex ethical code. In his book *Anthropological Intelligence* (2008), David H. Price argues that the postwar publication of *Chrysanthemum* "became the most famous American social-science contribution to the Second World War."

THEMES AND STYLE

Central to *The Chrysanthemum and the Sword* is that Japanese culture is founded on a deep belief in hierarchy and the conviction that everyone should "take one's proper station." Benedict argues, "Japan's confidence in hierarchy is basic in her whole notion of man's relation to the State and it is only by describing some of their national institutions ... that it is possible for us to understand their view of life." Knowing one's place in the Japanese hierarchy is accompanied by an extreme awareness of honor, virtue, and duty, which infiltrates every aspect of life. Benedict extensively describes the Japanese preoccupation with obligation and reciprocation, which she calls "the great network of mutual indebtedness." In addition, she discusses how the Japanese, who are extremely sensitive to failures and slurs, have a strong sense of shame and rigorously practice politeness to avoid shaming others.

Benedict achieves her rhetorical effect in *The Chrysanthemum and the Sword* by serving as a cultural translator who wishes to render the Japanese as human. She acknowledges the cultural challenge that the Japanese pose for U.S. citizens when she states, "The Japanese were the most alien enemy the United States had ever fought in an all-out struggle. In no other war with a major foe had it been necessary to take into account such exceedingly different habits of acting and thinking." Clifford Geertz, in his 1998 article "Us/Not-Us," observes that Benedict does not attempt to "unriddle Japan and the Japanese by moderating this sense of an oddly made world populated by oddly wired people, but by accentuating it." Indeed, Benedict discusses at length the wildly divergent characteristics peacefully coexisting in the Japanese personality: "The Japanese are, to the highest degree, both aggressive and unaggressive, both militaristic and aesthetic, both insolent and polite, rigid and adaptable, submissive and resentful of being pushed around, loyal and treacherous, brave and timid, conservative and hospitable to new ways." Benedict explains that these contradictory behaviors are permitted as long as hierarchical balance is maintained. Thus, she demonstrates how the Japanese people's "exceedingly different habits of acting and thinking" are actually quite logical and comprehensible.

Stylistically, Benedict's text is highly organized and powerfully expository, giving it a scientific quality. The thoroughness of her research is demonstrated in the abundance of empirical proof that she offers regarding all aspects of the culture, including sleeping, eating, sex, marriage, masculinity, drinking, and good and evil. Geertz contends that these "various assertions ... the unrelenting piling up of them, the one hardly dispatched before the next appears, is what give Benedict's argument its extraordinary energy." The author's argument, however, is also systematically and carefully constructed, giving her an air of authority. In an article published in the *American Journal of Sociology* in 1947, John A. Rademaker claims that Benedict's

Ruth Benedict's study *The Chrysanthemum and the Sword: Patterns of Japanese Culture* includes interviews with prisoners of Japanese internment camps in the United States. This photograph, dated 1942/1943, shows prisoners at such a camp. UNIVERSAL IMAGES GROUP/GETTY IMAGES.

study is "one of those rare books which sets forth the basic moral values of a national culture in a comprehensive pattern after careful and penetrating analysis of many facts of human relationships."

CRITICAL DISCUSSION

The Chrysanthemum and the Sword was embraced by the American public and well received by critics upon its publication. In a 1947 volume of *American Anthropologist,* A. L. Kroeber calls it "a book that makes one proud to be an anthropologist." He adds that the text "shows what can be done with orientation and discipline even without speaking knowledge of the language and residence in the country." Rademaker also lauds Benedict's text as providing "a dependable analysis of Japanese behavior" but argues that "there are points at which the analysis may be imperfect," especially because of the author's inability to visit Japan. In his review of *Chrysanthemum* in the *Harvard Journal of Asiatic Studies,* Gordon Bowles acknowledges the "orderly manner in which the data have been assembled" and the text's "incisive phrasing and keen logic," but he concludes that "the reader feels that only half the truth has been revealed…. While the stuff was most beautiful and while it was most excellently tailored, somewhere there was a lack of true fit in the garment finished for the Japanese."

Considered to be Benedict's most mature work, *The Chrysanthemum and the Sword* sought to persuade American citizens to renounce their preconceived notions about the Japanese in order to create a more peaceful world. The Japanese translation significantly influenced the country's consciousness and sparked an ongoing debate about the correct portrayal of Japanese culture. In a modern analysis of the book published in 2004, Sonia Ryang states, "In the postwar period it was a text that gave the Japanese a sense of relief; it explained Japan's defeat in the war and salvaged Japan and its cultural essence as something that did not have to be totally denied and discarded." Ryang also writes, "The ways in which *Chrysanthemum* has been read in Japan are indicative of changing self-perceptions of Japanese intellectuals as well as the general public, a self-perception which was then interactively fed back into the western discourse of Japan."

The Chrysanthemum and the Sword is generally regarded as setting the standard for personality and culture studies and continues to be discussed in studies of Japanese culture. In the essay "'A World Made Safe for Differences'" (2004), Christopher Shannon claims that *Chrysanthemum* is a "kind of cultural guidebook for American officials overseeing the reconstruction of Japan, [and] Benedict's book argues for a greater understanding and tolerance of all cultures as the key to preserving world peace." Some critics argue that Benedict generates this "greater understanding and tolerance" by comparing and contrasting Japan with the United States. According to Geertz, "Japan comes to look, somehow, less and less erratic and arbitrary while the United States comes to look, somehow, more and more so." He also states that the text is "organized from beginning to end in a look-unto-ourselves-as-we-would-look-unto-others manner." Other critics have been even harsher. C. Douglas Lummis, in the article "Ruth Benedict's Obituary for Japanese Culture" (2007), comments, "After some time I realized that I would never be able to live in a decent relationship with the people of that country unless I could drive this book, and its politely arrogant world view, out of my head."

BIBLIOGRAPHY

Sources

Benedict, Ruth. *The Chrysanthemum and the Sword*. New York: Houghton, 2005. Print.

Bowles, Gordon. Rev. of *The Chrysanthemum and the Sword,* by Ruth Benedict. *Harvard Journal of Asiatic Studies* 10 (1947): 237–41. Print.

Geertz, Clifford. "Us/Not-Us: Benedict's Travels." *Works and Lives: The Anthropologist as Author.* Stanford: Stanford UP, 1988. 102–28. Print.

Lavender, Catherine. "Ruth (Fulton) Benedict." *Twentieth-Century American Cultural Theorists.* Ed. Paul Hansom. Detroit: Gale Group, 2001. *Dictionary of Literary Biography.* Vol. 246. *Literature Resource Center.* Web. 1 Aug. 2012.

Lummis, C. Douglas. "Ruth Benedict's Obituary for Japanese Culture." *The Asia-Pacific Journal: Japan Focus.* 19 July 2007. Web. 10 Aug. 2012.

Ohnuki-Tierney, Emiko. *Kamikaze, Cherry Blossoms, and Nationalisms: The Militarization of Aesthetics in Japanese History.* Chicago: U of Chicago P, 2002. Print.

Price, David H. *Anthropological Intelligence: The Deployment and Neglect of American Anthropology in the Second World War.* Duke UP, 2008. Print.

Rademaker, John A. "*The Chrysanthemum and the Sword*: Patterns of Japanese Culture." *American Journal of Sociology* Sept. 1947: 156–58. *JSTOR.* Web. 10 Aug. 2012.

Ryang, Sonia. "Chrysanthemum's Strange Life: Ruth Benedict in Postwar Japan." *Japan Policy Research Institute Occasional Papers No. 32.* University of San Francisco Center for the Pacific Rim, July 2004. Web. 8 Aug 2012.

———. *Japan and National Anthropology: A Critique.* London: RoutledgeCurzon, 2004. Print.

Shannon, Christopher. "'A World Made Safe for Differences': Ruth Benedict's *The Chrysanthemum and the Sword.*" *Reading Benedict/Reading Mead: Feminism, Race, and Imperial Visions.* Ed. Dolores Janiewski and Lois W. Banner. Baltimore: Johns Hopkins UP, 2004. Print.

Further Reading

Banner, Lois W. *Intertwined Lives: Margaret Mead, Ruth Benedict, and Their Circle.* New York: Vintage, 2004. Print.

Di Leonardo, Micaela. *Exotics at Home: Anthropologies, Others, American Modernity.* Chicago: U of Chicago P, 1998. Print.

Fukui, Nanako. *From "Japanese Behavior Patterns" to "The Chrysanthemum and the Sword."* Tokyo: Kansai, 1995. Print.

———. "The Lady of the Chrysanthemum: Ruth Benedict and the Origins of *The Chrysanthemum and the Sword.*" *Reading Benedict/Reading Mead: Feminism, Race, and Imperial Visions.* Ed. Dolores Janiewski and Lois W. Banner. Baltimore: Johns Hopkins UP, 2004. Print.

Kent, Pauline. "Ruth Benedict's Original Wartime Study of the Japanese." *International Journal of Japanese Sociology* 3 (1994): 81–97. Print.

———. "Japanese Perceptions of *The Chrysanthemum and the Sword.*" *Dialectical Anthropology* 24.2 (1999): 181. Print.

Lummis, C. Douglas. *A New Look at "The Chrysanthemum and the Sword."* Tokyo: Shohakusha, 1982. Print.

Young, Virginia Heyer. *Ruth Benedict: Beyond Relativity, Beyond Pattern.* U of Nebraska P, 2005. Print.

Maggie Magno

COMMON SENSE

Thomas Paine

OVERVIEW

Thomas Paine's influential political pamphlet *Common Sense,* initially published on January 10, 1776, stirred a great number of colonists to support the still-fermenting American Revolution. Having arrived in America in 1774, Paine witnessed the nascent nation's reaction to the battles of Lexington and Concord on April 19, 1775, as well as the Battle of Bunker Hill on June 17, 1775. The pamphlet was written before the revolution had officially commenced, when Americans were divided about whether the colonies should reconcile with or declare independence from Great Britain. Political propaganda on the subject was widespread at the time *Common Sense* was published, but Paine distinguished himself from his fellow writers by relying on the premises of "simple facts, plain arguments, and common sense." Rather than utilize Latin phrases and philosophical quotations to impress an educated political elite, Paine employed simple language to convince a much broader audience. Paine's egalitarian aims were rewarded: his pamphlet was read more widely than any other publication in America during that period, yielding twenty-five editions in just one year.

Blending resonant biblical allusions with straight-forward political arguments, *Common Sense* unified opinion over the colonies' potential independence from England to an unprecedented extent. It stands as arguably the most successful piece of political propaganda in American history. Indeed, one might ask whether the American Revolution would have even taken place without the consensus-building effect of Paine's pamphlet.

HISTORICAL AND LITERARY CONTEXT

At the end of 1775, with the first battles of the war fresh in the minds of Americans, anger was in the air. Following England's enactment of the Sugar Act in 1764 and the Stamp Act in 1765—and even the more malicious 1773 Tea Act—dissent in the American colonies had been relatively moderate. The atmosphere grew more volatile, however, in the wake of the battles of Lexington, Concord, and Bunker Hill. Still, even as many colonists openly called for independence to be declared, a significant number of Americans remained either loyal to the crown (Loyalists) or undecided. Some Loyalists even took up arms against their fellow colonists, adding to the fraught and divisive political atmosphere as Paine prepared *Common Sense.*

When *Common Sense* appeared in January 1776, the trajectory of the conflict with Great Britain was far from clear. It had been six months since Bunker Hill, and although skirmishes with Loyalists persisted and many tempers smoldered, the debate over whether the colonies would attempt to reconcile with Britain or declare independence remained undecided. Paine, a man of letters who was well versed in the works of Enlightenment thinkers such as Isaac Newton and John Locke, was working at the time as an editor at *Pennsylvania Magazine* in Philadelphia. Having published nothing of his own, however, Paine was entirely unknown to the American public. That would change dramatically with *Common Sense.*

Common Sense sprang from the tradition of political pamphlets, which ranged from twenty to eighty pages. In his article "Thomas Paine and the Making of 'Common Sense,'" Craig Nelson calls pamphleteering "the most popular style of eighteenth-century publishing." *Common Sense* was among many notable pamphlets published on the question of American independence, including *Letters from a Farmer in Pennsylvania to the Inhabitants of the British Colonies* by John Dickinson (1768), *A State of the Rights of the Colonists* attributed to Samuel Adams (1772), and *A Summary View of the Rights of British America* by Thomas Jefferson (1774). Adopting a more egalitarian tone, *Common Sense* departs from—and, arguably, improves upon—the rhetoric employed in these other propagandist pamphlets.

The literary and cultural impact of *Common Sense* cannot be overstated. Paine's pamphlet drummed up popular support for the American Revolution, laying out literary themes that would be echoed in the Declaration of Independence. The pamphlet lifted its author to international prominence. A few years after its publication, as intellectual historian Laurence Dickey points out in his essay "Thomas Paine: Context, Text, and Presentism," "*Common Sense* came to figure prominently in French constitutional debates of the 1780s." However, Paine's political importance is by no means confined to the eighteenth century; his straightforward yet eloquent language still echoes today. In President Barack Obama's 2009 inaugural address, for example, he quoted the eighteenth-century pamphleteer.

❖ *Key Facts*

Time Period:
Late 18th Century

Genre:
Pamphlet

Events:
American Revolution

Nationality:
American

"POPERY" IN PAINE'S RELIGIOUS RHETORIC

Thomas Paine's *Common Sense* relies heavily on religious rhetoric to convince readers of the need for independence from Great Britain. In filling his pamphlet with biblical allusions and quotations—and even asserting that kingship is akin to "idolatry," a plan of the "Devil"—Paine targeted an American readership that was predominantly Protestant. He disparagingly equates the English monarchy with the Catholic Papacy, calling it "the Popery of government" and damning Loyalists who would use the terminology of "mother country" for harboring a "low papistical design."

In its use of the pejorative term "popery," Paine's pamphlet follows in a long tradition of anti-Catholic sentiment and rhetoric in early modern England. Among the most famous instances of anti-Catholic propaganda in England was the "Popish Plot." In 1678 Titus Oates allegedly uncovered a conspiracy to depose and murder King Charles II and overrun the country with a Catholic invasion from Ireland. Although Oates was ultimately declared a fraud, his propaganda set England aflame with anti-Catholic anger. Paine's decision to gear *Common Sense* toward a Protestant audience shows his awareness of the colonies' religious tenor and their English heritage of anti-Catholic propaganda.

THEMES AND STYLE

In *Common Sense,* Paine outlines how appeals to reason, the laws of nature, the colonies' commercial prowess, and even "the Almighty" all tend toward favoring independence over reconciliation. Placing plans for reconciliation with England in the realm of "something very ridiculous" and reiterating that "there is something very absurd in supposing a continent to be perpetually governed by an island," Paine places England's sovereignty over the colonies beyond the bounds of what reason, nature, or God would ordain, something not consonant with "common sense." He peppers his pamphlet with biblical allusions and even outright statements that both God and nature have "deserted" the sovereignty of the "Pharaoh of England," weaving his political cause neatly into the fabric of the Protestantism that was predominant in the colonies. In addition, Paine endeavors to play up not only the divinity of America's independence but also the people's practical ability to achieve such an end. He highlights how American commerce abroad, as well as the potential military resources of "tar, timber, iron, and cordage" at home, make the colonies fit for a defense against the British.

The phenomenal impact of *Common Sense* stems from its success in blending colonists' practical concerns about independence with their religious sensibilities and "common sense" views toward politics—all within, perhaps most importantly, the rubric of a simple voice. Other similar propagandist pamphlets also place religious, rational, and practical planks in their platforms, but none do so with prose as profound as Paine's. In "The Common Style of 'Common Sense,'" scholars Lee Sigelman, Colin Martindale, and Dean McKenzie provide a statistical analysis comparing *Common Sense* to fourteen other prerevolutionary pamphlets and conclude "that *Common Sense* was indeed stylistically unique; no other pamphleteer came close to matching Paine's combination of simplicity and forcefulness."

Though the simply stated argument in *Common Sense* made it accessible to a wide variety of people in the colonies, the pamphlet's true resonance comes from its emotional depth. Paine colors the quest for independence with religious shades—going so far as to say that "the reformation was preceded by the discovery of America, as if the Almighty graciously meant to open a sanctuary to the persecuted"—while also suggesting that "it is not in the power of Britain or of Europe to conquer America, if she do not conquer herself by *delay* and *timidity.*" In doing so, he implicates his readers in undermining a divine plan should they shrink from the cause of independence. This aspect of *Common Sense* struck a powerful chord in the deeply Protestant colonies.

CRITICAL DISCUSSION

Common Sense was an instant success, with demand for the pamphlet exploding within weeks of its release. In his biography *Tom Paine: A Political Life,* John Keane points out that by April 1776, just seven months after the initial release of the pamphlet, Paine claimed to have circulated 120,000 copies and would later boast that as many as 150,000 had been printed in America alone. Robert A. Ferguson, in his article "The Commonalities of *Common Sense,*" reports that George Washington dubbed *Common Sense* "unanswerable," saying it was "working a wonderful change … in the minds of many men," and that Benjamin Franklin likewise called the pamphlet's political impact "prodigious."

Beyond the influence it exerted in the buildup to the American Revolution, *Common Sense* has established a lasting literary legacy as a remarkable piece of prose. By breaking with eighteenth-century propagandist writing norms through his use of a simple style aimed at a broad readership, Paine set political rhetoric in America on a new path. Ferguson suggests that "the rhetorical patterns initiated in *Common Sense* have become intrinsic to American political speech … permanently embedded in the expressions of identity" in American politics.

There is a long history of scholarship on *Common Sense,* as well as on Paine. In recent years, linguistic and statistical analyses, such as the study in "The Common Style of 'Common Sense,'" have attempted to glean new insights into this oft-interpreted text. Additionally, intellectual historians such as Dickey have come to view Paine's work as illustrative of trends in the history of philosophy and of cross-pollination in political philosophy from both sides of the Atlantic. In addition, the man himself has been the subject of considerable biographical interest. Paine died somewhat ignominiously—due to a combination of his controversial religious views, expulsion from his native England, and even imprisonment in France during the Reign of Terror—and much scholarship over the past century has been devoted to redeeming his character. More recently, Keane's *Tom Paine: A Political Life* is notable for the way it melds biographical information with a scholarly treatment of Paine's political impact on both the United States and Europe.

A portrait of Thomas Paine, author of *Common Sense,* painted by Arthur Easton. PORTRAIT OF THOMAS PAINE (1737–1809) (OIL ON CANVAS), EASTON, A. (FL.C.1800)/LABOUR SOCIETY, LONDON, UK/THE BRIDGEMAN ART LIBRARY.

BIBLIOGRAPHY

Sources

Dickey, Laurence. "Thomas Paine: Context, Text, and Presentism." Rev. of *Tom Paine: A Political Life,* by John Keane. *Reviews in American History* 24.2 (1996): 216–25. Print.

Ferguson, Robert A. "The Commonalities of *Common Sense.*" *William and Mary Quarterly* 57.3 (2000): 465–504. Print.

Keane, John. *Tom Paine: A Political Life.* London: Bloomsbury, 1995. Print.

Nelson, Craig. "Thomas Paine and the Making of 'Common Sense,'" *New England Review* 27.3 (2006): 228–50. Print.

Paine, Thomas. *Common Sense.* Mineola: Dover, 1997. Print.

Sigelman, Lee, Colin Martindale, and Dean McKenzie. "The Common Style of 'Common Sense,'" *Computers and the Humanities* 30.5 (1996/1997): 373–79. Print.

Further Reading

Everton, Michael. "'The Would-Be-Author and the Real Bookseller': Thomas Paine and Eighteenth-Century Printing Ethics." *Early American Literature* 40.1 (2005): 79–110. Print.

Fruchtman, Jack, Jr. *Thomas Paine: Apostle of Freedom.* New York: Four Walls Eight Windows, 1994. Print.

Kaye, Harvey J. *Thomas Paine and the Promise of America.* New York: Hill and Wang, 2005. Print.

Larkin, Edward. *Thomas Paine and the Literature of Revolution.* Cambridge: Cambridge UP, 2005. Print.

Paine, Thomas. *Thomas Paine: Political Writings.* Ed. Bruce Kuklick. Cambridge: Cambridge UP, 2000. Print.

Rosenfeld, Sophia. "Tom Paine's *Common Sense* and Ours." *William and Mary Quarterly* 65.4 (2008): 633–68. Print.

Walker, Thomas C. "The Forgotten Prophet: Tom Paine's Cosmopolitanism and International Relations." *International Studies Quarterly* 44.1 (2000): 51–72. Print.

Elliott Niblock

DECLARATION OF INDEPENDENCE
Thomas Jefferson

❖ *Key Facts*

Time Period:
Late 18th Century

Genre:
Political Document

Events:
Founding of American
Republic

Nationality:
American

OVERVIEW

The *Declaration of Independence* (1776), written primarily by Thomas Jefferson, is an American political document that proclaims the independence of the thirteen British colonies in North America from rule by Great Britain. The *Declaration* lists grievances against King George III and asserts the colonists' natural and legal rights, among them the right to revolt against an unjust government. Written in a concise, official manner typical of a legal document, the *Declaration* is notable for its deductive argument and accessible language. With its classic rhetoric and logic, the document aims to lend credibility to the impending American Revolution. The phrasing is argumentative and persuasive, designed to justify the colonists' decision to revolt against King George III and to persuade other colonists to join the cause.

Drafted by Jefferson over seventeen days and heavily edited by the Second Continental Congress for two more, the *Declaration of Independence* was formally approved on July 4, 1776. That same day, Congress ordered several hundred copies to be printed and distributed all over the colonies. As the *Declaration* circulated throughout the colonies, rallies were held to read the new document aloud in order to reach those who could not read and to persuade those still uncertain about the necessity for colonial independence. By mid-August the *Declaration* appeared in British newspapers and soon after was translated and published throughout Europe. The document was quickly recognized as revolutionary and announced the arrival of the United States of America on the world political stage. Since 1776 the *Declaration of Independence* has become one of the most revered documents of American history and has inspired similar proclamations on behalf of other marginalized groups in the United States and abroad.

HISTORICAL AND LITERARY CONTEXT

Before the *Declaration* was written, the colonies had already been at war with Britain for more than a year, unable to resolve tensions over Parliament's authority in the colonies. In need of money to repay debts accrued from fighting in the Seven Years' War and to maintain English troops stationed in the colonies to defend against attacks by Native Americans, England began taxing the colonists on such items as glass, paint, and tea. The Stamp Act of 1765 required that printed material such as legal documents, newspapers, and other paper goods be printed on embossed paper printed in London and paid for with English currency. Many colonists were appalled at the Crown's attempts to raise money, maintaining that their lack of representation in Parliament made such heavy taxation unconstitutional and violated their natural rights as citizens. Citizens also voiced their dissent in the form of protests and effigy burnings. In 1774, when Parliament passed the Coercive Acts to reverse the trend of colonial resistance by reasserting Parliament as head of colonial government, members of the First Continental Congress assembled in Philadelphia to organize a boycott of British goods. Their petition to the king to repeal these acts was unsuccessful, and hostilities increased. The first skirmishes of the Revolutionary War took place in Massachusetts in Lexington and Concord in April 1775, and fighting would continue until 1783.

As the relationship between the colonies and Britain deteriorated, the Second Continental Congress appointed five men—Jefferson, John Adams, Roger Sherman, Benjamin Franklin, and Robert Livingston—to a committee responsible for drafting a statement expressing the colonists' case for independence. Jefferson took the lead in composing the preliminary version of the document, which was later revised by the committee before it was submitted to Congress. The *Declaration* was greatly informed by the ideas of the Enlightenment, which promoted the belief that humanity can be improved by discovering the "law of nature." Jefferson aimed to convince fellow colonists and the world at large of the colonies' moral and legal right to separate from Britain. To do so, he crafted the *Declaration* around the idea that the colonists were not rebels against an established political authority but were free men defending their imprescriptible rights from a tyrannical king.

American political literature in the late eighteenth century was growing increasingly concerned with independence. The most influential of these writings was Thomas Paine's *Common Sense* (1776). The pamphlet was the first document to express outright support for separation from Britain. Its widespread circulation, unassuming language, and frank assessment of the current political situation had a catalytic effect in swaying public opinion in favor of independence. The publication of *Common Sense* encouraged lively debate on the issue of independence, and Paine's language and philosophical ideas would inspire Jefferson's draft of the *Declaration*. Jefferson also modeled the document after the *Virginia Declaration of Rights,* written by George Mason on June 12, 1776. Jefferson borrowed key ideas from this earlier declaration, including the combination of natural rights and social contract theory for the basis of his argument and for the basic structure of his document. Philosophically the *Declaration*'s central idea that individuals enter into a government willingly, so long as it protects the natural rights of citizens, is greatly informed by John Locke's *Second Treatise of Government* (1689).

The day the *Declaration* was published, July 4, is commemorated as Independence Day, an important American holiday. Additionally, groups protesting perceived injustices have imitated the language and structure of the *Declaration* to rally public opinion around their cause. The earliest example of such imitation was the *Declaration of Sentiments* (1848), a call for women's rights, written by Elizabeth Cady Stanton. Keeping the basic structure and argument of Jefferson's *Declaration* intact, Stanton altered the phrasing to list the rights the political system had denied women. In 1963, in a notable historical moment leading up to the Civil Rights Act of 1964 and the Voting Rights Act of 1965, Martin Luther King Jr. delivered his well-known "I Have a Dream" speech, drawing heavily from the *Declaration of Independence*.

THEMES AND STYLE

Central to the *Declaration* is the idea that individuals possess natural rights and that the government, established by the people through a social contract, exists to protect these rights. The opening sentence announces the purpose of the document: to "declare the causes" of the separation from Britain and to chronicle the provocations that have made independence "necessary." According to the logic of Jefferson's argument, the colonists have a "right" and a "duty" to revolt against the king and to establish a new government that will abide the social contract theory and protect their natural rights.

In order to elucidate the necessity of independence, Jefferson relies on structure and deductive reasoning. The *Declaration* consists of five distinct parts: the introduction, the preamble, the indictment of George III, the denunciation of the British people, and the conclusion. The introduction sets up a general, universal dispute that elevates the situation from a petty colonial quarrel to a disturbance of the "Laws of Nature," significant in "the Course of human events." The *Declaration* begins with an appeal to philosophy and logic; rather than presenting an argument based on interpretations, Jefferson roots the document in observations. The preamble continues in this universal, philosophical tone, succinctly summarizing

THE RISE OF POLITICAL PARTIES AND THEIR EFFECT ON THE *DECLARATION OF INDEPENDENCE*

By the election of 1796, the American political system had become dominated by two political parties, the Federalists and the Democratic Republicans. The Federalist Party wanted a strong national government, and its members created a strong drive to draft and ratify the U.S. Constitution. The party split largely over disagreements with Alexander Hamilton's programs, including the Jay Treaty in 1794, which sought to settle loose ends remaining from the Revolutionary War. The Democratic Republicans claimed that developing a close economic relationship with Britain was Hamilton's attempt to undercut America's burgeoning republicanism. Jefferson was slandered and vilified by the Federalists, who saw him as a "snake in the grass" and who viewed his famous political document, the *Declaration of Independence,* as "the oily, wily language with which he lubricated his victims and applied his venom."

By the 1790s a stark difference in treatment of the *Declaration* was apparent in the Boston newspapers of the opposing political parties. The Republican *Independent Chronicle* celebrated the *Declaration* for its discussion of human rights and civil government and lauded the document as "our great American charter." Articles appearing in the Federalist *Columbian Centinel,* however, belittled Jefferson as "the scribe who penned the declaration" and berated "the seductive terms of Liberty and Equality." Campaigning for the presidency, Jefferson declared that "the spirit of 1776 is not dead, it has only been slumbering, the body of the American people is substantially republican." In contrast to the aristocratic Federalists, Jefferson and the Republicans posited themselves as the successors to and defenders of this revolutionary zeitgeist. With the election of Jefferson to the presidency of the United States in 1801, the Republicans' political ideals and view of the *Declaration* gained greater sway, while the Federalists lost favor.

ideas from Locke's *Second Treatise of Government.* Jefferson adapts Locke's concepts of the natural rights to life, liberty, and property, declaring that the colonists are entitled to the "unalienable rights" of "Life, Liberty and the pursuit of Happiness." Throughout the document he develops a syllogism—a tight deductive argument consisting of one major premise and one minor premise, leading to a logical conclusion. The major premise asserts that when a government seeks to reduce its people to living under despotism, "it is their right, it is their duty, to throw off such Government, and to provide new Guards for their future security." The minor premise is that the British king had denied the colonists' attempts to address these grievances civilly, thereby acting as a tyrannical ruler. Jefferson establishes logos and ethos in the introduction and preamble, and the longest section of the *Declaration* is an inductive proof of his minor premise, listing the

has," emphasizes the accumulation of complaints and accentuates the king's role as the prime conspirator against American liberty.

CRITICAL DISCUSSION

In the first decades after the publication of the *Declaration,* it was seen as primarily a product of the act of independence and not yet given its special place as one of the most esteemed documents of American history. David Ramsay's *The History of the Revolution* (1789) reflects this diminutive image of the *Declaration* as well as the limited knowledge of contemporaries regarding the document's inception. Ramsay's account mentions neither the committee appointed by Congress nor Jefferson's role in drafting the document and does not feature the preamble as prominently as one would expect from modern criticism. Instead Ramsay presents the *Declaration* as essentially "the act of the united colonies for separating themselves from the government of Great-Britain." This view would continue until the period of the 1790s to the 1820s, when critics began exploring the merits of the *Declaration* as a political document. As a writer for a Philadelphia newspaper stated in 1792, the *Declaration* is "not to be celebrated merely as affecting the seperation [sic] of one country from the jurisdiction of another; but as being the result of a rational discussion and definition of the rights of man, and the end of civil government."

Since Stanton's *Declaration of Sentiments* brought renewed attention to the ideas of human rights in 1848, the *Declaration* has become a principal document in the discussion of the natural rights of citizens. The *Declaration* has provided social movements seeking to expand freedom with a definition of civil rights, a precedent for political change, and an example of rhetoric aimed at protecting and promoting these ideals. Stanton and civil rights organizers of the twentieth century have stayed true to the spirit of the *Declaration* by engaging with its ideals but evolving it to more fully represent the process of democracy. Most notably, attention has been paid to the discrepancy in the opening lines, which state that "all men are created equal," and the practice of slavery. Abolitionists such as Frederick Douglass pointed out the hypocrisy of the new American democracy. In his famous speech from 1852, "What to the Slave Is the Fourth of July?" Douglass underlines the contradictions between the nation's ideals and practices regarding human rights. By the 1850s the *Declaration of Independence* had taken on a key role in the rhetoric of Abraham Lincoln, who believed that the framers of the *Declaration* included the problematic passage of the preamble as a first step toward the abolition of slavery and as future protection of the rights of individuals.

The *Declaration of Independence* is given great importance in political and philosophical discussions regarding the American Revolution and the change of political ideologies and organization such a fight represented. Specialized studies of the document often can

ways in which the king has stripped the colonists of their rights.

The wording of the *Declaration* is precise, resulting in a structural unity that achieves a stately and dignified tone reinforced through what was known as the Style Periodique of the eighteenth century. In this style a pace is created and maintained through word choices to give the impression of a cycle and a sense of completeness. Emphasizing the composition's musicality, the concluding word of each sentence is polysyllabic, allowing the sentence to resonate fully and elevate the aural reception of the piece. This rhetorical tactic was especially useful considering that a majority of Americans heard the *Declaration* as a speech, often at a gathering or political rally. In addition, in an appeal to pathos, the wording of the *Declaration* is distinctly negative. Utilizing anaphora, as in the repetition of the phrase "he has," to build momentum, Jefferson increases the emotional tenor to a crescendo near the end of the list of the king's offenses, where the king is described as showing "Cruelty & perfidy scarcely paralleled in the most barbarous ages" and is declared "totally unworthy [to be] Head of a civilized nation." The steady piling up of the injustices without explanation, coupled with the repetition of "he be divided into three overlapping groups: narrative, technical, and philosophical inquiries. John Hazelton's *The* Declaration of Independence: *Its History* (1970) is a technical study of the events immediately surrounding the composition and signing of the *Declaration* and of how the document was initially received. Hazelton situates conflicting evidence from the records of the Second Continental Congress and incorporates variant readings of the *Declaration* in order to demonstrate the level of active debate surrounding the act of separation from Britain. Carl Becker offers one of the most comprehensive studies of the political ideas contained in the *Declaration* in his book *The* Declaration of Independence: *A Study in the History of Political Ideas* (1922). Becker traces the philosophical roots of Jefferson's political document and argues that "the lineage [of the natural rights argument] is direct: Jefferson copied Locke and Locke quoted Hooker." Jefferson's reliance on Lockean philosophy is still widely accepted, but since the publication of Becker's book, there have been challenges to the philosophical origins of the *Declaration of Independence*.

BIBLIOGRAPHY

Sources

Becker, Carl L. *The* Declaration of Independence: *A Study in the History of Political Ideas.* New York: Harcourt Brace, 1922. Print.

Detweiler, Philip F. "The Changing Reputation of the *Declaration of Independence*: The First Fifty Years." *William and Mary Quarterly* 19.4 (1962): 557–74. Print.

Hazelton, John. *The* Declaration of Independence: *Its History.* New York: Da Capo, 1970. Print.

Jefferson, Thomas. *The Declaration of Independence. ushistory.org.* Independence Hall Association. Web. 11 July 2012.

Ramsay, David. *The History of the American Revolution.* 1789. Indianapolis: Liberty Classics, 1990. Print.

Further Reading

Goetsch, Paul, and Gerd Hurm, eds. *The Fourth of July: Political Oratory and Literary Reactions, 1776–1876.* Tübingen: Gunter Narr Verlag, 1992. Print.

Hardin, Joe Marshall. "The *Declaration of Independence* as a Text of Resistance: Textual Revisioning, Appropriation, and Demystification." *Readerly/Writerly Texts* 6. 1–2 (1998–99): 115–24. Print.

Lucas, Stephen E. "The Rhetorical Ancestry of the *Declaration of Independence*." *Rhetoric and Public Affairs* 1.2 (1998): 143–84. Print.

———. "Justifying America: The *Declaration of Independence* as a Rhetorical Document." *American Rhetoric: Context and Criticism.* Ed. Thomas Benson. Carbondale: Southern Illinois UP, 1989. Print. 67–130.

Maier, Pauline. *American Scripture: Making the Declaration of Independence.* London: Vintage, 1998. Print.

Whissell, Cynthia. "The US *Declaration of Independence*: Emotion, Style, and Authorship." *49th Parallel: An Interdisciplinary Journal of North American Studies* 9 (2002): n.p. Web. 11 July 2012.

Elizabeth Orvis

ENGLAND AND SPAIN, OR, VALOUR AND PATRIOTISM

Felicia Hemans

+ *Key Facts*

Time Period:
Early 19th Century

Genre:
Poetry

Events:
Peninsular War;
Napoleonic expansion
of France

Nationality:
English

OVERVIEW

England and Spain, or, Valour and Patriotism (1808) is a long poem by the English poet Felicia Hemans (née Felicia Dorothea Browne) that exhorts Britain to rescue Spain from the oppression of the French Empire, which had annexed Spain as part of the Peninsular War begun in 1807. Hemans's poem was one of a number of such poems to infuse the opportunistic British engagement on the Iberian Peninsula with the sentiment of noblesse oblige: According to the poet, the chivalric forces of "Albion" were selflessly coming to the aid of an imperiled ally. The Peninsular War would continue until 1812, when Napoleon's failed invasion of Russia forced a French withdrawal.

The second major work by Hemans, *England and Spain* initially startled her readers, many of whom were unused to militaristic sentiment in so-called women's poetry. However, despite poor distribution during its initial printing, *England and Spain* soon attracted the interest of the controversial poet Percy Bysshe Shelley, helping to establish Hemans as an author. Later works built her reputation as one of the leading female poets of the Romantic period, and her early verse found a wider readership when her collected poems were published shortly after her death. Her literary achievements bore great symbolic value for women's-rights activists in the late nineteenth century, and subsequent critics have found in Hemans a technically dexterous writer and a shrewd observer of literary tastes and trends. Nevertheless, today *England and Spain* is regarded, as noted by Paula Feldman in an article for *Keats-Shelley Journal,* as one of the poet's "apprentice works."

HISTORICAL AND LITERARY CONTEXT

England and Spain addresses a British citizenry harrowed by a series of continual wars with France. Beginning in 1792, the British Empire led at least four distinct attempts to curb the expansion of the post-revolutionary French state, whose military might Napoleon soon consolidated into the fabled Grande Armée. Britain would remain at war with France until 1814, assisted by seven successive coalitions of other European powers; the Peninsular War of the poem coincides roughly with the War of the Fifth Coalition. Having made little progress by land, the British Empire by 1808 turned to a chiefly naval strategy.

At the time of the poem's publication, Napoleon had succeeded in fragmenting and subjugating many of the German states to the east and Spain and Portugal to the southwest. His extraordinarily swift Prussian campaign (1806) would have been especially fresh in the memory of British citizens, and Hemans states that the late Prussian king Frederick the Great would be saddened and shocked at what had become of his realm. With the rebellion of the Portuguese in the summer of 1808, British forces finally had a point of entry for a land campaign. They formed an alliance with the Portuguese and Spanish armies, which the British proceeded to resupply, train, and reinforce. This coalition is repeatedly celebrated in the poem, with liberal references to Britain's fortuitous (and righteous) league with the Castilian (Spanish) people and, more generally, with the Iberian Peninsula.

Writing almost two decades into the coalition wars, Hemans was a relative newcomer to a much-poeticized series of conflicts. In some ways, she was more outspoken than her male peers. Notably, Hemans carries the element of martial patriotism in her work further than many other poets of the time—certainly further than Coleridge, whose "Fire, Famine, and Slaughter" (1798) expressed, according to Richard Foster Jones writing in "Eclogue Types in English Poetry of the Eighteenth Century," a "Romantic hatred of war," and thematized "the sorrow and desolation that hostile armies bring to a peaceful country." Wordsworth had decried Napoleon's expansionist policies in several of his 1807 *Poems* but stopped short of the valorizing call to arms that Hemans was to deliver.

Many of the formal traits of *England and Spain* would in turn characterize later war poems, though the work's most basic rhetorical gestures—such as reference to a mythic "Albion"—predate Hemans by centuries, and her contribution is therefore difficult to trace. Whatever their subject matter, most authors writing in the shadow of the Romantics were more apt to name Wordsworth or Coleridge than Hemans as being influential. Hemans did develop a considerable following in later life, but *England and Spain* (perhaps because of its warlike sentiment) never achieved the stature of her later volumes.

THEMES AND STYLE

The major argument of *England and Spain* is that the British-Spanish cause is one of liberty. The poem alludes to the sweetness of freedom and suggests that it is both the right and the duty of Britain to preserve the liberty of others. The poet regards Albion (an archaic name for Great Britain) as indeed the very birthplace of freedom and also suggests that as the "empress of the seas," Britain is the rightful guarantor of maritime commerce. The importance of preserving the dominance of British trade is a major theme of the poem. Hemans chooses allusions that simultaneously illustrate her point and suggest the impressive scope of British mercantilism. In one extended passage, the poet descants upon Britain's lack of natural resources, noting that despite the lack of native equivalents for "Parian marbles," "graceful cedars," or "trickling myrrh," the United Kingdom can supply itself with all these things via commerce—backed, of course, by a powerful navy.

Hemans further suggests the nobility of the British cause by yoking the present conflict to past martial achievements, both historical and mythical. In an age of cannon and cavalry, British soldiers in her poems more often wield the nobler weapons of their supposed ancestors, taking the field with "beamy spear and adamantine shield." Inherent in these ancient arms, for the poet, is a code of values extending through the chivalric age and privileging "honour's lofty soul." Against these heroes, France is seen as especially perfidious, having by "fraud achieved—e'en more than conquest won!" Thus Hemans at a stroke suggests the naturalness of armed combat as a solution to problems and implicates French politicking as a breach in the natural order.

In addition to historical and mythic battles, Hemans alludes to Greco-Roman and Christian religious tropes, consecrating the British cause as simultaneously the work of Mars and of Christ. The poet also personifies such qualities as Honour and Beauty, who celebrate British (and, to an extent, Spanish) victories, mourn the fallen, and console those left at home about the fate of their loved ones. A favored device in *England and Spain* is zeugma, which Hemans employs to suggest that British participation in the Peninsular War answers to both immediate political realities and abstract values. For example, the soldiers of Albion rally "the cause of JUSTICE and CASTILE to aid." Elsewhere, they are praised for being the first "the word of BRITAIN and of truth to wield."

CRITICAL DISCUSSION

Judging by its short print run and dismal sales, *England and Spain* had a small immediate readership; moreover, as Diego Saglia indicates in a 2007 article for *English Literary History,* the poem's "pro-military attitude shocked Hemans's patrons," leading her to attenuate that element of her work in later volumes. The poet's publishers only gradually acknowledged

"CASABIANCA" AND THE NAPOLEONIC WARS

Hemans would continue to take up the theme of war in individual poems, though none give as sustained a meditation on the subject as *England and Spain*. Her best-known poem, "Casabianca" (1826), diverges markedly from the unquestioned militarism of the earlier work, suggesting (if not fully presenting) the pathos and horror of war. The poem begins with the still-famous lines "The boy stood on the burning deck / Whence all but he had fled" and tells of a child, no more than thirteen years of age, who refuses to leave his post on a doomed ship during the Battle of the Nile (1798). Far from glorifying war as the freely chosen enterprise of heroic adults, the poem illustrates the boy's helplessness in the face of a strict and unthinking military discipline. Later generations of poets, for whom "Casabianca" was a standard memorization exercise in school, would find the same childlike vulnerability in the young soldiers of World War I. The extent to which Hemans deliberately aims to undercut her earlier, militant sentiments is unclear, even at the critical remove of two centuries. At the very least, Hemans refrains from the anti-French invective that characterizes the savage and perfidious Gauls of *England and Spain*: The boy in question, of "heroic blood" and gallant bearing, is the son of the French commander Luc-Julien-Joseph Casabianca.

the market for her work, and even after a third book Hemans was "still virtually unknown to the literary world," according to Feldman in her 1997 *Keats-Shelley Journal* article. Subsequent volumes, however, were both more widely read and better received, creating some interest in earlier books by Hemans. By the end of the nineteenth century, Hemans would become so emblematic of Romantic women's poetry in general that her picture graced the cover of even American anthologies.

Partly because of its limited audience during the war it described, *England and Spain* has been treated by later critics as important primarily in the context of Hemans's later, more famous work. In *PMLA,* Tricia Lootens suggests in a 1994 article that the work was a strong, early example of the poet's self-identification as a "national poet," developing themes of British moral and economic dominion that would resonate throughout her writing. David Rothstein, in a 1999 article for *Victorian Literature and Culture,* maintains that this process was taken to its extreme in *England and Spain,* which in his estimation "merely glorifies militant patriotism" compared to more nuanced later works. Rothstein notes, however, that Hemans was successful in avoiding the (then common) fate of the "poetess," whose subject matter is circumscribed by gender stereotypes. If Hemans's first major patriotic poem was too strident for some, it nonetheless demonstrated that war poetry is not a wholly masculine pursuit.

England and Spain also, as other literary scholars have discovered, helped to convince Hemans's publishers of her potential for a larger market. Paula Feldman offers a study of Hemans as an independent agent in the increasingly commercial (and magazine-driven) literary world of early nineteenth-century Britain. Exploring the poet's rise from the near-total obscurity of her earlier works (including *England and Spain*) to the great fame she enjoyed toward the end of her career, Feldman notes the poet's own developing knack for finding suitably popular topics and communicating with major publishers. *England and Spain,* read in this context, may be seen as an "apprentice work" not only in terms of rhyme and meter, but of the craft of earning a living as a poet.

BIBLIOGRAPHY

Sources

Feldman, Paula R. "The Poet and the Profits: Felicia Hemans and the Literary Marketplace." *Keats-Shelley Journal* 46 (1997): 148–76. Print.

Jones, Richard Foster. "Eclogue Types in English Poetry of the Eighteenth Century." *Journal of English and Germanic Philology* 24.1 (1925): 33–60. Print.

Kilcup, Karen L. "Embodied Pedagogies: Femininity, Diversity, and Community in Anthologies of Women's Writing, 1836–2009." *Legacy* 26.2 (2009): 299–328. Print.

Lootens, Tricia. "Hemans and Home: Victorianism, Feminine 'Internal Enemies,' and the Domestication of National Identity." *PMLA* 109.2 (1994): 238–53. Print.

Rothstein, David. "Forming the Chivalric Subject: Felicia Hemans and the Cultural Uses of History, Memory, and Nostalgia." *Victorian Literature and Culture* 27.1 (1999): 49–68. Print.

Saglia, Diego. "'A Deeper and Richer Music': The Poetics of Sound and Voice in Felicia Hemans's 1820s Poetry." *ELH* 74.2 (2007): 351–70. Print.

Further Reading

Guest, Harriet. *Small Change: Women, Learning, Patriotism, 1750–1810*. Chicago: U of Chicago P, 2000. Print.

Hemans, Felicia. *The Poetical Works of Felicia Hemans.* Boston: Phillips, Sampson and Co., 1849. Print.

Hoskins, James Thornton. *A Few Words on the Woman's Franchise Question.* London: Emily Faithfull, 1871.

Hutchings, Kevin, and Julia M. Wright. *Transatlantic Literary Exchanges, 1790–1870: Gender, Race, and Nation.* Burlington, VT: Ashgate, 2011. Print.

Saglia, Diego. "'O My Mother Spain!': The Peninsular War, Family Matters, and the Practice of Romantic Nation-Writing." *ELH* 65.2 (1998): 363–93. Print.

Sweet, Nanora, and Julie Melnyk. *Felicia Hemans: Reimagining Poetry in the Nineteenth Century.* New York: Palgrave, 2001. Print.

Michael Hartwell

FACUNDO

Civilization and Barbarism

Domingo Faustino Sarmiento

OVERVIEW

Facundo: Civilization and Barbarism (*Facundo: Civilización y Barbarie*), written by Argentine author Domingo Faustino Sarmiento in 1845, presents a dichotomy between the notions of civilization and barbarism in nineteenth-century Argentina. The creative nonfiction book reconstructs the life of the provincial Argentine leader Juan Facundo Quiroga, who was a *gaucho* (a "cowboy" from the Argentine pampas region). Facundo instilled fear in rural Argentina during the 1820s and 1830s, and Sarmiento's text offers a view of the development and modernization of Latin America during that period. Relying on melodramatic elements and description to drive home his criticism of both Facundo and the contemporary Argentine dictator Juan Manuel Rosas, Sarmiento criticizes the authoritarian leaders of his country as barbarians, advocating for a more cultured and civilized democratic leadership, which Sarmiento himself embodies.

Facundo was originally published in segments in 1845 in the Chilean newspaper *El Progreso* while Sarmiento, who had been forced out of Argentina by the Rosas regime, was living exile in Chile. Upon its publication, the work received mixed reactions that were generally aligned with readers' political leanings—those in support of Rosas's regime strongly condemned Sarmiento's work while more liberal individuals who favored democracy for Argentina's future viewed *Facundo* favorably. The book became representative of its author's political platform and was influential in the overthrow of Rosas in 1852 and the subsequent turn toward democracy in Argentina. Ultimately many of the ideals that Sarmiento espouses in his book came to fruition during his six-year presidency beginning in 1868. *Facundo* continues to be widely read and studied as a foundational work representative of the social, cultural, and political conflicts of nineteenth-century Latin America.

❖ *Key Facts*

Time Period:
Mid-19th Century

Genre:
Novel

Events:
Modernization of Latin America; Argentine independence; dictatorial rule of Argentina by Juan Manuel Rosa

Nationality:
Argentinian

An 1835 painting by Carlos Lezica depicting the assassination of Facundo Quiroga. Quiroga is the subject of *Facundo: Civilization and Barbarism*, by Argentine writer and politician Domingo Faustino Sarmiento. GIANNI DAGLI ORTI/THE ART ARCHIVE AT ART RESOURCE, NY.

PRIMARY SOURCE

EXCERPT FROM *FACUNDO: CIVILIZATION AND BARBARISM*

Today the Argentine Republic is the area of Spanish America whose outward manifestations have most come to the attention of the European nations, which often find themselves embroiled in its disorder, or else pulled, as to a vortex, toward its center where opposing elements swirl. France was on the brink of yielding to that attraction, and not without great effort of sail and oar, not without losing the rudder, did it succeed in removing itself and keeping its distance. Its most skilled politicians have not been able to understand anything of what they saw with their own eyes when they took a quick glimpse at the American power challenging their great nation. Seeing the waves of burning lava roaring in this great focus of intestine struggle, rolling, shaking, and crashing into each other, even those who think themselves most informed have said: "It is just a nameless, subaltern volcano, one of many that appear in America; soon it will be extinguished"; and then they have looked elsewhere, satisfied to have given a solution so easy and precise for social phenomena they have seen only superficially and grouped together. ...

Such is the task we have yet to realize in the Argentine Republic. It may be that so many good results will not be obtained right away, and that after so radical a subversion as the one Rosas has carried out, it may still take a year or more of wavering to get society back into its true balance. But, with the fall of that monster, we will at least start down the road leading to such a beautiful future, rather than getting further and further away every day under his disastrous impulse, and moving backward by giant steps into barbarism, demoralization, and poverty. Peru, no doubt, suffers the effects of its internal upheavals, but still its sons have not left for decades by the thousands, to wander through neighboring countries; no monster has risen up who surrounds himself with bodies, suffocates all spontaneity and all virtuous feeling. What the Argentine Republic needs above all, and what Rosas will never give, because it is no longer his to give, is that the lives, the property of men, not hang on an indiscreetly pronounced word, on the whim of the ruler. Given these two bases, security of life and of property, the form of government, the political organization of the state,

HISTORICAL AND LITERARY CONTEXT

Argentina gained independence from Spain in 1810, but when *Facundo* was published, the country was still divided into opposing factions and had yet to establish a unified national identity. Politically, Argentina was divided between the Unitarists, or Unitarians, who favored a centralized government and with whom Sarmiento identified, and the Federalists, who advocated for more autonomous regional leadership. In general terms this political division also represented a geographical divide between the countryside and the city. The capital city of Buenos Aires was closely connected to European culture and trade, and its urban values often clashed with those of the rural citizens of Argentina's southern countryside, including the pampas, or plains, region.

When Sarmiento composed Facundo in the 1840s, Rosas was at the reins of his Argentine dictatorial regime for a second time, a period of leadership that stretched from 1835 until 1852, when Sarmiento himself aided in Rosas's ousting. As a staunch Unitarist, Sarmiento had fought in the Argentine civil wars (1814–76) against Facundo, a political enemy who would later inspire the composition of *Facundo.*

As a result of his opposition to Rosas in the 1830s, Sarmiento was exiled to Chile in the early 1840s. *Facundo* responds directly to the history of authoritarian rule since Argentina's 1810 independence and denounces the repressive nature of the Rosas dictatorship through a criticism of Facundo's earlier leadership in the country.

During the early nineteenth century, *romanticismo* dominated Latin American literature. Partially influenced by European romanticism, this literary style was first exemplified by such Latin American poets as José María de Heredia of Cuba and Andrés Bello of Venezuela. Characterized by contrasts such as man versus nature, city versus countryside, medieval versus modern, romantic literature directly influenced Sarmiento's writing. Perhaps most notable was the work of his fellow Argentine Esteban Echeverria, whose writing and political ideology in such works as "La cautiva" (1837) and *El matadero* (written 1839, published 1871) had a clear impact on Sarmiento. The liberal political philosophy of such intellectuals as Echeverria and Juan Bautista Alberdi was fundamental for the development of Sarmiento's own political platform through his composition of *Facundo,* reflecting a similar advocacy of democracy and educational reform will come from time, events, circumstances. There is probably no people in America with less faith in a written pact, in a constitution, than the Argentines. Illusions are gone now; the Constitution of the Republic will be made imperceptibly, from within, without anyone having proposed it. Unitarist, federalist, or both, it must emerge from consummated deeds. …

Independent of these general motives for morality that belong to the human species at all times and in all countries, the Argentine Republic has elements of order that many countries in the world lack. One of the obstacles that blocks the calming of tempers in convulsive countries is the difficulty of calling public attention to new objectives that will remove that attention from the vicious circle of thought in which it exists. The Argentine Republic, fortunately, has so much wealth to exploit, so much novelty with which to attract people's spirits after a government like that of Rosas, that it would be impossible to upset the calm necessary to arrive at new goals. When there is a cultured government concerned with the interests of the nation, how many enterprises, how much

industrial movement! The pastoral peoples, busy propagating the merino sheep that produce millions and occupy thousands of men at every hour of the day; the provinces of San Juan and Mendoza, dedicated to raising silkworms, which, with government support and protection, within four years will lack enough workers for the agricultural and industrial tasks they require; the provinces of the north, devoted to the cultivation of sugarcane, of the indigo that is spontaneously produced; the river banks with free navigation that would give movement and life to the industries of the interior. Amid this movement, who will wage war? To achieve what? Only if there is a government as stupid as the present one, which treads on all these interests and instead of giving men work puts them in the army to wage war in Uruguay, Paraguay, Brazil, in sum, everywhere.

for modernizing Argentina. Sarmiento was part of the generation of 1837, a literary group that challenged Rosas's government.

Sarmiento's text was one of the first in a long tradition of Latin American *caudillo* novels that have been published since the mid-nineteenth century. Most notable among these are *El Señor Presidente* (1946) by Miguel Ángel Asturias, based on the presidency of the Guatemalan leader Manuel Estrada Cabrera; *I, the Supreme* (1974) by Augusto Roa Bastos, about the Paraguayan dictator José Gaspar Rodríguez de Francia; and *The Feast of the Goat* (2000) by Mario Vargas Llosa, about Rafael Leonidas Trujillo's dictatorship in the Dominican Republic. *Facundo* is also recognized as the most influential Latin American work of *romanticismo*, impacting later works of the same literary style. The book has been incorporated into the Latin American literary canon and, as a result, continues to be widely read and studied.

THEMES AND STYLE

Facundo embodies Sarmiento's war against dictatorships, especially that of Rosas, by contrasting an enlightened Europe, represented by Sarmiento and other educated men of the city, with the barbarism of

the rural gaucho and *caudillo* (a Latin American military leader or dictator), through the principal example of Facundo. By establishing this strong dichotomy, the author advocates for a liberal democratic government as the ideal alternative to the uncivilized rule of Latin American dictators. In his introduction Sarmiento writes that "Facundo—provincial, barbarous, brave, bold—was replaced by Rosas, son of cultured Buenos Aires without being so himself; by Rosas, traitorous, cold-hearted, calculating soul." The provincial is immediately aligned with the barbarous through the figure of Facundo, while Buenos Aires is described as cultured in direct contrast to Rosas's coldheartedness. Sarmiento's negative portrayal of the two dictators appeals to the reader's sympathy toward the victims of these two barbarous individuals, embodied by Sarmiento and his fellow Unitarists.

Sarmiento achieves the strong impact of his book by incorporating melodramatic and romantic elements in his description of Facundo and supporting his subjective portrayal with quotes, comparisons, and personal anecdotes: "Facundo possessed La Rioja as absolute master and arbiter: there was no voice but his, no concerns but his…. This was the same thing that Dr. Francia, Ibarra, Lopez, Bustos

DOMINGO FAUSTINO SARMIENTO: NINETEENTH-CENTURY ARGENTINE INTELLECTUAL

Domingo Faustino Sarmiento was an Argentine intellectual, politician, and writer who served as the seventh president of Argentina. Born on February 15, 1811, Sarmiento grew up in a modest environment and was influenced by his family's political activism. Before entering politics, he made his liberal political stance clear in his writing, through which he denounced the dictatorial brutality of such contemporary politicians as Juan Facundo Quiroga and Juan Manuel de Rosas. As a result, Sarmiento was exiled to Chile during the 1840s, during which period he wrote his most renowned work, *Facundo: Civilization and Barbarism,* and worked for *El Progreso* newspaper.

Sarmiento returned to Argentina after Rosas's fall, first serving in the Senate and later as president from 1868 to 1874. During his presidency, he ended the war with Paraguay and advocated for Latin American democracy and educational reform. He also contributed substantially to the modernization of Argentina through the establishment of a postal system and a train system. Following his presidency, Sarmiento continued to serve in different governmental positions for many years. He died from a heart attack on September 11, 1888, in Asunción, Paraguay.

had done … to destroy all existing rights in order to impose their own." Sarmiento draws parallels between the governance of other Latin American dictators and that of Facundo to emphasize the history of barbarous rule in the region and to illustrate the need for a civilized alternative. The book is written in the first person from the point of view of Sarmiento, who serves as both the narrator and the protagonist, giving a personal air to the text that reflects the real effects of the brutal dictatorship on individuals such as himself.

Facundo is characterized by an impassioned and irreverent tone that appeals to the emotions of its audience. In his author's note prior to the introduction, Sarmiento writes, "Toward the end of 1840 I was leaving my homeland, pitifully exiled, broken, covered with bruises, kicks, and blows received the day before in one of those bloody bacchanals of unruly soldiers." His colorful description of his run-in with his political opponents, whom he portrays once again as uncivilized, further reinforces the author's argument for a democratic alternative to the chaos that reigns in his country. Sarmiento's often candid and informal tone is contrasted by the author's incorporation of French quotes that precede each chapter, appealing specifically to an educated European audience whose political support he sought for his cause.

CRITICAL DISCUSSION

In the immediate aftermath of its publication, *Facundo* sparked much controversy regarding its portrayal of Argentina's political reality. Initial reactions by Latin American intellectuals included Valentín Alsina's criticism that the book misinterprets facts about Rosas and inadequately portrays the reality of Unitarist and Federalist relations. In her 1996 book *Facundo and the Construction of Argentine Culture,* Diana Goodrich quotes Alsina addressing Sarmiento directly: "You are setting out to write neither a romance, nor an epic, but a true social, political, and at times even military *history*…. That being the case, it is essential not to stray in the slightest … from historical accuracy and rigor." In the 1880s the text became canonized with the triumph of liberalism, whose proponents championed Sarmiento's foundational work.

While Sarmiento wrote numerous other books and essays during his lifetime, including *Conflictos y armonías de las razas en América* (Racial conflict and harmony in America; 1883), *Facundo* is his best-known and most highly regarded work. The work reintroduced the long-running Latin American intellectual debate on civilization versus barbarism, changing the terms on which the distinction was applied. The book's most obvious political influence was seen in Sarmiento's eventual presidency, which enabled him to apply many of the theories and ideals he had outlined in *Facundo* twenty years earlier. Sarmiento's book inspired other Latin American writers to examine and analyze dictatorship within the region, a trend that is reflected in the emergence of the "dictator novel" genre. This influence continues today and is evident in the predominance of dictator studies by scholars specializing in Latin American history, culture, and politics.

In their analysis of *Facundo,* many scholars have discussed the legacy of the civilization versus barbarism debate, which can be seen most prominently in the struggle for recognition of indigenous culture within Latin America. Goodrich explains in a 1992 article that "Sarmiento's program to do away with barbarism in order to proclaim the law of civilization has been aligned by his numerous enemies with the forces of modernization that have betrayed the quest for a native identity, one of many unresolved debates in Latin American politics and culture." Other scholars, such as Joseph A. Feustle Jr. in 1972 and Thomas Ward in 2007, have analyzed Sarmiento's work in comparison with later Latin American intellectuals, including José Martí, Eugenio María de Hostos, and Ezequiel Martínez Estrada.

BIBLIOGRAPHY

Sources

Goodrich, Diana S. *Facundo and the Construction of Argentine Culture.* Austin: U of Texas P, 1996. Print.

———. "From Barbarism to Civilization: Travels of a Latin American Text." *American Literary History* 4.3 (1992): 443–63. Print.

Sarmiento, Domingo Faustino. *Facundo: Civilization and Barbarism.* Trans. Kathleen Ross. Berkeley: U of California P, 2004. Print.

Further Reading

Criscenti, Joseph. *Sarmiento and His Argentina.* Boulder, CO: Lynne Rienner, 1993. Print.

Feustle, Joseph A., Jr. "Sarmiento and Martinez Estrada: A Concept of Argentine History." *Hispania* 55.3 (1972): 446–55. Print.

Jones, C. A. *Sarmiento: Facundo.* London: Grant & Cutler, 1974. Print.

Shaw, D. L. Rev. of *Sarmiento: Facundo,* by C. A. Jones. *Modern Language Review* 70.2 (1975): 443–44. Print.

Ward, Thomas. "From Sarmiento to Marti and Hostos: Extricating the Nation from Coloniality." *Revista Europea de Estudios Latinoamericanos y del Caribe/ European Review of Latin American and Caribbean Studies* 83 (2007): 83–104. Print.

Katrina White

THE FAERIE QUEENE

Edmund Spenser

✥ *Key Facts*

Time Period:
Late 16th Century

Genre:
Poetry

Events:
English Reformation;
defeat of the Spanish
Armada; reign of Queen
Elizabeth I

Nationality:
English

OVERVIEW

Published near the end of Queen Elizabeth I's reign, Edmund Spenser's epic romance *The Faerie Queene* pays homage to the virtue, chastity, beauty, and Protestant religious principles that Elizabeth attempted to embody as monarch. Written in highly structured verse, the six-book epic was published in two parts—the first three books were printed in 1590, the second three in 1596. Each book relates the story of a knight who represents one of several virtues: holiness, temperance, chastity, friendship, justice, and courtesy. The knights strive to defeat allegorical monsters; to protect defenseless figures; and to perform the will of Gloriana, the Faerie Queene. Even as the poem praises Queen Elizabeth's morality, English manners, and courtly behavior, it subtly critiques the monarch and her court, implying that they may not wholly embrace the Protestant ideals and virtues they claim to exhibit.

After the publication of the first three books, Elizabeth I rewarded Spenser with a stipend of £50 per year, and he completed the next three books. Although he had planned six more books featuring six new knights, he never completed them. As he reports in a letter to Sir Walter Raleigh, his goal in writing *The Faerie Queene* was "to fashion a gentleman or noble person in vertuous and gentle discipline" by using allegorical figures to convey moral truths from a Protestant perspective. At a time when English poets strove to create a national style, Spenser portrayed himself as a prominent poet who used fiction to produce thoughtful, well-behaved subjects for the queen. Today *The Faerie Queene* is known for its role in shaping English national identity and for its depiction of idealized Protestant subjects.

HISTORICAL AND LITERARY CONTEXT

During the 1580s and 1590s, when Spencer was composing *The Faerie Queene,* England was suffering political insecurity on two levels. Elizabeth, an aging monarch, had not married or produced an heir. Moreover, in 1588, Spain, a Catholic nation, sent an armada to attack English shores. Fears over succession and the tensions caused by the Spanish invasion were further intensified by the visit of the French Duke d'Alençon, a Catholic nobleman who tried to woo the queen. In response, English Protestant noblemen and the writers they patronized used pamphlets and pageantry to try to convince Elizabeth that she should avoid any form of Catholic alliance. They also hinted that she should send troops to assist nearby Protestant countries at war with Spain, such as the Netherlands.

As religious and nationalistic tensions overlapped and the threat of war loomed large in late-Elizabethan England, public writings became an essential tool in shaping the opinions of the literate classes. Because of the uncertainty caused by the queen's lack of a husband or an heir, writers needed to be careful about directly condemning any particular group of people; it was unknown which group might gain political power over England after the queen's death. Spenser, for example, was part of the entourages of two powerful Protestant earls—first the Earl of Leicester and then the Earl of Essex—and thus had to maintain a delicate balance between forwarding their agendas; praising the queen and the nation; and considering the reaction of potential future English monarchs, such as James VI of Scotland, whose mother was the Catholic Mary, Queen of Scots.

Allegory was a popular tool for Elizabethan writers in a politically sensitive landscape. Playwrights such as John Lyly turned to Greek and Roman literature for inspiration, dramatizing myths like that of Endymion. In Lyly's version of the Endymion myth, the moon simultaneously represents chastity, wisdom, and Elizabeth I. Multidirectional allegorical symbols not only offered interesting intellectual exercises but also protected a writer from accusations of overt political intervention. At the same time, allegory allowed writers to subtly praise or critique public figures or life at court. Honed in the period's pastoral works, such as the eclogues in Philip Sidney's *Old Arcadia* (1590) and Spenser's *Shepheardes Calender* (1579), the use of allegory peaked with Spenser's *Faerie Queene,* which deployed a single character (the Redcrosse Knight) to embody holiness, Christ, and England's patron saint, St. George.

Spenser's use of multifaceted symbolism had far-reaching effects on religious and national literature. John Milton used Spenser's portrayal of Error as a major inspiration for his description of Satan, Sin, and Death in *Paradise Lost* (1667). Spenser's Gothic overtones also influenced the way that English poet John Keats and other Romantic writers wrote about England's history. Spenser's influence continued into the modern era as writers such as Wilfred Owen read *The Faerie Queene* as escapist literature during World War I. Today Spenser's epic is frequently read as an example of nationalistic romance and of uniquely English style and structure.

THEMES AND STYLE

Because *The Faerie Queene* seeks "to fashion a gentleman," it places emphasis on defining what an English gentleman ought to do, say, and think to provide good service to the queen. Whereas Elizabethan courtiers were often shrewd, self-serving, and envious (in another work, Spenser compares minister of state Lord Burghley to a fox), *The Faerie Queene* describes idealized versions of knights who learn about and embody specific virtues in public and in private. Chief among these knights is Arthur, the ancient British hero-king who seeks to marry Gloriana. While other knights stumble and must be gradually educated, Arthur personifies "magnificence," which is "the perfection of the rest [of the virtues], and containeth … them all." As an English icon seeking to allegorically wed a representation of Elizabeth, Arthur personifies the epitome of national valor. By contrast, the fallibility of the other knights hints at the difficulty of perfectly embodying a single courtly virtue—let alone all of them.

The elaborate process of learning about and embodying a virtue is rhetorically mirrored in the complex organization of *The Faerie Queene*. Each book is divided into subunits called cantos, which contain a varying number of Spenserian stanzas. Each nine-line stanza contains eight lines of iambic pentameter and a closing line of hexameter, rhyming ABABBCBCC. The structure hearkens back to the rhyme royal used by English poet Geoffrey Chaucer but adds an Elizabethan twist with two additional lines of verse. In addition, Spenser uses first- and third-person narrators to combine the classical voice of epic poetry with the wandering, digressive English style of romance. This double-voiced narration guides the reader and the characters through dense, twisting sentences that aim to progressively educate them about a virtue. For example, when approaching a dark, scary cave, Una and the Redcrosse Knight fail to assess the situation properly, and Spenser's twisted syntax expresses their backward assessment: "Faire harbour that them seemes; so they in entred arre."

As a national poet, Spenser uses archaic British vocabulary and spelling to educate his audience about national virtues and literary history. Words like "eke" (also), "hight" (was named), and "quoth" (said) appeared old-fashioned even to Elizabethan ears. However, at the same time, the author frames himself as an heir of the Greco-Roman tradition, following Virgil's career by moving from "lowly Shepheards weeds" (pastoral poetry) to "sing of Knights and Ladies gentle deeds" in a courtly mode. By merging a Greco-Roman ethos with native English style, Spenser implies that English literature inherits and propagates ancient models of literature

EDMUND SPENSER: AN ENGLISHMAN IN IRELAND

As a member of the English bureaucracy living in Ireland, Edmund Spenser was both a rising young professional and an outsider to Elizabeth's court. After moving to Ireland to take a secretarial position early in his career, he created the poetic persona of Colin Clout to express his ambivalent feelings toward the court and the countryside. Although Ireland offered Spenser a chance to climb the social hierarchy and to eventually become a landowner and receive the Kilcolman estate, the relationship between English settlers and the native Irish was violent, and Spenser's home was incinerated during an uprising.

To defend the English position in Ireland, Spenser wrote *A View of the Present State of Ireland* (1596), also addressing the colony's upheaval in his other works. For example, Book Five of *The Faerie Queene* recounts a thinly disguised version of the British effort to "liberate" Ireland by means of warfare. Lady Irena, who represents peace, is rescued from the villain Grantorto by Knight Artegall, who represents justice. David Norbrook in *Poetry and Politics in the English Renaissance* (2002) points out that Spenser "regarded the Irish masses as not much superior to beasts" but hoped to influence them to embrace English culture through his writing. Although multiple perspectives on the Irish question emerge in *The Faerie Queene*'s nationalistic allegory, Spenser contained and censored their negative ramifications in order to promote the best possible image of England.

under the inspiration of Elizabeth I—the "Goddesse" and "Great Lady of the greatest Isle."

CRITICAL DISCUSSION

Because of its didactic goals and English style, *The Faerie Queene* won praise from Spenser's immediate contemporaries. Elizabethans such as Gabriel Harvey and Thomas Tresham lauded the "sweet" quality of the first three books, calling Spenser the unofficial poet laureate of England. In a 1753 entry in *Lives of the Poets,* Theophilus Cibber holds a more critical viewpoint: "Abundance betrays [Spenser] into Excess, and his Judgment is overborne by the Torrent of his Imagination." Samuel Taylor Coleridge, in an 1836 collection of his writings titled *Literary Remains,* praises the poet's descriptive style and acknowledges Spenser's role as a specifically English poet: "In Spenser we see the brightest and purest form of that nationality which was so common a characteristic of our elder poet … to glorify their country—to elevate England … this was their passion and object."

Socially and politically, the legacy of *The Faerie Queene* is mixed. While Elizabethan audiences may have enjoyed the work's syrupy praise of the monarch—in part because they knew how to read allegorically and to find deeper critiques of her policies—modern audiences may find the flattery sycophantic. The work

also is notorious for its unabashed portrayals of religious warfare: knights who kill "Saracens" (Muslims) or female beasts that represent the Catholic Church are framed as heroes. Although such portrayals may make modern audiences uncomfortable, these features, as Anne Lake Prescott and Hugh Maclean point out in *Edmund Spenser's Poetry* (1993), create fruitful material to analyze through the lenses of historical context, gender theory, and genre studies, allowing modern readers to explore early English perspectives on important religious and national issues.

Recent criticism has highlighted *The Faerie Queene*'s role in promoting English colonialism, particularly in an Irish context. In *Renaissance Self-Fashioning: From More to Shakespeare* (2005), Stephen Greenblatt argues that the "Bower of Blisse" episode in Book Two reflects a general fascination with the foreign and exotic, and he links these elements to the seductive power of idols and even poetry itself. Another frequent focus of *The Faerie Queene* criticism is the question of Spenser's engagement with poetic theory. For example, scholars discuss the influence of Italian and Spanish works on the text, analyzing how Spenser participates in and modifies the genre of the national epic from a European standpoint. Thus, as a compendious and descriptive allegorical text, *The Faerie Queene* provides a wealth of material on English poetics, Protestant culture, the cult of Queen Elizabeth, and the places where these topics intersect.

BIBLIOGRAPHY

Sources

Cibber, Theophilus. *The Lives of the Poets of Great Britain and Ireland.* Vol. 1. Middlesex: Echo Library, 2007. Web. 1 Sept. 2012.

Coleridge, Samuel Taylor. "Spenser." *Literary Remains.* Vol. 1. Ed. Henry Nelson Coleridge. Middlesex: Echo Library, 2007. 80–85. Web. 1 Sept. 2012.

"Edmund Spenser." *The Norton Anthology of English Literature.* Ed. M. H. Abrams and Stephen Greenblatt. 7th ed. New York: Norton, 2000. Print.

Greenblatt, Stephen. *Renaissance Self-Fashioning: From More to Shakespeare.* Chicago: U of Chicago P, 2005. Print.

Hadfield, Andrew. "Spenser, Edmund (1552?–1599)." *Oxford Dictionary of National Biography.* Oxford UP, 2004. Web. 1 Sept. 2012.

Norbrook, David. *Poetry and Politics in the English Renaissance.* Oxford: Oxford UP, 2002. Print.

Spenser, Edmund. *Edmund Spenser's Poetry.* Ed. Hugh Maclean and Anne Lake Prescott. 3rd ed. New York: Norton, 1993. Print.

Further Reading

Fogarty, Anne. "The Colonization of Language: Narrative Strategy in *A View of the Present State of Ireland* and *The Faerie Queene,* Book VI." *Spenser and Ireland: An Interdisciplinary Perspective.* Ed. Patricia Coughlan. Cork: Cork UP, 1989. 75–108. Print.

Hadfield, Andrew. "The Relevance of Spenser." *Modern Philology* 106.4 (2009): 686–701. Print.

Hammill, Graham, and Julia Reinhard Lupton. "Sovereigns, Citizens, and Saints: Political Theology and Renaissance Literature." *Religion and Literature* 38.3 (2006): 1–11. Print.

Lehnhof, Kent R. "Incest and Empire in *The Faerie Queene.*" *ELH* 73.1 (2006): 215–43. Print.

Montrose, Louis. "Spenser and the Elizabethan Political Imaginary." *ELH* 69.4 (2002): 907–46. Print.

Spenser, Edmund. *A View of the State of Ireland.* Ed. Andrew Hadfield, Willy Maley, and Sir James Ware. New York: Wiley-Blackwell, 1997. Print.

Nancy Simpson Younger

Opposite page:
Written during the reign of Queen Elizabeth I, *The Faerie Queen* is believed to be Edmund Spenser's celebration of his monarch. © CLASSIC IMAGE/ALAMY.

THE FEDERALIST

Alexander Hamilton, James Madison, John Jay

❖ *Key Facts*

Time Period:
Late 18th Century

Genre:
Essay

Events:
American Revolution;
writing of the
Constitution

Nationality:
American

OVERVIEW

Published in 1788 under the pseudonym Publius, *The Federalist* is a two-volume collection of eighty-five essays written by statesmen Alexander Hamilton, James Madison, and John Jay, to explain and defend the proposed Constitution of the United States. Seventy-eight of the *Federalist* essays had been previously published, from October 1787 to May 1788, in a number of newspapers in an effort to persuade American voters to ratify the newly written national charter. Delineating the imperfections in the existing Articles of Confederation, describing the reasoning behind the new governmental proposals, and answering the objections of critics, *The Federalist* became an enduring and influential treatise on the practical philosophy of politics.

The Federalist emerged in a time of political innovation and vigorous social debate, as writers, intellectuals, and social visionaries employed Enlightenment principles of scientific reasoning and humanitarian justice to argue for greater public participation in government. The independent spirit that led to the American Revolutionary War was a product of Enlightenment thinking, as was the innovative new government proposed by the Constitution drafted in 1787. The publication of the *Federalist* essays in a number of newspapers in New York and several other states reflected the contemporary assumption that most educated citizens were both competent and eager to take part in comprehensive political debate.

HISTORICAL AND LITERARY CONTEXT

After the signing of the Treaty of Paris, which ended the Revolutionary War in 1783, the sprawling new nation began the process of designing its independent government. The Continental Congress had begun work on a plan of self-governance by the time the *Declaration of Independence* was signed in July 1776. The Articles of Confederation adopted in 1781, however, proved insufficient to the complex task of uniting the disparate states under a national government strong enough to rein in interstate rivalries and flexible enough to support strongly felt state allegiances.

The loosely confederated states of the mid-1780s faced a number of problems. In the absence of a strong centralizing authority, trade relations among states were contentious, the monetary system was cumbersome and unstable, and both the treasury and the military had been weakened by years of war. In western Massachusetts, a farmers' debt crisis led to armed rebellion in January 1787 when Revolutionary War veteran Daniel Shays led thousands of militiamen in an attack on the federal arsenal in Springfield. New state constitutions set up widely divergent governments, from Pennsylvania, which expanded its electorate by removing the property requirement for voters, to South Carolina, which set such requirements so high that only 10 percent of white male voters were eligible to run for office. Fearful of the national economic effects of radical state constitutions and overwhelmed by increasing economic instability, many citizens began to speak out in favor of a stronger national government. From May to September 1787, state delegates met in Philadelphia to create a blueprint for a new government. Once finished, the U.S. Constitution required ratification by nine of the thirteen states, and it especially needed the support of the most powerful: Virginia, Pennsylvania, and New York. Concerned by an outpouring of antifederalist sentiment in New York newspapers, convention delegates Madison and Hamilton, along with statesman Jay, agreed to counter this opposition with a series of articles designed to persuade New York voters to accept the Constitution. Though there is some dispute over the authorship of the individual essays, it is generally agreed that Madison and Hamilton wrote the majority, with Jay authoring only five.

Political discourse flourished during the Enlightenment, as writers explored new systems of thought and developed innovative liberal theories of government. Values such as "life, liberty, and the pursuit of happiness," delineated in Thomas Jefferson's 1776 *Declaration of Independence,* replaced the pessimistic absolutism of earlier centuries. Writers such as John Locke (*Two Treatises of Government,* 1690) had pioneered the concept of representative government, and the Baron de Montesquieu had introduced the idea of separation of political powers in his 1748 work *The Spirit of Laws.* Scottish philosopher David Hume's 1739 *Treatise of Human Nature* developed the notion that politics and law could be governed by scientific principles. In America the persuasive pamphlets of journalist Thomas Paine had been a major force in promoting the cause of independence.

Addressed, "To the people of the State of New York," Hamilton, Madison, and Jay's essays were published in at least four New York newspapers and reprinted in journals in Virginia, Pennsylvania, Rhode Island, Massachusetts, and New Hampshire. Though it is unclear how many people actually read the essays as they were published, their thorough examination of the Constitution and cogent arguments in its favor have made *The Federalist* a document of lasting value in the general study of government and of the U.S. Constitution in particular. The essays are viewed as such an authoritative voice on the original meaning of the Constitution that they have been cited in more than 300 Supreme Court decisions.

THEMES AND STYLE

Publius begins the first essay with the central question of "whether societies of men are really capable or not, of establishing good government by reflection and choice, or whether they are forever destined to depend, for their political constitutions, on accident and force." Much of *The Federalist* is devoted to answering this question, first by examining the insufficiencies of the existing Articles of Confederacy, then by detailed explanation of the proposed Constitution, and last by countering the arguments of opponents. Within the central theme of the need for a strong national government to promote unity and gain international respect ("The national Government will be more wise, systematical, and judicious … with respect to other nations," *Federalist #3*), the authors devote careful attention to the division of powers that will keep such a centralized authority in check. As Madison states in the fifty-first, and perhaps most popularly known, essay, "In framing a government … the great difficulty lies in this: you must first enable the government to control the governed; and in the next place oblige it to control itself."

Recognizing the importance of rationality to their Enlightenment-era audience, the writers of *The Federalist* employ logical exposition and appeals to reason and judgment to plead their cause. "My arguments will be open to all and may be judged by all. They shall at least be offered in a spirit which will not disgrace the cause of truth" (*Federalist #1*). The first essay also introduces an appeal to the reader's self-interest by mentioning, "The additional security which its adoption will afford to the preservation of that species of government, to liberty, and to property." The Constitution arose out of the violent upheaval of revolution and the passion of new patriotism, and the writers spoke to those feelings as well. "Let me ask the man who can raise his mind to one elevated conception, who can awaken in his bosom one patriotic emotion" (*Federalist #40*). The authors also disarm their opponents by carefully raising and countering the foreseeable objections, "that the objectors may be disarmed of every pretext" (*Federalist #40*).

Though they were written in haste in order to promote the quick ratification of the new Constitution, the essays consist of language and syntax that had been

PERFECTING THE CONSTITUTION: THE BILL OF RIGHTS

In Essay 84 of *The Federalist,* Publius writes, "The most considerable of the remaining objections is that the plan of the convention contains no bill of rights." Although the author goes on to argue that the proposed Constitution's separation of powers provide ample protections for the rights of the individual, many antifederalists insisted that the lack of a clear listing of rights was a fatal flaw in the new document. Proponents felt that a bill of rights would not only force the government to respect fundamental rights but would also serve as an explicit reminder to citizens of what rights were due to a free people.

Many Americans supported the idea of a bill of rights, yet the framers of the Constitution had rejected every attempt to insert one, insisting that any list of guaranteed rights would necessarily be incomplete. Citizen rights would be amply protected, they maintained, by the very form of the proposed government with its specifically limited powers. At the same time *The Federalist* joined the debate over ratification, antifederalists such as Virginia's Patrick Henry and essayists under pseudonyms such as Brutus and Federal Farmer voiced the views of many who would not accept the new charter without a bill of rights. When ratification seemed threatened, federalist leaders promised that if the Constitution were accepted, they would support the introduction of a bill of rights in the form of a series of amendments. The Constitution was ratified on June 21, 1788. James Madison, Congressman from Virginia, proposed the promised amendments to the first U.S. Congress, and, after lengthy debate and revisions, the Bill of Rights became part of the Constitution on December 15, 1791.

carefully chosen throughout. The title itself is calculated, as the word "federalist" had been used previously to define those who supported a loose federation of individual states. Hamilton appropriated the term and used it to describe those who favored a powerful central government while maintaining strong state identities, astutely diffusing the conflict between national and state interests. The Latin pseudonym Publius was also chosen with purpose, as it formed a connection in the reader's mind between the authors and the classical ideals of the early Roman Republic, while also suggesting public service and the authors' intent to put aside their own identities in order to speak purely for the public good.

CRITICAL DISCUSSION

Though there are few records of public response to the *Federalist* essays, Ormond Seavey suggests in his essay about Madison in *American Writers of the Early Republic* (1985), "The popularity of the essays when they first appeared is evidenced by their appearance simultaneously in four of the five New York City papers." A February 1788 article in the New York *Independent Journal* announcing the publication of the collected essays praised the work: "The justness of the reasoning, the force of the arguments, and the beauty of

A portrait of Alexander Hamilton. PORTRAIT OF ALEXANDER HAMILTON (1757–1804) (OIL ON CANVAS), TRUMBULL, JOHN (1756–1843)/WHITE HOUSE, WASHINGTON D.C., USA/THE BRIDGEMAN ART LIBRARY.

the language … have justly recommended it to general applause." Though the Constitution was officially ratified in June 1788, *The Federalist*'s role in that outcome remains unclear. In addition to being published in New York, selected essays had been published in newspapers in Pennsylvania, Massachusetts, Virginia, and Rhode Island, where antifederalist sentiment was strong. Bound copies of *The Federalist* were distributed to the delegates at state ratification conventions. New Yorkers, to whom the essays had been directly addressed, sent a majority of antifederalist delegates to the state ratification convention but nonetheless ratified the new Constitution by a vote of thirty to twenty-seven. Though the actual effect of the essays on those who voted to ratify is still a matter of scholarly debate, many believe Hamilton, Madison, and Jay's articulate defense of the Constitution was a powerful factor.

If it was not conclusively persuasive in ratifying the Constitution, *The Federalist* did succeed in its aim to elucidate the political atmosphere and level of debate in the early United States of America. Jacob Cooke, who edited a 1961 edition of the collected essays, writes in its foreword, "*The Federalist,* the authoritative exposition of the Constitution, occupies an unrivaled place in our national political literature." In an essay in *Saving the Revolution* (1987), political analyst Murray Dry concurred, saying, "*The Federalist*'s full explanation of the Constitution's provisions, as well as its argument for a strong government, remain impressive and instructive today."

Judges, scholars, and political thinkers of all persuasions continue to read and analyze *The Federalist*'s arguments for the three-part representative republic delineated in the Constitution. Because the authors wrote anonymously and sometimes collaborated, debate

continues as to the exact attribution of many of the essays. In John Burt's analysis in *Raritan,* "The most interesting features of Federalist thought have to do with the suppression of 'faction,'" while James Jasinski, in a 1997 essay in *Rhetoric Society Quarterly,* discussed the collaborative format of the work as representative of the multiplicity of voices taking part in the early debates that formed the nation.

BIBLIOGRAPHY

Sources

Burt, John. "Tyranny and Faction in the *Federalist Papers.*" *Raritan* 13.2 (1993): 56–84. Rpt. in *Literature Criticism from 1400 to 1800.* Ed. Michael L. LaBlanc. Vol. 80. Detroit: Gale, 2002. *Literature Resource Center.* Web. 8 Aug. 2012.

Coenen, Dan T. "Fifteen Curious Facts about *The Federalist Papers.*" *Georgia Law.* 1 Apr. 2007. U of Georgia. Web. 9 Aug. 2012.

Cooke, Jacob, ed. Introduction. *The Federalist.* Middletown: Wesleyan UP, 1961. xi–xxx. Print.

Dry, Murray. "Anti-Federalism in *The Federalist*: A Founding Dialogue on the Constitution, Republican Government, and Federalism." *Saving the Revolution: "The Federalist Papers" and the American Founding.* Ed. Charles R. Kesler. New York: Free Press, 1987. 40–60. Rpt. in *Literature Criticism from 1400 to 1800.* Ed. Michael L. LaBlanc. Vol. 80. Detroit: Gale, 2002. *Literature Resource Center.* Web. 8 Aug. 2012.

Estes, Todd. "The Voices of Publius and the Strategies of Persuasion in *The Federalist.*" *Journal of the Early Republic* 28.4 (2008): 523+. *Literature Resource Center.* Web. 8 Aug. 2012.

Jasinski, James. "Heteroglossia, Polyphony, and *The Federalist Papers.*" *Rhetoric Society Quarterly* 27.1 (1997): 23–46. Rpt. in *Literature Criticism from 1400 to 1800.* Ed. Michael L. LaBlanc. Vol. 80. Detroit: Gale, 2002. *Literature Resource Center.* Web. 12 Aug. 2012.

Seavey, Ormond. "James Madison." *American Writers of the Early Republic.* Ed. Emory Elliott. Detroit: Gale Research, 1985. *Dictionary of Literary Biography.* Vol. 37. *Literature Resource Center.* Web. 8 Aug. 2012.

"To the People of America." *Independent Journal* 6 Feb. 1788: 3. *America's GenealogyBank.* NewsBank. Web. 10 Aug. 2012.

Further Reading

Ferguson, Robert A. "The Forgotten Publius." *Early American Literature* 34.3 (1999): 223. *Literature Resource Center.* Web. 8 Aug. 2012.

Furtwangler, Albert. *The Authority of Publius: A Reading of the "Federalist Papers."* Ithaca: Cornell UP, 1984. Print.

Kesler, Charles R., ed. *Saving the Revolution: The "Federalist Papers" and the American Founding.* New York: Free Press, 1987. Print.

Maggs, Gregory E. "A Concise Guide to the *Federalist Papers* as a Source of the Original Meaning of the United States Constitution." *Boston University Law Review.* BU. Web. 10 Aug. 2012.

Maier, Pauline. *Ratification: The People Debate the Constitution.* New York: Simon, 2011. Print.

Tina Gianoulis

THE HOME AND THE WORLD

Rabindranath Tagore

OVERVIEW

In 1916 Indian poet and novelist Rabindranath Tagore published his seventh novel, *Ghare Bāire,* in which he offers a critical—and controversial—assessment of the dangers of nationalism. In 1919 an English translation by his nephew Surendranath Tagore was published as *The Home and the World.* Set during the 1905 boycott of British goods known as the *Swadeshi* (self-sufficiency) movement, *The Home and the World* tells the story of Nikhil, an enlightened Bengali landowner who wants to free his country from British rule and to liberate his wife from traditional limitations on Indian women. He succeeds in coaxing his wife, Bimala, out of the women's quarters, only to have her become infatuated with Sandip, a charismatic and unscrupulous political activist. Bimala eventually sees through Sandip and recognizes her husband's greatness, but it is too late. Nikhil has been fatally wounded trying to quell the communal riots triggered by Sandip's version of nationalism. Attacked by Indian nationalists as pro-British propaganda, the novel explores the dark and destructive elements of nationalism, criticizing the extremism and terrorism that characterized early Indian nationalist activity.

Indian and Western readers had extremely different reactions to the novel. As Anita Desai explains in the introduction to the 1985 edition, Indian readers responded to the novel not as a work of fiction but as "a participant in the political storm that had gathered over India in the first decade of the century." Indian readers had strong reactions to the novel in part because Tagore is an emblematic figure in modern Indian culture and politics. Often compared to Russian novelist Leo Tolstoy and seen as a precursor to Mohandas Gandhi, Tagore was a leading member of the literary, cultural, and religious reform movement known as the Bengal Renaissance. Nevertheless, Indian nationalists accused Tagore of collaborating with the British. Many English readers, however, thought the book was a satire, while others mistakenly assumed Tagore's purpose in writing the novel was to explain contemporary India to the West. In 1913 Tagore was the first non-Westerner to receive the Nobel Prize in Literature and became an international literary celebrity, adding even more weight to his voice in India's political affairs. Today the book is generally acknowledged to be Tagore's masterpiece in the novel form.

HISTORICAL AND LITERARY CONTEXT

Ironically, the Indian nationalism that Tagore criticizes has its roots in Western education. Beginning in the 1830s, the British East India Company offered education to a small number of elite Indians, creating what historian Thomas Babington Macaulay in his collected works (*Macaulay, Prose and Poetry,* 1957) describes as a "class of persons Indian in blood and colour, but English in tastes, in opinions, in morals and in intellect." A large proportion of this class came from Bengal, where Calcutta, then the capital of British India, was located. Calcutta soon became the center of a thriving Indian intelligentsia. Following the Indian Mutiny of 1857, expanded opportunities for Western education and Queen Victoria's proclamation of equal opportunity for all races seemed to open the door to advancement. A generation of young Indians saw Western education as the path to jobs in law, journalism, education, and most importantly the Indian Civil Service, but they soon discovered that the door was less open than it appeared. Thwarted in their desire to play a larger role in India's government, the most politically conscious among them founded India's first nationalist organizations.

In 1905 British viceroy Lord Curzon divided Bengal into two provinces, leaving the Western-educated Bengali elite a minority in its homeland. Nationalist leaders, seeing the partition of Bengal as a case of divide and conquer, called for a boycott of British goods and institutions. At first, Tagore was a prominent participant in the Swadeshi movement, leading protest meetings, writing political pamphlets, and composing patriotic songs. Over time he became horrified by the movement's increasing violence, particularly communal violence between Hindus and Muslims. Despite bitter criticism, he withdrew from the movement in 1907, concentrating instead on experiments in economic development and education. According to Sumit Sarkar, author of the definitive study of the Swadeshi movement, *The Swadeshi Movement in Bengal 1903–1908* (2010), during this period Tagore "anticipated almost every basic principle of what later became a nation-wide mass movement of non-violent, non-cooperation under the dynamic leadership of Mahatma Gandhi."

Like Indian nationalism, the Indian novel was a by-product of Western education, which introduced

ABANINDRANATH TAGORE: BENGAL REVIVAL ARTIST

Rabindranath Tagore was not the only member of his family to play a formative role in modern Indian culture. His cousin Abanindranath Tagore (1871–1951) is widely considered the father of modern Indian art. In his early twenties, Abanindranath trained briefly in traditional European painting techniques. Under the influence of Dr. E. B. Havell, vice principal of the Government College of Art at Calcutta, and Japanese artist Okagura, he abandoned European painting styles in favor of painting derived from the Moghul and Rajput miniature traditions. In 1907 he founded the Oriental School of Art in Calcutta and was one of the leading figures in the Bengal revival movement. His paintings utilize traditional, folk, and popular materials in eclectic and often subversive ways.

the Indian middle classes to such authors as Sir Walter Scott and Charles Dickens, as well as to the British legal system. Bankimchandra Chatterji, a leading figure in the Bengal Renaissance and Tagore's direct literary progenitor, was the first to adapt the form to Indian subjects. Like Tagore, Chatterji made his name as a poet. He wrote his first novel in English; the fourteen that followed were written in Bengali and quickly translated into other Indian languages. According to Josna Rege in *The Oxford Encyclopedia of The Modern World* (2008), Chatterji "used historical settings to develop cultural nationalist themes and domestic settings to explore social issues such as widow remarriage; created vivid and complex characters, particularly women; and developed a modern Bengali prose style."

The historical Indian genre quickly became popular, thanks to what Mary Lago in *Rabindranath Tagore* (1976) describes as "Bengalis' increasingly strong desire to read about themselves, to have a literature that depicted daily life as they knew it." Political psychologist Ashis Nandy in *Return from Exile* (1998) sums up Tagore's primary role as "shaping the modern consciousness in India." Today he remains a towering literary figure, so well known in modern India that he is often referred to simply as Rabindranath or as Kabi the Poet.

THEMES AND STYLE

In *The Home and the World,* Tagore explores the dangers of nationalism, extremism, and terrorism, and the contradictory pulls of modernity and tradition, tracing their effect on the lives of three main characters as they move between the contradictory titular worlds. The story begins with Nikhil introducing his friend Sandip into the private quarters of his home and Bimala emerging from the sheltered world of home into the temptations of the world. Although British rule in India provides the context for the novel, the British themselves are no more

than what Nandy terms a "shadowy presence." Nevertheless, British rule shapes the narrative at every turn. Both Nikhil and Sandip are fundamentally shaped by Western ideas of nationalism and the desire to reshape Indian society in Western terms. The political disagreements are heightened by their rivalry over Bimala, who represents Bengal, a land torn between two visions of a Westernized, nationalist future. Both Nikhil and Sandip express their love for her as worship and frequently refer to her in terms that evoke Durga, the mother goddess. Sandip makes the equivalence specific when he declares, "My watchword has changed since you have come across my vision. It is no long Hail Mother but Hail Beloved." For Bimali, the experience is transformative: "I who before had been of no account now felt in myself all the splendour of Bengal itself…. Sandip babu made it clear how all the country was in need of me."

The novel is narrated in first person by the three main characters; in the Bengali version their accounts are described as "autobiographies." Also in this version the monologues are arranged in a structure that reflects the changing relationships between the main characters. This structure was not retained in the English translation, however, which is broken into chapters. Nevertheless, both versions of the novel begin and end with Bimala, whose transformations fuel the narrative action. The first-person accounts are written as introspective musings; change, action, and even dialogue are reported in monologue form rather than being fully articulated in the moment, thereby distancing the reader from the action and the primary characters from each other.

Despite the inherent drama of the story, the style of the novel is not particularly dramatic. Tagore seems to be more interested in the ideas than in the plot. Critical events take place offstage, told in only a line or two. This sense of distance is increased for the modern reader by Tagore's use of the lush, poetic, and highly rhetorical language typical of Bengali literature of the time. Bimala, for example, describes her emergence into the world in terms of the rivers that define the Bengali landscape: "So long I had been like a small river at the border of a village. But the tide came up from the sea, and my breast heaved; my banks gave way and the great drum beats of the sea were echoed in my mad current."

CRITICAL DISCUSSION

Critical reactions to the 1916 Bengali edition and the 1919 English translation of *The Home and the World* were so different that one might be forgiven for thinking that two different books were under review. (In fact, there were significant differences in structure and style between the two texts.) In India, though Tagore was still revered as a poet, the novel was widely read as an apologia for his rejection of the Swadeshi movement. Condemnation of the novel was so severe that Tagore published a defense of the work on two occasions. Reviewers of the English version—with the glaring exception of E. M. Forster—were mostly positive and even enthusiastic. Forster, himself a critic of

British rule in India, took Tagore to task for what he felt were the author's lapses in taste, his use of hackneyed situations, and his frequently vulgar writing, saying in a 1919 review for the *Athenaeum* that Tagore "meant the wife to be seduced by the World, which is, with all its sins, a tremendous lover; she is actually seduced by a West Kensington Babu."

Today Tagore is a celebrated figure throughout South Asia. He is generally considered the father of the modern Indian short story. His songs and poetry inspired Bangladesh in its battle for independence from Pakistan in 1971. India, Sri Lanka, and Bangladesh all chose songs by Tagore as their national anthems. Outside of India, he is known primarily as the first non-Westerner to win the Nobel Prize in Literature and as the subject of several films. In *Satyajit Ray: The Inner Eye* (1989), Andrew Robinson, filmmaker Satyajit Ray's biographer, goes so far as to claim, "If non-Bengalis know Tagore at all today it is mainly by virtue of Ray's interpretation of him on film."

Tagore's Nobel Prize—awarded for his poetry, not his novels—sparked a brief but intense period of popular and critical interest in his work in the West. However, Forster's damning review of *The Home and the World* and the widespread misconception of Tagore as an old-fashioned novelist caused Western interest in his prose fiction to decline, and his novels virtually disappeared for half a century. In the 1970s gender and subaltern scholars rediscovered his work, which led to a revived readership for all his novels—especially for *The Home and the World*. This interest intensified with the release of Ray's film version of *The Home and the World* in 1984.

Dancers perform to the music of Rabindranath Tagore during a 2010 festival to reintroduce his work to a UK audience.
© CLIFF HIDE NEWS/ ALAMY.

BIBLIOGRAPHY

Sources

Desai, Anita. Introduction. *The Home and the World*. Trans. Surendranath Tagore. New York: Penguin, 1985. Print.

Forster, E. M. "Tagore as a Novelist." *Athenaeum* 1 Aug. 1919: 687. Print.

Lago, Mary M. *Rabindranath Tagore*. Boston: Twayne, 1976. *Gale Virtual Reference Library*. Web. 4 Sept. 2012.

Macauley, Thomas Babington. "Minute of 2 February 1835 on Indian Education." *Macaulay, Prose and Poetry*. Ed. G. M. Young. Cambridge: Harvard UP, 1957. 721–29. Print.

Nandy, Ashis. "The Illegitimacy of Nationalism: Rabindranath Tagore and the Politics of Self." *Return from Exile*. Delhi: Oxford UP, 1998. Print.

Rege, Josna. "Novel: South Asia." *The Oxford Encyclopedia of the Modern World*. Vol. 5. Ed. Peter N. Stearns. New York: Oxford UP, 2008. 471–72. *Gale Virtual Reference Library*. Web. 2 Sept. 2012.

Robinson, Andrew. *Satyajit Ray: The Inner Eye*. London: Deutsch, 1989. Print.

Sarkar, Sumit. *The Swadeshi Movement in Bengal 1903–1908*. New Delhi: Permanent Black. 2010. Print.

Tagore Rabindranath. *The Home and the World*. Trans. Surendranath Tagore. London: Macmillan, 1919. Print.

Further Reading

Dasgupta, Subrata. *The Bengal Renaissance: Identity and Creativity from Rammohan Roy to Rabindranath Tagore*. Delhi: Permanent Black, 2007. Print.

Datta, P. K. *Rabindranath Tagore's* The Home and the World: *A Critical Companion*. Delhi: Permanent Black, 2003. Print.

Gordon, Leonard A. *Bengal: The Nationalist Movement, 1876–1940*. New York: Columbia UP, 1974. Print.

Kapadia, Novy. "The Contrasting Film and Novel Text of *Ghore Baire*." *Creative Forum* 21.1–2 (2008): 85. *Academic OneFile*. Web. 27 Aug. 2012.

Tagore, Rabindranath. *Gitanjali (Song Offerings): A Collection of Prose Translations Made by the Author from the Original Bengali*. New York: Macmillan, 1912. Print.

———. *Glimpses of Bengal, Selected from the Letters of Sir Rabindranath Tagore, 1885–1895*. London: Macmillan, 1921. Print.

Media Adaptation

The Home and the World. Dir. Satyajit Ray. Perf. Soumitra Chatterjee, Victor Banerjee, and Swatilekha Chatterjee. National Film Development Corporation of India (NFDC), 1984. Film.

Pamela Toler

LETTERS FROM GENERAL WASHINGTON TO SEVERAL OF HIS FRIENDS IN THE YEAR 1776

In Which Are Set Forth a Fairer and Fuller View of American Politics than Ever yet Transpired, or the Public Could Be Made Acquainted with through Any Other Channel

George Washington

❖ *Key Facts*

Time Period:
Late 18th Century

Genre:
Letter

Events:
American Revolution;
British capture of Fort
Lee

Nationality:
American

OVERVIEW

Letters from General Washington to Several of His Friends in the Year 1776: In Which Are Set Forth a Fairer and Fuller View of American Politics than Ever yet Transpired, or the Public Could Be Made Acquainted with through Any Other Channel is a collection of letters allegedly written by George Washington that was published in 1777. The letters were actually forged by an unknown author in an attempt to discredit Washington, who was serving as commander of the Continental army in the American Revolution (1775–83) when the letters first appeared. There are seven letters in the collection, addressed to Washington's wife, stepson, and farm manager, and they attempt to portray Washington as a whiny, cowardly British sympathizer. In truth, Washington was a fiercely loyal patriot, a savvy politician, and a brilliant military tactician. The author of the fabricated letters wrote them to sow doubt in the minds of colonists as to Washington's character and his loyalty to the colonies and to damage the morale of colonial forces that were already worn down, disheartened, and low on men and supplies.

Washington himself was amused by the clumsy fraud and did not think it worthy of comment. As a work of propaganda, the collection initially failed, but nearly twenty years later the American Republican Party utilized it with far more success. In a bitter dispute with the Federalists in 1796 over the Jay Treaty with Great Britain, the Republicans repeatedly presented the collection as proof that Washington was a British sympathizer, and this constant barrage eventually damaged Washington's reputation.

HISTORICAL AND LITERARY CONTEXT

During the fall and winter of 1776, the Continental army suffered a series of crushing defeats, caused primarily by supply shortages and low morale. The British, however, were well manned, well supplied, and motivated by an expectation that their recent victories would help end the war by Christmas. On November 20, 1776, the army of British general Charles Cornwallis laid siege to Fort Lee on the New Jersey shore of the Hudson River. It met with little resistance and stormed the fort easily. Once inside, according to the introduction to *Letters from General Washington,* Cornwallis's forces found a mixed-race man named Billy Lee who claimed to be General Washington's personal manservant. He said that Washington escaped in such haste that he left behind his possessions, one of which happened to be a small portmanteau containing seven personal letters.

General Cornwallis did indeed capture Fort Lee in November 1776, but the rest of the story, as told in the introduction to *Letters from General Washington,* is untrue. There was no Billy Lee, the portmanteau was a lie, and there were no letters found written by Washington. Early in 1777 a London bookseller published the fake letters as a pamphlet, along with the fabricated tale of their discovery as introduction. Most British reviewers saw through the deception, but the pamphlet still sold well enough to work its way over to the colonies and to be reprinted in British-occupied New York City.

Letters from General Washington was just one of many pieces of propaganda created during the war and in the years leading up to it. Both the colonists and the British produced artwork, slogans, and especially exaggerated or falsified news. Memorable slogans from the war include Patrick Henry's "Give me liberty or give me death," Nathan Hale's "I only regret that I have but one life to lose for my country," and "No taxation without representation." Although occurring five years before the beginning of the war, the Boston Massacre is an example of an event turned into a propaganda tool. The colonists chose to call the unfortunate killing of five individuals a "massacre" and embellished it in a multitude of ways, while Loyalists referred to it as the "Incident on King Street." Paul Revere created a colored engraving of the event, complete with numerous inaccuracies and exaggerations meant to inflame colonial tempers.

Even after *Letters from General Washington* was published in the colonies, it did not have the profound impact its author intended. Washington chose to merely ignore it in hopes that it would fade away. This proved unsuccessful as his opponents continued to slander him and point to his silence as confirmation of the authenticity of the letters. The letters continued to haunt Washington throughout his presidency. He finally chose to officially denounce them on March 3, 1797, his last full day in office. Once Washington retired, the letters were no longer of any serious political use, and they were forgotten. They did, however, serve as a precursor to a tactic of modern politics: propaganda masquerading as factual analysis, biography, or investigative reporting.

THEMES AND STYLE

The major theme of *Letters from General Washington* is that Washington is a man of little character and cannot be trusted. The seven letters that make up the collection include one to his wife, Martha; one to her son (his stepson), John Parke Custis; and five to his farm manager, Lund Washington (a distant cousin). In the first and most damaging letter, Washington is portrayed as a whining coward, still loyal to king and Crown. He supposedly writes, "I will not conceal it from you, that, at this moment, I feel myself a very coward." Later he asks, "Can you point out a way in which it is possible for me to resign, just now as it were, on the eve of action, without imputation of cowardice?" The letter to Martha portrays a man who is both a traitor to the colonies and an inattentive husband who has earned the mistrust of his wife. The letter begins, "You have hurt me, I know not how much, by the insinuation in your last [letter] that my letters to you have lately been less frequent, because I have felt less concern for you…. Why do you complain of my reserve? Or, how could you imagine that I distrusted either your prudence or your fidelity?" He also allegedly admits, "I love my king; you know I do: a soldier, a good man cannot but love him. How peculiarly hard then is our fortune to be deemed traitors to so good a king!" In the letters addressed to Lund, there is more reinforcement of doubts and fears and the temptation to simply give up: "Even from these very works which have inspired us with such confidence, I anticipate only misfortune and disgrace." The true author of the letters hoped to convince Americans that Washington was not worthy of their confidence.

By attempting to ruin Washington's character and image, the author of *Letters from General Washington* hoped that Americans would no longer trust or accept any form of leadership from Washington. Many of the letters paint a discouraged man, who does not really support separation from England: "I alone torment myself with thinking that everything is against us,"

WASHINGTON'S PERSONAL PAPERS

George Washington always understood the importance of written records. When he died, he left behind more than one hundred thousand manuscripts, including personal and formal letters, journals, diaries, and military communications. Unfortunately, everything ended up in the hands of family, friends, and acquaintances who did not recognize, or care about, the importance of preserving the documents for future generations. Washington's wife, Martha, burned all of her correspondence in 1802, a common act of widows and widowers at the time. Washington left the bulk of his papers to his nephew, Bushrod Washington, in his will. Rather than becoming a steward of the collection, Bushrod gave away thousands of papers, diaries, and other documents as a show of his celebrity.

In 1803 Chief Justice John Marshall convinced Bushrod to loan several large bundles of letters to him to use as reference for his five-volume biography of Washington. In 1827 Jared Sparks, a professor at Harvard who would later become president of the university, convinced Bushrod to give him a large portion of the remaining collection, which he used for research in writing his own biography on the first president. Unfortunately, Sparks did not maintain the order and condition of the documents in his care, rearranging many into groups and sequences he thought more fitting, giving away or simply throwing out any items he did not consider valuable, tearing pages out of diaries, and cutting Washington's signature out of letters to sell to souvenir hunters. One of the documents he cut to pieces was a draft of Washington's first inaugural address. It was more than sixty pages in length and only a third of it has ever been recovered. After Bushrod's death in 1879, his nephew, George Corbin Washington, sold what remained of the collection to the U.S. government.

and "I do not really wish for independence." Others ridicule numerous people in powerful positions. One letter refers to the governor of Virginia as a "madman," and another describes General Putnam, one of Washington's officers, as "very ignorant." The letters also question the sensibilities of Congress on more than one occasion.

The language used throughout the *Letters from General Washington* portrays a man who is uncertain of his own abilities and who constantly questions the actions of other Americans. This man speaks admiringly of the British and even repeats in more than one of the letters that he does not want independence from England. One particular sentence in the first letter, addressed to Lund, sets the tone of the entire collection and reflects the thoughts and beliefs of the author. It states, "We have overshot our mark; we have grasped at things beyond our reach: it is impossible we should succeed, and I cannot with truth, say that I am sorry for it; because I am far from being sure that we deserve to succeed." The essence of this sentence repeats over and over from one letter to the next.

An engraving depicting English troops landing in New York in 1776, the year before the spurious *Letters from General Washington* were published. FRENCH SCHOOL/THE BRIDGEMAN ART LIBRARY/GETTY IMAGES.

CRITICAL DISCUSSION

First published in London as a pamphlet in 1777, the collection of fake Washington letters received little if any response or credibility. One publication, the *Monthly Review,* declared, "We cannot look upon these letters as genuine, but we must pronounce them well written." The *Critical Review* went a step further, writing, "It is difficult to determine their authenticity from any intrinsic evidence. They contain no facts of a private nature, and they discover not only sentiment, but a correctness of composition." The collection was published in the colonies a year later, and it received the same lack of interest. In 1796 *Letters from General Washington* was republished as *Epistles, Domestic, Confidential and Official from General Washington* with the goal of humiliating and discrediting Washington, who was by then president of the United States, because he supported the Jay Treaty. Ratified by the U.S. Congress in February of that year, the treaty had angered many Americans for its conciliatory treatment of the British. Republicans aggressively promoted the new book, and their constant pressure and repeated lies eventually gained significant followers and damaged President Washington's public image and his emotional well-being.

Letters from General Washington may have been the first published work of propaganda about Washington, but it was not the last. Immediately after his death in 1799, a flood of biographies was published, portraying Washington as the hero of the age and recounting his life in every exaggeration and stereotype imaginable. One of the most popular of these, *The Life and Memorable Actions of George Washington* by Mason Locke Weems, was first released in 1800. It includes some of the most popular and creative lies that exist about Washington, including the story of him chopping down a cherry tree. Other fabulous tales in the book include Washington's prayer at Valley Forge on his knees in the snow, his rejection of the army's offer to make him king of the United States, and his pious references to God on his deathbed. Weems knew the tales were false, but he also knew that people would pay for good stories.

Ironically, for a published work that caused so much grief for the first president of the United States, little scholarly analysis of it exists. In the 1800s Weems's biography was not only popular but also influential. Many would-be profiteers used his formula to create their own biographies, most of which had less connection to reality than the Weems volume has. With each new book the stories became stranger and more provocative. Edward G. Lengel, in his 2011 book *Inventing George Washington,* explains how in the late 1800s "Washington was well on the way to transforming from an upstanding family man into a syphilitic rake." The lies and distortions were all made in the name of profit. Nearly a century passed before serious, factual works on Washington's life appeared.

BIBLIOGRAPHY

Sources

Donoughue, Bernard. *British Politics and the American Revolution.* New York: St. Martin's, 1964. Print.

Fitzpatrick, John C. *The George Washington Scandals.* Alexandria: Washington Society of Alexandria, 1929. Print.

Hamilton, Charles. *Scribblers and Scoundrels.* New York: Eriksson, 1968. Print.

Lengel, Edward G. *Inventing George Washington: America's Founder, in Myth & Memory.* New York: Harper, 2011. Print.

Twohig, Dorothy. "George Washington Forgeries and Facsimilies." *Provenance: The Journal of the Society of Georgia Archivists* 1 (1983): 1–13. *Papers of George Washington.* Web. 9 Aug. 2012.

Wood, Gordon S. "Rhetoric and Reality in the American Revolution." *William and Mary Quarterly* 23.1 (1966): 3–32. *JSTOR.* Web. 9 Aug. 2012.

Further Reading

Berger, Carl. *Broadsides & Bayonets: The Propaganda War of the American Revolution.* San Rafael: Presidio, 1976. Print.

Bloch, Ruth H. *Visionary Republic: Millennial Themes in American Thought, 1756–1800.* Cambridge: Cambridge UP, 1985. Print.

Chernow, Ron. *Washington: A Life.* New York: Penguin, 2010. Print.

Dunbar, Louise Burham. *A Study of "Monarchical" Tendencies in the United States from 1776 to 1801.* New York: Johnson Reprint, 1970. Print.

Grizzard, Frank E., Jr. *George Washington: A Biographical Companion.* Santa Barbara: ABC-CLIO, 2002. Print.

Lengel, Edward G. *General George Washington.* New York: Random, 2005. Print.

Schwartz, Barry. *George Washington: The Making of an American Symbol.* New York: Free Press, 1987. Print.

Washington, George. *George Washington: Writings.* New York: Library of America, 1997. Print.

Jim Mladenovic

LETTERS FROM MEXICO

Hernán Cortés

OVERVIEW

Written between 1519 and 1526, *Letters from Mexico* (*Cartas de relación*) includes official letters from Hernán Cortés to Spain's King Charles V that seek to reinforce and legitimize the explorer's conquest of "New Spain," a colony located in what today is Mexico. Adopting a formal tone that was customary for such reports (*relaciones*) by Spanish officials, Cortés's letters recount various events in his Mexican conquest, including his alliance with the Tlaxcalans, the *noche triste* ("sad night") in 1520 when his troops were slaughtered and run out of the Aztec capital of Tenochtitlán, a later reconquest of the city, and his ensuing governance of the territories. Cortés used the letters to present himself in a positive light and emphasize his control and authority over New Spain. After challenging royal orders upon undertaking the conquest, he wanted to regain favor with the king.

There are known to be five letters in all, but the first in the sequence was lost; thus, in most publications of the *Letters from Mexico,* the missing letter is replaced by one written by the municipality of Veracruz rather than by Cortés himself. The four letters written by Cortés were published in Spain during his lifetime and brought him much acclaim as a heroic conquistador. They reveal a great deal about Cortés in particular, such as his rivalries with other Spanish colonial officials, and about the life of a conquistador in general during Spain's conquest of Latin America and the Caribbean. In addition to having significant historical value, the letters are viewed as literary artifacts by modern-day scholars.

HISTORICAL AND LITERARY CONTEXT

Cortés arrived in the New World in 1504, only a few years after Christopher Columbus established the first Spanish settlement in the region, on the island of Hispaniola (the location of modern-day Haiti and the Dominican Republic). Spanish legislation and administration had not yet caught up to the reality of life in these uncharted lands, and Cortés and many other Spaniards aspiring to wealth and power sought to make names for themselves. As Cortés established himself as the secretary to Spanish explorer Diego Velázquez in Cuba, many of his fellow Spaniards ventured to neighboring areas; Juan Ponce de León conquered Puerto Rico in 1508, and Juan de Esquivel took Jamaica in

1509. In 1518 Cortés secured a position of leadership on an expedition of the Aztec civilization in what is now Mexico on the North American mainland. Before the expedition left Cuba, however, Velázquez withdrew his support and ordered the crew to disband, aggravating a grudge between the two Spaniards that only worsened in future years.

Departing for Mexico against Velázquez's orders, Cortés sought to conquer Mexico for himself. By mid-1519 Cortés had taken the city of Veracruz, circumventing Velázquez's power by invoking a *cabildo* (local government council) that positioned him directly under the orders of Charles V. By 1522 Cortés had razed the once-flourishing Aztec capital of Tenochtitlán and defeated the indigenous empire. Though Charles V appointed him governor of New Spain, Cortés faced many challenges to his power, such as rival conquistador Francisco de Garay's attempted conquest of northern Mexico. Cortés's later letters address his grievances and seek redress from the Spanish crown.

Letters from Mexico belongs to the tradition of the relaciones, which were formal reports written by Spanish officials. Relaciones, however, did not historically take the form of letters; instead, they were usually formatted as itemized accounts of services administered. Through their direct and candid address of the king, Cortés's lengthy narratives escape from the relaciones tradition and represent the emergence of a new literary genre that was, in a sense, a defense of the conquest of Latin America. One of Cortés's main goals was to persuade his audience of the righteous nature of his and his soldiers' actions. The enthusiastic tone of the writing harks back to the military narratives penned by Julius Caesar centuries earlier.

Because Cortés's letters were published soon after arriving in Spain, they contributed to his fame as a heroic, powerful leader of New Spain. Subsequent works chronicling Spanish conquest include Francisco Pizarro's "Cartas del Marqués Don Francisco Pizarro (1533–41)," which recounts his experiences in Peru, and Bernal Díaz de Castillo's *Historia verdadera de la conquista de la Nueva España* ("The True History of the Conquest of New Spain"; completed in 1568 and published in 1632), which record Cortés's expedition to Mexico and include the author's firsthand accounts. Cortés's letters were regarded as objective historical accounts of the Mexican conquest until the twentieth century, when the rhetoric surrounding such undertakings began to question the cruelty to and subjugation of the indigenous peoples.

THEMES AND STYLE

The purpose of *Letters from Mexico* is to emphasize acts that will further legitimatize Cortés's colonizing enterprise. In order to assuage any doubts the monarchy may harbor about him and to reaffirm his loyalty to the crown, Cortés devotes much of his letters to painstakingly proving how he has been misrepresented and betrayed by Velázquez. Describing how he confronted Spanish explorer Pánfilo de Narváez, whom Velázquez sent to Veracruz at the head of more than a thousand troops to sabotage Cortés's expedition, he writes in his second letter, "As I wished to avoid any disturbance, I thought it best to go by night without being observed if possible … and seize [Narváez] for I believed that once he was taken there would be no disturbance, because the others would be willing to follow justice, particularly since most of them had been forced to come by Diego Velázquez." By rationally presenting his case and portraying Narváez and Velázquez in a negative light, Cortés appeals to the Spanish king's morality and sense of justice.

Cortés conveys the legitimacy of his message through formal, judicious rhetoric. Written in the first person, the letters address the king with a respectful frankness that is intended to defend Cortés's honor and also appeal to the close personal relationship he believes he has established with the leader of Spain. In his fourth letter, he requests that the king intervene on his behalf regarding the sanctions imposed by the Spanish colonial administration on New Spain: "I might have gotten back at them for this in such a way that they would have been glad to revoke their mandates…. Yet in order to give no further opportunity to the tongues of those who have slandered me already, I have refrained from such action until Your Majesty be informed." In addition to drawing a clear picture of the injustice he perceives, Cortés incorporates thinly veiled threats that illustrate exactly what he is capable of doing in order to defend his colony.

Letters from Mexico is defined by an enthusiastic tone, though the letters also reflect the serious nature of his undertaking. To cast himself in a positive light, Cortés elevates the events surrounding his conquest to an almost mythical level. In his second letter he writes, "All that was lost … will shortly be regained, for each day many of the provinces and cities which had been subject to Mutezuma come and offer themselves as Your Majesty's vassals, for they see how those who do so are well received and favored by me, whereas those who do not are destroyed daily." Greatly simplifying his conflict with the various indigenous tribes, Cortés portrays himself as a benevolent and forgiving leader, emphasizing the ease with which he has scored

HERNÁN CORTÉS AND THE CONQUEST OF MEXICO

Hernán Cortés was a Spanish conquistador known for his conquest of the Aztec empire, as well as for founding colonial Mexico. He was born into the gentry in Medellín, Spain, around 1484 (the exact date is unknown), which enabled him to study law at the University of Salamanca. Abandoning his studies after two years, Cortés traveled to the island of Hispaniola in the Caribbean in 1504 to work as a notary. He served as secretary to Diego Velázquez during his conquest of Cuba and was assigned to lead an expedition to explore the coast of Mexico in 1518.

Despite strict orders to limit his expedition to trade and exploration, Cortés had a different objective in mind: to conquer the Aztec empire that dominated the region of modern-day Mexico. Upon his arrival on the Mexican coast, Cortés forged an alliance with enemies of the Aztecs, the Tlaxcalans. He was received peaceably in the Aztecs' capital city of Tenochtitlán, only to take their leader, Montezuma II, prisoner. Montezuma was eventually killed during an Aztec uprising against the Spanish, and Cortés struggled to subdue the indigenous community until finally defeating it in 1521. Cortés was then named governor of the territory, known as "New Spain," and ruled through 1526. After a failed expedition into Honduras, Cortés was removed from his post. He returned to Spain in 1540 and died there in 1547.

victories. It is now known, however, that the situation was actually much more drawn out than he led the Spanish crown to believe.

CRITICAL DISCUSSION

Cortés's first letters were published in Seville in 1522, and they were received by the Spanish public with awe and admiration. This sense of wonderment remained undiminished as the centuries passed. In the October 1843 issue of the *North American Review,* an article titled "Despatches of Hernándo Cortés" proclaims that Cortés's letters had "an interest of the same character with that of the Anabasis of Xenophon and the Commentaries of Caesar." Similar praise was registered in William H. Prescott's 1855 book *History of the Conquest of Mexico, with a Preliminary View of the Ancient Mexican Civilization, and the Life of the Conqueror Hernándo Cortés,* as he writes, "It will not be easy to find in the chronicles of the period a more concise, yet comprehensive, statement, not only of the events of [Cortés's] campaigns, but of the circumstances most worthy of notice in the character of the conquered countries."

Letters from Mexico contributed to a distorted, inaccurate understanding of the events surrounding the Mexican conquest that scholars have only recently begun to revise. Along with the chronicles of other Spanish participants in the conquest of Latin

Spanish conquistador Hernán Cortés makes Tenochtitlan ruler Montezuma a hostage upon arriving in Mexico in 1519. "HERNÁN CORTÉS MAKES MONTEZUMA A HOSTAGE IN 1519": (COLOUR LITHO), SPANISH SCHOOL/PRIVATE COLLECTION/PETER NEWARK AMERICAN PICTURES/THE BRIDGEMAN ART LIBRARY.

Letters from Mexico (2001), Anthony Pagden analyzes the conquistador's persuasive narrative approach, noting that "[Cortés] had to describe his actions, and in particular the less obviously legitimate of them, in the context of his longer-term achievements and objectives. His letters, then, are, at one level, an exercise in legitimation." The work of Matthew Restall in *Seven Myths of the Spanish Conquest* (2003) reflects a growing scholarly interest in the religious undertones of Cortés's correspondence. Restall observes that Cortés's letters "argued unambiguously that God had directed the Conquest of Mexico as a favor to the Spanish monarchy. The blessed status of Cortés himself was heavily implied; in one letter he uses the Spanish term *medio* (medium or agent), to describe his providential role."

BIBLIOGRAPHY

Sources

Clendinnen, Inga. "'Fierce and Unnatural Cruelty': Cortés and the Conquest of Mexico." *Representations* 33 (1991): 65–100. Print.

Cortés, Hernán. *Hernán Cortés: Letters from Mexico*. Trans. Anthony Pagden. London: Yale UP, 2001. Print.

"Despatches of Hernándo Cortés." *North American Review* 57.121 (1843): 459–90. Print.

Pagden, Anthony. "Introduction." *Hernán Cortés: Letters from Mexico*. London: Yale UP, 2001. xxxi–lxxi. Print.

Prescott, William H. *History of the Conquest of Mexico, with a Preliminary View of the Ancient Mexican Civilization, and the Life of the Conqueror Hernándo Cortés*. Boston: Phillips, Sampson, 1855. Print.

Restall, Matthew. *Seven Myths of the Spanish Conquest*. Oxford: Oxford UP, 2003. Print.

Further Reading

Fuentes, Carlos. "The Spanish Captain's Story." *Guardian Weekly* 135.26 (1986): 22. Print.

Morris, J. Bayard. "Introduction." *Hernándo Cortés: Five Letters 1519–1526*. George Routledge & Sons, 1928. ix–xlvii. Print.

Padrón, Ricardo. *The Spacious Word: Cartography, Literature, and Empire in Early Modern Spain*. Chicago: U of Chicago P, 2004. Print.

Rabasa, José. *Inventing America: Spanish Historiography and the Formation of Eurocentrism*. Norman: U of Oklahoma P, 1993. Print.

Todorov, Tzvetan. *The Conquest of America*. Trans. R. Howard. New York: Harper & Row, 1984. Print.

Wagner, Henry R. *The Rise of Fernando Cortés*. Los Angeles: The Cortés Society, 1944. Print.

Katrina White

America, the Cortés letters have been the subject of much scrutiny and controversy regarding the cruel manner in which the indigenous populations were treated. In her 1991 article in *Representations*, Inga Clendinnen remarks with irony on the true nature of Cortés's actions: "Cortés's strategy in the world had been to treat all men, Indians and Spaniards alike, as manipulable. That sturdy denial of the problem of otherness, usually so profitable, had here been proved bankrupt…. His privilege as victor was to survey the surreal devastation of the city … [reduced] to undifferentiated human wreckage."

Recent scholarship on *Letters from Mexico* has shifted away from the historical angle and toward its literary merit. In his introduction to *Hernán Cortés:*

Make Bright the Arrows
1940 Notebook
Edna St. Vincent Millay

OVERVIEW

Make Bright the Arrows: 1940 Notebook is a collection of patriotic war poems written in 1940 by Pulitzer Prize winner Edna St. Vincent Millay. Composed of twenty-four poems written about World War II, the collection argues for U.S. involvement in what most Americans considered a European war. Some of the poems employ an elegiac tone and lament European losses to German forces; in others, the tone is calm, as if Millay herself is reporting the devastation from firsthand observation. All support a U.S. declaration of war on Germany, and most include imagery of devastated landscapes, towns, and people. In a letter to her friend and contemporary George Dillon, Millay describes the collection as a "book of impassioned propaganda, into which a few good poems got bound up because they happened to be propaganda, too." As Millay told Dillon, her goal was to counter the isolationism that had pervaded American thinking after World War I.

Many of the poems in the collection were written and published singly and then compiled in *Make Bright the Arrows* a year later. After its publication, Millay, already a well-respected author, became even more popular despite the book's lukewarm reception among her peers. The work reflects a serious change in Millay's own politics. She had been an ardent pacifist during World War I; however, Adolf Hitler's radical politics angered her. *Make Bright the Arrows* argues that the United States is the only country that can stop him. One of Millay's most political books, the collection is notable for the aggressive stance it adopts in favor of American involvement in the war as it details the destruction of Europe.

HISTORICAL AND LITERARY CONTEXT

Although World War II officially began on September 1, 1939, with the German invasion of Poland, the United States did not enter the war until December 8, 1941. Because of the devastation of World War I and the Great Depression, the American government was hesitant to engage in what was perceived to be another European conflict. The United States watched from the sidelines as German forces invaded and occupied western European countries, including France,

the Netherlands, and Belgium. On July 10, 1940, the air conflict between Germany and England began. In what became known as the Battle of Britain, German air forces bombed British ships, towns, and defenses. Knowing that Hitler would control all of Europe if Britain fell, Millay was troubled by the continued neutrality of the United States.

As the title *Make Bright the Arrows* suggests, Millay advocates preparedness at a time when many Americans opposed another costly war, so soon after the massive casualties suffered during World War I. However, the number of civilians murdered by the Axis powers—as well as the German occupation—horrified Millay, and she felt that the United States should help the Allies defend Europe from Hitler's regime. *Make Bright the Arrows* focuses on the destruction of life in Europe, urging the United States to restore peace.

Before the United States entered World War II, many poets condemned Hitler's actions yet continued to express antiwar attitudes. They followed in the tradition of the World War I poets who contrasted the realities of war with the patriotic propaganda of the U.S. government. Millay's contemporaries, such as H. D., William Carlos Williams, and Marianne Moore, discussed the contradiction in preventing bloodshed with more bloodshed. Moore's poem "Keeping Their World Large" explores feelings of complicity in the European tragedy while acknowledging that sending American troops would result in more deaths. Similarly, "R.A.F.," by H.D., examines the moral consequences of fighting a war. Unlike her contemporaries, Millay does not discuss these problematic relationships; instead, her poems focus on the destruction of Europe and why it must be stopped.

Although she had decried World War I and participated in several antiwar rallies, by the late 1930s Millay was writing poetry that argued for U.S. participation in World War II, and the publication of *Make Bright the Arrows* defined her as a pro-war poet. Soon after *Make the Arrows Bright* was printed, Millay was commissioned by the Writers' War Board to produce propaganda poetry on assignment. A privately run organization, the Writers' War Board coordinated with the Council on Books in Wartime and the Office of War Information to produce pro-war publications.

Key Facts

Time Period:
Mid-20th Century

Genre:
Poetry

Events:
World War II

Nationality:
American

"THE MURDER OF LIDICE"

Two years after the publication of *Make Bright the Arrows: 1940 Notebook*, Edna St. Vincent Millay wrote her famous propaganda poem "The Murder of Lidice." The thirty-two-page ballad contrasts the peaceful life in a small Czech village with the assassination and deportation of all its citizens by German forces in 1942. Millay begins the poem by narrating the daily events in Lidice days before the massacre. The mood darkens as the villagers discuss the German occupation of what is now the Czech Republic. Millay describes in journalistic detail the day of the assassinations, offering individual accounts from characters in the poem. "The Murder of Lidice" offers a comprehensive description of the horrors of that day while questioning the lack of response from the United States to the atrocities committed by Germany. Even though the United States had officially entered World War II after the bombing of Pearl Harbor, British troops were doing most of the fighting on the European front.

Written as a commissioned piece for the Writers' War Board, "The Murder of Lidice" was widely read and quoted during World War II even though it received mixed critical reviews. The poem was intended to rouse popular support for the war by detailing the mass killings and deportations committed by Germany. More ragged in voice and disjointed in rhythm than Millay's love poems and sonnets, "The Murder of Lidice" is notable for its strident tone as it details the extermination of an entire village.

The strain of producing so much writing so quickly led Millay to suffer a nervous breakdown in 1946. In addition, her war poetry was not well received critically, and she published little poetry after the war. Although Millay's work was largely ignored until the late 1970s, twenty-first-century scholars have begun to note the historical significance of *Make Bright the Arrows*.

THEMES AND STYLE

In *Make Bright the Arrows* Millay objects to U.S. isolationism, which she viewed as irresponsible. Millay expresses concern about the expanding Nazi regime and Europe's inability to stop it. She also questions the morality of leaving England to fight alone. In "There Are No Islands Anymore," Millay reprimands the American public for its isolationist attitude. She states her agenda in the epigraph—"Lines Written in Passion and in Deep Concern for England, France, and my Own Country"—and then continues her argument in the first lines of the text.

> Dear Isolationist, you are
> So very, very insular!
> Surely you do not take offense?—
> The word's well-used in such a sense.
> Tis you, not I, sir, who insist
> You are an Isolationist.

The poem addresses the Isolationist directly and criticizes him for refusing to acknowledge the Nazi threat. The poem ends with a warning that the United States will be forced to fight alone if England and France are conquered.

Employing a variety of settings and tones, the collection as a whole contrasts American indifference with the events of World War II. The direct address in "There Are No Islands Anymore" mimics a news report as Millay narrates the large-scale effects of German occupation. Similarly, the tone of "And Then There Were None" is even-tempered as it discusses the Nazi regime's efficient deportation and planned extermination of European Jews. The first stanza uses the image of a game bird to represent the Jews. "Ten white ptarmigan / Perching in a pine; / Hitler gave his solemn oath: / And then there were nine." Each stanza marks a solemn countdown as Hitler kills each bird. In the end, only one bird remains, and Millay writes, "Hitler gave his solemn oath: / The race is now extinct." The poet does not hide her concerns from the reader. Millay stated that the poems in *Make Bright the Arrows* were "not poems, but posters." This strategy is especially effective in "And Then There Were None," with its short lines and imagery of birds being killed one at a time.

The emotional tenor of the collection is a mix of sadness and anger. Millay vacillates between reportage and grief as she accuses the American public of remaining apathetic to the war. The short poem "Memory of England" bemoans England's destruction by German air forces: "I am glad, I think, my happy mother died / Before the German airplanes over the English countryside / Dropped bombs into the peaceful hamlets that we used to / know—." The poem details the destruction of property and memories. Millay had visited England with her mother and considered the bombing of England a personal tragedy. In "Ballade of Lost Cities" she heightens the emotional tension by repeating the phrase "where are the towns of yesterday?," alluding to the cities that had fallen into the hands of the Nazis. The echoing cry mimics that of a lost child. Despite its elegiac tone, however, the poem concludes with an attack on the U.S. government for doing nothing. "President, why the lack of zest?— / Washington's safe— / who'd dare assay Boston, New York, the Middle-West? / *But where are the towns of yesterday?*" The solemn lyric turns accusatory at the very end, as Millay points a finger of blame at the United States.

CRITICAL DISCUSSION

Make Bright the Arrows was widely read and accepted by the American public, especially after the bombing of Pearl Harbor. The critical reception of the book was less positive. Although Millay had included the *1940 Notebook* subtitle as a warning that the poems were unpolished, many critics were confused by her overtly political themes and tone and scolded her for what

A sculpture by Marie Uchytilová memoralizing the children of Lidice murdered at Chełmno in reprisal for the assassination of Reinhard Heydrich. Two years after the publication of *Make Bright the Arrows: 1940 Notebook*, Edna St. Vincent Millay wrote her famous propaganda poem "The Murder of Lidice." TOMAS KRIST/LIDOVE NOVINY/ISIFA/GETTY IMAGES.

they considered a regression from her well-crafted sonnets and love poems. Writing in the March 1941 issue of *Poetry,* Jessica Nelson North criticizes the poem "The Crooked Cross" as "a weary piece of doggerel." However, she praises "An Eclipse of the Sun Is Predicted," calling it "moving." Poet Louise Bogan suggests that Millay's book was a "regression to the stock sentiments of the post–World War I era" and had seriously hurt the American poetic renaissance that had begun in 1912. Still others attacked Millay personally. The *Living Age*'s Eugene Jolas describes *Make Bright the Arrows* as "the expression of a poet whose conviction and sincerity are obvious, but whose creative spirit has burned out."

Scholars often refer to *Make Bright the Arrows* as a persuasive collection of patriotic poems that served as a bleak warning about the full threat of the Nazi regime. Despite this acknowledgement the book is not often taught in classrooms and does not enjoy the same recognition as many of Millay's earlier works, which include *Renascence, A Few Figs from Thistles,* and *Fatal Interview.* Filled with well-crafted love poems, sonnets, and witty critiques of gender politics, these books are viewed by scholars as more important than the propaganda poetry. In a 1982 article for the *Quarterly Journal of the Library of Congress,* Maxine Kumin writes, "It is astonishing how rapidly her writing career went into eclipse after World War II, and how little note has been taken, until quite recently, of the weight and importance of Edna St. Vincent Millay."

Make Bright the Arrows is seldom discussed in its own right. However, twenty-first-century scholars have begun to study the text in relation to the work of other female poets of the 1930s and 1940s. Critics also note the change in tone and emotion in Millay's political poetry during the period. In a discussion of the literary persona Millay adopted in her poems—that of "a speaker at once reverent, breathless, and naïve … the Girl"—Elizabeth Perlmutter notes that in *Make Bright the Arrows* "Millay turned increasingly to set pieces, political lyrics, and love poems still composed in the Girl's pastiche diction, though too many of them failed to achieve the freshness and breadth of emotion that the Girl had provided as a symbol in her earlier efforts." Perlmutter and other scholars express their concerns, just as Millay did, that the poems in *Make Bright the Arrows* were not as well-crafted in comparison to her previous work. The work can still be read as representing the instance when Millay's politics shifted. The poems also offer insight into American views of World War II and how Millay embraced an outspoken journalistic style in an attempt to change the isolationist attitudes of the American public.

BIBLIOGRAPHY

Sources

Kumin, Maxine. "'Stamping a Tiny Foot against God': Some American Women Poets Writing between the Two Wars." *Quarterly Journal of the Library of Congress* Winter 1982: 48–61. *JSTOR.* Web. 31 July 2012.

Millay, Edna St. Vincent. *Letters of Edna St. Vincent Millay.* Ed. Allan Ross MacDougall. New York: Harper, 1952. Print.

————. *Make Bright the Arrows: 1940 Notebook.* New York: Harper, 1940. Print.

North, Jessica Nelson. "Archer, What Target?" Rev. of *Make Bright the Arrows,* by Edna St. Vincent Millay. *Poetry* Mar. 1941: 389–91. *JSTOR.* Web. 31 July 2012.

Perlmutter, Elizabeth P. "A Doll's Heart: The Girl in the Poetry of Edna St. Vincent Millay and Louise Bogan." *Twentieth Century Literature* May 1977: 157–79. *JSTOR.* Web. 31 July 2012.

Further Reading

Clark, Suzanne. "The Unwarranted Disclosure: Sentimental Community, Modernist Women, and the Case of Millay." *Critical Essays on Edna St. Vincent Millay.* Ed. William Thesing. New York: Hall, 1993. 248–66. Print.

Emery, Noemie. "The Patron Saint of Pro-War Poetry." *Weekly Standard.* Weekly Standard, 13 Feb. 2003. Web. 31 July 2012.

Freedman, Diane F. *Millay At 100: A Critical Reappraisal (Ad Feminam: Women and Literature).* Carbondale: Southern Illinois UP, 1995. Print.

Milford, Nancy. *Savage Beauty: The Life of Edna St. Vincent Millay.* New York: Random, 2001. Print.

Nierman, Judith. *Edna St. Vincent Millay: A Reference Guide.* Boston: Hall, 1977. Print.

Thesing, William B. *Critical Essays on Edna St. Vincent Millay.* New York: MacMillan, 1993. Print.

Wetzsteon, Ross. *Republic of Dreams: Greenwich Village: The American Bohemia, 1910–1960.* New York: Simon, 2003. Print.

Wheeler, Lesley. *Voicing American Poetry: Sound and Performance from the 1920s to the Present.* Ithaca: Cornell UP, 2008. Print.

Hannah Soukup

Mein Kampf

Adolf Hitler

OVERVIEW

Mein Kampf, a two-volume book written by Adolf Hitler during his imprisonment in 1924, is a blend of autobiography and an exposition of Hitler's political and social ideologies. Although considered one of the twentieth century's most historically important texts, *Mein Kampf* is often described as poorly written, repetitive, and digressive. Its historic significance derives more from the far-reaching effects of its fanatical ideas than from its craftsmanship. Translated as *My Battle* or *My Struggle, Mein Kampf* traces the events that caused Hitler's intense hatred of democracy, communism, and Jews, although many critics believe some of the autobiographical details were manufactured to promote the rapid dissemination of his doctrine. Written like a guidebook for the Nazi Party and preying on the strong nationalistic and anti-Semitic sensibilities of the German people, the text claims Germans are members of a master race and outlines Hitler's program for making the nation into a world power. He writes that "the German Reich, as a state, should include all Germans … and lead them gradually and safely to a dominating position."

Initially published in 1925, the first volume of *Mein Kampf* was not warmly received by its German audience. After Hitler's release from Landsberg prison, he published the second volume in 1926, which sold only thirteen thousand copies in its first four years. Its dissemination increased, however, as Hitler rose to power. Insisting that each German citizen own a copy, the Nazi Party gave the book to newlyweds, railway officials, civil servants, and schoolchildren as a primer on race, genetics, and population. Foreign-language translations cropped up worldwide, although Hitler ensured that the most racist and inflammatory passages did not appear in copies outside of Germany until 1939. Some historians argue that the initial limited readership and abridged versions of *Mein Kampf* prevented the foreign audience from fully appreciating the horrors proposed by Hitler.

HISTORICAL AND LITERARY CONTEXT

The German government viewed World War I as a way to end disputes with rival countries, especially France, Russia, and the United Kingdom. Presented as Germany's opportunity to secure its place as a world power, the war was supported by the prevalently nationalistic public. Additionally, the Kaiser hoped that the war would unite Germany behind the monarchy and end the threat posed by the Social Democratic Party of Germany. However, as strict food rationing was introduced and mass casualties mounted, public enthusiasm for the war faded, leading to several uprisings and an attempted revolution. By the close of 1918, Germany had surrendered to the Allied forces and signed an armistice to end the fighting. The Kaiser abdicated his rule, and the Empire was replaced by the Weimar Republic, a government heavily criticized in *Mein Kampf.*

In 1919 Germany reluctantly signed the Treaty of Versailles, which required the country to take responsibility for the war, disarm and downsize its military, relinquish substantial territories, and pay significant reparations to certain countries. The terms led to severe economic losses and a deep bitterness among the people. Conservative and nationalist Germans criticized the signing of the treaty and blamed the Weimar Republic, socialists, communists, and Jews, who were accused of betraying Germany to its enemies during the war. It was on this stage that Hitler gained his foothold. In 1919 he joined an anti-Semitic political party that eventually became known as the National Socialist German Workers' Party (i.e., the Nazi Party). Hitler soon became the party's leader, garnered popular and fiscal support, and spearheaded a coup in 1923 to overthrow the German government. When the coup failed, Hitler was confined to the Landsberg prison, at which time he wrote *Mein Kampf.*

Mein Kampf draws largely on a tradition of social psychology, anti-Semitic texts, and theories of racial superiority and eugenics. Hitler's text is heavily influenced by French social psychologist Gustav Le Bon, whose book *The Crowd: A Study of the Popular Mind* (1895) theorizes that crowd behavior is influenced by emotion rather than intellect. Throughout *Mein Kampf,* Hitler makes use of this propagandistic theory by attempting to sway the German populace based on their emotions and fears, particularly their presumed hatred and innate suspicions of the Jews. Hitler may also have been influenced by French anthropologist and eugenics theorist Georges Vacher de Lapouge, whose book *The Aryan and His Social Role* (1899) asserts that the Nordic fair-haired Protestant is superior to all other races.

✣ *Key Facts*

Time Period:
Early 20th Century

Genre:
Manifesto

Events:
Versailles Treaty; foundation of the National Socialist German Workers' Party

Nationality:
German

YOUNG ADOLF HITLER

Adolf Hitler was born on April 20, 1889, in Braunau am Inn, Austria, near Germany's border. Hitler's ancestry was a source of embarrassment to him, often causing him to fabricate his personal history. Not only were his parents—Alois Hitler and Klara Pölzl—related as distant cousins, but his father was illegitimate and an alcoholic. Alois urged his son to find a secure government job, despite Adolf's inclinations to study art. After Hitler's father died in 1903, his mother allowed him to quit school to pursue his dream of becoming a painter.

When Klara died in 1907, Hitler moved to Vienna with the hope of attending the city's Academy of Fine Arts, to which he was twice denied entry. While living in Vienna, Hitler supported himself by selling his watercolor paintings and postcards. In *Mein Kampf*, Hitler portrays this period as one marked by severe poverty, when, in fact, he had a small inheritance and an orphan's pension that allowed him to live comfortably. During his time in Vienna, Hitler became interested in politics, often arguing with Marxists in cafés.

In order to avoid being drafted into the Austrian army, Hitler moved frequently in Vienna and immigrated to Germany in 1913. However, when World War I broke out in 1914, he volunteered for the German army. Hitler was greatly disheartened when he learned of Germany's surrender in 1918. This bitter disappointment spurred him to enter politics, thus beginning his unlikely career path from obscurity to infamy.

Both before and after World War II, *Mein Kampf* inspired a large body of scholarly works that not only criticized its form and content but also investigated its far-reaching impact. In *Books That Changed the World* (1956), Robert B. Downs laments, "It is the world's misfortune that Hitler's ideas did not expire with him. Their adherents are still numerous in Germany, while Communist governments have borrowed and are making extensive use of many of them." Today, Hitler's ideas live on in organizations devoted to racial purity, anti-Semitism, and the hatred of those of African and Middle Eastern descent. The "ethnic cleansing" seen in the Bosnian conflict in the 1990s reflected Hitler's doctrine.

THEMES AND STYLE

The central themes of *Mein Kampf* are that Germans are the Aryan, or master, race and all the indignities they have ever suffered have been inflicted by Jews. Hitler asserts that the Germans must purify and preserve their racial integrity by eliminating the Jews, who prey parasitically on others and are responsible for the evils of both extreme capitalism and Marxism. Hitler also argues that in order to become a significant presence on the world stage, Germany will require more Lebensraum, or living space, which it will obtain through the colonization of Eastern Europe and enslaving or eliminating the inferior Slavic race. According to Hitler, the acquisition of Eastern Europe is practically a moral imperative because it will save the Aryan race: "The *right* to acquire land and soil can become a *duty*, if without an extension of soil a great people appears doomed to destruction."

Mein Kampf achieves its rhetorical effect by appealing to the German people's innate sense of superiority while also preying on their established fears of the Jews. By repeatedly demonizing Jews, the text takes on an apocalyptical feel: "[the Jew] denies the State of all means of self-preservation, he destroys the basis of any national self-dependence and defense, he destroys the confidence in the leaders, he derides history and the past, and he pulls down into the gutter every thing which is truly great." As R. C. K. Ensor writes in "*Mein Kampf* and Europe," Hitler's outrageous claims about the Aryan race were "exceedingly well-suited for German consumption after the War ... it has long been an almost universal habit among Germans to regard themselves as a race naturally gifted above all other races." Hitler also weaves distorted religious allusions into his text to give credence to his self-stated status as an ordained savior-figure and to his fanatical ideas. For example, he writes, "I am acting in the sense of the Almighty Creator: *By warding off Jews I am fighting for the Lord's work.*" In "The Rhetoric of Hitler's *Battle*," Kenneth Burke describes Hitler's notions as "a bastardized or caricatured version of religious thought."

Stylistically, *Mein Kampf* is distinguished by its repetitiveness, verbosity, and disorganization. Dictated to several different typists, the book wanders from subject to subject. Max Lerner writes in "Some European Thinkers: Hitler as Thinker" that *Mein Kampf* "has all the marks of a book that has been talked. It is a congeries of unconnected fragments held together only by the sustained psychic tension of the speaker, rather than something set down reflectively with logic and inter-connection of its parts." In "Revolution and Revelation, Hitler's Model," Dorothy Thompson takes note of the book's repetition: "He hates 'dirt,' 'filth,' 'scum,' 'corruption,' 'pollution,' 'impurity.' It is amazing how often these words and their synonyms occur throughout the book." Lerner sees a method to this approach, stating that Hitler believed the continued iteration of a single idea would finally engender belief.

CRITICAL DISCUSSION

When the first volume of *Mein Kampf* was published in 1925, it was met with a tepid response from German reviewers. One of the earliest reviews, appearing in a conservative Berlin newspaper, states, "The reader looks for the fire of the spirit but only finds arrogance; instead of inspiration, he finds boredom; instead of love and enthusiasm, catchwords; instead of wholesome hatred, nothing but abuse." The book garnered international attention after Hurst and Blackett published the first unexpurgated English edition in 1939. Most critics attacked the poor aesthetics of the book.

For example, Thompson declares in a 1939 *New York Herald Tribune* article, "If the world is overthrown by this document and the man behind it, it is overthrown without benefit of grammar or literary style." However, some foreign critics warned against dismissing Hitler's text based solely on its dismal style. Ensor argues, "[Hitler] jumps from one topic to another … and yet it really is a very powerful book … its varied themes do cohere, and are masterfully bound together to form a single network of wide-reaching yet consistent argumentation."

Although the majority of Germans initially ignored *Mein Kampf,* it eventually became the bible of Nazism. Under the persuasion of Hitler and the Nazi Party, Germany and its allies devoted themselves to achieving the fanatical goals outlined in *Mein Kampf.* The consequences, as described by journalist Norman Cousins in Downs's *Books That Changed the World,* were horrific: "For every word in *Mein Kampf,* 125 lives were to be lost; for every page, 4,700 lives; for every chapter, more than 1,200,000 lives." In the decades since *Mein Kampf* was written, it has been the subject of an extensive body of criticism that has considered its legacy in historical, political, and sociological terms.

Much scholarship on *Mein Kampf* has focused on its rhetorical qualities, paying special attention to the propagandistic bent of the text. In "The Idol of the Tribe: *Mein Kampf,*" Philo M. Buck Jr. argues that although Hitler's ideas were not original, "his is the living imagination which lent them a new persuasiveness, and he it was who conveyed them to the imagination of the country, especially of the youth, and made them the message of a new gospel. One can learn a great deal about propaganda, its use and abuse, from *Mein Kampf.*" Indeed, Burke asserts that we must study and understand Hitler's arguments in order to "forestall the concocting of similar medicine in America." Scholars continue to investigate the propagandistic effect of *Mein Kampf.* Felicity Rash's *The Language of Violence* is a modern-day analysis of Hitler's linguistic and rhetorical devices, examining the glorification of the Aryan race and the demonization of the Jew. In dissecting Hitler's anti-Semitic imagery, Rash reveals how Hitler's discourse is the leading example of racist and totalitarian propaganda.

Adolf Hitler in 1899, at age ten (top row, center). *Mein Kampf* includes Hitler's political ideology as well as his autobiography. ADOLF HITLER AGED 10, TOP OF SCHOOL CLASS IV IN 1899, FROM 'A PICTORIAL LIFE OF HITLER,' BERLIN, 1935 (B/W PHOTO), AUSTRIAN PHOTOGRAPHER, (19TH CENTURY)/PRIVATE COLLECTION/PETER NEWARK PICTURES/THE BRIDGEMAN ART LIBRARY.

BIBLIOGRAPHY

Sources

Buck, Philo M., Jr. "The Idol of the Tribe: *Mein Kampf.*" *Directions in Contemporary Literature.* New York: Oxford UP, 1942. 219–38. Rpt. in *Twentieth-Century Literary Criticism.* Vol. 53. Detroit: Gale, 1994. *Literature Resource Center.* Web. 2 July 2012.

Burke, Kenneth. "The Rhetoric of Hitler's *Battle.*" *The Philosophy of Literary Form: Studies in Symbolic Action.* Berkeley: U of California P, 1973. 191–20. Rpt. in *Twentieth-Century Literary Criticism.* Vol. 53. Detroit: Gale, 1994. *Literature Resource Center.* Web. 2 July 2012.

Downs, Robert B. *Books That Changed the World.* New York: American Library Association, 1978. Print.

Ensor, R. C. K. "*Mein Kampf* and Europe." *International Affairs* (July-August 1939): 478–96. Rpt. in *Twentieth-Century Literary Criticism.* Vol. 53. Detroit: Gale, 1994. *Literature Resource Center.* Web. 2 July 2012.

Lee, Irving J. "General Semantics and Public Speaking: Perspectives on Rhetoric Comparing Aristotle, Hitler, and Korzybksi." *ETC: A Review of General Semantics* 62.1 (2005): 80+. *Literature Resource Center.* Web. 2 July 2012.

Lerner, Max. "Some European Thinkers: Hitler as Thinker." *Ideas Are Weapons: The History and Uses of Ideas.* New York: Viking, 1939. 356–74. Rpt. in *Twentieth-Century Literary Criticism.* Vol. 53. Detroit: Gale, 1994. *Literature Resource Center.* Web. 2 July 2012.

"*Mein Kampf* by Adolf Hitler." *Twentieth-Century Literary Criticism.* Ed. Laurie Di Mauro. Vol. 53. Detroit: Gale, 1994. 120–83. Gale, Cengage Learning Trial Site. Gale. *Literature Criticism Online.* Web. 7 July 2012

Rash, Felicity. *The Language of Violence: Adolf Hitler's Mein Kampf.* New York: Peter Lang, 2006. Print.

Thompson, Dorothy. "Revolution and Revelation, Hitler's Model." *New York Herald Tribune* 19 March 1939: 3. Rpt. in *Twentieth-Century Literary Criticism.* Vol. 53. Detroit: Gale, 1994. *Literature Resource Center.* Web. 2 July 2012.

Wenning, Elizabeth. "Adolf Hitler." *Contemporary Authors Online.* Detroit: Gale, 2005. *Literature Resource Center.* Web. 2 July 2012.

Further Reading

Bytwerk, Randall L. *Bending Spines: The Propagandas of Nazi Germany and the German Democratic Republic.* East Lansing: Michigan State UP, 2004. Print.

Caspar, C. "*Mein Kampf*—A Best Seller." *Jewish Social Studies* January 1958: 3–16. Rpt. in *Twentieth-Century Literary Criticism.* Vol. 53. Detroit: Gale, 1994. *Literature Resource Center.* Web. 2 July 2012.

Damon, Duane. *Mein Kampf: Hitler's Blueprint for Aryan Supremacy.* San Diego: Lucent Books, 2003. Print.

Ford, Michael. *Mein Kampf: A Translation Controversy.* United States: Elite Minds, 2009. Print.

Hackett, Francis. *What Mein Kampf Means to America.* New York: Reynal and Hitchcock, 1941. Print.

Herf, Jeffery. *The Jewish Enemy: Nazi Propaganda During World War II and the Holocaust.* Cambridge: Harvard UP, 2006. Print.

Marlin, Randall. *Propaganda and the Ethics of Persuasion.* Orchard Park: Broadview, 2002. Print.

McGuire, Michael. "Mythic Rhetoric in *Mein Kampf*: A Structuralist Critique," *The Quarterly Journal of Speech* (February 1977): 1–13. Rpt. in *Twentieth-Century Literary Criticism.* Vol. 53. Detroit: Gale, 1994. *Literature Resource Center.* Web. 2 July 2012.

Weber, Thomas. *Hitler's First War: Adolf Hitler, the Men of the List Regiment, and the First World War.* Oxford: Oxford UP, 2010. Print.

Media Adaptations

Mein Kampf. Dir. Erwin Leiser. Perf. Claude Stephenson, Louis Arbessier, and Heinrich Brüning. Minerva Film AB, 1960. Film.

Mein Kampf. Dir. Urs Odermatt. Perf. Götz George, Tom Schilling, and Anna Unterberger. 3 Sat, 2009. Film.

Maggie Magno

THE MOON IS DOWN

John Steinbeck

OVERVIEW

On assignment from the propaganda arm of the U.S. Foreign Information Service, John Steinbeck composed *The Moon Is Down* (1942) to encourage European resistance movements against the German military advance during World War II. Originally composed as a play and soon after adapted into a novella, *The Moon Is Down* describes the swift and efficient invasion of an unnamed and unsuspecting coastal mining town in northern Europe by unidentified foreign troops. The heavily outnumbered and formerly peaceable townspeople retaliate with a successful campaign of psychological warfare and sabotage. Their victory over the occupying forces symbolizes the U.S. government's goal of triumph over totalitarian aggression.

The Moon Is Down was an immediate best seller, but its publication—and the opening of the play on Broadway in April 1942—unleashed a furor of critical controversy in the United States, most of it focusing on Steinbeck's portrayal of the Nazis as flawed human beings rather than as depraved monsters. Although Steinbeck declines to specify the story's time, place, or combatants in order to evoke the universality of the threat of fascism, textual clues strongly suggest that he modeled the story on the Nazi occupation of politically neutral Norway in April 1940. In the occupied countries of Europe, the novella was an unqualified success, prompting the fascist governments of Germany and Italy to sentence to death anyone in possession of a copy. The work's underground circulation was such that Donald V. Coers, in an introduction to a 1995 edition of the novella, describes *The Moon Is Down* as "easily the most popular work of propaganda in occupied Western Europe."

HISTORICAL AND LITERARY CONTEXT

In the 1953 essay "My Short Novels," Steinbeck writes that he intended *The Moon Is Down* "as a kind of celebration of the durability of democracy" during World War II. At the time of its composition, German dictator Adolf Hitler's plot to overtake Europe was well under way in a series of rapid surprise attacks known as the blitzkrieg. German forces first invaded Austria in 1938, then Czechoslovakia in early 1939. With the invasion of Poland in September 1939, England and France declared war on Germany, Japan, and Italy.

However, France, Norway, Denmark, and the Netherlands surrendered to the Germans in 1940, and the following year Hitler's troops marched into the Soviet Union.

The Foreign Information Service sought to publish a work that would boost civilian morale. Steinbeck proposed a story about the imagined Nazi occupation of an American town, but the proposal was rejected for being potentially demoralizing to the American public. Steinbeck revised the setting to northern Europe and believed that the book might provide a blueprint for resistance in all Nazi-occupied countries. The play version of *The Moon Is Down* was completed on December 7, 1941, the day Japan conducted its surprise attack on American naval forces at Pearl Harbor, Hawaii. The title, drawn from William Shakespeare's *Macbeth,* signified the moral darkness that had enveloped Europe, though by the time of the novella's publication in March 1942, the title's meaning equally applied to the situation in the United States.

Unlike propaganda intended to provoke anger and outrage, *The Moon Is Down* portrays the enemy as human—vicious and ruthless but also scared, confused, and homesick. Before the war's outbreak, Steinbeck had established himself as a writer of social consciousness with a trio of works sympathetic to the plight of migrant workers—*In Dubious Battle* (1936), *Of Mice and Men* (1937), and *The Grapes of Wrath* (1939). Because *The Moon Is Down* appeared during some of the most desperate days of the war for Americans, critics argued that the circumstances demanded the same type of militancy Steinbeck had applied to the plight of the migrant workers. However, Steinbeck's European audience found his Nazis far more effective in rousing popular sentiment than the cold-blooded, maniacal Huns typical of the propaganda circulating on the continent.

Only after the war did Steinbeck and his critics learn of the extent of the book's impact abroad in terms of bolstering morale against the Nazis. After the surrender of Nazi Germany, *The Moon Is Down* became one of the first suppressed books brought back into the open in Europe. In 1946 King Haakon VII of Norway awarded Steinbeck the Liberty Cross, a medal previously bestowed only upon members of the Norwegian resistance. Close to one hundred editions of the novella have appeared worldwide, meriting the

+ *Key Facts*

Time Period:
Mid-20th Century

Genre:
Novel

Events:
World War II

Nationality:
American

THE MOON IS DOWN IN FILM

Twentieth Century Fox paid Steinbeck an unprecedented $300,000 for the rights to *The Moon Is Down,* four times what it had paid for his Pulitzer Prize-winning novel *The Grapes of Wrath.* Like *The Grapes of Wrath, The Moon Is Down* was scripted and produced by Steinbeck's friend Nunnally Johnson. Starring Cedric Hardwick as Colonel Lanser, Henry Travers as Mayor Orden, and Lee J. Cobb as Dr. Winter, the movie premiered in 1943 to generally positive reviews. Critics were pleased to discover that the Nazis of the film had been stripped of the qualities that had made them appear sympathetic in the novella and play. For example, Bosley Crowther observes in a 1943 *New York Times* review,

> Nunnally Johnson … has carefully corrected the most censurable features of the work … He has made Colonel Lanser, the Nazi despot of an invaded Norwegian mining town, a skeptic with respect to brutal measures but a cold and ruthless tyrant none the less. And he has wrung out such traces of defeatism as were apparent in the book and has sharpened with vivid incidents the horror of being enslaved.

Because of the changes, the film escaped the controversy that had plagued the novella and play. It was released in several European countries before and after the war ended.

work as much praise for its literary value as for its contribution to Nazi resistance during the war.

THEMES AND STYLE

The central thesis of *The Moon Is Down* is that democracy will always win over totalitarianism because a free people cannot be conquered against their will. Steinbeck models the resilient spirit of an ambushed village by depicting an underground resistance movement that sabotages the local mine and railway, limiting the enemy's access to coal. Despite severe punishments meted out by the enemy, the resistance gathers strength, and the invaders grow apprehensive living among people who detest them and who seem possessed of an indomitable will. The enemy's steely composure inevitably crumbles as the soldiers grow lonely and frustrated and suffer from paranoia and sleeplessness—symptoms of a deeply flawed, totalitarian ideology. When the townspeople completely destroy the mine with dynamite, Steinbeck depicts the futility of the enemy soldiers' situation as inevitable.

Steinbeck's principal rhetorical strategy is to establish a stark contrast between the oppressors and the oppressed through characters that embody the opposing philosophies of totalitarianism and democracy. One of Steinbeck's several experiments using a hybrid form known as the "play-novelette," *The Moon Is Down* consists mainly of action and dialogue, with limited description and virtually no analysis of the

events or the characters' thoughts. Nevertheless, Steinbeck is careful to show the damaging psychological effects of war on both sides of the conflict. The commanding officer of the enemy, Colonel Lanser, who faithfully carries out orders though he believes his high commander (ostensibly Hitler) to be deranged, represents a collectivist military bureaucracy. In contrast, the village's Mayor Orden embodies democracy and free will, allowing the people of the town to think for themselves and even referring to himself as "an idea conceived by free men."

Stylistically, Steinbeck portrays the contrast between political philosophies using clear, decisive, and balanced dialogue that asserts the certain failure of fascism. Mayor Orden's best friend, Dr. Winter, explains the enemy's misguided notion that arresting and executing the town's mayor will halt the resistance: "They think that just because they have only one leader and one head, we are all like that … but we are a free people; we have as many heads as we have people, and in time of need leaders pop up among us like mushrooms." His solid, unwavering tone is echoed by Orden, who, about to be executed, paints for Lanser a plain but profound vision of the triumph of democracy: "Free men cannot start a war, but once it is started, they can fight on in defeat. Herd men, followers of a leader, cannot do that, and so it is the herd men who win battles and the free men who win wars." Steinbeck crafts memorable, inspiring sentiments, void of emotional or ornamental language, to herald the inevitable victory of the forces of democracy, as epitomized in Dr. Winter's now-famous line from the story's conclusion, "The flies have conquered the flypaper."

CRITICAL DISCUSSION

Although the novella sold almost a million copies in its first year and the play had a successful road tour following its brief nine-week run on Broadway, critical reaction was divided between praise and outright hostility, prompting what Coers (1995) calls, "the fiercest literary battle of the Second World War." Steinbeck's humanization of the enemy elicited such a deluge of reviews, favorable and unfavorable, that *Newsweek* magazine, in April 1942, compiled a list of the attacks and counterattacks to clarify the debate. The following month the *New Republic* named the opposing critical camps the Green and Blue armies. Clifton Fadiman and James Thurber launched two of the most stinging assaults, charging that Steinbeck's sympathetic Nazis could not possibly help shore up the rage necessary to defeat the Germans. In "Two Ways to Win the War" (1942), Fadiman contends that Steinbeck's naïve belief in the power of democracy will puff up Allied troops with false optimism. However, John Chamberlain, in a review of the play, agrees with Steinbeck that the defenders of freedom will fight on to victory, making a portrayal of one-dimensional Nazi monsters unnecessary.

In this scene from the 1943 film adaptation of John Steinbeck's *The Moon Is Down*, Ingrid (played by Dorris Bowdon) is surrounded by enemy soldiers who have invaded her town. 20TH CENTURY FOX/THE KOBAL COLLECTION/ART RESOURCE, NY.

In the decades after the war, interest in the work's success as propaganda persisted. In *John Steinbeck As Propagandist: The Moon Is Down Goes to War* (1991), Coers uncovers a bulk of new evidence describing the vast, albeit illegal, distribution of *The Moon Is Down* in Western Europe and the tremendous momentum it supplied resistance movements. Scholars also have traced Steinbeck's distinction between herd men and free men, which appears in many of the author's works in various forms, as a derivative of a theory of group psychology developed by one of Steinbeck's closest friends and influences, the marine biologist and philosopher Ed Ricketts. In spite of the work's nominal purpose, the majority of contemporary critics have been inclined to assess *The Moon Is Down* in terms of its value as literature rather than as propaganda.

Although Steinbeck's characterization of the opposing forces in the novella remains a central issue of scholarly interest, the terms of the debate have shifted to how successful Steinbeck is in wedding ideology to content. In *The Moon Is Down*, some scholars contend, Steinbeck sacrifices credible characterization to the demands of ideology, creating a story so abstract that the reader finds it impossible to emotionally connect with either side. Richard Astro (1981), the leading academic expert on Steinbeck's philosophical perspective, argues, "*The Moon Is Down* is not really a war novel at all, nor is it antiwar. ... It is a failure as art not because Steinbeck failed to write a polemic about the horrors of Nazism, but rather because he was unable to relate abstract philosophical visions to concrete reality." Other retrospective analyses have praised Steinbeck's work for its insight into the psychology of war. Robert E. Mossberger observes, "Steinbeck was prophetically accurate in picturing the nature of the ultimate defeat. In his portrayal of the supposed conquerors admitting that in essence they have already been defeated by the relentless resistance of the supposedly conquered, there is considerable subtlety."

BIBLIOGRAPHY

Sources

Astro, Richard. "John Steinbeck." *American Novelists, 1910–1945.* Ed. James J. Martine. Detroit: Gale Research, 1981. Dictionary of Literary Biography 9. Web. 7 June 2012.

Chamberlain, John. Rev. of *The Moon Is Down,* by John Steinbeck. *New York Times* 6 Mar. 1942: 19. Web. 7 June 2012.

Coers, Donald V. *John Steinbeck As Propagandist: "The Moon Is Down" Goes to War.* Tuscaloosa: U of Alabama, 1991. Print.

———. Introduction. *The Moon Is Down.* By John Steinbeck. New York: Penguin, 1995. vii–xxiv. Print.

Crowther, Bosley. Rev. of *The Moon Is Down,* dir. Irving Pichel. *New York Times* 27 Mar. 1943: 8. Web. 7 June 2012.

Fadiman, Clifton. "Two Ways to Win the War." *New Yorker* 7 Mar. 1942: 52–53. Web. 7 June 2012.

Levant, Howard. "Three Play-Novelettes." *The Novels of John Steinbeck: A Critical Study.* Columbia: U of Missouri, 1974. 130–63. Print.

Mossberger, Robert E. "Steinbeck's War." *Critical Insights: John Steinbeck.* Ed. Don Noble. Pasadena: Salem, 2011. 275–309. Print.

Steinbeck, John. *The Moon Is Down.* New York: Penguin, 1995. Print.

———. "My Short Novels." *Steinbeck and His Critics: A Record of Twenty-Five Years.* Ed. E. W. Tedlock Jr. and C. V. Wicker. Albuquerque: U of New Mexico, 1969. 38–40. Print.

———. "Reflections on a Lunar Eclipse." *New York Herald Tribune* 6 Oct. 1963: 3. Print.

Thurber, James. Rev. of *The Moon Is Down,* by John Steinbeck. *New Republic* 16 Mar. 1942: 370. Web. 7 June 2012.

Further Reading

Astro, Richard. *John Steinbeck and Edward F. Ricketts: The Shaping of a Novelist.* Minneapolis: U of Minnesota, 1973. Print.

French, Warren. *John Steinbeck.* 2nd ed. New York: Twayne, 1975. Print.

Hays, Peter L. "Steinbeck's Plays: From Realism to Abstraction." *Studies in the Humanities* 1 Jun. 2004. *HighbeamResearch.* Web. 7 June 2012.

Lisca, Peter. *John Steinbeck: Nature and Myth.* New York: Thomas Crowell, 1978. Print.

Simmonds, Roy. *John Steinbeck: The War Years, 1939–1945.* Lewisburg: Bucknell UP, 1996. Print.

Media Adaptation

John Steinbeck's The Moon Is Down. Prod. and writ. Nunnally Johnson. Dir. Irving Pichel. Perf. Sir Cedric Hardwicke, Henry Travers, Lee J. Cobb, et al. United States: Released through Twentieth Century-Fox Film Corp., 1943. Film.

Janet Mullane

"NATIONAL SONG"

Sándor Petőfi

OVERVIEW

Sándor Petőfi's poem "National Song" (also translated as "National Ode"; alternately referred to by its first words as "Arise Magyar") pushed the radical youth of the city of Pest to take to the streets in what became known as the Hungarian national revolution of March 15, 1848. The six-stanza poem uses repetition, exhortation, and the contrast between ancient liberty and present subservience to call on the Hungarian nation to free itself from Austrian Habsburg rule. Issued in the rush of the "springtime of nations"—the national and social awakening then sweeping the European continent—it was representative of the agitation in a feudal, backward country for both national liberation and social justice. It calls out for faith and loyalty to overcome centuries of fear and bondage even in the face of death, thus putting mortal stakes on the decision of whether to take political action.

By the mid-nineteenth century, Hungary had been without sovereignty for more than three centuries after its defeat by forces of the Ottoman empire in 1526. Hungary was then gradually absorbed into the Habsburg empire, definitively by 1699, after Habsburg armies pushed the Turks back beyond the historic Hungarian lands. The Magyar (ethnic Hungarian) nobility had since been able to attain some measure of its ancient rights and privileges while oppressing and exploiting the peasants on its vast estates. The growth of a stratum of "lower nobility"—conscious of its historic national rights and responsibilities but increasingly impoverished and thus less invested in the status quo—along with a cultural revival in which literature was used to strengthen Hungarian identity and unity created the conditions for an antifeudal independence movement led by struggling scions such as Petőfi. Drought-caused famine and hardship, combined with the political hurricane emanating from Paris—where mass demonstrations in February 1848 led to the fall of the regime—produced the conditions ripe for the "National Song," which István Deák (1990) has called "the anthem of all Hungarian radicals" ever since.

HISTORICAL AND LITERARY CONTEXT

Starting in the 1820s, the French Revolution—Napoleon's forays across Europe in the name of rationalism and the liberation of oppressed nations—and literary Romanticism, which idealized the connection between individual and national suffering, had combined to unsettle the political and cultural landscape of the multinational Habsburg Empire. In Hungary, centuries of domination by the Austrian state, punctuated by the failure of various attempts at liberation and the social and economic domination of a corrupted feudal nobility over an impoverished peasant majority, spawned a movement for cultural renewal and modernization by what became known as the Reform Generation. Statesmen such as István Széchényi and Lajos Kossuth agitated for national autonomy, modernization, and the replacement of feudal structures. As elsewhere in the region, in the absence of political autonomy, writers and poets took on outsized stature as spokespeople for the national interest.

As the fateful year 1848 dawned, more moderate, generally wealthier aristocratic leaders were cautiously striving to consolidate a limited autonomy. However, in Pest-Buda (as Budapest was known before its unification in 1873), a more cosmopolitan population of students and workers, in addition to peasants in town for the large market fair, constituted a public interested in more thoroughgoing reform. As news of the upheavals in France reached Hungary at the beginning of March, Petőfi—a twenty-six-year-old former itinerant actor who had become a celebrated and influential poet and journalist—mobilized a number of his friends, including the writer Mór Jókai, in the group Young Hungary (later dubbed the March Youth) to push for more radical action. He wrote "National Song" on March 13, intending it for a reform banquet planned for the nineteenth. However, with news of the fall of the Habsburg government under pressure from radicals in Vienna, he chose to read it publicly on the morning of the fifteenth to intellectuals assembled at the Café Pilvax. Inspired by Petőfi's words, they spilled out into the streets; took over a local printing shop; and, ignoring the censorship regime, printed it, along with the group's list of demands formulated into the document "12 Points," by Jókai, in thousands of copies.

National movements for cultural revitalization in Eastern Europe were inspired by the literary Romanticism pioneered by Johann Wolfgang von Goethe and Friedrich Schiller in Germany and Lord Byron and Percy Bysshe Shelley in England. Petőfi thus fit into

✣ *Key Facts*

Time Period:
Mid-19th Century

Genre:
Poetry

Events:
Hungarian national revolution of 1848; "Springtime of Nations"

Nationality:
Hungarian

PRIMARY SOURCE

EXCERPT FROM "NATIONAL SONG"

Rise, Magyar! is the country's call!

The time has come, say one and all:

Shall we be slaves, shall we be free?

This is the question, now agree!

For by the Magyar's God above

We truly swear,

We truly swear the tyrant's yoke

No more to bear!

Alas! till now we were but slaves;

Our fathers resting in their graves

Sleep not in freedom's soil. In vain

They fought and died free homes to gain.

But by the Magyar's God above

We truly swear,

We truly swear the tyrant's yoke

No more to bear!

A miserable wretch is he

Who fears to die, my land, for thee!

His worthless life who thinks to be

Worth more than thou, sweet liberty!

Now by the Magyar's God above

We truly swear,

We truly swear the tyrant's yoke

No more to bear!

The sword is brighter than the chain,

Men cannot nobler gems attain;

And yet the chain we wore, oh, shame!

Unsheath the sword of ancient fame!

For by the Magyar's God above

We truly swear,

We truly swear the tyrant's yoke

No more to bear!

The Magyar's name will soon once more

Be honored as it was before!

The shame and dust of ages past

Our valor shall wipe out at last.

For by the Magyar's God above

We truly swear,

We truly swear the tyrant's yoke

No more to bear!

And where our graves in verdure rise,

Our children's children to the skies

Shall speak the grateful joy they feel,

And bless our names the while they kneel.

For by the Magyar's God above

We truly swear,

We truly swear the tyrant's yoke

No more to bear!

SOURCE: Eva March Tappan, ed. *The World's Story: A History of the World in Story, Song and Art,* Vol. VI: Russia, Austria-Hungary, The Balkan States, and Turkey, pp. 408–410. Boston: Houghton Mifflin, 1914.

a role of "national poet" modeled by such writers as Adam Mickiewicz in Poland. However, by the 1840s this literature in Hungary had become established and a bit tired. Petőfi's work had already moved beyond the abstracted, lone heroes of epic works (such as Mihaly Vörösmarty's "The Flight of Zalán" from 1825) to provide realistic and often satirical portraits of Hungarian village life, based on knowledge gained by his extended wanderings. With the escalation of the political situation, his poetry engaged more forthrightly with the pressing issues of the day. Thus verses such as "Italy," commemorating the Italian national struggle against the same Habsburg rulers, and "One Thought

Torments Me," hoping for a heroic death in the service of his cause, can be seen as precursors to the directness and force of the "National Song."

"National Song" and its immediate explosive impact gained iconic status as the distillation of the impulse for national freedom, catapulting Petőfi into a significant role in the heady politics of the national revolution. He engaged in political debates in the leading newspapers and journals; criticized the newly formed government for its timidity and ineffectiveness; and ran for a seat in parliament, an effort doomed by opponents' slander and political machinations. Especially in light of his subsequent death on the battlefield the

"TALPRA MAGYAR!"

following year—after Austrian forces had regrouped and engaged in an ultimately successful effort to reverse concessions to Hungarian autonomy—he became a political and literary hero rolled into one: the beacon of the nation's struggle. The uncompromising stance expressed in the ode famously inspired the celebrated modernist writer Endre Ady to press opposition to the monarchy in the last decade of its existence some sixty years later with the slogan "Petőfi doesn't bargain!" A century further on, in securely independent Hungary, schoolchildren still memorize the "National Song" to recite at celebrations of March 15, a national holiday.

THEMES AND STYLE

The central theme of "National Song" is the contrast between "our ancestors, who lived and died free," and the "slave land" that the current generation has allowed Hungary to become. Invoking the Romantic mantra of lost glories of the deep national past, Petőfi draws a direct line to the complacency he saw around him, even as the death knells of the old order seemed to be tolling. Though the exact nature of the duty to be performed is not specified—the accompanying "12 Points" enumerated demands for abolition of feudal privileges and broad autonomy for Hungary within the empire, alongside the core ultimatum of freedom

of the press—the mere act of rising "on your feet," as the poem opens, implies a cathartic redemption. The regular invocation of the "God of the Hungarians" bridges the gap between the ancient faith of the people and the modern task of building the nation, the ascendant deity of the age.

The key rhetorical strategy Petőfi employs is that of repetition. The last four lines of each of the six 8-line stanzas are the same: "For by the Magyar's God above / We truly swear / We truly swear the tyrant's yoke / No more to bear!" This position of relentless exhortation, what Lóránt Czigány in his 1986 study calls "the masterly use of the refrain," leaves the listener no place to hide from the imperative to seize the moment and act. The source and authority of the appeal is not explicit or justified, beyond the responsibility owed to the forefathers, but the imperative to serve the nation is all the more powerful for being anonymous, encapsulating the force of the role of national poet that Petőfi was in the midst of appropriating for himself. In addition, the alternation of patterns of word stresses and differing line lengths (what Enikő Molnár Basa, in her 1980 biography, calls "metrical mastery") and the use of monosyllabic words to produce a quick rhythm combine for an effect that compels the audience's identification with the cause.

THE SONG THAT WOULDN'T STOP SINGING

Like the ultraconservative and aristocrat-dominated interwar government before it, the post-World War II communist regime, established in 1948, tried to co-opt the legacy of Sándor Petőfi and the "National Song," with slogans such as "The heir of … Petőfi … the Hungarian Communist Party!" and "Arise, Magyars, the Fatherland calls!" However, after years of repression and the death of Soviet dictator Joseph Stalin in 1953, pressure began to build for change, inspired by that very legacy. Hungarian writers formed the "Petőfi Circle" and engaged in ever more lively and well-attended debates about issues of freedom of expression and national autonomy. On October 23, 1956, thousands of students marched to the massive Petőfi statue of 1882 on the bank of the Danube River in Budapest, chanting the "National Song" and demanding recognition of its "16 Points," modeled after the "12 Points" of March 15, 1848. This snowballed into the Hungarian revolution of 1956, which was crushed by a brutal Soviet-led invasion twelve days later.

Despite the bloody precedent, in the 1980s protesters demanding freedom and democracy again began leveraging the heritage of Petőfi. Demonstrators gathered each March 15 at the same statue and traced the same path as their 1956 predecessors—who themselves had been imitating Petőfi and his comrades' procession through Budapest's streets—and, again, recitations of the "National Song" featured prominently. Harassment by the authorities gradually gave way to tolerance, and on March 15, 1989, it was finally possible to commemorate the 1848 revolution freely and hope that its goals could finally be achieved, as the Communist Party carried out the preliminary steps of relinquishing power later that year.

"National Song" employs simple, direct language to make its point, compounding the impact of the recurring phrases and rhythms. Yet beneath the surface roils a complex stew of emotions, mobilizing the anger and shame accumulated through centuries of subjugation. Words such as *slave, damned,* and *pathetic* trigger deep associations of guilt and disgust vis-à-vis the rich culture and achievements of a people that had established its civilization in the Carpathian basin almost a millennium before. However, equally powerful words such as *honor* and *sainted* promise redemption to those who are willing to throw off the more recent degeneration and act.

CRITICAL DISCUSSION

"National Song" had a direct impact matched by few other poems in history; in the words of Gyula Illyés's 1963 biography of Petőfi (English translation published in 1973), what "began merely as a student demonstration … a poem … turned … into a historical occasion." Petőfi read it out several more times during the course of March 15, most famously on the steps of the National Museum. The growing crowds in effect took over the city, marking the Hungarian revolution; the day that is still commemorated as the national day of independence. "National Song" was reprinted in almost every other town in the country and translated into German, the official language of the empire. The full acceptance of the twelve points by the weakened monarchy less than a month later, on April 11, validated its force.

Petőfi's death, less than a year and a half after penning "National Song," at the hands of tsarist Russian forces aiding the Habsburg armies in putting down the Hungarian struggle, cemented his and the poem's status as national icons. Especially in the wake of the complete reversal of the April concessions and the execution of most of the surviving leaders of the independence movement, martyrdom was all that the nation had to show for its efforts—a fate that dovetailed with the tragic cast of the Romantic sensibility that had inspired them. Despite its grand, almost spiritual pretensions, it was a work written quickly and for maximum immediate practical effect. Thus, while it is a textbook example of the possibilities of poetry as mobilization, it has been little analyzed as literature; scholars have focused their attention on Petőfi's other, more substantial works, primarily his epic narrative poems, such as *A helység kalapácsa* (1844; *Hammer of the Village*), *János vitéz* (1845; *John the Hero*), and *Az apostol* (1848; *The Apostle*).

Especially given the nation's continuing struggles to achieve full-fledged independence—most Hungarians considered this status achieved only with the end of Soviet domination in 1989—scholars have mostly been loath to criticize too pointedly a work so beloved and central to national identity. George Gömöri, in the course of examining the parallels and connections between "National Song" and the work of Irish poet and patriot Thomas Moore in a 1990 article, does allow that it relies on a "somewhat banal contrast between the sword and the chain." Much more typical is hyperbolic praise such as that of Illyés: "high emotion runs through the six stanzas of this splendidly constructed poem like a six-pronged flash of lightning." However, it is difficult to argue with Czigány's conclusion: "no other poem has ever had such political significance in Hungarian history."

BIBLIOGRAPHY
Sources

Basa, Enikő Molnár. *Sándor Petőfi.* Boston: Twayne, 1980. Print.

Czigány, Lóránt. "Comet of the Revolution: Petőfi." *The Oxford History of Hungarian Literature: From the Earliest Times to the Present.* Oxford: Clarendon, 1986. 179–97. Print.

Deák, István. *The Lawful Revolution: Louis Kossuth and the Hungarians, 1848–1849.* New York: Columbia UP, 1979. Print.

Gömöri, George. "Petőfi—The Irish Connection." *A Journey into History: Essays on Hungarian Literature.* Ed. Moses M. Nagy. New York: Peter Lang, 1990. 115–23. Print.

Illyés, Gyula. *Petőfi.* Trans. G. F. Cushing. Budapest: Corvina, 1973. Print.

Mevius, Martin. "The Heirs of Kossuth, Petőfi and Táncsics (December 1944–January 1945)." *Agents of Moscow: The Hungarian Communist Party and the Origins of Socialist Patriotism 1941–1953.* Oxford: Clarendon, 2005. 87–110. Print.

Petőfi, Sándor. *Rebel or Revolutionary?: Sándor Petőfi as Revealed by his Diary, Letters, Notes, Pamphlets and Poems.* Trans. Edwin Morgan, G. F. Cushing, Thelma Dufton, László András, Gyula Kodolányi, and Mária Kőrösy. Budapest: Corvina, 1974. Print.

Further Reading

Cushing, George F. "The Role of the National Poet." Special Issue: "Hungarian Literature." *Review of National Literatures* 17 (1993): 59–80. Print.

Deák, István. "The Revolution and the War of Independence, 1848–1849." Ed. Peter F. Sugar, Péter Hanák, and Tibor Frank. Bloomington: Indiana UP, 1990. 209–34. Print.

Deme, László. "The Society for Equality in the Hungarian Revolution of 1848." *Slavic Review* 31:1 (1972). 71–88. Print.

Ewen, Frederic. "The Lyre and the Sword: Art and Revolution. 1. Hungary—July 31, 1849: Sándor Petőfi—The Poet as Warrior." *A Half-Century of Greatness: The Creative Imagination of Europe, 1848–1884.* Ed. Jeffrey Wollock. New York: New York UP, 2007. 256–75. Print.

Gerő, András. *Imagined History: Chapters from Nineteenth- and Twentieth-Century Hungarian Symbolic Politics.* Boulder: East European Monographs, 2006. 137–51. Print.

Lukácsy, Sándor. "Petőfi and the Revolution." *New Hungarian Quarterly* 14.50 (1973): 100–07. Print.

Sőtér, István. "From the Revolution of Poetry to Revolutionary Poetry." *The Dilemma of Literary Science.* Trans. Éva Róna. Budapest: Akadémiai Kiadó, 1973. 195–211. Print.

Rick Esbenshade

"ODES 3.2"

Horace

❖ *Key Facts*

Time Period:
1st Century BCE

Genre:
Poetry

Events:
Mounting tensions
with Parthia; Battle
of Carrhae; reign of
Augustus

Nationality:
Greek

OVERVIEW

Written by Quintus Horatius Flaccus in 23 BCE, "Odes 3.2" is a political poem that promotes the ideologies of the Roman emperor Augustus by praising the honest and simple life of a soldier, thus preparing the younger generation of Romans for the seemingly imminent war in the East against the Parthians. The work is one of the eighty-eight short poems that comprise Horace's magnum opus, *Odes 1-3*. He composed the poem in the majestic Alcaic meter, representing himself as the heir to Greek lyric poetry and expressing a philosophy of life with graceful precision. With an emphasis on traditional Roman virtues including loyalty, simplicity, and courage in battle, "Odes 3.2" has been criticized as a piece of war propaganda that attempts to atone for the humiliating defeat at the Battle of Carrhae and to justify Roman imperialism.

Augustus realized the importance of literature to his political career, so he gathered some of the greatest writers the world has ever known by means of his friend and advisor Maecenas. These writers included Virgil, Horace, Propertius, Livy, and Ovid. A complex patron-client system had existed and was continued under Augustus; for example, Maecenas gifted Horace a villa in the Sabine Hills (Sabine Farm) and, in return, the lyric poet sincerely praised Maecenas and promoted Augustine ideologies in his verse. Although the public's reception of the first three books of *Odes* disappointed Horace, Augustus responded with enthusiasm and commissioned him to produce a work for the Centennial Games. Horace's "Odes 3.2" has exerted a lasting influence on lyric poetry, having been praised for more than two millennia. However, it has also been sharply criticized in recent times as propaganda, particularly the famous gnomic line 13: *Dulce et decorum est pro patria mori* ("It's both sweet and noble to die for one's country").

HISTORICAL AND LITERARY CONTEXT

After fifty years of bloody civil wars, land confiscations, and proscriptions, Augustus ushered in the much-desired *Pax Romana* (Roman peace). He ensured both lasting peace within Rome and his own political success in three ways: he (1) defeated Antony at Actium in 31 BCE and achieved swift military victories in Spain and Illyria in 29 BCE,

(2) consolidated his position in claiming to restore the Republic in 27 BCE (although almost total control remained in his hands), and (3) introduced an extensive series of moral reforms in 28 BCE designed mostly to restore personal and social values among Rome's elites. These reforms were initially rejected, but they wound up passing in 18 BCE and 9 CE with the aid of poets such as Horace, who popularized Augustine policies.

At the time of *Odes'* appearance in 23 BCE, relations with Parthia had worsened and an eastern campaign appeared inevitable. Agrippa became commander in the East, and Augustus planned a visit to those provinces. In his commentary *The Third Book of Horace's Odes*, Gordon Williams concludes, "An Augustine youth can have no greater purpose than to prepare himself for the crusade against the Parthians, which so obsessed Romans mindful of several defeats." Pompey initially strained the relations between Parthia and Rome by seizing and partitioning disputed lands, and the ambitious Marcus Licinius Crassus followed this by waging war on Parthia. At the Battle of Carrhae in 53 BCE, Crassus was killed and the majority of his soldiers either died or were taken captive. Thus, vengeance was on the minds of many, and "Odes 3.2" promoted this bellicose sentiment.

Although there is much debate about the patron-client relationship in Rome, it appears that artists had an independent relationship with both Maecenas and Augustus and that they promoted Augustine ideologies with sincerity. After all, they greatly benefited from Augustine peace and clemency. Following the publication of his *Epodes* and *Satires 1-2*, Horace composed *Odes 1-3*. In particular, Horace's Roman *Odes* (3.1-3.6) promote the moral and political values of Augustus, which included education of the young, frugality, clemency, loyalty, and foreign conquest. These poems have, therefore, been singled out as an independent grouping and condemned by critics as propaganda. "Odes 3.2"—with the famous line, "It's both sweet and noble to die for one's country"—is both the most renowned and criticized of the Roman *Odes*.

Horace's *Odes* is considered by many to be the finest collection of lyric poetry ever written. Roman writers such as Propertius and Ovid were highly influenced by his poetic style, and Quintilian praised Horace as the only Roman lyric poet worth reading. Prudentius, the first great Christian poet, was inspired by Horace, and he Christianized the famous gnome in 3.2: it is a martyr's death that is "sweet and noble." Horace's literary impact continued through the Middle Ages and the Renaissance, and it is still felt today. Contemporary poets such as Michael Longley have imitated Horace, while Wilfred Owen and Ezra Pound criticized the use of the word "sweet" (*dulce*) in "Odes 3.2." There have been many fine commentaries and translations in recent years, and the distinguished classicist Phebe Lowell Bowditch provides valuable insights into the highly controversial topic of patronage in *Horace and the Gift Economy of Patronage*.

THEMES AND STYLE

Central to Horace's "Odes 3.2" is the idea that the true Augustine youth must realize the link between simplicity, virtue, and immortality. Horace begins the ode with the following stanza: "Let the sturdy boy learn through tough military experience to endure poverty as a friend, and let him harass the fierce Parthians, a horseman spreading fear with his sword." The simple and tough military way of life will help the boy toward virtue and lead him away from the "vulgar throng" and "sordid politics." Virtue leads to immortality, while punishment eventually catches up with the wicked. The Augustine elements emphasized in this poem are the moral education of the Roman youth, attack on political ambition, and Roman conquest. For these reasons, it has been labeled as Augustine propaganda. Furthermore, this propaganda was effective because it echoed traditional Roman values.

The person speaking in "Odes 3.2" is, in contrast to the autobiographical nature of Horace's *Epistles* and *Satires*, a prophet addressing the younger generation. It was the function of the Augustine poet to speak from a lofty position about important societal issues. In 3.1, the first Roman Ode, Horace makes the speaker's position clear: "I sing—as a priest of the muses—songs never before heard for boys and girls." The voice is the same throughout the Roman *Odes* (3.1-3.6). In "Odes 3.2," Horace writes, "Virtue opens a way to heaven for those who deserve not to die." This again is the prophet (*sacerdos musarum*)—a person inspired by the muses—reciting hortatory verse that promotes Augustine morality. The speaker, or Roman prophet, then reveals the secrets of immortality, a path achievable by means of Augustine morality.

Despite exhorting the reader to live according to certain values, "Odes 3.2" is characterized by its a graceful detachment. Influenced by Callimachean aesthetics of elegance and precision, Horace manipulates the Greek lyric meter of Alcaeus to his Latin verse

THE LIFE OF HORACE

Horace was born on December 8, 65 BCE, in Venusia, a town on the border of Apulia that was plagued by civil wars. His childhood shaped many of the attitudes expressed in his poetry. His father, a freedman and local official, sent him to Rome for the best possible education. Horace later studied in Athens at the Academy, which was presided over by the Epicurean enthusiast Theomnestus. After the assassination of Julius Caesar, he joined the army of Brutus and Cassius against the Triumvirs. He was on the losing side in the Battle of Philippi.

Horace returned to Italy when Octavian (Augustus) gave amnesty to those who had fought against him. By means of some influential friends, Horace secured an official post in the Roman Treasury. At this time, he began writing *Satires*, and in 38 BCE Virgil introduced him to Maecenas. Horace's success was immediate. He received the Sabine Farm from Maecenas, a small farm outside of Rome that inspired him to infuse his work with pastoral overtones. While writing about the traditional Roman way of life, Horace promoted the Augustine ideologies of simplicity, frugality, and a return to the countryside. Late in life he was offered the position of personal secretary to Augustus, but he turned it down. Horace died on November 27, 8 BCE, and was buried alongside Maecenas on the Esquiline. He is best remembered for his works *Satires, Epodes, Epistles,* and *Odes.*

in "Odes 3.2." Writing in a colloquial and "unpoetic" language, Horace utilizes hyperbaton—the artful arrangement of words by, say, separating a noun and an adjective—for special emphasis. His advice is philosophical, though the meanings of his lines are, at once, ambiguous and straightforward. For example, line 25 in "Odes 3.2" reads, "There is also a reward for reliable silence" (*est et fideli tuta silentio / merces*). His highly refined, unemotional style gives an air of authority to the speaker, who is promoting Augustus's virtues.

CRITICAL DISCUSSION

Although Horace was disappointed with the public's reception of *Odes 1-3*, the impact of the work can be measured not only by Augustus's positive response but also by those of his younger contemporaries Ovid and Propertius. Propertius, for example, appropriated material from Horace's *Odes*. In his essay "Ancient Receptions of Horace," Richard Tarrant notes the following about Propertius: "In his opening lines he recalls Horace's self-characterization in Odes 3.1.3 as the 'priest of the muses' (Musarum sacerdos) and his claim in 3.30.13-14 to have first adapted Greek lyric to Roman verse, and cheekily applies both attributes to himself an elegist." Ovid, who continuously borrowed from and referred to Horace's *Odes,* writes, "Horace with his many meters beguiled my ears." The ancients particularly admired

Beatus ille qui procul negotiis.

Horaz.

from lyric poetry as song to poetry which give lyric expression to complex thought. Their influence upon the development of modern lyric is thus enormous." In 1882 H. T. Pluss labeled "Odes 3.1-3.6" *die Romeroden,* or the Roman *Odes.* These six odes, in the Alcaic meter, lack both the levity and brevity of the other poems, and they heavily promote the political and moral ideologies of Augustus. Since then, many scholars have focused on the Roman *Odes* as a group because of these stylistic and thematic peculiarities.

There have been several trends in recent Horatian scholarship. Some contemporary critics, such as Daniel Garrison, have studied Horace's use of hyperbaton, while others have debated the structural unity of the Roman *Odes.* Williams goes so far as to contend that the study of the Roman *Odes* as a unit is "a waste of time." The most exciting trend has focused on the controversial subject of the patron-client relationship and its role in ancient Rome. Bowditch writes, "The triangular relationship of poet, patron, and 'public' audience must be interpreted in the social context of ancient Rome, where the exchange of goods and services provided for the ideological cohesion of a community." Horace's "Odes 3.2" was written to promote the Augustine ideals of courage and conquest, and no one in Roman history added more territory to the empire than Augustus. However, it is nearly impossible to measure exactly how much the Augustine poet Horace helped to achieve this expansion.

BIBLIOGRAPHY

Sources

Bowditch, Phebe Lowell. *Horace and the Gift Economy of Patronage.* Berkeley: U of California P, 2001. Print.

Garrison, Daniel. *Horace: Epodes and Odes.* Norman: U of Oklahoma P, 1991. Print.

Quinn, Kenneth. *Horace: The Odes.* London: Bristol Classical Press, 1996. Print.

Tarrant, Richard. "Ancient Receptions of Horace." *The Cambridge Companion to Horace.* Ed. Stephen Harrison. Cambridge: Cambridge UP, 2007. 277–290. Print.

Williams, Gordon. *The Third Book of Horace's Odes.* Oxford: Oxford UP, 1969. Print.

Further Reading

Grant, Michael. *History of Rome.* Englewood Cliffs: Prentice-Hall, 1978. Print.

Lowrie, Michèle. "Horace and Augustus." *The Cambridge Companion to Horace.* Ed. Stephen Harrison. Cambridge: Cambridge UP, 2007. Print.

———. *Horace's Narrative Odes.* Oxford: Oxford UP, 1997. Print.

Nisbet, R. G. M., and Niall Rudd. *A Commentary on Horace: Odes, Book III.* Oxford: Oxford UP, 2004. Print.

West, David. *Horace, Odes III: Dulce Periculum.* Oxford: Oxford UP, 2002. Print.

Woodman, A. J., and D. Feeny. *Traditions and Contexts in the Poetry of Horace.* Cambridge: Cambridge UP, 2002. Print.

Greg Bach

Horace's metrical virtuosity and verbal artistry. Quintilian praised Horace as "felicitously daring in his choice of words."

The numerous commentaries, translations, and critical works over the centuries attest to the aesthetic legacy of Horace's *Odes.* In his commentary *Horace: The Odes,* Kenneth Quinn writes, "Horace's *Odes* constitute one of the landmarks in the line of development

SELECTED WORKS
Ho Chi Minh

OVERVIEW

Ho Chi Minh's *Selected Works* (1960) contains a number of Ho's speeches and political addresses. The first part of the work offers essays concerning the collective Vietnamese response to French oppression in the early 1920s. Launched as part of a series of literary attacks on French colonials by Ho while he was living in Paris, these early essays acknowledge French control over the Vietnamese but refute the fundamental moral or cultural right of the French to that dominance by exposing their hypocrisy and ineptitude through satirical ridicule. In doing so, Ho effectively turns the tables on French authorities, exposing their unjustifiable assumptions of superiority to the Vietnamese.

From the very beginning of Ho's career as a revolutionary until his death in 1969, one of his most powerful revolutionary tools was his typewriter. The French began feeling the sting of his particular kind of narrative attacks while he was a young radical communist and nationalist in Paris, changing his name and address constantly to avoid being picked up by French agents who were always hot on his trail. Through his association with French radicals, Ho learned the power of the press, and in 1922 he founded his own journal, *Le Paria,* dedicated to the plight of the French colonial peoples. He also wrote scores of articles for other revolutionary journals, including *L'Humanité, La Vie Ouvrière,* and *La Correspondance Internationale.* These articles had an impact on political affairs in metropole France and on political affairs in colonial Vietnam, articulating Ho's basic rationale for resistance to colonial oppression. They helped set the stage for the Vietnamese people to eventually retake their country from the French, who had dominated the region since the late nineteenth century.

HISTORICAL AND LITERARY CONTEXT

In the 1880s France added the Chinese protectorates Tonkin and Annam to Cochin China. This tripartite area of control became part of the larger French colonial sphere of Indochina, but after World War II it was known as Vietnam. France retained control of Vietnam until 1945. After a short period of Japanese rule, Ho's Viet Minh soldiers conquered the area but then had to contend with French attempts to regain the former colony. With ongoing assistance from China but using their own battle tactics, the Viet Minh defeated France in 1954. Having supported and funded France, the

United States stepped in with a long conflict to continue what it saw as the fight to contain communism.

When Ho began writing his essays, Paris was already a breeding ground for Vietnamese radicalism. Wealthy Vietnamese families sent their sons to France for an education. They often became radicalized after attending meetings dedicated to socialist and communist ideology in what Ho biographer William Duiker has called the "Byzantine world of Vietnamese émigré politics in Paris." Ho agitated on behalf of underpaid and overworked factory and shipyard workers from colonial countries and was a founding member of the French Communist Party. Returning Vietnamese brought back ideas first encountered through articles penned by Ho, who had himself come to France by working on steamships through Asia, South America, the United States, and Europe.

Ho's Paris essays began a tradition of revolutionary writing focused on workers and peasants as both subjects of colonial abuse and the core of revolutionary efforts. Unlike Mao Zedong, Ho remained part of revolutionary struggle for most of his life and lacked the leisure that would have allowed him to engage in a wider philosophic scope. His work in relation to its specific target—colonial France—is thematically consistent with that of other international writers advocating resistance to colonialism. Frantz Fanon and Leopold Senghor in Africa, as well as Nuri as-Said and Bishara al-Khoury in the Arab world, developed the same sort of rhetorical stance in relation to their colonizers. All were reversing the paradigm of Westerners as bringers of civilization, instead insisting that Western civilization was built upon what Fanon calls "the sweat and the dead bodies of negroes, Arabs, Indians, and the yellow races."

Because Ho was both writer and political actor, it is impossible to disconnect his essays from his actions in the field. His work as part of Vladimir Lenin's Communist International Movement (COMINTERN) and his shared agenda with Mao in China gave him experience in radical hotbeds in Moscow, Berlin, and Southeast Asia. In 1941, with the help of the U.S. Office of Strategic Services, Ho started a guerilla warfare school on the Sino-Viet border. Its students emerged as leaders of the Viet Minh army that successfully battled Japan in 1945 and France in 1954, then fought the United States. All of these historic

✣ *Key Facts*

Time Period:
Mid-20th Century

Genre:
Speech/Essay

Events:
Rise of the Vietnamese independence movement; growth of anticolonialism

Nationality:
Vietnamese

THE CONFUCIAN EXAMS AND HO CHI MINH

The Han Emperor Wu Di (156 BCE-87 BCE) adopted a system of examinations based on the study of the five Chinese and the four Confucian classic texts to assign jobs to those who took the exams. This tradition lasted for nearly 2,000 years in China and for centuries in Vietnam. Ho Chi Minh's father, Nguyen Sinh Sac, reading a book while sitting on the back of a water buffalo, was noted by the Confucian Master Duong. Duong took the boy home, trained him, and married him to his daughter. Sac first sat for the Confucian Examinations in 1878 and did so again in 1891, 1894, 1895, and in 1898, failing several times, but he eventually earned the venerable *pho-bang,* or doctorate, second class. As a reward, his home village of Kim Lien gave him a house with two acres for cultivating rice. The villagers wished to throw him an expensive banquet too, but Sac asked instead that the meat for such a banquet be given to the poor. Like his father, the young Ho Chi Minh studied the Confucian classics, and though he never sat for the exams as his father had, he spent his life fighting for his own country's poor, ultimately establishing the Republic of Vietnam.

developments had their motives inscribed in Ho's essays, and in many ways their influence is enshrined in Vietnam, particularly its capital, Ho Chi Minh City.

THEMES AND STYLE

Ho's early essays focus on the plight of the Vietnamese at the hands of the French. "The Civilizers" (1922) and "The Colonial Abyss" (1923), for example, take a hard, sardonic look at colonizers whose "civilizing influence" results in oppression. The essays achieve believability by creating a sense of journalistic immediacy. The use of specific dates, times, and instances creates the impression of a special news flash reported by an eyewitness. In "Murderous Civilization" (1922) Ho reports that on April 2, at 4:30 p.m., a Vietnamese man employed for thirty-five years by the railroad is told by his supervisors to close the drawbridge, so he dutifully hoists a red flag. Then a different drunken government official orders him to open the bridge. Caught between conflicting orders, the old man hesitates, so is beaten unconscious. "Horribly burnt ... he dies after six days of atrocious suffering," Ho asserts, all the while animating the scene with fictional steam whistles from the boat, a mad Frenchman knocking over a red-hot brazier, and the red caution flag to which the beaten man points.

The collective intention of Ho's early essays is to rhetorically shift the moral high ground from the colonizing French to the Vietnamese people. In "Annamese Women and French Domination" (1922), he creates a scene of Vietnamese domesticity and innocence in order to show French barbarism disrupting it. After

French troops move through a small village, most villagers flee into the jungle, but a few trustingly remain: two old men, a maiden, a mother "suckling her baby," and an eight-year-old girl. They are accosted by drunken French soldiers seeking "money, spirits, and opium." One confused old man is hit on the head with rifle butts; the other is slowly roasted over a fire. The soldiers rape the maiden, the mother, and the eight-year old girl. The mother escapes with her baby and watches as a soldier slowly pushes his bayonet in and out of the girl's stomach. He then cuts off her head to steal her necklace. When the rest of the villagers return, they find the beheaded corpse of the disemboweled girl, her fist clenched under an "indifferent sky," and the roasted corpse of the old man "bloated, grilled, and golden."

Ho's emphasis on vivid images gives his essays their emotional power. His tone is consistently ironic and disdainful, denigrating the French as immoral while holding up the Vietnamese as exemplars of morality. Thus, while a Vietnamese employee fulfills his duties for years, French government workers are drunk in the afternoon, skipping work, and taking their government boats out on hunting larks. While villages are filled with serene and trusting elders, children, maidens, and young mothers, the French interlopers are armed, drunk, and violent. In *The Dehumanization of Art,* Jose Ortega y Gasset suggests that works such as Ho's, emphasizing specificity and visual imagery, offered audiences a "corporeality" and a "tactile" quality resulting in high emotional impact, so as works of propaganda, Ho's essays hit their mark.

CRITICAL DISCUSSION

Though there is no specific information regarding their immediate reception, the factual presentation in Ho's essays would have stretched the credulity of readers in 1960, when the Paris essays were first published as a collection. The impossibility of anyone in early 1920s Paris receiving such detailed and timely information from Vietnam as Ho reports would have been obvious. The technology, as well as the reporting venue that would have included such details, simply did not exist. Likewise, the logical presumptions of many essay details waver. It is unlikely that a drunken Frenchmen would cut off a head for a necklace, for example, if for no other reason than the item is easily taken without such horrific labor. Likewise, the slow, sexualized movement of the bayonet in and out of the eight-year-old girl's stomach can be construed as little more than a literary attempt to conflate one heinous act with another. The events, as reported, seem imagined.

Ho's essays of the 1920s constitute the juvenilia of a social and political pragmatist whose passionate desire to free his people from French colonial oppression started him on the long road to the presidency of the country he founded. As Jean Lacouture notes in *Vietnam: Between Two Truces* (1966), through Ho's actions and through his countless essays and political tracts, he became known to an ever-increasing readership as a living legend committed to his people and his nation. Likewise, his later essays, letters, and political tracts show an increasingly sophisticated awareness of the larger job of nation building that Ho had taken as his personal mission and of the wider public audience he needed to address. Consequently, they lack the vivid propagandist flamboyance of his early essays. But as ever, they carry in their words the same commitment as those penned by the bright-eyed young patriot showing up at all the socialist and communist meetings in Paris, speaking out on behalf of oppressed colonial peoples everywhere.

At the pinnacle of his success, biographies about Ho naturally began to appear. Though there is still relatively little scholarship about his essays, Lacouture offers one of the first comprehensive looks at Ho's life, and the scope has broadened with Duiker's *Ho Chi Minh* (2000) and Pierre Brocheux's *Ho Chi Minh: A Biography* (2007). Despite Ho's enduring status as a master political strategist and nation builder, no extensive critical examination of him as a writer and master propagandist has yet emerged.

North Vietnamese president Ho Chi Minh (1950). Some of his writings can be found in *Selected Works* (1960). © BETTMANN/CORBIS.

BIBLIOGRAPHY

Sources

Domenach, J. M. *La Propagande Politique.* Paris: U of France P, 1962. Print.

Duiker, William J. *Ho Chi Minh.* New York: Hyperion, 2000. Print.

Fanon, Frantz. *The Wretched of This Earth.* New York: Grove, 1963. Print.

Ho Chi Minh. *Selected Works.* 1962. New York: Prism Key, 2011. Print.

Lacouture, Jean. *Vietnam: Between Two Truces.* New York: Vintage, 1966. Print.

Ortega y Gasset, Jose. *The Dehumanization of Art.* Princeton: Princeton UP, 1968. Print.

Further Reading

Anderson, David, and John Ernst, eds. *The War That Never Ends: New Perspectives on the Vietnam War.* Lexington: UP of Kentucky, 2007. Print.

Bain, Chester. "Calculation and Charisma: The Leadership Style of Ho Chi Minh." *Virginia Quarterly* 49.3 (1973). Print.

———. "Ho Chi Minh: Master and Teacher." *Texas Quarterly* 16.3 (1973). Print.

Bradley, Mark. "Making Revolutionary Nationalism: Vietnam, America, and the August Revolution of 1945." *Itinerario* 23.1 (1999). Print.

Brocheux, Pierre. *Ho Chi Minh: A Biography.* New York: Cambridge UP, 2007. Print.

Chen, F. H. *Between East and West: Life on the Burma Road, the Tibetan Highway, the Ho Chi Minh Trail, and in the United States.* Niwot: U of Colorado P, 1996. Print.

Fall, Bernard. *Viet-Nam Witness, 1953–66.* New York: Praeger, 1966. Print.

MacMillan, Margaret. *Paris 1919: Six Months That Changed the World.* New York: Random House, 2003. Print.

Said, Edward. *Culture and Imperialism.* New York: Knopf, 1993. Print.

Robert Kibler

SONG OF ROLAND

❖ *Key Facts*

Time Period:
11th Century

Genre:
Poetry

Events:
Christian crusades
against Muslims in the
11th and 12th centuries;
spread of chivalric code
in Europe

Nationality:
French

OVERVIEW

The *Song of Roland* is the English title of *Chanson de Roland,* a French epic poem composed by an unknown author, probably during the eleventh century. It is considered the first great work of French literature and one of the most important surviving examples of the medieval epic. Although the story is set in the late eighth century—a period during which Charlemagne (c. 742–814) came to rule most of Europe—the poem actually reflects political issues and cultural conditions that were current at the time it was composed. Scholars identify various propagandistic elements in the *Song of Roland* that can be construed as promoting eleventh-century French goals, including the recruitment of combatants for the First Crusade, the idealization of the medieval code of chivalric conduct, and the need for a stronger monarchy in France.

Scholars also disagree about whether the *Song of Roland* was created by a single poet or was recorded in writing after a period of development as an oral composition. In either case, it was probably put into the form now known sometime around 1095, the year Christian forces began their first attempt to drive Muslims from the Holy Land. The poem is thought to be the earliest example of the *chanson de geste* (song of heroic deeds), a type of French epic poem that was widely composed and recited in France during the twelfth and thirteenth centuries. Popular among medieval audiences, the *Song of Roland* is still appreciated by modern readers for its vividly drawn hero, compelling battle scenes, and complex portrayal of the legendary Charlemagne.

HISTORICAL AND LITERARY CONTEXT

The *Song of Roland* is loosely based on a real event of 778, in which the rear guard of Charlemagne's forces, led by the warrior Roland, was attacked at Roncesvalles Pass in the northern Pyrenees, near the border between France and Spain. The assailants were almost certainly Basques—members of a local, non-Muslim ethnic group. At the time Charlemagne was king of the Frankish people, who were rapidly extending their influence in Europe. There are few historical references to the incident at Roncesvalles, which may have been a major defeat for the Franks or only a minor setback; in either case, it seems not to have had important consequences. Charlemagne became head of the

Holy Roman Empire in 800, and during the fourteen years he reigned as emperor, he created the geographic, political, and cultural foundations of Western Europe.

In the late eleventh century, there was a rise in religious enthusiasm among European Christians, as well as a power struggle between the church establishment and various political rulers. These factors led to the First Crusade (1096–99), a French-led military campaign against Muslim groups who controlled Jerusalem and surrounding areas of the Holy Land. Such a large military undertaking required support from both ordinary people and the aristocracy, and some scholars contend that the *Song of Roland* was intended to increase patriotic enthusiasm for the venture. It may be for this reason that the Basque attackers in the battle at Roncesvalles were replaced in the poem by Muslim assailants. Similarly, the depiction of Roland's ascent to heaven may have been meant as an encouragement for Christians to seek redemption by volunteering for the crusade.

The *Song of Roland* also reflects motifs that were becoming important in medieval culture, such as the ideal of the hero and the romance of chivalric warfare. For example, the poem transforms Hroudland, a man whose name was merely mentioned on a list of the dead at Roncesvalles, into the great warrior Roland, who becomes a martyr, sacrificing his life to defend the king. In the same way, and in keeping with the mythology that had grown up around Charlemagne over several centuries, the Frankish leader is depicted as a larger-than-life figure. The elevation of heroes to superhuman status was a typical characteristic of medieval epics, as seen in such noteworthy and roughly contemporaneous examples as Spain's *Poem of the Cid* and Russia's *Lay of Igor's Campaign.*

Although it is difficult to know exactly how effective the *Song of Roland* was in recruiting crusaders or spreading the chivalric ethos in the eleventh century, there is little doubt that it wielded other types of cultural and political influence in later times. In nineteenth-century France the poem was a widely known symbol of French spirit, and during the Franco-Prussian War of 1870–71 it became a kind of literary rallying cry. Decades later the poem was among the inspirations for J. R. R. Tolkien's *Lord of the Rings* (1954–55) trilogy. Although it is set in the fantasy world of Middle Earth, Tolkien's epic is viewed by some as a compelling critique of the mechanization of modern war. The character of Boromir, a knight who fights a doomed battle in the first volume of the trilogy, has been compared to the heroic Roland.

THEMES AND STYLE

The *Song of Roland*'s ninth-century story reflects eleventh-century values and dilemmas in ways that may be seen as either motivational or purely evocative. The poem's themes are developed in a complex and ambiguous manner. The portrayal of the un-Christian beliefs and practices of the "Saracens" (Muslims), for example, has led to the work's characterization as anti-Muslim in its message; the claim is mitigated, however, by the presence of admirable as well as despicable Saracen characters. There are also two ways of interpreting the tensions between Charlemagne and his finest knights, the Twelve Peers. The pivotal trial of Ganelon, who has betrayed Roland to the Saracens, upholds both the traditional role of family alliances (represented by the Peers' support for Ganelon) and the emerging paradigm of feudal hierarchies (represented by the single knight who fights for Charlemagne). These ambiguities make it challenging to determine what specific points of view—if any—the *Song of Roland* might have been promoting.

A key example of the *Song of Roland*'s rhetorical strategy can be seen in the thematic shift at midpoint from a focus on Roland as heroic protagonist to a focus on Charlemagne as a charismatic but conflicted leader whose rule is ultimately dependent on divine intervention. Roland's death serves as a turning point rather than a climax, adding dimensions not usually present in a simple tale of heroic self-sacrifice. The objections and accusations leveled against Roland by his friend Oliver, who urges Roland to summon help, further complicate the poem's message by forcing the audience to question Roland's motives; he refuses, and he and his entire regiment die. Similarly, discord among the Peers raise doubts about how powerful Charlemagne really is. Through both structure and dialogue, the *Song of Roland* reveals a level of meaning that goes beyond heroic action to explore political and ethical questions.

The *Song of Roland* was almost certainly composed for oral recitation, and its poetic effects were designed to engage an audience of listeners rather than a solitary reader. The auditory experience of the poem is shaped in several ways: its complex pattern of stressed syllables develops a rhythmic sound; its dramatic structure repeats the same scene several times with different details or from other viewpoints; and the listener learns about the characters through their actions, which gives the poem a quick pace and leaves an impression of sweeping scope. Although it is difficult to know exactly how people of the Middle Ages understood the *Song of Roland*, it seems likely that for typical audiences, the poem conveyed a strong sense

A CINEMATIC ROLAND

With its brave hero, charismatic king, revenge plots, and pitched battles, the *Song of Roland* would seem like a perfect film script. Yet only one adaptation of the story has reached the big screen—director Frank Cassenti's eccentric, artistic *La Chanson de Roland* (1978). In Cassenti's convoluted creation, Klaus Kinski (one of Europe's best-known actors at the time) plays a twelfth-century actor named Klaus who in turn plays the character of Roland in a performance of the eleventh-century poem about the ninth-century battle of Roncesvalles.

The film follows a band of storytellers who dramatize the tale of Roland for peasants travelling on a pilgrimage route. Along the way both players and peasants are attacked by bandits, beset by diseases, and threatened with starvation. Klaus/Roland becomes involved with the plight of the oppressed peasants and eventually sacrifices himself to help them. Beautifully photographed and remarkably attentive to period detail, the film is not about great battles, powerful knights, or allegiance to a king but about the spirit of Roland's story. Although the realities of poverty and injustice replace the threat of attacking armies, the protagonist is left with the same decision: whether to stand up for what he believes to be a righteous cause, no matter what the personal cost. By layering the elements of the Roland story in two time frames, Cassenti reveals the timelessness of its essential meaning.

of national pride and painted a vivid picture of heroic warriors, exotic enemies, and political intrigue.

CRITICAL DISCUSSION

There is no original manuscript of the *Song of Roland*, but there are a variety of partial copies, and there is one (the so-called "Oxford manuscript") that seems to be complete. This version of the poem, which probably dates from the middle of the twelfth century, contains around four thousand lines of Anglo-Norman French text and has served as the basis for most scholarship since it was identified in 1837. Although French commentators took a great interest in the poem during the nineteenth century, it did not become widely known in English until the second half of the twentieth century. Even then, critical discussion continued to focus on controversies over authorship, dating, and translation, and only gradually, as fundamental debates were resolved or exhausted, did scholars begin to explore the work in a larger literary and cultural context.

Interpretations of the *Song of Roland* differ widely, especially with respect to whether Roland should be considered a tragic hero in the classical sense (he refuses to summon help because he is arrogant and prideful) or a Christian knight who represents the chivalric ideal (he is willing to sacrifice himself in order to protect the king). These divergent views of the poem influenced many variants and translations of the Roland story that appeared throughout Europe

Illustration depicting Roland near death after the Battle of Roncesvalles © POODLESROCK/CORBIS.

of Roland would be seen not as "a depiction of heroic sacrifice or [an] articulation of precocious national sentiment" but rather as a text that concentrates and interconnects "questions of self and other, gender and genre, history and ideology."

BIBLIOGRAPHY

Sources

Cowell, Andrew. *The Medieval Warrior Aristocracy: Gifts, Violence, Performance, and the Sacred.* Woodbridge: Brewer, 2007. Print.

Haidu, Peter. *The Subject of Violence: The Song of Roland and the Birth of the State.* Bloomington: Indiana UP, 1993. Print.

Harty, Kevin J. *The Reel Middle Ages: American, Western and Eastern European, Middle Eastern and Asian Films about Medieval Europe.* Jefferson: McFarland, 1999. Print.

Keller, Hans E. "The *Song of Roland*: A Mid-Twelfth Century Song of Propaganda for the Capetian Kingdom." *Olifant* 3.4 (1976): 242–58. Print.

Kinoshita, Sharon. "'Pagans Are Wrong and Christians Are Right': Alterity, Gender, and Nation in the *Chanson de Roland.*" *Journal of Medieval and Early Modern Studies* 31.1 (2001): 79–111. Print.

Further Reading

Ashe, Laura. "'A Prayer and a Warcry': The Creation of a Secular Religion in the *Song of Roland.*" *Cambridge Quarterly* 28.4 (1999): 349–67. Print.

Cook, Robert Francis. *The Sense of the* Song of Roland. Ithaca: Cornell UP, 1987. Print.

Duggan, Joseph J., and Karen Akiyama, eds. *La Chanson de Roland-The Song of Roland: The French Corpus.* Turnhout: Brepols, 2005. Print.

Eisner, Robert A. "In Search of the Real Theme of the *Song of Roland.*" *Romance Notes* 14.1 (1972): 179–83. Print.

Kinoshita, Sharon. *Medieval Boundaries: Rethinking Difference in Old French Literature.* Philadelphia: U of Pennsylvania P, 2006. Print.

Pratt, Karen. *Roland and Charlemagne in Europe: Essays on the Reception and Transformation of a Legend.* London: King's College London Centre for Late Antique and Medieval Studies, 1996. Print.

Taylor, Andrew. *Textual Situations: Three Medieval Manuscripts and Their Readers.* Philadelphia: U of Pennsylvania P, 2002. Print.

Taylor, Philip M. *Munitions of the Mind: A History of Propaganda from the Ancient World to the Present Day.* Manchester: Manchester UP, 2003. Print.

Media Adaptation

The Song of Roland. Dir. Frank Cassenti. Perf. Klaus Kinski, Alain Cuny, and Dominique Sanda. France 3 (FR 3), 1978. Film.

Cynthia Giles

during the Middle Ages. That the basic outline of the tale could easily be adapted to suit the needs of a particular place and situation has inspired a strong trend in scholarship, as Hans E. Keller demonstrates in his 1976 article for *Olifant.*

While many contemporary scholars have focused on literary aspects of the *Song of Roland,* interest in the political dimensions of the work has also increased. Both Peter Haidu's 1993 book *The Subject of Violence: The Song of Roland and the Birth of the State* and Andrew Cowell's 2007 *The Medieval Warrior Aristocracy: Gifts, Violence, Performance, and the Sacred* opened new avenues of analysis, treating social subtexts of the poem and exploring its philosophical backgrounds. Sharon Kinoshita's influential 2002 article in *Journal of Medieval and Early Modern Studies* also expanded conventional views of the poem, moving away from familiar nineteenth-century paradigms. From this new perspective, Kinoshita argues, the *Song*

STARSHIP TROOPERS

Robert A. Heinlein

OVERVIEW

Starship Troopers (1959), a science fiction novel by Robert A. Heinlein, was written during the Cold War and envisions a future in which the world is run by a government composed of the military elite. The work is a coming-of-age story narrated by Juan Rico, an officer in the Terran Federation's Mobile Infantry who recounts his military training and education through a series of flashbacks. With scant plot and little character development, Heinlein's novel is remembered less for its literary achievements than for its overt celebration of militarism and its call for a more forceful U.S. foreign policy. It is generally regarded as the author's most controversial work.

Starship Troopers was originally intended to be part of a series for young adults, but Heinlein's longtime publisher, Scribner's, rejected the work due to its militaristic message. It wound up being serialized in the *Magazine of Fantasy & Science Fiction* in 1959 and was published in book form by G. P. Putnam's Sons later that year. Not only did it achieve great commercial success, but it also won the Hugo Award for Best Novel in 1960. *Starship Troopers* captures the Cold War anxiety in the United States in the 1950s and inspired both science fiction novels and movies, some of which are parodies. The favorable public reception to Heinlein's idiosyncratic views allowed him to expand beyond writing juvenile fiction in order to concentrate on novels with thinly veiled political messages aimed at a more mature audience.

HISTORICAL AND LITERARY CONTEXT

When the United States' World War II ally, the Soviet Union, took over most of Eastern Europe and began building and testing nuclear weapons, a postwar arms race ensued. The Chinese- and Russian-backed Korean War reinforced American fears of communist world domination, encouraging in some quarters the extreme pro-military views espoused by Heinlein.

These pro-military advocates were alarmed when President Dwight Eisenhower agreed in 1958 to a Soviet proposal to suspend nuclear bomb tests on both sides. Zealous anticommunists such as Heinlein were alarmed, and *Starship Troopers* represents his response to what he thought was a dangerous weakening of U.S. defenses.

Indeed, the Cold War sparked a number of anticommunist works. For example, the film *Invasion of the Body Snatchers* (1956), based on the 1954 novel *The Body Snatchers* by Jack Finney, depicts an alien invasion. In preparation for creating a society of uniformity and conformity, the aliens in the film replace humans with duplicates that lack all individuality. Some reviewers saw the film as an allegory of a Soviet takeover of the United States. Other cautionary films of the era, such as *I Married a Communist* (1949), *The Red Menace* (1949), and *I Was a Communist for the FBI* (1951), overtly uphold democracy and denounce communism. In this way, Heinlein was not the first to craft an anticommunist tale. However, his extreme pro-military themes in *Starship Troopers* were exceptional.

The success of *Starship Troopers* led Heinlein to publish a sequel in 1961, *Stranger in a Strange Land,* and it became the first science fiction book to appear on the best-seller list. In 1966 he published *The Moon Is a Harsh Mistress,* which details the decline of a libertarian utopia and is arguably his most political work. The book has had a substantial influence in the political realm of American libertarianism, where it is seen as a seminal text. A phrase that Heinlein popularized in the novel—"There ain't no such thing as a free lunch"—has since entered the American lexicon. Other writers have challenged the extremity of his political vision. For example, Harry Harrison's *Bill the Galactic Hero* (1965), depicting the adventures of a boy from an agricultural planet who joins the "Space Troopers," parodies *Starship Troopers.*

THEMES AND STYLE

Central to *Starship Troopers* is the transformation of the young, undisciplined, and privileged Rico into a noble, war-loving leader. The novel follows Rico through his military training, in which he is exposed to the philosophical justifications of a culture based on a military hierarchy. In the society imagined by Heinlein, a person must enlist in a national service to earn full citizenship and the right to vote. Important government jobs are reserved for military veterans, on the presumption that their training and experience have instilled in them morals and values that are not possessed by civilians. One of Rico's mentors explains to him the value of war and building up a strong

✤ Key Facts

Time Period:
Mid-20th Century

Genre:
Novel

Events:
Cold War; Cuban Missile Crisis; cessation of American nuclear testing

Nationality:
American

PAUL VERHOEVEN'S CINEMATIC ADAPTATION

In 1997 *Starship Troopers* arrived on the big screen, directed by Paul Verhoeven with a screenplay by Ed Neumeier. Neumeier and Verhoeven previously had worked together on *Robocop* (1987). Their vision of *Starship Troopers* centers on an intergalactic war story and utilizes numerous visual effects to play up the action and adventure. Verhoeven and Neumeier drop the anticommunist bent of Robert A. Heinlein's 1959 novel and highlight the wartime role of media as propaganda. Abandoning the book's first-person approach, Verhoeven frames his narrative through news coverage of the confrontation with the adversary.

Responding to the criticism of Heinlein's novel, specifically the charges of fascism, Verhoeven alters the protagonist from a Hispanic named Juan Rico to Johnnie Rico, played in the movie by an Aryan-looking Casper Van Dien. This casting choice helps the director explore and question the future of a society dictated by extreme militarism. The final result—a film that guts Heinlein's original political message and plays as a conventional war thriller—was not a success either commercially or critically.

military: "violence, naked force, has settled more issues in history than has any other factor." The mentor goes on to warn Rico—and the reader—of the danger of attempting to resolve conflicts peacefully, saying that individuals who "forget this basic truth have always paid for it with their lives and their freedom."

Heinlein structures his tale as a bildungsroman, or coming-of-age tale. Bookended with action sequences, the novel mostly occurs as flashbacks to Rico's youth that provide the structure of Heinlein's message. The story is told from Rico's vantage point, progressing from his initial exposure to the value of the military in high school to boot camp and cadet school to his contact and combat with extraterrestrials. Many of Rico's views on the military are influenced by his conversations with his high school mentor, Mr. Dubois, a former military officer who serves Heinlein's aim as a mouthpiece for many of the right-wing ideologies of the 1950s. Mr. Dubois and other teachers/mentors Rico encounters in his education demonstrate the validity of their arguments for militarism through mathematical proofs and symbolic logic, thereby nullifying any alternative suggestions from Rico and, in turn, the reader.

Heinlein's language in *Starship Troopers* is decidedly didactic. A large portion of the novel is spent in the protagonist's History and Moral Philosophy classroom, where his teacher, perhaps a stand-in for Heinlein, "heaps scorn on an inexcusable silly idea" that "violence never settles anything." By intercutting action sequences that capture the thrill of battle with

flashbacks to the education and training of the narrator, Heinlein outlines a way of life in which a boy can become a moral and honorable man. The horrors of the battlefield are deemphasized in favor of historical and philosophical justifications for militarism. The novel opens with an epigraph from an unknown platoon sergeant from 1918 who tells his soldiers, "Come on you apes! You wanta live forever?" This passage introduces the theme of the replaceable soldier and the value of laying down one's life in the name of national service, and it also captures the blunt, straightforward tone Heinlein employs throughout the novel.

CRITICAL DISCUSSION

Though *Starship Troopers* was a commercial success, it was also controversial. Discussing Heinlein's contributions to the genre of science fiction in his 1965 book *Heinlein in Dimension*, Alexei Panshin notes that the most glaring flaw in the author's work is his tendency to treat "his opinions as though they [are] facts." Panshin sees Heinlein's personal politics taking center stage to the degree that character development and plot construction become "completely subsidiary to the main business of his opinions-as-facts." One of the liveliest debates surrounding *Starship Troopers* occurred in *Proceedings of the Institute for Twenty-First Century Studies*. In the August 1959 issue, the editor, Theodore Cogswell, paired a lengthy quote from *Starship Troopers* with Wilfred Owen's poem "Dulce et Decorum Est," known for its horrific imagery of soldiers' deaths and as a condemnation of war. The piece initiated a critical conversation centered on art and propaganda that lasted for the next two years in the publication.

Starship Troopers is largely remembered for its pro-military, anticommunist viewpoints. It continues to be popular in certain circles, and Heinlein remains one of the most influential science fiction writers. Because of the range of themes he explores, the self-assuredness of his ideas and narrative tone, and his reader-friendly treatment of science-based threads, he is widely considered to be an innovator in the genre. In *Science Fiction after 1900: From the Steam Man to the Stars*, Brooks Landon writes, "Heinlein did more than any other figure in the twentieth century to popularize science fiction." He continues, "In a field swollen with success stories, major writers and significant innovators, Heinlein still stands out along with Arthur C. Clarke and Isaac Asimov as first among giants."

Despite such plaudits, most scholars have not embraced *Starship Troopers*. Critics have been quick to point out the dangerous implications of Heinlein's glorified portrayal of wartime and the military experience. In "The Temple of Boredom: Science Fiction, No Future," Luc Sante writes that Heinlein's work "approaches fascism" in its quest to express ideal, responsible government. M. Keith Booker writes in *Monsters, Mushroom Clouds and the Cold War: Science Fiction and the Roots of Postmodernism* that *Starship*

A still from the 1997 film adaptation of *Starship Troopers.* © TRISTAR PICTURES/COURTESY EVERETT COLLECTION.

Troopers is a "call to arms" and "a concerted attempt to indoctrinate the reader" into accepting the need for forceful foreign policy and the values of militarism. Leon Stover has published one of the few scholarly defenses of the novel, *Robert A. Heinlein,* in which he suggests that "the critics hated it" because "it is only by his dislike of the military that the liberal culture critic earns his credentials."

BIBLIOGRAPHY

Sources

Booker, M. Keith. *Monsters, Mushroom Clouds and the Cold War: American Science Fiction and the Roots of Postmodernism, 1946–1964.* Connecticut: Praeger, 2001. Print.

Brooks, Landon. *Science Fiction after 1900: From the Steam Man to the Stars.* London: Routledge, 2002. Print.

Gochenour, Phil. "Utopia of Pain: Adolescent Anxiety and the Ideology of Narrative in Robert A. Heinlein's *Starship Troopers.*" *New York Review of Science Fiction* 1 Jan. 2011: 8–12. Web. 20 July 2012.

Heinlein, Robert A. *Starship Troopers.* New York: G. P. Putnam's Sons, 1959. Print.

Panshin, Alexei. *Heinlein in Dimension: A Critical Analysis.* Chicago: Advent, 1968. Print.

Sante, Luc. "The Temple of Boredom: Science Fiction, No Future." *Harper's.* Harper's Oct. 1985: 69. Web. 21 July 2012.

Stover, Leon. *Robert A. Heinlein.* Boston: Twayne, 1987. Print.

Further Reading

Crim, Brian E. "'A World That Works': Fascism and Media Globalization in *Starship Troopers.*" *Film and History* 39:2 (2009): 17–25. Web. 24 July 2012.

Showalter, Dennis E. "Heinlein's *Starship Troopers:* An Exercise in Rehabilitation." *Extrapolation: A Journal of Science Fiction and Fantasy* 16 (1975): 113–24. Web. 19 July 2012.

Spark, Alasdair. "The Art of Future War: *Starship Troopers, The Forever War* and Vietnam." *Essays and Studies* 43 (1990): 133–65. Web. 24 July 2012.

Suvin, Darko. "Of Starship Troopers and Refuseniks: War and Militarism in U.S. Science Fiction, Part 1." *New Boundaries in Political Science Fiction.* Ed. Donald M. Hassler and Clyde Wilcox. South Carolina: U of South Carolina P, 2008. Web. 20 July 2012.

Wheat, David L., Jr. "The Alien Enemy Within." *New York Review of Science Fiction* 1 Sept. 2006: 8–18. Web. 24 July 2012.

Williams, Paul. "*Starship Troopers,* the War on Terror and the Spectacle of Censorship." *Science Fiction Film and Television* 2:1 (2009): 25–44. Web. 24 July 2012.

Media Adaptation

Starship Troopers. Dir. Paul Verhoeven. Perf. Casper Van Dien, Denise Richards, and Dina Meyer. TriStar Pictures, 1997. Film.

Elizabeth Orvis

"Swept and Garnished"

Rudyard Kipling

✥ *Key Facts*

Time Period:
Early 20th Century

Genre:
Short Story

Events:
Outbreak of World
War I; German attacks
on neutral villages in
Belgium

Nationality:
English

OVERVIEW

Published in the first few months of World War I, Rudyard Kipling's 1915 short story "Swept and Garnished" captures the growing English abhorrence of Germans and German combat tactics. An eerie combination of realist fiction, fable, and ghost story, "Swept and Garnished" suggests that those who are on the wrong side of war will be plagued with disease and disturbing hallucinations—not to mention God's wrath. Specifically, Kipling argues that Germans (who he terms "the Hun") are a callous people, prone to unnecessary violence in combat. The main character of the story, Frau Ebermann, is portrayed as selfish, ignorant, and unfeeling—the antithesis of the English citizenry. Although Kipling never explicitly states that English men and women should take part in the war effort against Germany, the story nevertheless serves as a thinly veiled call to arms.

"Swept and Garnished" was written in response to Germany's attack on neutral villages in Belgium, which involved the killing of many women and children. Such gruesome stories spurred the English to disseminate anti-German propaganda, and Kipling, who worked for Wellington House, the government's propaganda machine, was an integral part of this effort. The story, first published in *Century Magazine,* was one in a slew of increasingly impassioned works of propaganda—from songs to posters to pamphlets—that bombarded the English people during the war. Although less well known than Kipling's novels, children's books, and other short stories, "Swept and Garnished" was considered an important work during the heady early days of World War I and was widely reprinted. While many scholars disregard Kipling's war writings for their outright jingoism, "Swept and Garnished" paints a clear portrait of England's sense of cultural and moral superiority at the beginning of the conflict, before such ideals were obliterated by the horrors of modern warfare.

HISTORICAL AND LITERARY CONTEXT

At the outset of the war, both Axis and Allied forces were confident they would win quickly and decisively. News from the fronts, however, grew increasingly gruesome as the war raged on, due to widespread use of modern warfare techniques including chemical weapons, long-range rifles, tanks, and submarines. Before the war, many in the Western world were hopeful that the machine age—a new world of electricity, railroads, telephones, and sophisticated medical care—would bring about a golden era of progress, prosperity, and unparalleled human achievement. Instead, many were shocked to witness the use of humans' intellectual capabilities and mechanical prowess for brutal, modern warfare.

On August 4, 1914, Germany invaded France by way of neutral Belgium instead of attacking France on its defended eastern border. England—allies with Belgium—declared war on Germany the same day, and reports of German massacres against defenseless Belgians inundated England. "Swept and Garnished"—full of muted anger and ferocity—marks Kipling's artistic response to the attacks. From the start, Kipling, like many intellectuals of the time, was a vocal supporter of England's war effort, writing patriotic newspaper articles and various promilitary writings, including widely disseminated pamphlets. An expert at creating propaganda since the Boer War, Kipling worked for England's fledgling Bureau of Propaganda, lauding the English armed forces and praising English moral righteousness in the face of what he terms a "crazed and driven foe."

World War I produced a host of impassioned short stories, including work from literary greats Joseph Conrad, Edith Wharton, and D. H. Lawrence. Like "Swept and Garnished," fiction published early in the conflict had a patriotic tone; however, as the war turned increasingly grisly, the tenor changed. In England, due to the Defence of the Realm Act (1914), public disapproval of the military conflict was forbidden. Thus, if writers were opposed to war, they remained mostly quiet. Well known across the British Empire as a commentator on all things English, Kipling, although an occasional critic of England's military behavior in previous engagements, remained hawkish throughout the war, even after his son, John, died in combat in 1915. It was not until well after the close of World War I that Kipling expressed misgivings in "The Gardener," a mournful short story published in 1925.

"Swept and Garnished," along with Kipling's story "Mary Postgate" (1915), remain integral pieces of World War I propaganda literature and are often featured in war writing anthologies. Like most propaganda, "Swept and Garnished" was important during the war years but not widely read during peacetime. Although it is not particularly well regarded due to its narrow subject matter, Kipling's literary mastery is rarely disputed: he was awarded the Nobel Prize for Literature in 1907 and is often credited for popularizing the short story genre. Today he is best remembered for his short stories set in India, such as "The Bridge Builders" (1893); the novel *Kim* (1901); *The Jungle Book* (1894); and *Just So Stories* (1902), a handful of beloved children's tales.

THEMES AND STYLE

Beyond expressly attacking Germany as a cruel nation, "Swept and Garnished" explores how the atrocities of war surreptitiously invade and disturb the consciousnesses of all involved—even normal citizens. This idea is realized through the character of Frau Ebermann, who while at home sick with the flu envisions a series of frightening "dirty little children" overrunning her spotless personal space. Soon she realizes that these youngsters, whether ghosts or hallucinations, are Belgian children killed by German soldiers during the first attacks of the war. Although Kipling never overtly encourages his readers to enlist in the military or support the war effort, he nevertheless confronts them with vivid images of German atrocities and the innocent victims, personifying the consequences of denial and inaction through Ebermann, who can only shriek, "Go away! Go away!"

Throughout "Swept and Garnished," Kipling employs straightforward language, using concise diction, simple syntax, and candid dialogue. This rhetorical plainness contrasts with the content of the story, which includes supernatural visitations, panicked emotional states, and sickness-induced hysteria. The tension between the author's realistic tone and the increasing delirium of Ebermann creates a quick-paced, disturbing story, or what critic J. M. S. Thompkins in *The Art of Rudyard Kipling* (1965) calls "a hardly suppressed scream." Kipling's descriptions of Ebermann's well-cared-for and luxurious home replete with "yellow cut-glass handles of the chest of drawers" and "New Art finger-plates on the door" are at odds with the "parcel" of needy children that break in. The Bible verse (Matthew 12:43-45) from which "Swept and Garnished" takes its title is acutely ironic in Kipling's hands: although Frau Ebermann pretends that she is keeping her home and heart "swept and garnished" for God, she is horrified when her tranquility is threatened by those in need of her goodwill and compassion. Readers are left to assume that Ebermann, though not actually a soldier on the front lines, is still complicit in Germany's wartime slaughter and destruction.

The charged emotions present in "Swept and Garnished" spring from the friction between Frau Ebermann's lack of sympathy for Belgian children ("she had never been a child-lover in any sense") and the children's helplessness. By creating a dramatic situation in which a German woman demonstrates her selfishness and ignorance, Kipling obliquely mounts his propagandist argument, relying on the reader to independently interpret the implications of the story. Much of

THE CHILDREN'S STORIES OF RUDYARD KIPLING

Rudyard Kipling wrote fluidly in strikingly different genres, such as pamphlets, poems, and children's stories. However, to call *The Jungle Book* (1894), *Just So Stories* (1902), *Rewards and Fairies* (1910), and others simple "children's stories" is not quite accurate. Although these works were certainly written with children in mind, Kipling notes that he "worked the material in three or four overlaid tints and textures, which might or might not reveal themselves according to the shifting light of sex, youth, and experience." Part of the reason why his stories for children remain beloved a hundred years later is because they easily function on different intellectual levels—just as Mark Twain's *Huckleberry Finn* is an adventure story for kids as well as a critical portrait of nineteenth-century American life.

Indeed, books by Twain and Kipling that revolve around child protagonists have many key similarities. Although Twain's Huck lives on the banks of the Mississippi while Kipling's Mowgli lives in a jungle, each character is the focus of a bildungsroman, or coming-of-age tale, about a wild-hearted boy. Both Huck and Mowgli live outside the bounds of normal society, embark on adventures, and teach readers about how to make "normal life" in society more authentic and enjoyable.

"Swept and Garnished" consists of dialogue between Ebermann and the children, which grows increasingly frenzied and nonsensical as the story boils to a climax. In the final scene, in a clear homage to William Shakespeare's famous murderess from *Macbeth,* Ebermann is "on her knees, busily cleaning the floor" that is "all spotted with the [children's] blood." Kipling closes the tale with a clear suggestion that the German people—not just their military—are guilty of heartless hostility.

CRITICAL DISCUSSION

Initially published in *Century Magazine* in January 1915, "Swept and Garnished" was soon reprinted in other English journals, including *Nash's and Pall Mall Magazine* and *Scribner's Edition,* among others. In a 1917 article for the *Review of Reviews,* critic Norman Johnson Croom notes that the story is "moving in its simplicity." Although the short story itself did not receive more than a brief, passing mention after publication, Kipling was a conspicuous and vibrant presence in civic life during the war years, speaking at recruiting rallies; reporting from the battlefields in France; and penning strongly worded pamphlets, poems, and speeches. "Swept and Garnished" marks one offering among many from a prolific and established writer during World War I.

Attitudes toward "Swept and Garnished" shifted after the war primarily due to Kipling's political stance. As Celia M. Kingsbury notes in *For Home and Country: World War I Propaganda on the Home Front* (2010), "the

jingoism of much of [Kipling's] work is distasteful to contemporary readers." Indeed, many later critics, including George Orwell and Lionel Trilling, found Kipling's conservative and imperialist politics objectionable. Certainly, Kipling's outmoded worldview has prevented some readers from taking him seriously. Reviewer Walter Morris Hart takes another tack, noting in *Kipling: The Story-Writer* (1918) that "in spite of the strong tendency to moralize, in spite of the variety and certainty of opinion which we found to be characteristics of Kipling's work … he has found no clue to [life's] meaning." Nevertheless, Hart highlights the frequency with which Kipling's unwavering political certainty precludes some from understanding his work as more than a historical relic.

Although some critics dismiss Kipling's corpus of work due to its often misogynous and racist overtones, others glean authentic insight into the political, social, and emotional lives of the author and his contemporaries. Tracy E. Bilsing, for instance, argues in a 2000 essay for *WLA* that Kipling's war writings "reflect the innocence of the early war years, and … Kipling's own painful journey towards the truth and need for personal peace in the aftermath of the war." Moreover, she writes, "Kipling survives as a chronicler of the Great War" regardless of his political mores. Although "Swept and Garnished" is not the subject of a substantial body of scholarship, Kipling's life and work continue to command considerable scholarly investigation into the present day. In particular, his large body of work is important to students of fin de siècle colonialism, imperialism, and conflict; Edwardian England; and, of course, propaganda.

BIBLIOGRAPHY

Sources

Bilsing, Tracy E. "The Process of Manufacture: Rudyard Kipling's Private Propaganda." *WLA* 12.1 (2000): 76–100. *Literature Resource Center.* Web. 23 Sept. 2012.

Croom-Johnson, Norman. "Mr. Kipling's New Book." *Review of Reviews* 55.330 (1917): 589. Print.

Hart, Walter Morris. *Kipling: The Story-Writer.* Berkeley: U of California P, 1918. *Literature Resource Center.* Web. 23 Sept. 2012.

Kingsbury, Celia M. *For Home and Country: World War I Propaganda on the Home Front.* Lincoln: U of Nebraska P, 2010. Web. 27 Sept. 2012.

Thompkins, J. M. S. *The Art of Rudyard Kipling.* Lincoln: U of Nebraska P, 1965. Web. 27 Sept. 2012.

"World War I Short Fiction." *Short Story Criticism.* Vol. 71. Ed. Joseph Palmisano. Detroit: Gale, 2004. *Literature Resource Center.* Web. 25 Sept. 2012.

Further Reading

Booth, Howard J. *The Cambridge Companion to Rudyard Kipling.* Cambridge: Cambridge UP, 2011. Print.

Buitenhuis, Peter. *The Great War of Words: British, American and Canadian Propaganda and Fiction, 1914–1933.* Vancouver: U of British Columbia P, 1987. Print.

Gilmour, David. *The Long Recessional: The Imperial Life of Rudyard Kipling.* London: Murray, 2002. New York: Farrar, Straus & Giroux, 2002. Print.

Lackey, Michael. "E. M. Forster's Lecture 'Kipling's Poems': Negotiating the Modernist Shift from 'the Authoritarian Stock-in-Trade' to an Aristocratic Democracy." *Journal of Modern Literature* 30.3 (2007): 1–11. Web. 28 Sept. 2012.

Mallett, Phillip. *Rudyard Kipling: A Literary Life.* New York: Palgrave Macmillan, 2003. Print.

Matin, A. Michael. "'The Hun Is at the Gate!': Historicizing Kipling's Militaristic Rhetoric, from the Imperial Periphery to the National Center." *Studies in the Novel* 31.4 (1999): 432. *Literature Resource Center.* Web. 28 Sept. 2012.

Messinger, Gary. *British Propaganda and the State in the First World War.* Manchester: Manchester UP, 1992. Print.

Claire Skinner

Opposite page:
British World War I recruitment poster highlighting the atrocities in Belgium. © EVERETT COLLECTION INC./ALAMY.

"TRANSVAAL"

Algernon Charles Swinburne

OVERVIEW

Algernon Charles Swinburne's sonnet "Transvaal" (1899) served as a call for English mobilization in the Second Boer War (1899–1902), in which the British Empire fought against independent republics of European settlers for control of southern Africa. Published in the *Times* of London on October 9, 1899, the poem urged Englishmen to counteract Boer aggression almost before the war had begun, in order to protect the allegedly defenseless British colonists. Swinburne couched the conflict in terms of a moral battle between the dormant but undaunted valor of the English and the degeneracy of the Boer settlers, whom he described as "wolves" and "dogs." The poem was uncharacteristically vicious in sentiment for the cosmopolitan Swinburne and stood out even among other war poetry of the time for its no-quarter attitude.

Swinburne's poem appealed to an English public ready for war and largely in favor of British imperial expansion. Other English authors denounced "Transvaal" for its one-sided portrayal of the conflict, however, and the poet Thomas Hardy, who opposed the war, issued a series of literary rejoinders. Nor has the sonnet aged well, especially in light of the overwhelmingly civilian casualties of the war it advocated; some critics have even treated it as symptomatic of an overall decline in Swinburne's capabilities. "Transvaal" has had little influence on subsequent war poetry, which after the World War I largely sided with Hardy in taking into account the grim human toll of large-scale armed conflict. It is now regarded as an extreme specimen of the pro-war rhetoric that characterized a substantial portion of late Victorian literature.

HISTORICAL AND LITERARY CONTEXT

The Second Boer War was one outcome of the centuries-long European struggle for control of Africa. In the mid-1800s the British Empire had established a colonial presence on the Cape of Good Hope, and Boers (Dutch immigrants and their descendants) had settled much of inland southern Africa. The British formally recognized the independence of the Boer territories, but the 1877 annexation of the Transvaal Republic—which was located in the South African Republic, north of the Orange Free State—precipitated a brief Anglo-Boer conflict in 1880–81. This First Boer War lasted only three months before British troops were forced to withdraw.

The Transvaal once more became a zone of contention when rich gold deposits were discovered on the site of present-day Johannesburg. The Boer-controlled region soon played host to a substantial population of British immigrants, who gradually asserted their rights, first diplomatically and then in a series of failed uprisings. The conflict reached a head in 1899, when the Boers issued an ultimatum calling for the withdrawal of British troops from Transvaal borders; thus disregarded, the Boers declared war on October 11. Swinburne, as one of the leading English poets of the time, was all but required to make a patriotic statement on the matter. Other British literary voices, including most infamously Rudyard Kipling, joined him in calling for a swift and ruthless response.

Since its widespread adoption during the Elizabethan era, the sonnet form had frequently served as a vehicle for poetic rallying cries to the English public. William Wordsworth, writing nearly a century before Swinburne, put the sonnet to such use in "London, 1802," which mourned England's decline to "a fen / Of stagnant waters" and called for a return to the "manners, virtue, freedom, power" epitomized in the poetic vision of John Milton. Swinburne lays a quite similar charge of moral "stagnation" in "Transvaal," declaring that the English people have become mired in "sloth and doubt and treason" and now, at last, have an unmistakable call to action. Swinburne's war promises to efface doubts as to English national character and return the nation to a moral status that "brooked no wrong."

Many of the rhetorical gestures in "Transvaal" foreshadow tactics that would be used again in the propagandistic art and literature of World War I. For instance, the major crime of the Boers in Swinburne's poem is attacking the defenseless "women and … weanlings"; in the Great War, posters and poems abounded with depictions of physical threat to women and children. The reimagination of the enemy as animals likewise became a mainstay of British war posters, several of which depicted Kaiser Wilhelm II as a ravenous, tusked gorilla apt to trample homes and carry off women. Moreover, Swinburne's use of the sonnet as a literary emblem of "Englishness" (and a means of glorifying the British imperial project) would be carried further by the poets of that war, including most famously Rupert Brooke.

THEMES AND STYLE

"Transvaal" announces its main argument from the very first line: "Patience, long sick to death, is dead." The poet proceeds to assert that the appropriate time for British intervention in the Transvaal has long since passed and to appeal to readers' sense of shame in not having gone to war sooner; indeed, he voices his indignation that those at home could permit "sloth and doubt and treason" to stay their hand from righting such evident wrongs in southern Africa. Despite its publication at the war's very beginning, "Transvaal" adds to this sense of belated urgency by depicting the conflict as already well under way. It asserts that British civilian lives are under an imminent and inescapable threat, that the Boers' "war is waged where none may fight or flee."

The sonnet was written in the collective first person plural, the common mode of patriotic verse. Swinburne attempts to speak on behalf of an incensed public, assuming throughout that the audience already assents to his view of what must be done. Notably, the appeal of "Transvaal" is specifically to the English rather than to the more complex and more fractious collection of national interests known as Britain. This sense of national unity is cemented by reference to "Cromwell's England," which the poet reimagines as "a commonweal that brooked no wrong." Here Swinburne elides for effect the civil wars that produced "Cromwell's England," the infighting that vexed it, and its relatively short life before the restoration of the monarchy. But such elisions are necessary to project an image of total solidarity, in which only traitors would dare gainsay the poet's claims. It is on the strength of such a presumption that the poet can address the nation as a single entity in the closing line: "Strike, England, and strike home."

As the sonnet's imagery makes clear, the noble, unified "we" face an enemy who is cast not only as morally inferior but also as inhuman. Troublingly for many of Swinburne's critics, the speaker denies the personhood of the Boer settlers by comparing them to animals. In line 6, the Boers are "men like wolves set free," and by the poem's end they are not men at all but "dogs agape with jaws afoam" who must be "scourge[d] … Down out of life." Swinburne would amplify this pattern of canine imagery (and inflame the ensuing controversy) in his 1901 sonnet "On the Death of Colonel Benson," which referred to Boer children and mothers as "whelps and dams."

CRITICAL DISCUSSION

At the turn of the twentieth century, England seemed primed for such patriotic outbursts as "Transvaal." Literary historians have described the cultural climate of the time as, according to Kathryn R. King and William W. Morgan in *Victorian Poetry,* "aggressive

"BUT BY JINGO IF WE DO …"

Swinburne is among the many proponents of the Boer Wars (and later conflicts) to have been regarded in hindsight as "jingoistic." The humorous-sounding term denotes an aggressive, expansionist patriotism that has more recently come to be seen as a hallmark of early twentieth-century U.S. foreign policy. It is, however, originally an English expression, dating from an 1878 music-hall song written by G. W. Hunt and performed by G. H. MacDermott. The song's verses give a pugnacious view of the Russo-Turkish War, which the British Empire was prepared to enter on the side of the Ottoman Empire if Russia did not declare a truce. The chorus begins:

> We don't want to fight, but by Jingo if we do
> We've got the ships, we've got the men, we've got the
> money too.

The term "by Jingo" had long been used as a minced oath, but "MacDermott's War Song," as it is usually called, fixed in the minds of many the association between the innocuous phrase and an eagerness for war. While the British Empire never needed to deploy its "ships, men, and money" in the Russian conflict, those resources, and the nationalism that brandished them, would be deployed to devastating effect in 1899.

national arrogance … an almost mindless worship of power and force." Swinburne's call to arms was successful in feeding this sentiment, though its extremes of language were rebuked by several of his fellow writers. Almost immediately, W. H. Colby retorted, as quoted in *The Oxford Handbook of British and Irish War Poetry,* "Where are the dogs agape with jaws afoam? / Where are the wolves? Look, England, look at home." The poet and critic William Michael Rossetti, while an admirer of Swinburne's poetry in general, strongly opposed British escalation of the Boer conflict and wrote his own "Transvaal" sonnet to that effect. Likewise, Thomas Hardy, who was appalled in general by his countrymen's appetite for war, expressed in private letters his disappointment at the tone and sentiment of "Transvaal." Publicly he countered Swinburne's verse with his own pacifistic poems, which King and Morgan note depicted the pitfalls of a morally overconfident patriotism.

Removed from its immediate political impetus, "Transvaal" has come to be seen as an embarrassing foil to Swinburne's highly regarded early work. Cecil Y. Lang, editor of Swinburne's *Letters,* thus described the trajectory of the poet's career: "The most cosmopolitan of English poets was transformed into the most parochial and chauvinistic of British jingoes." King and Morgan note in retrospect that even among Boer War poetry (produced in great volume by "[Rudyard] Kipling, [William] Henley, [Alfred] Austin … and a host of lesser talents") Swinburne's "Transvaal"

A depiction of a battle during the Second Boer War: General Sir John French and his troops advancing to Kimberley under siege. THE ART ARCHIVE AT ART RESOURCE, NY.

distinguished itself for its "bloodthirsty turn of mind" and "particularly nasty … tone."

Possibly due to this dismal consensus regarding the poem's literary value, scholars have since turned their attention to representations of "Transvaal" in other literary works, which often provide trenchant critiques of their own. James Joyce's *Ulysses* has proven a touchstone for studies of this type, because it situates its commentary on Swinburne's poetry within a dense matrix of other cultural allusions. Barbara Temple-Thurston, in her 1990 essay in *James Joyce Quarterly*, notes that Swinburne serves as one of several points of reference for Joyce in his historical interpretation of the Boer War; the poet's symbolic value lies in depicting the "abhorrence" of warfare to Joyce and his alter ego, Stephen Dedalus. More recently still, in *Native Shakespeares: Indigenous Appropriations on a Global Stage* (2008), Thomas Cartelli observes the aptness and resonance of Joyce's comparison between Swinburne's Boer War poetry and the "bloodboltered" closing act of *Hamlet*.

BIBLIOGRAPHY

Sources

Arinshtein, Leonid M., and William E. Fredeman. "William Michael Rossetti's 'Democratic Sonnets.'" *Victorian Studies* 14.3 (1971): 241–74. Print.

Bevis, Matthew. "Fighting Talk: Victorian War Poetry." *The Oxford Handbook of British and Irish War Poetry.* Ed. Tim Kendall. New York: Oxford UP, 2007. 7–33. Print.

Cartelli, Thomas. "The Face in the Mirror: Joyce's *Ulysses* and the Lookingglass Shakespeare." *Native Shakespeares: Indigenous Appropriations on a Global Stage.* Ed. Craig Dionne and Parmita Kapadia. Aldershot: Ashgate, 2008. 19–36. Print.

King, Kathryn R., and William W. Morgan. "Hardy and the Boer War: The Public Poet in Spite of Himself." *Victorian Poetry* 17.1–2 (1979): 66–83. Print.

Lang, Cecil Y., ed. *The Swinburne Letters.* 6 vols. New Haven: Yale UP, 1959. Print.

Temple-Thurston, Barbara. "The Reader as Absentminded Beggar: Recovering South Africa in *Ulysses.*" *James Joyce Quarterly* 28.1 (1990): 247–56. Print.

Further Reading

Gosse, Edmund, and Thomas James Wise, eds. *The Complete Works of Algernon Charles Swinburne.* 20 vols. London: Heinemann, 1925–27. Print.

Hyder, Clyde K., ed. *Algernon Swinburne: The Critical Heritage.* Routledge, 2005. *Taylor & Francis e-Library.* Web. 6 July 2012.

Hyder, Clyde K. *Swinburne's Literary Career and Fame.* Durham: Duke UP, 1933. Print.

Rooksby, Rikky. *A. C. Swinburne: A Poet's Life.* London: Scolar Press, 1997. Print.

Saville, Julia F. "Swinburne Contra Whitman: From Cosmopolitan Republican to Parochial English Jingo?" *ELH* 78.2 (2011): 479–505. Web. 6 July 2012.

Michael Hartwell

"VITAI LAMPADA"

Sir Henry Newbolt

OVERVIEW

Written in 1892 and published in 1897 during the waning days of the Victorian era, "Vitai Lampada" is an inspirational poem by British writer, editor, and critic Sir Henry Newbolt (1862–1938). The Latin title, meaning "The Torch of Life," is taken from *De rerum natura,* by the Roman poet Lucretius, and refers to the torch that is passed from generation to generation. Newbolt's poem is a romanticized tribute to upper-class British spirit and to the ideas of fair play, pluck, and dedication to one's side, whether it is a team or a nation. With its glorification of British ideals, "Vitai Lampada" was comforting to a society on the verge of enormous change, and it became one of the archetypal poems of World War I. Its heartfelt refrain "Play up! play up! and play the game!" became one of the most frequently quoted lines of the day.

As the nineteenth century, with its transformative Industrial Revolution, drew to a close and the lead-up to a catastrophic world war began, British society experienced a mixture of imperial smugness and profound unease. The publication of "Vitai Lampada" coincided with Queen Victoria's Diamond Jubilee. Instantly popular and widely memorized, the poem captures a public spirit of patriotism along with a foreboding of terrible conflict and sacrifice. In its idealized depiction of the stouthearted British male, this propagandist poem promotes the values of steadfastness and devotion to duty that a nation needs from its citizens in times of war.

HISTORICAL AND LITERARY CONTEXT

Under the rule of Queen Victoria, the British Empire underwent a period of enormous growth between 1870 and 1900, facilitated by advances in communication, transportation, and weaponry. This expansion, which encompassed almost four million square miles around the world, was spurred by the economic need for access to goods such as tea, sugar, and raw cotton. In addition, British leaders felt the need to keep pace with the expansionist activities of France, Germany, and Russia in order to maintain a strong position in the tenuous European balance of power. A constantly shifting web of alliances created political instability and an international mood of anxiety before finally degenerating into the massively destructive conflict of World War I.

Prior to the publication of "Vitai Lampada," the British Empire faced many challenges, such as the Indian Mutiny in the East, the Boer Wars in southern Africa, and the 1885 defeat of English forces in the Sudan. (The battle in the Sudan inspired the following lines from the poem: "The sand of the desert is sodden red, —/ Red with the wreck of a square that broke.") Nonetheless, in 1894 the world traveler Lord Curzon, soon to be appointed viceroy and governor-general of India, called his nation's holdings "the greatest empire for good that the world has seen." This perception of the British that they were a noble, just, and civilizing influence was important to building and maintaining the empire. As a reassuring affirmation of national character, "Vitai Lampada" supported the British worldview.

Born in 1862 and educated at Clifton College preparatory school, Newbolt grew up immersed in the rhetoric of the "sporting" Englishman in the empire, where the ideal was to govern oneself and others with patrician fairness. Even people from the working class celebrated their British superiority with popular songs such as Leslie Stuart's "Soldiers of the Queen" (1881). Rudyard Kipling's patriotic stories and poems, such as "The English Flag" (1865), in which he weaves together exoticism and British condescension in rhythmic verse, established Kipling as the very epitome of the empire poet. Felicia Dorothea Hemans's poem "Casabianca" (1826) precedes Newbolt's poem in contrasting the horror of war with the "beautiful and bright" boy who sacrifices himself to his duty. Much of Newbolt's poetry, such as "Drake's Drum" (1897) and "The Song of the Guns at Sea" (1909), reflects this trend of equating patriotic militarism with nobility of spirit.

The campaign of mythmaking exemplified by "Vitai Lampada" was responsible for introducing to the language a number of enduring phrases and patriotic concepts, such as the title of Kipling's 1899 poem "The White Man's Burden." Newbolt's refrain in "Vitai Lampada" took its place in the language as well, and to many, the cry embodied the finest aspects of British culture and personality. The poem influenced several works, including *Scouting for Boys* by Robert Baden-Powell (1909) and "In Flanders Fields" by John McCrae (1915). Conversely, Newbolt's romanticization of the soldier's duty inspired a negative reaction

Key Facts

Time Period:
Late 19th Century

Genre:
Poetry

Events:
Industrial Revolution; expansion of the British Empire

Nationality:
English

THE OTHER SIDE OF THE OLD SCHOOL SPIRIT

Unlike Sir Henry Newbolt, many social analysts did not view the English system of elite public schools as the crucible of honor and nobility. "Public" in British education did not mean, as it did in the United States, open to all. Instead, it defined a small network of exclusive boarding and day schools that included Eton, Rugby, and St. Paul's. Public schools were started during the sixteenth century to offer education to the poor. By the mid-1800s, however, these institutions had been "reformed" to eliminate working-class students and were offering programs of education designed to turn the sons of the rising middle class into proper English gentlemen. Through physical deprivation, hazing, and fervent devotion to sport, public school students were taught the importance of conformity, obedience, self-sacrifice, and loyalty to the group.

George Orwell was a near-contemporary of Newbolt who had a much different view of public schools. In his autobiographical essay "Such, Such Were the Joys" (1952), Orwell says his life in a preparatory boarding school amounted to being "locked up ... in a hostile world ... of good and evil where the rules were such that it was actually not possible for me to keep them." Orwell's final assessment of the system is damning: "the characteristic faults of the English upper and middle classes may be partly due to the practice, general until recently, of sending children away from home as young as nine, eight or even seven."

in such works as Wilfred Owen's "Dulce et Decorum Est" (1917), which rails against poets who glorify war.

THEMES AND STYLE

Centered on themes of war and honor, "Vitai Lampada" is primarily a tribute to the very British virtue of "doing one's part" without regard for gain or glory and without question. Beginning with the comparatively inconsequential competition of a school cricket match and progressing to the bloody battlefield, Newbolt eulogizes the romanticized code of honor of the elite public school system [*see sidebar*]. Gains are made "not for the sake of a ribboned coat, / Or the selfish hope of a season's fame" but for "his Captain's hand on his shoulder," for the team, and for the sake of the game itself. War, though "a river of death," is likened to cricket, a noble game that demands one's best effort and has rules of honor that must be followed. Thus, Newbolt exhorts the reader to "play up!" (fight with valor) and "play the game!" (accept one's lot and do one's duty). The final message, echoed from the title to the last stanza, is one of continuity and tradition: the torch of duty and honor must be passed from one generation to the next.

Newbolt leads the reader along with a soldierly rhythm, from the mundane and familiar (the cricket match with its "bumping pitch") through the unimaginable ("the regiment blind with dust and smoke") to a glorious purpose ("This they all with a joyful mind / Bear through life like a torch in flame"). The poem begins on a note of eager suspense—"There's a breathless hush in the Close to-night"—that draws the reader in, and the tension mounts as the second verse opens with a bloody desert battle. It is the refrain "Play up! Play up! And play the game!" that relieves the tension, making the poem an anthem of hope, though neither the outcome of the cricket match nor the winner of the battle is revealed in the text. The goal is propagandist, to rally "the ranks," and the final verse offers exultant proof that sacrifice is rewarded by the perpetuation of cultural values.

Though the allusion of the poem's Latin title reveals Newbolt to be a product of the elite school system (he was an Oxford graduate) he praises, he makes his work accessible to the common people through the use of a pulsing rhythm, simple language, and a familiar sports metaphor. References to "school" and to the "schoolboy," along with the identification of war as just another game to be played, evince an innocence and purity that turn-of-the-century readers would have wanted to embrace.

CRITICAL DISCUSSION

"Vitai Lampada" was initially published in Newbolt's first book of poems, *Admirals All and Other Verses*. The small collection of patriotic verse resonated with a British public that was enamored of the mythology of the empire; the book sold twenty-one thousand copies in one year and made its author famous. Critics were moved by the poet's rosy nationalism. A reviewer in the *Globe* stated that he would "like to see these stirring verses in the hands of every high-spirited youth in the Empire," while the *Scotsman* found the verses to be "written in a sturdy, rhythmical speech, worthy of their high themes." Critic William Archer called Newbolt "a believer in the mission of England" and added that there is "nothing frothy ... nothing blusterous or insincere" about his patriotism, which Archer viewed as "[s]ad and earnest rather than thoughtlessly exultant." Though "Vitai Lampada" became Newbolt's most requested poem at recitations, the author did not see it as significant and was surprised by its success.

As defense of its empire and its network of European alliances led England into devastating war in 1914, a generation of schoolboys who had memorized "Vitai Lampada" marched off to fight. More than 700,000 of them would be killed. Newbolt's poem became both a rallying cry and a manifesto for a way of life that was fast disappearing. During the period between the two world wars, antiwar sentiment ran high, and the romantic patriotism of "Vitai Lampada" became a subject of ridicule and parody. Nevertheless, its place in British culture was solidified in 1934 when sculptor Gilbert Bayes carved the poem's refrain on the wall of Lord's Cricket Ground in London.

A 1896 etching, after a painting by William Barnes Wollen, depicting a match at Lord's Cricket Ground in England. In his 1892 poem "Vitai Lampada," Sir Henry Newbolt compares competing in cricket matches to participating in military actions. *CRICKET AT LORDS,* 1896 (COLOURED PHOTOGRAVURE), WOLLEN, WILLIAM BARNES (1857–1936) (AFTER)/ PRIVATE COLLECTION/ PHOTO © CHRISTIE'S IMAGES/THE BRIDGEMAN ART LIBRARY.

"Vitai Lampada" remains an essential expression of British sensibilities during the Empire and a representative example of pro-patriotism propaganda poetry. In "Henry Newbolt's Cultural Metrics," Meredith Martin praises the poem's success in using "the power of rhythm to inspire patriotic, military action." However, the most enduring legacy of "Vitai Lampada" may be its propagandist refrain. In "Playing the Game," Cecil Eby calls it "perhaps the most … influential cliché in the English-speaking world."

BIBLIOGRAPHY

Sources

Archer, William. "Henry Newbolt." *Poets of the Younger Generation.* London: Lane, 1902. 284–308. Print.

Eby, Cecil D. "Playing the Game." *The Road to Armageddon: The Martial Spirit in English Popular Literature.* Durham: Duke UP, 1988. 86–108. Print.

Evans, Eric. "A British Revolution in the 19th Century?" *BBC.* BBC, 17 Feb. 2011. Web. 8 July 2012.

Martin, Meredith. "Henry Newbolt's Cultural Metrics." *The Rise and Fall of Meter: Poetry and English National Culture, 1860–1930.* Princeton: Princeton UP, 2012. 122–29. Print.

Nelson, James G. "Henry (John) Newbolt." *British Poets, 1880–1914.* Ed. Donald E. Stanford. Detroit: Gale, 1983. *Literature Resource Center.* Web. 9 July 2012.

Wheen, Francis. "Play Up! Play Up! And Play the Game!" *New Statesman & Society* 31 May 1996: 23+. *General Reference Center GOLD.* Web. 10 July 2012.

Further Reading

Betjeman, John. "Sir Henry Newbolt After a Hundred Years." *Listener* 67 (28 June 1962): 1114–15. Print.

Faulkner, Peter. "Newbolt, Kipling and 'The Lordliest Life on Earth.'" *Durham University Journal* 86.2 (1994): 253–57. Rpt. in *Poetry Criticism.* Vol. 91. Ed. Michelle Lee. Detroit: Gale, 2008. *Literature Resource Center.* Web. 10 July 2012.

Hattersley, Roy. *The Edwardians.* New York: St. Martin's, 2005. Print.

Kernahan, Coulson. "Henry Newbolt." *Six Famous Living Poets.* London: Butterworth, 1922. 97–107. Print.

Murdoch, Brian. *Fighting Songs and Warring Words: Popular Lyrics of Two World Wars.* London: Routledge, 1990. Print.

Perkins, David. *A History of Modern Poetry, from the 1890s to the High Modernist Mode.* Cambridge: Harvard UP, 1976. Print.

Richards, Jeffrey. "Popular Imperialism and the Image of the Army in Juvenile Literature." *Popular Imperialism and the Military: 1850–1950.* Ed. John M. MacKenzie. New York: St. Martin's, 1992. 80–108. Print.

Tina Gianoulis

"THE WAR PRAYER"

Mark Twain

✣ *Key Facts*

Time Period:
Early 20th Century

Genre:
Short Story

Events:
Spanish-American
War; annexation of the
Philippines

Nationality:
American

OVERVIEW

"The War Prayer," a short story written by Mark Twain (1835–1910), responds to American popular support of the annexation of the Philippine Islands in 1899. It bitingly condemns the propaganda that encouraged unquestioning patriotism and religious fervor, common justifications for war. Twain uses irony and hyperbole to illustrate the point that humanism and Christianity's teaching of love are incompatible with the conduct of war. Set in an unnamed Christian country, "The War Prayer" portrays a town in the grip of war fever. Invigorated by the prospect of battle, the people celebrate with a patriotic parade and a church service to invoke God's blessing and enlist help to conquer the enemy. An aged stranger then arrives, claiming that God sent him to reveal the implications of the congregation's appeal for His partisanship and its implicit component of begging that innocent people be made to suffer and die. The congregation dismisses his speech as the ramblings of an unstable mind. Twain's story acts as a reminder of the grim realities of war that lurk behind the rhetoric and national symbols used to drum up support.

Originally written in 1905, "The War Prayer" was not published in full until 1923, thirteen years after Twain's death. It was originally rejected by *Harper's Bazaar* in 1905 as unsuitable for a women's magazine, and friends and family discouraged Twain from seeking publication elsewhere, fearing that the piece would be labeled sacrilegious and hurt his career. Writing to his friend Dan Beard, to whom he had read the story, Twain lamented, "I don't think the prayer will be published in my time. None but the dead are permitted to tell the truth." Excerpts first appeared in a 1912 biography written by Albert Bigelow Paine, Twain's close friend and literary executor. When the story was published in Paine's collection of Twain's fiction, *Europe and Elsewhere,* it was recognized for its indictment of the bloodlust that masquerades as patriotism in wartime, a message that has continued to be relevant to the wars fought throughout the twentieth century and beyond.

HISTORICAL AND LITERARY CONTEXT

Twain wrote "The War Prayer" in 1905, at a time when he was increasingly discouraged with America's quest to become an imperial power at the turn of the twentieth century. Expanding its power through military adventures, the United States fought the Spanish-American War in 1898 to "free" Cuba from Spanish rule. The war ended with the Treaty of Paris, signed on December 10 of that year, which gave the United States colonial authority over Cuba, the Philippines, Guam, and Puerto Rico. This new development was justified with the ideology of (in the words of the procolonialist writer Rudyard Kipling) "the white man's burden," turning it into a righteous civilizing mission. Fighting continued for another decade, however, in what was known first as the Philippine Rebellion and later as the Philippine-American War. When it became clear that the United States had no intention of giving up control over the area after driving out the Spanish, Twain became disillusioned, and he responded by publishing a series of angry articles condemning American imperialism.

Twain was not alone in the feelings of outrage that inspired "The War Prayer." A group of concerned citizens, including the steel magnate and philanthropist Andrew Carnegie and the philosopher William James, began to speak out against U.S. imperialism. The Anti-Imperialist League was formally founded on November 19, 1898, to protest the Spanish-American War and fight against the adoption of an enlarged imperial agenda. Returning to the United States in 1900 after working in Europe, Twain quickly became one of the most outspoken and influential opponents of imperialism and soon joined forces with the Anti-Imperialist League. In January 1901 he agreed to serve as vice president of the league. Opposition to the Philippine-American War became a major focus of his organizational and literary career for the remainder of his life.

In "The War Prayer" Twain responds in part to Kipling's poem "The White Man's Burden" (1899), which proposes that white people are obliged to promote cultural development in less-developed areas of the world. This line of thinking became a justification for cultural imperialism at the beginning of the twentieth century. "The War Prayer" also draws on Henry David Thoreau's opposition to the Mexican-American War in his 1849 essay "Civil

Disobedience," in which he reminds Americans that by supporting the government blindly, they become complicit in immoral acts. During Twain's involvement with the Anti-Imperialist League, he wrote several political essays that were released as pamphlets through the organization. In the January 1901 edition of the *North American Review,* Twain published "To the Person Sitting in Darkness," his most popular anti-imperialist essay, challenging the ideology of "the white man's burden" as applied to the Boxer Rebellion (1900) in China.

In the time since its full publication in 1923, "The War Prayer" has gained recognition for its poignant critique of dangerous rhetoric in times of war. One notable aspect of the story's construction is the lack of clear indicators of time or place, allowing for its themes to be applied to contemporary conflicts. In the 1960s the story experienced a resurgence in popularity as part of the growing opposition to the Vietnam War. Since that time, U.S. military invasions in the Middle East in the late twentieth century and the early twenty-first century also revived interest in "The War Prayer."

THEMES AND STYLE

Infuriated that a war of "liberation" had become a war of imperialism, Twain wrote his "prayer" in order to illuminate the hypocrisy of merging religion and war and to warn against the dangers of insincere religion and blind patriotism. He takes to task religious sentiments that, most markedly during wartime, fail to uphold their purported doctrine of peace and instead foster nationalism and a desire to dominate and convert. Twain's stranger points out that even simple-seeming prayers carry with them a darker side: "Is it one prayer? No, it is two—one uttered the other not. ... Ponder this— keep it in mind. If you beseech a blessing upon yourself, beware! lest without intent you invoke a curse upon a neighbor at the same time." The story keeps the identity of the story's prophet ambiguous: does Twain really intend to represent an angel, or could the messenger be death, Twain himself, or all of the above? The mystery of their originator makes the words more significant.

"The War Prayer" is notable for Twain's use of satire, particularly irony, as the primary rhetorical vehicle for his critique of propaganda. Of the two major satirical tactics, both named after Roman satirists, Twain's work can be characterized as Juvenilian—abrasive and sarcastic in confronting what it sees as social evil—rather than Horatian, which uses humor and often sympathy in addressing perceived folly. The congregation's prayer for victory reflects the dualistic nature of irony, which says one thing but means another. The narrator's zealous description of the events is followed by the stranger's monologue, consisting mostly of his prayer. The

"THE WAR PRAYER" RECREATED IN VISUAL CULTURE

Twain's storytelling in "The War Prayer" is so well crafted and the message so immediately palpable that it has been recreated in various theatrical and film versions that have become a part of U.S. popular culture. In April 2007 Lyceum Films released a ten-minute film adaptation (retaining Twain's original title) that stars Tim Sullivan as the preacher and Jeremy Sisto as the stranger. Also in 2007 journalist Markos Kounalakis produced and directed an animated film adaptation titled "The War Prayer." Both endeavors translated Twain's classic story into the language of contemporary visual culture, connecting it to wider audiences and promoting its message for future generations.

The 1981 made-for-television movie *The Private History of a Campaign That Failed,* directed by Peter H. Hunt, dramatizes Twain's 1885 short story of the same name, which was inspired by his brief experience in the pro-Confederate Missouri State Guard during the Civil War. The plot follows a group of teenage soldiers who go to the battlefield without proper training and lack an understanding of the reason for the war. The film concludes with the arrival of a ghost who delivers "The War Prayer" as an antiwar epilogue.

congregation's inability to understand what the stranger reveals about their religious fervor indicates a level of inoculation against critical thinking, which propaganda relies on and that is especially dangerous in wartime. Twain's Juvenilian pessimism comes out in the story's final line, in which the crowd dismisses the stranger as a lunatic "because there was no sense in what he said."

Twain opens the story with the declaration, "It was a time of great and exalting excitement. The country was up in arms, the war was on, in every breast burned the holy fire of patriotism." This beginning builds anticipation for the reader, reinforced through alliteration. War is understood as part of the country and the individual's righteous destiny. That it is "a glad and gracious time" implies that the opportunity to wage war on behalf of one's country is a divine gift to be met with gratitude. Opposition is quashed through threats of violence rather than met with logic and intellect; patriotism is based on blind emotion. The stranger's prayer also utilizes alliteration but to achieve a vastly different tone. His grave sermon intends to puncture the congregation's euphoria, using reminders of the gruesome realities of war to confront their conscience. His stark monologue halts the story's momentum. In this section Twain repeats "help us" anaphorically, juxtaposing the Christian plea for divine aid and images of the enemies' suffering.

An 1899 cartoon depicting the Philippines and other territories as stubborn children being schooled by Uncle Sam. The chalkboard on the wall reads, "The U.S. must govern its new territories with or without their consent until they can govern themselves." Mark Twain's story "The War Prayer" is a critique of the 1899 American annexation of the Philippines. © WORLD HISTORY ARCHIVE/ALAMY.

CRITICAL DISCUSSION

Because of Twain's decision not to pursue publication of "The War Prayer" during his lifetime, early critical reactions to the story are virtually nonexistent. Since 1923 it has been reprinted many times, becoming widely accessible to general audiences. The story is often overlooked in the American literary canon, however, and is one of Twain's lesser-known works.

"The War Prayer" has been important to peace activists, especially during the Vietnam War and the U.S.-led wars against Iraq. Antiwar websites frequently include the work on suggested reading lists. In the 1960s, as antiwar sentiments increased as a result of the escalation of the Vietnam War, Mark Twain's publisher released "The War Prayer" as a self-contained piece. The volume contained stark line drawings by John Groth (1902–1988), an artist and combat veteran of World War II. This edition revived interest and encouraged continued scholarship of the work as a prime example of literature that critiques the rhetoric and propaganda of wartime.

With an increased focus today on Twain's later career, critics have responded to Twain's insecurity about preserving his crafted public image as a humorist and Southern gentleman while being true to the politically engaged, often angry individual underneath. Further attention to this duality, as Alan Gribben argued in "The Importance of Mark Twain" (*American Quarterly*, 1985), has led to a greater appreciation of Twain's full canon. Twain expert Jim Zwick has called for more scholarship concentrating on the works by Twain that make us uncomfortable and that have been overshadowed by his humorous writings. In *Mark Twain's Weapons of Satire* (1992), Zwick argues that "The War Prayer" and much of Twain's later anti-imperialist writing has largely been ignored as a result of America's repression of its imperialist history. To promote continued study of Twain's literary works, the University of California Press and the Bancroft Library launched the *Mark Twain Project Online* in October 2007. The digital collection features critical editions of Twain's writings as well as a collection of his letters and notebooks. In addition, the University of California's online *Journal of Transnational American Studies* has reprinted a special issue of *Mark Twain Studies* (vol. 2, published in Japan and edited by Shelley Fisher Fishkin and Takayuki Tatsumi) titled "New Perspectives on 'The War Prayer'—An International Forum" to promote global discussion of the work.

BIBLIOGRAPHY

Sources

Budd, Louis J. *Mark Twain: Social Philosopher*. Columbia: U of Missouri P, 2001. Print.

Gribben, Alan. "The Importance of Mark Twain." *American Quarterly* 37.1 (1985): 30–49. Print.

Lock, Helen. "Twain's Rhetoric of Irony in 'The War-Prayer.'" *Journal of Transnational American Studies* 1:1 (2009): n. pag. American Cultures and Global Contexts Center, U of California, Santa Barbara. Web. 21 June 2012.

Twain, Mark. "The War Prayer." *Europe and Elsewhere*. New York: Harper, 1923. Print.

Zwick, Jim. *Mark Twain's Weapons of Satire*. New York: Syracuse UP, 1992. Print.

Further Reading

Britton, Wesley. "Mark Twain and Tom Paine: 'Common Sense' as Source for 'The War Prayer.'" *Conference of College Teachers of English Studies* 54 (1989): 132–49. Print.

Fishkin, Shelley Fisher. "'None but the Dead Are Permitted to Tell the Truth': Mark Twain's Missives to the Future." *American Secrets: The Politics and Poetics of Secrecy in the Literature of the United States.* Ed. Eduardo Barres-Grela and José Liste-Noya. Madison, NJ: Fairleigh Dickinson UP, 2011. 17–36. Print.

Foner, Phillip S. *Mark Twain: Social Critic.* New York: International, 1973. Print.

Geismar, Maxwell, ed. *Mark Twain and the Three Rs: Religion, Revolution and Related Matters.* Indianapolis, IN: Bobbs-Merrill, 1973. Print.

Kiskis, Michael J. "'The War-Prayer': Samuel Clemens and 9/11." *Journal of Transnational American Studies* 1.1 (2009). Print.

Media Adaptation

The War Prayer. Dir. Michael A. Goorjian. Perf. Kristen Clement, Thomas Dekker, and Emmy Farese. Lyceum Films, 2007. Film.

Elizabeth Orvis

THE WEALTH OF NATIONS
Adam Smith

✣ *Key Facts*

Time Period:
Late 18th Century

Genre:
Philosophical tract

Events:
Seven Years' War;
birth of capitalism; the
Enlightenment

Nationality:
Scottish

OVERVIEW

Adam Smith's *The Wealth of Nations* was published in 1776 as a philosophical tract that attempted to explain how society could be more harmonious and the population wealthier by following free-market economics. In doing so, Smith laid the foundation for modern capitalism and the formal study of economics. His work is divided into five "books" that discuss labor, money, the nature of corporate stocks, the system of economics in place at the time, and how governments get money to operate. Although Adam Smith may have been a philosopher, he wanted his readers to know his theories were based on rational, scientific inquiry that offered a new and better way of thinking about how economies worked.

Smith was pleasantly surprised when his work started to influence the wealthiest and most important people of Great Britain. In the decades after publication, many British leaders tried to reorder the British Empire's economy according to Smith's notion of the "Invisible Hand of the Market." Previously, the empires of Europe were mercantilists in nature; they tried to control the flow of raw materials from their colonies to their homelands, where they would then use these materials to manufacture more complex goods to sell at home and abroad for a profit. For example, merchants would take lumber from New England and send it to England, where it would be made into furniture to be sold to someone in New England. Ideally, this would enrich the empire and keep colonies dependent. Smith's system sought to free trade from restrictions so that it would be governed by the self-regulating market (the "invisible hand") rather than by the government, which might not operate according to the best interests of society.

HISTORICAL AND LITERARY CONTEXT

Smith lived during the Enlightenment, an intellectual movement that believed the world behaved rationally and could, through logic, be understood in its entirety. Philosophers tried to understand why humans behaved as they did, how nature worked, and how people could improve themselves according to these new ideas. Smith was born in Scotland and attended the University of Glasgow, where a certain strain of Enlightenment thinking was forming. This strain was more interested in practical and provable knowledge than in coming up with grand theories for how the universe worked, a trend more popular in continental Europe, particularly France.

Great Britain had won the Seven Years' War (also known as the French and Indian War) in 1763 but had incurred massive debts. The British Parliament and Prime Minister Charles Townshend were desperate to find a way to pay back these debts, which piqued Adam Smith's interest in writing a book to help the British Empire operate more efficiently. Additionally, changes in the price of food led to Smith attempting to determine why prices for goods rise and fall.

Adam Smith's writing is very similar to that of other Enlightenment philosophers who conveyed their ideas in the form of dialogue. Although Smith was well versed in the writings of many different philosophers, it was his teacher at Glasgow University, Francis Hutcheson, who instructed him in moral philosophy. Before writing *The Wealth of Nations,* Smith had examined human behavior in his *Theory of Moral Sentiments* and had concluded that human greed would not destroy society because most people could restrain themselves from becoming too greedy. Other influences were Bernard Mandeville's *The Fable of the Bees,* and the writings of David Hume.

In the decade following the initial publication of *The Wealth of Nations,* the book came to be regarded as one of the most important and influential works on economic thought ever published. In that time, *The Wealth of Nations* was translated into French and German and it was reprinted three times in English. Adam Smith would work on two more editions before his death in 1790. Perhaps only the works of Karl Marx in the 1840s or John Maynard Keynes in the 1930s had a similar effect on the way people thought about how nations should structure their economies.

THEMES AND STYLE

The main idea discussed in *The Wealth of Nations* is that free trade would create societies that are more stable and offer greater freedoms than societies based on the rule of an absolute monarch or religious leader. Many people worried that human nature, if not controlled by some authority, would destroy society through its inherent greed and violence. Smith sought to calm these fears by arguing that an individual "by pursuing his own interest he frequently promotes that of the society more effectually than when he really intends to promote it." Smith had to convince Great Britain not only that his economic theory was sound but also that a society ordered around his economic theories would be better than the existing society.

As a moral philosopher, Smith bases his entire work on a series of rational claims and real-world examples. Unlike some types of propaganda, Smith does not try to appeal to the emotions of the reader but uses logic to convince the reader that he is correct. For example, in the first chapter Smith claims that division of labor has made the greatest impact on the productivity of labor. To prove this, Smith spends several pages discussing what effect the division of labor has had on certain industries; why it is advantageous to divide jobs among people rather than have one person do everything; and how this division of labor allows for greater prosperity. This argument unfolds in a logical order: A statement is made; Smith proves it; and he then uses this point to prove subsequent ones.

The effect of this approach is that Smith's expository writing style makes for dry reading. Smith, a professor, used his lecture notes as the basis for his book, so reading *The Wealth of Nations* is reminiscent of a classroom lecture. Edmund Burke said that "the style of the author maybe sometimes thought difficult, but it must be remembered that the work is didactic, that the author means to teach, and teach things that are by no means obvious." Smith attempts through logical discussions to lead the reader to conclude that his arguments and the reasoning that underpin them are incontrovertible.

CRITICAL DISCUSSION

Upon publication, the public received Smith's work as a substantial body of philosophical thought, though its impact was more muted than it might have been in Britain owing to the start of the American Revolution. The influential English writer Horace Walpole and others dismissed Smith's work as being repetitive and poorly written. The first intellectually substantial criticism of Smith came in 1777 from the Scottish philosopher James Anderson, who, in *An Enquiry into the Nature of the Corn Laws,* criticizes some of Smith's conclusions about rent and price fluctuations. However, members of the prestigious Royal Society, dedicated to the scientific pursuit of knowledge, were overwhelmingly supportive of Smith's work and its conclusions. Edmund Burke, a conservative member of Parliament, was a Smith supporter and proclaimed Smith's work to be new, profound, and original.

Despite some early criticism of Smith's conclusions, *The Wealth of Nations* found widespread acceptance in Western Europe. For almost two hundred and fifty years, Smith's work has formed the basis of economic discussion for academics, political leaders, and social theorists. Even Karl Marx, the primary intellectual force behind socialism and communism, used Smith's Labor Theory of Value as a basis for his

ADAM SMITH AND THE ROLE OF SELF-INTEREST

A major area of philosophical inquiry that Adam Smith was concerned with was what constitutes moral behavior. For Smith, the establishment of a free-market system was a moral issue. Critics have argued that he meant to replace decision-making based on morals or virtue with decision-making based solely on economic considerations, as expressed in Smith's view that "the butcher, the brewer, or the baker" produce goods to make money, not out of kindness.

Before and for several decades after the publication of Smith's *The Wealth of Nations,* society generally held that individuals should not act out of self-interest. One of the principal components of republicanism was that a man was to act according to the public good even if it meant that his private interests would be harmed. Smith's most controversial idea was that self-interest could serve the public good. For example, if a man who knows how to build roads wanted to make money, he might ask the government to allow him to construct and operate a toll road. Ideally, the man would enrich not only himself but also his community by providing a new and improved transportation route, facilitating increased trade. Nevertheless, the economic role of self-interest has remained a controversial subject, particularly in periods of economic unrest.

theories about the proletariat, even as he criticized Smith's basic assumptions about the equalizing power of free trade. By the early twenty-first century—after the fall of the Soviet Union and the move by the Chinese government under Dong Xiaoping toward greater economic freedom—every major country had, to a greater or lesser extent, accepted Smith's idea that economic freedom helps to create a more stable and prosperous society.

After a period of modern backlash, criticism of *The Wealth of Nations* in recent years has become more favorable with a resurgence of conservative appreciation of capitalism. In the 1960s and 1970s, many leftist scholars perceived Smith to be either naive in his belief that human greed could be controlled or that he did not care about workers and those who opposed capitalism. Scholars since the late 1990s have looked upon Smith more favorably, believing that he was concerned that the public had not taken to heart his admonishments that government should create a publicly funded education system and provide for the poor. During Smith's lifetime, the British government stopped subsidizing food prices in accordance with the "Invisible Hand" of the market, leading to widespread famine and suffering. Much of the current debate about Adam Smith and *The Wealth of Nations* revolves around the extent to which Smith believed in the virtue of the free market and whether the corporate capitalism dominant in economically advanced nations of

A statue of Adam Smith outside St. Giles' Cathedral in Edinburgh, Scotland. © ALAN WILSON/ALAMY.

the world today truly adheres to Smith's vision for how free markets can bring about a more harmonious and prosperous society.

BIBLIOGRAPHY

Sources

Fitzgibbons, Athol. *Adam Smith's System of Liberty, Wealth, and Virtue: The Moral and Political Foundations of* The Wealth of Nations. Oxford: Clarendon, 1995. Print.

Force, Pierre. *Self-Interest before Adam Smith: A Genealogy of Economic Science.* Cambridge: Cambridge UP, 2003. Print.

Griswold, Charles L., Jr. *Adam Smith and the Virtues of Enlightenment.* Cambridge: Cambridge UP, 1999. Print.

Hume, David. "Of Refinement in the Arts." *Commerce, Culture, and Liberty: Readings on Capitalism Before Adam Smith.* Ed. Henry C. Clark. Indianapolis, IN: Liberty Fund, 2003. 358–70. Print.

Mandeville, Bernard. "The Fable of the Bees." *Commerce, Culture, and Liberty: Readings on Capitalism before Adam Smith.* Ed. Henry C. Clark. Indianapolis, IN: Liberty Fund, 2003. 203–18. Print.

Ross, Ian Simpson. *The Life of Adam Smith.* Oxford: Clarendon, 1995. Print.

Smith, Adam. *The Wealth of Nations.* New York: Barnes and Noble, 2004. Print.

Werhane, Patricia H. *Adam Smith and His Legacy for Modern Capitalism.* Oxford: Oxford UP, 1991. Print.

Further Reading

Depew, David, Jr. "Adam Smith and Edmund Burke: Texts in Context." *Poroi: An Interdisciplinary Journal of Rhetorical Analysis and Invention* 7.1 (2011): 1–35. Print.

Evensky, Jerry. *Adam Smith's Moral Philosophy: A Historical and Contemporary Perspective on Markets, Law, Ethics, and Culture.* Cambridge: Cambridge UP, 2005. Print.

Fleischacker, Samuel. "Adam Smith's Reception among the American Founders." *The William & Mary Quarterly* 59.4 (2002): 897–924. Print.

———. *On Adam Smith's* Wealth of Nations: *A Philosophical Companion.* Princeton: Princeton UP, 2004. Print.

Hanley, Ryan Patrick. *Adam Smith and the Character of Virtue.* Cambridge: Cambridge UP, 2011. Print.

Kennedy, Gavin. "Adam Smith and the Role of the Metaphor of an Invisible Hand." *Economic Affairs* 31.1 (2011): 53–57. Print.

Milgate, Murray, and Shannon C. Stimson. *After Adam Smith: A Century of Transformation in Politics and Political Economy.* Princeton: Princeton UP, 2009. Print.

O'Rourke, P. J. *On* The Wealth of Nations. New York: Atlantic Monthly, 2007.

Phillipson, Nicholas. *Adam Smith: An Enlightened Life.* New Haven, CT: Yale UP, 2010. Print.

Rothschild, Emma. *Economic Sentiments: Adam Smith, Condorcet, and the Enlightenment.* Cambridge, MA: Harvard UP, 2001. Print.

Sen, Amartya. "Uses and Abuses of Adam Smith." *History of Political Economy* 43.2 (2001): 257–71. Print.

Whitmore, Richard. "Adam Smith's Role in the French Revolution." *Past & Present* 175.1 (2002): 65–89. Print.

Adam Carson

Parties and Factions

ANIMAL FARM

George Orwell

OVERVIEW

British novelist George Orwell's *Animal Farm* (1945) is an allegorical fable that indicts the communist betrayal of the ideals of the 1917 Bolshevik Revolution. On its surface a children's tale about an animal rebellion on a farm, the book is formulated so that the events of the barnyard revolt exactly parallel many of the key events of Russian history in the quarter century following the revolution. *Animal Farm,* however, also functions symbolically on levels beyond its attack on the oppressive totalitarian regime of Soviet leader Joseph Stalin (1929–53), containing larger moral lessons about the betrayal of revolutions generally and the abuses of power that transcend particular historical circumstance.

Written between November 1943 and February 1944, *Animal Farm* was initially rejected by several British and American publishers as too harsh a criticism of the Soviet Union, then a World War II ally. By the time the novel finally appeared on August 17, 1945, the war in Europe was over, and Stalin had already begun to consolidate his power through the forceful takeover of several Eastern European countries. In this climate Orwell's warnings about the insidiousness of Soviet totalitarianism struck a nerve. *Animal Farm* was an immediate best seller in Orwell's native England as well as in the United States. As Cold War tensions escalated in the 1950s between the democratic West and the Soviet Union and its satellites, the popularity of the novel soared. *Animal Farm* has since sold more than twenty million copies in dozens of languages worldwide. It remains one of the world's best-selling and most widely studied novels.

HISTORICAL AND LITERARY CONTEXT

Orwell wrote *Animal Farm* to expose the myth of Soviet communism and to warn of how easily the ideals of socialism could be corrupted by totalitarian regimes. In the aftermath of the overthrow of the Russian czar in February 1917, control of the Russian government was seized by the Bolsheviks, the radical left wing of the Russian Social-Democratic Workers' Party, which renamed itself the Communist Party in 1918 and established the Union of Soviet Socialist Republics (USSR) four years later. The Bolshevik Revolution had been dedicated to abolishing the classism of imperial rule. It had promised to improve the standard of living of the Russian peasants and working class and to confer upon them localized power. Conditions for the common people, however, had steadily declined under the rule of Stalin. His plan to collectivize Russia's farms to finance an aggressive program of industrial development had resulted in the deaths of millions of peasants by slaughter or starvation. Political dissent of any kind was outlawed. It is estimated that roughly twenty million people were exiled to the forced labor camps known as the Gulag during a series of purges meant to eliminate traitors to the regime.

Despite the abundant evidence substantiating Orwell's distrust of Stalinism, many Western intellectuals were inclined to overlook Stalin's transgressions because of the Soviet army's successes at repelling the Nazi forces of German dictator Adolf Hitler during World War II. At war's end, however, as Stalin's armies marched into Eastern Europe, Western attitudes toward the Soviet Union turned hostile. "Ironically," John Rodden writes in his introduction to *Understanding Animal Farm* (1999), "*Animal Farm* now seemed to be a prophetic book, ahead of its time. Orwell seemed to have predicted the collapse of Allied alliance and unveiled the Soviet dictatorship as the new enemy of Western democracy."

Orwell felt compelled to transmit his moral warnings about the abuses of power in the guise of an innocent animal story because he believed, as he once wrote, "This business of making people *conscious* of what is happening outside their own small circle is one of the major problems of our time, and a new literary technique will have to be evolved to meet it." Orwell set up the structure of *Animal Farm* to blend two genres popular since classical times: the allegory, a figurative treatment of one idea under the semblance of another, and the beast fable, a story that uses the misadventures of animals to expose the vices and follies of humans. *Animal Farm* is frequently compared to the masterpieces of political allegory of the eighteenth century—principally French writer Voltaire's *Candide* (1759) and Anglo-Irish author Jonathan Swift's *Gulliver's Travels* (1726)—for its dramatization of the corruption of utopian ideals. As a classic of anti-Soviet propaganda, critics cite as its nearest rivals Orwell's own dystopian novel of pervasive government surveillance, *1984* (1949), and Hungarian-born novelist Arthur Koestler's powerful symbolic critique of Stalin's growing paranoia and the brutality of his purges, *Darkness at Noon* (1940).

+ *Key Facts*

Time Period:
Mid-20th Century

Genre:
Novel

Events:
Rise of Stalinism

Nationality:
English

ORWELL IN THE SPANISH CIVIL WAR

When the Spanish Civil War broke out in 1936, Orwell volunteered to fight for the Republican army against the Nationalists of General Francisco Franco. By the middle of 1937, however, Orwell had grown disillusioned by the infighting among the anarchist and communist factions of the Republican forces. In *Homage to Catalonia* (1938), his firsthand account of the war, he bitterly complained that the workers' revolution had been betrayed by the Soviet-backed Communist Party of Spain (PCE), which had arrested and imprisoned or executed many of the militia of his own anarchist group, representatives of the Workers' Party of Marxist Unification. Orwell and his wife, who was working in Barcelona, barely escaped the purges by the PCE.

Biographers often trace the origins of *Animal Farm* to Orwell's inside knowledge of communist maneuverings in Spain, which to his mind were not geared to liberating Spain from Franco but to spreading and consolidating Stalin's power by any means. Orwell's essay "Why I Write" (1946) exists as confirmation: "The Spanish war and other events in 1936-7 turned the scale and thereafter I knew where I stood. Every line of serious work that I have written since 1936 has been written, directly or indirectly, against totalitarianism and for democratic socialism, as I understand it."

The anti-Soviet propaganda of *Animal Farm* has been frequently invoked on the world political scene, especially in the period preceding the official dissolution of the USSR in 1991. In the early years of the Cold War, *Animal Farm* circulated in Eastern Europe, the Ukraine, Korea, and elsewhere in underground editions sponsored by the U.S. Central Intelligence Agency (CIA). It became required reading in high schools throughout the United States and Britain, and in 1954, at the height of the hearings conducted by U.S. senator Joseph McCarthy to root out communist sympathizers, the CIA released an animated film version of *Animal Farm* for classroom distribution. In 1981 *Animal Farm* was serialized in the Nicaraguan newspaper *La prensa* to show how the Soviet-backed Sandinista revolution had been corrupted. The book was banned in the Soviet Union until the late 1980s; its first official publication there was considered a testament to the credibility of the cultural thaw known as glasnost. Even as the Cold War recedes in memory, scholars insist on the timeless relevance of *Animal Farm*'s themes of justice, equality, freedom, and power. New editions, authoritative study guides, and critical companions to the book are regularly released. A made-for-television version was released in 1999, and stage productions continue to tour worldwide.

THEMES AND STYLE

Animal Farm satirizes the failure of the Bolshevik Revolution to create a democratic socialist state while warning that all revolutions degenerate into totalitarianism through the abuses of power. For purposes of allegory, Orwell wrote his plot so that it is synonymous with the aftermath of the revolution. At the same time, he used the form of the beast fable as a general strategy of personification, drawing on conventional identifications of animals with certain human characteristics. The setting of the narrative, Manor Farm, owned by the drunken and abusive Mr. Jones, is the equivalent of prerevolutionary Russia under the leadership of the czar. In an incident meant to parallel the revolutionary days of 1917, the animals revolt and run Mr. Jones off his land. The animals intend to create a utopian community based on a principle of equality. But, in illustration of one of the book's major themes—the societal tendency to class stratification—the pigs (the Bolshevik elites), under the leadership of the tyrannical boar Napoleon (Stalin), establish control over the farm. Claiming superior intellect, the greedy and nonproductive pigs manipulate the simpler animals (the working class) into performing all the useful labor on very low rations. Those who do not conform run afoul of Napoleon's dogs (Stalin's secret police), and some are publicly executed (Stalin's purges). The loyal and hardworking cart horse, Boxer, is a powerful reminder of the dangers of blind submission to authority, another prominent theme. Boxer's naive belief in the good intentions of the ruling pigs—his mantra is "Napoleon is always right"—consigns him to suffer the full extent of their tyranny. By the end of the story, the pigs are walking upright and wearing Mr. Jones's clothing. They play poker and drink to excess with humans while the rest of the animals remain as disenfranchised and oppressed as they were before the revolt.

In addition to criticizing dictators for using violence to control their subjects, Orwell targets the use of propaganda as an instrument of terror in totalitarian regimes. The fat porker Squealer, Napoleon's minister of propaganda, manipulates language to excuse all the pigs' actions. A "brilliant talker" who "could turn black into white," Squealer twists the rules of logic and confuses the less intelligent animals with his eloquence. He employs impenetrable statistical jargon to convince them that their lives are improving, brainwashes them with the repetition of catchy slogans, and threatens the return of Mr. Jones if they do not comply with his demands. In one of his most devious moves, he secretly changes the rules of the farm, the Seven Commandments, to benefit the pigs, most famously altering Commandment 7—"All animals are equal"—to read, "All animals are equal, but some animals are more equal than others."

Orwell's attack on propaganda is part of his larger strategy to examine the relationship between language and truth. He uses the simple language and form of the children's fairy tale to draw readers into a fantasy realm more emotionally compelling than the real world. At the same time, the symbolic

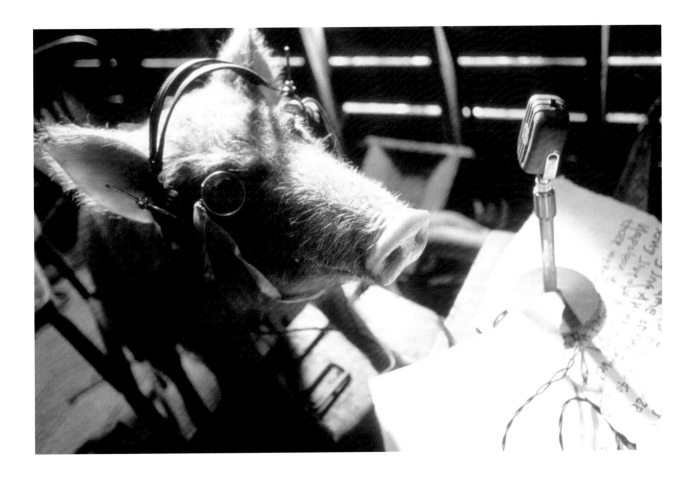

import of his allegory depends to a great extent on dramatic irony. Orwell employs a naive, third-person narrator who recounts the tale with precision and directness, refraining from commenting on the action. The tension created between what the narrator knows but refuses to tell and what the reader recognizes as the truth sets Orwell's political message more clearly in relief.

CRITICAL DISCUSSION

When *Animal Farm* was first published, critics were unanimous in their praise of the book's seamless fusion of ideological and artistic purpose. The response to its political message was divided, however, with critics on the far right arguing that Orwell should have been even harsher in his criticisms of Stalin and critics on the far left suggesting that Orwell was a disillusioned revolutionary overly pessimistic about the future of socialism. Among the first critics to attach significance to *Animal Farm* beyond its immediate historical context was Arthur M. Schlesinger Jr. In the *New York Times Book Review* for August 25, 1946, Schlesinger notes:

> Orwell writes absolutely without coyness or whimsicality and with such gravity and charm that 'Animal Farm' becomes an independent

creation, standing quite apart from the object of its comment. The qualities of pathos in the tale of the betrayal of the animals—in the account, for example, of Boxer, the faithful horse—would compel the attention of persons who never heard of the Russian Revolution.

Orwell's earliest American critics, many of them less familiar with his socialist politics than their British counterparts, tended to read *Animal Farm* exclusively as a critique of Russian communism, failing to grasp—or deliberately ignoring—its attack on capitalism. The subsequent widespread dissemination of *Animal Farm* in the mass media in support of specific political agendas, both conservative and radical, contributed to some general misunderstandings about the work. *Animal Farm* has even been subjected to revisionism. The 1954 CIA-sponsored film version, for example, altered the ending so that the pigs are overthrown by the other animals, thus making the forces of anticommunism appear stronger.

The fiftieth anniversary of the publication of *Animal Farm* was recognized with a new illustrated edition and an outpouring of critical commentary. It is considered a credit to Orwell's literary imagination that the work supports analysis on a variety of different levels. Among the most frequently studied issues related to the text are its literary influences, biographical and historical context, pedagogical impact, persuasive strategies, interpretation of Marxist economics, and thematic links to *1984*. A number of scholars have argued that, although Orwell failed to predict the triumph of free-market capitalism, his lessons about safeguarding freedoms are even more applicable in the twenty-first century than they were in his own time. In an introduction to a new edition of *Animal Farm* published in 2000, Malcolm Bradbury defines its legacy: "[We] have all lived or risk living somewhere close to Animal Farm…. It is one of the great modern political allegories, and the story it tells, of innocent and necessary revolution turning into dictatorship and betrayal, is not just a striking piece of political intelligence but a fundamental modern myth."

BIBLIOGRAPHY

Sources

Bradbury, Malcolm. Introduction. *Animal Farm.* By George Orwell. London: Penguin, 2000. v–xv. Print.

Orwell, George. *Animal Farm.* London: Penguin, 2000. Print.

Rodden, John. Introduction. *Understanding Animal Farm: A Student Casebook to Issues, Sources, and Historical Documents.* Ed. John Rodden. Westport, CN: Greenwood, 1999. xvii–xxvi. Print.

Schlesinger, Arthur M., Jr. Rev. of *Animal Farm,* by George Orwell. *New York Times Book Review* 25 Aug. 1946. Print.

Further Reading

Bloom, Harold, ed. *Modern Critical Interpretations: Animal Farm.* Philadelphia: Chelsea House, 1999. Print.

Hitchens, Christopher. *Why Orwell Matters.* New York: Basic, 2002. Print.

Orwell, George. "Why I Write." *George-Orwell.org.* Web. 11 June 2012.

Rai, Alok. *Orwell and the Politics of Despair.* Cambridge: Cambridge UP, 1988. Print.

Rodden, John. *The Politics of Literary Reputation: The Making and Claiming of "St. George" Orwell.* New York: Oxford UP, 1989. Print.

Media Adaptations

Animal Farm. Dir. Joy Batchelor and John Halas. Perf. Gordon Heath and Maurice Denham. Halas and Batchelor Cartoon Films, 1954. Film.

Animal Farm. Dir John Stephenson. Perf. Pete Postlethwaite and voice of Kelsey Grammer. Hallmark Entertainment and TNT, 1999. TV Movie.

Janet Mullane

BEWARE THE CAT

William Baldwin

OVERVIEW

Beware the Cat is an anti-Catholic satire written in support of the English Reformation by William Baldwin in 1553 but not printed until 1570. A series of interconnected stories about a kingdom of talking cats that takes the form of a debate about the ability of animals to reason, *Beware the Cat* stands apart from other anti-Catholic satires—indeed, from other fiction—of its day by virtue of its novelistic structure and sophisticated narrative strategy. Baldwin employs a frame narrator, identified as G. B., to shed doubt on the veracity of the fantastic tales introduced by pedantic scholar Master Gregory Streamer, thereby mounting an attack on the superstition of Catholic observance.

Composed toward the end of the reign of the boy king Edward VI (1547–53), the first English monarch raised as a Protestant, *Beware the Cat* was suppressed with Edward's death in July 1553 and the accession of Catholic Queen Mary, known later as "Bloody Mary" for her persecution of Protestants. *Beware the Cat* was finally published in 1570, several years after Baldwin's death (c. 1563). A printer, an editor, a translator, a philosopher, a dramatist, a poet, and a satirist, Baldwin was recognized by his contemporaries as a man of great learning. However, with the exception of *Mirror for Magistrates* (1559), an anthology of didactic verse stories, all of Baldwin's writings fell into obscurity by the eighteenth century. Through the efforts of William A. Ringler and other scholars in the late twentieth century, the reputation of *Beware the Cat* was resurrected. It is now considered Baldwin's most important work and is the earliest-known original piece of long prose fiction in the English language. It is relevant to modern audiences as a seminal text in the development of the novel and as a reflection of Renaissance ideas about the production and transmission of knowledge.

HISTORICAL AND LITERARY CONTEXT

The English Reformation began during the reign of Henry VIII (1509–47) and was part of the Protestant Reformation inaugurated by German priest Martin Luther. For Henry VIII this was more a political dispute than a religious one: he wanted the Catholic Church to dissolve his marriage to Catherine of Aragon. Pope Clement VII refused to grant Henry's request for annulment or divorce, so the king renounced Catholicism and removed England from papal control. Henry was succeeded by his nine-year-old son, Edward VI, whose brief reign saw sweeping reforms requiring the abolition of all observances based solely on church tradition and not found in the text of the Bible, including veneration of idols, granting of indulgences, transubstantiation of the mass, and other practices. Edward VI's successor, Queen Mary, restored Catholicism as England's national religion, but the next monarch, Elizabeth I (1558–1603), reinstated the Anglican Church, or Church of England.

The publication history of *Beware the Cat* is tied to the fortunes of Edward Whitchurch's London printing house. Although biographical information on Baldwin is scant, it is known that he was an assistant to Whitchurch for six years, between 1547 and 1553, and that Whitchurch was also dissatisfied with Catholicism. With King's Printer Richard Grafton, Whitchurch published books in support of the Reformation—bibles, primers, common prayer books—as well as several texts by Baldwin. Whitchurch ceased printing operations and went into hiding on the accession of Queen Mary, whose prohibition against anti-Catholic propaganda barred the immediate publication of *Beware the Cat.* The book was not published until 1570, when it appeared in two separate editions.

In his 1981 essay in *Huntington Library Quarterly,* Critic Steven Gresham notes that *Beware the Cat* is typical of Protestant reform literature of its day in its adoption of the "commonplace strands of anti-Catholic satire: allusions to the cruelty and gluttony of the pope; attacks on transubstantiation; similarities drawn between witchcraft and unwritten verities; and vignettes of superstitious priests." *Beware the Cat* also followed conventions in its inclusion of several genres, including proverbs, hymns, letters, and beast fables. The work does, however, place an unusual level of demand upon the reader to discriminate between the judgments of Streamer and those of G. B. (a stand-in for Baldwin, who was sometimes referred to by the first name Gulielmus). In his review of the work in *Criticism,* Terence N. Bowers observes, "The book is one of a number of anti-Catholic satires that appeared

❖ *Key Facts*

Time Period:
Mid-16th Century

Genre:
Satire

Events:
English Reformation; reign of Edward VI

Nationality:
English

VAGARIES OF THE MONARCHY

Beginning in the late 1540s, William Baldwin was a printer's assistant in London to Edward Whitchurch, who, along with John Day, Richard Grafton, and William Seres, was among the most prominent publishers of anti-Catholic propaganda during the reign of Protestant King Edward VI. Whitchurch, fearing reprisals upon the accession of Catholic Queen Mary to the throne in 1553, went into hiding, but not before deeding the contents of his printing establishment—which he later recovered through an intermediary—to two stationers. Day, Seres, and Grafton, by contrast, were briefly imprisoned by Queen Mary for their printing activities in 1554.

In Whitchurch's absence, his offices were taken over by Catholic printer John Wayland. Baldwin, a violent opponent of Catholicism, was politically astute enough to hide his Protestant beliefs during the reign of Mary. He ceased publishing original works but continued to work as a printer, first for Wayland and then for Thomas Marshe, whose offices were raided by Queen Mary's government in 1558 under suspicion of heresy. Upon the accession of Elizabeth I that same year, Baldwin was free to publish again. He was ordained a deacon late in life and is thought to have died in 1563, most likely from the plague.

during Edward VI's outspokenly Protestant reign; but unlike the majority, which were crude pieces of invective, *Beware the Cat* makes a far more sophisticated critique."

In 1988 Ringler and Michael Flachmann published a modern edition of *Beware the Cat* that helped convince literary scholars of the work's undeserved obscurity. Ringler and Flachmann detail Baldwin's many narrative innovations, arguing that *Beware the Cat* deserves recognition as the first English novel, a distinction that had long been reserved for George Gascoigne's *The Adventures of Master F. J.* (1573). While the genre debate continues, *Beware the Cat* is widely discussed as a work of historical and aesthetic importance in the transition from oral to print culture.

THEMES AND STYLE

Beware the Cat satirizes the superstitions underlying Catholic belief. However, the narrative complexity of the work creates subtexts that are broader in implication about the production and transmission of knowledge. The narrative begins with a December 1552 conversation among theater people about a production of Aesop's fables. Among the group are G. B. and Streamer, who disagree on the ability of animals to reason. G. B. is skeptical, citing learned philosophers. Streamer references his own experience to argue the contrary along with stories he has heard and a description of his success mixing a potion that enables him to understand the voices of cats. *Beware*

the Cat consists of G. B.'s transcription of Streamer's oration, framed by G. B.'s commentary. According to Arthur F. Kinney in his essay in *Humanist Poetics* (1986), "The complicated game of narrative wordplay and wit takes us through one story into the next to discover finally that to believe Streamer means to believe in all the legendary traditions claimed by the Roman Church—and just those traditions opposed by the Protestants under Edward VI." The theme of superstition is more overarching, as Bowers explains: "Embodied in [the] rather ridiculous question about animals ... is an important debate concerning different notions about the ground and nature of our knowledge—one sense-based, the other text-based.... A stable society, *Beware the Cat* implies, is one composed of a literate populace whose knowledge comes not from what it hears or 'experiences,' but from what it reads."

Baldwin employs diverse rhetorical strategies that confuse truth and reality and require his audience to reconcile opposing meanings. He populates the story with real people, including himself and his writing collaborator Master Ferrers, but disrupts the verisimilitude by introducing the fictional Streamer. The miraculous stories of cats, including a section devoted to Mouse-slayer, who is brought to court for cat infractions, are laced with references to Catholic observances, calling into question the foundations of Catholicism. The tales are glossed by the commentary of G. B., who destabilizes his own objectivity by admitting that he has ordered the narrative and annotated Streamer's oration. Adding to the confusion is the embedded character of Streamer's anecdotes. The stories told second- and third-hand emphasize the speculative quality of the Catholic faith and the unreliability of its oral transmission.

The language of *Beware the Cat* draws the audience's attention away from what is being said to how it is being said. Baldwin gives the tales an air of plausibility but repeatedly collapses their logic, often through the marginal notes, which are by turns evaluative, parodic, irrelevant, or misrepresentative, as when Streamer reports that a boy spit out his potion, calling it "a cat's turd," and G. B. remarks, "Strange things are delectable." Further, Streamer's convoluted, pompous speech is nearly incomprehensible, and his solemn retelling of mixing the potion of kite's heart and hare's kidneys under auspicious astrological conditions is full of comical inaccuracy, revealing that he in fact concocted a serum meant to aid in the understanding of birds, not cats.

CRITICAL DISCUSSION

The reception of *Beware the Cat* is little documented. The text was reissued in 1584 and 1652, and Ringler records that it was popular enough among Elizabethans to have been used as a reference for William

Shakespeare and Thomas Nashe. The reasons for its subsequent neglect remain undetermined, but critics speculate that the significance of Baldwin's complex rhetorical framework may have been lost on an audience relatively unfamiliar with printed texts. According to Ringler and Flachmann, the work had been so erased from literary memory by the nineteenth century that "no history of the novel, from John C. Dunlop in 1814 to Paul Salzman in 1985, pays any attention to Baldwin."

Beware the Cat is today considered significant for its style and content. As scholar Renate Leder defines its importance, "The pungent satire of Catholic superstition echoes contemporary positions propagated in Protestant polemics, while its intricate narrative structure and textual challenges to the authorial position serve as generic markers of the novel." Modern critics have focused on Baldwin's complex narrative strategy as it reflects his understanding of the possibilities of the print culture to manipulate reader response.

Scholars frequently note that Baldwin was in the vanguard of those attempting to shape a literate Protestant culture. According to Bowers, "Although readers may at first find this text, with its dizzying array of fantastic stories, to be incomprehensible and uncontrolled … it is a highly wrought satire that playfully explores the psychological and social effects of textual and oral communication and the potential role of the printed book in society." Given that Baldwin exposes the unreliability of the oral transmission of knowledge associated with Catholicism to promote the text-based Protestant epistemology, critics have frequently discussed *Beware the Cat* in conjunction with Renaissance humanist ideals of critical thinking. In her 1989 piece in *Style,* Nancy C. Gutierrez explains: "According to Renaissance critical theory, a text was not merely a product crafted by the author, but an experience—the experience of reading—through which process the reader would be persuaded to ethical activity that would irrevocably change his moral life." As numerous analyses of *Beware the Cat*'s complex rhetorical structure illustrate, the process of reading, as construed by Protestantism, placed high expectations on the reader to distinguish the valid from the invalid. For this reason, *Beware the Cat* has been judged a very early contribution to the field of reader-response theory, which regards the reader's interpretive practice as vital to the meaning of a text.

BIBLIOGRAPHY

Sources

Baldwin, William. *"Beware the Cat": The First English Novel.* Ed. William A. Ringler and Michael Flachmann. San Marino: Huntington Library, 1988. Print.

Bowers, Terence M. "The Production and Communication of Knowledge in William Baldwin's *Beware the Cat*: Toward a Typographic Culture." *Criticism* 33.1 (1991): 1–29. *Literature Resources from Gale.* Web. 5 Aug. 2012.

Gresham, Stephen. "William Baldwin: Literary Voice of the Reign of Edward VI." *Huntington Library Quarterly* 44.2 (1981): 101–16. *JSTOR.* Web. 9 Aug. 2012.

Gutierrez, Nancy C. *"Beware the Cat*: Mimesis in a Skin of Oratory." *Style* 1 (1989): 49–69. *Literature Resources from Gale.* Web. 4 Sept. 2012.

Kinney, Arthur F. *"Aliquid Salis*: Narrative Wordplay and Gascoigne's *Adventures of Master F. J." Humanist Poetics: Thought, Rhetoric, and Fiction in Sixteenth-Century England.* Amherst: U of Massachusetts P, 1986. 89–120. Print.

Leder, Renate. "Fanciful Fictions: The Fashioning of Authorship in Two Elizabethan Novels." MA thesis. U of Utrecht. 2007. Web. 5 Aug. 2012.

Ringler, William A. *"Beware the Cat* and the Beginnings of English Fiction." *Novel: A Forum on Fiction* 12.2 (1979): 113–26. *Literature Resources from Gale.* Web. 5 Aug. 2012.

English Queen Mary I in a 1554 painting by Hans Eworth. Mary's Catholicism meant that William Baldwin's anti-Catholic novel *Beware the Cat* was not published until after her reign. QUEEN MARY I, 1554 (OIL ON OAK), EWORTH OR EWOUTSZ, HANS (FL.1520–74)/ SOCIETY OF ANTIQUARIES OF LONDON, UK/THE BRIDGEMAN ART LIBRARY.

Further Reading

Bonahue, Edward T., Jr. "'I Know the Place and the Persons': The Play of Textual Frames in Baldwin's *Beware the Cat.*" *Studies in Philology* 91.3 (1994): 283–300. *Literature Resources from Gale.* Web. 9 Aug. 2012.

Klawitter, George. "Hearing People Talk Naturally in Elizabethan Prose Fiction." *A Search for Meaning: Critical Essays on Early Modern Literature.* Ed. Paula Harms Payne. New York: Peter Lang, 2004. 7–22. Print.

Lucas, Scott C. *"A Mirror for Magistrates" and the Politics of the English Reformation.* Amherst: U of Massachusetts P, 2009. Print.

Masten, Robert. "'The Cat Got Your Tongue': Pseudo-Translation, Conversion, and Control in William Baldwin's *Beware the Cat.*" *Translation and Literature* 8.1 (1999): 3–27. *JSTOR.* Web. 9 Aug. 2012.

Moore, Steven. "The Renaissance Novel: English." *The Novel: An Alternative History, Beginnings to 1600.* New York: Continuum, 2010. 343–90. Print.

Smith, Bruce R. "Mapping the Field." *The Acoustic World of Early Modern England.* Chicago: U of Chicago P, 1999. 30–48. Print.

Janet Mullane

THE CANTOS

Ezra Pound

OVERVIEW

The Cantos, a multivolume work of lyric poetry published in several installments between 1925 and 1969, is widely regarded as the magnum opus of American poet Ezra Pound. The poems take up a sweeping variety of topics, articulating Pound's political and aesthetic views through a pageant-like array of styles and personae. *The Cantos* draws on a remarkable range of earlier texts, from classical Greek poetry to the writings of U.S. president John Adams; in doing so, the poems establish a sense of continuity between the heroic figures of ancient myth and the Renaissance and Enlightenment thinkers Pound admired. *The Cantos* serves as the formal expression of Pound's desire to create a "poem to include history"; more infamously, the poems use this same network of cultural references to justify, even to celebrate, Pound's Fascist ideology and strident anti-Semitism. The poet frequently arranged historical leaders into two camps: a noble, judicious party that he gradually identified with the Fascist cause, and a cravenly materialistic party that he would identify with Allied leaders and the Jewish conspiracy he presumed to have supported them.

The most forceful reaction to Pound's work came with the 1948 publication of *The Pisan Cantos,* which despite its overt declarations of racism was awarded the 1949 Bollingen Prize by the United States Library of Congress. The award committee's decision sparked a debate, still ongoing, about the limits of craft and technique in establishing the worth of a literary work. Today *The Cantos* is mainly the province of specialists and literary historians due to the poems' multilingual content and frequent abstruse allusions. *The Cantos* remains significant, however, for its tremendous influence on many major poets of the late twentieth century. The poems' formal iconoclasm, rich and fragmentary network of allusions, and cross-cultural interpretation of history have informed the work of such writers as Galway Kinnell and Charles Olson.

HISTORICAL AND LITERARY CONTEXT

Pound's *Cantos* "includes" (to use the poet's term) a view of history in which, roughly speaking, the interests of judicious rulership have been continually opposed to those of reckless material gain. This conflict is cyclical: Pound perceived the ills of financial speculation in periods as diverse as fifteenth-century

Siena (Cantos 42–44), eighteenth-century London (40), and medieval China (55). Furthermore, Pound was a prolific translator of Western classics, which he often saw as foreshadowing his own political views. The poet's opposition to the "unnatural increase" of interest-based lending may be traced as far back as the *Politics* of Aristotle. Finally, Pound's own experience of World War I, in which many of his friends and literary associates were killed, led to an entrenched suspicion of the motives underlying U.S. and British national politics.

Few passages in Pound's work speak more directly to a historical moment than the "Italian Cantos" (72–73), written during World War II. At the time of their composition, Pound had spent a period of three years delivering propagandistic speeches on behalf of the Italian Fascist Party. These speeches, in addition to rallying support for Fascism, denounced U.S. president Franklin D. Roosevelt and UK prime minister Winston Churchill. Moreover, they defamed groups that Pound saw as opposed to the Fascist cause, including Jews and communists. The "Italian Cantos" furthered this project by couching many of the same insults in historical or literary terms. Thus the conflict between Fascists and communists is reflected in the rivalry between two medieval Italian factions: the (for Pound) noble Ghibellines and the perfidious Guelphs (72). He would reprise these charges in English in *The Pisan Cantos,* wherein he mourned the Axis dead and denounced the Rothschild family in frankly racist terms (Canto 74).

Literary antecedents of Pound's work are numerous, but a major point of reference may be found in the *Divine Comedy* of Dante Alighieri. Pound explicitly followed the Dantean model in the "Italian Cantos," which adopt the Italian language and partially share Dante's rhyme scheme. More significantly, these cantos inherit Dante's technique of invoking the ghosts of history to serve as spokesmen for the poet's political views. Pound cast the recently deceased Fascist intellectual F. T. Marinetti as a heroic spirit who wished to forgo paradise in order to continue fighting; he also rehabilitated the figure of Ezzelino da Romano, an Italian warlord whom Dante had consigned to hell but whom Pound considered a national icon. The utility of Pound's laudatory portraits of Fascist and "proto-Fascist" figures was quickly recognized; portions of

✣ Key Facts

Time Period:
Early to Mid-20th Century

Genre:
Poetry

Events:
World War II; rise of fascism in Italy

Nationality:
American

RADIO ROME AND THE COMPOSITION OF *THE PISAN CANTOS*

The Pisan Cantos are notorious not only as one of the great powder kegs of literary politics but also for the unusual circumstances of their production. During World War II, Pound had declared himself in favor of the Fascist party in Italy, expressing his support in a series of inflammatory speeches for Radio Rome. These speeches, whose treasonable nature remains debatable, derided the American cause and made veiled calls for the assassination of President Franklin D. Roosevelt. Consequently, when American forces occupied Italy in 1945, Pound was arrested and interned at an American camp north of Pisa. It was during this confinement that Pound, sometimes writing from an open-air steel cage, produced his draft of *The Pisan Cantos*. In 1946 Pound was declared unfit to stand trial and relocated to a federal psychiatric hospital, where he completed and published *The Pisan Cantos* and two subsequent volumes.

For nearly all students of Pound, the portion of his career represented by the Radio Rome speeches constitutes a discomfiting "suspension" of his poetic work. Some historians, however, including Conrad Rushing, maintain that the treasonable potential of Pound's speeches has been overstated; had the poet been brought to trial, Rushing speculates, Pound would likely have received a light sentence—or none at all.

Canto 72, along with all of Canto 73, appeared in early 1945 issues of *La Marina Repubblicana*, a Fascist periodical, as what Patricia Cockram calls "parable[s] for the cause."

The influence of *The Cantos* on subsequent literature has been profound, especially among American poets of the post-World War II generation. In his 1992 study *The ABC of Influence: Ezra Pound and the Remaking of American Poetic Tradition*, Christopher Beach notes that during Pound's lifetime, many poets (among them Robert Creeley, Denise Levertov, and Allen Ginsberg) "recurred to Pound in forming their sense of poetic inheritance and in establishing their own poetic theories." Many of these figures, individually or as part of the Black Mountain School, gave rise to an influential aesthetic heritage of their own.

THEMES AND STYLE

Critics have been frustrated in their attempts to detect an overall theme, plot, or other structure that could satisfactorily include all 120 cantos. Pound's technique is rather to interweave a series of political, aesthetic, and historical preoccupations, ranging from principles of good governance to laments at the abuse of language by the press. An additional challenge for Pound scholars is the fact that many of the thematic traits in Pound's work are ideological—and they represent an ideology singularly unattractive to most readers. For instance, Pound's sustained opposition to usury not infrequently devolves into a set of broadly anti-Semitic accusations. Prominent among these, to the consternation of critics, is the recurring allegation that a Jewish conspiracy has engineered the system of financial speculation for their own profit.

As might be expected of a work almost a half century in the making, *The Cantos* displays a gamut of approaches to match a range of sometimes self-contradictory viewpoints. Moreover, it is not always clear that Pound aims to convince the reader of anything: at times the speaker appears utterly uninterested in the reader's acceptance, or even comprehension, of what is being said. A favored technique is the culling of quotations from historic personages who seem to agree with Pound's claims. For instance, Pound locates a precedent for his poetic motto "Make it new!" in a phrase supposedly engraved on the bathtub of Shang dynasty emperor Ch'eng T'ang (Canto 53). Earlier, the "Adams Cantos" (62–71), largely drawn from the writings of American founding father John Adams, portray a leader of great intellectual integrity and, as if incidentally, with more than a passing resemblance to Benito Mussolini (Canto 38). Pound often extends this appeal to authority by contrasting well-rounded leaders (e.g., Thomas Jefferson) with those, such as the Medicis, who are callously concerned with monetary riches (Canto 21).

The speaker of Pound's poems often adopts recognizable styles that both enhance the authority of the speaker and satirize the source of that authority. Canto 1 explicitly mimics both the plot and the cadence of Homer's *Odyssey* (Book 11), with appeals to the Greek gods and the prophet Tiresias. Later, in Canto 45, the speaker embarks on an extended Biblical declamation against usury, a practice which "blunteth the needle in the maid's hand / and stoppeth the spinner's cunning." He also frequently shifts among languages, sometimes making a sustained digression beyond the confines of English. The so-called China Cantos (52-61), for example, often juxtapose untranslated Chinese characters with English text; Cantos 72 and 73 are written entirely in Italian. With these gestures, the speaker aims to establish both the universality of the issues he addresses and his cultural authority to address them.

CRITICAL DISCUSSION

The Pisan Cantos (1948) served to galvanize critical opinions surrounding Pound's work as a whole. Controversy arising from the 1949 Bollingen Prize decision gripped the American literary press for much of the following year. The poems contained some frankly racist passages but, more troubling for postwar Americans, they also, as Ronald Bush notes, "lamented the passing of fascist and Nazi collaborators." Moreover, the poet's character became the target of attacks, as he had been arraigned for treason, only to escape on an insanity defense. Even as the furor over the award died down, *The Pisan Cantos* were seen to raise disturbing issues that would persist well beyond their immediate political context. William Barrett, writing in 1949 at the height of the controversy, posed the essential question in this way: "How far is it possible, in a lyric poem, for technical embellishment to transform vicious and ugly matter into beautiful poetry?"

In the wake of the *Pisan Cantos* controversy, the question of whether and to what extent *The Cantos* in general were "Fascist" documents vexed Pound studies for decades. As late as 1978, John Lauber deemed the entire suite of *Cantos* a "Fascist epic" and pointed to the catalog of "enemies of civilization" already in progress in Pound's early work (Cantos 14-16). A year later, however, David Murray directly contested this judgment, claiming that Lauber had merely provided a "detailed recital of Fascist elements" rather than any evidence that the poems represented a coherent ideology. Debates of this nature continued in subsequent years. Andrew Parker, writing in 1982–83, identified Pound as "a persistently embarrassing problem for the institution of literary criticism" and called for critical assessments of Pound that accounted for both his poetics and his ideology.

Criticism since the 1980s has, in fact, challenged the assumption that Pound's work, even in the infamous *Pisan Cantos,* espoused a fixed ideological position, "Fascist" or otherwise. Ronald Bush, writing in 1995, declared that the "protracted, complex, and fractured process" attested by Pound's manuscripts suggested that such a coherent framework might never be found, whatever propagandistic purpose individual cantos might serve. It is this view of *The Cantos*—as the fragmented chronicle of an individual mind at work, rather than a unified ideological tract—that has prevailed into the twenty-first century.

Ezra Pound photographed in the 1920s. COURTESY EVERETT COLLECTION.

BIBLIOGRAPHY

Sources

Barrett, William. "Comment: A Prize for Ezra Pound." *Partisan Review* 16.4 (1949): 344–47. Print.

Beach, Christopher. *The ABC of Influence: Ezra Pound and the Remaking of American Poetic Tradition.* Berkeley: U of California P, 1992. Print.

Bush, Ronald. "Modernism, Fascism, and the Composition of Ezra Pound's *Pisan Cantos.*" *Modernism/modernity* 2.3 (1995): 69–87. Print.

Cockram, Patricia. "Collapse and Recall: Ezra Pound's Italian Cantos." *Journal of Modern Literature* 23.3–4 (2000): 535–544. Print.

Lauber, John. "Pound's *Cantos*: A Fascist Epic." *Journal of American Studies* 12.1 (1978): 3–21. Print.

Murray, David. "A Reply to John Lauber's 'Pound's *Cantos*: A Fascist Epic.'" *Journal of American Studies* 13.1 (1979): 109–13. Print.

Parker, Andrew. "Ezra Pound and the 'Economy' of Anti-Semitism." *boundary 2* 11.1–2 (1982–83): 103–28. Print.

Further Reading

Doob, Leonard W., ed. *"Ezra Pound Speaking": Radio Speeches of World War II.* Westport, CT: Greenwood P, 1978. Print.

Cookson, William. *A Guide to the "Cantos" of Ezra Pound.* Rev. and expanded. New York: Persea, 2001. Print.

Heyman, Clemens David. *Ezra Pound: The Last Rower.* New York: Viking, 1976. Print.

Kappel, Andrew. "The Reading and Writing of a Modern *Paradiso*: Ezra Pound and the Books of Paradise." *Twentieth Century Literature* 27.3 (1981): 223–46. Print.

Kenner, Hugh. *The Pound Era.* Berkeley: U of California P, 1973. Print.

McGann, Jerome. "The *Cantos* of Ezra Pound: The Truth in Contradiction." *Critical Inquiry* 15.1 (1988): 1–25. Print.

Pearlman, Daniel. "The Anti-Semitism of Ezra Pound." *Contemporary Literature* 22.1 (1981): 104–15. Print.

Stoicheff, Peter. *The Hall of Mirrors: "Drafts & Fragments" and the End of Ezra Pound's "Cantos."* Ann Arbor: U of Michigan P, 1995. Print.

Media Adaptation

Pound, Ezra. *Ezra Pound Reads His Cantos.* New York, N.Y.: CMS Records, Inc., 1971. DVD.

Michael Hartwell

THE CLANSMAN

An Historical Romance of the Ku Klux Klan

Thomas Dixon Jr.

✤ *Key Facts*

Time Period:
Early 20th Century

Genre:
Novel

Events:
Reconstruction; second
wave of Ku Klux Klan
activity

Nationality:
American

OVERVIEW

Thomas Dixon Jr.'s 1905 novel *The Clansman: An Historical Romance of the Ku Klux Klan* is a work of propaganda that criticizes the role of radical Republicans in rebuilding the post-Civil War South, while romanticizing the Ku Klux Klan as the region's savior. The book chronicles the intersecting lives of the Stonemans and the Camerons, two families on opposite sides of the political divide. Austin Stoneman is a powerful northern politician bent on punishing the South. Richard Cameron is an upstanding southern doctor wrongly accused in the conspiracy to assassinate U.S. president Abraham Lincoln. The families are brought together when children Elsie Stoneman and Ben Cameron meet and fall in love and Elsie's brother Phil falls for Ben's sister. As the parallel romances unfold amid the social and political chaos of Reconstruction, Ben finds purpose in the Ku Klux Klan and oversees the killing of Gus, a former slave guilty of raping a white woman. Elsie comes to understand and appreciate the southern cause, and the novel ends with the couple poised for a future in which "Civilisation has been saved, and the South redeemed from shame."

The Clansman was an immediate, popular success, selling 40,000 copies in less than two weeks. Some commentators criticized Dixon for exploiting painful national wounds for personal gain. After the novel was adapted for the stage, it drew protest from African American communities around the country. Today the novel is best known though D. W. Griffith's 1915 film adaptation, *The Birth of a Nation,* and is regarded as a driving force behind the culturally prevalent stereotype of African American men as sexual predators.

HISTORICAL AND LITERARY CONTEXT

The Clansman draws on the history of the South in the aftermath of the Civil War (1861–1865). During Reconstruction (1865–1877) there was significant political debate over the direction that rebuilding should take. The Lincoln administration hoped to expedite the process by focusing on reconciliation, but radical Republicans feared that former Confederates would quickly return to power. Therefore, these Republicans sought a comprehensive approach to restructuring southern politics and institutions and wanted to offer freed slaves a quick path to enfranchisement. One of the most prominent of these Republicans was U.S. congressman Thaddeus Stevens, whom Dixon acknowledges as the model for Austin Stoneman.

When *The Clansman* was published in 1905, racial and regional tensions were high. However, the Ku Klux Klan, formed by Confederate army veterans in 1865, was losing influence. The book's publication helped to reignite interest in the group, though membership did not increase dramatically until after the release of *The Birth of a Nation* (1915), which gave rise to what is generally considered the second wave of Klan activity. Membership peaked in the mid-1920s, expanding significantly in the North and in the South. Ultimately, however, Dixon disagreed with the direction of the new Klan, and in a 1923 speech for the American Unity League at the Century Theatre in New York, he condemned the organization for moving away from the spirit of its founders and for embracing violence and anarchy.

The Clansman is part of a tradition of propagandistic fiction that examines antebellum slavery and racial conflict. Because of the growing popularity and respectability of the novel as a literary genre, such fiction provided an accessible and appealing means of disseminating political messages. Among the best-known works in this tradition is Harriet Beecher Stowe's 1852 antislavery novel *Uncle Tom's Cabin,* which is sometimes referred to as the antithesis of *The Clansman.* Dixon places *The Clansman* within the context of contemporary debates over race, explaining in his note to the reader that the book is "the second of a series of historical novels planned on the Race Conflict." The first volume, *The Leopard's Spots* (1902), chronicles the life of southerner Charlie Gaston during a period that spans the end of the Civil War and the rise of the Ku Klux Klan during the aftermath.

Following the success of *The Clansman*'s 1905 debut, Dixon adapted the work as a play, which debuted later that year and drew outrage and protest nearly everywhere it was performed. Dixon's sequel, *The Sins of the Father,* was published in 1912. Collectively, Dixon's works—while not well known to modern audiences—have had a substantive and lasting impact on American culture. Clare Eby suggests in a 2001 article in the *African American Review* that Richard Wright's novel

Native Son (1940), the story of a poor African American man tried and executed for the accidental killing of a white woman, may be read, in part, as a response to the stereotype of the African American as beast, which Dixon's work helped to create.

THEMES AND STYLE

The central theme of *The Clansman* is that the Ku Klux Klan is one of few forces of protection against the imminent threat that freed slaves pose to white southerners, the southern way of life, and the purity of the white race. The threat of African American violence is most clearly illustrated by the freed slave Gus, whose brutal, racialized rape of Ben's childhood sweetheart, Marion Lenoir ("the black claws of the beast sank into the soft white throat and she was still"), causes the young woman and her mother to commit suicide. Dixon depicts African Americans as animalistic—easily led but incapable of holding power without descending into corruption— while he lionizes Lincoln as a sympathetic figure who hoped to relocate African Americans and to preserve America as an Aryan country. He warns readers that radical Republicans' reckless advocacy of rights for freed slaves threatens the North as well as the South and that if freed slaves are given social and political equality, the country will become a debased "mulatto" nation.

As a work of propaganda, *The Clansman* succeeds by appealing to fear and uncertainty at a time when Americans were experiencing significant cultural, demographic, and political changes. Dixon uses a bifurcated rhetorical strategy to justify southern readers' fear and resentment of African Americans and to warn northern readers of the perils of integration. He describes an alleged situation in which "a Negro electorate controlled the city government, and a gang of drunken negroes, its sovereign citizens, paraded streets at night firing their muskets unchallenged and unmolested." He depicts African American legislators giving themselves pay increases to cover their gambling losses and laments that these criminals are already "booked for judges of the Supreme Court." By contrast, he paints the Ku Klux Klan as a force of protection and safety in a time of transition and fear and as an organization marked by tradition and procedure and steeped in the romance of the old South and of ancient Scotland.

Stylistically, *The Clansman* is notable for its attempt to realistically embody the Reconstruction-era South. In his note to the reader, Dixon explains that he has "sought to preserve in this romance both the letter and the spirit of this remarkable period." To this end, he provides numerous historical details, including references to songs commonly sung by soldiers during the Civil War, a depiction of the Lincoln assassination and its aftermath, and detailed descriptions of the disguises worn by Ku Klux Klan members. These embellishments add strength to the work as propaganda, suggesting that the author is equally meticulous in his description of the African Americans and Klan members of the period.

THE CLANSMAN AND THE BIRTH OF A NATION

Following the immense success of Thomas Dixon Jr.'s novels, American director D. W. Griffith gave the author a substantial sum for the film rights to *The Clansman*. Griffith's *The Birth of a Nation,* in which African American characters are played by white actors in blackface, premiered in February 1915. Although it received wide praise as an aesthetically innovative work that used its musical score to great advantage, the film immediately drew protests from the National Association for the Advancement of Colored People (NAACP), which worked to educate the public about the inaccuracies in Griffith's movie.

Dixon, who had befriended future U.S. president Woodrow Wilson while studying at Johns Hopkins University, persuaded Wilson to screen *The Birth of a Nation* at the White House for the president, members of his cabinet, and members of the Supreme Court. After Americans perceived that Wilson had sanctioned the film, Griffith's work quickly gained a wide audience. Millions of Americans are believed to have seen it in its first year of release, and by 1931 the film had earned $18 million, a nearly unparalleled accomplishment at the time. Controversy continued, however, as several cities banned showings. Today Griffith's film is considered one of the most controversial ever made and has been the subject of an extensive body of scholarship that far exceeds the criticism devoted to Dixon's novel.

CRITICAL DISCUSSION

An immediate success, *The Clansman* helped to reinvigorate interest in the Ku Klux Klan. The novel is generally credited as the original source of the burning cross imagery popularly associated with the modern Klan. In an article in *Cinema Journal,* Russell Merritt (1972) writes, "Dixon rode the back of current fears spawned by the large migration of southern Negros to northern cities, the waves of immigrants pouring in from Eastern Europe, and the abiding popularity of alarmist social theories." He suggests that Dixon was a consummate master of propaganda and that Dixon's vision of "Reconstruction became a testing ground to see what the Negro was really like when left to roam at large." Not all segments of society welcomed Dixon's work, particularly after it was adapted for the stage and became the subject of outrage and protest from African American communities in numerous cities.

As *The Birth of a Nation* became widely known for its racism, Dixon's novel fell into critical neglect. Scholars feared associating their name with the controversial text. When they did write about the novel, it was generally in relation to Griffith's better-known film. Beginning in the 1980s, however, a new body of criticism on *The Clansman* emerged. Since that time, critics have viewed Dixon's work through a wide range of critical lenses, including critical race theory and whiteness studies, cultural history, and film history and theory.

D.W.
GRIFFITH'S
- AMERICAN INSTITUTION -
THE BIRTH OF A NATION
"THE SUPREME PICTURE OF ALL TIME"
NEW YORK MAIL
MAY 2ᴺᴰ 1921

Poster for *The Birth of a Nation*, D. W. Griffith's 1915 film adaptation of *The Clansman*. EPOCH/THE KOBAL COLLECTION/ART RESOURCE, NY.

in Literature and Language examines the role of Lydia Brown, Austin Stoneman's mulatto housekeeper, suggesting that the novel's "racial and gender concerns converge" in this "tawny leopardess."

BIBLIOGRAPHY

Sources

Biggio, Rebecca Skidmore. "Violent Fraternities and White Reform: The Complementary Fictions of Albion Tourgée and Thomas Dixon." *Arizona Quarterly* 67.2 (2011): 73–100. Print.

Bynum, Tara. "'One Important Witness': Remembering Lydia Brown in Thomas Dixon's *The Clansman*." *Texas Studies in Literature and Language* 52.3 (2010): 247–65. Print.

Dixon, Thomas, Jr. *The Clansman: An Historical Romance of the Ku Klux Klan.* New York: Doubleday, Page & Co., 1905. Print.

Eby, Clare. "Slouching toward Beastliness: Richard Wright's Anatomy of Thomas Dixon." *African American Review* 35.3 (2001): 439–58. Print.

Magowan, Kim. "Coming between the 'Black Beast' and the White Virgin: The Pressures of Liminality in Thomas Dixon." *Studies in American Fiction* 27.1 (1999): 77–102. Print.

Merritt, Russell. "Dixon, Griffith, and the Southern Legend." *Cinema Journal* 12.1 (1972): 26–45. Print.

Ruiz-Velasco, Chris. "Order out of Chaos: Whiteness, White Supremacy, and Thomas Dixon, Jr." *College Literature* 34.4 (2007): 148–65. Print.

Further Reading

Davenport, F. Garvin. "Thomas Dixon's Mythology of Southern History." *Journal of Southern History* 36.3 (1970): 350–67. Print.

Dixon, Thomas, Jr. *The Leopard's Spots.* New York: Doubleday, Page & Co., 1902. Print.

Gillespie, Michele K., and Randal L. Hall, eds. *Thomas Dixon Jr. and the Birth of Modern America.* Baton Rouge: Louisiana State UP, 2006. Print.

Inscoe, John C. "*The Clansman* on Stage and Screen: North Carolina Reacts." *North Carolina Historical Review* 64.2 (1987): 139–61. Print.

Kinney, James. "The Rhetoric of Racism: Thomas Dixon and the 'Damned Black Beast.'" *American Literary Realism, 1870–1910* 15.2 (1982): 145–54. Print.

MacLean, Nancy. *Behind the Mask of Chivalry: The Making of the Second Ku Klux Klan.* New York: Oxford UP, 1994. Print.

Stokes, Melvin. *D. W. Griffith's* The Birth of a Nation: *A History of "The Most Controversial Motion Picture of All Time."* Oxford: Oxford UP, 2007. Print.

Thomas, Brook. "The Clansman's Race-Based Anti-Imperialist Imperialism." *Mississippi Quarterly* 62.1–2: 303–34. Print.

Media Adaptation

The Birth of a Nation. Dir. D. W. Griffith. Perf. Lillian Gish, Mae Marsh, and Henry B. Walthall. Epoch Producing Corporation, 1915. Film.

Greta Gard

One strand of critical response to Dixon's novel considers it in the context of the literary tradition from which it emerged. Writing in *Arizona Quarterly,* Rebecca Skidmore Biggio (2011) compares Dixon's works to those of Albion W. Tourgée, a carpetbagger, whose novel *A Fool's Errand* (1879) is a largely autobiographical account of his experiences as a northerner in the Reconstruction-era South. Biggio suggests the authors' opposing viewpoints "exemplify postwar cultural negotiations concerning the place of violence in political participation." The growth of critical race and whiteness studies also has spurred resurgent interest in *The Clansman*. For example, Kim Magowan's 1999 article in *Studies in American Fiction* considers the gendering of racial tensions in Dixon's novel: "White men consequently find themselves oscillating between two roles Dixon intends to be distinguishable: the black male rapist and the white female rape victim." Similarly, Tara Bynum's 2010 article in *Texas Studies*

"EL MATADERO"

Esteban Echeverría

OVERVIEW

The short story "El matadero" ("The Slaughter House") was written by Argentine author Esteban Echeverría about 1838. The story is a political allegory that focuses on the perceived clash between civilization and barbarism that Echeverría identified as being at the heart of the problems surrounding nineteenth-century Latin American reality. Written in a foreboding, emotional tone that conveys a sense of urgency to his Argentine readership, "El matadero" portrays the city of Buenos Aires, representative of Argentine society in general, as directly threatened by the barbaric influences of despotic rule under the perceived uncultured traditions of rural Argentina. Taking place in a slaughterhouse in the city of Buenos Aires during a meat shortage in the city, the story describes the escape of a bull from the chopping block and the pursuit by the butchers, as well as the later attack and murder of a passing unitarist by the dictator's henchmen (the Mazorca).

"El matadero" was not published until 1871, when it appeared in the Argentine magazine *Revista del Río de la Plata* after being discovered by statesman and poet Juan María Gutiérrez following Echeverría's death. Emerging as it did during the formation of a liberal press promoted by the unitarist presidency of Domingo Faustino Sarmiento (1868–74), "El matadero" received a warm reception by editors of the progressive Argentine magazines and newspapers of the period. "El matadero" is exemplary of the virulent propaganda against the dictatorship of political and military leader Juan Manuel de Rosas that circulated during the late 1830s and 1840s, especially among leftist intellectuals exiled from the country who sought refuge in the progressive cultural spheres of Latin American metropolises such as Montevideo, Uruguay. Because of the short story's late publication date, however, the political ideals of "El matadero" did not affect the politics of Argentina in the 1840s or directly affect the dictatorship of Rosas, as was Echeverría's aim. Nevertheless, the story has become one of the most influential narratives in the history of Latin American literature.

HISTORICAL AND LITERARY CONTEXT

Although Argentina gained independence from Spain nearly thirty years prior to Echeverría's composition of "El matadero," the country was sharply divided into two opposing factions and was trying to develop a national identity. The political sphere was separated into the federalists, who advocated for more autonomous regional leadership and backed the Rosas government, and the unitarists, who sought a centralized, democratic government and with whom Echeverría identified. The country's political division was also generally reflective of a geographic divide between the urban and rural areas of Argentina. The rural Argentine culture and traditions of those residing in Argentina's southern Pampas (plains) region were disdained by citizens of the capital city of Buenos Aires, who identified with European culture and values more closely than those of their own countrymen.

When Echeverría first composed "El matadero" in about 1838, Rosas had returned to his position as governor of the Buenos Aires province for the second time during a period of dictatorship that lasted from 1835 to 1852. An outspoken unitarist, Echeverría denounced Rosas's regime in his writing and cultural involvement in Buenos Aires during the 1830s. A founding member of the Asociación de Mayo ("May Association") literary movement that sought to represent the harsh reality of contemporary Argentina, Echeverría was exiled along with some of his fellow members, including statesman and writer Sarmiento and political thinker Juan Bautista Alberdi, in the early 1840s. It is possible to read "El matadero" as a direct denunciation of the repressive Rosas dictatorship, which was noted for its uncivilized, barbaric nature.

Echeverría is recognized as one of the first *romanticismo* writers in Latin America, a movement that heavily influenced the literature of the region during the early nineteenth century. Partially inspired by European romanticism, which French poet Victor Hugo described as "liberalism in literature," Echeverría employed this literary style as a vehicle for communicating his strong anti-Rosas politics. Echeverría's work combined *romanticismo* with another literary style of the period, *costumbrismo*. *Costumbrismo* focused on representing the quotidian lifestyle and mannerisms of the local people, often from a satirical perspective, which Echeverría employed to construct his critical political allegory. In "El matadero," he combines these two literary influences with the anti-Rosas and antidictatorial rhetoric that was being circulated in Latin America during the period by intellectuals such

✦ *Key Facts*

Time Period:
Mid-19th Century

Genre:
Short Story

Events:
Repressive dictatorship of Juan Manuel de Rosas; political divide between federalists and unitarists in Argentina

Nationality:
Argentine

ESTEBAN ECHEVERRÍA: ACTIVIST IN EXILE

Born on September 2, 1805, José Esteban Antonio Echeverría was influenced from an early age by European art and culture and spent five influential years in Paris beginning in 1825. Upon returning to Buenos Aires in 1830, he became involved in the literary scene, publishing his first poems in the newspapers *La gaceta mercantil* and *El diario de la tarde*. His first book, *Elvira o la novia del Plata* (Elvira, or silver bride), emerged in 1832 to a warm reception. Echeverría's 1837 narrative poem "La cautiva" (The captive woman) published in his poetry collection *Rimas,* has been recognized as the first romantic work written in the Spanish language.

A staunch unitarist, Echeverría was devoted to the overthrow of Argentine dictator Juan Manuel de Rosas and was forced into exile in 1840 as a result of his politics. The author settled in Montevideo, Uruguay, in 1841, but he never became fully involved in that country's literary scene. In 1846 Echeverría published *El dogma socialista* (The socialist dogma) based on the credo of the earlier Argentine movement known as the Asociación de Mayo ("May Revolution"), of which he had helped found. He died in Montevideo on January 19, 1851, and today is regarded as the father of *romanticismo* in Latin America and as an important nineteenth-century political activist in the region.

as Alberdi and Sarmiento to achieve his powerful message.

While the posthumous publication of "El matadero" did not allow for the narrative to directly influence Argentine politics during Echeverría's lifetime, the short story had a lasting impact on the debate surrounding civilization and barbarism. There is also a clear dialogue between the work of Echeverría and Sarmiento, a fellow unitarist who in 1845 published his groundbreaking *Facundo: Civilization and Barbarism,* which promotes urbanization and denounces Rosas. The two authors had met and established an intellectual dialogue when Sarmiento visited Montevideo in the early 1840s. Echeverría's analysis and reflection on life in Buenos Aires directly influenced the work of many Argentine authors, especially of the *costumbrismo* tradition, including *Buenos Aires desde setenta años atrás* (Buenos Aires from seventy years ago; 1908) by José Antonio Wilde and *La gran aldea* (The big village; 1884) by Lucio V. López. Echeverría's tradition of representing life and politics in Argentina through a critical gaze has been carried on by later generations of Argentine writers, including Tomás Eloy Martínez, Alicia Kozameh, and Alicia Partnoy, all of whom present denunciations of the military regime during the Argentine Dirty War (1976–83), when thousands of citizens were killed or "disappeared."

THEMES AND STYLE

The main message of "El matadero" is a criticism of Rosas's regime as an unwanted legacy of the barbaric and antiquated Spanish colonial rule that the Argentine people had worked so hard to escape during their struggle for independence only a few decades earlier. Echeverría associates the negative influence of colonialism with the ignorant, uneducated lifestyle of the Pampas, represented by the sadistic cruelty of the butchers and the uncouth crowd that fight over the scraps left over from the slaughter. The author draws a direct parallel between the animals brutally butchered at the slaughterhouse and the unitarists who endured the cruelty of Rosas's repressive dictatorial rule. "Nearby, two Negro women were dragging along the entrails of an animal. A mulatto woman carrying a heap of entrails slipped in a pool of blood and fell lengthwise under her coveted booty … All a representation in miniature of the savage ways in which individual and social conflicts are thrashed out in our country." Echeverría deliberately emphasizes the link between sexual and racial difference and barbarism in his description of the multitude, the majority of whom are female and of mixed or African race. This link between race and barbarism was a common trope in the anti-Rosas propaganda created by Echeverría and other writers of his generation.

Echeverría achieves the power of his criticism through his construction of a moral binary between good-unitarist and evil-federalist, combined with the use of authorial intrusion—for example, when Echeverría disrupts the narrative to address his reader directly. Written in the third person, the narrative clearly demonizes the uncivilized mob of the slaughterhouse while sympathizing with the unitarist victim's cultured morale. "'The Unitarist cur!' 'The son of a bitch!' … The Unitarist was a young man, about twenty-five years old, elegant, debonair of carriage, who, as the above-mentioned exclamations were spouting from these impudent mouths, was trotting toward Barracas, quite fearless of any danger ahead of him." The slaughterhouse mob and the Mazorca who lurk nearby, representative of the federalists, are immediately portrayed as the aggressors, whereas the unitarist's superior "carriage" and values render him the innocent and undeserving victim of the federalists' wrath. With the construction of such a clear binary, Echeverría—in his simplistic black-and-white vision—accomplishes a direct denunciation of the representatives of the dictator's repressive violence, thus contributing to the growing anti-Rosas propaganda of the period.

Echeverría employs rural slang and extensive dialogue throughout "El matadero" to convey a tone of foreboding that foreshadows the tragic destiny of the unitarists in Argentina if the cruel ways of Rosas are not stopped. The direct contrast between the unitarist's cultivated speech ("Infamous executioners, what do you want to do with me?") and the crass jargon of the slaughterhouse crowd ("'The whip will tame him.' 'Give him a good pummeling!' 'First the cowhide and scissors.' 'Otherwise to the bonfire with him!'") further highlights the inferiority of the naive masses who blindly follow the clearly inhumane tactics of reigning despot Rosas. Later answering the federalist judge's question about wearing the required insignia in honor of the "Restorer" (Rosas), the unitarist condescendingly proclaims, "Insignia becomes you, slaves, but not free men." The use of terms such as "slaves" and "executioners" by the unitarist to interpellate the attackers further emphasizes the barbarism of the pro-Rosas factions, functioning as propaganda not only against Rosas but also against federalists in general.

CRITICAL DISCUSSION

Echeverría's narrative quickly gained fame as an exemplary short story of the *romanticismo* style following its 1871 publication. Fellow Argentine writer Gutiérrez was the first critic to study the work of Echeverría in-depth, editing and annotating *Obras completas de Echeverría* (The complete works of Echeverría) in 1874. Gutiérrez praised the political vision and historical value of Echeverría's work, noting the literary elements employed by the author in his detailed annotation of "El matadero," including a framing of bright, red-toned colors that highlighted the bloody nature of the slaughterhouse, as well as Echeverría's portrayal of the unitarist as a victim not only of the federalists but also of his own personal dignity and culture. Unfortunately, Gutiérrez's analysis, as well as those of other contemporary critics, was only published in Spanish. As William H. Katra notes in *The Argentine Generation of 1837: Echeverría, Alberdi, Sarmiento, Mitre* (1996), however, Sarmiento had his concerns with Echeverría's vision of Argentina in "El matadero," aligning the author more with barbarism than civilization: "Echeverría is the poet of desperation, the shout of culture trampled on by the horses of the pampa ... Poor Echeverría!"

Along with Echeverría's 1846 *El dogma socialista* (The socialist dogma), "El matadero" is regarded as his most important political work. The majority of the writers of his generation regarded him as their mentor, and he left his political and literary legacy specifically in the hands of Alberdi, to whom he communicated the same in a letter dated October 1, 1846, as scholar Olsen A. Ghirardi notes in his 2005 speech at Academia Nacional de Derecho y Ciencias Sociales de Córdoba. The direct political involvement of fellow writers Alberdi and Sarmiento—the latter of whom ascended to the Argentine presidency in the post-Rosas period—carried on, in part, Echeverría's political goals of democratization. In a more visual interpretation, María Luisa Bemberg's critically acclaimed 1984 film *Camila* rescues many of the same themes from "El matadero," exploring the clash between civilization and barbarism in Argentina during the Rosas regime.

Argentine postage stamp with a portrait of Esteban Echeverría, author of "El matadero." © HIPIX/ ALAMY.

More than a century after its initial publication, "El matadero" continues to be widely recognized and studied for its realistic portrayal of a gruesome period in Argentine history. Many scholars have addressed the issue of race in Echeverría's narrative; Katra notes, "Several of the writings of the 1837 militants ... [including] Echeverría's "El matadero" ... understandably contain explicit racial overtones when they allude to the struggle waged for decades against the hated Rosas regime. The above serves to explain in large part the disgust, fear, and even hatred exhibited by all the 1837 activists." While race forms part of the larger debate of civilization versus barbarism, other scholars have focused on the intellectual polemic more broadly.

BIBLIOGRAPHY

Sources

Echeverría, Esteban. "The Slaughterhouse." *The Argentina Reader: History, Culture, Politics.* Ed. G. Nouzeilles and G. Montaldo. Trans. A. Flores. Durham: Duke UP, 2002: 107–14. Print.

Ghirardi, Olsen A. "El legado de Esteban Echeverría." Academia Nacional de Derecho y Ciencias Sociales, Córdoba, Argentina. 6 Sept. 2005. Web. 13 Sept. 2012.

Goodrich, Diana S. *Facundo and the Construction of Argentine Culture.* Austin: U of Texas P, 1996. Print.

Katra, William H. *The Argentine Generation of 1837: Echeverría, Alberdi, Sarmiento, Mitre.* Madison: Fairleigh Dickinson UP, 1996. Print.

Skinner, Lee. "Carnality in 'El Matadero.'" *Revista de Estudios Hispanicos* 33 (1999): 205–226. Print.

Further Reading

Echeverría, Esteban. *La Cautiva.* 6th ed. Ed. Leonor Fleming. Madrid: Cátedra, 1999. Print.

———. *Obras completas de D. Esteban Echeverría.* Ed. Juan Maria Gutierrez. Buenos Aires: Casaralle, 1874. Print.

Jitrik, Noé. *Esteban Echeverría.* Buenos Aires: Centro Editor de América Latina, 1967. Print.

Masiello, Francine. *Between Civilization and Barbarism: Women, Nation, and Literary Culture in Modern Argentina.* Lincoln: U of Nebraska P, 1992. Print.

Weber, David J., and Jane M. Rausch. *Where Cultures Meet: Frontiers in Latin American History.* Wilmington: SR, 1994. Print.

Wilson, Jason. "Writing for the Future: Echeverría's 'El Matadero' and Its Secret Rewriting by Jorge Luis Borges and Adolfo Bioy Casares as 'La Fiesta del Monstruo.'" *Forum for Modern Language Studies* 43.1 (2007): 81–92. Print.

Katrina White

MAO II
Don DeLillo

OVERVIEW

Don DeLillo's tenth novel, *Mao II,* published in 1991, compares novelists with terrorists, examining the interaction of mass media and individualized voices, of icons and iconoclasts. It does so primarily through the figure of Bill Gray, a popular but reclusive author who has long been working on a massive novel that he never intends to finish. The complex plot of the book treats Gray's circle of acquaintances, including his assistant Scott—who hopes to keep Gray from publishing for fear of how a mass audience will affect the integrity of Gray and his work—and Karen Janney, a former follower of Sun Myung Moon and a romantic interest for both Gray and Scott. On the surface, Scott and Karen represent the extremes of individualism and collectivism, respectively, but as DeLillo delves into their psychologies as well as that of Gray, this division becomes increasingly complicated and the question of how to affirms one's individualism when "the future belongs to crowds" becomes increasingly challenging.

Mao II was well received by critics. It went on to win the PEN/Faulkner Award and was nominated for a Pulitzer Prize in 1992. In the years that followed publication, the novel assumed even greater import as the widening impact of terrorism on the global stage led many to see DeLillo, and especially *Mao II,* as particularly prescient. The novel stands as a reaction to escalating global terror but precedes by two years the first terrorist attack on the World Trade Center and by nine years the September 11 attack that destroyed the center's twin towers, greatly amplifying the threat of terrorism among Americans.

HISTORICAL AND LITERARY CONTEXT

The late 1980s and early 1990s were a period of great global political turmoil, and many Americans experienced a shift in focus with regard to world affairs. Communist regimes began to collapse throughout Europe, most symbolically manifested in the 1989 dismantling of the Berlin Wall and culminating in the 1991 collapse of the Soviet regime. The culturally defined enemy of U.S. policy faded but was quickly replaced by a new theater for conflict: the Middle East. Long an area of tension, the Middle East became the new bane of U.S. foreign policy, and in 1991 U.S. forces entered the region in a major way: the Persian Gulf War with Iraq, waged in response to Iraq's invasion of

oil-rich Kuwait. This new theater, however, came with a new kind of enemy. Traditional armed forces of the region could not hope to measure up to the sheer size and firepower of the U.S. military, but the country's military presence was met with guerilla-style fighting and increased use of terror attacks. Although terrorism was nothing new, it now replaced the Red Menace of the Cold War as the great boogeyman of the American psyche.

Mao II engages with these new conditions by focusing on the component of terrorism that sets it apart from traditional or even guerilla warfare. Terrorism is not merely about attacking one's enemy but about making a statement in doing so. It is the expression of a worldview, the creation of a narrative, and the novel explores this by comparing the creative process of writers with acts of terror. Gray comments on the "curious knot that binds novelists and terrorists," suggesting that the latter replace the former with their own "raids on consciousness." However, DeLillo does not allow writers and terrorists to become simply interchangeable, as the novel focuses on the contrast between individual and mass thinking and concentrates on the role of mass media. Bill Gray eschews the public spotlight; terrorists depend on it to disperse their message.

Like DeLillo's other novels, *Mao II* is typically characterized as postmodernist fiction, and similar to many other postmodern novels, it uses this examination of mass media as a means to ask larger questions about the certainty of our understanding of our world, suggesting that what we take as our reality is closer to a narrative construct than anything that could be called objective. Additionally, David Foster Wallace has suggested that DeLillo's writing is a cutting-edge harbinger of the kind of fiction being written by younger authors, which he dubs "Image-Fiction" and which involves the "strategic deployment of pop-cultural reference" in its treatment of contemporary themes.

Critic Emma Brockes notes in her 2003 piece in the *Guardian* that "practically every successful male novelist of the past 10 years claims DeLillo as an influence." Among these are such notables as Wallace, Jonathan Franzen, Jonathan Lethem, and Chuck Palahniuk. *Mao II* was published in the midst of DeLillo's most celebrated period—after *White Noise* (1985) and *Libra* (1989) and before *Underworld* (1997)—and

❖ *Key Facts*

Time Period:
Late 20th Century

Genre:
Novel

Events:
Fall of the Berlin Wall; collapse of the Soviet Union; Iraqi invasion of Kuwait; rise of terrorism as a geopolitical threat

Nationality:
American

SALMAN RUSHDIE: AN INSPIRATION

In addition to being influenced by the photographic ambush of J. D. Salinger, Don DeLillo has also cited Salman Rushdie as an inspiration for *Mao II*. Rushdie, a British Indian writer, published three acclaimed novels between 1975 and 1983, including the Booker Prize-winning *Midnight's Children* (1981). His fourth novel, *The Satanic Verses* (1988), received critical praise, with some critics calling it Rushdie's finest novel yet, but it also provoked great controversy in some parts of the world because of what opponents characterized as blasphemous treatment of both Islam and its prophet Muhammad. A number of countries with large Muslim populations banned the novel, and in February 1989 the spiritual leader of Iran, Ayatollah Khomeini, issued a *fatwa* (Islamic ruling) calling for the death of Rushdie.

In the wake of the novel's publication and Khomeini's fatwa, which has been perceived by some as an orchestrated media event devised by the Ayatollah, riots broke out, bookstores were firebombed, and those associated with the book in any way were threatened and assaulted. Rushdie himself was forced into hiding and was kept under constant police protection, though the controversy also increased sales of the book tremendously, pushing it to the top of best-seller lists. Although the direct threat to Rushdie has diminished somewhat over the years, Iran has stated that the fatwa will remain in effect permanently.

became one of his most influential novels. DeLillo has been lauded for his ability to think in large terms about a particular historical moment. It is perhaps because of this sense of historicity that his novels, none more so than *Mao II,* have been seen as prophetic. Indeed, the events of September 11, 2001, eerily resonated with the themes of the book and even with specific scenes, as when photographer Brita Nilsson and Gray debate the merits of the World Trade Center towers immediately before turning their discussion to terrorism.

THEMES AND STYLE

Mao II opens with a mass marriage at New York's Yankee stadium of Sun Myung Moon's followers, including Karen. The scene cuts to the heart of the novel, presenting the tension between what DeLillo has described as "the polar extremes of … the arch individualist and the mass mind." The novel seems to suggest that the future looks bleak for the individualist in this age of mass thinking, mass media, and mass reproduction. DeLillo also weaves a number of other related thematic threads through the work, including the power of images. "Mao II" refers to Andy Warhol's silkscreen portrait of Mao Zedong, which like much of that artist's work speaks to the ease with which images can be reproduced and multiplied. DeLillo has admitted to being inspired by two photographs that represent "polar extremes":

one of the mass wedding in Yankee Stadium and one of the reclusive J. D. Salinger—upon whom Gray is loosely based—who appears outraged at having been ambushed by photographers.

Despite these large, culturally sweeping concerns, the narrative of *Mao II* tends to be intimate. History looms large, but the story is one largely composed of pairs or small groups in conversation in private spaces. Notably, however, as Gray is coaxed into a more public role—whether for publicity, to aid in a hostage release, or simply for aesthetic reasons—the settings of the book likewise become more public. Although Gray is the presumptive central character of the novel, DeLillo shifts the focus with each chapter, rotating through various characters, including terrorist Abu Rashid, such that the ultimate point of view of the novel is collective, despite the stubborn individualism of many of the characters.

DeLillo has long been celebrated for his distinctive literary style, which is in many ways a mixture of styles. He can switch from a raw, stripped-down style reminiscent of Ernest Hemingway or Raymond Carver to a lusher, descriptive style. Yet whichever mode he enters, the distinctive DeLillo voice cuts through. This voice has often been described as particularly philosophical and aphoristic. As Brockes suggests, "A DeLillo sentence can scan like an epigram from the self-help industry…. But while the rhythm of a DeLillo soundbite soothes, its sentiment subverts the reader's expectations like a malevolent fortune cookie." This style, which Brockes calls "the language of advertising," is quite evident in *Mao II* and has led some critics to bemoan the distance that one feels from DeLillo's characters. "If one remains less moved by *Mao II* than engaged and impressed," writes Lorrie Moore in her review for the *New York Times,* "that is the contract a reader must often make with a book by Mr. DeLillo; he is seldom an emotional writer." *Mao II* can almost be read as a series of images, leaving the emotional response largely in the hands of the reader, with limited authorial manipulation.

CRITICAL DISCUSSION

Following *White Noise* and *Libra,* the expectations for *Mao II* were high. For many critics *Mao II* met those expectations, providing yet another work to cement DeLillo's reputation. Reviews were generally positive, though even some positive reviewers expressed misgivings about the dispassionate tone. Writing for the *New York Review of Books,* critic Robert Towers notes that "the main conflicts are ideological rather than personal. Bill Gray is movingly and convincingly described, but in action he is much less persuasive." However, the shortcomings were, by and large, secondary to the lauding of the novel for its insights into modern media and global politics and its stylistic deftness. The work was shortlisted for a number of literary awards, including the Pulitzer, and won the PEN/Faulkner Award in 1992.

As celebrated as the novel might have been upon its publication, the intervening years seem only to have strengthened its reputation. In *The Cambridge Companion to Don DeLillo* (2008), John N. Duvall suggests that *Mao II*'s "speculations on terrorists and the cultural role of terrorism … , it is retrospectively clear, provided us with a frame of reference for beginning to process the post-9/11 world years before the terrorist attacks on America." Indeed, the novel, topical though it is, has not dated—and has instead garnered a growing interest in—its treatment of the mechanics of terrorism. The work also has drawn attention to the way the media play a role in terrorism, manipulated by the perpetrators thereof and shaping popular characterization of circumstances, global and personal, newly defined by the specter of terrorism.

Words such as "prophetic" and "prescient" often appear in discussions, scholarly and otherwise, of DeLillo's *Mao II*. The September 11 attacks sparked a new interest in *Mao II,* with many critics reexamining Gray's notion of terrorism as a dominant form of narrative discourse in the late twentieth century. This approach to the novel remains predominant among critics, but scholars have also addressed the themes that resonate most profoundly through the full body of DeLillo's fiction: commodification of culture, the power of mass media, and the role of the artist and author in modern life. These topics, of course, are intimately bound with one another, and DeLillo offers few easy determinations, neither condemning the shallowness of images nor valorizing the writer as a heroic figure. As such, *Mao II* provides ground for much scholarly debate, both about the novel and the larger cultural situation that informs it.

BIBLIOGRAPHY

Sources

Brockes, Emma. "View from the Bridge." *Guardian.* Guardian News and Media, 23 May 2003. Web. 20 Aug. 2012.

DeLillo, Don. *Mao II.* New York: Penguin, 1991. Print.

Duvall, John N., ed. *The Cambridge Companion to Don DeLillo.* Cambridge: Cambridge UP, 2008. Print.

Moore, Lorrie. "Look for a Writer and Find a Terrorist." Rev. of *Mao II,* by Don DeLillo. *New York Times.* The New York Times Company, 9 June 1991. Web. 20 Aug. 2012.

Passaro, Vince. "Dangerous Don DeLillo." *Conversations with Don DeLillo.* Ed. Thomas DePietro. Jackson: UP of Mississippi, 2005. 75–85. Print.

Towers, Robert. "History Novel." Rev. of *Mao II,* by Don DeLillo. *New York Review of Books.* NYREV, 27 June 1991. Web. 20 Aug. 2012.

Wallace, David Foster. "E Unibus Pluram: Television and U.S. Fiction." 1990. *A Supposedly Fun Thing I'll Never Do Again.* Boston: Little, Brown, 1997. 21–82. Print.

Further Reading

Cowart, David. *Don DeLillo: The Physics of Language.* Athens: U of Georgia P, 2002. Print.

DePietro, Thomas, ed. *Conversations with Don DeLillo.* Jackson: UP of Mississippi, 2005. Print.

Kavadlo, Jesse. *Don DeLillo: Balance at the Edge of Belief.* New York: Peter Lang, 2004. Print.

Olster, Stacey, ed. *Don DeLillo: Mao II, Underworld, Falling Man.* London: Continuum, 2011. Print.

Osteen, Mark. *American Magic and Dread: Don DeLillo's Dialogue with Culture.* Philadelphia: U of Pennsylvania P, 2000. Print.

Rowe, John Carlos. "*Mao II* and the War on Terrorism." *South Atlantic Quarterly* 103.1 (2004): 21–43. Print.

Marc Oxoby

THE MOZI

Mo Di

✢ *Key Facts*

Time Period:
4th Century BCE

Genre:
Philosophy

Events:
Founding of the Mohist
School of philosophy;
disintegration of the
Chinese feudal system

Nationality:
Chinese

OVERVIEW

The Mozi, a fourth-century BCE philosophical work attributed to the Chinese thinker Mo Di (c. 470 BCE–c. 391 BCE), is one of the first argumentative texts in Chinese thought. It articulates serious criticism of the early forms of Confucianism, a rival philosophical movement and school. The text, which is arranged systematically, differs from Confucian approaches in that it does not base its argument on the authoritativeness of the received wisdom embodied in traditional thought. Instead, it employs a state consequentialist methodology to determine and value what is most beneficial to the state and its people. This state consequentialism was justified through appeals to heaven, which, Mohists believed, was committed to the benefit of all people. By questioning the benefit of typical Confucian rituals that favor the upper class, such as a mandated three-year mourning period for a deceased parent, Mo Di argues for the implementation of a social philosophy that would benefit the working class, the social group to which he belonged and for whom he was a vocal advocate.

Mo Di, the founder of the Mohist School of philosophy, was the first major Chinese thinker to challenge the precepts of Confucius, who justified and rationalized the traditional institutions and arts of the Zhou dynasty. During the fourth century BCE, Mo Di's fame equaled that of Confucius, and his school of philosophy was widely popular among the middle and lower classes—those who did not have the economic means for the ceremonial music and elaborate public rituals espoused by Confucius and thus considered them wasteful and useless. Although the philosophy of Mo Di has not had the lasting significance of that of Confucius, his systematic treatise, *The Mozi,* is one of the most important books in the history of classical Chinese thought.

HISTORICAL AND LITERARY CONTEXT

As early as the seventh century BCE, during the decline of the Zhou dynasty, China witnessed the beginning of the disintegration of the feudal system. This led to the scattering of educated nobles and officials throughout China, many of whom maintained their livelihood by becoming private teachers. By the fourth century BCE, one of these teachers, Confucius, had become the most recognized thinker and

teacher in the Ru school, which had formed out of the Chinese literati and advocated the cultivation of human-heartedness and a sense of justice, as well as adherence to a tradition of rituals and ceremonies. Following Confucius's death, his students and followers recorded his teaching in the *Analects of Confucius,* a text that would contribute to the school's increasing importance during the pre-Qin period.

The Mozi consists of writings that were composed over a considerable period of time, from the late fifth-century BCE to the early part of the third-century BCE. The earlier parts of the text were composed by Mo Di himself, whereas later portions were written by Mohists over the decades and even centuries that followed. Mo Di is thought to have belonged to the social stratum of artisans and reportedly worked as a carpenter when he was a young man. Commoners such as Mo Di considered wasteful the luxuries and rituals of the political elites courted by Confucius. It was from this perspective that Mo Di criticized Confucius's rationalization of traditional aristocratic socio-political institutions.

Although it certainly contained elements of propaganda, *The Mozi* was composed primarily as a philosophical tract that would oppose Confucius and the institutions he supported. As such the text's primary influences were the teachings of Confucius, which were compiled by his students in the *Analects.* Much of the *Analects* are attributed to Confucius though they were actually compiled by his followers, and many scholars, such as Chris Fraser, in his piece on Mohism in the *Stanford Encyclopedia of Philosophy,* argue that "the *Mozi* is not a single composition or work, in the modern sense, but an anthology of diverse writings probably composed at different times, by different writers or editors. No part of the anthology purports to be from the hand of Mo Di himself."

Although *The Mozi* only exercised significant cultural influence for a few hundred years—a relatively small period of time in the history of Chinese philosophy—the Mohist School was a powerful political force and represented the first philosophical opposition to Confucianism, as well as opposition to other philosophical movements such as Daoism and Legalism. According to Arthur Waley in *Three Ways of Thought in Ancient China,* "The Mohists were an organized body, under the strict control of a leader known as the Grand Master, who enforced absolute obedience to an exacting code of honour and self-sacrifice." Although the political and philosophical influence of the Mohist school has long since waned, *The Mozi* is considered one of the most important treatises in the history of Chinese philosophy.

THEMES AND STYLE

Two philosophical ideas are central to *The Mozi*: First, the work espouses a mode of inquiry that seeks to evaluate social institutions and rituals on the basis of their usefulness in generating and maintaining the state's welfare. Second, it incorporates an ethics of impartial caring for all that Mo Di argues is a logical extension of the aforementioned state consequentialism. This emphasis on usefulness appeals to and serves to benefit working-class people of China for whom extensive mourning rituals, for example, are economically unfeasible. In the section titled "Exalting Worthiness I," Mo Di articulates the negative form of this utilitarian argument, claiming that "kings, dukes, and great officers" have failed in establishing a wealthy state and a numerous population because they have not been "'utilizing ability' in their governing." By implementing a methodology that evaluates the consequences or benefit to the state of any action, Mo Di argues that the state will better achieve prosperity. Similarly, *The Mozi*'s ethic of impartial caring for all is in part economic, arguing that it is mutually beneficial for people to care for others regardless of their relationship to them.

The Mozi achieves much of its rhetorical force through the evocation of historical precedence. Many of the arguments in the text begin with variations of the following: "In Ancient times, kings, dukes and great men …" By appealing to these ancient examples, Mo Di forms a historical argument and grants his own philosophy a sense of historical continuity. *The Mozi* also achieves its rhetorical aims by consolidating a sense of unity around figures of authority and the concept of universal benefit. In the section "Exalting Unity I," Mo Di argues that order is achieved by obeying "village heads" or "rulers of the state," whose authority is granted via the "Sons of Heaven." With regard to unity through mutual benefit, Mo Di's second argument against offensive warfare, for example, claims that regardless of who wins a battle, both sides lose because they have wasted resources. It is mutually beneficial, Mo Di argues, to avoid warfare.

Stylistically, *The Mozi* is distinguished by its systematic formality. By organizing the text into an enumerated series of arguments, Mo Di seeks to portray the comprehensive nature of his philosophy. The sections of the "core" are often arranged in triads, such as "Exalting Worthiness I, II, and III" or "Condemning Offensive Warfare I, II, and III." The unadorned, repetitive style is also more accessible to the very people whom the text supports: the working class. Indeed, in *Disputers of the Tao* (1989), A. C. Graham attributes the

DAODEJING

Another fundamental text in the history of Chinese religion and philosophy, *Daodejing* was composed in the sixth century BCE by the Chinese thinker Laozi. According to legend, Laozi saw that the Zhou Dynasty was in decline and decided to exile himself from his country. The border guard asked the old man to write down his thoughts, and the work he produced, *Daodejing,* became one of the most influential texts in Chinese philosophy, eventually becoming, along with the works of the philosopher Zhuang Zhou, one of the founding texts of Chinese Daoist philosophy.

The multiple interpretational valences make a succinct explanation of the book difficult. The work itself suggests the ineffability of its subject matter, saying that "the *dao* that can be spoken is not the eternal *dao.*" The text has been read as a political, religious, philosophical, and even military treatise, and, as with many texts of Chinese antiquity, the complications of translating the work from classical Chinese further cloud the issue. The title alone has been translated in various ways, but generally *dao* means "the way," as in a path, and *de* is similar to the Western idea of "virtue." The hundreds of translations and scholarly studies of the text attest not only to its historical importance but also to its continued philosophical relevance in both China and the West.

text's style to Mo Di's social standing, suggesting that "the notoriously graceless style of early Mohist writing, ponderous, humourless, repetitive, suggests the solemn self-educated man who writes only for practical purposes and has no opportunity to polish his style as an adviser to princes." Although this repetitive style can make the text difficult to read, it allows Mo Di to articulate multiple arguments in support of his claims.

CRITICAL DISCUSSION

Although much of the history surrounding *The Mozi* and its progenitor is obscured by the paucity of historical texts, there does seem to be general consensus that Mohism, the school founded by Mo Di was, along with Confucianism, one of the two main philosophical movements in China from roughly 400 BCE to 200 BCE. In his introduction to *The Mozi,* Ian Johnston quotes the Chinese scholar Youlan Feng on the importance of the movement's teacher: "Mo Zi is one of the most important figures in Chinese history, a man whose name was constantly linked with that of Confucius from the Warring States period down to the beginning of the Han dynasty." Mencius, a fourth-century BCE Confucian teacher, appointed himself the task of opposing Mo Di and his teachings, specifically that of impartial caring for all.

Despite being primarily a philosophical and religious text, *The Mozi* has often been regarded as a sociopolitical tract that advocates for class equality. In the *Fundamentals of Chinese Philosophy,* Laurence C. Wu argues that "in Mo Zi's mind, an ideal society is

Some commentators have focused on the text's importance for broader scholarly discourse on specific periods in Chinese history. In "Introduction: Reconsidering *The Mozi*?" Franklin Perkins claims that understanding the text "is an essential element of understanding Warring States philosophy." In "Mengzi's Inheritance, Criticism, and Overcoming of Moist Thought," Weixiang Ding explores *The Mozi*'s influence on Confucianism. Owen Flanagan also focuses on the relationship between Confucians and Mohists, arguing that Mohists incorporate the Confucian concept of moral emulation but also insist that rationality plays an important role in human motivation. Dan Robins notes the political and social agenda of the Mohist school and hints at *The Mozi*'s nature as propaganda in his essay, "The Moists and the Gentleman of the World," arguing that the Mohists, "engaged in philosophy not to hash out issues with other philosophers, but to challenge the customs and rulers of their time."

BIBLIOGRAPHY

Sources

Feng, Youlan. *A Short History of Chinese Philosophy.* New York: MacMillan, 1948. Print.

Fraser, Chris. "Mohism." *Stanford Encyclopedia of Philosophy.* 2002. Ed. Edward N Zalta. Stanford University. Web. 26 Nov. 2012.

Graham, A. C. *Disputers of the Tao.* La Salle: Open Court, 1989. Print.

The Mozi. Trans. Ian Johnston. New York: Columbia UP, 2010. Print.

Perkins, Franklin. "Introduction: Reconsidering *The Mozi*?" *Journal of Chinese Philosophy* 35.3 (2008): 379–83. Wiley Online Library. Web. 5 Nov. 2012.

Robins, Dan. "The Moists and the Gentlemen of the World." *Journal of Chinese Philosophy* 35.3 (2008): 385–402. Wiley Online Library. Web. 5 Nov. 2012.

Waley, Arthur. *Three Ways of Thought in Ancient China.* Stanford: Stanford UP, 1982. Print.

Wu, Laurence C. *Fundamentals of Chinese Philosophy.* New York: UP of America, 1986. Print.

Further Reading

Ding, Sixin. "A Study on the Dating of Mozi Dialogues and the Mohist View of Ghosts and Spirits." *Contemporary Chinese Thought* 42 (2011): 39–87. Print.

Hoobler, Dorothy, and Thomas Hoobler. *Confucianism.* New York: Facts On File, 2009. Print.

Laozi. *Tao Te Ching (Daodejing).* Trans. William Scott Wilson. Boston: Shambhala, 2010. Print.

Loy, Hui-chieh. *The Moral Philosophy of the Mozi "Core Chapters."* Berkeley: U of California Berkeley, 2006. Proquest. Web. 5 Nov. 2012.

———. "The Word and the Way in Mozi." *Philosophy Compass* 6.10 (2011): 652–62. Wiley Online Library. Web. 5 Nov. 2012.

Tanner, Harold. *China: A History.* Indianapolis: Hackett, 2009. Print.

a welfare state of material sufficiency where the basic material needs of the people are satisfied." Although the text certainly generated a significant philosophical school and countless adherents over a 200-year period, it exercised little lasting influence on Chinese thought, as evinced by Johnston's claim that "*The Mozi* has been a sadly neglected work, both in China itself over two millennia, and in the West since early Chinese philosophy first became a subject of significant interest in the 19th century."

Greg Luther

THE MUSES ARE HEARD

Truman Capote

OVERVIEW

Originally published in the *New Yorker* in 1956, Truman Capote's *The Muses Are Heard* reflects on the time the author spent with an American opera company touring Russia during the winter of 1955. Later published as a travel book, *The Muses Are Heard* is written in a witty and engaging style that weaves facts and observations in the manner of a fictional narrative. The first part of the book, titled "When the Cannons Are Silent," introduces the cast members during a briefing in a West Berlin rehearsal hall and describes the troupe's laborious three-day train trip to Leningrad. The second part, "The Muses Are Heard," focuses on five days of rehearsal and the December 26 performance of the opera *Porgy and Bess* (1935). By exploring the cultural differences between the United States and the Soviet Union, and the political implications behind *Porgy and Bess,* Capote portrays the anticapitalist and anticommunist sentiments on both sides of the Cold War divide.

Capote's first book-length work of nonfiction, *The Muses Are Heard* garnered much critical acclaim. It also marked the author's first foray into a new genre of literary nonfiction, what he referred to as the "journalistic novel." Reaction among members of the opera company he had traveled with was less than enthusiastic: they had assumed he would paint the show in a positive light and were disappointed to read his humorous, often ironic account of the production. Several critics were surprised to learn that sections of the text were fictionalized, perhaps to surreptitiously inject the author's perspective on the events. Nevertheless, the journalistic novel form proved popular, leading Capote to pen one of his most famous works, *In Cold Blood: A True Account of a Multiple Murder and Its Consequences* (1966).

HISTORICAL AND LITERARY CONTEXT

Set in Cold War Russia, *The Muses Are Heard* explores the Soviet Union under the leadership of Nikita Khrushchev, who took power in 1953 shortly after the inauguration of U.S. president Dwight D. Eisenhower and the death of Soviet dictator Joseph Stalin. Tensions between the United States and Soviet Union eased somewhat as Khrushchev announced his plans for de-Stalinization and peaceful coexistence with the West. Under his leadership, the Soviet Union engaged in a series of cultural exchanges with the United States, allowing artists and performers from both countries to travel abroad and display the "reality" of life on the other side of the Iron Curtain.

Sponsored by the U.S. Department of State, the 1955 performance of *Porgy and Bess* in Russia by the Everyman's Opera Company was an effort to show that the United States did not have a "Negro problem," as Soviet propaganda purported. The show, which features an African American cast, depicts life in a southern black community, an unusual subject for communist Russia. Capote in his own writing tried to avoid appealing to the anticommunist hysteria that had swept the United States during the early 1950s, fueled by U.S. senator Joseph McCarthy's communist witch hunts. Instead, the author wished to connect with readers who had yet to hear a shrewd, unbiased take on the propaganda game between Russia and the United States.

Before writing *The Muses Are Heard,* Capote honed his skills by experimenting with an eclectic mix of genres. His early works include articles for the *New Yorker,* nonfiction travel essays, short story collections such as *A Tree of Night* (1949), plays such as *The Grass Harp* (1952), and screenplays such as *Beat the Devil* (1953). This interest in a range of journalistic and fictional styles, and adaptation of his work to the stage and screen, eventually led him to create the highly visual, detailed genre of the nonfiction novel.

The technique was so successful that it inspired his successors to bend genre conventions even further. Many writers experimented with Capote's form, agreeing with the author's argument that nonfiction novels should be free of first-person narration and any mention of the author. A few such forays into the nonfiction novel include Hunter S. Thompson's 1966 *Hell's Angels,* Norman Mailer's *Armies of the Night* (1968), and Tom Wolfe's 1968 *The Electric Kool-Aid Acid Test.* Toward the end of the twentieth-century, the nonfiction novel waned in popularity and was replaced by personalized forms of writing such as the memoir and the extended essay. Nevertheless, Capote's work in *The Muses Are Heard* and *In Cold Blood* mark the pioneering of an important genre in American literature.

❖ *Key Facts*

Time Period:
Mid-20th Century

Genre:
Travel Book

Events:
Cold War; Red Scare; Warsaw Pact

Nationality:
American

PORGY AND BESS: POLITICAL OPERA

First performed in 1935, the American folk opera *Porgy and Bess* takes place in the early 1920s on Catfish Row, a fictitious setting based on the real Cabbage Row in Charleston, South Carolina. Based on DuBose Heyward's novel *Porgy* (1925), with music written by George Gershwin and lyrics by DuBose Heyward and Ira Gershwin, the story centers on the life of Porgy, an African American beggar living in the slums, and his efforts to save beautiful Bess from her violent boyfriend, Crown, and a drug dealer known as Sportin' Life. Many African Americans reacted with ambivalence to the opera's rendering of black stereotypes. Nevertheless, the opera's songs, such as "Summertime," which has been recorded more than 25,000 times, became popular hits and later Broadway standards.

Behind the opera, which Capote watched dozens of times in order to write *The Muses Are Heard,* lie complex political messages that flew in the face of the Cold War-era Russian establishment. In the novel, Capote notes that the opera, "when slipped under the dialectical microscope, proves a test tube brimming with the kind of bacteria to which the present Russian regime is most allergic." He also pays close attention in his writing to the fact that *Porgy and Bess* "sings out loud that people can be happy with plenty of nothin', an unwelcome message indeed" in communist Russia.

THEMES AND STYLE

The Muses Are Heard focuses on several key themes, such as the power of propaganda and the fear of the unknown to obscure cultural realities. Through what has been termed the "human interest" element of the book, Capote allots more attention to the stories of his traveling companions than to the local culture and customs of Russia. He exposes Americans' anti-Russian sentiments through character sketches, showcasing the personalities of the different members of the opera company, such as Leonore Strunsky, the wife of *Porgy and Bess* lyricist Ira Gershwin; columnist Leonard Lyons; coproducer and director Robert Breen; and actors Bruce Jackson and Helen Thigpen. Capote describes a moment in which the cast has its first encounter with native Russians and proceeds to "stare … as though amazed, and rather peeved, to discover Russians had two eyes correctly located." Through the characters' subsequent words and actions, Capote renders the cultural differences between Russia and the United States, revealing both Russians' and Americans' inability to see their own shortcomings.

Rhetorically, Capote uses dialogue between his traveling companions to voice his personal perceptions about American and Russian culture. In so doing, he avoids explicitly intruding on the text as a narrator, which would complicate the text's status as a work of nonfiction. For example, a cast member named Walmsley, referring to anti-Russian propaganda in the United States, quips, "Believe me, sir, the Russians know as much about the Negro situation as you do. And they don't give a damn one way or another. Except for statements, propaganda, anything they can turn to their own interests." By showing how Walmsley's perceptions are as heavily controlled by propaganda as he believes Russians' are, Capote tacitly directs the reader toward the irony inherent in American's feelings of cultural superiority.

The Muses Are Heard uses humorous and satirical language to describe the characters and episodes that Capote encounters on his excursion. Because there are so many different Americans on the trip, he captures the intricacies of their voices and the subtle idiosyncrasies of their actions. Each character is written about with a different tone—from the serious tenor reserved for Ambassador Bohlen and his wife to the repulsive, hyperbolic depiction of the Russian Orlov. Through these numerous voices, Capote paints a wide range of anti-Russian and anti-American sentiments, including his own perspective on the events. In a way, despite his efforts to mask his narrative voice, his shrewd sense of humor becomes a character in the story, poking fun at the foolish nature of both the American and Russian characters.

CRITICAL DISCUSSION

The Muses Are Heard was well received among readers. Its success can be attributed to its status as the first nonfiction novel and to Capote's deadpan delivery, which avoids taking anything, including the text itself, too seriously. In a 1958 *New York Times* article, critic Mark Slonim describes the novel's effect: "*The Muses Are Heard* is not a chronicle or a diary or a travelogue…. It is a record made by a brilliant writer in a casual, almost flippant manner—but with such freshness, with such light strokes and subtle innuendos, that the book reads like a highly enjoyable, charming story." In the review Slonim pinpoints the characteristic of the book that would fuel the success of subsequent nonfiction novels—the author's highly engaging and readable style.

The success of the journalistic novel launched a new genre centered on experimental nonfiction. In *Music for Chameleons* (1975), Capote explains how *The Muses Are Heard* inspired his later literary nonfiction work: "*The Muses Are Heard* had set me to thinking on different lines altogether: I wanted to produce a journalistic novel, something on a large scale that would have the credibility of fact, the immediacy of film, the depth and freedom of prose, and the precision of poetry." Although *In Cold Blood* has eclipsed *The Muses Are Heard* in terms of popularity and critical acclaim, the latter has nevertheless been praised for its role in breaking genre conventions. Author Kenneth T. Reed in *Truman Capote* (1981) acknowledges that the book "provided Capote with the kind of reporting opportunity for which he was looking at that point in his career, and with a chance to put shape and sense into an otherwise unheralded experiment in the arts."

Current scholarship on *The Muses Are Heard* tends to focus on Capote's perceptions of American-Soviet relations as voiced through his characters. In *Capote: A Biography* (1988), Gerald Clarke writes that Capote casually puts his own thoughts into the mouths of his characters, as when the character Priscilla Johnson refers to the cast as a "second-rate company." Clarke also reveals that Capote invented the passage about the Norwegian businessmen, perhaps to interrupt the story with his own opinions. Reed notes that it was impossible for Capote to completely avoid espousing anti-Russian sentiments in his writing, however—or to completely filter them through the cast of characters he traveled with—because of his awareness of the "supposed inferiority of Russian manners and political values."

Truman Capote, author of *The Muses Are Heard,* photographed in 1966. © BETTMANN/CORBIS.

BIBLIOGRAPHY

Sources

Capote, Truman. *The Muses Are Heard, an Account.* New York: Random House, 1956. Print.

Chiasson, Lloyd. "Truman Capote." *American Literary Journalists, 1945–1995: First Series.* Ed. Arthur J. Kaul. Detroit: Gale Research, 1997. 29–39. *Dictionary of Literary Biography.* Vol. 185. *Literature Resource Center.* Web. 31 July 2012.

Clarke, Gerald. *Capote: A Biography.* New York: Simon and Schuster, 1988. Print.

Garson, Helen S. "Truman Capote." *American Novelists since World War II: Sixth Series.* Ed. James R. Giles and Wanda H. Giles. Detroit: Gale Group, 2000. *Dictionary of Literary Biography.* Vol. 227. *Literature Resource Center.* Web. 31 July 2012.

Reed, Kenneth T. *Truman Capote.* Boston: Twayne, 1981. *Twayne's United States Authors Series.* Vol. 388. *The Twayne Authors Series.* Web. 31 July 2012.

Slonim, Mark. "Ivan and Porgy." *New York Times* 2 Dec. 1958: n. pag. Print.

"Truman Capote." *Contemporary Authors Online.* Detroit: Gale, 2010. *Literature Resource Center.* Web. 31 July 2012.

Further Reading

Capote, Truman. *In Cold Blood: A True Account of a Multiple Murder and Its Consequences.* New York: Random House, 1966. Print.

Goad, Craig M. "Truman Capote." *American Novelists since World War II: First Series.* Ed. Jeffrey Helterman and Richard Layman. Detroit: Gale Research, 1978. *Dictionary of Literary Biography.* Vol. 2. *Literature Resource Center.* Web. 1 Aug. 2012.

Heyward, DuBose. *Porgy.* New York: George H. Doran, 1925. Print.

Long, Robert Emmet. *Truman Capote, Enfant Terrible.* New York: Continuum, 2008. Print.

Rosenmeier, Rosamond. "The New Journalists." *Tom Wolfe.* Ed. William McKeen and Clenora Hudson-Weems. New York: Twayne, 1995. *Twayne's United States Authors Series.* Vol. 650. *The Twayne Authors Series.* Web. 1 Aug. 2012.

Steinbeck, John. *Once There Was a War.* New York: Viking, 1958. Print.

Anna Deem

OBSERVE THE SONS OF ULSTER MARCHING TOWARDS THE SOMME

Frank McGuinness

❖ *Key Facts*

Time Period:
Late 20th Century

Genre:
Play

Events:
World War I; Catholic-Protestant conflict in Ireland; rise of the IRA

Nationality:
Irish

OVERVIEW

Frank McGuinness's play *Observe the Sons of Ulster Marching towards the Somme* follows eight volunteers for the 36th Ulster Division in World War I (1914–18) as they prepare to participate in the first battle of the Somme, an Allied offensive in France that took place from July 1 to November 13, 1916, and saw some of the bloodiest fighting in history. The play opens in 1969 and develops in flashbacks from the perspective of the sole survivor among the group, Kenneth Pyper, now an aged Loyalist, embittered by his own survival and struggling to find meaning in the wasted lives of his friends. The battle of the Somme operates as a metaphor for the seemingly endless religious strife in Northern Ireland, with special relevance for the contemporary reality of the Troubles, the violent confrontations that had been raging since the late 1960s between the Catholic minority in Northern Ireland, backed by the Irish Republican Army, and the Protestant majority, backed by various paramilitary groups.

While *Observe the Sons of Ulster* breaks no new ground in exploring the past to explain the present, its perspective is unusual: McGuinness, a Catholic from County Donegal in the Republic of Ireland, uses the play to uncover the motivations of the Protestant Unionists (who wanted to preserve Northern Ireland's union with Britain) from Northern Ireland who are his characters. Upon its premiere on February 18, 1985, at the Peacock Theatre in Dublin, the capital of the Republic of Ireland, at the height of the Troubles, *Observe the Sons of Ulster* generated considerable controversy, with critics debating whether the play was a rigorous indictment of Ulster Protestantism or a more generous act of remembrance that sought to separate the myth of Unionism, founded on centuries of triumphalist anti-Catholic rhetoric, from its reality. Overwhelming acclaim ensured the play's transfer to the main stage of Dublin's Abbey Theatre in December 1985. A London production opened the following year, and the play has since been revived frequently on stages worldwide.

HISTORICAL AND LITERARY CONTEXT

In *Observe the Sons of Ulster,* the first battle of the Somme emerges as a defining moment for the Protestant Ulster consciousness. The battle, which claimed 80 percent of the 7,000-member 36th Ulster Division on its first day, came to represent a heroic blood sacrifice for the Union, one equal but opposite to that of the Irish rebels who had participated the previous April in the Easter Rising, a failed insurrection against British control of Ireland. As the play illustrates, the Ulster men who enlisted to fight in World War I were motivated more by their opposition to Home Rule—which would grant Ireland internal autonomy, though it remained a part of the British Empire—than they were by any resolve to vanquish the Germans. The battle of the Somme is represented in its wider historic significance as well, as McGuinness traces the fierce rivalry between the Protestants and the Catholics back to the late-seventeenth-century Battle of the Boyne, where King James II, a Roman Catholic, lost the English throne to the Dutch Protestant William of Orange. At the same time, the violence of World War I reverberates through Ireland's subsequent twentieth-century history: the political separation in 1921 of Northern Ireland, which remained loyal to the British monarchy, from the rest of the country; the home-ruled Irish Free State; and the eruption of the Troubles in the late 1960s because of the Unionist/Protestant discrimination against the Nationalist/Catholic minority in Northern Ireland.

On one level, full of the anti-Catholic jingoism that had inspired the Ulster volunteers for battle, *Observe the Sons of Ulster* was perceived by some at the time of its opening in Dublin to squarely lay the blame for Ireland's ongoing religious strife on the bigotry of the Protestants. The play was more widely understood, however, to be nonpartisan, an attempt by the Catholic McGuinness to humanize the Protestants and to use their past to understand, and perhaps remedy, the present.

Observe the Sons of Ulster partakes of the renewed interest in Ulster's history that was prompted by the onset of the Troubles. McGuinness has acknowledged his debt to A. T. Q. Stewart's 1977 historical survey, *The Narrow Ground,* which emphasizes the power of the folk memories of the past, especially the Orange tradition dating back to the battle of the Boyne, in shaping the contemporary Ulster identity. McGuinness was also influenced by his recent discovery of the near-total annihilation of the Ulster volunteers at the Somme, an event whose memory had been erased in

Catholic Ireland. His effort in the play to see both sides of the Catholic/Protestant rivalry is a feature common to much of his later dramatic output, as well. Among his many plays, however, *Observe the Sons of Ulster* is most often compared with *The Carthaginians* (1988), which uses the historical relations between Rome and Carthage as a metaphor for the hostilities between Britain and the Catholics of Northern Ireland that erupted in Bloody Sunday, a violent clash that left unarmed civil rights protesters dead at the hands of the British army in Derry, Northern Ireland, on January 30, 1972. In their emphasis on the ambiguities of the conflicts addressed, as well as on individual and collective trauma rather than historical fact, both plays have been discussed as worthy successors to Sean O'Casey's famous play about Ireland's involvement in World War I, *The Silver Tassie* (1928).

Because of its political pluralism, writes Ben Francombe in his article "Frank McGuinness" (2011), *Observe the Sons of Ulster* "embrace[d] the conciliatory spirit that had started to infiltrate the seemingly deadlocked conflict in the North." *Observe the Sons of Ulster* was in fact revived at the Abbey Theatre in 1994 to mark the declaration of a cease-fire in Northern Ireland. It has been, however, the play's deeper meanings—its universal messages about misguided heroics and the complexities of male bonding in times of catastrophe—that have resonated with international audiences in its many revivals and have most contributed to the play's reputation as one of the finest antiwar dramas of the twentieth century.

THEMES AND STYLE

Observe the Sons of Ulster examines the motivations of the Ulster men who enlisted and fought in World War I with an eye to better understanding the Troubles and deconstructing a history of sectarianism propelled by hollow and dangerous folk memory. McGuinness makes it clear that the soldiers of his story, with the exception of Pyper, initially joined up in the belief that their bravery in battle would secure a British victory and therefore British control over Ireland. As the play progresses, however, and the seven dead appear as ghosts of Pyper's memory on stage, the cultural myth of Ulster loyalism gives way to more personal forms of bonding that humanize the soldiers.

McGuinness exposes the destructive nature of the Ulster heroics with two principal strategies. First, he frames the main action of the play, which follows the eight men as they perform their military duties, with the reflections of Pyper, the sole survivor among the group. Second, he dramatizes the erosion of the anti-Catholic posturing and Protestant unanimity that at first unites the young men as their resolve crumbles in the face of reality. The two-act play is divided into four scenes. The first, "Remembrance," is Pyper's prologue, which provides a gloss on what is to follow, revealing him to inhabit an "Ulster that lies in rubble at our feet" because of the religious strife that World

"WE WERE NEVER TOLD"

Frank McGuinness was born in Buncrana, County Donegal, on July 29, 1953, and attended Donegal schools through the 1960s. Situated on the border of Northern Ireland, County Donegal was once part of the Ulster province but was split off when the Republic of Ireland was established in 1921. Despite the physical proximity, McGuinness has confessed that he knew little of Ulster's history or culture until he began lecturing at the University of Ulster in Coleraine in the late 1970s. It was around this time that he became aware of the tremendous sacrifice made by the men of the 36th Division at the first battle of the Somme, where more than 5,500 Ulster soldiers died on the first day of fighting. McGuinness was shocked and angered that this history had been erased in Catholic Ireland. According to McGuinness's friend Myles Dungan—himself a champion of the forgotten Southern Nationalists who fought in World War I—McGuinness adopted the mantra "We Were Never Told" during the course of writing *Observe the Sons of Ulster Marching towards the Somme*. In an essay in the *Irish Times* commemorating the ninetieth anniversary of the battle of the Somme, Dungan stated that the implications of the refrain did not become clear to him until he attended a performance of *Observe the Sons of Ulster*, which he described as "an electrifying and chastening experience. Something that meant so much to Ulster Unionists meant precisely nothing to a Southern Nationalist."

War I clearly did not halt. "Initiation" brings the men together in training camp, where they are united by their swaggering Ulster pride. This scene establishes Pyper's role as an outsider. An artist and homosexual from an upper-class family who claims to detest his Ulster background and to have joined the war effort because he wants to hasten his own death, Pyper succeeds in goading the men into reflecting on their political and religious certainties in "Pairing," a scene that couples the soldiers in four separate conversations that all take place during a period of leave after five months of duty. Through these talks, full of fear and doubt, the men form strong emotional bonds, realizing that they are in the end fighting for no other cause than for each other. They grow as individuals, including the nilhist Pyper, who is transformed by his love for a fellow soldier, a blacksmith from Fermanagh. The Ulster myth appears strikingly empty in "Bonding," the play's climax, in which the men reenact the Battle of the Boyne and exchange Orange sashes only to march into a bloodbath, leaving Pyper alone to grow old contemplating the absurdity of their cause.

While *Observe the Sons of Ulster* celebrates the courage of the Ulster soldiers and lifts their sentiments above mere prejudice, its tone is primarily one of remorse for the vapid heroics that have kept Ireland in a perpetual state of siege. The anti-Catholic rhetoric of the men progressively loses its resonance in the face of their terror and what the audience knows to be historical

Lalor Roddy in a scene from the 1996 Royal Shakespeare Company production of *Observe the Sons of Ulster Marching towards the Somme.* © ROBBIE JACK/CORBIS.

inevitability. But McGuinness directs audience interpretation early on by establishing the divide between political jingoism and private sacrifice in Pyper's prologue, where the old man lashes out at the Protestant God and the soldiers' blind belief in the Ulster cause: "We claimed we would die for each other in battle. To fulfill that claim we marched into the battle that killed us all. That is not loyalty. That is not love. That is hate. Deepest hate. Hate for one's self. We wished ourselves to die and in doing so we let others die to satisfy our blood lust." It is this inheritance of self-hatred that plagues Pyper over the course of his adult life.

CRITICAL DISCUSSION

Observe the Sons of Ulster played to enthusiastic audiences in its initial run and was honored with several awards, perhaps most significantly the Ewart-Biggs Peace Prize, established in large part to promote reconciliation in Ireland. David Nowlan's *Irish Times* review of the Abbey's original production, as quoted in Helen Lojek's 2007 article "*Observe the Sons of Ulster*: Historical Stages," labeled the play "one of the most comprehensive attacks ever made in the theatre on Ulster Protestantism" and thereby ignited a protracted debate in the letter columns of the paper. Most critics disagreed with Nowlan's estimation, praising *Observe the Sons of Ulster* as a brave attempt at cross-cultural understanding.

Subsequent runs of *Observe the Sons of Ulster* outside Ireland—throughout Europe and Australia in the 1990s and in the United States in the early 2000s—were welcomed for the universality of the play's antiwar message, while revivals at home continued to generate enthusiasm for McGuinness's efforts at bridge building. Maeliosa Stafford, an established theater director in Ireland who staged a production of *Observe the Sons of Ulster* for the Festival of Sydney 1990, spoke for many Irish reviewers in declaring that McGuinness "uses this play as his olive branch, it is the way he can deal with horror and sectarian violence, by presenting a play like this and showing the views of those on the other side of the fence." Lojek records that by the time *Observe the Sons of Ulster* reached the New York stage at Lincoln Center in February 2003, "Its relevance to US history seemed so compelling that one reviewer suggested the play be retitled *Observe the Sons and Daughters of America Marching Towards Iraq*." The play has also resonated with audiences as an emblem of the hate speech that currently divides Muslims and Christians.

Observe the Sons of Ulster has generated a large quantity of academic criticism, much of it focusing on McGuinness's view of history and the strategies he employed to get audiences to identify with men whose values they do not understand or do not share. Critics have judged the play to be consistent with modernist interpretations of World War I that expose the hollowness of combat rhetoric. But McGuinness's method of exploding the Ulster cultural myth—his use of the outsider Pyper as an "Other" to investigate difference—is considered especially innovative. The play has been the subject of a number of studies examining how Pyper's homosexuality helps shift the progress of the play away from the specifics of history and public experience toward the personal and the universal. In her article "Watch Yourself," Susan Cannon Harris suggests that the theme of homosexuality is central to McGuinness's deconstruction of historical myth. She writes, "McGuinness's work, by foregrounding the issue of sexual orientation, suggests that the restrictive structures that define political opposition are dependent on those that uphold the distinction between hetero- and homosexuality, and that by subverting one of these structures it might be possible to subvert the others."

BIBLIOGRAPHY

Sources

Dungan, Myles. "Fighting Amnesia." *Irish Times*, 2006. Web. 22. Jan. 2013.

Francombe, Ben. "Frank McGuinness." *British and Irish Dramatists since World War II: Third Series.* Ed. John Bull. Detroit: Gale Group, 2011. *Dictionary of Literary Biography.* Vol. 245. *Literature Resource Center.* Web. 13 Aug. 2012.

Harris, Susan Cannon. "Watch Yourself: Performance, Sexual Difference, and National Identity in the Irish Plays of Frank McGuinness." *Genders* 28 (1998). Web. 10 Aug. 2012.

Lojek, Helen. "*Observe the Sons of Ulster*: Historical Stages." *Echoes Down the Corridor: Irish Theatre—Past, Present, and Future.* Ed. Patrick Lonergan and Riana O'Dwyer. Dublin: Carysfort, 2007. 81–94. Print.

McGuinness, Frank. *Observe the Sons of Ulster Marching towards the Somme.* London: Faber, 1986. Print.

Nowlan, David. "Observe the Sons of Ulster Marching Toward the Somme at the Peacock." *Irish Times* 19 Feb. 1985: 10. Print.

Sommer, Elyse. Rev. of *Observe the Sons of Ulster Marching Towards the Somme*, by Frank McGuinness. Dir. Nicholas Martin. Lincoln Center, Mitzi E. Newhouse Theater, New York, NY, 2003. *CurtainUp*, 2003. Web. 22 Jan. 2013.

Stafford, Maeliosa, with Aine de Paor. "Druid in Oz." *Theatre Ireland* 24 (1990–91): 46–49. *JSTOR.* Web. 4 Aug. 2012.

Further Reading

Brown, Terence. "From the Somme to Armageddon." *Fortnight* 18–31 March 1985: 23–24. *JSTOR.* Web. 4 Aug. 2012.

Herron, Tom. "Dead Men Talking: Frank McGuinness's *Observe the Sons of Ulster Marching towards the Somme.*" *Eire-Ireland: A Journal of Irish Studies* 39.1–2 (2004): 136+. *Literature Resource Center.* Web. 4 Aug. 2012.

Hill, Jacqueline. "Art Imitating War? *Observe the Sons of Ulster Marching towards the Somme* and Its Place in History." *Etudes irlandaises* 34.1 (2009): 37–52. Print.

Kiberd, Declan. "Frank McGuinness and the Sons of Ulster." *Yearbook of English Studies* 35 (2005): 279+. *Literature Resource Center.* Web. 5 Aug. 2012.

Lojek, Helen. *Contexts for Frank McGuinness's Drama.* Washington, DC: Catholic U of America P, 2004. Print.

Pine, Emilie. "The Tyranny of Memory: Remembering the Great War in Frank McGuinness's *Observe the Sons of Ulster Marching towards the Somme.*" *Irish University Review* 40.1 (2010): 59+. *Literature Resource Center.* Web. 4 Aug. 2012.

Media Adaptation

Observe the Sons of Ulster Marching Towards the Somme. Dir. Patrick Hoffman. Perf. Richard Easton, Dashiell Eaves, Christopher Fitzgerald, et al. New York, © 2003. Videocassette.

Janet Mullane

POEMS FOR SPAIN

Stephen Spender, John Lehmann

✤ *Key Facts*

Time Period:
Mid-20th Century

Genre:
Poetry

Events:
Spanish Civil War; rise of Franco; growing tension between communism and fascism

Nationality:
English

OVERVIEW

Poems for Spain (1939), edited by Stephen Spender and John Lehmann, is an anthology of English poetry (with some Spanish verse in translation) that expresses solidarity with the Popular Front during the Spanish Civil War (1936–1939) and condemns Francisco Franco's Nationalist regime for instigating and perpetuating the conflict. Some of the era's most famous poets, including W. H. Auden, Louis MacNeice, and Pablo Neruda, contributed to the work, along with many less well-known writers. The poems are stylistically diverse but serve to depict what Spender termed the "long, crushing, and confused process of defeat, which the democratic principle has been undergoing." More generally, they represent an ongoing exploration of the relationship between literature and active politics, a tension sometimes addressed explicitly and sometimes implicit in the dynamic of the poetry.

Though the poems were written during the war, the collection was published after the decisive Nationalist victory of 1939—a fact that seriously curtailed their efficacy as articles of literary propaganda. Moreover, critics of the "thirties poets" recognized in their Spanish Civil War writings a jingoistic strain uncomfortably reminiscent of World War I. Novelist George Orwell remarked that "the literary history of the thirties seems to justify the opinion that a writer does well to keep out of politics." A few individual works from the book transcend this critical apathy, most notably Auden's "Spain," which is now considered the iconic English poem of the Spanish Civil War. The book as a whole is remembered as a milestone in the ongoing conversation among the influential "Auden group" of poets (Auden, Spender, MacNeice, and C. Day-Lewis) and as a testament to literary and artistic voices silenced by the war.

HISTORICAL AND LITERARY CONTEXT

Poems for Spain anthologized literary reactions to the Spanish Civil War, which officially began in July 1936. Tensions between the left-wing Popular Front and the right-wing Nationalists erupted in a military coup that originated in northern Africa and quickly spread to the Iberian Peninsula. Many observers saw in the war an inevitable clash between the emergent political systems of communism and fascism; many more were appalled by reports of mass executions and political murders. As the conflict wore on, the Nationalist force extended its control from the northern and southwestern edges of Spain to encompass the nation as a whole.

By the time *Poems for Spain* went to press, the Nationalists had won the war; Franco declared victory in April 1939. Many of the poems, however, were written earlier and thus both reflect immediate experiences of the war and issue urgent calls for its cessation. Several British authors, including Spender and Auden, had spent time in Spain as fighters in the international brigades or as war reporters; poet John Cornford was killed near Córdoba at the war's outset. The British literati in general strongly favored the Popular Front, an allegiance they expressed in publications such as *Left Review.* Moreover, a burgeoning communist presence in the United Kingdom attracted many writers who saw in Franco's regime a political and moral archenemy.

Spender and Lehmann cast the political import of *Poems for Spain* in terms of other historic conflicts and the literary response thereto. In his introduction, Spender invokes the "greatest of the English war poets," Wilfred Owen, who famously declared, "All a poet can do to-day is warn." Where Owen sought to warn about "the pity of war" and to provide an antidote to militant patriotism, Spender offers a call to arms, a "warning that it is necessary for civilization to defend and renew itself." Spender further invokes William Wordsworth, who had seemingly anticipated *Poems for Spain* in his reaction to an earlier war. Like Wordsworth, who had upheld the Spanish cause against Napoleonic invasion, Spender (along with the other contributors) invokes, in the name of a timely cause, the "fundamental, political and moral ideas of liberty, justice, freedom."

Poems for Spain confirms the existence of a strong communist undercurrent in British literature; contributors Margot Heinemann and Sylvia Townsend Warner went on to have influential, politically active careers. The collection also serves as a sort of closing statement for the 1930s as a literary epoch. In a 1943 piece for *Poetry,* David Daiches describes the book as "the final stage of [the] brief but important cycle" of 1930s poetry, a period he characterizes (the contributions of female poets to *Poems for Spain* notwithstanding) as an expression of "the doomed hopes and justified fears of the young men" of that decade. Daiches also offers an explanation for the subsequent generation's break with the 1930s poets: the grimly prophetic earlier work had come all too true during World War II, leaving little to say but a distasteful "I told you so."

THEMES AND STYLE

Nearly all of the *Poems for Spain* speak to a preoccupation with the horrors of war, which are almost invariably blamed on Nationalist forces and their international supporters. Central to many poets' depiction of the conflict is the idea that Spain—its people, its culture, even its landscape—was caught totally off-guard by the magnitude and suddenness of the war; a number of poems carry this idea to the ominous conclusion that England would face a similar fate. Relatively few of the poems directly address the matter of British involvement in the war, generally arguing that the United Kingdom must intervene before the fascist plague spreads further. Notable in this regard is Edgell Rickword's satirical address "To the Wife of Any Non-Intervention Statesman," which declares, "Spain bleeds, and England wildly gambles / To bribe the butcher in the shambles."

The techniques employed in *Poems for Spain* are as diverse as the writers themselves. A number of distinct approaches are demarcated by the book's sections, which bear such titles as "Satire," "Romances," and "Lorca." In "Lorca," three poems mount a grimly specific appeal to the volume's literary audience. These funereal compositions cast poet Federico García Lorca as a representative victim of the Franco regime; his assassination exemplifies a dangerous Nationalist attitude toward writers and intellectuals. In his poem "Lorca," Geoffrey Parsons writes, "The Fascists have only one answer for a poet— / Their stuttering lead syllables prevent repartee." This premise—that the Nationalist agenda is inimical to poetry and to art in general—is repeated throughout the book.

The language and tenor of the poems vary from one author to another. Many of the poems give vent to indignation at the sheer human cost of the war; bitter sarcasm is common, as in Rex Warner's "Arms in Spain," which accuses the Italian Fascist Party of supporting the Nationalist offensive "Lest the hand should be held at last more valuable than paper, / lest man's body and mind should be counted more than gold." Others express sorrow at the passing of a simpler way of life, as does Ruthven Todd in "Poem for Joan Miró," which depicts prewar Spain as a paradise of pastoral beauty. Still others, such as Charles Donnelly (whose poem "The Tolerance of Crows" was penned shortly before his own death in the war), attempt to match the impersonal force of war with a coolly disciplined style, enumerating the origins of death in "problems on maps, well-ordered dispositions, / Angles of elevation and direction."

PAINTERS OF THE SPANISH CIVIL WAR

Some of the *Poems for Spain* eulogize works of art by Pablo Picasso and Joan Miró—the two Spanish artists most closely associated with the Spanish Civil War—with prescience and sensitivity. Albert Brown, in "From a Painting by Picasso," mourns the "pure tints in the sky of life," which war threatens to destroy with a "black sudden daub of despair," and imagines with dread the war's toll on the women of Picasso's portraits. Miró's work is likewise eulogized in a poem by Ruthven Todd, who recognizes that the "peasant pots," "dry brown hare," and "magic farm" of the painter's 1920s work will be unable to greet him upon his return. By 1937, many of the early works of these artists—Picasso's cafes and cityscapes, Miró's geometric farmlands—had fallen victim to the war.

Picasso and Miró survived the war to resume their internationally acclaimed work. Indeed, Picasso produced one of his greatest masterpieces, the richly allegorical mural *Guernica* (1937), at the height of the conflict. Picasso's painting depicts the terror of a German bombing raid in the Basque country and speaks more generally to the war's potential to destroy lives and derange landscapes. The work was commissioned for the 1937 Paris International Exposition by a Spanish Republican government facing its imminent overthrow. Miró's starkly foreboding mural *The Reaper* (1937) was produced for the same occasion, though its political connotations are less evident.

CRITICAL DISCUSSION

Poems for Spain did more to cement the artistic reputation of its authors than to advocate for political change. Individual poems in the volume were well regarded as literature if not as historical reportage. As early as 1940, Orwell recognized Auden's "Spain" as "one of the few decent things that have been written about the Spanish war," though he took the poet to task for the casual "amoralism" of some of his descriptions. Critical discussion of the book was soon curtailed, as Daiches reports—World War II brought about a changing of the poetic guard, ushering in the short-lived New Apocalypse movement and the "violent mythopoeic faculty" of Dylan Thomas.

Subsequent criticism of *Poems for Spain* has established the work's place in the development of the political views of the Auden group. The poets' public procommunist and antifascist commitments in *Poems for Spain* were often undercut by subsequent publications, in which more private views were revealed. Lee Bartlett, editor of a 1980 collection of Spender's letters, regarded the poet's work during the *Poems for Spain* period as evidence of a "growing 'engagement' with the general plight of the poor, the unemployed, the oppressed." The same volume, however, reveals Spender's often vehement distaste for those

A Spanish Civil War poster promoting support for the International Brigades, military units made up of antifascist volunteers from different countries. British poet Stephen Spender was one such volunteer. 'THE INTERNATIONAL BRIGADES AT THE CORE OF THE POPULAR ARMY HELP DEFEND YOUR WEALTH AND HOMELAND,' REPUBLICAN POSTER (COLOUR LITHO), SPANISH SCHOOL, (20TH CENTURY)/ PRIVATE COLLECTION/ PETER NEWARK MILITARY PICTURES/THE BRIDGEMAN ART LIBRARY.

very groups; Robert C. Manteiga, writing in *Modern Language Studies* in 1989, considers this proof that Spender was "a true bourgeois with little tolerance for people of a different social class."

Poems for Spain stands as one of the major compilations of the Spanish Civil War. In "Doing Business with Totalitaria" (2006), Marina Mackay notes that the Spanish Civil War is, for literary historians, "conventionally the first stop after the high modernist 1920s." Several authors of *Poems for Spain* expressed their political stances more clearly and directly in the *Left Review* and the somewhat infamous pamphlet *Authors Take Sides on the Spanish War* (1937). Moreover, those contributors who remain

widely read owe their fame chiefly to earlier writings. Auden's "Spain" again constitutes the major exception. In a 1972 piece for *Albion,* Christopher Bone notes that it is still "generally considered to be the best poem in the English language concerning the Spanish Civil War." However, acclaim for Auden's poem among later critics has been less universal. In *Dividing Lines: Poetry, Class, and Ideology in the 1930s* (1991), Adrian Caesar affirms contemporary critiques of the politically noncommittal "Spain" and suggests that other poets, such as Rex Warner and John Cornford, more nearly approached the anthology's stated goal.

BIBLIOGRAPHY

Sources

Bone, Christopher. "W. H. Auden in the 1930s: The Problem of Individual Commitment to Political Action." *Albion: A Quarterly Journal Concerned with British Studies* 4.1 (1972): 3–11. Print.

Caesar, Adrian. *Dividing Lines: Poetry, Class, and Ideology in the 1930s.* Manchester UP, 1991. Print.

Daiches, David. "Contemporary Poetry in Britain." *Poetry* 62.3 (1943): 150–64. Print.

Mackay, Marina. "'Doing Business with Totalitaria': British Late Modernism and Politics of Reputation." *ELH* 73.3 (2006): 729–53. Print.

Manteiga, Robert C. "Politics and Poetics: England's Thirties Poets and the Spanish Civil War." *Modern Language Studies* 19.3 (1989): 3–14. Print.

Orwell, George. "Inside the Whale." *Inside the Whale and Other Essays.* London: Victor Gollancz, 1940. Print.

Spender, Stephen. *Letters to Christopher: Stephen Spender's Letters to Christopher Isherwood, 1929–1939.* Ed. Lee Bartlett. Santa Barbara: Black Sparrow Press, 1980. Print.

Further Reading

Auden, W. H., et al. *Authors Take Sides on the Spanish War.* London: Left Review, 1937. Print.

Monteath, Peter. *Writing the Good Fight: Political Commitment in the International Literature of the Spanish Civil War.* London: Greenwood P, 1994. Print.

Spender, Stephen. *The Thirties and After.* New York: Random House, 1978. Print.

Symons, Julian. *The Thirties: A Dream Revolved.* Revised ed. London: Faber and Faber, 1975. Print.

Wilkinson, James D. "Truth and Delusion: European Intellectuals in Search of the Spanish Civil War." *Salmagundi* 76/77 (1987–88): 3–52. Print.

Michael Hartwell

REFLECTIONS ON THE REVOLUTION IN FRANCE

Edmund Burke

OVERVIEW

Published in 1790, Edmund Burke's *Reflections on the Revolution in France* is an aggressive philippic against the French Revolution and a passionate defense of tradition and custom against violence and radical change. The revolution, which began in 1789, threatened not only to topple the French monarchy but to destabilize other European governments as well. As interest in democracy and ideals of equality and freedom gained momentum among the British populace, the ruling class grew concerned that England might also fall to revolutionary fervor. Ostensibly a reply to Charles-Jean-François Depont, a French friend of Burke's who had solicited the author's opinion on the events across the English Channel, *Reflections* is a stern warning to educated English citizens about the dangers that radical political change, such as that advocated by French republicans, posed to the smooth running of nations in general and to the social fabric of Great Britain in particular.

Burke wrote *Reflections* near the end of a career in Britain's Parliament that had lasted almost three decades. While serving in the House of Commons, he was often involved in efforts to limit the authority of the Crown in favor of the rights of citizens as enshrined in the English Constitution. Indeed, he was sympathetic with American revolutionaries in their conflict with the British monarchy. Thus, his angry attack on the French Revolution in *Reflections* came as a surprise, and, although the work was a great success, selling nineteen thousand copies within six months, it received much hostile criticism. At least fifty responses, many of them overtly critical, were penned in the years following the publication of *Reflections,* with Thomas Paine's *Rights of Man* (1791) becoming the most popular. Many writers referred to Burke as an "ingenious madman," and he was lampooned in France and in numerous political cartoons. Even some of his political allies, such as Charles James Fox, were forced to concede that his indictment was excessive. Nevertheless, many of his pronouncements proved correct as the revolution progressed, and he is today regarded as one of the most important English writers on the French Revolution and as an extremely prescient, if not prophetic, voice amid the turbulence of the early 1790s.

HISTORICAL AND LITERARY CONTEXT

Reflections details Burke's outrage at the French for their lack of deference to traditional institutions, as well as his fear that the extremism of French republican principles would result in a democratic tyranny. Although he conceded that the French monarchy was far from perfect (King Louis XVI had been accused of bankrupting the country and of other abuses of power), Burke argued that the wholesale eradication of the monarchy, an institution that had served France well, showed precipitous and gross disrespect. England's Glorious Revolution, which ended the reign of King James II in 1688, was for Burke an appropriate model for overthrowing a monarch; its purpose was to restore liberties and to protect established institutions, not to destroy national traditions and to promote radical ideologies. For similar reasons, Burke was accepting of the American revolutionaries' establishment of a republican government: the institutions of such a government were already largely in place and functioning in colonial America, and so the revolution there lacked the radical element he found so abhorrent in revolutionary France.

The events of 1789 resuscitated a spirit of radicalism in Great Britain that had been quiet throughout the 1780s, inaugurating an era of panic and concern. A slew of pamphlets from radical British publishers increased the unease of political elites such as Burke. For them, the spread of French revolutionary principles necessitated a strong defense of the existing English government, especially given that embers of revolution continued to smolder in the country. In *Reflections,* Burke discusses the potential threat of radical British religious dissenters and amateur philosophers, whose French counterparts had been the prime movers of the revolution in their country.

Reflections appeared during an early phase of a larger historical-literary phenomenon known as the revolution debate or the pamphlet war of the 1790s. During this period, England witnessed a tremendous outpouring of political literature related to the French Revolution. Like much of the political writing of the day, *Reflections* addresses English politics as much as it does French affairs. Many of Burke's arguments respond directly to those advanced by Richard Price in his *Discourse on the Love of Our Country,* a sermon delivered in 1790, which Burke felt smacked of French revolutionary ideas. Burke's

❖ *Key Facts*

Time Period:
Late 18th Century

Genre:
Treatise

Events:
French Revolution;
American Revolution;
growth of liberal
democracy

Nationality:
Irish

EDMUND BURKE AND THE AMERICAN REVOLUTION

Shortly after the publication of *Reflections,* Thomas Jefferson remarked, "The Revolution of France does not astonish me so much as the revolution of Mr. Burke." Jefferson was referring to an apparent intellectual inconsistency that many of Burke's opponents also noted: some fifteen years before he denounced the French Revolution, Burke had defended the American Revolution. However, a number of crucial differences between the two revolutions partially account for his seemingly contradictory opinions.

In an address to Parliament, Burke explained that Americans, through their fight for freedom, learned "order, submission to command, and a regard for great men," which the French lacked. He also noted that Americans already had a strong republican government, which meant that the changes they sought had been much less drastic than those sought in France. In addition, several events that strongly affected Burke's thinking intervened between the American and French Revolutions. The violence of the Gordon Riots in England in 1780, for example, alerted many to the potential destructiveness of an angry mob, and the Regency Crisis in 1788, occasioned by the debilitating illness of King George III, raised awareness of the potential dangers of even a temporary loss of centralized political leadership.

vicious critique was predicated on an exaggerated characterization of Price's radicalism, reflecting the vitriol and extremism of the heated political climate of the period.

Burke's characterization of Price and his pronouncements about the spread of French radicalism had a long afterlife in counterrevolutionary British political writing. After the French Revolution became more violent and France declared war on Britain in 1793, travesties of Enlightenment intellectuals' writings became common, and the popular critiques of Burke's *Reflections* gave way to an outpouring of conservative writing. However, unlike Burke with his elaborate rhetorical posturing, writers such as Hannah More, Arthur Young, and Samuel Horsley employed simple language to convey Burkean sentiments to middle- and lower-class readers. Burke's influence as a conservative writer has persisted, and he is today considered one of the foundational figures of modern British conservatism.

THEMES AND STYLE

The central theme of *Reflections* is that traditional customs and institutions, such as the law, the church, and even the monarchy, constitute the fabric of society and bind a nation together; therefore, change, when necessary, should be gradual, not swift and violent. Burke writes, "It is with infinite caution that any man ought to venture upon pulling down an edifice which has

answered in any tolerable degree for ages the common purposes of society, or on building it up again without having models and patterns of approved utility before his eyes." The French, he notes, lack such models and patterns and instead have relied on abstract principles and "pretended rights" of "theorists" in order to construct a new government. For him, such an approach is misguided because it fails to consider "all examples of antiquity … precedents, charters, and acts of parliament" or to respect a government that has proved its "usefulness over time."

As a series of reflections in epistolary form, with no chapter divisions or subject headings, *Reflections* lacks formal structure. This absence of discernible form, however, allows Burke to write in a variety of rhetorical styles. The text moves seamlessly from a dramatic, highly stylized eulogy of Marie Antoinette ("I saw the queen of France … [N]ever lighted on this orb … a more delightful vision … just above the horizon … glittering like the morning star") to shorter, plainer statements of principle ("On this scheme of things, a king is but a man, a queen is but a woman; a woman is but an animal, and an animal not of the highest order"). As David Duff has noted, this blending of styles gives the text a natural feel that functions as a formal analogue to Burke's characterization of the nation as an organic continuum from past to future.

The stylistic oscillations of *Reflections* are matched by shifts in language, marking the contrasts between the people of England and France. Burke describes his ideal state (Britain) in terms of a smooth-running, familial entity ("we have given to our frame of polity the image of a relation in blood"), while he excoriates the French revolutionaries for being antipathetic, violent, and unnatural ("Everything seems out of nature in this strange chaos of levity and ferocity."). He calls France a "monstrous tragi-comic scene" where all the "decent drapery of life" has been "rudely torn off." Whereas the British feel "love, veneration, admiration, or attachment" for their government, the French subscribe to a "barbarous philosophy" that condones the kidnapping and degradation of the royal family. At its most basic, the state is, for Burke, "a partnership between those who are living, those who are dead, and those who are to be born," a contract of quasi-divine importance that should be immune to the whims of the revolutionaries' "cold hearts and muddy understandings."

CRITICAL DISCUSSION

Reflections was an immediate success; seven thousand copies sold in its first week of availability, generating a flurry of passionate written responses, both positive and negative, which often mention Burke in the title (such as those by Joseph Priestley and Catharine Macaulay). Many of Burke's admirers responded effusively, including British author and politician Edward Gibbon, who is reported to have said, "I admire his

Promis'd Horrors of the French INVASION, — or — Forcible Reasons for negociating a Regicide PEACE. Vide. The Authority of Edmund Burke.

Promis'd Horrors of the French Invasion, a 1796 print by British caricaturist James Gillray, projects the feared impact of France's revolutionary ideals. *PROMIS'D HORRORS OF THE FRENCH INVASION, PUBLISHED BY HANNAH HUMPHREY, 1796 (COLOURED ENGRAVING), GILLRAY, JAMES (1757–1815)/© COURTESY OF THE WARDEN AND SCHOLARS OF NEW COLLEGE, OXFORD/THE BRIDGEMAN ART LIBRARY.*

eloquence, I approve his politics, I adore his chivalry." Even King George III is said to have remarked, "it was a book which every gentleman ought to read." However, detractors such as Paine, Mary Wollstonecraft, and Brooke Boothby attacked Burke for romanticizing tradition and the ruling elite. In *A Vindication of the Rights of Men* (1790), Wollstonecraft's famous response to *Reflections,* she scathingly refers to Burke's "servile reverence for antiquity, and prudent attention to self-interest."

Although Burke endured a barrage of criticism in the early 1790s, by 1793 his "critics were silenced," as noted by John Whale, because many of his predictions about the bloody course the revolution would take proved correct. His pronouncements confirmed the importance of British ministries in the early decades of the nineteenth century. As the British political landscape changed, two seemingly opposed political factions sought to claim the author as one of their own. Burke, dubbed in the 1830s the patron saint of conservatism, also appealed to Victorian liberals. The anthologizing of his writings throughout the nineteenth century gave rise to what J. C. D. Clarke calls a "usable" and adaptable Burke. Recognized as an important prose writer who straddled the gap between the Enlightenment and Romanticism, Burke remains a focus of critical interest.

Burke's *Reflections* has attracted scholarly attention from a wide variety of disciplines and approaches. Critics interested in the literature of the Romantic period and in British political history, for example, have frequently treated Burke as what Kevin Gilmartin describes as a "benchmark of the conservative temperament" in the 1790's. While the politics of *Reflections* are thus often at the forefront of many critical discussions, the work's literary dimensions have not been ignored. Questions of genre and structure in particular have been the focus of recent attention; David Duff, for instance, has described the work as a "generically hybrid text which combines a huge range of expressive modes." Burke's elaborate defense of all things British (constitution, customs, and way of life) has also made *Reflections* a fertile site for discussions of nationalism and national identity. Thus, Tom Furniss notes that Burke's *Reflections* develops a "reactionary nationalism," an idea of British-ness predicated on a love for (and preservation of) the country's longstanding sociocultural order that contrasts with the destructive "revolutionary nationalism" of France. Burke's efforts to consolidate a British identity by means of his characterization of the French as a barbaric "other" have even led some critics to examine *Reflections* in terms of the larger dichotomy between East and West, Orient and Occident, Asia and Europe. Spurgeon Thompson, for example, examines

Reflections in the context of later eighteenth-century travel writing and declares it a "foundational text for … Eurocentrism."

BIBLIOGRAPHY

Sources

Burke, Edmund. *Reflections on the Revolution in France.* Ed. L. G. Mitchell. New York: Oxford UP, 2009. Print.

Butler, Marilyn, ed. *Burke, Paine, Godwin, and the Revolution Controversy.* New York: Cambridge UP, 1984. Print.

Clarke, J. C. D. Introduction. *Reflections on the Revolution in France.* Ed. Clarke. Stanford: Stanford UP, 2001. 23–122. Print.

Duff, David. "Burke and Paine: Contrasts." *The Cambridge Companion to British Literature of the French Revolution in the 1790s.* Ed. Pamela Clemit. New York: Cambridge UP, 2011. 47–70. Print.

Gilmartin, Kevin. "Counter-revolutionary Culture." *The Cambridge Companion to British Literature of the French Revolution in the 1790s.* Ed. Pamela Clemit. New York: Cambridge UP, 2011. 129–44. Print.

Rakove, Jack N. "Why American Constitutionalism Worked." *Reflections on the Revolution in France.* By Edmund Burke. Ed. Frank M. Turner. New Haven: Yale UP, 2003. 248–67. Print.

Thompson, Spurgeon. "Edmund Burke's *Reflections on the Revolution in France* and the Subject of Eurocentrism." *Irish University Review* 33.2 (2003): 245–62. *JSTOR.* Web. 26 June 2012.

Whale, John, ed. Introduction. *Edmund Burke's* Reflections on the Revolution in France: *New Interdisciplinary Essays.* Manchester: Manchester UP, 2000. 1–17. Print.

Wollstonecraft, Mary. *A Vindication of the Rights of Men.* London: J. Johnson, 1790. Print.

Further Reading

Blakemore, Steven, ed. *Burke and the French Revolution: Bicentennial Essays.* Athens: U of Georgia P, 1992. Print.

Deane, Seamus. "Burke and the Enlightenment." *The French Revolution and Enlightenment in England.* Cambridge: Harvard UP, 1988. Print.

De Bruyn, Frans. *The Literary Genres of Edmund Burke: The Political Uses of Literary Form.* New York: Oxford UP, 1996. Print.

Dwan, David, and Christopher Insole, eds. *The Cambridge Companion to Edmund Burke.* New York: Cambridge UP, 2012. Print.

Furniss, Tom. "Cementing the Nation: Burke's Reflections on Nationalism and National Identity." *Edmund Burke's* Reflections on the Revolution in France: *New Interdisciplinary Essays.* Ed. John Whale. Manchester: Manchester UP, 2000. 145–67. Print.

Gilmartin, Kevin. *Writing against the Revolution: Literary Conservatism in Britain, 1790–1832.* New York: Cambridge UP, 2007. Print.

Hodson, Jane. *Language and Revolution in Burke, Wollstonecraft, Paine, and Godwin.* Aldershot: Ashgate, 2007. Print.

Howard, Darren. "Necessary Fictions: The 'Swinish Multitude' and the Rights of Man." *Studies in Romanticism* 47.2 (2008): 161–78. *JSTOR.* Web. 26 June 2012.

O'Brien, Conor Cruise. *The Great Melody: A Thematic Biography of Edmund Burke.* Chicago: U of Chicago P, 1992. Print.

Alex Covalciuc

THE RICE SPROUT SONG

Eileen Chang

OVERVIEW

Eileen Chang's 1955 novel *The Rice Sprout Song* explores the internal lives and relationships of a family suffering during the era of communist land reform in southern China. Chang offers a cutting critique of 1950s communist ideology by stoking her readers' sense of injustice over the sufferings of the novel's characters rather than by employing an authoritative narrative voice or taking an overt political stance. The protagonist Gold Root and his family—as well as the communist officials, or "cadres," who constantly interfere in their lives—are rendered intensely realistic and relatable through Chang's attention to the smallest human details.

The U.S. government commissioned Chang to write *The Rice Sprout Song* as a kind of expose intended to increase anticommunist sentiment in the United States and abroad. The novel was received well in the United States largely because it reinforced American perceptions of Chinese communism. After serving its political purpose in the United States, and having been banned in mainland China, the novel drifted into near-obsolescence until Columbia University professor C. T. Hsia resuscitated Chang's work in 1961, famously hailing her as "the best and most important writer in Chinese today." Since then, Chang's writing has influenced scores of Chinese writers. The legacy of *The Rice Sprout Song,* however, goes beyond what the book says about communism in China in the 1950s. An examination of the conditions surrounding the text's production and reception also reveals much about the political agenda of the United States during this period.

HISTORICAL AND LITERARY CONTEXT

Prior to the twentieth century, the majority of China's population lived as farming peasants, suffering frequently from hunger and other miseries under a feudal system in which the wealthy elite lived sumptuously off of the backbreaking labor of the poor. These conditions worsened during the Japanese invasion and the Chinese civil war of the 1940s. This long history of poverty proves essential in understanding the Chinese Communist Party's rise to power during the mid-1940s under Chairman Mao Zedong. Mao's communist policies and programs shaped the political and economic conditions of mid-century China and also brought about large-scale changes in traditional Chinese cultural and artistic values.

By the early 1950s, the Communist Party had thousands of propagandists working in Shanghai in order to bolster popular support for the dramatic changes it endorsed. Meanwhile, the United States Information Agency (USIA) also enlisted many writers to help in its Cold War against communist governments such as China's. The USIA had been recently expanded by President Dwight D. Eisenhower, as those in power began to realize that in an information age, the imperialist project of spreading democracy depended largely on the skillful use of words to summon support both at home and abroad. The U.S. government's commissioning of Chinese literary authors was adopted as a relatively new strategy with the belief that it would be particularly useful in bolstering anticommunist feeling in the West and perhaps even in reorienting the Chinese value system to comply with America's political and economic aims. The Rice Sprout Song, which depicts the wretchedness and desperation provoked by the widespread food shortages in once-bountiful southern China during the land-reform era, is one of two propaganda novels written by Chang on USIA commission. The other is Naked Earth (1956).

Although The Rice Sprout Song is technically a piece of propaganda, most critics find it far superior to most novels of its kind, including those of her contemporaries in China. This is largely because Chang's critique of communism feels more implicit than explicit; her exquisite detailing of the lives of common people engages reader sympathy far more effectively than do the minimal descriptions of flat characters often found in overtly political fiction. In this respect, The Rice Sprout Song bears the influence of the celebrated Chinese writer Lu Xun, whose work displays a nuanced understanding of politics. The title of Chang's novel is, in part, a response to a series of modern yangko ("rice sprout") operas, such as The White-Haired Girl (1945), produced for the Communist Party during the 1940s as a means of garnering support from peasants for communist policies and reforms.

Chang has been lauded more in China for her prewar, modernist short fiction than for her expert demonstration of how abstract politics impacts the personal lives of the powerless in the realist *The Rice*

Key Facts

Time Period:
Mid-20th Century

Genre:
Novel

Events:
Communist Revolution in China; Cold War

Nationality:
American

THE PERSONAL TRAGEDIES OF EILEEN CHANG

The tragic sensibility that defines the fiction of Eileen Chang (1920–1995) may have been informed by her unhappy childhood and difficult adult life. Chang was born into a high-class but dysfunctional family. When she was a child, her mother left Chang's father after he had become an opium addict and taken a concubine. Chang visited her mother when Chang was old enough to do so, but her father became jealous and locked her in the house. Eventually, Chang escaped to live with her mother.

Chang planned to attend the University of London, but because Europe was at war, she instead went to the University of Hong Kong. When Japan invaded Hong Kong in 1941, her studies were again compromised by war. Returning to Shanghai, she began writing the early works that made her popular in the 1940s, but she soon lost favor, perhaps in part because of her brief marriage to Hu Lancheng, who was branded a traitor for collaborating with the Japanese. Chang moved to the United States in 1955 and married an American screenwriter, Ferdinand Reyher, in 1956, but he died in 1967. Chang ended up living the rest of her life as a recluse in Los Angeles, still writing but without much publishing success. She died in 1995 without ever having returned to her homeland.

Sprout Song. However, her propaganda pieces had some influence on the Chinese Scar Literature of the 1970s, which attacks the later brutalities of Mao's Cultural Revolution, though these works are more simplistic and optimistic than Chang's. Much Chinese fiction of the 1990s, such as Yu Hua's best seller *To Live* (1993), echoes Chang's *The Rice Sprout Song* in both style and subject matter.

THEMES AND STYLE

The Rice Sprout Song explores the effects of hunger on human behavior and how the communist land reform of the 1950s actually worsened rather than improved the plight of China's peasant class. The obsessive and secretive relationship toward food that developed among poor farmers and communist officials alike demonstrates the level of denial that was required in order for the Communist Party to justify the continuation of its reforms in mainland China. Throughout the novel, the communist cadres generate celebratory and hopeful statements that sound good but fail to feed the people. Nevertheless, to avoid communist persecution, the poor must pretend, in the words of the character Big Aunt, that "everything is fine now! The poor have turned!"

Chang's omniscient third-person narration creates the illusion of objectivity, masking the novel's true function as anticommunist propaganda. Nevertheless, Chang's novel makes clear that communism

leads to scarcity by stifling individual freedom and motivation. She emphasizes this notion in her depictions of the communist cadres, who constantly deny that the peasants are starving and invade their privacy. Chang also explicitly calls attention to communism as empty rhetoric, such as when she notes how the cadres "fell into these familiar phrases without hesitation." However, rather than sacrificing the seeming objectivity of the narration by portraying the communist cadres as wooden, Chang utilizes skillful and frequent shifts in perspective that offer humanizing insights into the thoughts, feelings, and doubts of communist officials.

Chang's careful wording and phrasing choices have a subtle, haunting quality, making the text feel more like a timeless human tragedy than political propaganda. Gold Root's sister, Gold Flower, looks statuesque in her opening role as a bride: "there was about her an air of unreality, and oddly, of permanence." Later, watching his newly returned wife, Moon Scent, Gold Root is reminded of "some obscure goddess in a broken down little temple." The visiting Communist Party propaganda writer Ku, watching Moon Scent punish her daughter, Beckon, for begging for food, sees "something primeval in her exaggerated, theatrical exhibition of horror and distress." This theatrical quality renders the starvation grotesque, as in the last scene when the peasants are forced to celebrate a plenty that does not exist by performing the traditional dance of *The Rice Sprout Song* under the watchful eyes of communists who had shot several insurgent peasants the previous day. The final observation adds to the feeling of tragic universality, as Chang notes that "under the immense open sky the sound [of gongs and symbols] was muffled and strangely faint." By salting the realism of the narrative with this theatricality, Chang manages to soften the glaring political causes of tragedy, thereby creating an elegant and effective masque for the text's propagandist motivations.

CRITICAL DISCUSSION

Critical accounts of *The Rice Sprout Song*—and of the history of modern Chinese fiction in general—tend to vary depending on the political orientation of the critic. As Christopher Lee notes in *The Semblance of Identity: Aesthetic Mediation in Asian American Literature,* the book "has lived, as it were, different lives in different languages as it circulated among different publics." Shortly after writing *The Rice Sprout Song* in 1955, Chang left for the United States, realizing that her writing would no longer be welcomed in Maoist China. Her once-celebrated short fiction, detailing the personal lives of middle-class women in pre-communist, Japanese-occupied Shanghai, was now considered "bourgeois," and her political novels were banned in mainland China until the 1990s. *The Rice Sprout Song* did draw considerable interest in Hong Kong and Taiwan, and in the United States it was lauded by *Time*

China Land Reform, communist propaganda from 1951 depicting a new ox being brought to a communal farm. The Rice Sprout Song, commissioned by the U.S. Information Service, contradicts such images, describing instead hardship and starvation caused by the reforms. © MARY EVANS PICTURE LIBRARY/ ALAMY.

magazine as "the most authentic novel so far of life under the Chinese Communists." Nevertheless, it was largely forgotten by Americans after its political goals had been served.

Once Hsia offered his high praise of Chang in 1961—noting in particular The Rice Sprout Song's elegant, "classic" narrative structure and how the depictions of personal tragedies are reminiscent of those captured by writers such as Katherine Porter, Eudora Welty, and Flannery O'Connor—her writing drew the attention of critics Leung Ping-Kwan, Rey Chow, and Nicole Huang, among others. Early critics admired Chang's fiction for its evocative mixture of Eastern culture and Western psychology. Many recent scholars laud the book for its humane, profound depictions of the ordinary, non heroic people from the era it addresses.

Scholarly examinations of Chang's work have taken a more political bent in recent years. Though Chinese critics have paid more attention to her short fiction, other commentators have focused on her anticommunist novels and their role as propaganda. Lee emphasizes that The Rice Sprout Song was perceived—and inaccurately so—in the United States as an autobiographical, ethnographic text offering rare, secret information about communist China. Asian American literature scholar Richard Jean So has discussed Chang's propagandist work in even more detail, putting The Rice Sprout Song in the historical context of the "literary information warfare" that was so prevalent in the Cold War era.

BIBLIOGRAPHY

Sources

Chang, Eileen. The Rice Sprout Song: A Novel of Modern China. Berkeley: U of California P, 1998. Print.

"Eileen Chang (1921-)." Short Story Criticism. Vol. 28. Ed. Anna Sheets. Detroit: Gale, 1998. 18–47. Gale Cengage Learning. Web. 13 July 2012.

"Eileen Chang (1920–1995)." Twentieth-Century Literary Criticism. Vol. 184. Ed. Thomas J. Schoenberg and Lawrence J. Trudeau. Detroit: Gale, 2007. 100–54. Print.

Goldblatt, Howard. "The Rice Sprout Song." The China Quarterly 159 (1999): 760–61. Print.

Lee, Christopher (Christopher Ming). The Semblance of Identity: Aesthetic Mediation in Asian American Literature. Stanford: Stanford UP, 2012. Print.

Louie, Kam, ed. Eileen Chang: Romancing Languages, Cultures and Genres. Hong Kong: Hong Kong UP, 2012. Print.

Wang, David Der-Wei. "Forward." The Rice Sprout Song: A Novel of Modern China. Berkeley: U of California P, 1998. vii–xxv. Print.

Further Reading

Chi, Pang Yuan, and David Der-Wei Wang, eds. Chinese Literature in the Second Half of a Modern Century: A Critical Survey. Bloomington: Indiana UP, 2000. Print.

Chow, Rey. Modern Chinese Literary and Cultural Studies: Reimagining a Field. Durham: Duke UP, 2000. Print.

Feuerwerker, Yi-tsi Mei. Ideology, Power, Text: Self-Representation and the Peasant "Other" in Modern Chinese Literature. Palo Alto, CA: Stanford UP, 1998. Print.

Hsia, C. T. *A History of Modern Chinese Fiction.* New Haven: Yale UP, 1971. Print.

Lee, Leo Ou Fan. *Shanghai Modern: The Flowering of a New Urban Culture in China, 1930–1935.* Cambridge: Harvard UP, 1999. Print.

Leung Ping-Kwan, "Two Discourses on Colonialism: Huang Guliu and Eileen Chang on Hong Kong of the Forties." *Boundary 2* 25.3. (1998): 77–96. Print.

Wang, David Der-Wei. *The Monster that Is History: History, Violence, and Fictional Writing in Twentieth-Century China.* Berkeley; Los Angeles: U of California P, 2004. Print.

Media Adaptation

"The Rice Sprout Song." Studio One in Hollywood. Columbia Broadcasting System (CBS). WABI-TV, Bangor. 15 Apr. 1957. Television.

Sarah Gardam

SEVEN INTERPRETIVE ESSAYS ON PERUVIAN REALITY

José Carlos Mariátegui

OVERVIEW

José Carlos Mariátegui's collection *Seven Interpretative Essays on Peruvian Reality* was published in Lima in 1928, after each piece had appeared separately in the periodicals *Mundial* and *Amauta*. As an early Marxist interpretation of Latin American history, each of the seven essays focuses on a different aspect of Peruvian society: "Economic Evolution," "The Problem of the Indian," "The Problem of Land," "Public Education," "The Religious Factor," "Regionalism and Centralism," and "Literature on Trial." In his introduction, Mariátegui, who concurrently founded the Socialist Party of Peru (later the Communist Party of Peru), denies that he is "an impartial, objective critic" and freely proclaims his "avowed and resolute ambition: to assist in the creation of Peruvian socialism," which he envisions as an indigenous movement that would not follow the European model.

Mariátegui's activism began in 1918 when he launched a leftist newspaper, *La Razón,* which espoused socialist ideas, especially the reform of universities, support for labor unions, and an eight-hour work day. His central thesis in *Seven Interpretive Essays,* which was a culmination of his early writing, was that the Spanish Conquest had usurped the natural order of life in Peru and Latin America, creating an underclass of native peoples who must now find the strength to cast off the yoke of Western oppression and reclaim their rightful place at the center of their nation's culture, politics, and economy. In "The Problem of the Indian" and "The Problem of Land," for example, he chastises the *latifundistas*—large landowners—for oppressing the nation's peasants through their feudal-like policies. The solution, he believed, would be a collective situation based on the traditional practices of the native Incas. Likewise, the other essays argue for reform based on pre-Spanish traditions. The book's impact was immediate and long-lived. It can be construed as one of the Socialist Party's founding documents as well as a romantic treatise on Peruvian history and myth that inspired the *indigenismo* movement. Although occasionally criticized for its heterodoxy, *Seven Interpretive Essays* remains one of the most important Marxist analyses produced in Latin America and has inspired generations of Peruvian activists.

HISTORICAL AND LITERARY CONTEXT

By the turn of the twentieth century, most of Spain's New World colonies had extricated themselves from colonial rule. But after independence the colonial elites—exclusively Spanish in their ancestry—became the national elites, and society remained divided by class and ethnicity, with Indians occupying a place in society below that of mestizos. Governments were formed by rival families of the ruling classes and came to power through sham elections or military coups. During the same period, socialism was rapidly spreading from European intellectual circles to the populist-minded intellectuals in countries from Mexico to Argentina. Following World War I, the colonial and postcolonial peoples of Asia, Africa, and Latin America, galvanized by the success of the 1917 Bolshevik Revolution, formed leadership cadres and brought communism to their own countries.

Mariátegui's leftist writings as a journalist during this time drew the ire of President Leguía, and Mariátegui was effectively forced out of the country in 1919. He spent the next three years in Europe, primarily in Italy, where he witnessed the birth of the Italian Communist Party and the ascent of Benito Mussolini. For several months he was the houseguest of the eminent philosopher and historian, Benedetto Croce. Croce guided him through the works of Karl Marx and introduced him to the writings of Georges Sorel, whose 1908 *Reflections on Violence*—an inspiration to both Marxists and fascists—convinced Mariátegui of the power of myth in building a revolutionary consciousness.

When he returned to Peru in 1923, Mariátegui allied himself with Victor Raúl Haya de la Torre, the leader of the American Popular Revolutionary Alliance (APRA) and the leading Peruvian intellectual of the twentieth century. In 1928 Mariátegui founded the Socialist Party of Peru, which later became the Peruvian Communist Party, as a direct result of having published *Seven Interpretive Essays.* A cultural shift was then underway: *modernismo*—an aesthetic movement that blended romanticism, symbolism, and Parnassianism (which advocated "art for art's sake")—was sweeping the intellectual classes, students were protesting, and workers were forming trade unions. The

Key Facts

Time Period:
Early 20th Century

Genre:
Essay

Events:
Aftermath of World War I; spread of modernist aesthetics and Marxist ideology in South America

Nationality:
Peruvian

MARIÁTEGUI, MODERNISM, AND MYTH

José Carlos Mariátegui's use of mythology in incorporating Peru's indigenous peoples into a specifically Peruvian brand of socialism came partly from his intuition and partly from studying European modernism at the source. Visually, modern art ransacked the totems of "primitive" peoples for their evocative potency. Anthropologists, such as Sir James Frazer in *The Golden Bough* (1890), deconstructed myths as a framework for intellectual and artistic activity in cultures around the world. The psychologist Carl Jung explored myths as dramatic embodiments of each culture's emotional development. Most relevant for Mariátegui, however, was his encounter with the work of George Sorel and Sorel's insistence that social movements need a myth at their heart—i.e., the "myth of the general strike"—to gain popular support. "The soul of the Indian," said Mariátegui, in a footnote to "The Problem of the Indian" in *Seven Interpretive Essays*, "is not raised by the white man's civilization or alphabet but by the myth, the idea, of the Socialist revolution. The hope of the Indian is absolutely revolutionary. That same myth, that same idea, are the decisive agents in the awakening of other ancient peoples or races in ruin."

time was ripe for political reform, and Mariátegui understood that communism would never succeed as a European import.

A passionate modernist himself in literature and the graphic arts, Mariátegui was well situated to attract and hold the attention of the Peruvian cultural elite. A devotee of Irish novelist James Joyce, Spanish artist Pablo Picasso, and founder of psychoanalysis Sigmund Freud, he proposed a mythological framework for the struggle for social justice, and he drew upon the potent images and symbols of pre-Colombian art for his periodicals, posters, and banners. His principal magazine, the journal *Amauta* (1926–1930)—a native word meaning *master*—always included woodcuts of native art. Writing in the September 1928 issue of *Amauta,* Mariátegui stated: "Certainly, we do not wish that Socialism in America be a tracing and a copy. It must be a heroic creation. We must, with our own reality, in our own language, bring Indoamerican socialism to life."

THEMES AND STYLE

The main theme of the *Seven Interpretative Essays* is, in the words Jaime Hanneken, that of "forging a path of socialist revolution in Peru through the political and economic empowerment of its indigenous population." As Mariátegui himself puts it in the seventh and most militant essay, "Literature on Trial": "Man's spirit is indivisible and it must be so to achieve plenitude and harmony. I declare without hesitation that I bring to literary exegesis all my political passions and ideas, although in view of the way this word has

been misused, I should add that my politics are philosophy and religion." As suggested in the collection's title, the essays are not necessarily historically factual; Mariátegui's purpose was to foment socialist activism by reimagining Peru's past within a mythological framework.

Inspired by romanticism, the prose of *Seven Interpretive Essays* is highly emotional. In the sixth essay, "Regionalism and Centralism," he writes in colorful terms about the grandeur of the land: "The Andes advance to the sea, converting the coast into a narrow cornice dotted with ports and coves and forcing the cities into the sierra." Mostly, however, he addresses his reader plainly and directly, with a no-nonsense, almost brutal, confidence in the facts at his command. "The problem of the Indian is rooted in the land tenure system of our economy," he states flatly. "Any attempt to solve it with administrative or police measures, through education or by a road building program, is superficial and secondary as long as the feudalism of the gamonales [landowning bosses] continues to exist." Believing that native Peruvians must be empowered and brought into the socialist movement as the equals of the Spaniards and mestizos, Mariátegui asserts that

> the assumption that the Indian problem is ethnic is sustained by the most outmoded repertory of imperialist ideas. The concept of inferior races was useful to the white man's West for purposes of expansion and conquest. To expect that the Indian will be emancipated through a steady crossing of the aboriginal race with white immigrants is an anti-sociological naivete that could only occur to the primitive mentality of an importer of merino sheep.

These quotations, with their tone of palpable frustration with the ignorance and stupidity of the governing classes, make it obvious whom he conceives his readers to be—his fellow socialists and anyone else who has suffered at the hands of the ruling classes, especially the peasants, their urban counterparts, and the middle classes. Like the romantic he is, he uses many rhetorical styles to get his point across. He cajoles, he exhorts, he mocks, he reasons. After dismantling with ironclad logic all previous solutions to "the Indian problem," he returns to his original theme: "The new approach locates the problem of the Indian in the land tenure system."

CRITICAL DISCUSSION

The initial reaction to the *Seven Interpretative Essays on Peruvian Reality* was lukewarm; many news outlets ignored the book completely. Within a few years, however, Mariátegui's essays came to be seen as inspirational and original. When he died at age 35, just two years after the *Seven Essays* was published, the editors of his journal *Amauta* wrote that "Mariátegui, his memory, his life, his work belong to the proletariat.

In *Seven Interpretive Essays on Peruvian Reality* (1928), José Carlos Mariátegui discusses the indigenous people of Peru, like these Quechuan weavers. © TOPFOTO/THE IMAGE WORKS.

His life is our example, his work an unbreakable affirmation, his cadaver a protest." *Seven Interpretative Essays on Peruvian Reality* is essential for understanding Marxism as it developed in Peru, and it foreshadowed many of the ideas Mariátegui developed further in his *Defense of Marxism,* published serially in *Amauta* around the same time.

Mariátegui's essays guided generations of Peru's political activists. It was a guiding document in the 1968 Peruvian revolution led by Juan Velasco Alvarado, whose concept of *Peruanismo* was inspired at least partly on Mariátegui's call for justice for the economically disadvantaged. Later, the Maoist Communist Party of Peru adopted the name "The Shining Path" from one of Mariátegui's maxims: "Marxist-Leninism is the shining path to the future," and the United Mariáteguista Party was formed in 1984 by the merger of several leftist parties. In 2001 Alejandro Toledo was elected president of Peru and served until 2006. Born into a peasant family of Quechua heritage, Toledo represents the fulfillment of Mariátegui's ideals, becoming the nation's first indigenous president.

Mariátegui's varied interests, including socialism, political science, modern art and literature, mythology, and psychology, have provided scholars with many areas of research. In 1978 the Mexican author José Aricó wrote that the *Seven Interpretative Essays on Peruvian Reality* "remains, fifty years after its publication, the only really significant theoretical work of Latin American Marxism." Twenty years later, Penelope Duggan and Michael Löwy praised Mariátegui's strain of romanticism in *Seven Interpretive Essays* and called him "not only the most important and most inventive of the Latin American Marxists but a thinker whose work, in its power and originality, is of universal significance." According to biographer Jorge Basadre, Mariátegui's *Seven Interpretive Essays* "linked history to the drama of the present and the imponderables of the future" in a "methodical approach to national affairs that disdained pedantry, excessive details, and rhetoric."

BIBLIOGRAPHY

Sources

Aricó, José. "Mariátegui and Latin American Marxism." *Socialismo y Participación* 5 (1978): 16. Print.

Basadre, Jorge. Introduction. *Seven Interpretive Essays on Peruvian Reality.* By José Carlos Mariátegui. Trans. Basadre. Austin: U of Texas P, 1971. *Marxist Internet Archive.* Web. 30 Oct. 2012.

Duggan, Penelope, and Michael Löwy. "Marxism and Romanticism in the Work of Jose Carlos Mariategui." *Latin American Perspectives* 25.4 (1998): 76+. *General OneFile.* Web. 23 Sept. 2012.

Hanneken, Jaime. "Jose Carlos Mariategui and the Time of Myth." *Cultural Critique* 81 (2012): 1+. *Academic OneFile.* Web. 24 Sept. 2012.

Mariátegui, José Carlos. *Seven Interpretative Essays on Peruvian Reality.* Trans. Jorge Basadre. Austin: U of Texas P, 1971. *Marxist Internet Archive.* Web. 24 Oct. 2012.

Pita, Alfredo. "Jose Carlos Mariategui (1894–1930): Witness to an Age." *UNESCO Courier* Dec. 1994: 48. *General OneFile.* Web. 25 Sept. 2012.

Subirats, Eduardo. "Mariategui, Latin American Socialism, and Asia." *World Review of Political Economy* 1.3 (2010): 517+. *Academic OneFile.* Web. 24 Sept. 2012.

Further Reading

Galindo, Alberto Flores. *In Search of an Inca: Identity and Utopia in the Andes.* Trans. Hiatt Willie and F. Walker. New York: Cambridge UP, 2010. Print.

Löwy, Michael, ed. *Marxism in Latin America from 1909 to the Present: An Anthology.* Trans. Michael Pearlman. Atlantic Highlands: Humanities, 1992. Print.

Mariátegui, José Carlos. "Ethics and Socialism." *Defensa del Marxismo,* 1930. Trans. first published in *Tricontinental, Theoretical Organ of the Executive Secretariat of the Organization of Solidarity of the Peoples of Africa, Asia and Latin America* 3 (Nov.-Dec. 1967): 20–27. Marxist Internet Archive. Web. 24 Oct. 2012.

———. *The Heroic and Creative Meaning of Socialism.* Ed. and trans. Michael Pearlman. Atlantic Highlands: Humanities, 1996. Print.

———. *History of the World Crisis,* 1924. Trans. Juan R. Fajardo, 1998. *Marxist Internet Archive.* Web. 24 Oct. 2012.

Sorel, Georges. *Reflections on Violence.* Trans. T. E. Hulme. New York: Collier, 1961. Print.

Wachtel, Nathan. *The Vision of the Vanquished: The Spanish Conquest of Peru through Indian Eyes, 1530–1570.* New York: Barnes and Noble, 1977. Print.

Gerald Carpenter

"SPAIN"

W. H. Auden

OVERVIEW

W. H. Auden's poem "Spain," published in 1937, addresses one of the major conflicts of the time, the Spanish Civil War. In "Spain" Auden provides a survey of human history—past, present, and future—that achieves a remarkably sweeping scope in the space of ninety-two lines. The Spanish Civil War (1936–39) lies at the center of the poem, and Auden identifies this conflict as the defining struggle of human history up to this moment. Urging readers to take action in support of the anti-fascist fighters loyal to the embattled Spanish Republic, Auden depicts the war in Spain as a critical turning point in history, and he suggests that hope for a brighter future depends on the audience's response.

"Spain" was a popular success upon its initial publication, and it made a significant impact as propaganda for the cause it advocated—all proceeds from its sale were donated to aid groups working in Spain. Auden's poetic contribution to the Spanish Republican cause was one of the most notable among many others, as the Spanish Civil War became a cause célèbre for leftist artists and intellectuals in Britain. Yet "Spain" soon became the target of intense opprobrium from critics such as George Orwell, who condemned it as a politically naive exercise that blithely ignored the fact that both sides in the Spanish war were guilty of atrocities. Auden, who had often expressed doubt that poetry could make a difference in the real world, eventually regretted writing a poem that so earnestly attempted to do just that. Later in his life, he prohibited publishers from including "Spain" in his collected works.

HISTORICAL AND LITERARY CONTEXT

Spain became a republic in 1931, when the unpopular King Alfonso XIII was overthrown. The republic's last democratically elected government was dominated by liberals and moderate socialists. Conservative elements in Spanish society, including landowners, military officers, and Catholic clergy, opposed this government, and in 1936 right-wing army officers led by Francisco Franco revolted. Franco's rebellion set off a civil war, with forces loyal to the Republican government fighting against Franco's Nationalist forces for control of Spain. The Nationalists acquired the support of Nazi Germany and fascist Italy, and the Soviet Union provided aid to the Republicans. The democracies of Great Britain and France, meanwhile, tried to stay neutral.

While the British government refused to intervene in the Spanish conflict, many British citizens took sides. Writers and artists in particular were publicly divided over the war in Spain. Left-leaning writers, including Auden, strongly supported the Republicans, while a smaller number supported Franco. Artists and intellectuals with leftist or socialist sympathies sought to make material contributions to the Republican cause, with many using their talents to produce propaganda on its behalf. British poets and artists who supported the Spanish Republic played a key role in raising money for the cause and in recruiting soldiers for the International Brigades (foreign sympathizers who fought for the Republic). Early in the conflict, some writers, including John Cornford and Julian Bell (who both died in battle), as well as Orwell, even volunteered to fight in the International Brigades themselves.

Auden was one of many poets who vocally supported the Republicans, and by the beginning of 1937 he wanted to take a more active part in the conflict. Auden visited Spain in early 1937, apparently with the intention of volunteering to serve as an ambulance driver, though he never did so. Auden's only contribution to the cause in Spain "was to make a few propaganda broadcasts" on the radio, "which he soon realized [had] no purpose because most of his listeners understood no English." Disillusioned, he returned to England. Many other British poets had written propaganda poems to promote the Republican cause, and Auden—one of the country's best-known young poets—chose to produce his own contribution to this rapidly growing body of literature.

"Spain" was an effective contribution to pro-Republican propaganda efforts in Britain, yet it was controversial in its own time, and its legacy has proved ambiguous. Many critics regard it as one of Auden's greatest poems, but Auden himself felt differently. Later in his career, he turned away from writing about political subjects and rejected the highly politicized "Spain." By 1964 he would only permit the poem's publication if the editor agreed to include a note calling it "trash which he is ashamed to have written."

✣ Key Facts

Time Period:
Early to Mid-20th Century

Genre:
Poetry

Events:
Spanish Civil War

Nationality:
English

THE INTERNATIONAL BRIGADES

Although the governments of Britain, France, and the United States declared neutrality in the Spanish Civil War, many left-leaning citizens of these countries wanted to help the Republic in its fight against fascism. Tens of thousands of foreigners volunteered to fight for the Republic, and they were organized into units known as the International Brigades. French volunteers made up the largest contingent. German and Italian exiles opposed to the fascist regimes in their home countries were also well represented. Thousands of Americans and Canadians joined as well. The largely American Abraham Lincoln Battalion became one of the best-known units of the International Brigades, seeing action in many battles and suffering heavy casualties.

The Brigades' effectiveness was undermined, though, by their subordination to agents of the Communist International who answered to Joseph Stalin's Soviet Union. Not all of the volunteers were communists, but political cadres loyal to Stalin coerced them to espouse Stalinist orthodoxy. Deviation from the Stalinist party line could result in execution, in grim repetition of the purges occurring in the Soviet Union at the same time. The Brigades were withdrawn from Spain in 1938, when it was clear the Republic was doomed and the Western allies' appeasement of Adolf Hitler made it necessary for Stalin to protect his own geopolitical interests by reaching an understanding with Nazi Germany.

THEMES AND STYLE

The dominant themes of "Spain" are the urgency of the struggle for the Spanish Republic and the conflict's status as a turning point in history. The poem progresses from an opening description of humanity's past to a concluding invocation of a desired future, with a present defined by "the struggle" at the center. Fittingly for a poem written to raise money for the Republican cause, Auden also argues that the struggle's outcome depends not on the intervention of supernatural forces but on the actions and decisions of those reading or listening to the poem.

Auden emphasizes the struggle's urgency with the refrain "today the struggle," coupled with repetitions of "yesterday" and "tomorrow." The poem begins with a sweeping overview of the past achievements of civilization: "yesterday the invention / Of cart-wheels and clocks, the taming of / Horses. Yesterday the bustling world of the navigators." In his repetitions of "yesterday," Auden seemingly depicts a world becoming progressively better. But he argues that enjoyment of the fruits of progress must be sacrificed for the struggle: "Yesterday the classic lecture / On the origin of Mankind. But to-day the struggle." After the struggle has been won, Auden suggests, artistic pursuits and leisure activities can be resumed: "To-morrow for the young the poets exploding like bombs, …/ To-morrow the bicycle races / Through the suburbs on

summer evenings. But to-day the struggle." Through the poem's structure, Auden powerfully argues that past and future must be subordinated to a struggle on which both depend.

The tone of "Spain" is rather dispassionate, as Auden relies on the logical force of the structure rather than an emotional appeal to achieve his desired effect. The poem's speaker expresses an attitude of resolute but resigned commitment to the grim necessity of the struggle instead of real enthusiasm. The speaker's language takes on emotional force only in the act of ventriloquizing the (misguided) appeals of others for divine or other supernatural intervention in the struggle. These others cry out, "Intervene. O descend as a dove or / A furious papa or a mild engineer, but descend," only for the force they petition to reply that they must take action on their own: "I am your choice, your decision. Yes, I am Spain." Significantly, the section that concludes by admonishing the audience that "I am your choice, your decision" occurs at the center of the poem, which then turns to a wistful entertainment of possibilities for the future; perhaps Auden's detached approach is meant to imply that clear and rational action serves the struggle more effectively than passion.

CRITICAL DISCUSSION

"Spain" first appeared as part of a sixteen-page pamphlet published by Faber & Faber in May 1937; the poem became a useful propaganda tool for British supporters of the Spanish Republic. It was "sold for a shilling, with all proceeds to go to Medical Aid for Spain," and speakers at pro-Republican demonstrations read the poem to the crowds. However, "Spain" was soon targeted by critics who denounced the poem's naive representation of military life and its seemingly uncomplicated endorsement of violence. Orwell, who had served in combat in Spain and had nearly been murdered by communist agents who were ostensibly on the same side he was, specifically lambasted the line urging "the conscious acceptance of guilt in the necessary murder." He wrote derisively, "Mr. Auden's brand of amoralism is only possible if you are the kind of person who is always somewhere else when the trigger is pulled."

Perhaps in response to such criticism, Auden revised the poem and retitled it "Spain 1937." He changed the line that had infuriated Orwell to "the conscious acceptance of guilt in the fact of murder" and made several other revisions that distanced the poem's speaker from partisanship in the struggle he described. Auden's dissatisfaction with "Spain" is often taken to represent an important turning point in his career, a moment when he chose to turn away from politics. Although this view is highly contested among critics, it remains influential in shaping the reception of "Spain."

Some mid-twentieth-century critics viewed "Spain" as an unfortunate lapse on Auden's part, a moment when he mistakenly turned away from the properly timeless and universal subject matter of poetry to write propaganda for a momentary political cause. More recent critics such as Stan Smith and Loris Mirella tend to challenge this view, while Peter Collier, in his essay in *Visions and Blueprints* (1988), defends the poem's focus on current events by arguing that "Spain" is "an occasional poem in the best sense.... The occasion is a turning-point in modern history, with enormous moral and political consequences for Britain and the rest of Europe, as well as for Spain." Some modern critics, following in Orwell's footsteps, condemn Auden's naive view of war. Peter Firchow, however, in *W. H. Auden: Contexts for Poetry* (2002), defends Auden's use of words such as "murder" by arguing that, even though Auden was a noncombatant, he tries to expose the realities of war by rejecting euphemistic descriptions of its violence.

BIBLIOGRAPHY

Sources

Anderson, James M. *The Spanish Civil War: A History and Reference Guide.* Westport: Greenwood, 2003. Print.

Auden, W. H. *Spain.* London: Faber & Faber, 1937. Print.

Collier, Peter. "The Poetry of Protest: Auden, Aragon and Eluard." *Visions and Blueprints: Avant-garde Culture and Radical Politics in Early Twentieth-Century Europe.* Ed. Edward Timms and Peter Collier. Manchester: Manchester UP, 1988. 137–58. Print.

Firchow, Peter Edgerly. *W. H. Auden: Contexts for Poetry.* Newark: U of Delaware P, 2002. Print.

Mirella, Loris. "Realigning Modernism: Eliot, Auden, and the Spanish Civil War." *Modern Language Studies* 24.3 (1994): 93–109. *JSTOR.* Web. 14 Sept. 2012.

Orwell, George. "Inside the Whale." *The Collected Essays, Journalism and Letters of George Orwell: An Age Like This 1920–1940.* Vol. 1. Ed. Sonia Orwell and Ian Angus. New York: Harcourt, Brace & World, 1968. 493–526. Print.

Smith, Stan. "Missing Dates: From 'Spain 1937' to 'September 1, 1939.'" *Literature and History* 13.2 (1987): 155–74. *JSTOR.* Web. 14 Sept. 2012.

Further Reading

Bryant, Marsha. *Auden and Documentary in the 1930s.* Charlottesville: U of Virginia P, 1997. Print.

Emig, Rainer. *W. H. Auden: Towards a Postmodern Poetics.* New York: St. Martin's, 2000. Print.

Grass, Sean C. "W. H. Auden, from 'Spain' to 'Oxford.'" *South Atlantic Review* 66.1 (2001): 84–101. *JSTOR.* Web. 14. Sept. 2012.

Hecht, Anthony. *The Hidden Law: The Poetry of W. H. Auden.* Cambridge: Harvard UP, 1993. Print.

Izzo, David Garrett. *W. H. Auden Encyclopedia.* Jefferson: McFarland, 2004. Print.

Manteiga, Robert C. "Politics and Poetics: England's Thirties Poets and the Spanish Civil War." *Modern Language Studies* 19.3 (1989): 3–14. *JSTOR.* Web. 14. Sept. 2012.

Mendelson, Edward. *Early Auden.* London: Faber & Faber, 1981. Print.

Preston, Paul. *The Spanish Holocaust: Inquisition and Extermination in Twentieth-Century Spain.* New York: Harper, 2012. Print.

Watson, George. "Facing Unpleasant Facts: George Orwell's Reports." *Sewanee Review* 96.4 (1988): 644–57. *JSTOR.* Web. 14. Sept. 2012.

John Walters

Bullet holes at the site of executions in Barcelona during the Spanish Civil War. W. H. Auden's poem "Spain" is considered one of the significant literary works from the war. © VINCENT ABBEY/ALAMY.

"SPRING SILKWORMS" AND "THE SHOP OF THE LIN FAMILY"

Mao Dun

✥ *Key Facts*

Time Period:
Early 20th Century

Genre:
Short Story

Events:
May Fourth Movement;
establishment of Chinese
Communist Party; Second
Revolutionary Civil War;
Japanese invasion of
China

Nationality:
Chinese

OVERVIEW

In 1932 Chinese writer Mao Dun published the short stories "Spring Silkworms" and "The Shop of the Lin Family," which both chronicle the economic and political changes during the Chinese Civil War of 1927 through 1936 and the Japanese invasion of Shanghai. In "Spring Silkworms," Mao Dun, which is a homophone for the Chinese term for "contradiction" and the pen name of Shen Yanbing, writes about peasants who sacrifice their time, money, and health to raise silkworms. In "The Shop of the Lin Family," Mr. Lin is financially ruined as he struggles to keep his shop open amid the fighting in Shanghai. Both stories combine elements of traditional Chinese literature, Russian and French literature, and Chinese vernacular as well as Chinese Communist Party ideals. Through this mix of forms, Mao Dun hoped that his "literature may take upon itself a great and important task: to awaken the masses of the nation and give them strength."

Mao Dun, who wrote thirteen novels and more than one hundred short stories in addition to essays and literary reviews, worked in the 1920s as a propaganda writer for the Guomindang government and the Chinese Communist Party. "Spring Silkworms" and "The Shop of the Lin Family" reflect his pro-revolution stance and his support of the Chinese Communist Party during the Chinese Civil War and Japanese imperialism. However, his stories transcend political propaganda and reflect the tension between his leftist ideology and May Fourth Movement thinking. This balance becomes especially apparent in "Spring Silkworms," through his critique that the farmers will never be able to wear the silk they help produce, and in his creation of the traditional and anti-foreign character Old Tongbao, whose feudal consciousness Mao Dun criticizes.

HISTORICAL AND LITERARY CONTEXT

During the Second Revolutionary Civil War, the Chinese Communist Party fought against Chiang Kai-shek's ruling Guomindang Party to establish democratic rights for laborers. Established in 1921, the Party worked with the Guomindang until 1927, when Chiang purged the Guomindang of communist members and arrested and killed workers and students with communist sympathies in Shanghai. Mao Zedong, who later became the head of the People's Republic of China, vied for control of the Chinese Communist Party after the split. In the midst of the civil war, the Japanese invaded China's northeast provinces in 1931 and attacked Shanghai in early 1932.

Mao Dun published both "Spring Silkworms" and "The Shop of the Lin Family" in 1932 in the midst of this political turmoil. In "Spring Silkworms," Mao Dun focuses on a poor rural family dedicated to the difficult task of raising silkworms only to discover that the market for cocoons has collapsed due to the Japanese occupation and the worldwide economic depression. Thus, he demonstrates how both imperialism and capitalism have harmed the peasant class through no fault of their own. The Japanese invasion, specifically the January 28 Incident, also inspired Mao Dun to write "The Shop of the Lin Family," in which a shopkeeper falls deep into debt as the Shanghai market collapses and Japanese goods are banned. These stories showed the plight of ordinary people under the rule of the Guomindang, as well as the hardships caused by the Japanese invasion, to demonstrate the need for revolution.

Following the May Fourth Incident of 1919, writers sought to realistically portray issues of social justice and championed the study of other countries' ideas and cultures. Chinese writer Lu Xun, although not an avowed political writer, was interested in portraying a Marxist viewpoint in his work. He translated Western works into Chinese and wrote short stories and essays that were critical of Chinese society and could be construed as encouraging a cultural revolution. His 1918 short story, "Kuangren riji," or "Diary of a Madman," is credited with introducing Chinese realism and literature written in Chinese vernacular, which greatly influenced Mao Dun's writing style and that of his contemporary Lao She, who wrote *Rickshaw Boy* and the play *Teahouse*. Mao Dun spent time with other May Fourth Movement writers, including Yeh Sheng-t'ao, the author of one of the first May Fourth-era novels, *Ni Huan-Chih*. According to David Der-wei Wang in *Fictional Realism in*

Twentieth-Century China (1992), Western writers, most notably Leo Tolstoy and Émile Zola, also inspired Mao Dun's device of combining recent historical events with the "psychological and behavioral changes" experienced by people living through them. Tolstoy's *War and Peace* (1869), for example, explored the effect of the French invasion of Russia on members of the tsarist ruling class, and Zola's panoramic Rougon-Macquart novels explored life in France during the Second French Empire, from 1852 to 1870.

Mao Dun stopped writing fiction after 1949, when he became the first Minister of Culture for China. Although his later writing, mainly propaganda tracts and literary theories, lacked the art of his creative fiction, stories such as "Spring Silkworms" and "The Shop of the Lin Family" demonstrate a unique combination of Western and Chinese literary traditions. Like Tolstoy and Zola, he pays attention to his characters' psychological and behavioral experiences, but he also incorporates the instructive nature of literature popular during the Qing dynasty and that was inspired by Buddhism and Confucianism. Further evidence of this integration of seemingly competing ideologies is Mao Dun's use of literary techniques, which make his texts more human and at times ambivalent. Writing fiction about events that were still occurring give his works a journalistic feeling.

THEMES AND STYLE

Both "Spring Silkworms" and "The Shop of the Lin Family" show the inability of the working classes to prosper under Guomindang rule. While Mao Dun illustrates the necessity for China to move from the traditions of Confucianism and the Guomindang toward the reformations desired by the Chinese Communist Party, the stories also impart a feeling of nostalgia and respect for the old ways of life in China. In "Spring Silkworms," Old Tung Pao's family expends all of their money and energy on raising silkworms, even though "there was no guarantee of their earning any return." The communist message of the story denounces the treatment of peasants under imperialism and the feudal landlord system, but Mao Dun also writes in a way that honors the hard work, optimism, and traditions of the peasants. In "The Shop of the Lin Family," Mao Dun again writes in a sympathetic tone for the plight of the working class while criticizing the Guomindang; he also portrays the human side of capitalism. Although Mr. Lin vows to "charge first-grade prices for second-rate merchandise" to recuperate his debts, he cannot resist giving favored customers discounts or allowing them to buy goods on credit.

The third-person narration of both stories reveals Mao Dun's journalism background and provides the stories with an authoritative tone. At the end of "Spring Silkworms," he writes: "That's the way it happened. Because they raised a crop of spring silkworms, the people in Old Tung Pao's village got deeper into

THE HIGH RISK OF SERICULTURE

"Spring Silkworms" focuses on the process of sericulture, which is the raising of silkworms to produce raw silk. Sericulture was a demanding and time-consuming job most often done by peasants living on rented land. The first stage of silk production was to incubate the silkworm eggs, and the farmers sometimes strapped the eggs to their bodies to keep them warm. After the eggs hatched, the larvae required immense amounts of mulberry leaves that the farmers piled on feeding trays. These feedings lasted for days, meaning the peasants had to tend to the worms around the clock, assuring they had enough to eat and keeping the feeding trays clean.

Once the worms increased in size, they spent several days building cocoons by secreting liquid from two glands. The liquid hardens when exposed to air. When the worms finished building their cocoons, the farmers dropped them in boiling water to kill them so they would not exit the cocoons and damage the silk thread. Even after the laborious process, farmers like Old Tung Pao's family were not guaranteed a good return when they sold the raw silk at market, and each year they ran the risk of wasting their time and money on the process.

debt." This didacticism clearly states the hardship for the silkworm farmers and reinforces Mao Dun's belief that the intellectual community should instruct the uneducated and poor classes in revolution. His authoritative tone, however, reveals his diversion from a strict Communist Party message. He wanted to create political writing that was also artistic and objective. He attempts to reflect on the time period from a variety of perspectives and to use forms of literature from both China and the West.

Mao Dun's adept use of the vernacular adds to the realism of his stories and also shows that his characters are ordinary people who are powerless under the Guomindang and the Japanese. The worms in "Spring Silkworms" are referred to as "little darlings" and "grubs." These terms help readers unfamiliar with silkworms to understand the emotional energy the family expends on their high-maintenance crop. Mao Dun's use of colloquial language to villainize Guomindang members and other authority figures helps readers relate to the characters' desperation and promote the revolution. In "The Shop of the Lin Family," a Guomindang official is described as "a hateful swarthy pock-marked fellow" who leers at Mr. Lin's teenage daughter like "a hungry dog." This unsavory characterization represents the threat of the party to all Chinese people.

CRITICAL DISCUSSION

Both stories were praised by other writers when first published in 1932, although Chinese Communist Party members were displeased with their lack of a

A Chinese woman and a pile of silkworm pupae at a Beijing market. Struggling Chinese silkworm farmers appear in Mao Dun's "Spring Silkworms," a story that has been published with another of his stories, "The Shop of the Lin Family."

© BLICKWINKEL/ALAMY.

into mere pawns of callous fortune." Nonetheless, Hsia calls Mao Dun's characterization of the peasants in "Spring Silkworms" "a loving portrayal" that "transforms the supposed Communist tract into a testament of humanity." Wang points out that Mao Dun's middle-class, educated background limited his understanding of the proletariat. Like many other May Fourth writers, he was comfortable writing for other intellectuals, although "Spring Silkworms," and two other companion stories, "Autumn Harvest" and "Winter Ruin," all deal with the plight of the peasant. Even his novel *Midnight,* which focuses on the bourgeois in Shanghai, includes a subplot about a peasant uprising.

In addition to their artistic achievements, "Spring Silkworms" and "The Shop of the Lin Family" have elements of reportage literature. In his piece on Mao Dun in *Chinese Fiction Writers,* Charles A. Laughlin defines reportage literature as "consciously literary texts that narrate 'real people and real events' with a view to documenting social problems and momentous historical changes." Mao Dun does this by writing about the changes occurring during the civil war and Japanese invasion as they were happening. The stories continue to resound with audiences; "Spring Silkworms" was adapted as a silent film in China in 1933 and "The Shop of the Lin Family" was filmed in China in 1959. In 1998 the British Film Institute chose *Spring Silkworms* as one of their 360 all-time classic films from around the world.

clear revolutionary message. In *Realism and Allegory in the Early Fiction of Mao Tun* (1986), Yu-Shin Chen explains that Mao Dun's fiction was "minutely analyzed and criticized" by party members, especially Ch'u Ch'iu-po and Ch'ien Hsing-ts'un. "Spring Silkworms" was criticized as sentimentalizing prerevolutionary days, while "The Shop of the Lin Family" showed too much sympathy for a bourgeois shopkeeper.

Although communist officials initially disliked the stories, they later were among only a few of Mao Dun's stories that were approved as following Maoist principles. According to C. T. Hsia in *A History of Modern China,* the stories are some of the best of the time period and genre. He writes that "Spring Silkworms" "comes nearest to transcending the inherent limitations of the proletarian genre" but that neither story explores "the enormity of oppression and destitution without reducing human beings

BIBLIOGRAPHY

Sources

Bell, Lynda S. "Of Silk, Women, and Capital: Peasant Women's Labor in Chinese and Other Third World Capitalisms." *Journal of Women's History* 11.4 (2000): 82. *ProQuest.* Web. 23 Oct. 2012.

Chen, Yu-Shin. *Realism and Allegory in the Early Fiction of Mao Tun.* Bloomington: Indiana UP, 1986. Print.

Hsia, C. T. *A History of Modern China.* 3rd ed. Bloomington: Indiana UP, 1999. Print.

Laughlin, Charles A. "Mao Dun." *Chinese Fiction Writers, 1900–1949, Dictionary of Literary Biography,* Vol. 328. Ed. Thomas Moran. Detroit: Gale, 2007. *Literature Resource Center.* Web. 4 Oct. 2012.

Laughlin, Charles A. "Narrative Subjectivity and the Production of Social Space in Chinese Reportage." *Boundary 2* 25.3 (1998): 25. *Academic Search Complete.* Web. 4 Oct. 2012.

Mao, Dun. *Spring Silkworms and Other Stories.* Trans. Sidney Shapiro. Hong Kong: Chinese UP, 1979. Print.

Wang, David Der-wei. *Fictional Realism in Twentieth-Century China: Mao Dun, Lao She, Shen Congwen.* New York: Columbia UP, 1992. Print.

Further Reading

Anderson, Marston. *The Limits of Realism: Chinese Fiction in the Revolutionary Period.* Berkeley: U of California P, 1990. Print.

Dun, Mao. *Midnight.* New York: AMS, 1979.
    Print.

Lu, Xun, and William A. Lyell. *Diary of a Madman
    and Other Stories.* Honolulu: U of Hawaii P, 1990.
    Print.

Stevens, Sarah E. "Figuring Modernity: The New Woman
    and the Modern Girl in Republican China."*NWSA
    Journal* 15.3 (2003): 82+. *Literature Resource Center.*
    Web. 4 Oct. 2012.

Media Adaptations

Chun Can. Dir. Bugao Cheng. Perf. Ying Xiao, Yuexian Yan,
    and Jianong Gong. Mingxing Film Company, 1933. Film.

The Lin Family's Shop. Dir. Shui Hua. Perf. Xie Tian.
    Guangzhou Beauty Culture Communication, 1959. Film.

Lin Jia Pu Zi. Dir. Choui Khoua. Perf. Shu Chen, Tao
    Han, and Bin Lin. Beijing Film Studio, 1959. Film.

Kathryn Molinaro

SWEET AND SOUR MILK

Nuruddin Farah

✣ **Key Facts**

Time Period:
Late 20th Century

Genre:
Novel

Events:
Rule of Major General
Mohamed Siad Barre
as military dictator and
President of Somalia;
establishment of Somali
Revolutionary Socialist
Party; invasion of the
Ogaden region of
Ethiopia

Nationality:
Somali

OVERVIEW

Nuruddin Farah's *Sweet and Sour Milk* (1979) follows a Somali health officer, Loyaan, as he searches for answers in his twin brother's mysterious death, possibly at the hands of the government that employed him. The first novel in Farah's trilogy, *Variations on the Theme of an African Dictatorship, Sweet and Sour Milk* depicts the turmoil of life under the oppressive regime of the General, head of a regime whose abusive practices reverberate in the families and social relationships of its citizenry. Peppered with poetic language and metaphor, the novel delineates the "fight over the dead soul" of Soyaan, whose dissidence has been recast as loyal servitude by the government likely responsible for his death.

Published ten years into General Mohamed Siad Barre's rule, *Sweet and Sour Milk* drew the ire of the Somali government and sealed Farah's exile. Written in Rome and published in England, the novel also marked the arrival of the first Somali novelist of significance to emerge onto the international literary scene. While Farah's temporary residency in the West may have helped shape his already evident modernist sensibilities, the key themes in *Sweet and Sour Milk* and the novels that followed place the author's chief interests firmly in Africa. Important less as a historically accurate depiction of 1970s Somalia and more as an exploration of the ripple effect of oppression through the family and social institutions of postcolonial society, *Sweet and Sour Milk* raises questions about the human response to tyranny.

HISTORICAL AND LITERARY CONTEXT

The Republic of Somalia was created in 1960 when the British-controlled State of Somaliland merged with the formerly Italian-controlled Trust Territory of Somalia to form the Somali Republic. The British- and Italian-established government retained power until 1969, when President Abdirashid Ali Shermarke was assassinated by one of his bodyguards, and Major-General Mohamed Siad Barre of the Somali Army seized power. In the years that followed, Barre and his government eliminated the parliament, Supreme Court, and the constitution. In 1976 Barre established the Somali Revolutionary Socialist Party with which he sought to combine scientific socialism with Islamic principles in his governance of Somalia. A year later he provoked hostilities with an incursion into the long-contested Ogaden region of Ethiopia, complicating Somalia's international standing and bringing hardship to its citizens, who were simultaneously being affected by drought.

While the early years of Barre's rule brought increased literacy to Somalia, by the late 1970s war and poverty were decimating the middle class and its social and cultural institutions, including universities. The government effectively controlled the flow of information in the country, heavily censoring newspaper, radio, and television reporting. The threat of prison or worse for those who opposed the country's one-party system caused an exodus of writers and intellectuals, with many continuing their work from the safety of Europe, the United States, or elsewhere in Africa. The government censored Farah's serialized Somali language novel, *Tallow Waa Telee Ma* (1974). When he was traveling several years later, he learned that the government had dubbed his novel *The Naked Needle* (1976) treasonous and that returning to Somalia likely would mean incarceration or death.

In *Variations on the Theme of an African Dictatorship* trilogy, *Sweet and Sour Milk* was followed by *Sardines* (1981) and *Close Sesame* (1983). The cycle deals with the horror of life under the figure of the General, who takes on something of a mythic cast throughout the novels, each of which contains characters who are part of the revolutionary group to which Soyaan belonged in the first novel. In *Sardines,* journalist Medina chooses a life of solitude after having been ousted from her job for publishing news stories unfavorable to Barre. In her solitude, she begins to translate world literature into Somali. The final novel, *Close Sesame,* follows Deeriye, once an esteemed tribal leader, who laments that his long struggle against colonial powers—rather than bring freedom to Somalia—laid the groundwork for a regime as repressive and violent as those who came before them.

Farah's earlier work put him firmly in the government's sights. *Sweet and Sour Milk,* which was published while he was traveling, made it virtually impossible for Farah to return to Somali. He spent almost twenty years in exile. Barre was overthrown in 1991, but Farah did not return to his native country until 1996. As of late 2012, the author resides in South Africa and continues to write about Somalia. Most commentators count the dual facts of his homeland and his exile as defining influences on Farah's body of work.

THEMES AND STYLE

Sweet and Sour Milk exposes the manner in which the Somali government ruthlessly controls the lives and speech of its citizens, even after their deaths. The novel opens with the death of Soyaan, who has fallen ill after eating a meal at which an untrustworthy government minister was present. At Soyaan's bedside when he draws his last breath, his twin brother, Loyaan, suspects murder and vows to solve the mystery of his brother's death. His investigation reveals Soyaan's participation in clandestine dissident activities, strengthening his belief that Barre's government is responsible, a belief that is heightened by Soyaan's posthumous rehabilitation and designation as a hero, whose dying words were, "Labor is honor and there is no General like Our General." Loyaan knows, of course, that his brother made no such statement, which, in its approximation of the Islamic creed, slyly equates the General with God, the opposite of Soyaan's beliefs. When Loyaan attempts to correct the false stories being circulated about his brother, a bureaucrat at the death registry informs him that Soyaan's file cannot be amended—that, even dead, Soyaan is "a property of the state."

Farah makes use of classic elements of the political thriller to underline the danger Loyaan faces as he examines Soyaan's life, sifting clues to determine why and by whom he was killed. Loyaan is naive in the workings of the shadowy anti-government organizations with which his brother was involved, and the clues he finds, such as the diatribe on the scrap from Soyaan's pillowcase, seem ominous. Moreover, Loyaan is unsure about various other characters' identities and allegiances. Late in the novel, when confronting the government minister he suspects may be involved in his brother's death, lines from Soyaan's pillowcase scrap return to him— "They were at my neighbor's yesterday. When will my turn come?"

While *Sweet and Sour Milk* is often noted for its modernist elements, the novel makes use of poetic language and metaphor that echo Somalia's tradition of oral poetry. Ali Ahad points out that under Barre's censorship, "in the best tradition of Somali political conflict, an important part of propaganda against the regime was played by oral poetry." The epigraphs that introduce each chapter resemble prose poems and introduce the themes of the chapter. Often centered on young children or animals, these passages contain elements of violence and disorder repeated in the action that follows. There are, for instance,

"two cats in a brawl over a dead rat's meat," a brawl ending with the victor walking away "majestically," abandoning "a dead rat and a fallen rival." The chapter that follows introduces the news reports of Soyaan's death, with the government fighting to claim his corpse in service of their socialist propaganda. The terrible waste of Soyaan's death is made poignant by the arrival of Soyaan's mistress and their son, whom she brings to "share the love … Soyaan left behind."

CRITICAL DISCUSSION

Winner of the English Speaking Union Literary Award in 1980, *Sweet and Sour Milk* expanded Farah's reputation outside of Africa. The West gave the novel favorable reviews. Writing on the trilogy for the *New York Times*, William Ferguson praised the novels as "feverishly lyrical; Mr. Farah has given us a powerful political statement that moves constantly toward song." Salman Rushdie, himself the subject of death threats following the publication of his novel *The Satanic Verses*, has called Farah "one of the finest of contemporary African novelists."

Scholars have described *Sweet and Sour Milk* as the first Somali novel to be widely read in the West, its portrait of the educated, urban Somali in contrast to the oft-reported portrayals of a famine-ravished nomadic life and violence. Further, Farah, who won the 1998 Neustadt Prize, has been credited with helping to put East African literature on the world literature map at a time when other regions in Africa received far more scholarly attention. In *The Columbia Guide to East African Literature since 1945*, Simon Gikandi and Evan Mwangi describe Farah's work as "an important bridge in the literary history of East Africa," spanning the gap between "the generation of writers who emerged during decolonization" and "those who came of age during the period of postcolonial failure and crisis."

PRIMARY SOURCE

EXCERPT FROM *SWEET AND SOUR MILK*

Clowns. Cowards. And (tribal) upstarts: these are who I work with. The top civil service in this country is composed of them. Men and women with no sense of dignity, nor integrity; men and women whose pride has been broken by the General's Security; men and women who have succumbed and accepted to be humiliated. Are you married? Do you have children? How many? Five? A wife and a mistress? Plus the tribal hangers-on who have just arrived and whom you support? Listen to the knock on your neighbour's door at dawn. Hearken: the army boots have crunched grains of sand on the road leading away from your house. Listen to them hasten. When will your turn come? Yesterday was your colleague's turn. You saw his wife wrapped in tears, you saw how she averted her eyes. Does she know where they have taken her husband? She goes from one police station to another. The police know who she is, and what she is seeking, but no one will tell her anything. She won't return home, in fact she cannot bear to: she has four small children to face and somehow feed. What has he done? What has her little clerk of a husband done? But what have all the others done, what have the thousands who languish in prisons done? The methods of the General and of the KGB are not dissimilar, I can tell you that. Instructions: Know who do not know you. Plant seeds of suspicion in every thinking brain and hence render it 'unthinking.' I remember what a friend of mine once said to another: 'Raise your children, but not your voice nor your head. To survive you must clown. You must hide in the convenience of a crowd and clap. Don't put your neck out; why do that? There must be millions like you who are suffering the same ill-treatment. When in the company of the newly groomed upstarts (the

Sweet and Sour Milk has been analyzed as a standalone novel, as part of the *Variations on the Theme of an African Dictatorship,* and in conjunction with Farah's body of work as a whole. Much scholarship traces postcolonial themes and tropes in the novels, particularly as they relate to the author's modernism. In his 1988 essay in *World Literature Today,* Gikandi conjectures that "Farah is attracted to modernism and modernist style because its unfinished and fragmented nature seems to parallel the narrative of the postcolonial state, while its reflexivity and circularity provide him with a language of social critique." Others have investigated *Sweet and Sour Milk*'s exploration of family relationships as they replicate the power dynamics created by totalitarian regimes. More recent scholarship traces the evolution of Farah's treatment of Somalia as it parallels the changing face of the country, which, like Farah's role as novelist, has undergone a number of shifts in the decades since *Sweet and Sour Milk* brought his tale to the world.

BIBLIOGRAPHY

Sources

Ahad, Ali. "Could Poetry Define Nationhood? The Case of Somali Oral Poetry and the Nation." *Journal of Historical and European Studies* 1 (2007): 51–57. Print.

Farah, Nurrudin. *Sweet and Sour Milk.* St. Paul: Graywolf, 1979. Print.

Ferguson, William. "In Short: Fiction." *New York Times.* The New York Times Company, 12 June 1992. Web. 14 Sept. 2012.

Gikandi, Simon, and Evan Mwangi. *The Columbia Guide to East African Literature since 1945.* New York: Columbia UP, 2007. Print.

Gikandi, Simon. "Nuruddin Farah and Postcolonial Textuality." *World Literature Today* 72.4 (1988): 753–58. Rpt. in *Contemporary Literary Criticism.* Ed. Jeffrey W. Hunter. Vol. 137. Detroit: Gale Group, 2001. *Literature Resource Center.* Web. 15 Sept. 2012.

Rushdie, Salman. "Nuruddin Farah." *Imaginary Homelands: Essays and Criticism 1981–1991.* Granta Books, 1991. 201–02. Rpt. in *Contemporary Literary Criticism.* Ed. Jeffrey W. Hunter. Vol. 137. Detroit: Gale Group, 2001. *Literature Resource Center.* Web. 15 Sept. 2012.

Sullivan, Grace. "Variations on the Theme of Somalia." *San Francisco Review of Books* 18.1 (1993): 39. Rpt. in *Contemporary Literary Criticism.* Ed. Jeffrey W. Hunter. Vol. 137. Detroit: Gale Group, 2001. *Literature Resource Center.* Web. 14 Sept. 2012.

Further Reading

Adam, Ian. "The Murder of Soyaan Keynaan." *Emerging Perspectives on Nurrudin Farah.* Ed. Derek Wright. Trenton: Africa World Press, 2003. Print.

Bardolph, Jacqueline. "Brothers and Sisters in Nuruddin Farah's Two Trilogies." *World Literature Today* 72.4 (1998): 727–32. Rpt. in *Contemporary Literary Criticism.* Ed. Jeffrey W. Hunter. Vol. 137. Detroit: Gale Group, 2001. *Literature Resource Center.* Web. 14 Sept. 2012.

Dasenbrock, Reed Way. "Nuruddin Farah: A Tale of Two Trilogies." *World Literature Today* 72.4 (1998): 747–52. *Literature Resource Center.* Web. 14 Sept. 2012.

men whom the General's sense of tribal priorities have supplied with the unquestioned authority to do what they please, when and where they please), make sure your profile is kept low. Take my counsel seriously, don't detect the note of cynicism in what I've just said. Clowns. Cowards. And upstarts.' Well, well. They trot the unprincipled line of the General's régime. I say: let's together humour the General. Let us sing his astral titles. The withered hope of a dream leafy as autumn. Our throats have pained, the latest encomium is too long to give an encore to. Listen to the knock on your neighbour's door at dawn. Hearken: the army boots have crunched grains of sand on the pavement by your window. Listen to them hasten. Listen to the revving of the engine. They've taken another. When will your turn come? The wife doesn't switch the electric lights off. The brightness of dawn overpowers them in the end. The sun will have sent her on her fearsome errand. She gives the morning terror to the brother of the detainee. The brother has himself once been imprisoned for nine months without trial. He has been through water—and other primitive methods of torture. The triumph of fear over anger engages his pensée, whereas the flames of rage indulge the understanding sympathy of the sister-in-law. Will he do something to avenge his brother's unfair detention? 'Go home and don't worry' is all he says. 'I will supply your needs, will pay for the children's school fees.' Listen to his heart reject the reasoning of his head. See the expression on his face harden. Hearken: the cry of naked hunger is in the wind.

Farah, Nurrudin. *Sardines.* St. Paul: Graywolf, 1981. Print.

———. *Close Sesame.* St. Paul: Graywolf, 1983. Print.

Hawley, John C. "Nuruddin Farah—Tribalism, Orality, and Postcolonial Ultimate Reality and Meaning in Contemporary Somalia." *Ultimate Reality and Meaning* 19.3 (1996): 189–205. Rpt. in *Contemporary Literary Criticism.* Ed. Jeffrey W. Hunter. Vol. 137. Detroit: Gale Group, 2001. *Literature Resource Center.* Web. 14 Sept. 2012.

Wright, Derek. *Emerging Perspectives on Nuruddin Farah.* Trenton: Africa World Press, 2002. Print.

Daisy Gard

Venice Preserv'd, or, a Plot Discovered

Thomas Otway

✧ *Key Facts*

Time Period:
Late 17th Century

Genre:
Play

Events:
Restoration of the
English monarchy;
conflict between Whigs
and Tories

Nationality:
English

OVERVIEW

Venice Preserv'd, or, a Plot Discovered, a tragic play by English dramatist Thomas Otway that was first performed in 1682, depicts the unraveling of a conspiracy against the Venetian Senate when a man is forced to choose between loyalty to his wife and his fellow conspirators. As the play begins, Jaffeir, a destitute Venetian nobleman, is persuaded by his friend, Pierre, to join a clandestine uprising against the corrupt senate. To prove his loyalty to the conspiracy, Jaffeir places his wife, Belvidera, in the care of the rebels, but after their leader, Renault, attempts to rape her, Belvidera persuades Jaffeir to inform on his erstwhile cohorts. Jaffeir confesses to the senate after being falsely assured that the lives of his fellow conspirators will be spared, and he eventually makes restitution with Pierre for this betrayal by killing him, thus saving him from an ignominious execution. Jaffeir then kills himself, and Belvidera goes insane and dies shortly thereafter. The play's numerous allusions to the factional strife of the English Restoration period (1660–1685) allow it to serve uniquely as both a commentary on the divided loyalties that accompany civil discord and as a spirited piece of propaganda that attacks the enemies of Otway's own political party.

Despite a number of politically motivated condemnations, *Venice Preserv'd* was one of the most successful tragedies of Restoration drama. It was jubilantly received by Otway's political allies (the Duke of York, later to become King James II, attended an early performance, as did the current king, Charles II) and by theatergoers in general. As its topicality faded, it remained popular until well into the nineteenth century (albeit often in bowdlerized form) for its dramatic pathos, as well as for its general air of cynicism about government and idealism.

HISTORICAL AND LITERARY CONTEXT

After a brief period of parliamentary rule following the English Civil War (1642–1651), the ascension of the previously exiled Charles II to the throne in 1660 heralded the restoration of the English monarchy. Nonetheless, the power struggle between the king and his parliament—a struggle that, a decade earlier, had culminated in the execution of Charles I, the new king's father—remained unresolved, and was exacerbated by the king's libertinism and Catholic sympathies versus the Puritanical and anti-Catholic outlook of most parliamentarians. This political division led to the emergence of two opposing political parties. Supporters of the king were eventually designated as Tories, and his opponents were called Whigs.

Venice Preserv'd arrived on the heels of a major Tory victory: the king had recently dissolved parliament in order to defeat the contentious Exclusion Bill, which was inspired in part by fraudulent reports of a "Popish Plot" to assassinate the king and slaughter Protestants and would have legally prevented his openly Catholic brother, James, the Duke of York, from ascending to the throne upon Charles's death. Furthermore, the bill's chief supporter, the 1st Earl of Shaftesbury, had been arrested and tried for high treason—albeit unsuccessfully, though he was eventually forced to flee the country for fear of a second trial and conviction. Otway, an outspoken Tory, presented *Venice Preserv'd* in part as a celebration of the bill's defeat, a fact reflected by the play's conspiratorial themes, its explicit endorsement of Charles and his brother in the prologue and epilogue, and its vicious and overt caricaturing of Shaftesbury in one of its characters (a corrupt, lascivious senator called Antonio, so named to play off of Shaftesbury's first name, Anthony).

Otway's play emerged from a literary milieu that emphasized wit and satire and demonstrated political partisanship. Tory authors such as Otway, Aphra Behn, and John Dryden traded jeremiads with Whig authors such as Elkanah Settle and Thomas Shadwell, the latter of whom famously caricatured Otway and his colleagues in his 1682 satire "The Tory Poets," which received an even more damning response later that year in Dryden's mock-heroic portrait of Shadwell, "Mac Flecknoe." *Venice Preserv'd,* in its conscientious engagement with the politics of the time, has its closest analogue in Dryden's allegorical poem *Absalom and Achitophel* (1681-1682), which likewise deals with the Popish Plot, the Exclusion Bill, and the controversy over Charles's royal successor, though Otway's play is less straightforwardly allegorical.

As one of the most popular tragedies of the Restoration, *Venice Preserv'd,* along with Otway's previous play, *The Orphan,* helped to usher in the era of the "she-tragedy" in the late seventeenth and early eighteenth centuries, a genre so named for its focus on the sufferings of tragic heroines such as

Belvidera. The play's political elements, meanwhile, carried on a tradition of drama-based social commentary that can be observed today in such political theater as Harold Pinter's later work, which is similarly concerned with skullduggery and the misuse of power.

THEMES AND STYLE

A principal theme of *Venice Preserv'd* is the human cost of living in a society characterized by political disloyalty and rebellion. The plot is essentially an interlocking series of betrayals, a state of affairs that is presented as inevitable in a society where "one Venetian / Trusts not another" and "A factious, giddy, and divided Senate / Is all the strength of Venice." Jaffeir and Belvidera are psychologically tormented by their conflicting loyalties, unable to take any course of action without breaking faith in some way. Otway implicitly ties this theme of pervasive disloyalty to the antiroyalist machinations of Whig politicians, designating them as responsible for England's morally corrupt, politically fragmented society.

Otway achieves this rhetorical goal through a combination of explicit didacticism and politically charged metaphor. The prologue and epilogue are blunt in their contempt for Whigs and support for the monarchy, asserting of Charles II to "let each brave heart / Rouse and unite to take his injured part." Meanwhile, by setting his play in a republic rather than a monarchy, Otway is able to equate both the rulers and the rebels of the play with the Whig party, thereby negatively portraying both sides of the power divide without running the risk of offending his fellow Tories. The corrupt senate (particularly the cartoonishly loathsome character of Antonio) thus represents the Tory perception of Whigs as greedy, entitled politicians, while the rebellious conspiracy (especially the vicious, brutal Renault) represents the complementary Tory perception of Whigs as seditious plotters intent on undermining the monarchy.

Stylistically, *Venice Preserv'd* tends toward a rather histrionic emotional register, as is typical of Restoration drama. Written primarily in blank verse, the play is full of dialogue that in Otway's time would have been considered elegant and sensitive but may strike modern readers as overwrought, as when Jaffeir laments his betrayal of Pierre by saying, "Love, pity, fear, and mem'ry how I've wronged him, / Distract my quiet with the very thought on't, / And tear my heart to pieces in my bosom." This type of sentiment, hyperbolic though it may now seem, effectively foregrounds the pathos of Otway's portrayal of the attempt to live a moral life within a fatally compromised society and adds a note of passionate intensity to the play's political attack on Whig ambition and intrigue. The play's few comic scenes, which largely focus on Antonio's sadomasochistic interactions with Pierre's mistress Aquilina, are even more

THE POPISH PLOT

During the period from 1678 to 1681, much of England was seized by a paroxysm of anti-Catholic hysteria when a disreputable former clergyman named Titus Oates gave sworn testimony of a vast Jesuit conspiracy to assassinate the king and install his Catholic brother, the Duke of York, the presumptive heir to the throne, as a puppet ruler in order to effect a massacre of Protestants and a papal takeover of England. Oates's claims were not taken very seriously by the king, who had Catholic leanings and eventually converted on his deathbed. However, Parliament, already fairly anti-Catholic in sentiment, devoted much time and energy to investigating Oates's assertions, which led to the execution of over a dozen innocent men.

Oates's allegations were eventually discredited and he was convicted of perjury. In the meantime, however, the widespread concern about a possible Catholic takeover of England led to the parliamentary introduction of the Exclusion Bill, which would have explicitly prevented the Catholic Duke of York from becoming king. It was this bill that consolidated the split between the two English political parties and established their respective names: the opponents of the bill were referred to as Tories, while its supporters were called Whigs.

overstated. At one point Antonio tells her, "I'll give thee this t'other purse to let me be a dog—and to use me like a dog a little," then follows through at some length. These scenes, in addition to conveying the supposed depths of senatorial corruption and depravity, also amount to a character assassination of Antonio's real-life model, the aforementioned Whig leader Shaftesbury.

CRITICAL DISCUSSION

Venice Preserv'd was an immediate critical and popular success, despite the disapprobation of Whig commentators. Dryden, the most prominent literary critic of the Restoration period, esteemed it enough to compose two special prologues for when the Duke and Duchess of York attended performances. The play's blatant partisanship won it many powerful admirers. As Roswell Gray Ham remarks in *Otway and Lee: Biography from a Baroque Age,* "it was almost officialized as the Tory paean of triumph" upon its viewing by the king. Of course, that same partisanship also provoked a fair amount of hostility from Otway's political enemies. For example, an anonymous 1682 satire, quoted in Ham's biography, complains that "every Blockhead that can please the Court / Plucks up a Spirit, and turns Poet for't." None of these attacks significantly damaged *Venice Preserv'd*'s success, which endured long after the political situation that inspired the play had ended.

Although *Venice Preserv'd* is among the most noteworthy literary manifestations of the Tory

reaction to the Exclusion Bill and its attendant controversies, its subsequent influence is probably ascribable to the more universal elements of its plot, which have allowed it to seem relevant to a wide variety of historical situations and be co-opted by ideologues on opposite sides of the political fence. Indeed, the play was banned in London in 1777 for its supposed sympathy toward republicanism, an ironic turn of events given Otway's staunch opposition to that ideology. Aline Mackenzie Taylor's 1950 study *Next to Shakespeare,* which analyzes the play's lengthy stage history, observes that *Venice Preserv'd* has been "most popular when political feeling was most strongly partisan." This testifies to the play's ability to simultaneously transcend and invite political affiliation.

Modern scholarship of *Venice Preserv'd* often focuses on the relationship between the play and its political context, and especially on its vagaries as a piece of Tory partisanship. That the play was received as such is not in doubt, but the extent of its political agenda, as well as the precise way in which that agenda is promulgated, is a subject of some controversy. Susan J. Owen, for example, argues in the essay "Drama and Political Crisis" that the play's supposedly straightforward Toryism is compromised by "the universal nastiness of the world of the play, and the absence of heroic

possibilities." She adds that "the outlook is too close to nihilism to be compatible with fervent Toryism." Other critics, such as Kerstin P. Warner in *Thomas Otway,* explore the psychological ramifications of the play's emotionally extreme characters.

BIBLIOGRAPHY

Sources

Ham, Roswell Gray. *Otway and Lee: Biography from a Baroque Age.* New Haven: Yale UP, 1931. Print.

Otway, Thomas. *Venice Preserved.* Ed. Malcolm Kelsall. Lincoln: U of Nebraska P, 1969. Print.

Owen, Susan J. "Drama and Political Crisis." *The Cambridge Companion to English Restoration Theatre.* Ed. Deborah Payne Fisk. Cambridge: Cambridge UP, 2000. 158–73. Print.

Taylor, Aline Mackenzie. *Next to Shakespeare.* Durham: Duke UP, 1950. Print.

Warner, Kerstin P. *Thomas Otway.* Boston: Twayne, 1982.

Further Reading

Gruber, Elizabeth. "'Betray'd to Shame': *Venice Preserved* and the Paradox of the She-Tragedy." *Connotations* 16.1–3 (2006/2007): 158–71. Print.

Hughes, Derek. "Human Sacrifice on the Restoration Stage: The Case of *Venice Preserv'd.*" *Philological Quarterly* 88.4 (2009): 365–84. Print.

Kewes, Paulina. "Otway, Lee and the Restoration History Play." *A Companion to Restoration Drama.* Ed. Susan J. Owen. Oxford: Blackwell, 2001. 355–77. Print.

Leissner, Debra. "Divided Nation, Divided Self: The Language of Capitalism and Madness in Otway's *Venice Preserv'd.*" *Studies in the Literary Imagination* 32.2 (1999): 19–31. Print.

Luis-Martínez, Zenón. "'Seated in the Heart': *Venice Preserv'd* between Pathos and Politics." *Restoration and 18th Century Theatre Research* 23.2 (2008): 23–42. Print.

Munns, Jessica. *Restoration Politics and Drama: The Plays of Thomas Otway, 1675–1683.* Newark: U of Delaware P, 1995. Print.

Owen, Susan J. *Restoration Theatre and Crisis.* Oxford: Clarendon, 1996. Print.

Solomon, Harry M. "The Rhetoric of 'Redressing Grievances': Court Propaganda as the Hermeneutical Key to *Venice Preserv'd.*" *ELH* 53.2 (1986): 289–310. Print.

James Overholtzer

WHAT IS THE THIRD ESTATE?

Emmanuel-Joseph Sieyès

✛ **Key Facts**

Time Period:
Late 18th Century

Genre:
Pamphlet

Events:
French Revolution

Nationality:
French

OVERVIEW

Published in 1789 in an atmosphere of economic uncertainty and vehement national debate about representative government in the months before the onset of the French Revolution, the Abbé Emmanuel-Joseph Sieyès's pamphlet *What Is the Third Estate?* (*"Qu'est-ce que le tiers état?"*) calls for fundamental change to the Estates-General, France's prerevolutionary legislative body. The pamphlet poses a series of rhetorical questions about privilege, social utility, the common good, and the national constitution as it argues for expanding the people's legislative power. The text asserts that the people's will is the source of political power and calls on the lower classes to demand the political rights that are justly theirs.

What Is the Third Estate? was widely read and carried enormous political influence in 1789. Its publication brought Sieyès fame and a position of authority among the leaders calling for government reforms. In *Rhetoric of Bourgeois Revolution* (1994), historian William Sewell calls it "the most influential pamphlet of the thousands published in the months leading up to the French Revolution." Many of the pamphlet's central ideas were incorporated as policy at the Estates-General that summer. Although Sieyès did not intend for his writings to lead to the arrest and beheading of the king, *What Is the Third Estate?* joined the chorus of fomenting discontent that would eventually explode in the revolution of July 1789 and France's unstable and violent political history of the late eighteenth and nineteenth centuries.

HISTORICAL AND LITERARY CONTEXT

Sieyès wrote *What Is the Third Estate?* in an atmosphere of angry disappointment after the Parlement of Paris, France's most powerful prerevolutionary court, dashed hopes for change to the Estates-General. The Estates-General was composed of three separate orders: one for representatives of the clergy; a second for the aristocracy; and a third for the Third Estate, which represented everyone else—that is, the vast majority of the population. Each order cast a single, collective vote on legislative decisions; thus the aristocracy and clergy held two-thirds of the legislative seats. Since they generally voted as a bloc, the first and second orders had a de facto veto power over the initiatives of the Third Estate. After deliberations about changing the Estates-General, the Parlement in September 1788 decided to uphold the traditional structure. This decision ignited Sieyès's rhetorical verve.

France was in the midst of financial and political turmoil in 1788 when King Louis XVI convened the Estates-General. The fact that it was meeting at all was exceptional. The Estates-General was not a regularly convening body as are the national legislatures of today. The Estates had last met in 1614 during the regency of Louis XIII. However, the summer of 1786 marked the beginning of fiscal and political crisis for Louis XVI. The French state was facing bankruptcy, and, at least in principal, the Estates-General had to approve all new taxation laws. Still, the king was hesitant to convene the Estates-General because of the political risk involved. As Sewell explains, "calling the Estates-General threatened to unleash an avalanche of stored-up grievances" and "demands that the Estates be granted the right to meet regularly, which might transform them into something like the British Parliament." Ultimately, though, the king had little choice and called on the Estates-General for help raising new revenue in July 1788.

What Is the Third Estate? appeared in January 1789, as the Estates-General prepared to meet in May. During this lead-up period, Sieyès's text was part of an "unending succession" of publications that criticized the aristocracy while demanding reform to the parliamentary procedures of the Estates-General. Sieyès was not the only writer responding to the political crisis, and in the pamphlet he often extends and responds to arguments of other writers.

What Is the Third Estate? became a focal point in debates about the Estates-General. Sieyès had long been an anonymous ecclesiastical scholar in Chartres. By 1789 he had become a militant defender of the Third Estate, but he himself was not part of the popular order; as a member of the lower clergy (indicated by the title *abbé,* which means "abbot"), he was part of the First Estate. *What Is the Third Estate?* quickly vaulted him into a prominent political role. He became an important voice at the Estates-General and then the National Assembly. He later played a role in the coup that brought Napoleon Bonaparte to power in 1799. Though it would take nearly a century, Sieyès's conception of representative government ultimately became central to the modern French state.

THEMES AND STYLE

In *What Is the Third Estate?* Sieyès explains the nature and origins of political representation and calls for a redistribution of power that would give the Third Estate its just and legitimate voice in the legislative body. He took a more radical stance than most of the pamphleteers on voting procedure at the Estates-General. Reformers were commonly demanding three changes: (1) that the Third Estate have an equal number of representatives as the other orders, (2) that these representatives truly come from the ranks of the Third Estate—Sieyès charges that nobles often bullied the Third Estate into electing members of the aristocracy—and (3) that the vote count at the Estates-General be a total tally of votes by the individual representatives. For Sieyès these demands were not enough. In one of the more inflammatory passages, he violently asserts that the clergy and aristocracy are a "frightful disease devouring the living flesh of the [political] body." In his view, this useless and harmful growth has no legitimate right to represent France: "They have become the real enemies of common interest. They cannot therefore be entrusted with the task of providing for it."

As the title *What Is the Third Estate?* indicates, rhetorical questions are central in Sieyès's persuasive strategy. The text opens with a series of three questions about the political role of the Third Estate. "1. What is the third estate? *Everything.* 2. What, until now, has it been in the existing political order? *Nothing.* 3. What does it want to be? *Something.*" These questions are also the titles of the first three chapters, in which Sieyès supports and elaborates his initial answers. In those chapters he introduces a series of more detailed questions. For instance, he opens the first chapter by asking, "What does a nation need to survive and prosper?" His answer: "It needs *private* employments and *public* services." Sieyès then develops this point with a description of the French workforce. In stark contrast with the two privileged orders, the Third Estate provides the overwhelming majority of the country's socially useful work and fulfills the most burdensome public service tasks. They are therefore everything to the nation. They in fact are the nation and should be central in the legislative process. "The so-called utility of the privileged order for performing public service" on the other hand, "is no more than an illusion."

Sieyès's tone in this back-and-forth monologue varies in emotional tenor. At times his rhetorical questions are neutral and instructional. The question about national prosperity simply frames the subject Sieyès will discuss in the first chapter. Yet he quickly and often ramps up his discourse with highly charged emotional language and mocking sarcasm that expose his opponents' views as absurd. He hammers home his points by presenting them as obvious and simple ideas that anyone will understand: "If it is claimed, therefore, that one of the properties of the French constitution is that two hundred thousand individuals out of a total number of twenty million citizens amounts to

CAHIERS DE DOLÉANCES

The term *cahiers de doléances* often appears in the original French in historical discussions of the Estates-General of 1789. Translated into English, this term means "grievance log" or "list of grievances." As the central line of communication between the local authorities and the king, these cahiers played an important role in the French legislative system of the monarchy before the revolution. When electors met in each region to choose their representatives to the Estates-General, they drew up cahiers de doléances that their representatives were charged with presenting at the Estates-General. When the legislature convened, one of its major tasks was to compile a general list from the cahiers sent by each region. There was debate at the time about whether the representatives were bound by these local grievances during the legislative process.

The cahiers de doléances offer modern scholars an abundant source of documentation on the attitudes and events that led to the creation of the National Assembly and the eventual overthrow of the French crown. In 1930 the French Ministry of Education commissioned a catalog of the cahiers. American scholar Beatrice F. Hyslop compiled the first edition of this catalog, published in 1933 and later supplemented by her in 1952.

two-thirds of the common will; the only answer is that this amounts to claiming that two and two makes five."

CRITICAL DISCUSSION

What Is the Third Estate? and Sieyès in his new political role had an immediate and profound impact on the course of the revolution. In his writings and as a representative elected to the Estates-General, he developed an argument about the national "constitution." In the prerevolutionary context, the term "constitution" referred to both a document that dictated the fundamental structures of government and more generally to that fundamental structure or composition of the government itself. Because supreme executive power derives from a mandate from the masses, only the will of the people could legitimately decide upon the founding document and the general composition of the national government. According to Sieyès, the nation had not chosen the constitution of the Estates-General, and the Third Estate "had the authority to declare themselves the country's legitimate national assembly … and elaborate a constitution on their own." On June 17, 1789, they did just that by ratifying a resolution Sieyès himself had drafted. The modern French National Assembly was born.

Long-term reception of Sieyès fluctuated from the fame and prominence of the revolutionary era to relative obscurity during much of the nineteenth century. The restoration of the Bourbon monarchy in 1815 drove Sieyès into exile and made his conception of popular sovereignty a dangerous and subversive idea. Civil

Jacques-Louis David's 1817 portrait of Emmanuel-Joseph Sieyès, author of *What Is the Third Estate?* The pamphlet had an immense influence on the popular thinking that contributed to the outbreak of the French Revolution. *EMMANUEL JOSEPH SIEYÈS (1748–1836) 1817 (OIL ON CANVAS), DAVID, JACQUES LOUIS (1748–1825)/ FOGG ART MUSEUM, HARVARD UNIVERSITY ART MUSEUMS, USA/ BEQUEST OF GRENVILLE L. WINTHROP/THE BRIDGEMAN ART LIBRARY.*

BIBLIOGRAPHY

Sources

Baker, Keith Michael. *Inventing the French Revolution: Essays on French Political Culture in the Eighteenth Century.* Cambridge: Cambridge UP, 1990. Print.

Champion, Edme. "Introduction." *Qu'est-ce que le tiers état?* Au siège de la sociéte. Paris: 1888. I–XIII. *Internet Archive.* Web. 22 Sept. 2012.

Frank, Stephanie. "The General Will beyond Rousseau: Sieyès's Theological Arguments for the Sovereignty of the Revolutionary National Assembly." *History of European Ideas* Sept. 2011: 337–43. *SciVerse.* Web. 22 Sept. 2012.

Laquièze, Alain. "La Réception de Sieyès par la doctrine publiciste française du XIXème et du XXème siècles." *Electronic Journal of Constitutional History* Sept. 2005. *REDiris.* Web. 9 Oct. 2012.

Sieyès, Emmanuel-Joseph. *Qu'est-ce que le tiers état?* Paris: Au siège de la sociéte, 1888. *Internet Archive.* Web. 22 Sept. 2012.

Sewell, William H. *Rhetoric of Bourgeois Revolution: The Abbé Sieyès and* What Is the Third Estate? Durham: Duke UP, 1994. Print.

Sonenscher, Michael, ed. and trans. *Sieyès: Political Writings.* Indianapolis: Hackett, 2003. Print.

Further Reading

Bronislaw, Baczko. "The Social Contract of the French: Sieyès and Rousseau." *Journal of Modern History* 60 Supplement: *Rethinking French Politics in 1788* (1988): S98–125. *JSTOR.* Web. 22 Sept. 2012.

Chisick, Harvey. "The Pamphlet Literature of the French Revolution: An Overview." *History of European Ideas,* 17.2–3 (1993): 149–66. Print.

Forsyth, Murray. *Reason and Revolution: The Political Thought of the Abbé Sieyès.* New York: Leicester UP, 1987. Print.

Furet, Francois, and Mona Ozouf, eds. *A Critical Dictionary of the French Revolution.* Trans. Arthur Goldhammer. Belknap P of Harvard UP: Cambridge, 1989. Print.

Kaiser, Thomas, and Dale Van Kley, eds. *From Deficit to Deluge: The Origins of the French Revolution.* Stanford: Stanford UP, 2011. Print.

Sonencher, Michael. *Before the Deluge: Public Debt, Inequality, and the Intellectual Origins of the French Revolution.* Princeton: Princeton UP, 2007. Print.

law scholars in the late nineteenth and early twentieth reestablished his reputation as a crucial revolutionary thinker. Edme Champion's introduction to the 1888 centennial edition provides an overview of nineteenth-century reception of *What Is the Third Estate?* and contemporary historian Alain Laquièze has done a detailed study of the changing perceptions of Sieyès.

What Is the Third Estate? remains a canonical document in historical studies of the French Revolution. It provides modern-day readers with a view of the political tensions that exploded into the recurrent civil wars and coups of late-eighteenth- and nineteenth-century France. In contemporary scholarship Sewell has examined the pamphlet to explore the dynamic interactions of written texts and social and political culture. Scholars Keith Michael Baker and Stephanie Frank, among others, have written about tensions between Jean-Jacques Rousseau's conception of the social contract and Sieyès's conception of political representation and the general will.

Nicholas Snead

WHEN HEAVEN AND EARTH CHANGED PLACES
A Vietnamese Woman's Journey from War to Peace

Le Ly Hayslip

OVERVIEW

Le Ly Hayslip's memoir *When Heaven and Earth Changed Places: A Vietnamese Woman's Journey from War to Peace* (1989) recounts a life torn between the insurmountable contradictions of war. Born in central Vietnam under French colonial rule, Phung Thi Le Ly, along with her devout Buddhist family and her village, is caught up first in Ho Chi Minh's fight for liberation from the French, then in the civil war between Ho's communist Viet Cong fighters and the Republican forces of the South Vietnamese, and finally in the "American war" after U.S. forces become active in the conflict. As she grows up, young Le Ly works for the Vietcong and is forced to cooperate with the French, Americans, and South Vietnamese. She is then sentenced to death as a traitor by the Vietcong and suffers torture, rape, and abuse from men on all sides of the conflict. Yet she survives with dignity, strength, and a determination to seek healing and promote peace. Aimed at an American audience, including Vietnam veterans, Hayslip's chronicle persuasively authenticates the Vietnamese perspective and demonstrates that she and her people were fighting for neither democracy nor communism but for independence.

When Heaven and Earth Changed Places was published in the United States fourteen years after the Vietnam War ended. A devastated U.S. citizenry, both military and civilian, was still attempting to come to terms with the losses sustained during the long conflict. Hayslip's was one of the first Vietnamese accounts of the conflict written in English (with the help of writer and editor Jay Wurts). Despite being uncompromising in its revelations of brutality and injustice, it avoids bitterness and blame, which made it accessible and popular in the United States. *When Heaven and Earth Changed Places* puts a human face on a largely unknown enemy and issues a much-welcomed call for understanding and reconciliation.

HISTORICAL AND LITERARY CONTEXT

Hayslip's memoir emerged from decades of colonization and war in Vietnam. After the Japanese occupation of Indochina during World War II, the French attempted to retake their former holdings in the region. Despite Ho's eventual victory over the French in 1954, Western powers partitioned the country at the Geneva Conference, claiming it was a first step toward national autonomy. Soldiers from the Communist Democratic Republic of Vietnam in the north joined a strong liberation movement in South Vietnam, and a bitter civil war broke out when the United States backed the South Vietnamese government. The United States steadily increased its involvement until, by 1968, 540,000 American soldiers were deployed in Vietnam. Escalating U.S. intervention, the draft, repeated military failures, and brutal images of the conflict in the media made U.S. involvement unpopular and divisive on the home front, as hundreds of thousands joined antiwar protests. American troops were finally withdrawn in 1973, and the war officially ended in 1975 when the South Vietnamese surrendered in Saigon. The scars left by the conflict at home and abroad are deep and enduring.

Hayslip was five years old when resistance forces overwhelmed the French and was twenty-one when she escaped her war-torn country in 1970 as the wife of an American civilian contractor. In 1986 she returned to her homeland to try to locate her relatives and to make peace with her past. Because relations between Hayslip's two nations had not normalized, she was obliged to enter Vietnam through Thailand, hiding her identity from the Communist government. Revisiting the transformed landscapes of her youth and learning the horrifying stories of family members long presumed dead spurred her to work on her memoir. Through recounting the story of her life, which also represents a history of the modern conflicts in Vietnam, she became part of a larger healing process related to the American experience of the Vietnam War.

In the decades following the withdrawal of U.S. troops from Vietnam, literary works of trauma and survival gradually emerged, including such autobiographies as Vietnam veteran and antiwar activist Ron Kovic's *Born on the Fourth of July* (1974) and U.S. Marine veteran and journalist Philip Caputo's *A Rumor of War* (1977), both of which describe the disillusionment and anguish particular to the Southeast Asian conflict. Although Hayslip's memoir echoes similar concerns, her position as a Vietnamese American, woman, and noncombatant is unique: much post-Vietnam War American literature has focused only on how American soldiers suffered and experienced the conflict,

Key Facts

Time Period:
Late 20th Century

Genre:
Memoir

Events:
Vietnam War and its aftermath

Nationality:
Vietnamese

GLORIA EMERSON: VIETNAM AUTHOR

Although Le Ly Hayslip's memoir *When Heaven and Earth Changed Places* undoubtedly broke new ground in the exploration of the costs of the Vietnam War, it was not the first work by a woman to explore alternative perspectives of the conflict. Gloria Emerson, born in New York City in 1929, left a wealthy but dysfunctional family during the 1950s to become a journalist, working her way up from fashion reporter on the women's page to foreign correspondent. In 1956 she traveled to Vietnam, during the waning days of French rule. As the war escalated in the late 1960s, she asked editors at *The New York Times* to send her to Vietnam again.

She returned to the site of the conflict in 1970 and braved battles, helicopters, and guerillas to cover the effects of the war on civilians and soldiers from all sides. In 1976 she published a unique and comprehensive book of interviews titled *Winners and Losers: Battles, Retreats, Gains, Losses, and Ruins from the Vietnam War*. Just before her death in 2004, she composed her own obituary, explaining that she had "wanted to go back to write about the Vietnamese people and the immense unhappy changes in their lives, not a subject widely covered by the huge press corps who were preoccupied with covering the military story."

with the Vietnamese remaining invisible or serving only as a backdrop for assessments of the political and military role of the United States. A later example of such a work is Robert S. McNamara's candid 1995 memoir *In Retrospect: The Tragedy and Lessons of Vietnam*.

When Heaven and Earth Changed Places brought Americans face to face with Vietnamese civilians, particularly peasants, providing insight into the struggles of a people under fire and affording Americans the opportunity to view themselves through Vietnamese eyes. Vietnamese American Nguyen Thi Thu Lam's *Fallen Leaves* (1989), published the same year, offers a female experience of the wars from a middle-class viewpoint. Other works by Vietnamese-born writers about events of the war include Tran Van Dinh's *Blue Dragon, White Tiger: A Tet Story* (1983), Bao Ninh's *The Sorrow of War: A Novel of North Vietnam* (1991), Nguyen Qui Duc's memoir *Where the Ashes Are: The Odyssey of a Vietnamese Family* (1994), and Andrew X. Pham's *The Eaves of Heaven: A Life in Three Wars* (2008). Hayslip published a sequel, *Child of War, Woman of Peace*, in 1993. When influential film director Oliver Stone combined the sequel with *When Heaven and Earth Changed Places* in his 1993 movie *Heaven and Earth*, Hayslip's audience grew.

THEMES AND STYLE

Hayslip encapsulates her novel's overriding message of healing and reconciliation, as well as her purpose for recording her life experiences, in a plea to

her American audience, particularly veterans: "I ask you to read this book and look into the heart of one you once called enemy." Without accusation, she condemns war, of which she says, "Children and soldiers have always known it to be terrible." She reveals a people physically and morally crushed by conflict while making war itself her only real villain. As her father sadly advises her when she rails against her sister's forced marriage to a Republican official, "Don't hate Chin—and don't hate Ba for marrying him. Hate the war for what it did to them both." Her brutal experiences lead to cynicism about causes and ideology and to a resolute focus on survival. She must make a decision: "I promised myself, I would only flow with the strongest current and drift with the steadiest wind—and not resist. To resist you have to believe in something." Hayslip does manage to retain her belief in the commonality of human experience, ending the book on a note of hope: "We have time in abundance … to repeat our mistakes. We only need to correct them once, however … to break the chain of vengeance forever."

One of Hayslip's most effective narrative techniques is leaping through time, breaking up her exposition of wartime experiences with flash-forwards to her return to Vietnam in 1986. These jumps in chronology remind the reader of the narrator's survival and maturation, juxtaposing her anger, despair, and cynicism as a young woman with the more measured voice of the older Hayslip. Extending this rhetoric of transformation to illustrate the ways in which opposites can resolve into a whole and repair differences, she contrasts the physique of the Americans with that of the Vietnamese, American military masculinity with natural Vietnamese femininity, the powerful with the powerless, the destroying with the nurturing. Yet, in the spirit of her Buddhist faith and need for healing, she is determined to reunite these opposites: "Anger can teach forgiveness, hate can teach us to love and war can teach us peace."

Although it describes a period of violent chaos and oppression, the overall tone of *When Heaven and Earth Changed Places* is life affirming and frank. Hayslip openly acknowledges her faults and failures while describing the betrayals she experiences. Vietnamese words and phrases are scattered throughout the text to draw readers into the culture and life of her people, as are frequent references to Buddhist tradition and philosophy, and Vietnamese folk tales and maxims. For example, she frequently repeats the analogy, "By sticking together, the tiny ants can carry the elephant," to describe the relationship between the Vietnamese people and the mammoth U.S. forces. One of the most persuasive of the recurring folktale images is that of the woman warrior. Determined to emulate the legendary warrior's skill as a fighter, Hayslip realizes that her most important work is "to bring forth and nourish life, and to defend it with a warrior's strength."

A Vietnamese woman carries a basket of vegetables past a building ruined during the Vietnam War. © EYE UBIQUITOUS/ ALAMY.

CRITICAL DISCUSSION

American critics and readers welcomed Hayslip's compelling depiction of the effects of war on her life and her gently insistent antiwar perspective. Scholars received it as a groundbreaking work of personal history. Rachel Klayman, an editor who recommended the manuscript for publication, called it a classic along the lines of *The Diary of Anne Frank* (1947) and Mark Mathabane's autobiography of apartheid, *Kaffir Boy* (1986). In 1989 *When Heaven and Earth Changed Places* appeared on the front page of *The New York Times Book Review,* where David K. Shipler writes, "Remarkably, Ms. Hayslip never slides into bitterness, although she has good cause … she manages so gracefully to transcend politics, keeping her humaneness as the focus." Lynne Bundesen (1989) of the *Los Angeles Times Book Review* writes the book "should be required reading in military colleges and in high schools and universities looking for broader, more personal interpretations of geo-politics." Hayslip has revealed that she was subjected to virulent negative responses to her book from anti-Communist Vietnamese refugees in the United States, some of whom threatened violence and called her a whore, a Vietcong, and a betrayer, focusing only on certain details of her story.

Nevertheless, *When Heaven and Earth Changed Places,* which has been reprinted several times and translated into seventeen languages, still resonates deeply in both U.S. and Vietnamese society. Scholar Renny Christopher features Hayslip in her academic study *The Viet Nam War / The American War: Images and Representations in Euro-American and Vietnamese Exile Narratives* (1995) as the Vietnamese American author who has received the most critical attention. Christopher has fostered debate over the definition of the personal and political in the memoir, rejecting a claim made by Shipler that the book "transcends politics." Christopher counters, "Hayslip describes in detail the politics of civil war and class conflict." She writes that despite the author's personal description of her memoir as a story of human experience rather than politics, war memoirs are by nature political. After the book's publication, Hayslip established the East Meets West Foundation, which works through such projects as the Mothers Love Pediatric Clinic and Peace Village Medical Center to solve the deep societal problems resulting from many years of war, and the Global Village Foundation, which focuses on community development within Vietnam.

Feminist scholars have pointed out another distinctive aspect of the work. Bundesen writes, "[T]he private side of any war is rarely told, and [the memoir] is, supremely, the woman's side … Hayslip gives us the point of view of Any woman, combining her autobiography with an eyewitness account of Vietnam's history over the last forty years." In a 2001 essay in *Haunting Violations: Feminist Criticism and the Crisis of the "Real,"* Leslie Bow sides with those who view the book as necessarily political, stating that its impact stems from the immigrant experience: "Hayslip's position as an Asian female immigrant is intrinsic to the narrative's political message."

BIBLIOGRAPHY

Sources

Bow, Leslie. "Third-World Testimony in the Era of Globalization: Vietnam, Sexual Trauma, and Le Ly Hayslip's Art of Neutrality." *Haunting Violations: Feminist Criticism and the Crisis of the "Real."* Ed. Wendy Hesford and Wendy Kozol. Urbana: U of Illinois P, 2001. 169–94. Print.

Bundesen, Lynne. Rev. of *When Heaven and Earth Changed Places,* by Le Ly Hayslip. *Los Angeles Times* 25 June 1989: 4. Print.

Christopher, Renny. *The Viet Nam War / The American War: Images and Representations in Euro-American and Vietnamese Exile Narratives.* Amherst: U of Massachusetts P, 1995. Print.

Hayslip, Le Ly, with Jay Wurts. *When Heaven and Earth Changed Places: A Vietnamese Woman's Journey from War to Peace.* New York: Doubleday, 1989. Print.

Shipler, David K. "A Child's Tour of Duty." Rev. of *When Heaven and Earth Changed Places,* by Le Ly Hayslip. *New York Times Book Review* 25 June 1989: 1. *General Reference Center Gold.* Web. 4 Sept. 2012.

Whitney, Craig R. "Gloria Emerson, Chronicler of War's Damage, Dies at 75." *New York Times.* 5 Aug 2004: A21. Print.

Further Reading

Emerson, Gloria. *Winners and Losers: Battles, Retreats, Gains, Losses, and Ruins from the Vietnam War.* New York: Random, 1976. Print.

Hayslip, Le Ly, with James Hayslip. *Child of War, Woman of Peace.* New York: Doubleday. 1993. Print.

Hoffman, Eva. Rev. of *When Heaven and Earth Changed Places,* by Le Ly Hayslip. *New York Times* 17 May 1989: C21. Print.

Kempley, Rita. "Nine Questions for … Le Ly Hayslip; *Heaven and Earth*'s Inspiration: On War & Peace, Movies & Karma." *Washington Post* 2 Jan 1994: G2. Print.

Kolko, Gabriel. *Anatomy of a War: Vietnam, the United States, and the Modern Historical Experience.* New York: New Press, 1994. Print.

McMahon, Robert J. "Changing Interpretations of the Vietnam War." *The Oxford Companion to American Military History.* New York: Oxford UP, 1999. 767–68. Print.

Simson, Maria. "Vietnam Memoir Gets New Life via Hollywood." *Publishers Weekly* 27 Sept. 1993: 28. *Literature Resource Center.* Web. 1 Sept. 2012.

Stephens, Rebecca L. "Distorted Reflections: Oliver Stone's *Heaven and Earth* and Le Ly Hayslip's *When Heaven and Earth Changed Places.*" *Centennial Review* 41.3 (1997): 661–69. Print.

Media Adaptation

Heaven and Earth. Dir. Oliver Stone. Perf. Tommy Lee Jones, Joan Chen, Hiep Thi Le. Warner Bros. Films, 1993. Film.

Tina Gianoulis

SOCIAL CLASSES

DUMB LUCK
Vu Trong Phung

OVERVIEW

Dumb Luck, a satirical novel by Vu Trong Phung, was first published in Tonkin (known as northern Vietnam today) in 1936. Its English version, translated by Nguyen Nguyet Cam and Peter Zinoman, appeared in the United States in 2002. The novel's success derives primarily from its effective exposure and condemnation of extraordinarily ignominious human activities: the decadent lifestyles, social corruptions, and mindless aping of Western fads in modern, urban Vietnamese society in the early twentieth century. The novel focuses on the life of the picaro-like protagonist, Red-Haired Xuan, who interacts and socializes with various upper-class urbanites in Hanoi and whose artfulness, sophistry, and deception metamorphose him from an orphaned, homeless vagabond into an honorable national hero. The language that the characters use in their conversations throughout *Dumb Luck* is urbane, comic, witty, and also lewd. The appearance of some French vocabulary in their speeches indicates the influence of French language and culture upon the colonized Vietnamese.

Vietnam was a colonial dependency of France from 1858 to 1945. Under French occupation many members of the Vietnamese elite were educated in France, and many others gained access to French culture through colonial schools, books, magazines, and newspapers written in French. In the early twentieth century, commercialism, materialism, and capitalism exercised a significant impact upon the half-feudal, half-colonial Vietnamese society. Those who zealously idolized French culture and civilization wanted to Westernize and modernize Vietnam through social reforms. *Dumb Luck* satirically criticizes the Vietnamese urbanites who became ludicrous puppets and caricatures of their own too-often pseudo-ideologies and who generated cultural turbulence in Vietnamese society through their shallow, superficial understanding of Western civilization. *Dumb Luck* long has been considered a gem in modern Vietnamese literature, and in today's climate of globalization and cultural exchange, the work still merits praise for its critique of social disruptions that occur with the homogenization of traditional cultures into transnational or global systems.

HISTORICAL AND LITERARY CONTEXT

In the 1920s French Indochina witnessed the emergence of various political, intellectual, and ideological movements. The mandarins traditionally trained in Confucian philosophy were replaced by a new group of intellectuals educated under the French colonial system in Vietnam. The French colonists desired to create a new Vietnamese identity for the Vietnamese peoples—the "yellow gentlemen" who would appreciate French cultural values and mores and who would emulate French criteria of deportment in a civilized society based on French norms. Thus, the language, history, and literature of France were integrated into the domestic educational system to produce a generation of French-educated Vietnamese who could communicate in French and fill clerical and staff positions in offices operated by French-owned enterprises.

Dumb Luck was published during a period in which the Self-Strength Literary Group was promoting the idea that "progressive renovation of external forms will trigger the progressive renovation of our spirit." Vu was skeptical of this group's goal of Europeanization. Words such as "civilization," "women's rights," "progress," "modernity," and "Europeanization" recur throughout the novel, signaling the obsession with the French culture of liberty, equality, and feminism that so enchanted many Vietnamese of that era. They believed that the values of French urban culture should replace those of the indigenous Vietnamese agrarian culture. The characters in *Dumb Luck* represent several social levels, but most of them construct their identities through pretension; hypocrisy; affected cosmopolitan sensibility; and even decadent, lustful fashion in order to be considered "civilized" and "sophisticated" citizens. Vu expresses sharp disdain toward these superficial vogues practiced by a group of wealthy urbanites in Hanoi; he sardonically vituperates against them for their absurdities and obscenities.

Dumb Luck is considered to be the first Vietnamese satire that directly addresses the ugliest flaws in the social realities of the upper and ruling class of the colonial period. Thus, Vu neither implies nor hints at criticism, as previous Vietnamese authors had done in their critiques of that society. Although Vu lived for only twenty-seven years (1912–39), he witnessed rapid changes in Vietnamese society and perceived the social ills that derived from them, such as materialism; capitalism; the decline of filial piety; and the moral

⁜ *Key Facts*

Time Period:
Mid-20th Century

Genre:
Novel

Events:
French colonization of Vietnam

Nationality:
Vietnamese

VU TRONG PHUNG: REALIST AUTHOR

Vu Trong Phung was born into a poor family. At the age of fifteen he had to give up his formal education to earn a living. As a disciplined, hardworking person he became frustrated and chagrined with the urban Europeanization movement, which was compared to an aggressive storm that blew all of the dirtiest foreign trash into Vietnam, destroying Vietnamese traditional and cultural values. He lived in a humble, tiny garret amid the degenerating society of colonial Hanoi. His anger at social corruption and human immorality led to his pessimism, because he felt impotent and confused with life's injustice and absurdity.

In a 1937 interview with the *Bac Ha Journal,* he stated straightforwardly that he had lost his faith in society. He felt suffocated and disgusted by the stench of a rotten society dominated by money, materialism, greed, and lust. He observed that many youths idolized hedonism and debauchery and that they were intellectually too lazy to think critically. His responsibility as a realist author was to expose the obscenities of human foibles and the immorality of a so-called "civilized" society so that no one would be deceived by the ostentatious veneer over an underlying decadent modernity.

degeneration witnessed by such social ills as adultery, cuckoldry, and lasciviousness. Ironically, all of these problems are accepted as characteristics of modernity. Vu's other works, including "From Theory to Practice," "To Be a Whore," and *The Industry of Marrying Europeans,* also deride people who adore materialism and foreignness. During the same period, Nguyen Cong Hoan (1903–77) also wrote several short stories scornfully criticizing the upper-class people who had sacrificed their humanity to greed and selfishness, including "The Teeth of an Upper-Class Family's Dog," "Filial Piety: Paying Tribute to Mom," and "Two Bastards."

Dumb Luck establishes Vu's reputation as a pioneering Vietnamese modernist who satirically portrays Vietnamese colonial society during its transition into the modern period, catalyzed by the power of money and the appeal of French-influenced customs. Some expressions used by the novel's characters have entered spoken Vietnamese as comic colloquialisms. Subsequent Vietnamese authors of significance, including Nguyen Hong and Nguyen Tuan, have acknowledged Vu as a true master of satire. Realists and naturalists such as Ngo Tat To, Nam Cao, and Bui Hien followed Vu in his addressing the ugly social realities of the Vietnam of their time.

THEMES AND STYLE

Dumb Luck denounces the moral degeneration in the semifeudal, semicolonial urban society of Vietnam during its transition toward a capitalistic modernity in which people abandon their traditional moral values to embrace the licentious lifestyles promoted by materialism and greed. Vu's novel asks readers to reexamine their moral and ethical standards of behavior closely. He satirizes the obscenity, grotesqueness, and absurdity of a culturally turbulent society. For example, chapter fifteen, "The Happiness of a Family in Mourning," exposes many ugly blemishes. The funeral of Grandpa—Mr. Civilization's father—becomes a boisterous carnival in which female relatives show off their trendy, provocative clothes; adolescents flirt overtly with each other; and the family displays its wealth and sophistication for the public to envy: "There were all sorts of fashionable men and women—flirting, courting, gossiping, teasing, arranging trysts, and making each other jealous—all the while maintaining the appropriately sorrowful expressions of mourners at a funeral." On the one hand, Vu derides his characters, but on the other hand, he suggests that, in order to maintain their sanity in such trying times, readers must laugh at these caricatures of themselves presented so artfully in situations of foregrounded decadence and perversion.

Vu skillfully employs the device of exaggeration to achieve greater comic, ironic, and satiric effects in his narrative, but his exaggeration is not far removed from the reality of the life he satirizes. For example, during Grandpa's funeral, his unchaste niece, Miss Snow, wears "a long, see-through dress over a bra with black lace trim that [reveals] her underarms and the top half of her breasts." Her intentionally revealing mourning outfit elicits carnal responses from many visitors, despite her ostensible innocence. Another rhetorical device that the author uses effectively is paradox. The title of chapter fifteen, mentioned above, is paradoxical: the death of a family member leads to his family's happiness. Tides of civilization and Europeanization are associated with "waves of venereal disease," lust, cuckoldry, and "rubber breasts." Mr. Civilization mistakes Red-Haired Xuan's "stupidity" for "a combination of courtesy and modesty," while Red-Haired Xuan is, in fact, "the defiler of [Mr. Civilization's youngest sister's] virginity," an uneducated opportunist, and generally a "bastard." Thus, exaggeration and paradox help Vu satirize a decadent society that is losing the battle between the "old" and the "new"—a society on the edge of moral collapse.

The narrative tone throughout *Dumb Luck* is consistently arch and ironic. The conversations among the characters reveal deep but transparent levels of pretense, hypocrisy, and vulgarity. For instance, Mrs. Deputy Customs Officer claims to be a "civilized woman," although she is a "horny" nymphomaniac and a "passionate adherent of nudism" who finds joy in being ravished. She tells Red-Haired Xuan that she does not "discriminate" against the working class, but she calls her own people—the Annamese—"stupid" and "pathetic." Vu's novel is unarguably a diatribe against the ostentation and ignobility of urbanites during a period of cultural transition and decline.

CRITICAL DISCUSSION

Before the August Revolution of 1945, Vu and his works received contradictory reviews and criticism, primarily due to the author's prurient language and pornographic descriptions. A member of the Self-Strength Literary Group criticized him for using obscenities, for showing no respect for his readers, and for his depressing pessimism. However, Vu was praised for his insightful observations of social realities and for his bravery in condemning the power of the wealthy class who luxuriated in depravity. He was an anti-romantic, believing that literature should be used as a weapon, as a means to express an author's anger and frustration at life's absurdities. In a 1942 review of Vu's major novels, Vu Ngoc Phan calls *Dumb Luck* a picaresque novel without much high value because the characters are unrealistic. This critic also faults Vu for his overreliance on sexuality, which is used as a resolution for all conflicts in the novel; for his "conservative attitude; and for his failure to address a specific moral path that one should follow.

Controversies about *Dumb Luck* primarily resulted from the author's complex but inconsistent political perspectives, the critics' lack of understanding of the author and their misinterpretations of Vu's works, and the standards of political correctness set for Vietnamese socialist literature. From 1958 to 1987, due to several political events such as the Vietnam War, the reunification of Vietnam in 1975, and the postwar Vietnam culture, Vu and his works generally experienced severe criticism by socialist critics from the north—*Dumb Luck* was effectively banned in the Democratic Republic of Vietnam from 1960 to 1975 and in the unified Socialist Republic of Vietnam from 1975 to about 1982. The author was only fully rehabilitated after 1986. For example, some socialist writers, such as poet Nguyen Dinh Thi, note that nowhere in Vu's works can we find an honest portrayal of a working-class person, a laborer, or a farmer. However, in the late 1980s critics started to interpret *Dumb Luck,* as well Vu's other novels, from a less conservative point of view, acknowledging him as the master of Vietnamese satire. His significant position in Vietnamese literature now is unarguably recognized. In his essay in *So Do: Tac pham va du luan* (2002), Do Duc Hieu states that behind Vu's acerbic laughter at the absurd and the grotesque is his humanism. Do continues, sardonically, by stating that *Dumb Luck* derides Europeanization, a political trick designed by Western colonists to civilize the barbaric peoples in the East. The novel exposes the ridiculous deception masked under the feudalistic and colonial regime's demagogic policies, as well as its cunning, malicious agendas.

Since 1990, scholarship on *Dumb Luck* and other works by Vu has flourished. Critics have begun to recognize the positive message behind his apparent pessimism: the novel contains educational values and

A young woman carrying bananas in Hanoi, Vietnam, the setting for the life of Xuan in *Dumb Luck.* © MARTIN PUDDY/ CORBIS.

represents a permanent warning. For example, in his piece in *Vu Trong Phung: Mot tai nang doc dao* (2000), Nguyen Dang Manh emphasizes the author's hatred of social injustice and corruption under the French, demonstrating his desire to annihilate all social ills to build a just and rational society. *Dumb Luck* is a satire that directs laughter at human foibles, but it also teaches its readers to weigh imported vogues so that they will not become ridiculous pseudo-practitioners of values that do not promote the indigenous culture that is life affirming for the native population. Most of the criticism on Vu and *Dumb Luck* exists in Vietnamese, with few Western scholars writing about it since its publication in English in 2002. Sheridan Prasso of the *Los Angeles Times* notes that Vu is "a brilliant and prolific satirist who has been compared to Balzac." According to James Banerian, writing in *World Literature Today, Dumb Luck* is "worthwhile for its unique and comical look at Hanoi in social transition," and the English version captures the original humor, irony, and sarcasm effectively.

BIBLIOGRAPHY

Sources

Banerian, James. Rev. of *Dumb Luck,* by Vu Trong Phung. *World Literature Today* 77.2 (2003): 95. Print.

Do, Hieu Duc. "Nhung lop song ngon tu trong *So Do*" [Waves of Language in *Dumb Luck*]. Ed. Ton Thao Mien. *So Do: Tac pham va du luan* [Dumb Luck: Text and Criticism]. Hanoi: NXB Van Hoc, 2002. 270–88. Print.

Nguyen, Manh Dang. "Vu Trong Phung va niem cam uat khong nguoi" [Vu Trong Phung and His Ceaseless Anger]. *Vu Trong Phung: Mot tai nang doc dao* [Vu Trong Phung: A Unique Talent]. Ed. Mai Huong. Hanoi: NXB Van Hoa-Thong Tin, 2000. 92–98. Print.

Prasso, Sheridan. "When Tradition and Modernity Knock Heads." Rev. of *Dumb Luck,* by Vu Trong Phung. *Los Angeles Times.* Los Angeles Times, 12 Jan. 2003. Web. 3 Oct. 2012.

Vu, Phan Ngoc. "Vu Trong Phung." *Nam Cao; Vu Trong Phung.* Khanh Hoa: NXB Tong Hop Khanh Hoa, 1991. 77–89. Print.

Vu, Trong Phung. *Dumb Luck.* Trans. Nguyen Nguyet Cam and Peter Zinoman. Ed. Peter Zinoman. Ann Arbor: U of Michigan P, 2002. Print.

Further Reading

Cooper, Nicola. *France in Indochina: Colonial Encounters.* London: Berg, 2001. Print.

Marr, David G. *Vietnamese Tradition on Trial, 1920–1945.* Berkeley: U of California P, 1984. Print.

Thanh, Le, and Peter Zinoman. "We Interview Mr. Vu Trong Phung about the Novels *The Storm* and *To Be a Whore.*" *Michigan Quarterly Review* 44.1 (2005): 73–78. Print.

Zinoman, Peter. "Provincial Cosmopolitanism: Vu Trong Phung's Foreign Literary Engagements." *Travelling Nation-Makers: Transnational Flows and Movements in the Making of Modern Southeast Asia.* Ed. Caroline S. Hau and Kasian Tejapira. Singapore: National U of Singapore P, 2011. 126–52. Print.

Vu, Trong Phung. *Luc Xi: Prostitution and Venereal Disease in Colonial Hanoi.* Trans. Shaun Kingsley Malarney. Honolulu: U of Hawaii P, 2011. Print.

———. *The Industry of Marrying Europeans.* Trans. Thuy Tranviet. Ithaca: Cornell University Southeast Asia Program Publications, 2005. Print.

Quan Ha

THE FACTORY SHIP

Takiji Kobayashi

OVERVIEW

The Factory Ship, sometimes translated as *The Cannery Boat* or *The Crab-Canning Boat*, is a short novel written by the Japanese author Takiji Kobayashi and published in 1929. The novella describes the life of a sailor onboard a Japanese crab-canning boat and depicts severe working conditions in graphic terms. Often considered one of the most important works of literature to emerge from the short-lived proletarian literary movement in Japan, *The Factory Ship* is a work of social realism intended to evoke anger and disgust at the social injustices perpetuated in its pages. In vivid images of abhorrent conditions and striking contrasts between the lives of the workers and their bosses, Kobayashi treats class struggle as a microcosm and advocates Marxist class analysis and worker solidarity as a political solution to the problems facing modern Japan.

The Factory Ship was initially published as a serial in the May and June issues of the Japanese literary magazine *Senki*. It generated an enthusiastic response from readers and was soon after translated into English, French, Russian, and German. However, government officials in Japan felt threatened by the subject matter and Kobayashi's call to action and immediately banned the book from further distribution. *The Factory Ship* would not be published until after World War II. Since then it has continued to shock audiences with scenes of torture that have prompted discussions on labor laws and human rights violations. The novel experienced a jump in sales in 2008 during Japan's economic recession. Because of its overt political message, *The Factory Ship* continues to garner scholarly attention and contribute to worthwhile social and political discussion in Japan and internationally.

HISTORICAL AND LITERARY CONTEXT

In the 1920s proletarian literature emerged as Japan's most important literary movement as authors responded to deteriorating working conditions and economic hardships faced by the working poor. With the withdrawal of Western products from the international market during World War I, Japan's economy enjoyed a boom and rapid development of monopoly capital that lasted only as long as the war. By 1920 the bubble collapsed, and Japan experienced a series of recessions and minor banking crises. The Tokyo earthquake of 1923 further aggravated its sluggish economy, and the 1927 financial crises pulled the Japanese market into a depression even before the stock market collapsed in New York in 1929. While one-quarter of the banks in Japan faltered during the crises, rural areas were hit hard by the plummeting value of rice and silk in the market.

Japan's postwar recession contributed to the proliferation of Marxist scholarship, especially in the field of economics. A group of socialist activists, including Hitoshi Yamakawa and Kazuo Fukumoto, established the Japanese Communist Party, which was subject to intense persecution and repression by the police and military. In March 1928 (and again in April 1929), thousands of suspected communists were arrested and imprisoned unless they recanted their allegiance to communist ideology. Kobayashi responded to the mass arrests, interrogations, and trials in his story "March 15, 1928"—also published in 1929 in *Senki* and which depicted graphic scenes of interrogation and torture by police. Later in 1928 Kobayashi began writing *The Factory Ship* after reading a newspaper account of abysmal working conditions and brutal treatment of workers onboard the canning ship *Hakuai Maru*. The exposé prompted Kobayashi to undertake research on the working conditions on canning boats, including interviewing former and current workers.

The tendency toward Marxist thought and class awareness expressed itself in literary forms in the latter half of the 1910s. Sukeo Miyajima's novel *Miner* (1916) chronicles the resistance of a miner against his boss's tyranny and presents a theory about the struggle for anarchist revolution. Later, in 1924, Hatsunosuki Hirabayashi and Suekichi Aono launched the literary magazine *Literary Front*, which would become a primary organ for the burgeoning movement known as proletarian literature, or Taisho workers literature, named for the Taisho period in Japanese history (1912–26) during which a new consciousness arose regarding workers' rights. *Literary Front* published such notable works as Yoshiki Hayama's *The Prostitute* (1925), which takes up the theme of sexual labor to consider the intersections of class and gender as they affect both male and female workers.

Kobayashi's bold decision to portray the brutal conditions of the workingman in the face of government repression of Marxist theory and communist

✣ Key Facts

Time Period:
Early 20th Century

Genre:
Novella

Events:
Japanese economic crisis; Tokyo earthquake of 1923; founding of the Japanese Communist Party and rise of Japanese proletarian literature

Nationality:
Japanese

THE FACTORY SHIP AND MODERN AUDIENCES: FILM AND GRAPHIC NOVEL ADAPTATIONS

The resurgence in popularity of Takiji Kobayashi's *The Factory Ship* in 2008 can be traced to a few important events that expanded interest in him from a tiny circle of devoted readers and literary scholars. A Takiji Library was established as a centralized source of information related to Kobayashi's works. It also sponsored the publication of ten books, including a manga version of *The Factory Ship,* in order to attract a younger readership. The graphic novel contains striking images that bring Kobayashi's words to life and make the novel's message clearer and more accessible to the next generation.

Following the success of the visual adaptations of *The Factory Ship,* blockbuster director Sabu announced his decision to create another film adaptation of the classic novel. In 1953 So Yamamura had released the first cinematic adaptation of *The Factory Ship,* which won the award for best cinematography the following year at the Japanese Film festival, Mainichi Film Concours. Sabu's version (2009) keeps the original title but makes significant changes, most notably the decision to provide character names and develop individual characteristics through backstories provided through flashbacks. One man, Shinjo, emerges from the mass of sailors as a leader. In choosing to call attention to Shinjo, Sabu subverts Kobayashi's intention to highlight solidarity and collective action to instead emphasize individual responsibility. In a 2010 interview with Stefan Steinberg, Sabu claims that this decision was made to bring the movie to a larger audience and was aimed at encouraging individualism in a culture that is sometimes too willing to conform. Shying away from the bold political and social engagement of the novel, Sabu contends that he didn't want to promote collectivism too much because "it often becomes violent." His movie, then, is less a plea for revolution or a call to arms than an endorsement of "the individual who becomes more responsible for him/herself."

activity inspired a genre of literature but ultimately contributed to his untimely death. Upon its publication, *The Factory Ship* was banned, and one particular passage involving a less-than-favorable depiction of the emperor earned Kobayashi six months in jail. In 1933 he was arrested again, this time for attempting to meet with a member of the Communist Party, and died from injuries sustained while in police custody. His death at age thirty shocked fellow writers and activists, and the incredible brutality he suffered served as a warning to like-minded individuals. The state's continuing censorship and violent repression forced many progressives to withdraw from public political engagement, while the genre of proletarian literature withered after Kobayashi's death.

THEMES AND STYLE

The Factory Ship presents a microcosm of the working conditions of capitalism through the struggles of workers onboard a fishing boat and the hardships they must endure. Thematically, the novella departs abruptly from the topics taken up in the traditional literature preceding it. In his introduction to the 1973 edition of the text, Frank Motofuji contends that, until the first decade of the twentieth century, the peasant appeared very seldom in Japanese literature, and when he did, he was usually an object of derision and scorn. Kobayashi breaks from this trend by presenting a fuller representation of modern Japanese society, unafraid to tackle controversial situations and subject matter. He examines the relationships that exist between workers, the direct supervisors acting as middle management, and the capitalist bosses whose orders the managers carry out and takes his examination as far as the emperor, whose imperialist regime has facilitated the growth of capitalism and the exploitation of workers. These relationships are presented without ambiguities to provide an honest and realistic treatment of exploitative practices occurring in industrial societies.

In portraying the working conditions, Kobayashi opts to emphasize the collective state rather than individual psychological reactions. Writing about his work, he says that he has "rejected all attempts at depicting character or delving into psychology" in order to present the group of workers as a "collective hero" rather than individual heroes with unique interests. This is also done by not giving individual workers names, instead referring to people as "the student" or "the head fisherman," so that the members of the working class in their entirety emerge as heroes of the story. Kobayashi's love of cinema, especially the films of Charlie Chaplin, is evident in the pages of *The Factory Ship,* where techniques such as close-ups and montages give the reader a visual experience. These techniques also encouraged later adaptations of *The Factory Ship* into films and Japanese comic books.

Kobayashi's passionate desire to right social injustices comes across in his writing, in which he highlights inequities to promote sympathy with the common, working man. Metaphors likening the workers to animals are common; one man looks like "a dead louse" while another is referred to in likeness to an octopus, because "to keep itself alive, the octopus will eat its own tentacles, if it must." Juxtaposed with a description of a malnourished worker as "a rib cage barely covered with skin" are those of the superintendent and the captain, who regularly drink beer together and whose hands are "dimpled like a plump woman's."

CRITICAL DISCUSSION

After *The Factory Ship* was published, Kobayashi's stark and realistic portrayal of working life connected with readers and alarmed government officials in Japan. While readers identified with the realistic representation of hard labor, critics were less than enthusiastic with Kobayashi's narrative choice to eschew individual psychology. In his review of *The Factory Ship* in

Fishing for crabs off Japan's northern island, Hokkaido, in 1979. Takiji Kobayashi's *The Factory Ship* is about the crew of a crab-fishing ship. © MICHAEL S. YAMASHITA/ CORBIS.

Tokyo Asahi Shinbun in June 1929, Kurahara Korehito simultaneously commends the work as one of the greatest novels to be released to date while warning of the danger of burying the individual in the group. He insists that proletarian writers are not justified in forgoing the individual for the group because "the materialistic view of history by no means denies the role of the individual in history and society." Kurahura maintains that if Kobayashi had been able to depict the psychology and characters of individuals "as representatives of each class and stratum," the overall effect would have made *The Factory Ship* "even more splendid."

The Factory Ship sheds much-needed light on the often oppressive and exploitative working conditions within a capitalist society. Since its publication in 1929, the work has been regarded as one of the greatest examples of the Japanese proletarian novel and has enjoyed a rise in popularity in the past decade. Upon the economic downturn in 2008, sales of *The Factory Ship* jumped to more than 500,000 and landed the novel at number thirteen on the best-seller list. Critic Norma Field, who has studied the renewed interest in *The Factory Ship,* asserts in her 2009 piece in the *Quarterly Changbi* that it stems from "a hunger for collectivity and activism amid the loneliness and cynicism produced by neoliberal callousness." She argues that Kobayashi's attention to the overlapping concerns with class systems, imperialism, and colonialism in his novel's examination of exploitation and resistance continues to be relevant today.

The Factory Ship has been widely regarded as a milestone in proletarian literature. Scholars such as Motofuji assert that Kobayashi "merits our attention as the representative writer of an important literary movement in modern Japan." In the past two decades, the number of international scholars investigating Japanese proletarian literature has grown from a few exceptional scholars to dozens of students and intellectuals working in diverse areas. These scholars and members of the public gathered in 2003, 2004, and 2005 for an international symposium hosted by the Shirakaba Bungakukan-Takiji Library in Tokyo to discuss Kobayashi and fellow proletarian writers. In her 2006 essay in *Positions: East Asia Cultures Critique,* Heather Bowen-Struyk finds in the stories of proletarian writers, such as *The Factory Ship,* a willingness to engage with social issues motivated by "the possibility of revolution amidst glaring inequality" in a way that strikes a chord with contemporary issues.

BIBLIOGRAPHY

Sources

Bowen-Struyk, Heather. "Guest Editor's Introduction: Proletarian Arts in East Asia." *Positions: East Asia Cultures Critique* 14.2 (2006): 251–78. *The Asia-Pacific Journal: Japan Focus.* Web. 30 Aug. 2012.

Field, Norma. "Commercial Appetite and Human Need: The Accidental and Fated Revival of Kobayashi Takiji's Cannery Ship." *Quarterly Changbi* Spring 2009. *The Asia-Pacific Journal Japan Focus.* Web. 24 Aug. 2012.

Karlsson, Mats. "Kurahara Korehito's Road to Proletarian." *Japan Review* 20 (2008): 231–73. *JSTOR.* Web. 24 Aug. 2012.

Motofuji, Frank. "Translator's Introduction." *The Factory Ship and the Absentee Landlord.* Takiji Kobayashi. Trans., Frank Motofuji. Tokyo: U of Tokyo P, 1973. Print.

Steinberg, Stefan. Interview with Sabu. *World Socialist Website.* International Committee of the Fourth International, 3 Mar. 2010. Web. 30 Aug. 2012.

Further Reading

Bowen-Struyk, Heather. *Rethinking Japanese Proletarian Literature.* Ann Arbor: U of Michigan P, 2001. Print.

Field, Norma, and Heather Bowen-Struyk. *Literature for Revolution: An Anthology of Japanese Proletarian Writings.* Chicago: U of Chicago P, 2012. Print.

Kurahara, Korehito. Rev. of *The Factory Ship*, by Takiji Kobayashi. *Tokyo Asahi Shinbun* June 1929. Print.

Keene, Donald. *Modern Japanese Literature: From 1868 to the Present Day.* New York: Grove, 1956. Print.

Viglielmo, Valdo H. "An Aspect of the Japanese Novel." *Poetics of the Elements in the Human Condition: The Sea.* Ed. Anna-Teresa Tymieniecka. Holland: D. Reidel, 1985. Print.

Media Adaptations

Kanikosen [*The Factory Ship*]. Dir. So Yamamura. Perf. So Yamamura, Masayuki Mori, and Sumiko Hidaka. Gendai Productions, 1953. Film.

Kanikosen [*The Factory Ship*]. Dir Sabu [Hiroyuki Tanaka]. Perf. Ryuhei Matsuda, Mitsuki Tanimura. Dub, IMJ Entertainment, Imagica, 2009. Film.

Elizabeth Orvis

GOD'S BITS OF WOOD

Ousmane Sembène

OVERVIEW

God's Bits of Wood (1960), a historical novel by Senegalese writer and filmmaker Ousmane Sembène, chronicles the effects of the 1947–48 Dakar-Niger railway strike on West African colonial society. Originally published in French as *Les bouts de bois de Dieu,* the book opens with Dakar-Niger railroad workers voting to strike for the same higher wages and family stipends earned by white workers. Angered by the demands, the French railroad officials cut off water to workers' homes and use physical violence to coerce them into cooperation. The turning point arrives when the women of Thiès march on Dakar in a protest that draws so much attention that the railroad's management is forced to open negotiations. A nationally publicized speech delivered by the strikers' spokesman Ibrahima Bakayoko causes the strike to expand across West Africa, forcing the railroad to surrender. Although Bakayoko is the heroic leader, the true heroes are the common men who rise against the railroad to demand their rights and the women who fight to keep their families from starvation. Viewing the strike primarily as a class struggle, Sembène created a story in which the African proletariat overcomes an oppressive system controlled by European bureaucrats and the collaborating African elite.

God's Bits of Wood is the author's third and most famous novel. Considered Sembène's masterpiece, it remains one of the most celebrated novels produced in twentieth-century Africa for its moving account of the power of ordinary people. In *Contemporary African Writers,* Abdul-Rasheed Na'Allah notes, "Many young people who read [*God's Bits of Wood*] conclude that every African has a duty to save their communities from the perpetual enslavement of Africa by global powers." Translated into English in 1962, *God's Bits of Wood* is frequently examined in world literature classes in the West. It is also widely read in Senegal and Mali, where the strike occurred.

HISTORICAL AND LITERARY CONTEXT

Although the French had been a constant presence in Senegal since 1659, their efforts to colonize Senegal did not become a full-scale campaign until the nineteenth century. With the slave trade on the decline, commodity production came into demand. In the 1850s the French established a series of forts along the Senegal River, subjugating native kingdoms along the way. The development of the railroad allowed the French to conquer Mali (French Sudan). The French increased their economic foothold through forced labor and imprisonment. Other than minimal attempts to provide health and educational services, little was done to improve the lives of West Africans.

The construction of the Dakar-Niger Railway began in 1883 and was completed in several stages over the next forty years. The railroad connected the Niger River with the port of Dakar, which allowed raw materials to be transported to France and, eventually, around the world. The railroad was supervised by European technicians and administrators who enjoyed generous salaries, health and vacation benefits, an allowance for their families, and bonus pay for working overseas. Africans hired to perform construction and unskilled labor on the railway were denied these same benefits and had no job security or opportunity for advancement. Skilled African workers had some degree of job security and benefits but were never paid equal wages for the same work performed by white employees. In 1947 transportation came to a halt across French West Africa when the railroad workers on the Dakar-Niger line staged a five-month strike to obtain the same rights as their French counterparts. After a bitter strike the railroad agreed to the demands of the workers, who returned to their jobs on March 19, 1948. The victory is celebrated as a turning point in West Africa's anticolonial struggle.

During World War II Sembène was drafted into the French colonial army. Upon completion of his military service, Sembène returned to Senegal, where he found the capital Dakar in a state of turmoil: the indigenous people were loudly voicing their dissatisfaction with the exploitative nature of colonialism. In 1947 Sembène participated in the railroad workers' strike on the Dakar-Niger line, but he left for France before its successful conclusion. Deeply affected by the experience, the author later drew on the events he had witnessed to create *God's Bits of Wood.* The author took up permanent residence in Senegal once it had achieved independence from France in 1960—the same year he published *God's Bits of Wood.* Writing in *Research in African Literatures,* James A. Jones notes, "The story of an African victory over French administrators resonated during a year in which eight French

Time Period:
Mid-20th Century

Genre:
Novel

Events:
Dakar-Niger railway strike; growth of anticolonialist movement

Nationality:
Senegalese

THE FATHER OF AFRICAN CINEMA

Although Ousmane Sembène first made his mark as a novelist, he turned from literature to film soon after completing *God's Bits of Wood* in 1960. The first movie he made, *Borom Sarret,* appeared in 1963, and his next came out five years later. Called *Mandabi* (1968), Sembène's second feature had the distinction of being the first African film made in an African language. During a long career that lasted until his death in 2007, Sembène made a number of influential films, establishing himself as "the father of African cinema," according to critic A. O. Scott in a tribute published in the *New York Times* after Sembène's death.

A communist as well as an artist, Sembène was as critical of Africa's postindependence leadership as he had been of the continent's colonial oppressors. His style and subject matter range widely in his ten feature-length movies, and he worked in Wolof, Diola, French, and other languages. Some of his best-known films, such as *Xala* (1974) and *Ceddo* (1977), are satires that skewer the hypocrisies of contemporary politicians. He also produced touching, humane explorations of contemporary African life. Among these was *Moolaadé* (2004), which portrays women who rebel against the tradition of female genital mutilation. Scott writes, "It is hard to overstate his importance, or his influence on African film and also, more generally, on African intellectual and cultural self-perception."

West African colonies became independent." The book is frequently compared to Émile Zola's social realist novel *Germinal* (1885).

Sembène distinguished himself as a pioneering novelist during the colonial and postcolonial eras and was one of the first African writers to give significant attention to women's issues. His creations regularly center on the conflict between Africa and colonialism as well as exposing the political systems that hold back African social and economic progress. A socialist with a desire to reach the grassroots, Sembène strove to make his works intelligible to ordinary people. He eventually turned to filmmaking as a means of reaching a broader audience. Despite frequent censorship of his works in Senegal, Sembène has been acknowledged with many awards and has gained widespread viewership for his films in Africa and abroad.

THEMES AND STYLE

Central to *God's Bits of Wood* is the strikers' devotion to pursuing social justice. While striking to improve their financial situation, the workers are also fighting for racial equality by demanding equal benefits for employees regardless of race. The character Mamadou Keita summarizes the workers' grievances: "Why should they be paid more? ... And when they are sick, why should they be taken care of while we and our families are left to starve?" The deeply racist railroad official Dejean feels he can not compromise with the strikers because "to give in on the question of family

allowances ... would amount to recognition of a racial aberrance, a ratification of the customs of inferior beings. It would be giving in, not to workers but to Negroes." Throughout the novel Sembène acknowledges the ugliness of racism but implies that the real problem is classism. In a confrontation with Dejean, Lahbib argues, "[You] do not represent a nation or a people here, but simply a class. We represent another class, whose interests are not the same as yours."

In *God's Bits of Wood* the author achieves his rhetorical effect by casting the common people as the true heroes of the story. Sembène's story illustrates how large numbers of people from different ethnic groups, generations, and genders working together can bring about great change. Although several individuals distinguish themselves as heroic figures in the strike, the victory is won through community action. For example, the strikers' wives overcome their superstitions and petty animosities to support each other in finding food and water for their families. In one notable scene the women of Dakar hold off a police cavalry charge with torches.

A fictional novel based on historical events, *God's Bits of Wood* is defined stylistically by its realism. Jones states, "In order to present a complete narrative of the struggle from oppression to equality, Sembène condenses fourteen years of labor history into a single year. Nevertheless, Sembène's narrative conforms to the official record in most important aspects." Jones cites an interview in which Sembène describes his right as an artist to "reveal a certain number of historical facts that others would like to keep hidden.... Wolof society has always had people whose role it was to give voice, bring back memory, and project towards something." In addition to general historical accuracy, Sembène describes in great detail the lives of colonial Africans, such as the women's cooking responsibilities and the activity occurring at public water taps. Although many elements of the novel are fictionalized, the realistic tone leads the reader to believe that the author's ultimate goal of a united Africa may indeed be accomplished.

CRITICAL DISCUSSION

Hailed as an example of socialist realism, *God's Bits of Wood* was lauded by critics for successfully portraying the economic and social concerns of the labor union as well as the individual issues of the railway workers and their families. Jones quotes a reviewer for the *Times Literary Supplement* who noted, "Sembène Ousmane has in abundance ... the ability to control a wide social panorama, without once losing sight of, or compassion for, the complexity and suffering of individuals." Jones also quotes Meredith Tax writing in the *Voice Literary Supplement*: "In [Sembène's] best-known book, *God's Bits of Wood* ... modern history, tribal customs, ordinary lives, great scenes of mass battle, and several love stories are thrown together in a marvelous stew that simmers and boils with life."

In the author's dedication to *God's Bits of Wood,* Sembène indicates his intent was to celebrate the victory of the West African labor movement and illustrate that the strike "was not in vain." While French archive documents present Africans as an undifferentiated mass, Sembène's narrative creates a sense of African unity. Writing in the late 1950s during a time when Africans were preparing to vote on their independence from France, Sembène attempted to "evoke a collective memory of African unity," according to Jones. He adds, "If his novel complicates [social historians'] work by influencing the African collective memory of the strike, it also provides a challenge to colonial attempts to manufacture a collective memory."

Most critics agree that the collective movement in *God's Bits of Wood* offers a sense of hope for positive societal change. In *An Introduction to the African Prose Narrative,* Augustine Mensah states, "*God's Bits of Wood* is a novel about change … in the end we see a society which is renewed and regenerated." Mensah also notes, "This renewal is brought about not by the manipulations of some wise and superior agent, but through the collective inner workings of the people themselves." Many modern scholars contend that Sembène's story treats issues of race but only insofar as it informs class struggle. In *Literature of Africa,* Douglas Killam argues Sembène "is concerned especially with the wide disparity between rich and poor, exploiter and exploited, considerations that overlap race." Killam also notes Sembène's preoccupation with "conditions—economic, political, social, and cultural—in the present and how these may be altered to improve the present, lead to a better future, and especially, to rectify the wide disparity in the quality of lives of those whose labor for little reward creates wealth, privilege, and power for the few."

BIBLIOGRAPHY

Sources

Jones, James A. "Fact and Fiction in *God's Bits of Wood.*" *Research in African Literatures* 31.2 (2000): 117. *Literature Resource Center.* Web. 2 Oct. 2012.

Killam, Douglas. "Chapter 5: Sembène Ousmane: *God's Bits of Wood* (1962)." *Literature of Africa.* Westport: Greenwood, 2004. Print.

Mensah, Augustine. "The Uses of History: Three Historical Novels from West Africa." *An Introduction to the African Prose Narrative.* Ed. Lokangaka Losambe. Trenton: Africa World, 2004. Print.

Na'Allah, Abdul-Rasheed. "Sembène Ousmane." *Contemporary African Writers.* Ed. Tanure Ojaide. Detroit: Gale, 2011. *Dictionary of Literary Biography. Literature Resource Center.* Web. 2 Oct. 2012.

Scott, A. O. "A Filmmaker Who Found Africa's Voice." *New York Times.* New York Times, 12 June 2007. Web. 3 Dec. 2012.

Sembène, Ousmane. *God's Bits of Wood.* Trans. Francis Price. Garden City: Doubleday, 1962. Print.

Tax, Meredith. "Pop Goes the Novel: Historical Fiction Seizes Power." *Voice Literary Supplement* December 1985. Print.

Further Reading

Diop, Papa Samba. "Les bouts de bois de Dieu; La letter et l'illusion. *Le français aujourd'hui: Mélanges offerts à Jurgen Olbert.* Ed. Gilles Dorion, Franz-Joseph Meissner, Janos Riesz, and Ulf Mielandt. Frankfurt-am-Main: Moritz Diesterweg, 1992. 449–65. Print.

Fall, Khadi. *Ousmane Sembène's Roman "Les bouts de bois de Dieu."* Frankfurt am Main: Verlag fur Interkulturelle Kommunikation, 1996. Print.

Habiyakare, Thadée. *De l'assommoir aux bouts de bois de Dieu: Le monde de travail vu par Émile Zola et Sembène Ousmane.* Villeneuve d'Ascq: Presses Universitaires du Septentrion, 1998. Print.

Harrow, Kenneth W. "Art and Ideology in *Les bouts de bois de Dieu*: Realism's Artifices." *French Review* 62 (1989): 483–93. Print.

Makonda, Antoine. *Les bouts de bois de Dieu, de Sembène Ousmane: Étude critique.* Paris: F. Nathan, 1985. Print.

Njoroge, Paul Ngigi. *Sembène Ousmane's* God's Bits of Wood. Nairobi: Heinemann Educational, 1984. Print.

Ojo, S. Ade. "Revolt, Violence and Duty in Ousmane Sembène's *God's Bits of Wood.*" *Nigeria Magazine* 53.3 (1985): 58–68. Print.

Maggie Magno

Author Ousmane Sembène at the FESPACO Film Festival in Ouga, Burkina Faso, 1991. © CAROLINE PENN/CORBIS.

A HAZARD OF NEW FORTUNES

William Dean Howells

✧ *Key Facts*

Time Period:
Late 19th Century

Genre:
Short Story

Events:
Proliferation of
periodicals; Haymarket
Square Riots; the
Gilded Age

Nationality:
American

OVERVIEW

First published in 1889 in *Harper's Weekly,* William Dean Howells's *A Hazard of New Fortunes* injects social and economic struggles into the middle-class world of literary realism. Told from the viewpoint of literary editor Basil March, the novel follows characters such as the German socialist Berthold Lindau, the proslavery Colonel Woodburn, and the capitalist Jacob Dryfoos as they interact through the periodical *Every Other Week.* Through his role at the paper, the once-insulated March meets socially disdained nouveau riche, poor, and ethnically marginalized individuals, realizing how close to and how complicit he is with such social injustices.

A Hazard of New Fortunes is Howells's third piece (of nine) following the lives of Basil and Isabel March. Though welcomed by a public that was fond of the March characters and well received critically for its attention to social justice, *Hazard* was quickly forgotten until the end of the twentieth century when interest in the novel, particularly its focus on social issues and literature's role therein, was renewed. *Hazard* is notable for its attention to the impact of periodicals and popular novels on society. It also grapples with the labor- and class-related aftershocks of the American Civil War, depicting a violent streetcar strike—inspired by the Haymarket Riots of 1886—in the streets of New York City.

HISTORICAL AND LITERARY CONTEXT

Periodicals were reaching farther into the nation at the end of the nineteenth century, creating a cohesive "imagined community" bound by common readership, ideas, and a metropole unfettered by distance. As the century progressed, it became easier, cheaper, and thus more practical than ever before to produce—and to purchase—reading materials. Periodicals such as *Hazard*'s *Every Other Week* allowed less well-known individuals to voice opinions: American activists and writers were taking advantage of the increasingly democratic forums of periodicals. As literacy rose, newspapers and magazines took on voices from multiple social strata, with rapid circulation facilitating a more inclusive national dialogue than before. As discussion mounted, so too did social frictions. Increasingly, those excluded from the growing American conception of "us" rose against their marginalization.

The 1880s were rife with the social and economic legacies of the Civil War as well as the effects of the Second Industrial Revolution, the Gilded Age, and a worldwide labor movement incited by the rise of thinkers such as Leo Tolstoy, John Ruskin (both of whom are read by Lindau in *Hazard*), Henry George, and Karl Marx. For Howells, these issues were compounded by the execution of anarchists involved in the Chicago Haymarket Square Riots of 1886, an event that is fictionalized in the streetcar strike of *Hazard.* Spurred to action, Howells attempts to effect awareness of social injustices through literature in *Hazard.* Its gentle, reader-friendly ending belies the author's political side, which is revealed in personal records and in his later involvement with the American Anti-Imperialist League, the National Association for the Advancement of Colored People, and women's suffrage.

The novel's title, drawn from William Shakespeare's *King John,* signals a long literary history connecting migration, war, and economic exploitation. It also underscores the immigrant spirit inherent to *Hazard* and, both Shakespeare and Howells suggest, to the evolution of a nation—despite some characters' pretensions otherwise. Following the tradition of Rebecca Harding Davis's *Life in the Iron-Mills* (1861), an early realist exposé of the oppressive impact of industrialization on the working class, and inspired by works by Stephen Crane, Henry James, and Mark Twain, Howells had been investigating morality and social issues for some time, writing on the then-new consequences of divorce in *A Modern Instance* (1881), studying the American businessman in *The Rise of Silas Lapham* (1885), and focusing on labor in *Annie Kilburn* (1888).

Howells continued to weigh socialism against capitalism in *The Quality of Mercy* (1892) and *A Traveler from Alturia* (1894) and to examine the relationship of the self to society in *An Imperative Duty* (1893). Narrowly following *Hazard, Criticism and Fiction* (1891) defends realism, with Howells writing: "Let [fiction] portray men and women as they are.... Let it leave off painting dolls and working them by springs and wires." Eventually, his drawing room realism prepared the way for grittier works of naturalism; novels such as Theodore Dreiser's *Sister Carrie* (1900) and Frank Norris's *McTeague* (1899) returned to many of the threads of *Hazards* while focusing on a swath of society beyond the white middle class.

THEMES AND STYLE

Issues of social responsibility and willful blindness are at the heart of *Hazard*. These issues are personified in character foils such as the philanthropic Conrad Dryfoos and his money-worshipping father. Further, Howells deploys realism to depict New York's poor as clearly (though less fully) as he does the comfortable middle class, magnifying the equal importance of each class through their paralleled visibility. By drawing attention to the realities of the poor, *Hazard* suggests Howells's own readers ought to face the suffering of others rather than ignore or, worse, comfortably enjoy such misfortune as "picturesque." The Marches begin to realize how blithe their previous social tourism has been when, finding themselves in a rundown neighborhood, they note that there are people who "have to spend their whole lives in it … with no hopes of driving out of it, except in a hearse." Faced with this realization, they can no longer take a "purely aesthetic view of the facts" and understand that ignoring discomfiting realities at home is as "absurd" or "selfish" as going to the theater (or reading romances) to remain blind to their fellow New Yorkers.

Hazard uses illustrations to expand and complicate its readers' purviews beyond that of Basil March, extending their views of themselves and of others. For example, the fourteenth section (chapter 7 of part 2) in *Hazard*'s original *Harper's Weekly* serialization is accompanied by an image captioned, "Lindau furiously interrupted. 'Yes, when they have gathered their millions together from the hunger and cold and nakedness and ruin and despair of hundreds of thousands of other men, they "give work" to the poor!'" On one side, a strongly lit Lindau raises a passionate fist toward a shadowy March at the other; such details give greater credence to Lindau's socialist ideals than to March's tacit silence while triangulating the reader as a participant/witness between the two men. Moreover, by originally publishing *Hazard* as a serial, Howells highlighted its realist elements: juxtaposed with news and sketches of real people and laden with real-life corollaries, *Hazard* could straddle the bar of fiction, paralleling its plot's movements to its readers' lives during its run.

Language joins the other elements of *Hazard* to foster the sense of veracity central to realism. March's staid, regular diction makes him a relatable oasis in a sea of dialects: from Fulkerson's Western slang to the Woodburns' deep southern drawls to Lindau's German-inflected English, *Hazard* is as much a linguistic sketch of the melting pot of New York as a series of social sketches, its chaotic structuring mirroring the chaos of the modern city, its multiplicity of voices giving depth to its socially disparate characters. Readers are reminded of Lindau's American

HOWELLS, SERIAL ILLUSTRATIONS, AND SOCIAL REALISM

Despite the tendency of *Harper's Weekly* to illustrate its texts and *Hazard*'s own preoccupation with elements of magazine production, including art, nineteen of the novel's thirty-four segments were serialized without William Allen Rogers's drawings. Of those, none ventured beyond characters into wider social elements, even though *Hazard*'s focus was on social justice and Rogers was the magazine's political cartoonist. Moreover, as the novel progressed and its political footing strengthened, its illustrations were reduced in both size and number. Soon after *Hazard* transitioned to book form, the drawings disappeared altogether. Howells's growing reliance on a "photographic school of fiction"—verbal rather than visual "pictures"—and the preponderance of illustrations in humorous rather than serious works could be at the heart of these changes.

Over his career, Howells's wife and daughter (among others) periodically illustrated his texts; he even proposed writing an accompaniment to his brother-in-law's art. That few of his works were ultimately illustrated can be partially attributed to the tendency of the *Atlantic Quarterly*, his literary home, to illustrate far less than other periodicals rather than to a personal aversion to illustrations. Howells's interest in the relation of images to text, especially the intersection of traditional illustrations and developing photographic technologies with social realism, grew steadily throughout the nineteenth and twentieth centuries.

credentials when, waving his Union Army wound, he invokes the Gettysburg Address to compare abolitionists and labor reformers, marrying his socialist ideas with firmly American precepts: "All the roadts and mills and mines and landts shall be the beople's [sic] and be ron *by* the people *for* the people." At the same time, the Everyman March's fluency in German and his desire to have his children learn it serve to incorporate Lindau's heritage into the American landscape. Language becomes unifying rather than divisive, emphasizing its role in socioeconomic reformation.

CRITICAL DISCUSSION

The public reacted well to *A Hazard of New Fortunes* and its "distinctly American" humor, though many found Howells's move from the drawing room to its surrounds bracing. Contemporary reviewers praised it for truly capturing the inner workings of the oft-passed but unknown masses of New York and for its dramatic depiction of the strikes; one reviewer for the *Critic* (January 1890) declared it Howells's salvation against staying at a "'jelly-fish' level," a sentiment echoed by another of the *Literary World*, who finds "he has nobly beaten his crochet-hook into a spear, and does manly work in strong and competent fashion."

Author William Dean Howells writing at his desk in his home in Martinsville, Ohio. © LEBRECHT MUSIC AND ARTS PHOTO LIBRARY/ALAMY.

Though regarded as a turning point in Howells's aspirations for realism's increasingly democratic possibilities, critics such as Kenneth Warren have argued Howells's intersecting social worlds still girder rigid social stratifications. Others are more optimistic, finding that *Hazard*'s wide swath of characters allows greater communication and negotiations across groups rather than solely relying on a top-down power structure. Still, as Amy Kaplan elucidates in *The Social Construction of American Realism* (1988), the street car strike implicates Howells's characters as ultimately distanced from street-level reality, undercutting realism's ability to bring about social cohesion, especially when *Hazard*'s sociocultural intersections occur mainly by chance rather than intention.

As part of its recent resurgence, *A Hazard of New Fortunes* figures prominently in works unraveling the relationship between mass media, the public, and corporations; studies on the effects of urban capitalism and the city on the nation; and the social effects of corporate personhood and what Gib Prettyman, in his 2003 essay in *American Literary Realism,* calls "commercial idealism." Labor and its relationship to the legacy of the Civil War, too, are still commonly tied to *Hazard* because, as Andrew Rennick writes in his piece for *American Literary Realism,* "the war performs a structural function for the novel itself." Additionally, *Hazard*'s focus on an editor and the workings of a periodical and the characters themselves, including Conrad Dryfoos's tragic death, have spurred many biographical readings between *Hazard* and Howells's own life, friends, and sorrows.

BIBLIOGRAPHY

Sources

Cheyfitz, Eric. "A Hazard of New Fortunes: The Romance of Self-Realization." In *American Realism: New Essays.* Ed. Eric J. Sundquist. Baltimore: Johns Hopkins UP, 1982: 42–65. Print.

Howells, William Dean. *Criticism and Fiction.* New York: Harper and Brothers, 1891. *Google Book Search.* Web. 16 Aug. 2012.

Kaplan, Amy. *The Social Construction of American Realism.* Chicago: U of Chicago P, 1988. Print.

"Mr. Howells's "Hazard of New Fortunes." Rev. of *A Hazard of New Fortunes* by William Dean Howells. *Critic: A Weekly Review of Literature and the Arts* 11 Jan. 1890. *ProQuest.* Web. 14 Aug. 2012.

Prettyman, Gib. "The Next Best Thing: Business and Commercial Inspiration in *A Hazard of New Fortunes.*" *American Literary Realism* 35.2 (2003): 95–119. *JSTOR.* Web. 19 Aug. 2012.

Rennick, Andrew. "'A Good War Story': The Civil War, Substitution, and the Labor Crisis in Howells's *A Hazard of New Fortunes.*" *American Literary Realism* 35.3 (2003): 247–61. *JSTOR.* Web. 14 Aug. 2012.

Rev. of *A Hazard of New Fortunes* by William Dean Howells. *Literary World: A Monthly Review of Current Literature* 18 Jan. 1890: 21. *ProQuest.* Web. 14 Aug. 2012.

Warren, Kenneth W. *Black and White Stranger: Race and American Realism.* Chicago: U of Chicago P, 1993. Print.

Further Reading

Blake, Linnie. "William Dean Howells and the City of New York: A Hazard of New Writing." *Studies in the Literary Imagination* 41.1 (2008): 1–19. *Literature Online.* Web. 19 Aug. 2012.

Clayton, Owen. "London Eyes: William Dean Howells and the Shift to Instant Photography." *Nineteenth-Century Literature* 65.3 (2010): 374–94. *JSTOR.* Web. 21 Apr. 2012.

Howells, William Dean. "The Strong Government Idea." *Atlantic Monthly* Feb. 1880: 273–77. *Making of America.* Web. 16 Aug. 2012.

Johnson, Joel A. *Beyond Practical Virtue: A Defense of Liberal Democracy through Literature.* Columbia: U of Missouri P, 2007. Print.

Kaplan, Amy. "The Knowledge of the Line: Realism and the City in Howells's *A Hazard of New Fortunes.*" *PMLA* 101.1 (1986): 69–81. *JSTOR.* Web. 09 Aug. 2012.

Nettels, Elsa. *Language, Race, and Social Class in Howells's America.* Lexington: UP of Kentucky, 1988. Print.

Prettyman, Gib. "The Serial Illustrations of *A Hazard of New Fortunes.*" *Resources for American Literary Study* 27.2 (2001): 179–95. *Project Muse.* Web. 10 Aug. 2012.

Katherine Bishop

HEARTBREAK HOUSE
A Fantasia in the Russian Manner on English Themes
George Bernard Shaw

OVERVIEW

Written by George Bernard Shaw, the play *Heartbreak House: A Fantasia in the Russian Manner on English Themes* (1919) tells the story of a group of wealthy aristocrats on the eve of World War I. Ellie Dunn and her father are invited to a dinner by Captain Shotover, an aging capitalist who believes that Europe has fallen into global conflict because of the amorality and frivolity of society. Most of the characters' interactions focus on petty interpersonal conflicts and childish games instead of the looming war. The play climaxes in a bombing raid that almost destroys the house; however when the danger passes, the bored and ineffectual characters are left simply feeling somewhat disappointed. By examining the questionable moral compass of European political leaders and the malaise of the aristocracy, the play draws on the comedy of manners style that Russian dramatists such as Anton Chekhov made popular.

Written from 1913 to 1916, *Heartbreak House* was not published until after the end of World War I. Shaw, acutely aware of the real-life threat of the air raids dramatized in the play's third act, purposely delayed publication of the work, believing the written word to be—as he writes in the preface to the play—"a greater military danger than poison, steel, or trinitrotoluene." Although the play was performed soon after the end of the war, it proved to resonate more with audiences during World War II. Coupled with its lengthy preface, the play makes clear the author's contempt for wealthy aristocrats who are more concerned with leisure, love, and literature than with the politics of the day. Using the metaphor of a ship, *Heartbreak House* is a portrait of a vain ruling class that has failed to steer a nation in turmoil away from the brink of destruction.

HISTORICAL AND LITERARY CONTEXT

When Shaw began writing *Heartbreak House* in 1913, World War I had not yet begun, though the chain of events leading up to the war had already been set in motion. A series of European defense alliances and disputes in Morocco and Albania had created a heated climate of militarism and nationalism. Tensions between Austria-Hungary and Serbia continued to intensify, culminating in the 1914 assassination of Austrian archduke Franz Ferdinand by a Bosnian-Serb nationalist, marking the start of World War I. However,

the European ruling classes were largely detached, idly playing in what Shaw in his preface to the play calls an "overheated drawing-room atmosphere."

Although he completed *Heartbreak House* in 1916, several years before the war ended, he did not publish it until peace talks had begun in 1919. Morale in England had been low during the conflict, and prowar propaganda in the form of postcards and posters proved crucial to rallying public support. British propaganda played upon the sympathies of the nuclear family, portraying men who enlisted as protectors of their wives and children. Shaw, a supporter of the war effort, wrote propaganda to defend the cause, although he disagreed with the jingoistic tenor of many prowar fanatics. When the war ended and the Covenant of the League of Nations was drafted, the movement toward peace and world government did little to stunt the playwright's criticism of the ruling elite. He writes in the preface, "the orators of the front bench can edify or debauch an ignorant electorate at will. Thus our democracy moves in a vicious circle of reciprocal worthiness and unworthiness."

Shaw's play is based on other early-twentieth-century dramas that trained a critical eye on the aristocracy. He modeled *Heartbreak House* particularly on the work of Russian authors such as Leo Tolstoy and Anton Chekhov. In several works Tolstoy examines the causes of war and the amorality of the upper class, and Chekhov's play *The Cherry Orchard* (1904) focuses on a dying aristocracy, which Shaw in his preface describes as "helpless wasters of their inheritance" with a "habit of living in a vacuum." Central to both plays is the failure to preserve the nuclear family, a theme echoed in British propaganda of World War I urging British soldiers to protect and defend their families.

Since its publication, *Heartbreak House* has influenced a variety of other wartime writings because of its applicability to a variety of conflicts and eras. It has been adapted for stage and screen, including as a 1985 film starring Rex Harrison and Amy Irving and as a 2006 BBC movie. In the twenty-first century, the play has seen several stage revivals, perhaps owing to the popularity of the Occupy movement and the belief that the wealthiest one percent of the population has failed to wield political power for the common good.

✣ Key Facts

Time Period:
Early 20th Century

Genre:
Play

Events:
Franco-Prussian War; Austro-Hungarian invasion of Serbia; World War I

Nationality:
English

THE PLAYS OF GEORGE BERNARD SHAW

George Bernard Shaw was a prolific playwright who penned more than fifty plays and a handful of other works. He received the Nobel Prize in Literature in 1926. He is perhaps best known for his play *Pygmalion* (1912), which served as the basis for the musical *My Fair Lady* (1956). The story of Eliza Doolittle, a Cockney girl who is transformed into a society lady, exhibits Shaw's predilection for social commentary, particularly about the false nature of society's upper crust. Like many of his other works, *Pygmalion* can be viewed as a comedy and as a deep social critique.

Shaw also turned a critical eye on society in several of his other plays, including *The Apple Cart* (1928), in which he examines the politics at play between a king and a prime minister at odds in their beliefs about how to rule the country. *Man and Superman* (1903) depicts a Don Juan-type character who is fleeing from a woman desperate to marry him. Critics have compared both plays to *Heartbreak House* for their representation of Shaw's ability to simultaneously write comedy and social commentary. His comedies of manners remind readers that beneath the surface of social interactions lie complex meanings and unsettling social truths.

THEMES AND STYLE

The central theme of *Heartbreak House* is that a nation, like a ship at sea, will sink in the storms of conflict if it lacks a responsible ruling elite at the helm. Shaw describes Heartbreak House as a room "built so as to resemble the after part of an old-fashioned high-pooped ship, with a stern gallery." The owner, Captain Shotover, is described as a seafaring man, an "ancient but still hardy man with an immense white beard, in a reefer jacket with a whistle hanging from his neck." As an embodiment of the ruling class, he repeatedly demonstrates his ineptitude and senility, often walking about in a cloud of confusion. Although he criticizes the younger generation for the sorry state of the world, he also recognizes his complicity. When the house survives the bombing raid at the end of the play, the sense lingers that the aristocrats will continue their doomed voyage without having learned any lesson about their role in the conflict.

Shaw achieves his social commentary by offering a sharp contrast between the follies at play in Heartbreak House and the burgeoning war outside its walls. The conversations between the characters are often petty and childish, such as when Hesione's "beautiful black hair" is revealed to be a wig. Ellie, who believes herself to be in love with Hesione's husband, bemoans the revelation and desperately plumbs it for meaning: "Oh! Even the hair that ensnared him false! Everything false!" Meanwhile, the "distant explosion" that is heard outside fails to provoke such a passionate response from any of the characters. Several of the aristocrats are even depicted sleeping: Ellie falls asleep while reading and later she hypnotizes Boss Mangan into a trance by stroking his head. Like the frivolous conversations, the characters' languor stands in stark contrast to the booming war outside.

Despite the play's lighthearted banter, *Heartbreak House* is woven with a dark and ominous tone. Shaw's pessimism is palpable. Although the dialogue reflects the melodramatic orations the characters are used to reading in literature, their words fail to capture the meaning of the events outside. By the end of the play, when the characters can no longer ignore the explosions, Shotover in a rare moment of clarity announces, "the judgment has come. Courage will not save you; but it will show that your souls are still live." However, once the shots subside, Hector, Hesione's husband, can only proclaim the world "damnably dull … again."

CRITICAL DISCUSSION

Published in 1919 and first performed by the New York Theatre Guild in 1920, *Heartbreak House* was not an immediate success with critics and audiences. According to Robert Bryden in *The Cambridge Companion to George Bernard Shaw* (1998), the lack of enthusiasm was "surely the result of the fact that it was never played as it was designed to be played, in wartime." However, when the play was reintroduced at the Cambridge Theatre in London in 1943, World War II audiences, keenly aware of the causes and horrors of war, were much more receptive to the play's themes and social criticisms.

Theater companies have continued to revisit *Heartbreak House,* particularly during times of war, because of the play's incisive commentary on wartime politics and stern warning of catastrophe if social leaders do not remain vigilant. In a 2006 review for the *New York Times,* Charles Isherwood explains the continued relevance of Shaw's work: "With the world seemingly on endless edge these days, and with plenty of Americans feeling disengaged from the circus of our cultural and political discourse, Shaw's bracing analysis of a civilization in decline seems more valuable than ever." Isherwood points to the perennial applicability of the play's climax, an "unsettling and dispiriting image: well-groomed humanity greeting its own destruction with an inviting smile."

Scholars have frequently discussed *Heartbreak House* in the context of other plays of the day. Taking a cues from the play's subtitle and Shaw's introduction, critics have compared the work to Chekhov's plays, particularly *The Cherry Orchard,* which deals with the failures of an aristocracy clinging to its lavish lifestyle in defiance of the rapidly changing outside world. In particular, scholars tend to highlight the devastating results of society's inaction. In *Critical Essays on George Bernard Shaw* (1991), Frederick P. W. McDowell traces this theme throughout Shaw's works: "*Heartbreak House* looks forward to *The Apple Cart* (1929) and the other plays which follow it in the admission that in some contingencies violence can be condoned, and is preferable to inaction: the inhabitants of Heartbreak House have deliberately chosen at the end of the play the holocaust they could with prudence evade." In *Shaw: The Annual Bernard Shaw Studies* (2003), Christopher Innes contrasts the theme of a doomed society with the utopian visions of Shaw's contemporaries such as H. G. Wells, whose writing helps to shape the detached fantasy world in which the inhabitants of Heartbreak House live.

BIBLIOGRAPHY

Sources

Bryden, Robert. "The Roads to Heartbreak House." *The Cambridge Companion to George Bernard Shaw.* Ed. Christopher Innes. Cambridge: Cambridge UP, 1998. 180–194. Print.

Gullace, Nicoletta F. "Sexual Violence and Family Honor: British Propaganda and International Law during the First World War." *American Historical Review* 102.3 (1997): 714–47. *JSTOR.* Web. 1 July 2012.

Innes, Christopher. "Utopian Apocalypses: Shaw, War, and H. G. Wells." *Shaw: The Annual Bernard Shaw Studies.* Ed. Gale K. Larson and MaryAnn K. Crawford. University Park: Pennsylvania State UP, 2003. 37–46. Print.

Isherwood, Charles. "British Gentry, Fiddling while the Abyss Looms." Rev. of *Heartbreak House,* by George Bernard Shaw. *New York Times* 12 Oct. 2006. Web. 27 June 2012.

Laurier, Joanne. "The Shaw Festival's 50th Season: George Bernard Shaw's *Heartbreak House.*" *World Socialist Web Site.* International Committee of the Fourth International, 23 July 2011. Web. 29 July 2012.

McDowell, Frederick P. W. "Technique, Symbol, and Theme in *Heartbreak House.*" *Critical Essays on George Bernard Shaw.* Ed. Elsie B. Adams. New York: Hall, 1991. 85–104. Print.

Shaw, George Bernard. *Heartbreak House, Great Catherine, and Playlets of the War.* New York: Brentano's, 1919. Print.

Further Reading

Chekhov, Anton. *The Complete Plays.* New York: Norton, 2006. Print.

Gibbs, A. M. *Heartbreak House: Preludes of Apocalypse.* New York: Twayne, 1994. Print.

Roy, Emil. "G. B. Shaw's *Heartbreak House* and Harold Pinter's *The Homecoming*: Comedies of Implosion." *Comparative Drama* 41.3 (2007): 335–48. Print.

Shaw, George Bernard. *The Apple Cart: A Political Extravaganza.* London: Constable, 1930. Print.

Strauss, E. *Bernard Shaw: Art and Socialism.* London: V. Gollancz, 1942. Print.

Weintraub, Stanley. *Journey to Heartbreak: The Crucible Years of Bernard Shaw, 1914–1918.* New York: Weybright and Talley, 1971. Print.

Media Adaptations

"Heartbreak House." Great Performances. Dir. Anthony Page. Perf. Rex Harrison, Amy Irving, and Rosemary Harris. Public Broadcasting Service (PBS). 16 Apr 1985. Television.

"Heartbreak House." BBC Play of the Month. Dir. Cedric Messina. Perf. John Gielgud, Siân Phillips, and Barbara Murray. British Broadcasting Corporation (BBC). 19 May 1977. Television.

Lisa Kroger

Diana Rigg and Rex Harrison in a 1983 production of *Heartbreak House* at the Theatre Royal, London. © JEROME YEATS/ALAMY.

"In the Slums of Glasgow"

Hugh MacDiarmid

❖ *Key Facts*

Time Period:
Early 20th Century

Genre:
Poetry

Events:
Rapid industrialization
and urbanization;
interwar economic crisis

Nationality:
Scottish

OVERVIEW

Hugh MacDiarmid's "In the Slums of Glasgow" (1935) forms one of a constellation of poetic perspectives on the mixture of overcrowding, unemployment, and poverty besetting Scotland's largest city after World War I. The poem was published in *Second Hymn to Lenin and Other Poems* as part of a planned "Red Lion" sequence on Glasgow life. Compared to other poems in this volume, however, its political content is slight. Although the poet takes the slums as his point of departure, the most of the poem is an ecstatic freeverse meditation on the essential oneness of humanity and is inspired by elements of Hindu mysticism. The poet lays claim to "a glorious awareness / of the inner radiance" that includes the slum dwellers but also extends to "high and low … rich and poor."

Largely overshadowed by MacDiarmid's more politically charged work in the same volume, "In the Slums of Glasgow" nonetheless served to draw back the curtain on urban poverty in Scotland and to connect MacDiarmid's often esoteric art with a pressing contemporary issue. Considered in isolation from MacDiarmid's larger body of work, "In the Slums of Glasgow" is sometimes critiqued as expressive of escapism or denial, but it has also been praised as an example of MacDiarmid's dexterity with poetic form. "In the Slums of Glasgow," for most scholars, achieves its greatest significance in context, as one approach to the complex problem of reconciling urgent social crises with a contemplative philosophical stance.

HISTORICAL AND LITERARY CONTEXT

In the nineteenth century, Scotland had experienced a period of rapid industrialization that drew much of the population to its urban centers and established Glasgow as the "Second City of the Empire." This surge of urbanization resulted in poor living conditions for many and created, alongside unprecedented growth in the textile and mining industries, a massive labyrinth of slums. For MacDiarmid's contemporary Edwin Muir, who moved to Glasgow in 1901, these were hellish places that threatened to encroach upon the comparably Edenic rural Scotland he had left behind. A brief World War I industrial boom, especially in the shipping industry, further drove migration to the country's major shipbuilding cities, with Glasgow at their center. Shortly after the end of the war, however, the country experienced an economic depression that persisted through the 1930s.

MacDiarmid (given name: Christopher Murray Grieve) was one of a number of Scottish authors to champion communism as a possible remedy for the economic crisis. He officially joined the Communist Party of Great Britain in 1934, a year before "In the Slums of Glasgow" was published. MacDiarmid's poetry shows a tendency to intermingle political preoccupations with a wide range of philosophical and aesthetic detours. He most nearly approaches a propagandistic tone in his series of "Hymns to Lenin," which celebrate the Soviet leader as a Christ figure while not exculpating him for the evils attending his rise to power. The second such hymn was published separately in 1932 and rereleased as part of a booklength collection, *Second Hymn to Lenin and Other Poems,* in 1935. Here, as in his previous works, MacDiarmid provided a variety of poetic perspectives on the nature and significance of the poverty experienced by many Scots. "In the Slums of Glasgow" transposes the poet's egalitarian worldview to the realm of a largely abstract spirituality.

MacDiarmid bore a sometimes contentious relationship to the famous English exponents of literary modernism. On the one hand, much of his work espoused a strong literary nationalism, expressed most notably by his use of the Scots language rather than English in nearly all of his early poetry; on the other hand, MacDiarmid shared with T. S. Eliot, Ezra Pound, and others a penchant for incorporating a wide range of learned allusions into his verse. "In the Slums of Glasgow" is in English, with brief detours into ancient languages but no Scots; it presents a striking parallel to Eliot's own adoption of Sanskrit terms to signal transcendent experiences and ideals. Donald Wesling (1980) pointed out a further stylistic similarity between MacDiarmid's poem and Eliot's *The Waste Land,* noting that both "disorient the reader" with "hallucinative" strings of rhyming nonsense syllables.

MacDiarmid is widely regarded as the key figure of a twentieth-century Scottish renaissance in literature but "In the Slums of Glasgow" played a minor part at best within this revolution. Much more influential was *A Drunk Man Looks at the Thistle* (1926), which is widely considered to be MacDiarmid's masterpiece and showcases at considerable length his ability to modulate among languages and metrical patterns.

THEMES AND STYLE

"In the Slums of Glasgow" expresses the speaker's belief in the underlying unity of human beings and the nonduality of the universe itself. The slums of Glasgow serve largely as a ready example of (or occasion for) this realization; in pursuit of his theme, the poet sometimes seems to look through the slum tenants and their surroundings rather than at them. Speaking of his realization of the "seamless garment," the speaker notes that "it was easier to do this in the slums … life is more naked there, more distinct from mind." He draws a few other instances of slum life into his poem: the mothers "concerned only for the highest possible vitality of her children" and the lovers who surrender to an "unprudential / Guideless life-in-death of the ecstasy they share." These are counterbalanced, however, by MacDiarmid's detection of the same thematic unity in geological and biological processes and in the protean nature of water.

As early critics noted in other of MacDiarmid's poems, "Slums" employs a language designed more to capture the speaker's experience with lyrical clarity than to convince the reader of his views. The poet narrates a process of revelation and transformation in which he discovers that "these dogmas are not as I once thought true nor as afterwards false / But each the empty shadow of an intimate personal mood." The speaker never appears "in-scene" with the slum dwellers he describes, instead describing them in largely categorical terms. Indeed, apart from the emphasis of the title, the slums of Glasgow appear more as one of several leitmotifs than as the major subject of the poem.

MacDiarmid's use of rhyme and stanza serves as a formal analogue to the mounting emotional intensity of the poem, lending an overall structure to his wide-ranging observations. The basic pattern is an eight-line stanza with a rhyme on alternating lines. At the poem's very beginning these stanzas almost read as conventional accentual-syllabic verse: "I have caught a glimpse of the seamless garment / And am blind to all else for evermore." Successive stanzas retain the rhyme scheme, but the lines lengthen and loosen until meter is wholly obscured, as in the catalog of "individuality, conjunction, disjunction, priority, posteriority" that comprises part of one line. Eventually the poet reaches the triumphant conclusion that Philosophy has set "her victorious foot / On the withering flower of the fast-ageing world," and the remainder of the poem comprises a "quiet trance" in which soft-spoken lines alternate with couplets of nonsense syllables. Finally, the "great heart of Glasgow" retires, leaving only sound: "Duddadam dadade dudde dadadadadadodadah."

SYNTHETIC SCOTS, SYNTHETIC ENGLISH

The early 1930s was a period of transition for MacDiarmid, stylistically as well as politically. In 1922 the poet, previously writing as Christopher M. Grieve, had first adopted his now-famous pseudonym and begun his project of writing in (and attempting to revive literary use of) the Scots language. In a conscious break from the earlier Scots poet Robert Burns, MacDiarmid assembled his "synthetic Scots" from old literary texts and disparate regional dialects, making liberal use of English when a native word could not be found. The experiment ultimately proved an enduring critical success, culminating in MacDiarmid's masterwork, the epic-length Scots poem *A Drunk Man Looks at the Thistle* (1926).

"In the Slums of Glasgow" provides a relatively mild expression of MacDiarmid's second great linguistic project, the "synthetic English" he adopted briefly and intensely circa 1932. As Kenneth Buthlay (1982) notes, MacDiarmid worked during this period in an idiom rich with scientific jargon and copious borrowings from ancient and modern languages. The poet nominally abandoned his synthetic English project at about the time *Second Hymn to Lenin and Other Poems* (1935) went to press; however, many of the qualities that characterized this experimental period, including a search for "recondite elements of the English vocabulary," persisted in attenuated form well into MacDiarmid's later work.

CRITICAL DISCUSSION

At the time of its publication "In the Slums of Glasgow" was often overlooked in favor of the more controversial political material in the same volume. *Second Hymn to Lenin and Other Poems* was more widely discussed for its use of satire, which *Poetry* magazine reviewer Horace Gregory (1937) praised as "virtuosic." The "anti-poetic" language that marks portions of "Slums" was another point of note for critics, but they usually cited it in the context of other poems, including the title work. Tellingly, Gregory noted "times … when [MacDiarmid's] virtuosity misleads him" and a tendency in the longer poems (perhaps including "Slums") to fail "to discriminate between the force of his personal convictions and the need to present them to the reader."

As early as 1940 *Second Hymn to Lenin and Other Poems* was understood as an important component of MacDiarmid's work; James G. Southworth praised its "provocative and substantial" subject matter. However, for many critics "In the Slums of Glasgow"—as a valorization of slum life rather than a critique of its causes—lacked the force of other works (some by MacDiarmid) that treated the problem of poverty on explicitly political grounds. Like many of MacDiarmid's Scots lyrics, the poem

Scottish poet Hugh MacDiarmid, author of "In the Slums of Glasgow." © MARY EVANS PICTURE LIBRARY/ALAMY.

trajectory. Donald Wesling (1980) notes MacDiarmid's ability to "mute the signification of words and to exaggerate the seeming autonomy of the system of sounds" in the poem's closing stanza. He also suggests that this final refusal to rhyme befits a "long meditation on poverty." Béatrice Duchateau (2012) briefly incorporates "In the Slums of Glasgow" into her discussion of the longer, recently discovered "Glasgow 1938"; the first poem shows that "the essence of life survives in the slums," but the later work reproves this optimism, asserting that "the eyes of the slum people are too weak a source of light for the salvation of Scotland."

BIBLIOGRAPHY

Sources

Bold, Alan. "Here Comes Everyscot." *Fortnight* 318 (1993): 24–26. Print.

Buthlay, Kenneth. *Hugh MacDiarmid (C. M. Grieve)*. Revised ed. Edinburgh: Scottish Academic Press, 1982. Print.

Duchateau, Béatrice. "Urban Scotland in Hugh MacDiarmid's Glasgow Poems." *Études Écossaises* 15 (2012): n.p. Web. 20 July 2012.

Gregory, Horace. "A Contrast in Satires." *Poetry* 49.5 (1937): 282–85. Print.

Morse, Samuel French. "Four Generations." *Poetry* 112.2 (1968): 131–37. Print.

Southworth, James G. "Hugh MacDiarmid." *The Sewanee Review* 48.1 (1940): 105–18. Print.

Wesling, Donald. *The Chances of Rhyme: Device and Modernity*. Berkeley: U of California P, 1980. Web. 20 July 2012.

Further Reading

Daiches, David. "Hugh MacDiarmid and Scottish Poetry." *Poetry* 72.4 (1948): 202–18. Print.

Fraser, Russell. "Edwin Muir's Other Eden." *The Sewanee Review* 108.1 (2000): 78–92. Print.

MacQueen, John, and Tom Scott, eds. *The Oxford Book of Scottish Verse*. Oxford: Clarendon, 1966. Print.

Riach, Alan, and Michael Grieve, eds. *Hugh MacDiarmid: Selected Poetry*. Manchester: Carcanet, 2004. Print.

Michael Hartwell

found itself compelled to answer critical charges of unintelligibility: Samuel French Morse (1968) opined that "the astounding range of MacDiarmid's knowledge" was ultimately an insufficient substitute for poetic skill. Written a decade after the poet's best-known Scots work, "Slums" also came to be seen as an early instance of the "synthetic English" that Mac-Diarmid would later adopt. These experiments won the praise of some modernists but frustrated a wider readership: Alan Bold (1993) notes that even at the end of the twentieth century, MacDiarmid persisted in the public imagination as "Scotland's great unpopular Poet-Intellectual."

Today "In the Slums of Glasgow" is generally valued as an exemplar of MacDiarmid's handling of poetic form and diction rather than for any political

"JOHANNESBURG MINES"

Langston Hughes

OVERVIEW

Langston Hughes's 1928 poem "Johannesburg Mines," a brief and straightforward piece about the role of poetry in discussing the exploitation of native Africans in the mines of South Africa, foreshadows Hughes's 1930s essays and poems, which were published in periodicals such as *International Literature, Crisis, New Masses,* and *Opportunity.* Best known as a Harlem Renaissance poet, Hughes wrote a wide collection of essays and poetry in the 1930s asserting his support of workers' rights around the world. First labeled a "proletarian poet" by Margaret Larkin after the release of his 1927 poetry collection *Fine Clothes to the Jew,* Hughes cemented that reputation in the 1930s. In *Critical Essays on Langston Hughes* (1986), Edward J. Mullen writes this was the "turbulent decade that had compelled his transformation from the blues poet extraordinaire of the Harlem Renaissance to the radical voice of the proletariat masses."

Hughes, the first African American to make a living entirely from writing, incorporates aspects of jazz and blues into his Harlem Renaissance-era poetry about working class African Americans. Although this technique was not always met with positive reception, most critics welcomed Hughes's style. Writer Alain Locke applauded his ability to represent the duality required for African Americans living in a still-segregated country. In the 1930s Hughes expanded his writing about working-class African Americans to include workers from around the world. Critics reviewed very little of Hughes's 1930s writing, although these pieces had a large impact on Hughes's personal life, including leading to him testifying in front of Joseph McCarthy's Senate Permanent Subcommittee on Investigations. His radical essays and poems are still less well-known than his work in the 1920s, but they nonetheless show that Hughes was a writer aware of his power and was willing to speak up for those who could not speak for themselves.

HISTORICAL AND LITERARY CONTEXT

The gaiety and excess of the 1920s abruptly halted when the stock market crashed in October 1929, marking the beginning of the Great Depression. Around the world, unemployment numbers soared. The popularity of the Communist Party, already ruling the Soviet Union, increased as jobless men and women looked for alternative governing solutions in the midst of the economic devastation. In the United States, Jim Crow laws continued to maintain segregation and discrimination against blacks. This persisting racism was best exemplified in the 1931 Scottsboro case in which nine African American teenage boys were falsely accused of raping two women on a train. The American Communist Party helped the accused with their case, a major step in recruiting African Americans to join the party.

Hughes's publishing of "Johannesburg Mines" in 1928 reflects the connection he felt with Africa and with international issues of class and race, foreshadowing his 1930s writings. Throughout the 1920s, native African workers in South Africa's diamond and gold mines went on strike against white mine owners to protest low wages and unfair working conditions. When he wrote "Johannesburg Mines," Hughes had traveled to several countries in Africa, although not South Africa. As a high school student, Hughes read *The Liberator,* a socialist magazine produced by Max Eastman, but he did not openly embrace communism until the Scottsboro trial. As countries around the world moved deeper into the Depression, he expanded on the themes of anticapitalism and workers' rights begun in poems such as "Johannesburg Mines" and those in *Fine Clothes to the Jew.*

Hughes's 1930s pieces reflect the race consciousness present in his Harlem Renaissance writing as well as the influence of earlier poets who wrote about the working class. Hughes's 1921 poem "A Negro Speaks of Rivers" highlights his pride in his African ancestry, and his 1926 essay "The Negro Artist and the Racial Mountain" puts forth his belief that art by African Americans should reflect their racial background. Lorenzo Thomas cites Chicago poet and newspaper reporter Carl Sandburg as an influence on Hughes's writing style. Just as Sandburg portrayed the dialect and experiences of immigrants and the working class, like Walt Whitman before him, Hughes also attempted to capture a particular vernacular to represent workers internationally. As Hughes traveled in the 1930s to Cuba, Haiti, and the Soviet Union, among other countries, he met many people who would inspire his poems and essays.

Although Hughes distanced himself from communism in the 1940s and 1950s, he continued to use his craft for social activism, including writing about the civil rights movement in the United States. However, his writing after the 1930s was less overtly political and aggressive. Hughes wrote about his time

❖ *Key Facts*

Time Period:
Early 20th Century

Genre:
Poetry

Events:
Increased race consciousness associated with the Harlem Renaissance in America; increased consciousness of workers' rights and popularity of socialism worldwide; labor strikes in South African gold and diamond mines

Nationality:
American

THE SCOTTSBORO BOYS

In March 1931 a group of white teenagers fought with nine African American teenagers on a train in Alabama. The white young men were kicked off the train, and the black young men were arrested for assault and later accused of raping two white women who were also on the train. What followed were sensational trials, held in Scottsboro, Alabama, in which all-white juries sentenced eight of the nine black teenagers to death. The youngest boy, who was 12, was not given a death sentence.

The NAACP and American Communist Party both offered to take on the cases after the first ruling. The American Communist Party ultimately appealed the eight cases on behalf of the teenagers, whom the media nicknamed the Scottsboro Boys. Even though the cases were tried three times, including twice in the U.S. Supreme Court, and one of the women testified that she had fabricated the rape story, the teens were still found guilty of rape and given prison sentences. Of the nine Scottsboro Boys, seven served prison terms. However, the case is credited with bringing an end to all-white juries in the United States.

in the Soviet Union for a series of columns in the *Chicago Defender* in the 1940s. Christopher C. De Santis in *Langston Hughes and the Chicago Defender: Essays on Race, Politics, and Culture, 1942–1962* (1995) explains that in these columns Hughes "retained his commitment to representing the dreams and frustrations of oppressed people" but that his writing "lost much of the radical edge" that characterized his 1930s pieces.

THEMES AND STYLE
In "Johannesburg Mines" Hughes expands his focus on issues of race in the United States to encompass class disparities in countries around the world. The poem shows Hughes's insistence that a writer must address international issues, such as the power of the working classes under various governments and militaries, and capitalism. He believed that these institutions maintained both racial and class oppression. In a 1937 essay for the *Baltimore Afro-American,* he reported from the Spanish Civil War, siding with the Republicans, that "illiterate African colonials" who fought for the Nationalists were "only further aiding the rebel guards to tighten more surely their grip of despotism on Africa as well as on Spain." For Hughes, politics of race and class were intertwined across national borders.

Hughes uses "Johannesburg Mines" to examine the way poetry works in political contexts. After he explains that there are "240,000 / Native Africans working," he asks the reader, "What kind of poem / Would you / Make out of that?" This rhetorical question encourages a metareading of the poem and forces the reader to critique the effectiveness of political poetry. He answers his own question by crafting a poem from his knowledge of South African workers and by presenting the facts. However, the rhetorical question,

which halts the poem in the middle before repeating the number of South African miners, projects the sense that the poem is unfinished. This technique encourages the reader to consider whether poetry can truly portray such injustices. Soviet critic Lydia Filatova, in a 1933 essay for *International Literature,* sees Hughes as "first of all … a poet of the Negro proletariat" who should therefore write in what might be termed a "black vernacular." He refused to abide by rules based on his race and nationality or based on particular ideas of aesthetics. In much of his social writing, he identifies with the workers and urges for change. Formally, he ignores restrictions on writing, thus turning literature, a tool of production in itself, over to the workers.

"Johannesburg Mines" and Hughes's other political writings are also characterized by a straightforwardness that makes them accessible to the international working class on whose behalf he speaks. The simplicity and repetition of "Johannesburg Mines" not only lays bare the extensive inequality present in that industry but does so without references unfamiliar to his audience. He lets the number—"240,000 natives / Working in the / Johannesburg mines"—speak for itself in a dispassionate tone that illustrates the stark reality of the miners' circumstances. He also writes in a conversational way to represent the bond that workers from around the world share. A singular international language does not exist, but Hughes uses onomatopoeia in his essay "Swords over Asia" to create a type of universal understanding. He inserts "Boom!" throughout the essay as he beseeches "the workers [to] pull down the War-makers—destroy their governments—and turn their battleships into yachts to use on summer holidays." The repetition of exclamation marks both in this essay and others imparts a performative aspect resembling a workers' rally. This punctuation, just like his rhetorical question in "Johannesburg Mines," serves as a call to action for his readers.

CRITICAL DISCUSSION
Hughes's 1930s essays and poetry received little notice in the United States, and "Johannesburg Mines" seems to have elicited no reviews. Alain Locke, writing in 1933 for *Opportunity,* reviewed Hughes's *Scottsboro Limited,* a one-act play and four protest poems, writing that Hughes "turns more and more in the direction of social protest and propaganda." Foreign audiences more readily welcomed Hughes's 1930s essays and poetry. Aspiring artists around the world, including Senegalese poet Léopold Sédar Senghor and French poet Aimé Césaire, credited Hughes's writing with inspiring their own. Filatova, although she criticizes his writing style for not speaking the "language" of the "Negro masses," expresses appreciation that Hughes uses "his writings as a weapon in the struggle against capitalism for the emancipation of toiling Negroes and toiling humanity in all countries."

Hughes's outspoken essays and poetry of the 1930s haunted his reputation for years. His essays on the Scottsboro trials, particularly "Cowards from the Colleges," which criticized black middle- and upper-class organizations for their lack of support for the Scottsboro young men, caused a nearly decade-long riff between Hughes and the NAACP. In 1953 he was called to a hearing in front of McCarthy's Senate Permanent Subcommittee on Investigations over his alleged "un-American" acts, stemming mainly from his writing inspired by his 1932 yearlong stay in the Soviet Union. He had to outline the period in which he sympathized with the Soviets, a loyalty apparent in essays such as his 1933 "Moscow and Me," in which he writes: "Moscow and freedom! The Soviet Union! The dream of all the poor and oppressed—like us—come true." Although Hughes traces his radicalism as only during the 1930s, writer Faith Berry states that his social and class awareness spanned his entire career.

Hughes's writing in general did not receive academic attention until the 1960s, and Berry was one of the first to recognize his essays in her 1973 collection *Good Morning Revolution.* Although Hughes's 1930s writing is still largely unknown, De Santis writes that Hughes's essays are especially urgent because he "used the essay form as a vehicle through which to comment on the contemporary issues he found most pressing at various stages of his career." In explaining why Hughes's social writing has been overlooked, biographer Arnold Rampersad cites his rejection of recognized forms, "a radical and revolutionary act," which leads to the work being "called 'protest' literature and consigned to the literary attic."

Poet Langston Hughes.
© EVERETT COLLECTION
INC./ALAMY.

BIBLIOGRAPHY

Sources

De Santis, Christopher C. *Langston Hughes and the Chicago Defender: Essays on Race, Politics, and Culture, 1942–1962.* Chicago: U of Illinois P, 1995. Print.

Filatova, Lydia. "Langston Hughes: American Writer." *International Literature* 1 (1933): 93–107. Web. 4 Oct. 2012.

Hughes, Langston. *Essays on Art, Race, Politics, and World Affairs.* Vol 9. Ed. Christopher C. De Santis. Collected Works of Langston Hughes. Columbia: U of Missouri P, 2002. Print.

———. "Hughes Finds Moors Being Used as Pawns by Fascists in Spain." *Baltimore Afro-American,* 30 Oct. 1937: 1–3. Web. 4 Oct. 2012.

Hughes, Langston, Arnold Rampersad, and David E. Roessel. *The Collected Poems of Langston Hughes.* New York: Knopf, 1994. Print.

Locke, Alain. "Black Truth and Black Beauty: A Retrospective Review of the Literature of the Negro for 1932." *Opportunity,* Jan. 1933: 14–18. Web. 4 Oct. 2012.

Mullen, Edward J. *Critical Essays on Langston Hughes.* Boston: Hall, 1986. Print.

Thomas, Lorenzo. "'It Is the Same Everywhere for Me:' Langston Hughes and the African Diaspora's Everyman." *Montage of a Dream: The Art and Life of Langston Hughes.* Eds. John Edgar Tidwell and Cheryl R. Ragar. Columbia: U of Missouri P, 2007. 181–94. Web. 20 Sept. 2012.

Further Reading

Dawahare, Anthony. "Langston Hughes' Radical Poetry and the 'End of Race.'" *Nationalism, Marxism, and African American Literature Between the Wars: A New Pandora's Box.* Jackson: UP of Mississippi, 2002. Web. 20 Sept. 2012.

Foley, Barbara. *Spectres of 1919: Class and Nation in the Making of the New Negro.* Urbana: U of Illinois P, 2003. Print.

Hughes, Langston. "My Adventures as a Social Poet." *Phylon* 8.3 (1947): 205–12. Print.

Hughes, Langston, Arnold Rampersad, and David E. Roessel. *Fight for Freedom and Other Writings on Civil Rights.* Columbia: U of Missouri P, 2001. Print.

Hughes, Langston, and Faith Berry. *Good Morning Revolution: Uncollected Social Protest Writings.* Westport: Hill, 1973. Print.

Peddie, Ian. "'There's No Way Not to Lose': Langston Hughes and Interracial Class Antagonism." Ed. Valerie Babb. *Langston Hughes Review* 18 (2004): 38–55. Print.

Scott, Jonathan. *Socialist Joy in the Writing of Langston Hughes.* Columbia: U of Missouri P, 2006. Print.

Young, Robert. "Langston Hughes's Red Poetics and the Practice of 'Disalienation.'" *Montage of a Dream: The Art and Life of Langston Hughes.* Eds. John Edgar Tidwell and Cheryl R. Ragar. Columbia: U of Missouri P, 2007: 181–94. Web. 20 Sept. 2012.

Kathryn Molinaro

LES MISÉRABLES

Victor Hugo

OVERVIEW

Victor Hugo's 1862 novel *Les Misérables* is the story of several different characters in early nineteenth century France and the hardships they encounter. Centering on the character Jean Valjean, an ex-convict, and his story of redemption, Hugo comments on the societal injustices created by the unrelenting laws at the time. Categorized as historical fiction, *Les Misérables* begins in 1815 and culminates with the June Rebellion, a failed attempt by young Parisian Republicans to overthrow the monarchy on June 5 and 6, 1832. The "us versus them" thematic elements in the novel paved the way for later legal and social reform in France, serving as propaganda-laden evidence that exposed Parisians to the injustices of a monarchy government.

Upon its publication, Hugo described *Les Misérables* as "moving around a great soul, which is the incarnation of all the social misery of the time." The title roughly translated from French into English is "the miserable." Hugo used the social and political unrest of nineteenth-century France to inform his work, using Valjean's unjust legal issues as a catalyst to depict the suffocating monarchy as seen from the point of view of the common man. A large-scale publicity campaign and Hugo's reputation as an accomplished poet made *Les Misérables* an instant commercial success, achieving his lifelong interest in accurately portraying the struggles of the poor and speaking out against the monarchy to bring about much-needed social and political change.

HISTORICAL AND LITERARY CONTEXT

Before the June Rebellion of 1832, France was in a steadily increasing state of unrest. The period from 1827 to 1832 was marked with economic problems as well as food shortages, poor harvests, cost-of-living increases, and general discontent among the French social classes. Cholera added to the turmoil when an outbreak all over Europe in the spring of 1832 resulted in more than 18,000 deaths in Paris alone. After the deaths of two notable Parisians—politician Casimir Pierre Périer, the Orleanist party President of the Council, and General Jean Maximilien Lamarque, who showed sympathy for the lower class—several failed rebellions occurred against the government from groups such as the Legitimists. Using the death of Lamarque as an excuse, the Republicans, a group

of students, led an uprising that resulted in the June Rebellion against the monarchy rule.

Hugo began writing *Les Misérables* in the second half of the 1840s as France's monarchial rule was coming to an end, culminating in the Revolution of 1848, which led to the French Second Republic. Although the story is rooted in past events, its themes of social and political unrest resonated with the strife that was still felt by the lower social classes in France upon its publication. Hugo was giving them a voice with his writing and in reality with the various speeches that he presented in the Chamber of Peers, the upper house of the French legislature, where he spoke out against the French legal system and the unjust discrimination of the poor.

Influenced by epic pieces of fiction such as Homer's *Iliad* and *Odyssey* and John Milton's *Paradise Lost*, Hugo also drew inspiration for *Les Misérables* from the Romantics of the era, including Alphonse de Lamartine; Alfred de Musset; Charles Nodier; Alfred-Victor, Count de Vigny; and his greatest literary inspiration, François-René de Chateaubriand. Hugo's previous writings also led to his interest in the struggles of the lower class that drove *Les Misérables,* including his depiction of commoners as a political force in 1831's *The Hunchback of Notre-Dame* and society's unfair treatment of the poor in 1829's *The Last Day of a Condemned Man.*

Press releases ran for six months before publication of *Les Misérables,* and copies of the book sold out within hours of its release. Since 1862 the novel has been translated into numerous languages and has been adapted for film, television, theater, radio, animation, and games. Perhaps its most well-known adaptation is the musical of the same name, which opened in Paris in 1980. Known colloquially as "Les Mis" or "Les Miz," the musical was the second-longest-running musical in the world in 2012 as well as the second-longest-running musical in London's West End theater district.

THEMES AND STYLE

In *Les Misérables* Hugo uses the lives of fictional characters to expound on his own interest in the struggles of the poor and how they overcame the hardships they were dealt. To make his readers sympathize with the horrible conditions endured by the lower class, Hugo sets the tone of the novel with his message clearly spelled out in the preface:

> So long as there shall exist, by reason of law and custom, a social condemnation, which, in the face of civilization, artificially creates hells on earth, and complicates a destiny that is divine, with human fatality; so long as the three problems of the age—the degradation of man by poverty, the ruin of woman by starvation, and the dwarfing of childhood by physical and spiritual night—are not solved; so long as, in certain regions, social asphyxia shall be possible; in other words, and from a yet more extended point of view, so long as ignorance and misery remain on earth, books like this cannot be useless.

With this bold opening statement Hugo is openly admitting that *Les Misérables* is a work of propaganda that he is using to expose society to the problems of the poor that he feels are being overlooked.

Hugo uses dense passages and lengthy sentences to depict the purpose behind the novel, which he details in its preface. Weaving multiple plots and characters together, *Les Misérables* is considered one of the longest novels of all time, with 365 chapters and 1,900 pages in the original French edition. The complex length and structure of Hugo's diction lends itself to the nature of his subject by affixing a severity and weight to the text, such as in the following passage:

> Can human nature be so entirely transformed inside and out? Can man, created by God, be made wicked by man? Can a soul be so completely changed by its destiny, and turn evil when its fate is evil? Can the heart become distorted, contract incurable deformities and incurable infirmities, under the pressure of disproportionate grief, like the spinal column under a low ceiling? Is there not in every human soul a primitive spark, a divine element, incorruptible in this world and immortal in the next, which can be developed by goodness, kindled, lit up, and made to radiate, and which evil can never entirely extinguish.

The same sentiments written in one or two sentences may not have conveyed the depth of the character's anguish. By using rhetorical questions in succession, Hugo forces readers to ponder society's unfair treatment of the poor.

To carry out his themes, Hugo uses a dramatic tone and formal diction that make some passages read like a speech. A line such as "Let us never fear robbers nor murderers. Those are dangers from without, petty dangers. Let us fear ourselves. Prejudices are the real robbers; vices are the real murderers. The great dangers lie within ourselves. What matters it what threatens our head or our purse! Let us think only of that which

VICTOR'S HUGO ROAD TO *LES MISÉRABLES*

Victor Hugo, who turned sixty in 1862 when *Les Misérables* was published, drew upon a multitude of life experiences while writing his ambitious novel. Born in 1802 in Besançon, Hugo lived in France for most of his life until he was exiled in 1851 due to Napoleon III's coup d'état. During his exiled period, Hugo lived in Brussels and then hopped around the Channel Islands, first moving to Jersey and then Guernsey. He moved back to France in 1873 and remained there until his death in 1885.

The inspiration behind *Les Misérables* came from Hugo's childhood during an era of political chaos. Two years after Hugo's birth, Napoleon became emperor, and the Bourbon monarchy was reinstated before Hugo turned eighteen. His parents also held differing political and religious views, which resulted in a tumultuous home life. Before he began writing novels, Hugo first proved himself to be an accomplished poet, publishing five volumes of poetry between 1829 and 1840. After reading François-René de Chateaubriand, he began to emulate the famed French Romantic writer and started drafting early ideas for *Les Misérables* in 1830.

threatens our soul" could have been plucked from one of Hugo's own speeches in the Chamber of Peers. Again, the author has his characters detail the need for social and political reform, and he uses tone and diction to express the severity of these issues.

CRITICAL DISCUSSION

Although *Les Misérables* was an instant success, it was also met with a great deal of criticism, especially from Hugo's peers. Gustave Flaubert found "neither truth nor greatness" in the novel, while Charles Baudelaire, contrary to the positive review he gave the book in a newspaper, said that it was "tasteless and inept." *Les Misérables* also struck a nerve with the French realists, who criticized Hugo for his proclivity to romanticize life instead of portraying it objectively. The realists went on to publish several books that were written as a statement against the romantic writers, including *Germinal* by Émile Zola, *Madame Bovary* by Flaubert, and *Une Vie* by Guy de Maupassant.

Since its publication *Les Misérables* has become one of the most popular books of all time, hailed for being among the first of its kind to comment openly on political and social strife. Critic Anne-Sophie Cerisola writes in her 2012 overview of the novel, "*Les Misérables* is a blend of epic, myth, dramatic and lyrical components; grotesque and sublime; satire and romance; comedy and tragedy; realism and romanticism which led many critics to describe the novel as a 'monster.' Maybe it is, and yet, it still makes people dream." Cerisola hypothesizes that the controversy

Illustration of Jean Valjean holding Cosette in his arms in a scene from Victor Hugo's *Les Misérables*. © LEBRECHT MUSIC AND ARTS PHOTO LIBRARY/ ALAMY.

Whatever the reason for the book's popularity, there is no denying the overwhelming praise it has received for its moral purpose and ambition. Hugo's work helped create a culture receptive to books that call for social and political reform, pushing authors to write about what they believe in.

over the novel's challenging syntax and subject matter was what led to the staying power of *Les Misérables*. Hugo did not make things easy on his readers; he forced them to struggle with the text, and ultimately the text won them over.

As *Les Misérables* moved on to become the canonized text that it is today, critics continue to explore how it became so popular. In a 1995 overview of the book, writer Myrto Konstantarakos wonders whether the work was actually as popular as it seems, noting that most French schools are hesitant to include the novel in their curricula. However, Jean-Paul Sartre notes that while most of the Romantic writers claimed that they were writing "for the people," Hugo was the only Romantic writer to "reach his intended audience." Moreover, the publication of *Les Misérables* has been referred to as a turning point in literature, shifting the era of Romanticism into the era of realism.

BIBLIOGRAPHY

Sources

Cerisola, Anne-Sophie. "An Overview of *Les Misérables*." Detroit: Gale, 2012. *Literature Resource Center*. Web. 9 Aug. 2012.

"Explanation of: 'Les Misérables' by Victor Hugo." *LitFinder Contemporary Collection*. Detroit: Gale, 2010. *LitFinder for Schools*. Web. 10 Aug. 2012.

Harsin, Jill. *Barricades: The War of the Streets in Revolutionary Paris*. New York: Palgrave, 2002. Print.

Hugo, Victor. *Les Misérables*. New York: Modern Library, n.d. Print.

Konstantarakos, Myrto. "*Les Misérables*: Overview." *Reference Guide to World Literature*. Ed. Lesley Henderson. 2nd ed. New York: St. James, 1995. *Literature Resource Center*. Web. 10 Aug. 2012.

"Nineteenth-Century Social Protest Literature Outside England." *Nineteenth-Century Literature Criticism*. Ed. Lynn M. Zott. Vol. 124. Detroit: Gale, 2003. *Literature Resource Center*. Web. 9 Aug. 2012.

"Victor (Marie) Hugo." *Gale Online Encyclopedia*. Detroit: Gale, 2012. *Literature Resource Center*. Web. 9 Aug. 2012.

Further Reading

Artes, Skyler. "Victor Hugo's Paris: Reviving Palingenesis." *French Forum* 35.1 (2010): 1+. *Literature Resource Center*. Web. 10 Aug. 2012.

Hugo, Victor. *The Hunchback of Notre-Dame*. New York: Dodd, Mead, 1947. Print.

Hugo, Victor, and Geoff Woollen. *The Last Day of a Condemned Man*. London: Hesperus, 2002. Print.

Nash, Suzanne. "Vargas Llosa, Mario. The Temptation of the Impossible: Victor Hugo and *Les Misérables*." *Nineteenth-Century French Studies* 36. 3–4 (2008): 359+. *Literature Resource Center*. Web. 10 Aug. 2012.

Ousselin, Edward. "Victor Hugo's European Utopia." *Nineteenth-Century French Studies* 34. 1–2 (2005): 32+. *Literature Resource Center*. Web. 10 Aug. 2012.

Media Adaptation

Les Misérables. Dir. J. Stuart Blackton. Perf. William V. Ranous, Maurice Costello, and Hazel Neason. Vitagraph Company of America, 1909. Film.

Les Misérables. Dir. Tom Hooper. Perf. Hugh Jackman, Russell Crowe, and Anne Hathaway. Working Title Films, 2012. Film.

Anna Deem

"LIFE IN THE IRON-MILLS"

Rebecca Harding Davis

OVERVIEW

"Life in the Iron-Mills," a short story by Rebecca Harding Davis, was published anonymously in the *Atlantic Monthly* in 1861 and recounts the tragic life of a worker in Virginia's iron industry who is subjected to horrific working conditions. The worker, named Hugh Wolfe, shares living quarters with his cousin Deb in conditions of extreme poverty. In his limited spare time, Hugh carves sculptures from korl, a waste product of iron smelting. One day, five visitors to the mill, including the mill owner's son, come across Hugh's sculpture of a crouched woman, and the subsequent conversation about his artistic endeavors leads to fateful consequences for Hugh and Deb. Combining gritty realism with romantic idealism, the story dramatizes social-class divisions and renders the middle-class reader complicit in the oppression of working-class laborers.

"Life in the Iron-Mills" was well received, despite calling into question the middle-class ideology of the cult of domesticity: the idea that women, from their separate sphere, could heal the wounds of industrial society. *The Atlantic* published the story anonymously, generating much speculation about the work, particularly regarding the author's gender. The story's stark style helped inspire the development of American literary realism.

HISTORICAL AND LITERARY CONTEXT

From her middle-class home in Wheeling, located in an iron-smelting region of what was then Virginia, Davis witnessed the progress of industrialization. Before the outbreak of the U.S. Civil War in 1861, the movement to abolish slavery had been accelerating and the Underground Railroad made use of the Ohio River to help slaves escape. Quakers applied Christian teaching in the fight against slavery; these religious principles also inspired the incipient movement for women's rights and suffrage. Many activists for women's rights also supported temperance, believing alcohol caused men to neglect their duties and abuse their families.

"Life in the Iron-Mills" shows industrialization leading to a new kind of labor for the white race, which problematized ideas about race and gender. Most of the nonblack industrial workers were immigrants from Great Britain, Ireland, and Germany. (The protagonists of the story are from Wales.) These immigrants struggled to maintain their white identity against the ruling-class gaze, which categorized them as belonging to an inferior race. Although women were supposed to be the ministering angels who brought comfort and healing, they were too degraded by these conditions to be of much help, as is illustrated by the relationship between Hugh and Deb.

Much popular fiction of the nineteenth century, both in England and the United States, revealed injustice and oppression. The best-selling American novel of the century, *Uncle Tom's Cabin* (1852) by Harriet Beecher Stowe, appeals to readers' emotions while showing that even a woman's moral suasion could not resolve the injustices created by slavery. In England, Mary Gaskell and Charles Dickens wrote novels that delved into the underside of urban, industrial life, revealing the cruelty of economic conditions. Karl Marx's *Communist Manifesto* (1848) explained how capitalism was inextricably based on workers' oppression. It was the writing of Nathaniel Hawthorne, however, that inspired Davis from an early age, and she drew on his material to develop her idea that ordinary objects—such as the home where the characters live and the sculpture that Hugh Wolfe creates—reveal truths of the human heart.

"Life in the Iron-Mills" received critical approval when it appeared in the *Atlantic Monthly*. One year later Davis completed the novel *Margret Howth,* which was also popular. A successful decade followed: she married an admirer and met with Hawthorne before his death. As realism became the dominant literary style, fiction focused on class and character, and featured precise attention to realistic detail. Authors who would later become famous for this style include William Dean Howells and Mark Twain, as well as women such as Sarah Orne Jewett. Davis continued to write through her years of marriage and motherhood, in a variety of genres, always focusing on the downtrodden. At the time of her death in 1910, she was eulogized by the *New York Times* as the mother of her journalist son and, only incidentally, as the author of "Life in the Iron-Mills." Her work was forgotten until 1972, when the Feminist Press reprinted the story with an essay by Tillie Olsen.

❖ *Key Facts*

Time Period:
Mid-19th Century

Genre:
Short Story

Events:
Industrialization; growth of social reform movements

Nationality:
American

The Iron-Rolling Mill, an 1875 painting by Adolph Menzel. In "Life in the Iron-Mills" Rebecca Harding Davis depicts the bleak conditions facing the workers of mills and factories across the United States. *THE IRON-ROLLING MILL* (OIL ON CANVAS), 1875, MENZEL, ADOLPH FRIEDRICH ERDMANN VON (1815–1905)/NEUE NATIONALGALERIE, BERLIN, GERMANY/THE BRIDGEMAN ART LIBRARY.

THEMES AND STYLE

"Life in the Iron-Mills" shows humans degenerating into animals through dehumanizing industrial work. For instance, the Welsh miners "when they are drunk … neither yell, nor shout, nor stagger, but skulk along like beaten hounds" and sleep in "kennel-like rooms." The well-to-do visitors who tour the mill embody different false approaches to the situation. Kirby, the mill owner's son, simply wishes that workers could be replaced by machines. The Yankee reporter is a professional spectator, whereas Mitchell, a "thorough-bred gentleman" and friend of Kirby's, "accompanied them merely for amusement." When Doctor May, another visitor, sees Hugh Wolfe's sculpture of a woman, he praises it for its anatomical detail and encourages Hugh with the American ideal of the self-made man: "Make yourself what you will. It is your right." The doctor is unable to offer Hugh material assistance, but the suggestion that money offers a solution leads Deb to steal Mitchell's wallet—a crime for which Hugh is found guilty. Before he can be taken to prison, he slashes his wrist with a piece of tin. A Quaker woman arrives after Hugh's suicide, promising Deb that he will be buried not in the mill town but out by trees. Deb, after three years in prison, comes out to join her and seek healing in the natural world.

The story begins and ends within a framework of a journey from the house where the Wolfe family had lived in the past. An anonymous narrator directly addresses the reader, a technique more often associated with a sentimental style rejected by later realists. Davis, however, adds a new, harsh tone that challenges readers to choose their moral stance. Early on, he explains to his readers: "I am going to be honest. This is what I want you to do. I want you to hide your disgust, take no heed to your clean clothes, and come right down here with me,—here, into the thickest of the fog and mud and foul effluvia. I want you to hear this story. There is a secret down here, in this nightmare fog, that has lain dumb for centuries: I want to make it a real thing to you. "Her emphatic style and graphic imagery mingling with romantic passages unsettles and implicates readers, forcing them to consider their own positions regarding race, gender, and class.

Melodramatic events, culminating in Hugh's graphic suicide, evoke an emotional response meant to arouse Christians to consider what their religion demands: pity for Hugh and Deb, as well as anger at an unjust and cruel capitalist system in need of reform. Allusions to the Bible resonate throughout the text; readers familiar with phrases such as "What must we do to be saved?" must grapple with that question coming from the face of Hugh's grotesque sculpture. The laborers speak in dialect, a trait of regionalist literature. Their English speech, conveyed by alternate spellings and elisions that make it difficult to parse, emphasizes the unbridgeable divide between the workers and those who rule over them. This divide, the text reminds us, was referred to in Jesus's parable of Dives and Lazarus, in which the rich man is condemned for eternity.

CRITICAL DISCUSSION

When it appeared in the *Atlantic Monthly,* "Life in the Iron-Mills" received critical acclaim and initiated Davis's successful writing career. Because the story was published anonymously and the narrator was unidentified, readers initially debated the gender of the author. Her identity was eventually revealed, and a letter from an admirer, newspaper editor L. Clarke Davis, led to their marriage. Prolific writer Elizabeth Stuart Phelps, whose article on the death of female workers in the Lowell mills appeared a few years later in the *Atlantic Monthly*, wrote that she learned how to connect with readers from her encounter with "Life in the Iron-Mills."

Although a single story cannot be credited with crafting the labor movement, "Life in the Iron-Mills" exposed workers' inhumane conditions and coincided with the process of labor organization. Conditions for most workers have since steadily improved, though occupations such as iron smelting remain dangerous. Today, many college programs in labor studies include "Life in the Iron-Mills" as an early and powerful example of an American text that examines working conditions.

Rediscovered as a feminist text in 1972 because Davis broke new ground for women writers with her realistic descriptions of topics considered out of bounds for females, recent scholars also explore how the text grapples with race and gender. Caroline S. Miles, in an *American Transcendental Quarterly* article, examines the story's presentation of the male body and masculinity, arguing that "descriptions of the white male body, some of them grotesque and alarming, inundate Davis's counter-narrative of picturesque classlessness and laboring bliss, and function as a way of making tangible the elusive and unwritten construction of class and of whiteness." Reading the text from the perspective of white studies, Eric Schocket notes in an article in *PMLA* that the korl woman, "rising out of the soot and blackness and gesturing with outstretched white arms toward the sky … is nothing so much as a racial figure for working-class possibility. And standing as she does in the center of what we have come to consider the germinal text of American industrial fiction, she casts a long white shadow that we have yet to see fully."

BIBLIOGRAPHY

Sources

Davis, Rebecca Harding. "Life in the Iron-Mills." *The Atlantic Monthly* 7.42 (1861). *Cornell Digital Library.* Web. 9 July 2012.

Miles, Caroline S. "Representing and Self-Mutilating the Laboring Male Body: Re-Examining Rebecca Harding Davis's 'Life in the Iron Mills.'"*American Transcendental Quarterly* 18.2 (2004): 89–104. Rpt. in *Short Story Criticism.* Vol. 109. Detroit: Gale, 2008. *Literature Resource Center.* Web. 30 June 2012.

Phelps, Elizabeth Stuart. "Stories That Stay."*Century Magazine* 81 (1910): 118–24. *Unz.org.* Web. 1 July 2012.

Schocket, Eric. "'Discovering Some New Race': Rebecca Harding Davis's 'Life in the Iron Mills' and the Literary Emergence of Working-Class Whiteness." *PMLA* 15.1, Special Topic: Rereading Class (2000), 46–59. *JSTOR.* Web. 4 July 2012.

Further Reading

Curnutt, Kirk. "Direct Addresses, Narrative Authority, and Gender in Rebecca Harding Davis's 'Life in the Iron Mills.'"*Style* 28.2 (1994). *Academic Search Complete.* Web. 6 July 2012.

Douglas, Ann. *The Feminization of American Culture.* New York: Knopf, 1977. Print.

Harris, Sharon. *Rebecca Harding Davis and American Realism.* Philadelphia: U of Pennsylvania P, 1991. Print.

Lasseter, Janice Milner. "The Censored and Uncensored Literary Lives of Life in the Iron-Mills." *Legacy* 20.1/2 (2003): 175–90.

Olsen, Tillie. "Biographical Interpretation."*Life in the Iron Mills,* by Rebecca Harding Davis. New York: Feminist P, 1972. Print.

Pfaelzer, Jean. *Parlor Radical: Rebecca Harding Davis and the Origins of American Social Realism.* Pittsburgh: U of Pittsburgh P, 1996. Print.

Roediger, David R. *Wages of Whiteness: Race and the Making of the American Working Class.* London: Verso, 1999. Print.

Silver, Andrew. "'Unnatural Unions': Picturesque Travel, Sexual Politics, and Working-Class Representation in 'A Night under Ground' and 'Life in the Iron-Mills.'"*Legacy* 20.1/ 2 (2003): 94–117. Rpt. in *Short Story Criticism.* Vol. 109. Detroit: Gale, 2008. *Literature Resource Center.* Web. 30 June 2012.

Tichi, Cecilia, ed. *Life in the Iron-Mills* by Rebecca Harding Davis. Bedford Cultural Editions. Boston: Bedford, 1998. Print.

Robin Morris

MEET ME ON THE BARRICADES

Charles Yale Harrison

✤ *Key Facts*

Time Period:
Early 20th Century

Genre:
Novel

Events:
Rise of fascism; outbreak
of Spanish Civil War;
Stalinist purges; rise
of communism in the
United States

Nationality:
Canadian

OVERVIEW

Meet Me on the Barricades (1938) is a highly stylized novel of fantasy and political satire by the Canadian American journalist Charles Yale Harrison. Using a format that combines a stream-of-consciousness flow with theatrical spates of dialogue, *Barricades* tells the story of two days in the life of Peter Herbert Simpson, a mild-mannered symphony oboist who spices up his humdrum existence with a rich and detailed inner fantasy world. A romantic leftist, disillusioned by the less-than-noble underpinnings of idealistic revolutions around the world, Simpson escapes into a number of heroic roles as a dashing revolutionary and advisor to world leaders. As Comrade Piotr Simpson, he has a torrid affair with the lovely Russian Natasha and ideological conversations with Joseph Stalin and Vladimir Lenin. As Compañero Pedro Simpson, he is a captain in the Republican forces combating General Francisco Franco in the Spanish Civil War. Interspersed with swashbuckling fantasy are Simpson's more mundane discussions with his friends, such as the reporter Roy Darrell, who presents a more jaded perspective on revolutionary fervor. In *Meet Me on the Barricades,* Harrison portrays a world that is awash with propaganda, and his protagonist is vulnerable to these influences.

Written during the turbulent period between the two world wars, *Meet Me on the Barricades* was described by an early reviewer as "iconoclastic" in its examination of popular political movements in Russia, Spain, and the United States. Innovative in style and in its mocking approach to commentary, Harrison's novel ruthlessly lampoons idealism, cynicism, and the idea of the sacrosanct in politics, but it does not offer solutions. Rather, the chaotic, uproarious narrative re-creates the atmosphere of a perplexing era and an Everyman who wants desperately to be a hero. In a 1938 review of the book, Eugene Lyons speculates that Harrison's critiques are aimed at the "pompous propagandists who bedevil meek and well-meaning creatures with their lies and quarrels."

HISTORICAL AND LITERARY CONTEXT

The decades between the end of World War I in 1919 and the beginning of World War II in 1939 marked a period of political upheaval and societal anxiety. The Western world had been devastated by what had been dubbed the War to End All Wars. Though the success of the 1917 communist revolution in Russia gave support to progressive leftist movements in other nations, including a rise in communist fervor in the United States, many people had lost faith in democratic government. This sentiment grew with the hardships resulting from a severe worldwide economic depression that began in 1929 and lasted about ten years. By the mid-1930s, socialist idealism had come under attack by right-wing nationalist political parties in Germany, Italy, and Spain. The leaders of these movements—Adolf Hitler, Benito Mussolini, and Francisco Franco, respectively—appealed to citizens with promises of order, stability, and a return to former national glory.

Meet Me on the Barricades, therefore, was published at a time when leftist movements were experiencing political and ideological setbacks on the world stage. In the case of Spain, national elections held in February 1936 succeeded in bringing a coalition of leftist groups called the Popular Front to power, and it formed a progressive reformist government. About four months later, however, a group of right-wing generals under the leadership of Franco launched a rebellion against the Popular Front government, leading to years of bloody civil war before the defeat of the leftist Republicans by Nationalist forces. In the Soviet Union, communist ideology remained strong, but government policies of repression and purges of dissidents disillusioned many who looked to the socialist state for leadership in just, humane governance. The period from 1936 to 1938 would become known in the Soviet Union as the years of the "great terror," when purges initiated by Stalin against opposition leaders led to widespread persecution and execution of "enemies of the people" throughout the country. Many pacifists and political progressives, such as Harrison's hero Simpson, found these betrayals of their ideals painfully disheartening. Through his novel Harrison criticizes the political propaganda machines, exposing their destructiveness and manipulations.

Literature from the period between the world wars reflects a number of cultural trends, as writers explored the devastating effects of war. Robert Graves's memoir *Goodbye to All That* (1929) provides a deeply personal account of the wartime experiences of a British soldier, while *The Great Gatsby* (1925), written by F. Scott Fitzgerald, explores the frenetic escapism prevalent in U.S. society after World War I. Harrison's own first novel, the pacifist *Generals Die in Bed* (1930), offers a Canadian perspective on the conflict. The interwar period was also a time of literary innovation as a number of modernists experimented with unorthodox styles and formats in their work. James Joyce's stream-of-consciousness novel *Ulysses* (1922) may have inspired Harrison's experimental style in *Barricades,* and *Mrs. Dalloway* (1925) by Virginia Woolf was influential in its expansion of the experiences of a single day into a novel.

Though *Meet Me on the Barricades* is one of Harrison's lesser-known works, the issues of disillusionment and helplessness it examines have remained significant. Ted Allan, another Canadian writer, covers some of the same ground in his more utopian *This Time a Better Earth* (1939), about the Spanish Civil War. Harrison himself believed that *Barricades* influenced one of the great humorists of the decade. In 1947 he approached the writer James Thurber, charging that Thurber had stolen from *Barricades* the idea for his famous story "The Secret Life of Walter Mitty" (1939). Though the similarities between Mitty's heroic fantasy life and Simpson's are obvious, Thurber denied ever having read Harrison's book, and nothing more came of the matter.

THEMES AND STYLE

Simpson, Harrison's hero in *Meet Me on the Barricades,* asks the question that forms the author's central juxtaposition of political passion and disenchantment: "Is there nothing left for me but to live my life out tooting an oboe, or for the world to go from generation to generation under the eternal burden of oppression and injustice?" Though Simpson longs to join the great revolutionaries of the past and perform heroic deeds, his real world is too limited by banality, and the world stage seems dominated by compromise and betrayal. Simpson struggles through a "gluey sea of propaganda, floundering from ideology to ideology." The critic Bernard Wolfe suggests that the novel "is inspired by a hatred for … treachery and a fear that the gullible Simpsons [of the world] will again swallow the fatal pills of patriotism prepared by the imperialists and sugar-coated by their hired publicists." Even within Simpson's own fantasies, the lure of destructive power is strong: "He turns and looks behind him and sees marching ranks of steel-helmeted troops carrying rifles with fixed bayonets…. He blinked and came to with a start…. This is militarism, not revolution. My God, I was in the wrong daydream!" Finally, though Harrison gently mocks Simpson's heroic pretensions, he does not condemn Simpson's idealism, asserting, "To laugh is not enough, and to sneer in bitterness and cynicism out of great knowledge is still less."

Meet Me on the Barricades has little plot beyond Simpson's fantastic inner life; nevertheless, Harrison's innovative story has a captivating entertainment value

THE PRACTICAL RADICAL: A PIONEER IN HOUSING ISSUES

Charles Yale Harrison was a journalist and publicist as well as a novelist, and in the years between the two world wars, he became one of the first members of the press to address the issue of public housing. An American by birth, Harrison spent his early years in Canada, serving in the Royal Montreal Regiment during World War I before returning to the United States to work as a journalist in New York. His leftist social conscience led him to examine issues of fairness in housing, and in 1937 he published a series of groundbreaking pamphlets on the subject, titled *Housing Becomes a National Issue, Housing Confronts Congress, What Price Subsidy!* and *A Housing Tale of Two Cities, London and New York.*

Harrison served as director of public relations for the New York City Housing Authority from 1934 until 1938, when he left to take a job with the Federal Housing Administration. Though he was one of the earliest proponents of public housing initiatives, his achievements did not impress his more radical colleagues, who accused him of compromising his principles in order to advance his career. An angry exchange of letters in the Marxist journal the *New International* ended with a scathing criticism of Harrison for his "achievements in ballyhooing the phony Roosevelt housing program in order to grease the ways for the war policy of the Fourth New Deal."

that draws in readers and gives the novel persuasive power. Much of the tale is told in dialogue, giving Simpson's encounters with historic figures immediacy and humor. In one of the most compelling allegories in the novel, Earl Browder, head of the U.S. Communist Party from 1930 to 1945, meets his earlier (and more ideologically radical) self with resulting hilarity. The Browder from 1937, "in top hat, cutaway coat, lavender striped trousers; a respectable supporter of democracy," is so incensed by the Browder of 1932, "in a proletarian leather jacket," that he throttles him. Simpson's real-world friends, Ascaso the Spanish musician and Darrell the jaded journalist, serve as a kind of Greek chorus, grounding Simpson in reality during their drunken discussions.

Harrison's stream-of-consciousness narrative gives *Barricades* a tempo that is sometimes breathtaking, sometimes mystifying: "Life and death, a terrible question. A smartly dressed crowd. Robles. Morituri te salutamus. Mr. Fischer's experiences in Spain. He is dead. Executed by men. Latin." The descriptions are terse but evocative, as when Harrison details Pedro Simpson's uniform: "He wears a red beret, pulled smartly over his right eye, a snugly fitting khaki tunic." Throughout, the tone is poignantly comic, with obvious affection for the hapless progressives represented by Simpson and merciless satire for those who have betrayed his ideals.

Sixtieth-anniversary celebration of the International Brigades of the Spanish Civil War (1996). The protagonist of Charles Yale Harrison's *Meet Me on the Barricades* (1938) imagines himself as a member of the International Brigades. © DUSKO DESPOTOVIC/ SYGMA/CORBIS.

CRITICAL DISCUSSION

Meet Me on the Barricades was greeted with respect by critics who admired Harrison's early work in *Generals Die in Bed.* Lyons of the *Saturday Review* recommends the novel as a "brief, witty, highly intelligent book … an effective mental purgative for intellectuals suffering from political dyspepsia and ideological constipation." Harold Strauss, writing for the *New York Times,* calls Harrison "the bull in the china shop of radical political faiths," stating that the author's failure to provide positive solutions turns "what was intended as devastating satire into a stumbling sort of tragedy." Other reviewers agree that *Barricades* ultimately fails as a political statement. R. L. Duffus of the *New York Times* observes that "one reads it with interest and lays it down with a vague dissatisfaction…. The book lacks the final decisive stroke." Similarly, a reviewer for the *Pittsburgh Press* concludes that "there is nothing to be deduced from the book apparently, except that Harrison again is asking, 'Where do we go from here?' but he asks the question most interestingly."

By the end of the twentieth century, Harrison's innovative political satire was not widely read, and fewer than a hundred copies remained in library systems in North America. However, it remains an eloquent statement of a unique political perspective at a distinct time in history, articulating the angst of committed leftists and pacifists watching helplessly as fascism gained strength and the world marched inexorably toward another global war. The novel also stands as an example of early-twentieth-century modernity in writing, combining interwar cynicism with utopian fantasy in a stream-of-consciousness narrative that echoes the work of James Joyce and foreshadows the political allegory of George Orwell.

By the twenty-first century, *Meet Me on the Barricades* was little discussed among scholars, most of whom preferred Harrison's earlier work *Generals Die in Bed.* Caren Irr describes *Barricades* as "more cautious in its leftism" than Harrison's previous writing and notes that although the novel is set in New York City, it has little sense of place and that "location [is] merely a vacant place in which ideas echo." Nils Clausson points out that "although Harrison has virtually disappeared from American literary history, he has fared slightly better among critics of Canadian literature."

BIBLIOGRAPHY

Sources

"Charles Yale Harrison, James Burnham, and Max Shachtman Correspondence (January/February 1939)." *New International* 5.2 (1939): 60+. *Marxists Internet Archive.* Web. 26 Sept. 2012.

Clausson, Nils. "Charles Yale Harrison's 'Little-Known Minor Masterpiece': *Generals Die in Bed,* Modernism, and the Canon of World War I Fiction." *War, Literature and the Arts: An International Journal of the Humanities* 23.1 (2011): n. pag. *Literature Resources from Gale.* Web. 25 Sept. 2012.

Duffus, R. L. "Oboe Players Don't Die in Bed." Rev. of *Meet Me on the Barricades,* by Charles Yale Harrison. *New York Times* 5 Mar. 1938: 15. *ProQuest Historical Newspapers.* Web. 22 Sept. 2012.

Irr, Caren. *The Suburb of Dissent: Cultural Politics in the United States and Canada.* Durham, NC: Duke UP, 1998. Print.

Lyons, Eugene. "Caspar Milquetoast Joins the Revolution." Rev. of *Meet Me on the Barricades,* by Charles Yale Harrison. *Saturday Review* 12 Mar. 1938: 5. Print.

"'Meet Me at Barricades' Lifts Veil on Spanish Revolt." Rev. of *Meet Me on the Barricades,* by Charles Yale Harrison. *Pittsburgh Press* 13 Mar. 1938: 10. Web. *Google News.* 24 Sept. 2012.

Strauss, Harold. "A Political Satire and Fantasy." Rev. of *Meet Me on the Barricades,* by Charles Yale Harrison. *New York Times* 6 Mar. 1938: 87. *ProQuest Historical Newspapers.* Web. 22 Sept. 2012.

Wolfe, Bernard. "Red Fantasy." Rev. of *Meet Me on the Barricades,* by Charles Yale Harrison. *New International* 4.4 (1938): 126–27. *Marxists Internet Archive.* Web. 4 Oct. 2012.

Further Reading

Aaron, Daniel. *Writers on the Left: Episodes in American Literary Communism.* New York: Columbia UP, 1992. Print.

Harrison, Charles Yale. *Generals Die in Bed: A Story from the Trenches.* Toronto: Annick, 2002. Print.

———. *Thank God for My Heart Attack.* Austin, TX: Holt, Rinehart and Winston, 1968. Print.

Kutulas, Judy. *The Long War: The Intellectual People's Front and Anti-Stalinism, 1930–1940.* Durham, NC: Duke UP, 1995. Print.

Tina Gianoulis

MOTHER

Maxim Gorky

❖ *Key Facts*

Time Period:
Early 20th Century

Genre:
Novel

Events:
Repressive rule of Tsar
Alexander III; First
Congress of the Russian
Social Democratic Labour
Party (RSDLP); failure of
1905 Russian Revolution

Nationality:
Russian

OVERVIEW

Mother, a novel written by Maxim Gorky in 1907, traces an uneducated woman's journey from political disinterest to socialist activism in a Russian manufacturing city. Based on a strike in Gorky's childhood hometown, Nizhny Novgorod, and written in a realist style, the narrative reflects the collective experiences of an emerging Russian working class that hopes for a new political reality. When her son Pavel is arrested after a street demonstration, Pelegueya Nilovna takes on his revolutionary work. Gorky conveys the former peasants' purposeful defiance of tsarist laws as they struggle against factory owners, police, and religious leaders. By conveying the dimension and depth of the Russian working class, the novel calls into question earlier Russian literary works that focused solely on the lives of the aristocracy and the bourgeoisie. In doing so, Gorky's novel reflects the liberating changes in the character of the working classes inspired by Russia's revolutionary movement.

By the time he wrote *Mother,* Gorky had already been persecuted as a revolutionary writer and Bolshevik propagandist. After the collapse of the 1905 Revolution (in which he was an active participant), Gorky was forced to leave Russia, so he wrote the novel in exile, starting in the United States and finishing in Capri, Italy. The novel reflects Gorky's evolution as a practitioner of neorealism, as he sought to create an artistic chronicle of class struggle and the revolution. The book resonated with the new society that would emerge after the successful October Revolution of 1917; while not free of idealization, the novel introduced a "journalistically expressed political indignation," according to Gorky biographer Moissaye Joseph Olgin. Despite this idealization of its proletariat subjects, Gorky's *Mother* was a compelling portrait of an uneducated woman as she awakens to the promise of socialism.

HISTORICAL AND LITERARY CONTEXT

In the mid-nineteenth century, hopes were high within the peasant class for increased rights and representation within the Russian Empire's tsarist government. Tsar Alexander II issued a series of liberal reforms, beginning with the Emancipation Manifesto of 1861, which freed serfs and allowed them the rights to marry without consent, to own property, and to own a business. These reforms included unfair land distribution, however, and proved to be disadvantageous for peasants and led to civil unrest. The Populist, or *Narodnik,* movement sought to abolish the monarchy and distribute land among the peasants. The 1877 suppression of a Narodnik uprising led to the formation of anarchist revolutionary groups. When Alexander II was assassinated, his successor, Alexander III, moved away from liberal reform to support a reactionary antidemocratic government.

As *Mother* suggests, by 1907 these political setbacks had not diminished Russians' belief in social protest and political literature as a path to a Marxist socialist government. Gorky had already used his literary talents to expose tsarist control of the press and had written political plays such as *The Lower Depths* (1902). Following the failed 1905 revolution and his exile, Gorky aligned himself with Vladimir Lenin's Bolshevik wing of the Russian Social Democratic Labour Party (RSDLP). Optimistic about the promise of a Bolshevik government, the exiled author wrote *Mother* to demonstrate the rewards of the class struggle for those who resisted the tsarist regime.

At the start of the twentieth century, Russian fiction was emerging from its critical realist tradition. Ivan Turgenev's *Sketches from a Hunter's Album* (1852) was the first work to depict the peasant as a rational being capable of dreams and pragmatic behavior. Leo Tolstoy was more idealistic; in *War and Peace* (1869) he suggested that the peasant had a higher moral wisdom than a nobleman. However, Anton Chekhov's story "Peasants" (1897), drawn from his experiences as a doctor during a cholera epidemic and famine, caused an uproar among the Populist intelligentsia who objected to the portrayal of peasants coarsened by poverty. Marxists, however, applauded the story for its depiction of how the capitalist town had caused the downfall of the village, according to Orlando Figes in *Natasha's Dance, A Cultural History of Russia* (2002). The horrific realities of famine, rape, and beatings in Ivan Bunin's short stories resonated strongly with Gorky's own grim experiences, which influenced his alignment with Bolshevik politics.

Mother first gained international notoriety when tsarist censors banned it, and it fast became the template for socialist realism fiction, a form Gorky perceived as a marriage of nineteenth-century critical realism and Bolshevik ideals. Later novels elaborated on Gorky's heroic narrative, including Dmitry Furmanov's *Chapaev* (1923) and Fedor Gladkov's *Cement* (1925). German modernist Bertolt Brecht drew from Gorky's novel when he wrote *The Mother* (1932), one of his Lehrstücke, or "learning plays," that was a critique of capitalism. Joseph Stalin's representatives promoted Gorky's socialist realism at the First Congress of the Writers' Union in 1934 as a portrayal of Soviet life as it would become, "conforming to the Party's narrative of socialist development," according to Figes. Although revered throughout the Soviet Union for his contribution to Russian literature, in the post-Soviet era Gorky is most remembered for his role as an intellectual rather than for the artistry of his writing.

THEMES AND STYLE

Central to *Mother* is the transformation of the unschooled Nilovna, "the mother," as she becomes an active participant in socialist causes. Countering the prevailing Russian literary tradition of the time, the desires and dilemmas of Gorky's proletariats make them compelling central characters. Chapter one reveals the workers' mental state: "None of them, it seemed, had either the time or the desire to attempt to change this state of life." Nilovna initially mistrusts the socialists who assemble at her house, and she warns her son, "You must be on the watch with people; they all hate one another. They live in greed and envy." However, as she interacts with the socialists, she begins to see them as individuals unified by their activism but distinct in motivation and behavior. Gorky demonstrates that the intellect and spirit of the working class are as formidable as those of the upper classes by showing Nilovna awakening to the significance of her own actions.

Gorky establishes his socialist agenda by progressing from generalizations to realistic details about the hardships of the activists' lives. He presents the novel's world through third-person limited omniscient narration, restricting the reader's observations to Nilovna's world, but not to her consciousness. Her social circle—and the novel itself—expands through her son Pavel's activism. The emotional impact of Pavel's arrest is conveyed most acutely when Nilovna reflects that this lively world may now be closed off to her. "During the last years she had become accustomed to live constantly in the expectation of something momentous, something good…. Now he was gone, everything was gone." The grimy, "smoke-covered faces" of factory workers are contrasted with those of the activists, who are "melancholy" but often smile in enthusiasm for the social changes they hope to make. Through Nilovna's discovery of a vocabulary and a purpose in activism, *Mother* demonstrates the importance of education and protest for the betterment of the lower classes.

Stylistically, the novel reflects a humanist indignation about injustices toward the working class and

MAXIM GORKY: CONFLICTED BOLSHEVIK

Maxim Gorky was the pen name of Alexei Maximovich Peshkov, born in 1868 in Nizhny Novgorod. His invented last name combined the Russian words for "wretched" and "bitter," qualities that characterized the writer's impoverished childhood and resulting social conscience. His parents died when he was nine, and at twelve he went to live with his grandmother. As a youth, Gorky found himself in violent altercations with other peasants, and he attempted suicide in 1887. These experiences informed his prolific body of work, which included short stories, memoirs, criticism, political pamphlets, novels, and plays. Gorky's name became associated with Marxism when agitators adopted lines from his "Song of the Stormy Petrel" as their rallying cry. He first met Lenin in the offices of the Marxist magazine *New Life*; their nearly twenty-year association was characterized by the uneasy interplay between artist and authoritarian politician.

The prolific writer fled Russia in 1905 and remained in exile until 1913; he later participated in the October Revolution of 1917. Gorky published criticisms of Bolshevik authoritarian policy in *Untimely Thoughts* (1918) and left the Soviet Union for Italy in 1922. Stalin convinced the author to return in 1932, a publicity coup for the Soviets. But the reconciliation was short-lived. Gorky was placed under house arrest in 1934 and died under mysterious circumstances in 1936.

empathy for their shortcomings. Their living conditions lead to a "lurking malice" that is nearly impossible to counteract; men are "exhausted with toil," drink to excess, and "break into bloody quarrels." But Gorky is attentive to their inherent nobility. His novel begins with degradation, but the prose gathers power in moving from the inchoate "obscure depths" of Nilovna's past to specific instances of proletariat outrage, sadness, calm, and agency. As Gorky ennobles his working-class figures, he carries on the humanist project and attitudes first found in novels of Tolstoy, who was a populist advocate. *Mother* also serves as counterpoint to Gorky's own work. In his early short stories such as "Chelkash" (1894), he turned to real-life prototypes in the search for heroic characters who could be elevated as subjects of protest. Gorky's earlier novels *Foma Gordeev* (1899) and *The Three of Them* (1900) reflect intense hostility toward the tsarist regime, but with *Mother* he intended "to sustain the failing spirit of opposition in the dark and threatening forces of life," according to Gorky biography F. M. Borras.

CRITICAL DISCUSSION

Already a writer of international importance, Gorky achieved further notoriety as a Bolshevik advocate when he published *Mother*. A government press committee deemed that Gorky had propagated a "work that advocates serious violations of the law … and calls

Political activist and author Maxim Gorky. Born Alexei Maximovich Peshkov, he began writing under the name Gorky, which translates to "bitter," a reflection of his feelings toward Russia. © LEBRECHT MUSIC AND ARTS PHOTO LIBRARY/ALAMY.

Mother is most often discussed today as a novel conveying the Bolshevik struggle. Scholars focus on the complex relationship between Gorky's artistic agenda and Lenin's political agenda. Eric J. Klaus, for example, in his 2003 essay *Germano-Slavica,* notes the author's "humanism, the symbiotic interplay of intellect and activity, a teleological mission, as well as the negative aftertaste of coercion." Stefan Morawski, writing in *Science and Society,* considers Lenin's praise of artistic independence as "bound up with the needs of the moment and the tactics of the fight to win Gorky." In his 1975 piece in *The Positive Hero in Russian Literature,* Rufus Mathewson notes the success of the heroic model Gorky established in *Mother,* which includes "two formulas often found in later Soviet fiction: the conversion of the innocent, the ignorant, or the misled to a richer life of participation in the forward movement of society; and the more important pattern of emblematic political heroism in the face of terrible obstacles." Other commentators note that *Mother* is favored over his more artistically successful works. According to Harold B. Segel in *European Writers* (1990), *Mother* was "adulated out of all proportion in the Soviet Union, both because of its subject and because of Vladimir Lenin's enthusiasm for it,"

BIBLIOGRAPHY

Sources

Borras, F. M. *Maxim Gorky, The Writer.* Oxford: Clarendon, 1967. Print.

Figes, Orlando. *Natasha's Dance, A Cultural History of Russia.* New York: Picador, 2002. Print.

Gorky, Maxim. *Mother.* New York: Citadel, 1947. Print.

"Gorky's 'Mother'; A True and Pathetic Study of Human Nature." *New York Times.* New York Times Company, 25 May 1907. Web. 2 Oct. 2012.

Kaun, Alexander Samuel. *Maxim Gorky and His Russia.* New York: J. Cape & H. Smith, 1931. Print.

Klaus, Eric J. "The Formula of Self-Formation: Bildung and Vospitanie in Goethe's Wilhelm Meister's Apprenticeship and Gorky's Mother." *Germano-Slavica* 14 (2003): 75+. *Literature Resource Center.* Web. 2 Oct. 2012.

Levin, Dan. *Stormy Petrel: The Life and Work of Maxim Gorky.* London: F. Muller, 1967. Print.

Lukacs, Georg. "Maxim Gorky 1868–1936: Eulogies from His Funeral on the Red Square." Trans. S. D. Kogan. *International Literature* 8 (1936). Rpt. in *Red Flag, Journal of the CP (MLM)* 1 (2007). *Marxists Internet Archive.* Web. 26 Sept. 2012.

Mathewson, Rufus W., Jr. "Lenin and Gorky: The Turning Point." *The Positive Hero in Russian Literature.* 2nd ed. Palo Alto: Stanford UP, 1975. 156–76. Rpt. in *Twentieth-Century Literary Criticism.* Ed. Scot Peacock. Vol. 67. Detroit: Gale Research, 1997. *Literature Resource Center.* Web. 13 Sept. 2012.

Morawski, Stefan. "Lenin as a Literary Theorist." *Science and Society* 29.1 (1965): 2–25. Rpt. in *Twentieth-Century Literary Criticism.* Ed. Scot Peacock. Vol. 67. Detroit: Gale Research, 1997. *Literature Resource Center.* Web. 13 Sept. 2012.

for riots and acts of rebellion," as Henri Troyat notes in *Gorky* (1989). Within Russia, the magazine in which the first part of *Mother* appeared was confiscated and destroyed; the second part of the novel was heavily censored, but underground versions circulated internationally. In 1907 a *New York Times* reviewer wrote that through Gorky, "we are made to mingle with the little band of revolutionists…. Through [*Mother*] we know her people." Georgi Plekhanov, who established the first Russian-language Marxist political group, wrote that "from an artist like Gorky … even the most learned sociologist may learn something," as quoted in Olgin. Lenin himself saw the book's flaws but applauded it nonetheless as being "useful," according to Dan Levin in *Stormy Petrel* (1967).

Mother is considered a milestone in the development of the Soviet novel. Gorky was noted for combining the humanist approach of earlier Russian novelists with a social conscience. With *Mother,* he established himself as the father of socialist realism, a state-approved heroic style that presented an idealized Soviet reality. In 1938, two years after Gorky's death, Valery Zhelobinsky adapted Gorky's novel for an opera. The Marxist and literary historian Georg Lukacs eulogized the writer as "a staunch defender of Socialist culture against fascist barbarity in our times, [who] also fought constantly for the cultural needs and the intellectual development of the oppressed proletariat."

Olgin, Moissaye Joseph. *Maxim Gorky, Writer and Revolutionist.* London: M. Lawrence, 1933. Print.

Segel, Harold B. "Alexei Maximovich Peshkov." *European Writers: The Twentieth Century.* Ed. George Stade. Vol. 8. New York: Charles Scribner's Sons, 1990. *Scribner Writers Series.* Web. 13 Sept. 2012.

Troyat, Henri. *Gorky.* Trans. Lowell Bair. New York: Crown, 1989. Print.

Further Reading

Gorky, Maxim. *Reminiscences of Leo Nicolayevitch Tolstoi.* Trans. S. S. Koteliansky and Leonard Woolf. London: Hogarth, 1920. Print.

Hare, Richard. *Maxim Gorky, Romantic Realist and Conservative Revolutionary.* London: Oxford UP, 1962. Print.

Luker, Nicholas, ed. and trans. *An Anthology of Russian Neo-realism: The "Znanie" School of Maxim Gorky.* Ann Arbor: Ardis, 1981. Print.

Scherr, Barry P. "The Young Novelist." *Maxim Gorky.* Boston: Twayne, 1988. *The Twayne Authors Series.* Web. 2 Oct. 2012.

Media Adaptations

Mat. Dir. Aleksandr Razumnyj. Perf. Ivan Bersenev, Vladimir Karin, and Ludmila Sychova. 1920. Film.

Mother. Dir. I. Pudovkin. Phot. A.N. Golovnia. Written by N. Zarkhi and V. I. Pudovkin. Minneapolis, MN: Festival Films, 1926. Film.

Karen Bender

MOTHER COURAGE AND HER CHILDREN

Bertolt Brecht

❖ *Key Facts*

Time Period:
Mid-20th Century

Genre:
Play

Events:
German invasion of
Poland; World War II

Nationality:
German

OVERVIEW

Bertolt Brecht wrote the play *Mother Courage and Her Children* (1941), which chronicles the tragic story of the antiheroic, entrepreneurial matriarch Anna Fierling, in response to Germany's 1939 invasion of Poland, which marked the beginning of World War II. The play, set during the Thirty Years' War (1618–48), follows Fierling and her three children as she pulls a wagon across Europe, selling provisions to warring Protestant and Catholic armies. Although she is enthusiastic about the war and the booming economy, her profiteering leads to the deaths of her children. Her condition illustrates Brecht's message that a world economy driven by capitalism breeds constant war, which in turn feeds on working-class consumers enslaved to the capitalist machine. The play, one of Brecht's first successful solo experiments with a new style of drama known as epic theater, employs an episodic plot structure, coarse colloquial language, incidental music, and a distant historical setting in order to make a sociopolitical commentary on the evils of German capitalism under the Third Reich.

Staged by a group of German communist refugees in Switzerland to protest Adolf Hitler's tyranny, *Mother Courage* opened at Zürich's Schauspielhaus on September 19, 1941. Only months before the show debuted, Brecht, who had fled his home country of Germany for Denmark in 1933, expatriated to the United States. The Swiss production impressed American playwright Thornton Wilder, whose attendance at the premiere led to an American translation of the play. But lingering anti-German sentiment and the play's procommunist tenor prevented it from being performed in the United States. Brecht finally revived *Mother Courage* when he returned to East Berlin in 1949. The play found considerable commercial success amid the postwar devastation of the Soviet-occupied city. Subsequent European tours earned the playwright an international reputation, leading to the widespread proliferation of his epic theater techniques and political ideology.

HISTORICAL AND LITERARY CONTEXT

Before Hitler seized control of Germany in 1933, the Communist Party of Germany (KPD) was the largest in Europe outside the Soviet Union. However, party members' influential presence in the German parliament was perceived as a threat to Hitler's National Socialist German Workers' Party. On February 27, 1933, Nazi officials reported that a fire at the Reichstag (the German parliamentary building) was part of a communist plot to overthrow the government. The government outlawed the KPD, and party members were arrested and sent to concentration camps. Now with a Nazi majority in parliament, the Third Reich began a military campaign to regain the European territories taken from Germany under the terms of the Treaty of Versailles (1919).

When *Mother Courage* was first staged, the Nazi invasions across Europe showed few signs of slowing. The United States had not yet entered the war, and the Soviet Union had only recently signed a mutual assistance agreement with Britain. The belief that the World War I armistice had been signed by criminals and supported by Jews and communists to undermine the German state persisted in Germany. Brecht, in exile because of the Marxist and propagandistic plays he wrote during the 1920s and early 1930s, eventually moved to Sweden, where he wrote *Mother Courage* as a warning to nations that continued to trade with Germany despite Hitler's dangerous ambitions.

Although Brecht had experimented with the propagandistic genre of expressionism in his revolution-themed play, *Drums in the Night* (1922), he and colleagues such as Erwin Piscator believed that expressionism's focus on idealistic protagonists who sought to change humanity through spiritual revelation was ill-suited to political theater under a fascist regime. Instead, they pursued a new, militant form of proletarian drama, which they called epic theater. The new style integrated film clips, life-size puppets, popular music, and theatrical machinery to disrupt the spectator's experience and encourage intellectual engagement. After collaborating with Piscator on such productions as *Hoppla, We're Alive!* (1927) and *The Good Soldier Schweik* (1928), Brecht diverged from Piscator's documentary style in favor of allegorical plays. Brecht's most successful works include *The Three-Penny Opera* (1928), *Señora Carrar's Rifles* (1937), and *Fear and Misery of the Third Reich* (1938), which use everyday interactions to offer insights into large-scale social and economic problems.

Brecht's political exile prevented him from producing much of his theatrical work until the end of World War II, but the success of his epic theater experiments made him one of the most influential theater practitioners of the twentieth century. Like his theoretical writings, his productions were meticulously documented and have been studied by directors as a model for effective political theater. Many artists have emulated his dramatic writing style. Peter Weiss's groundbreaking play *Marat/Sade* (1964) employs Brecht's dialectical approach to address the moral conflict between socialism and capitalism, and Tony Kushner uses similar tactics to confront attitudes toward communism, religiosity, homosexuality, and AIDS in his Pulitzer prize-winning play *Angels in America* (1993). Today, critics celebrate *Mother Courage* as an exemplar of dramaturgy that embodies Marxist ideology.

THEMES AND STYLE

The central theme of *Mother Courage* is that commerce, like war, benefits the rich while seducing the working classes into a depraved condition akin to slavery. Like many members of the KPD, Brecht believed that the Nazi party was a front for elite German industrialists and that Nazi leaders were disingenuous in their promise of prosperity for the middle class. As a working-class figure, Mother Courage curses the savageries of combat but embraces the economic opportunity that war provides. She observes that armed conflict is simply "the continuation of business by other means … instead of cheese, it's now with lead." She represents a "great living contradiction," as the shrewd business deals that she brokers to provide for her family are the same transactions that ultimately get them killed. Although many audiences pity Mother Courage for her seemingly inescapable misfortune, Brecht has stated that she is unambiguously guilty in her capitulation to and partial embrace of a deeply flawed system.

Brecht uses numerous theatrical strategies, described in his 1948 theoretical essay "A Short Organum for the Theatre," to create what he called *Verfremdungseffekt*. Often translated as "alienation" or "defamiliarization effect," the term describes a strategy to expose the socially constructed nature of reality by letting audiences see the human and technological modes of production that illusionist theater attempts to obscure. For example, during performances of the play, stagehands perform scenic changes in full view of the audience; musicians' instruments are visibly lit; and narration, song, and direct address interrupt the flow of action. Brecht uses scenic titles, projections, and summary reports to disrupt suspense and narrative continuity and to invoke a Marxist critique of the way capitalism misdirects workers'

MOTHER COURAGE AND HER COLLABORATORS

With the publication of *The Life and Lies of Bertolt Brecht* (1994), German literary scholar John Fuegi began a contentious debate over the authorship of Brecht's plays, claiming that many were written by several of his mistresses, most notably Elisabeth Hauptmann, Margarete Steffin, and Ruth Berlau. In her 1985 memoir, Berlau affirms that the three women at various times collaborated on manuscripts with Brecht but insists that the partnerships were inspired by Marxist notions of the collective. Although there is ample evidence that the women Fuegi references indeed collaborated on many of Brecht's well-known plays, historians and linguists have determined that many of Fuegi's most tendentious claims, which concern financial exploitation of the three women, are largely exaggerated.

Steffin, a German actress, is widely acknowledged to have played a central role in the writing of *Mother Courage and Her Children*. She even arranged a sham marriage with a Danish citizen so she could remain in Denmark and write with Brecht during his exile. When the Nazi advance forced Brecht and his wife to seek asylum in the United States in 1939, however, Steffin accompanied them only as far Moscow, where she tragically died from tuberculosis while awaiting her exit visa.

interests through an elaborate, illusory economic and social power structure.

Mother Courage also combines several linguistic techniques to heighten the sense of alienation that pervades the play. It pairs dialogue written in coarse, colloquial speech with occasional rhyming couplets delivered directly to the audience in order to force actors to demonstrate their characters rather than inhabit them. Despite attempts to limit the audience's empathy for the characters, however, the play is not entirely devoid of affect. Poignant images, such as a silent scream that overwhelms Mother Courage as she hears her son being executed offstage while she haggles over his ransom, provoke a powerful response in stark contrast to the work's otherwise distant tone. This tension between intimacy and alienation, reality and illusion, encourages the audience to examine the implicit ideological agenda that underlies Brecht's work.

CRITICAL DISCUSSION

Mother Courage, which premiered in a Zürich community of German exiles, received praise from critics for its revolutionary style and political immediacy. Hungarian literary critic and onetime Marxist tastemaker György Lukács praises *Mother Courage* for maintaining a cogent Marxist message through its touching characterization and stark reality. In spite of the warm reception, Brecht was irritated by critics' references to Mother Courage's psychology, and he

without the play's original context, modern audiences cannot engage with heavy-handed politicization. However, others have adapted the play to suit alternative ideologies; for example, many European and American troupes adapted it as an allegory of the human condition during the Vietnam War. The first African adaptation was licensed in 1995, with Ugandan revolutionaries staging a production titled *Maama Nalukalala* and translated into their native Laganda.

While the volume of scholarship concerning Brecht's theoretical and dramatic writings peaked between the 1960s and the 1980s, historians, literary critics, and theater practitioners continue to study the author as a playwright and a theoretician. Many early studies focus on the translation and interpretation of Brecht's epic theater practices in relation to the Berliner Ensemble's many *Modellbücher,* or model books, which photographically document each scene moment by moment. Since John Willett collected nearly all of Brecht's theoretical writings on the theater into the comprehensive *Brecht on Theatre: The Development of an Aesthetic* (1964), scholars have increasingly analyzed Brecht's political ideologies to discern the playwright's beliefs about communist philosophies and to place his work in relation to radical feminist theory.

BIBLIOGRAPHY

Sources

Berlau, Ruth. *Living for Brecht: The Memoirs of Ruth Berlau.* Trans. Geoffrey Skelton. Ed. Hans Bunge. New York: Fromm, 1987. Print.

Brecht, Bertolt. "A Short Organum for the Theatre." *Brecht on Theatre: The Development of an Aesthetic.* Ed. and trans. John Willett. New York: Hill, 1964. 179–208. Print.

———. *Mother Courage and Her Children.* Trans. John Willett. Ed. John Willet and Robert Manheim. New York: Arcade, 1994. Print.

Fuegi, John. *The Life and Lies of Bertolt Brecht.* London: HarperCollins, 1994. Print.

Honegger, Gitta. "Gossip, Ghosts, and Memory: *Mother Courage* and the Forging of the Berliner Ensemble." *Drama Review* 52.4 (2008): 98–117. *Project MUSE.* Web. 13 June 2012.

Leach, Robert. "Mother Courage and Her Children." *The Cambridge Companion to Brecht.* 2nd ed. Ed. Peter Thomson and Glendyr Sacks. Cambridge: Cambridge UP, 2006. 128–38. Print.

Thomson, Peter, and Vivien Gardner. *Brecht: Mother Courage and Her Children.* Plays in Production. Cambridge: Cambridge UP, 1997. Print.

Further Reading

Barthes, Roland. "Seven Photo Models of *Mother Courage.*" *Drama Review* 12.1 (1967): 44–55. Web. 7 Jun 2012.

Esslin, Martin. *Brecht, A Choice of Evils: A Critical Study of the Man, His Work, and His Opinions.* 4th ed. London: Methuen, 1984. Print.

Martin, Carol, and Henry Bial, eds. *Brecht Sourcebook.* London: Routledge, 2000. Print.

famously rewrote large sections of the play to make his protagonist less empathetic. However, the resultant increase in moral ambiguity led communist critics to complain that the play lacked a positive party message, as Mother Courage fails to learn any lesson from her tragic losses. Brecht's caustic reply is characteristic of his disdain for the East German Communist leaders: he retorts that what matters to society is not whether Mother Courage learns a lesson but whether audiences learn to see things differently.

Since the play's legendary 1949 production and subsequent European tour (between 1951 and 1955), the work has been lauded as a masterpiece of twentieth-century political drama applicable to several political contexts. According to theater historian Robert Leach in *The Cambridge Companion to Brecht* (2006), *Mother Courage* remains an "almost programmatic illustration of this alternative kind of dialectical theater because its power derives precisely from the relationship between the material, the technique, and the function." Although *Mother Courage* is still frequently produced around the world, many contemporary productions have rejected the application of Brecht's theatrical practices because

Oesmann, Astrid. *Staging History: Brecht's Social Concepts of Ideology.* Albany: State U of New York P, 2005. Print.

Willett, John. *Brecht in Context: Comparative Approaches.* London: Methuen, 1998. Print.

Media Adaptations

Mother Courage and Her Children. Perf. Flora Robson, Olive McFarland. British Broadcasting Corporation, 1959. Television Movie.

Mother Courage and Her Children. Dir. Peter Palitzsch, Manfred Wekwerth. Perf. Helene Weigel, Angelika Hurwicz. Constantin Film, 1961. Film.

Mother Courage and Her Children. Dir. George C. Wolfe. Tran. Tony Kushner. Cast Meryl Streep, Kevin Kline, Austin Pendleton, et al. New York, © 2006. Videocassette.

Sara Taylor

NORTH AND SOUTH

Elizabeth Gaskell

✛ **Key Facts**

Time Period:
Mid-19th Century

Genre:
Novel

Events:
Industrialization; growth
of economic and social
disparity

Nationality:
English

OVERVIEW

Elizabeth Gaskell's 1855 novel *North and South* presents a critique of industrialization and its effects on Victorian society, particularly the working poor. *North and South* tells the story of Margaret Hale and her experiences in the fictional town of Milton, a northern industrial city based on Manchester, England. Having grown up in the south, Margaret is forced to move with her family after her father, a vicar, breaks with the Church of England. Shocked by the poverty in the north, Margaret feels called to help the workers in a nearby cotton mill but discovers that their situation is as complicated as her own relationship with the mill's owner, John Thornton. Blending social critique with more traditional romantic elements, *North and South* appealed to a broad readership.

Gaskell lived during an era of rapid changes, with industrialization having profound consequences in England, economically and socially. With the growth of urban areas and advances in printing, newspapers and magazines did a brisk business, and writers such as Charles Dickens and Wilkie Collins regularly published their fiction in serial form. *North and South,* which originally appeared in Dickens's *Household Words,* garnered a mixed response from critics of the day. Dickens himself was critical as her editor and as a reader. In the mid-twentieth century Gaskell's work began to enjoy a reevaluation, and she has since gained traction as a significant figure in Victorian literature.

HISTORICAL AND LITERARY CONTEXT

The Industrial Revolution, which most historians date to the mid-eighteenth century, brought substantial changes to the economic and social order of England. Machine-based manufacturing and steam power technology contributed to rapid growth in productivity, especially in the textile industry, which was one of the first to become mechanized. As factories came into existence as a major source of employment, cities grew around them. Manchester, which was nicknamed "Cottonopolis," was one of the earliest industrialized cities, with significant textile manufacturing occurring from the 1780s.

By 1850 Manchester boasted more than one hundred cotton mills, employing thousands of workers, including children. Starting around 1819 the British government passed legislation to regulate child labor and workday length, but in the 1850s children as young

as nine could still work ten-hour days. Living conditions for factory workers were often cramped and dirty and a breeding ground for disease. Friedrich Engels, in his *The Condition of the Working-Class in England in 1844,* felt unequal to describing "the filth, ruin and uninhabitableness, the defiance of all considerations of cleanliness, ventilation and health" he observed around the cotton factories in Manchester. Gaskell, who lived in Manchester from her marriage in 1832 onward, was well acquainted with the plight of the poor.

In the mid-nineteenth century, British literature, and particularly novels, enjoyed a period of great popularity. Writers such as Dickens produced plot-driven works calibrated to entertain a broad audience, but they also included social commentary dealing with the challenges of the era, especially those faced by the poor. *Oliver Twist,* Dickens's 1838 novel about an orphan boy on the mean streets of London, dealt with urban squalor and child labor, among other issues. Dickens, who had himself been forced to work in a shoe-blacking factory as a child, had a great deal of influence on other writers of the era in terms of helping to popularize novels with marked social concerns and in his role as an editor, first of *Household Words* and then of *All the Year Round,* which he also published. Dickens's novel *Hard Times,* which appeared in *Household Words* in 1854 just before *North and South,* dealt with many of the same themes. Indeed, Gaskell's writing was directly influenced by Dickens and the need to prevent too much overlap between the two novels.

North and South is one of the last novels in the "industrial genre," with George Eliot's *Felix Holt* the only work of significant note written after Gaskell's. The novel also marks a change for Gaskell, who followed it with her controversial biography, *The Life of Charlotte Brontë,* the publication of which provoked threats of litigation from still living parties described in the book. Gaskell was forced to issue a retraction in *The Times,* and to sanction a withdrawal of the second edition from sale. Gaskell's fiction after *North and South* shifted away from factory settings, although Gaskell's class concerns remain evident and a ripe subject for contemporary scholarship.

THEMES AND STYLE

North and South is often considered an example of the "condition-of-England" novel, which sought to reveal the misery that industrialization brought to the lower classes. In the novel Margaret Hale, new to Manchester and shocked by the city's filth, sets about trying to help the poor she encounters. Startled by the angry response she receives from those she offers to aid, she attempts to educate herself and in the process becomes involved in the affairs of Marlborough Mill and its manager, John Thornton, as well as Nicholas Higgins, a representative for the fledgling worker's union. As the story unfolds, Gaskell brings to life the devastating consequences of factory work on workers, especially through the character of Higgins's daughter Bessy, who is dying of consumption brought on by poor ventilation in the mills.

Gaskell makes use of an omniscient narrator with access to multiple characters' thoughts and feelings to illustrate the daily impact of factory life across social strata. Access to the character's inner lives demonstrates that the social upheavals radiating outward from the factory are mirrored in the emotional lives of everyone concerned. And interestingly, as scholar Jill Matus points out, Gaskell's revelation of the suffering of all, women and men, lower class and middle class, "bring[s] home the double standard of her culture's way of coding the exhibition of overwhelming emotion as feminine and working-class." Matus points to the example of Mr. Hale preferring Thornton rather than Margaret, accompany him to his wife's funeral. Although it is Margaret's mother's funeral, it is against convention for her to attend. Margaret speculates that this is because middle-class women are expected to keep their emotions in check while "poor women go and don't care if they are seen overwhelmed with grief." Middle-class men may also be overwhelmed with emotion, in her reading, and Margaret thinks that poor women have the right idea.

Gaskell's critique of industrial conditions develops through her realism, as she describes in plain language the conditions of life in Milton, affording her middle-class readers a view of factory life as her heroine encounters it. Higgins and his daughter speak in the working-class dialect of Manchester, and Margaret herself is scolded by her mother for picking up slang from striking workers. In addition, Gaskell employs a didactic tone as she develops, through dialogue, various points of view on key issues such as workers' rights.

CRITICAL DISCUSSION

North and South was much read in its original serialized form, although critical reactions were mixed. A review in *The Athenaeum* boldly stated "[this year] will produce few better tales than *North and South*." A significant strand of criticism, however, most often from male reviewers, held that women were unable to fully grasp the nature of industrialization and its attendant problems, urging "Mrs. Gaskell" to spend more time focusing on the part of the novel of traditionally female provenance, the romance.

Susan Hamilton notes that, following Gaskell's sudden death in 1865, critics' urge to "identify Gaskell's writing achievement almost exclusively with

HOUSEHOLD WORDS

Launched in March of 1850, Charles Dickens's *Household Words* weekly magazine published original fiction and journalism taking on the social issues of the day. While it addressed many issues affecting the poor, the magazine, at two pence, was mainly aimed at the middle class. The magazine employed a small cadre of "staff" writers, including Dickens's good friend Wilkie Collins, who wrote anonymous pieces in the style of Dickens. *Household Words* also published fiction from other Victorian authors, ninety of whom were women. One of the first writers Dickens contacted for submissions was Elizabeth Gaskell. He had admired her novel *Mary Barton: A Manchester Life* and proposed that she serialize another novel in his magazine. The first issue of *Household Words* included her story *Lizzie Leigh,* which described the life of a young prostitute in Manchester.

Household Words was printed until 1859 when a dispute between Dickens and his publishers, Bradbury and Evans, led Dickens to start another journal, *All the Year Round,* of which he would be the sole proprietor. Over the course of its publication, *Household Words* had been quite successful, earning Dickens a respectable income and helping to further the careers of several fledgling writers, including Gaskell. In addition to many short stories, Gaskell published what would later become *Cranford* and, more famously, *North and South.*

a single title has yielded a critical reputation deeply riven into opposed streams of writing: the 'social problem' novels … and the novels of provincial life." This division would factor into her relative obscurity or treatment as a "minor Victorian" or "woman writer" until the mid- to late twentieth century. During the 1970s and 1980s Gaskell's work received renewed attention, especially from feminist scholars who were interested in the elements of domestic and social critique in Gaskell's work. Gaskell's fiction also attracted new popular attention, and Gaskell joined the company of Austen, Eliot, and Trollope in having novels made into lavish BBC "heritage dramas." Hamilton sees these productions as fulfilling "a palliative function for late twentieth- and early twenty-first century British society alarmed by intensified class division and increasing globalization."

North and South has been discussed as a work that speaks for itself and as a work that speaks to Gaskell's development and ultimate importance as a writer and part of the Western literary canon. Patricia Johnson analyzes *North and South* as a "fusion" of industrial novel and bildungsroman that "dramatizes the ways in which the public domain and the private sphere interpenetrate each other and make it impossible to separate social issues, such as class and gender roles, from psychological issues, such as sexuality and maturity." In Johnson's reading, all of the characters in the novel are struggling to grow and develop, and that growth is interdependent between characters and across

Elizabeth Gaskell, English novelist and author of *North and South.* © LEBRECHT MUSIC AND ARTS PHOTO LIBRARY/ ALAMY.

multiple facets of each character's life. Elizabeth Starr, meanwhile, suggests that Gaskell, by setting her novels in factories and meeting rooms, conceived of them as being part of the public dialogue surrounding industrialization. Moreover, "recognizing Gaskell's efforts to find a place for her fictional work in the midst of urban commerce and industry" will "require readers and critics to reconsider popular conceptions of a reassuringly domestic, self-effacing, and properly maternal Elizabeth Gaskell," thus defeating earlier evaluations of Gaskell in this line.

BIBLIOGRAPHY

Sources

Engels, Friedrich. *The Condition of the Working-Class in England in 1844. Internet Modern History Sourcebook.* Fordham University. Web. 13 July 2012.

Hamilton, Susan. "Gaskell Then and Now." *The Cambridge Companion to Elizabeth Gaskell.* Ed. Jill Matus. Cambridge: Cambridge UP, 2007. Print.

Johnson, Patricia E. "Elizabeth Gaskell's North and South: A National Bildungsroman." *The Victorian Newsletter* 85 (1994): 1–9. *Literature Resource Center.* Web. 13 July 2012.

Matus, Jill. Introduction. *The Cambridge Companion to Elizabeth Gaskell.* Ed. Jill Matus. Cambridge: Cambridge UP, 2007. Print.

Rev. of *North and South,* by Elizabeth Gaskell. *The Athenaeum* 7 Apr. 1855: 403. *Literature Resource Center.* Web. 13 July 2012.

Starr, Elizabeth. "'A Great Engine for Good': The Industry of Fiction in Elizabeth Gaskell's *Mary Barton* and *North and South.*" *Studies in the Novel* 34.4 (2002): 385–402. *Literature Resource Center.* Web. 13 July 2012.

Further Reading

Barchas, Janine. "Mrs. Gaskell's *North and South*: Austen's Early Legacy." *Persuasions: The Jane Austen Journal* 30 (2008): 53+. *Literature Resource Center.* Web. 13 July 2012.

Brown, Pearl L. "From Elizabeth Gaskell's *Mary Barton* to her *North and South*: Progress or Decline for Women?" *Victorian Literature and Culture* 28.2 (2000): 345–58. *Literature Resource Center.* Web. 13 July 2012.

Hotz, Mary Elizabeth. "'Taught by Death What Life Should Be': Elizabeth Gaskell's Representation of Death in *North and South.*" *Studies in the Novel* 32.2 (2000): 165–84. *Literature Resource Center.* Web. 13 July 2012.

Lansbury, Coral. "Chapter 4: *North and South.*" *Elizabeth Gaskell.* Boston: Twayne, 1984. Twayne's English Authors Series 371. *The Twayne Authors Series.* Web. 12 July 2012.

Meckier, Jerome. "Parodic Prolongation in *North and South*: Elizabeth Gaskell Revaluates Dickens's Suspenseful Delays." *Dickens Quarterly* 23.4 (2006): 217–28. *Literature Resource Center.* Web. 13 July 2012.

Weiss, Barbara. "Elizabeth Gaskell: The Telling of Feminine Tales." *Studies in the Novel* 16.3 (1984): 274–87. *Literature Resource Center.* Web. 13 July 2012.

Media Adaptation

North and South. Dir. Brian Percival. Perf. Daniela Denby-Ashe, Richard Armitage, and Tim Pigott-Smith. British Broadcasting Corporation (BBC), 2004. TV Series.

Daisy Gard

PLUMES

A Folk Tragedy

Georgia Douglas Johnson

OVERVIEW

A one-act drama first produced in 1928 at both the Harlem Experimental Theatre in New York and the Cube Theatre in Chicago, *Plumes: A Folk Tragedy* (1927) was written by Harlem Renaissance poet, playwright, and short story writer Georgia Douglas Johnson (c. 1880–1966). Published under the pen name John Temple and set at the dawn of the twentieth century, the play focuses on the efforts of a poor, black, widowed mother to save her ill child; at the same time, however, she plans an all-but-inevitable funeral for the girl. *Plumes* is a key example of early African American folk drama. The genre arose in response to virulent white bigotry that portrayed African Americans as lazy, uncultured, and amoral. Seeking to refute and combat racist stereotypes—including those promulgated in the nineteenth- and early twentieth-century blackface minstrel shows that sparked the Harlem Renaissance (at the time called the New Negro movement)—folk dramas incorporated music, dance, and shared myth to depict the strength and depth of black culture and ethics. Johnson's play in particular attempted to represent and include women in the larger political project of the artistic renaissance.

Johnson was one of the most prolific, well-known, and respected African American woman writers of the 1920s and 1930s Harlem Renaissance, a period during which social thought and artistic expression flourished in her community. Originally from Georgia, she served as a leading organizer of the movement, which stressed that African Americans could best combat racism by producing art with themes of racial pride and social determination while condemning institutionalized racism. Johnson differed from her male counterparts in exploring motherhood, love, and the oppression of women. *Plumes* won first prize in a 1927 literary contest sponsored by the National Urban League's magazine *Opportunity* and was well received by Johnson's colleagues and audience. Through her poetry, plays, and short stories, she became a vital critic of African American and female oppression.

HISTORICAL AND LITERARY CONTEXT

Johnson's work was written against the backdrop of significant early twentieth-century social breakdowns in the United States as well as a dramatic increase in white supremacist thought and writing. The previous century's Civil War and emancipation had brought African Americans freedom from slavery but not from oppression, poverty, and racism. Beginning in 1910 the Great Migration brought more than a million blacks from the rural South to industrial cities of the North and Midwest, where they competed for low-status jobs with established immigrant communities. Civil rights legislation of the mid- to late 1800s proved ineffective. Overcrowding and the disillusionment of African American World War I veterans, who came home to continued discrimination, led to brutal race riots and lynchings across the country in 1919. An economic boom in the 1920s, when Johnson produced many of her most important poems and plays, fueled urbanization until the stock market crash in 1929. General economic decline impacted all Americans, but those at the margins were struck hard by the Great Depression that followed.

Around the time that *Plumes* was published and staged, multiple works had appeared claiming that blacks lacked the intelligence and morality to ever properly integrate into American society. Contradicting what amounted to racist propaganda, the Harlem Renaissance of the 1920s and 1930s developed and encouraged a sense of cultural pride among African Americans. Within this vital movement, playwrights countered the caricatures of blackface performances by featuring black actors portraying the complex emotions of everyday life. Although almost every writer of the movement took up the themes of racial oppression and inequality, the inequities within the African American community went largely ignored. Women were still viewed as maids, seamstresses, cooks, and childcare providers. A number of female writers emerged during the renaissance, however, expressing their individuality and describing the experience of being both African American and female. Johnson was earliest and foremost among them.

Such folk dramas as *Plumes* were heavily influenced by the intellectual work of Howard University professor Alain Locke and scholar and civil rights activist W. E. B. Du Bois. The two took very different approaches to the genre. Johnson was a friend and

❖ Key Facts

Time Period:
Mid-20th Century

Genre:
Play

Events:
Great Migration; Great Depression; beginning of the Harlem Renaissance

Nationality:
American

THE GEORGIA DOUGLAS JOHNSON SATURDAY EVENING SALON

Many critics believe that Johnson may have equaled or surpassed the importance of her literary work with the vital role she played as the hostess and organizer of the weekly S Street Salon. In the early 1920s, writer Jean Toomer approached Johnson about holding weekly conversations among leading African American critics, writers, and thinkers in Washington, D.C., where she spent the majority of her life. Soon after her husband's death in 1925, Johnson began welcoming intellectuals into her home as a way of joining together as a community in supporting one another's work, studying their craft together, and celebrating and discussing African American culture and politics. Among the many attendees of these salons were Toomer, Zora Neal Hurston, Langston Hughes, Eulalie Spence, Anne Spencer, Richard Bruce Nugent, Gwendolyn Bennett, Alain Locke, Jessie Redmon Fauset, May Miller, Angelina Weld Grimké, and Marita Bonner. Johnson also used her home as a "halfway house" for those in need. A number of literary organizations and gathering places in the Washington, D.C., area continue to foster communication and community among African American writers and artists, all with roots in Johnson's Saturday salons.

admirer of Locke, who believed that African American theater should focus on the humanity of its subjects. According to Will Harris's 1994 article "Early Black Women Playwrights and the Dual Liberation Motif," however, Johnson was also dedicated to Du Bois's conviction that "art (and especially theater) was crucial for countering stereotypes still plaguing the race, and for establishing inspirational models for a progressive people." All art, in Du Bois's mind, should be propaganda. Receiving encouragement from Locke and the man who first inspired her to write, poet William Stanley Braithwaite, Johnson managed to combine both ideologies. Her folk dramas, aimed at African American audiences, sought to reconstruct black identity and self-worth by encouraging pride in black history, traditions, and culture. Johnson also wrote explicitly politicized plays designed for white audiences, such as *A Sunday Morning in the South* (1925) and *Blue-Eyed Black Boy* (c. 1930). These treated the subject of lynching in an attempt to shape broader public opinion about violence against blacks.

Although much of her work remained unpublished during her lifetime, and some of her writings were lost after her death, Johnson is now recognized as a major figure in the Harlem Renaissance. In addition to her role as a writer, she promoted the general advancement of African American culture and status, inviting leading intellectuals, artists, critics, and writers into her home for weekly readings and discussions. Her poetry and plays have been especially vital to

African American literary and historical writers, particularly such feminists as Toni Morrison and Johnson scholar Judith L. Stephens. Atlanta University awarded Johnson an honorary doctorate in 1965, the year before her death, and in 2010 she was inducted posthumously into the Georgia Writers Hall of Fame. The discovery of a handful of Johnson's missing works has led to a reexamination of her writing and legacy.

THEMES AND STYLE

Plumes explores the conflicts built into maternal love, the contradictory social expectations in the African American community, and the efforts of black women to hold some power in an overwhelmingly oppressive world. Charity Brown lives in a humble cottage in the rural South, where she sits with her friend Tildy discussing the completion of a white dress that her very sick daughter, Emmerline, has long desired. The two women gently debate the length of the hem, knowing that the dress, intended for social use, will likely serve as a funeral shroud. Meanwhile, an ornate funeral procession passes, complete with plumed horses, a luxury Charity resolves to have in order to make her daughter's funeral respectable. The doctor arrives and offers some hope, however, in the form of an operation that would cost fifty dollars—the exact amount needed for the plumed horses. The play's themes are brought into sharp focus when Charity's decision, easily resolved if it could be based on love, becomes a social and moral dilemma. In a 1997 introduction to the author's *Selected Works,* Claudia Tate writes that Charity's confusion over her priorities emphasizes "Johnson's steadfast conviction that only love can preserve human dignity." Johnson believed that women's natural instincts—if they were allowed to follow them—would be crucial to ameliorating racism and sexism. Finally, the play also touches on traditional African American spiritualism—an important subject in folk drama—in displaying the seriousness with which the women take Tildy's reading of coffee grounds; the women's distrust of the doctor; and the symbolism of the white dress, which might either serve as a celebration of joy or as a burial garment.

The contrast between *Plumes*'s humble setting and its title is an example of Johnson's use of irony as a rhetorical strategy. The play thwarts audience expectations by evoking positive images of beauty, wealth, and social status, while the action is focused on poverty, helplessness, and death. Charity's difficulty in deciding between possibly saving her daughter's life and giving her a respectable funeral heightens the irony of her situation. The author's decision to keep Emmerline offstage is further evidence of the metaphoric substance of her play. In ensuring that the audience hears the girl's anguish as something coming from afar, Johnson exposes the cultural silencing of the suffering and marginalization of African Americans, particularly women and girls.

The impact of *Plumes* relies on the emotionally charged tenor of the language, which conveys the direness of Charity's situation. When the doctor chides her for her indecision about proceeding with the operation, the fraught mother insists, "I do love my child. My God, I do love my child. You don't understand…." Just as important to Johnson was the use of realistic vernacular: the play is written in the colloquial black dialect of the post-Civil War South. Charity, who has already buried her husband and other daughter, explains her motives to Tildy for desiring the plumed horses, saying, "I made up my mind the time Bessie went that the next one of us what died would have a shore nuff funeral." In employing both these tactics, the author hoped that her realistic and multifaceted presentation of African American lives and troubles would help eliminate biases by drawing on universal emotions.

CRITICAL DISCUSSION

Although Johnson was initially known as a poet, her plays increasingly supported her literary reputation, especially as they became more overtly political in their treatment of discrimination and sexism. Throughout the 1920s many of Johnson's contemporaries—notably Braithwaite, Locke, and Du Bois (although he sometimes criticized Victorian and traditional elements in her poetry)—lauded her literary endeavors as first-rate examples of their genres. Some commentators faulted her for her use of colloquial language, however, arguing that it contributed to negative views of blacks. After the Harlem Renaissance ended, her significance to the movement was ignored for decades in academic and literary discussion. A rise in cultural studies in the later twentieth century led to a vast reexamination of African American writers of the period. *Plumes* in particular is one of the most often cited examples of African American folk drama from the renaissance and has maintained a strong reputation among scholars.

Johnson has recently been viewed as a serious champion of social determination against both institutionalized racism and sexism. Stephens argues in *The Plays of Georgia Douglas Johnson* (2006) that in her fight against bigotry, the author's dramas "shift the focus away from black people as 'primitive,' toward a consideration of the uncivilized (primitive) institution of slavery, its far-reaching effects, and how post-emancipation African Americans must deal daily with its consequences." Well-known Harlem Renaissance theater scholar David Krasner also comments on Johnson's achievements in this realm, addressing her influence on the African American theater world. In his 2002 study *A Beautiful Pageant,* Krasner maintains that Johnson "made a compelling case for an indigenous black theatre and supplied empirical evidence that ordinary black people have values, conscience, and the skills to make these facts evident." Exploring Johnson's examination of gender inequities, Harris notes that one of the most important aspects of the author's oeuvre is a "focus on black women working,

MRS. G. D. JOHNSON

American poet Georgia Douglas Johnson, who also wrote a number of plays, including *Plumes.* SCHOMBURG CENTER, NYPL/ART RESOURCE, NY.

and seemingly entrapped, in domestic situations. But the circumstances under which the protagonists perform their labor, and the manner in which their work is portrayed, lifts domesticity beyond the trivial and reinvests it with significance."

The dominant trend in current studies of *Plumes* is feminist in nature. Scholars have found it essential to see Johnson's feminism in context—to understand her work within the constraints of the time period during which she lived and worked. In "Folk Plays, Home Girls, and Back Talk" (1995), Megan Sullivan discusses the voice *Plumes* has given to women of the early twentieth century in their attempt to respond to the male-dominated Harlem Renaissance. Tate specifies that Johnson "refused to subscribe to a patriarchal sexuality that designated women as male property." In our current cultural climate, *Plumes,* along with the broader body of work Johnson left behind, is studied less for what it depicts and concludes about race than for its unique example of strong, pro-feminine themes in an environment of masculine supremacy.

BIBLIOGRAPHY

Sources

Harris, Will. "Early Black Women Playwrights and the Dual Liberation Motif." *African American Review* 28.2 (1994): 205. *General OneFile.* Web. 13 July 2012.

Krasner, David. *A Beautiful Pageant: African American Theatre, Drama, and Performance in the Harlem Renaissance 1910–1927.* New York: Palgrave, 2002. *Google Books.* Web. 8 Aug. 2012.

Stephens, Judith L. "Art, Activism, and Uncompromising Attitude in Georgia Douglas Johnson's Lynching Plays." *African American Review* 39. 1–2 (2005): 87–102. Web. 25 Aug. 2012.

———. *The Plays of Georgia Douglas Johnson: From the New Negro Renaissance to the Civil Rights Movement.* Urbana: U of Illinois P, 2006. Print.

Sullivan, Megan. "Folk Plays, Home Girls, and Back Talk: Georgia Douglas Johnson and Women of the Harlem Renaissance." *CLA Journal* 38.4 (1995): 404–20. Print.

Tate, Claudia, ed. Introduction. *Selected Works of Georgia Douglas Johnson.* By Georgia Douglas Johnson. xvii–xxxvii. New York: Hall, 1997. Print.

Further Reading

Bower, Martha Gilman. *Color Struck under the Gaze: The Pathology of Being in the Plays of Johnson, Hurston, Childress, Hansberry, and Kennedy.* Westport: Greenwood Press, 2003. Print.

Brown-Guillory, Elizabeth, ed. *Wines in the Wilderness: Plays by African American Women from the Harlem Renaissance to the Present.* New York: Praeger, 1990. Print.

Gates, Henry Louis, Jr., ed. *Selected Works of Georgia Johnson.* New York: Hall, 1997. Print.

Henderson, Dorothy F. *Georgia Douglas Johnson: A Study of Her Life and Literature.* Diss. Florida State U, 1995. Ann Arbor: UMI, 2002. Print.

Perkins, Kathy A. *Strange Fruit: Plays on Lynching by American Women.* Bloomington: Indiana UP, 1998. Print.

Raynor, Sharon D. "The World of Female Knowing According to Georgia Douglas Johnson, Playwright." *CLA Journal* 45.2 (2001): 231–23. Print.

Shockley, Ann Allen. *Afro-American Women Writers 1746–1933: An Anthology and Critical Guide.* New Haven: Meridian, 1989. Print.

Stephens, Judith L. "*And Yet They Paused* and *A Bill to Be Passed*: Newly Recovered Lynching Dramas by Georgia Douglas Johnson." *African American Review* 33 (1999): 519–22. Print.

Tolson, Melvin B. *The Harlem Group of Negro Writers.* Westport: Greenwood Press, 2001. Print.

Wall, Cheryl A. *Women of the Harlem Renaissance.* Bloomington: Indiana UP, 1995. Print.

Colby Cuppernull

"Preamble to the Constitution of the IWW"

Thomas J. Hagerty

OVERVIEW

The "Preamble to the Constitution of the IWW," authored by Thomas J. Hagerty in June 1905, announces the formation of the International Workers of the World (IWW), a Chicago-based organization bent on dismantling capitalism by uniting individuals on the basis of their economic disadvantage and exploitation rather than by trade or political affiliation. The brief preamble is written in an emphatic voice and advances three key themes. The first is that no mutual interests exist between the working class and the employing class. The second is that existing trade unions have been slow to respond and are ineffective against the growing power of monopolistic, industrial capitalism. The third is that only through class solidarity and seizure of the means of production can the working class improve conditions. The preamble is designed to undermine the power of trade unions and electoral politics by positing industrial unions as the only viable solution to the problems of the working class.

Hagerty's preamble is one of his few works—and one of his last—but is his best known. It was quickly and enthusiastically embraced by the radical labor movement, and its adoption codified a militant stance against craft unionism and capitalism. The preamble has had a lasting influence on the IWW, whose members are known as Wobblies, and it is still included as part of the organization's principles. The preamble and its predecessor, "The Manifesto of the Industrial Workers of the World," hold symbolic resonance because they were produced in Chicago, the site of the Haymarket Affair of 1886, the Pullman Strike of 1894, and the fight for the eight-hour workday. The preamble laid the foundation for modern industrial unions and articulated the complexities faced by workers negotiating for competitive wages in an economy reliant upon mass production that required fewer and fewer skilled workers.

HISTORICAL AND LITERARY CONTEXT

In the 1880s the growth of class-consciousness and increasing affinity for the ideals espoused by anarchists and socialists were subdued by the shocking bombing at a labor rally in Chicago's Haymarket Square on May 4, 1886. The affair killed eleven, injured dozens, and led to the hasty executions of those allegedly responsible.

However, violent labor disputes, coupled with the rise of unskilled, mass production jobs that eroded union power and deflated wages, led to a re-emergence of class-consciousness in the early twentieth century. The demand for a labor movement that better served the interests of the working class also emanated from dissatisfaction with the extant labor organizations, especially the American Federation of Labor (AFL), which had displaced the earlier Knights of Labor and the Western Labor Union. Opponents criticized the AFL as an extension of the bourgeoisie, and many felt it had suppressed strikes too often or colluded with management against the interests of workers.

When Hagerty, William D. "Big Bill" Haywood, Eugene V. Debs, Daniel DeLeon, Lucy Parsons, and other supporters of the radical labor movement converged on Brand Hall in Chicago on June 27, 1905, for the Founding Convention of the IWW, the Russian Revolution of 1905 had already begun with a series of general strikes. The founders of the IWW saw themselves as part of a global labor movement, and the events in Russia marked the dawn of a new age in labor consciousness and tactics. Hagerty's preamble aimed to capitalize on this momentum and to convince the seventy delegates, representing approximately fifty thousand workers, to restructure their craft unions into industrial unions.

Organizations traditionally express their founding ethos with a preamble. The 1878 preamble to the constitution of the Knights of Labor argues that wealth is becoming increasingly concentrated and that intervention is necessary to ensure equitable distribution of income. It predicts the "pauperization" of the working class, which would fuel Hagerty's more militant preamble a quarter-century later. The Knights of Labor preamble aims to secure a larger portion of wealth for the working class by advocating for legislation placing stricter regulations on how workers would be compensated. It outlines fifteen aims, which include the creation of a Bureau of Labor statistics, equal pay based on gender, and an end to child labor for those under the age of fourteen. By contrast, the precursor to Hagerty's preamble, the "Manifesto of the Industrial Workers of the World," argues against seeking legislative reforms and instead advocates revolution. For Hagerty, any other course of action would be inadequate to confront the evolving power and reach of the capitalists.

⁜ Key Facts

Time Period:
Early 20th Century

Genre:
Manifesto

Events:
Haymarket bombing in Chicago; First Russian Revolution; increasingly violent and highly publicized labor disputes in the United States; spread of socialist ideology; founding convention of the IWW

Nationality:
American

THE MYSTERIOUS DEMISE OF THOMAS HAGERTY

Reverend friar Thomas J. Hagerty was an American Roman Catholic priest and founding member of the Industrial Workers of the World (IWW). His career as a union activist, public speaker, and author was short-lived, and almost nothing is known about his life prior to his completion of seminary training in 1895. As early as 1892, he began to reconcile Marxist theory with church doctrine, but his views brought him into conflict with the Catholic church. In 1902 he abruptly left his parish in New Mexico and became more deeply involved in the labor movement. He spoke before the joint convention of the Western Federation of Miners and Western Labor Union in Denver and spent time in mining camps with Eugene V. Debs recruiting miners for the American Labor Union.

Eventually his tenure with the Catholic church was terminated for espousing increasingly revolutionary views. In 1904 he became editor of the American Labor Union's monthly publication, *Voice of Labor.* Because of this position, he was invited to the January 1905 conference that led to the creation of the IWW that same summer. Shortly after appearing alongside Daniel DeLeon at an IWW membership meeting in Milwaukee in 1905, however, Hagerty inexplicably disappeared from the movement. He was rediscovered by IWW songwriter and poet Ralph Chaplin living under the name Ricardo Moreno in Chicago and working as a Spanish teacher and oculist. The exact date of his death and his activities after 1920 remain unknown, but his bombastic rhetoric that fueled the creation of the IWW still inspires radicals today.

The publication of Hagerty's aggressive and overtly Marxist preamble anticipated the growing influence of socialism in the United States in the period leading up to World War I. Although Hagerty disappeared from the radical movement after 1905, his literary legacy persisted. The novels *The 42nd Parallel* (1930) and *1919* (1932) by American writer John Dos Passos recount the emergence of the IWW and allude to Hagerty's ideas. The socialist magazine *Seven Arts* and the poems of socialist activist Arturo Giovannitti reflect the ordinary language and confrontational style used in the preamble. More recently, Hagerty's vision for a social movement founded on class solidarity can be heard in the cry of the Occupy Wall Street protestors who emerged in September 2011, "We are the ninety-nine percent."

THEMES AND STYLE

Central to Hagerty's preamble is the portrayal of wealth inequality as an unrelenting battle between the working class and the employing class. He contrasts the deplorable conditions faced by many workers with the privileged lives led by a few employers. The employing class has "all the good things in life" while "millions of working people" suffer from "hunger and want." The preamble continues its war metaphor by calling for solidarity in a class "struggle." Workers are told to "take possession of the earth and the machinery of production" and to end the wage system. Hagerty strategically deploys inflammatory rhetoric as a means to compel individuals to abandon entrenched trade unions for his emerging industrial union, the IWW.

Hagerty's preamble disputes prevailing ideology, arguing that workers and management have mutual interests in a system that can be gradually reformed. The text begins in the third person with the emphatic declaration that "the working class and the employing class have nothing in common." It later shifts to the first-person plural to explain how the current system of trade unions is "unable to cope" with changing arrangements of power. This shift to first person subtly implies agreement between the speaker and the audience. This implied agreement is a rhetorical move meant to convince trade union representatives to convert their organizational structures to that of industrial unions.

Stylistically, the preamble uses verbs that convey conflict and phrases that underscore the erosion of the power of the working class. Hagerty implies that workers are already at war, for "there can be no peace" until conditions are improved. Workers must "take," "abolish," "struggle," and overthrow the existing system as an "army of production." He argues that trade unions have misled workers into believing that they have shared interests with those in power. Consequently, power has become concentrated into "fewer and fewer hands" that control the "management of industries." Hagerty's radical language bears greater resemblance to the words of August Spies or Albert Parsons—the Chicago anarchists of the 1880s who were hanged following the Haymarket bombing—than the leaders of traditional labor unions. Spies anticipated Hagerty's language when he wrote, "machinery involves a great accumulation of power, and always a greater division of labor in consequence."

CRITICAL DISCUSSION

After the publication of the preamble, Hagerty disappeared from public view; however his text came to characterize the ethos of the IWW. In a 1912 article in the *Atlantic Monthly* about the successful IWW-backed textile strike in Lawrence, Massachusetts, Lorin F. Deland states that the "famous preamble … has been called a vicious document." John Martin, writing about the Lawrence Strike in *The Independent* in 1912, quotes the preamble to explain that the IWW "fight[s] only in an irreconcilable conflict between employer and workman." V. F. Calverton's *The Liberation of American Literature* (1932) echoes this sentiment, describing the IWW as a "menacing thorn" for many employers. Paul F. Brissenden in an essay published in *University of California Publications in Economics* (1918) explains that daily

A meeting of the IWW in support of a strike in 1914. © BETTMANN/ CORBIS.

newspapers mocked the IWW acronym by interpreting it variously as the "I Won't Works," the "I Want Whiskey Brigade," and "Irresponsible Wholesale Wreckers."

The preamble became Hagerty's lasting legacy. Robert Doherty, writing a 1962 article for *Labor History*, remarks that Hagerty's "role in the founding of the IWW is even more impressive when one considers the relatively short time he had spent in the labor and radical movement." A few years before the 1905 convention, Hagerty was a Roman Catholic priest in New Mexico. His harsh critique of trade unions and demand for workers to unify and seize the means of production anticipated the sit-down strike and other direct action tactics used in contemporary social movements. Paul Buhle in a 2005 article for *Monthly Review* agrees with this assessment, writing that the "Wobblies were not wrong to call for solidarity as labor's strength, and they espoused a revolutionary, emancipatory doctrine still unrealized today." The IWW's call for class solidarity and desire for societal transformation lives on in the Arab Spring and the Occupy Wall Street movement. The Arab Spring, for a time, unified individuals across a broad range of political and economic beliefs in the Middle East, ending the thirty-year administration of Egypt's Hosni Mubarak after eighteen days of public demonstrations. Similarly, the Occupy Wall Street movement brought together a diverse coalition to overtake public space.

Hagerty's writings, including the preamble, remain relatively unexamined, although the preamble is routinely mentioned in discussions about the founding convention of the IWW. Melvyn Dubofsky explores Hagerty's "Manifesto of Industrial Workers of the World" for its vexing contradictions and illuminates how it led to the publication of the preamble. Buhle investigates the role of the IWW as a vehicle of industrial socialism, explaining that "the Wobblies projected ... the rule of direct economic democracy *sans* the political state." Their future vision for society arose from another of Hagerty's key contributions, Hagerty's wheel, a framework for a new society with industrial unions at its core.

BIBLIOGRAPHY

Sources

Brissenden, Paul F. "The Launching of the Industrial Workers of the World." *University of California Publications in Economics.* Vol. 4. Ed. Carl C. Plehn. Berkeley: U of California P, 1918. Print.

Buhle, Paul. "The Legacy of the IWW." *Monthly Review* 57.2 (2005): 13–27. *Academic Search Premier.* Web. 29 Sept. 2012.

———. *Marxism in the USA.* London: Verso, 1987. Print.

Calverton, V. F. *The Liberation of American Literature.* New York: Scribner's, 1932. Print.

Deland, Lorin F. "The Lawrence Strike: A Study." *Atlantic Monthly* May 1912: 694–705. Web. 25 Oct. 2012.

Doherty, Robert E. "Thomas J. Hagerty, the Church, and Socialism." *Labor History* 3.1 (1962): 39–56. Web. 2 Oct. 2012.

Dubofsky, Melvyn. "The Origin of the IWW." *John Dos Passos's USA: A Documentary Volume.* Dictionary of Literary Biography 274. Detroit: Gale Group, 2003. Print.

Martin, John. "The Industrial Revolt at Lawrence." *Independent* March 1912: 491. Print.

Spies, August. "Address of August Spies." *The Accused, The Accusers: The Famous Speeches of the Eight Chicago Anarchists in Court When Asked If They Had Anything to Say Why Sentence Should Not Be Passed upon Them. On October 7th, 8th, and 9th, 1886, Chicago, Illinois.* Chicago: Socialistic Publishing Society, 1886. *Chicago Historical Society Haymarket Affair Digital Collection.* Web. 26 Oct. 2012.

Further Reading

Dubofsky, Melvyn. *We Shall Be All: A History of the Industrial Workers of the World.* Ed. Joseph A. McCartin. Chicago: U of Illinois P, 2000. Print.

Green, James R. *The World of the Worker: Labor in Twentieth-Century America.* Chicago: U of Illinois P, 1998. Print.

Kimeldorf, Howard. *Battling for American Labor: Wobblies, Craft Workers, and the Making of the Union Movement.* Berkeley: U of California P, 1999.

Lee, Frederic. *Radical Economics and Labor.* Ed. Frederic S. Lee and Jon Bekken. New York: Routledge, 2009. Print.

Proceedings of the First Convention of the Industrial Workers of the World. Ann Arbor: U of Michigan Library, 1905. Print.

Renshaw, Patrick. *The Wobblies: The Story of the IWW and Syndicalism in the United States.* Chicago: Dee, 1999. Print.

Thompson, Fred W., and Jon Bekken. *The Industrial Workers of the World: Its First One Hundred Years: 1905 through 2005.* Cincinnati: Industrial Workers of the World, 2006. Print.

Mark Casello

THE PURGATORY OF SUICIDES

Thomas Cooper

OVERVIEW

The Purgatory of Suicides (1846) by Thomas Cooper is an epic poem that takes up the cause of the Chartists, a group of working-class protesters active from 1838 to 1848 in pursuit of electoral and parliamentary reform. Starting with the basic conceit of a Dantean journey among the ghosts of suicides, the poem draws together the author's increasingly pessimistic commitment to Chartist ideals, his religious skepticism, and an aesthetic frequently characterized by critics as peculiarly "high-cultural" given his stated audience. The poet does considerably more than reiterate the values of the traditional epic, however; he also undercuts the epic idealization of a unified national history, reinterprets the past to show the injustice of contemporary class relations, and argues that the time has come for major political change.

By 1850 Cooper's epic was already a well-known text, though its far-flung allusions and somewhat abstruse vocabulary give every indication of having missed his ostensible working-class readership. For similar reasons, however, it served Chartist ends as a demonstration that literary aptitude (as characterized by the elite) was by no means a class-bound trait; newspapermen and pamphleteers frequently praised the poem as a success story, focusing on Cooper's humble beginnings as a shoemaker and his subsequent self-education. During the twentieth century and following, much criticism of *The Purgatory of Suicides* has centered on the interplay between its style and its politics, with some scholars arguing that the poem effectively "sells out" to middle-class expectations even as others defend the work for its knowing subversion of those expectations. This tension is a common theme in Chartist literature, and *The Purgatory of Suicides,* as a major representative poem, provides ample ground for exploring it. Penned in the course of a nearly three-year term in Stafford Gaol, *The Purgatory of Suicides* remains Cooper's most famous work.

HISTORICAL AND LITERARY CONTEXT

Cooper's opening injunction "Slaves, toil no more!" is a response to the frustrated efforts of the Chartists, who had sought by any means available to win greater political representation for the British working classes. The movement was officially inaugurated via a "People's Charter," published in 1838, demanding the establishment of elections by secret ballot and the extension of the franchise to all adult males. Moreover, the Chartists wished to remove impediments to working-class participation in Parliament. At the time, parliamentary seats were unpaid and available only to property holders, effectively blocking those of modest means from serving. The Chartists' plight was systematically ignored by the political elite, leading in 1842 to a general strike and, in some regions, violent protests.

It was in just such a protest—the Staffordshire Pottery Riots—that Cooper was implicated, leading to his imprisonment and thus to his composing *The Purgatory of Suicides.* As a Chartist leader, Cooper had encouraged the participants in the general strike, but he maintained that his speeches (partly reprinted as verse in *The Purgatory of Suicides*) had stopped short of countenancing violence or destruction of property. This claim notwithstanding, Cooper was imprisoned in Stafford Gaol from 1842 to 1845, for a term of thirty-five months. In the preface to his poem, Cooper credits his jail time with providing the impetus and occasion for his pessimistic epic. His term at Stafford also contributed to both a political and a spiritual disillusionment, and his desire not to repeat the experience may have motivated his partial retirement from politics. Chartism as a distinct movement was definitively quashed in 1848, when Parliament reacted to a mass meeting of reformers by banning public assemblies and enacting strict antisedition laws. The major goals of the People's Charter would be achieved at much greater length, with universal male suffrage not gained until 1918.

Cooper was conscious that a "Chartist rhymer" was unlikely to incur a great deal of sympathy among London literary critics. He drew upon numerous canonical works in setting the style and themes of his epic. *The Purgatory of Suicides* displays an obvious formal debt to Edmund Spenser, borrowing the Elizabethan poet's famed nine-line stanza and the archaizing practice of using medieval "Spenserian" words. Echoes of Dante's *Inferno* are evident as well, especially in the poem's ambivalent attitude toward the suicides. Critics have also seen the imprint of John Milton's *Paradise Lost,* which the poet had partly committed to memory, in what Stephanie Kuduk calls Cooper's "political reformulation of British history."

⁜ *Key Facts*

Time Period:
Mid-19th Century

Genre:
Poetry

Events:
Growth of Chartism; the Staffordshire Pottery Riots

Nationality:
English

THE STRIKE AND RIOTS OF 1842

The general strike and subsequent Pottery Riots of 1842 were among the most notable mass actions to be associated with the Chartist movement. The term Pottery Riots is associated with a region of Staffordshire known as the Potteries for its historical concentration of that trade, but the riots are now believed to have begun, as did the strikes before them, in the coal-mining industry. In the summer of 1842, responding to what would later be termed the Six Year Depression (1837–1843), mine owners began issuing drastic (and sometimes illegally sudden) pay cuts. When the colliers refused the new terms, they were often locked out, leading to a stalemate between labor and capital. This conflict spread to become a general strike, paralyzing the coal industry throughout the English Midlands and, by summer's end, halting regional pottery production as well. Allegations of police abuse led to vandalism, first in the village of Burslem and then in the neighboring town of Stoke, engulfing police stations and private residences alike. Cooper, as one of the organizers of the strike, was on scene when a similar riot erupted in Hanley on August 15. Mere hours before the arrival of the cavalry, he delivered the "seditious and conspiratorial" opening line of *The Purgatory of Suicides*: "Slaves, toil no more!"

While Cooper's commitment to the working-class cause would continue in one form or another until his death in 1892, *The Purgatory of Suicides* marked an extended foray into a more literary and less overtly political mode for the poet. The poem is itself formally conservative, with few strong stylistic markers whose influence might readily be detected in a successor work. Without question, however, *The Purgatory of Suicides* contributed to a greater awareness of working-class literature in the late nineteenth century, having made an elegant case for workingmen as participants in a national literary culture.

THEMES AND STYLE

The Purgatory of Suicides is an extended poetic argument that all history takes the form of a human striving for liberty and that Chartism is the necessary and worthy culmination of this trend. In relating this contemporary problem to similar struggles in classical Greece, biblical Egypt, and a host of other times and places, Cooper builds the case that the freedoms demanded by the British laborers are universal human rights, not concessions to be made at the whim of the ruling class. The poem also takes up the relationship between the "tyranny" of organized religion and the enforcement of class relations, expressing skepticism at the direction that Christianity in particular has taken. When the poem was written, Cooper was a nonbeliever in the Christianity then practiced by the majority of his British contemporaries. He was also skeptical of the avowed social and spiritual aims of institutional Christianity, which he saw as an instrument of oppression for the working classes he represented. In *The Purgatory of Suicides*, Cooper denounces institutional Christianity as a "monster faith." The suicides of the poem's title serve both as a demonstration of the desperate measures to which oppressed peoples have been driven and as a warning against succumbing to despair.

Cooper cites an otherworldly vision as the immediate cause for his poem, claiming that his writing follows from a sojourn among the ghosts of those who took their own lives. Before launching into this mythological mode, however, Cooper introduces the poem's main concern by calling for the modern-day "slaves" of England's mines and factories to "toil no more" and, somewhat more controversially, for them to "go forth, and tame the proud!" Cooper's focus on suicide and the futility of life seems at first to be at odds with his political message, but as the narrator converses with shades from the various empires of the past, he sees the historical excuses given for tyranny confronted and refuted. In an exchange typical of the early books of the poem, a deceased Chinese emperor avers that "faith and fear, fable and prodigy" are needful to maintain order among the common people; to this declaration a spectral Mark Antony replies (with characteristic emotion) that those who are "sunk in the stagnancies of custom old" are little better than cowardly dogs.

In the preface, Cooper sets himself the stylistic task of balancing popular appeal and literary ornamentation, but the work systematically favors the latter. A desire for a broad readership does not prevent Cooper from using a broad range of mythical allusions and "fine old words" derived from biblical, Homeric, and Elizabethan sources. Moreover, those literary references that Cooper sees fit to gloss in the second edition are approached with the assumption that names such as Sardanapalus and Appius Claudius will be "familiar to the most unclassic reader." The result is a text that is largely inaccessible to working-class men and difficult even for those of the middle class, much like other such reformist writings that failed to appreciate the skills and tastes of their potential audiences.

CRITICAL DISCUSSION

The first edition of *The Purgatory of Suicides* was evidently somewhat slow to sell. Cooper prefaced the 1847 second edition with an equivocal appeal to "my own order, the Working-Class" and attempted to lower the price of the reissued volume, which he dubbed the "People's Edition." Gregory Vargo explains that in the years following this new edition, Cooper's work "made [him] a minor celebrity in the world of middle-class literary reformers," and in 1860 the pamphleteer W. Ormond conferred upon the poem "lasting and imperishable fame." Quite apart from the poem's contentious status as Chartist propaganda, Cooper's passage on the psychological horrors inflicted by

"Plug Plot Riot in Preston," illustration, 1842. Chartist leaders such as Thomas Cooper led labor strikes across England that year; he was imprisoned for his role in the strikes and wrote *The Purgatory of Suicides* while in prison. "PLUG PLOT RIOT IN PRESTON," ILLUSTRATION FROM 'THE ILLUSTRATED LONDON NEWS,' AUGUST 1842 (ENGRAVING), ENGLISH SCHOOL, (19TH CENTURY)/ PRIVATE COLLECTION/THE BRIDGEMAN ART LIBRARY.

religion—especially a belief in hell—was widely cited in the religious debates of the mid-nineteenth century. In 1858 the pamphleteer George Lucas accused Cooper of "blundering theology" for *Purgatory*'s attack on "monstrous thing[s] derived from an old monster faith," while George Sexton, writing as "Melampus" in 1863, took the opposite side of the debate, suggesting that the same skeptical "words" would "remain true to all time."

Critics have frequently observed in *The Purgatory of Suicides* a reflection of a class tension generally inherent in Chartist literature, which represented working people but was often aimed, via its style and body of cultural references, at a middle-class readership. Sally Ledger, in a 2002 study, cites the epic as "the most extreme example of the high-cultural, anti-populist trend within Chartist poetry." Moreover, as Vargo notes, the erudition in *The Purgatory of Suicides* may have been partly counterproductive: when wealthier readers upheld Cooper's self-help as an alternative to political agitation, the "hard-won classical education so proudly on display" may in fact have obscured the plight of the many cobblers, potters, and farriers who could never hope to achieve literary fame.

Literary scholars have also maintained that Cooper's "high-cultural" poetics proved useful, if not vital, to his political goals. Mike Sanders, in a 2006 essay, asserts that Cooper chose his style partly to make a point to upper- and middle-class readers; like other Chartist poets, he "argued that the capacity of the working classes both to recognize and produce good poetry demonstrated their fitness for the franchise." Kuduk suggests that even seemingly "highbrow" elements of the work are frequently subverted or reinterpreted, as when the poet "appropriates" the Spenserian stanza (and the epic form in general) "to criticize those

same institutions" that epics customarily celebrate. In Kuduk's view, Cooper succeeds in "continually connecting the immediate political concerns and realities of his day to philosophical and historical insights."

BIBLIOGRAPHY

Sources

Kuduk, Stephanie. "Sedition, Chartism, and Epic Poetry in Thomas Cooper's *The Purgatory of Suicides*." *Victorian Poetry* 39.2 (2001): 164–87. *Project MUSE*. Johns Hopkins University. Web. 8 Aug. 2012.

Ledger, Sally. "Chartist Aesthetics in the Mid Nineteenth Century: Ernest Jones, a Novelist of the People." *Nineteenth-Century Literature* 57.1 (2002): 31–63. *JSTOR*. Web. 8 Aug. 2012.

Lucas, George. *"Blundering Theology": Plain Words Addressed to Mr. Thomas Cooper, with Notes and Comments on His Recent Lectures and Sermons, Delivered in Newcastle, July 12th to July 18th, 1858.* Gateshead: R. Jackson, 1858. *Cowen Tracts. JSTOR.* Web. 8 Aug. 2012.

Ormond, W. *Inceptions: Fragments.* Bristol: J. B. Taylor, 1860. *Bristol Selected Pamphlets. JSTOR.* Web. 8 Aug. 2012.

Sanders, Mike. "'A Jackass Load of Poetry': *The Northern Star*'s Poetry Column 1838–1852." *Victorian Periodicals Review* 39.1 (2006): 46–66. *Project MUSE*. Johns Hopkins University. Web. 8 Aug. 2012.

Sexton, George. *The Doctrine of Eternal Torment Refuted.* London: George Abington, 1863. *Bristol Selected Pamphlets. JSTOR.* Web. 8 Aug. 2012.

Vargo, Gregory. "A Life in Fragments: Thomas Cooper's Chartist Bildungsroman." *Victorian Literature and Culture* 39.1 (2011): 167–81. Print.

Further Reading

Armstrong, Isobel. *Victorian Poetry: Poetry, Poetics, and Politics.* New York: Routledge, 1993. Print.

Boos, Florence S. "The Poetics of the Working Classes." *Victorian Poetry* 39.2 (2001): 103–10. *Project MUSE.* Johns Hopkins University. Web. 8 Aug. 2012.

Gilbert, Pamela K. "History and Its Ends in Chartist Epic." *Victorian Literature and Culture* 37.1 (2009): 27–42. Print.

Maidment, Brian. *The Poorhouse Fugitives: Self-taught Poets and Poetry in Victorian Britain.* Manchester: Carcanet, 1987. Print.

Scheckner, Peter, ed. *An Anthology of Chartist Poetry: Poetry of the British Working Class, 1830s–1850s.* London: Associated UP, 1989. Print.

Vicinus, Martha. *The Industrial Muse: A Study of Nineteenth-Century British Working-Class Literature.* New York: Barnes and Noble, 1974. Print.

Weiner, Stephanie Kuduk. *Republican Politics and English Poetry, 1789–1874.* New York: Palgrave Macmillan, 2005. Print.

Michael Hartwell

THE RAGGED-TROUSERED PHILANTHROPISTS

Robert Tressell

OVERVIEW

The Ragged-Trousered Philanthropists (1914), originally subtitled "Being the Story of Twelve Months in Hell, Told by One of the Damned, and Written Down by Robert Tressell," is an English novel bemoaning the lack of political awareness among the impoverished—and often unemployed—working classes of the early twentieth century. Writing under the penname Tressell, Robert Noonan (born Robert Croker), an Irishman who spent twelve years in South Africa and alternately experienced relative wealth and poverty in his own life, died penniless, his novel still unpublished. Although epic in scope, the story focuses on a group of house-painters who argue about the causes of poverty, which they believe is self-inflicted. To their astonishment and outrage, their new coworker Frank Owen assures them that the culprit is money. Owen, whom Tressell styles as a prophet, proceeds to demonstrate how the capitalist system, aided by government and religious authorities, allows the rich to exploit powerless and complicit workers, basically presenting Karl Marx's theory of economics and the concept of a socialist society, or "co-operative commonwealth," as the cure.

At the time of the novel's appearance, increasingly discontented workers and progressives were challenging the strict social class system of the Edwardian era. Severely edited to remove its radical politics, the work was published in 1914 in North America and England for liberal middle-class audiences and again in 1918 in a cheap version for working-class readers. After reaching the Soviet Union in 1920 and Germany in 1925, it was reissued in England in 1941 and published in its entirety in 1955. The novel was successful on each new appearance, with sales only suffering during the patriotic fervor of World War I. Before and after the war, the trade union movement and liberal reformers adopted the book as a sort of bible. Decades later, a World War II-era British audience, consisting largely of those in the military, turned toward the Labour Party, which won landslide victories in 1945 and even elected two communists to Parliament. Many scholars and historians count *The Ragged-Trousered Philanthropists* as a major influence on the election results.

HISTORICAL AND LITERARY CONTEXT

The second phase of the Industrial Revolution, which lasted roughly from the 1860s through the

Edwardian era (1900–1910), brought mechanization, mass production, and an increased insistence on efficiency to factory workers and laborers. It also brought the opportunity for wealth to the business and middle classes, the consolidation of financial power among the small number of wealthy citizens, a laissez-faire attitude to government, and a widening of the gap between the rich and the working class. The rigid social structure gave way to the prospect of upward mobility, creating a new dream for the vast majority of the populace in Britain and its colonies, countries rich in resources where native peoples and poor immigrant whites vied for scarce means. Most labored in substandard working conditions, were treated and even abused as inferiors, and lived in poverty. Many supported capitalism and believed themselves to be both lucky and undeserving.

The Ragged-Trousered Philanthropists sprang from both the experience of continued industrialization and the increased activism of the Progressive Era, which beginning in the 1890s saw workers and liberals from other classes organizing for reform. Recognizing that the innovations in industry had done nothing to improve the lives of the laboring masses—and, in fact, had exacerbated their problems—the progressives demanded the passage of laws regulating industry and guaranteeing workers' rights. Socialism gained ground during this time, and the Labour Party, founded in 1900, began to accrue influence. As a painter, decorator, and budding socialist in South Africa, Tressell achieved some political influence, serving as a trades council secretary and helping found Irish brigades to fight against British imperialism in the Boer War of 1899 to 1902. After returning to England, he joined the Social Democratic Federation (SDF), Britain's first Marxist socialist party, in 1906.

Partly because people who worked for a living were assumed to be inherently less interesting, few novelists portrayed working-class characters before the twentieth century. The main exception was Charles Dickens, who had grown up in poverty. Writing from about 1837 to 1870, during and after the first stage of the Industrial Revolution, Dickens focused on the injustices the poor faced on a daily basis. Reassessing *The Ragged-Trousered*

Key Facts

Time Period:
Early 20th Century

Genre:
Novel

Events:
Rise of Marxism; Second Industrial Revolution; growth of the Labour Party

Nationality:
English

PRIMARY SOURCE

EXCERPT FROM *THE RAGGED-TROUSERED PHILANTHROPISTS*

"Money is the real cause of poverty," said Owen. ...

Owen opened his dinner basket and took from it two slices of bread, but as these were not sufficient, he requested that anyone who had some bread left would give it to him. They gave him several pieces, which he placed in a heap on a clean piece of paper, and having borrowed the pocket knives they used to cut and eat their dinners with from Easton, Harlow, and Philpot, he addressed them as follows:

"These pieces of bread represent the raw materials which exist naturally in and on the earth for the use of mankind; they were not made by any human being, but were created by the Great Spirit for the benefit and sustenance of all, the same as were the air and the light of the sun." ...

"Now," continued Owen, "I am a capitalist; or rather, I represent the landlord and capitalist class. That is to say, all these raw materials belong to me. It does not matter for our present argument how I obtained possession of them, or whether I have any real right to them; the only thing that matters now is the admitted fact that all the raw materials which are necessary for the production of the necessaries of life are now the property of the Landlord and Capitalist class. I am that class: all these raw materials belong to me."

"Good enough!" agreed Philpot.

"Now you three represent the Working Class: you have nothing—and for my part, although I have all these raw materials, they are of no use to me—what I need is—the things that can be made out of these raw materials by Work: but as I am too lazy to work myself, I have invented the Money Trick to make you work *for* me. But first I must explain that I possess something else besides the raw materials. These three knives represent—all the machinery for production; the factories, tools, railways, and so forth, without which the necessaries of life cannot be produced in abundance. And these three coins"—taking three halfpennies from his pocket—"represent my Money Capital." ...

Owen proceeded to cut up one of the slices of bread into a number of little square blocks.

Philanthropists in London's *The Guardian* in 2011, Howard Brenton comments, "vivid scenes among the bosses on the town council read like a berserk Dickens." The economic situation in early twentieth-century Britain, seeming no better, led to a number of writers to advocate socialism. Tressell undoubtedly read Friedrich Engels's *The Condition of the Working Class in England* (published in English in 1887), which documents the horrific conditions in the slums and the overwork and impoverishment of the workers, particularly children.

On the cutting edge of socialism in its time, Tressell's novel is considered seminal in documenting and promoting the birth of a working-class consciousness and is credited with converting thousands to socialist doctrines. George Orwell, a famous fan of the novel, cited it as a key influence on his autobiographical *Down and Out in Paris and London* (1933). While *The Ragged-Trousered Philanthropists* is not commonly read today as a work of literature, it is still taught in the context of political writing and has inspired many live productions, including television (1967) and radio (2008, 2009, and 2010) adaptations by the BBC and stage plays, the first premiering in 1978, with revivals touring throughout the 1980s and 1990s and as recently as 2012. Trade unions and socialist and Marxist groups continue to promote the book and its vision.

THEMES AND STYLE

Despite targeting business owners as greedy, unprincipled, and corrupt, Christians as hypocritical, and the capitalist system as innately unjust, the thematic focus of the novel is the "ragged-trousered philanthropist," who gives his work away for nothing. Ignorant and stunted in their potential, the workers allow their "betters" to dictate their thoughts and actions and assume they deserve no more than they are getting, which is nothing, once the system takes their paltry wages back in exchange for minimal food and shelter. A character named Crass insists that "ther's plenty of 'em wot's too lazy to work" and that education "jus' puts foolish ideas into people's 'eds." Owen, the novel's socialist hero, rails against the downtrodden, who "go about gasping for breath, and telling each other that the likes of them could not expect to have air to breathe unless they had the money to pay for it." Their respect for the bosses' rules is greater than their loyalty to each other. If a worker commits an infraction, Owen says, his fellows "all fall upon him in the name of law and order, and after doing your best to tear him limb from limb, you'll drag him, covered with blood, in triumph to the nearest Police Station and deliver him up to 'justice.'"

"These represent the things which are produced by labour, aided by machinery, from the raw materials. We will suppose that three of these blocks represent—a week's work. We will suppose that a week's work is worth—one pound: and we will suppose that each of these ha'pennies is a sovereign." …

Owens now addressed himself to the working classes as represented by Philpot, Harlow and Easton.

"You say that you are all in need of employment, and as I am the kind-hearted capitalist class I am going to invest all my money in various industries, so as to give you Plenty of Work. I shall pay each of you one pound per week, and a week's work is—you must each produce three of these square blocks. For doing this work you will each receive your wages; the money will be your own, to do as you like with, and the things you produce of course will be mine, to do as I like with. You will each take one of these machines and as soon as you have done a week's work, you shall have your money."

The Working Classes accordingly set to work, and the Capitalist class sat down and watched them.

as soon as they had finished, they passed the nine little blocks to Owen, who placed them on a piece of paper by his side and paid the workers their wages.

"These blocks represent the necessaries of life. You can't live without some of these things, but as they belong to me, you will have to buy them from me: my price for these blocks is—one pound each."

As the working classes were in need of the necessaries of life and as they could not eat, drink or wear the useless money, they were compelled to agree to the Capitalist's terms. They each bought back and at once consumed one-third of the produce of their labour. The capitalist class also devoured two of the square blocks, and so the net result of the week's work was that the kind capitalist…had more than doubled his capital…As for the working classes, Philpot, Harlow and Easton, having each consumed the pound's worth of necessaries they had bought with their wages, they were again in precisely the same condition as when they started work—they had nothing.

Dialogue and monologue, or lecture, appear plentifully in the novel as rhetorical strategies. Tressell uses argument and persuasion to communicate Owen's points to his disbelieving and often derisive compatriots. It is most often the narrator who reports Owen's frustrations and reveals his scathing criticisms and bitterness. This technique allows the novelist to address and involve the reader without maligning Owen in front of the other characters. Tressell also uses a variety of approaches to render his didactic intentions readable. Owen delivers a particularly vivid and now-famous hands-on demonstration of the workings of capitalist economics that Tressell names "The Great Money Trick." Temporarily recruiting his skeptical coworkers to the cause, Owen has the men cut pieces of bread into three parts. Each must give two parts to his employer, keeping one for himself. Then, he must pay the one he has kept for basic necessities, leaving him exactly where he started, while the bosses end up with a huge surplus.

The Ragged-Trousered Philanthropists is by turns highly comic, tragic, naturalistic, and even farcical, attributing outrageous opinions to Owen's colleagues in colloquial language. The overall tone is charged with discontent and sometimes desperation, emphasizing the precarious circumstances of the characters. Alluding

to his own desperate attempts to avoid the workhouse and provide for his daughter, Tressell writes, "As Owen thought of his child's future, there sprang up within him a feeling of hatred and fury against his fellow workmen … who, having lived in poverty all their lives, considered that what had been good enough for them was good enough for their children." His pessimistic assessment of the workers ("They were the enemy … No wonder the rich despised them and looked upon them as dirt") did not impede the book's great success.

CRITICAL DISCUSSION

In the author's preface, included in the 1955 edition and those that followed, Tressell writes, "My main object was to write a story full of human interest and based on the happenings of everyday life … There are no scenes in the story that I have not either witnessed myself or had conclusive evidence of … Because it is true it will probably be denounced as a libel." Dave Harker, writing for *TUC History Online* in 2003, quotes Thomas Richards, the book's original publisher, as calling the book "damnably subversive" and "extraordinarily real." Reaction to the novel's first printing was remarkably positive, given its mainly middle- and upper-class readership; the later edition, aimed at the British working class, received a passionate response.

ROBERT TRESSELL: PERPETUAL OUTSIDER

Robert Tressell (1870–1911) was illegitimate, Irish, and a tradesman, all of which counted against his chances for social and material success. Born in Dublin, he searched for a financially stable and politically honorable life in Cape Town and Johannesburg, South Africa, and in Hastings, England, before deciding to emigrate to Canada. Tressell was already well educated and multilingual when he changed his name and left home at sixteen, repulsed by the fact that his family's money came from absentee landlordism, a common practice that drained the income from rural areas to the wealthy in the cities. In South Africa he left his marriage because his wife was unfaithful, and he took his daughter Kathleen with him. His work in the building trades eventually brought him a measure of financial stability, but upon returning to Britain, he was barely able to make ends meet, even working extra jobs.

His constant worry about financial ruin and about being unable to support Kathleen caused his political commitment to waver at times. When he contracted tuberculosis and could no longer work or actively pursue politics, he turned to writing. After his book was rejected by several publishers, he tried to burn it, but Kathleen saved it and was later able to get it published. She eventually carried out his dream of emigrating to Canada after Tressell died in Liverpool at the age of forty-one and was buried in a mass grave with other paupers.

By 1954 the book had gone through twenty-two printings in its severely abridged form. The unabridged 1955 version has appeared in more than sixty new editions and reprintings. The slaughter that occurred in World War I and the October 1917 Russian Revolution brought the book an even more fervent audience. All told, *The Ragged-Trousered Philanthropists* has easily sold more than one million copies.

After communism failed to achieve its goals in the Soviet Union, socialists and other progressives continued to promote reforms avidly, convincing countries across Europe to establish universal education, health care, and social welfare. In fact, the 1955 complete edition of *The Ragged-Trousered Philanthropists* was produced by a Communist Party publisher. For a while, Tressell's ideas came to be seen as less drastic and treacherous. Harker wrote in 2003 that the book's "socialist ideas remain very relevant to those of us prepared to put them into practice in these increasingly anti-capitalist and anti-imperialist times." Although the novel's main popularity has been with ordinary readers, academics have often analyzed it. Some dismiss the novel on the grounds that it reads as a rant or a screed rather than as a well-crafted work of fiction, but most admire the strength of the story and its persistence as somewhat of an underground classic, able to draw in a still-vibrant readership.

Recent scholarship views the novel mainly through the lens of British imperialism. Although the topic does not appear explicitly in the story—aside from the workers' support of protectionist policies against foreign laborers—critics assert that Owen champions anticolonialist attitudes. Jonathan Hyslop's 2001 article for *History Workshop Journal* argues that since the majority of Tressell's working life was spent in South Africa, he was eminently able to portray English working conditions "with a starkness that would not have been possible from inside British society." Tressell's personal heritage is critical to modern readings of the work. In a 2002 essay for *Journal of Commonwealth Literature,* scholar Julie Cairnie writes, "[P]lacing emphasis on class *and* colonialism modifies Tressell's life story and challenges conventional readings of his text." She concludes that the work "reveals the entanglement of domestic and imperial politics, the troubled relationship between England and South Africa, and draws an implicit analogy between the British working class and the South African poor whites."

BIBLIOGRAPHY

Sources

Brenton, Howard. "Rereading: Howard Brenton on *The Ragged Trousered Philanthropists* by Robert Tressell." *London Guardian.* Guardian News and Media, 4 Feb. 2011. Web. 21 Sept. 2012.

Cairnie, Julie. "Imperial Poverty in Robert Tressell's *The Ragged-Trousered Philanthropists.*" *Journal of Commonwealth Literature* 37.2 (2002): 175–94. *JSTOR.* Web. 27 July 2012.

Harker, Dave. Rev. of *The Ragged-Trousered Philanthropists,* by Robert Tressell. *TUC History Online.* Trades Union Congress, 29 May 2003. Web. 27 July 2012.

Hyslop, Jonathan. "A Ragged Trousered Philanthropist and the Empire: Robert Tressell in South Africa." *History Workshop Journal* 51 (2001): 64–86. *JSTOR.* Web. 27 July 2012.

McSmith, Andy. "Robert Tressell: Return of the Working-Class Heroes." *London Independent.* The Independent, 22 June 2010. Web. 21 Sept. 2012.

Tressell, Robert. *The Ragged-Trousered Philanthropists.* Boston: Indy, 2012. Print.

Further Reading

Ball, F. C. *One of the Damned: Life and Times of Robert Tressell.* London: Weidenfeld, 1973. Print.

Cairnie, Julie, and Marion Wells, eds. *Revisiting Robert Tressell's Mugsborough: New Perspectives on* The Ragged-Trousered Philanthropists. London: Cambria, 1998. Print.

Harker, Dave. *Tressell: The Real Story of* The Ragged-Trousered Philanthropists. London: Zed, 2003. Print.

Kirk, John. *Twentieth-Century Writing and the British Working Class.* Cardiff: U of Wales P, 2003. Print.

Mitchell, Jack. *Robert Tressell and* The Ragged Trousered Philanthropists. London: Lawrence, 1969. Print.

Smith, David. *Socialist Propaganda in the Twentieth-Century British Novel.* New York: MacMillan, 1978. Print.

Media Adaptations

The Ragged-Trousered Philanthropists. Dir. Christopher Morahan. Perf. Kenneth Benda, Christopher Benjamin, and Janne Blair-Stewart. British Broadcasting Corporation (BBC), 1967. TV Movie

The Ragged-Trousered Philanthropists. Dir. Julian Webber. Cast Ray Collins, Steve Hofvendahl, Ellen Mareneck et al. New York, 1986. VHS.

Colby Cuppernull

SUBJECT INDEX

Bold volume and page numbers (e.g., **3:269–272**) refer to the main entry on the subject. Page numbers in italics refer to photographs and illustrations.

C

I

J

K

women's rights, **2:**39

Zong massacre, **1:**37, 38

See also Abolitionist movement;
Civil War (America, 1861–1864)

Slavery in Massachusetts (Thoreau),
2:124

Slaves

freed, **2:**250–252, *252*

freed children of, **1:**3

fugitive, **1:**3, **3:**169–172

narratives, **2:**53

relocation to Africa, **1:**6, **2:**85–87,
92, 93, 94, **3:**288

Slavic Review (journal), **3:**308

Sleep teaching (Hypnopedia), **3:**7

Slonim, Mark, **2:**264

Slovic, Scott, **1:**286

Slovo, Gillian, **2:**47

Slow Violence (Nixon), **2:**103

SLP (Socialist Labor Party), **3:**112

Slums, **1:**105–108, *107,* **2:**326–328,
328

See also Poverty

Small, Helen, **1:**136

A Small Place (Kincaid), **1:**74, 75

Small Soviet Encyclopedia, **3:**347

The Smell of It (Ibrahim), **3:**321

Smith, Adam, **1:**67, **2:**234–236, *236*

Smith, Allen, **1:**289

Smith, Brian, **3:**78

Smith, Gerrit, **1:**3

Smith, John Raphael, **1:** *39*

Smith, Joseph F., **3:**352

Smith, K. E., **3:**155

Smith, Michael B., **1:**139

Smith, Stan, **2:**287

Smith, T. V., **1:**353

Smithsonian (magazine), **3:**354–355

Smoke Signals (film), **2:**32, 34

Smoking, **3:**49–52, *51*

Smuts, Jan, **2:**17

SNCC (Student Nonviolent
Coordinating Committee), **1:**49

Snow (Pamuk), **1:**245–246

Snyder, Gary, **1:**242

So, Richard Jean, **2:**279

So Do: Tac pham va du luan (Do),
2:311

Sobrino, Jon, **3:**256

Socarrás, Carlos Prío, **1:**232

*The Social Construction of American
Realism* (Kaplan), **2:**322

Social contract, **2:**302

Social controls, **3:**7–10

*Social Darwinism in American Thought,
1860–1915* (Hofstadter), **1:**334

Social ecology, **3:**76–78, *78*

Social psychology, **3:**77

Social realism

The Factory Ship (Kobayashi),
2:313–316, *315*

A Hazard of New Fortunes
(Howells), **2:**320–322

Pale Fire (Nabokov), **1:**177–180,
179

Red Crag (Lo and Yang),
3:350–351

Socialism

Atlas Shrugged (Rand), **3:**268

vs. capitalism, **2:**320

Ender's Game (Card), **3:**79

The Iron Heel (London), **3:**112–114,
114

The Jungle (Sinclair), **1:**127–130, *127*

Looking Backward (Bellamy),
3:115–119, *117*

market economics, **3:**86

News from Nowhere (Morris),
3:120–122, *122*

Orwell, George, **2:**242, **3:**79, 123

"Preamble to the Constitution of
the IWW" (Hagerty), **2:**358

The Public and Its Problems
(Dewey), **1:**351, 352

*Seven Interpretative Essays on
Peruvian Reality* (Mariátegui),
2:281–284, *283*

Shaw, George Bernard, **3:**54

The State and Revolution (Lenin),
3:306–309, *308*

Utopia (More), **3:**135

The Socialist Dogma (El dogma socialista)
(Echevarría), **2:**254, 255

Socialist Labor Party (SLP), **3:**112

Socialist Party of America, **1:**127, 129

Socialist Party of Peru, **2:**281

Socialist realism, **3:**137

Socialist Standard (journal), **3:**113

Socialist Voice (newspaper), **3:**112

Society for Effecting the Abolition of
the Slave Trade, **1:**37, 38

Society for Individual Rights, **1:**20

Society for Promoting Christian
Knowledge (SPCK), **1:**314–316, *316*

Society for the Diffusion of Useful
Knowledge, **3:**163

Society of Friends. *See* Quakers

The Society of the Spectacle (Debord),
3:73

*Sociology for the South; or the Failure of
Free Society* (Fitzhugh), **3:**289

Socrates, **1:**232

Soderlund, Gretchen, **1:**357

Soft science fiction, **3:**70

*Sol Plaatje: South African Nationalist
1876–1932* (Willan), **1:**254

The Soldier (Brooke), **1:**23, **3:**228

Soldiers, unknown, **1:**198

Soldiers of the Queen (Stuart), **2:**227

Solidarity, **1:**50

Somalia, **2:**292–295, *293*

*Some European Thinkers: Hitler as
Thinker* (Lerner), **2:**196

*Some Questions about the Guerrillas in
Brazil* (Marighella), **1:**282

Somersett's Case (1772), **1:**37

Somme, Battle of, **2:**266–269, *268*

Sommerstein, Alan, **2:**110

Somoza Debayle, Anastasio, **2:**98

Somoza García, Anastasio, **1:**117, **2:**98

*Sonallah Ibrahim and the (Hi)story of the
Book* (Mehrez), **3:**323

Song, Choan-Seng, **3:**211, 212

Song of Protest (Cien sonetos de amor)
(Neruda), **1:**116–118

Song of Roland (Chanson de Roland),
2:214–216, *216*

Song of the Stormy Petrel (Gorky),
2:343

Songs

"Battle Hymn of the Republic"
(Howe), **2:**137–139, *139*

"We'll Meet Again," **3:**57–59, *59*

World War I, **3:**229

Songs of Experience (Blake), **3:**153–155,
155

W

AUTHOR INDEX

The author index includes author names represented in *The Literature of Propaganda*.
Numbers in **Bold** indicate volume, with page numbers following after colons.

A

Abbey, Edward, **1**: 285

Achebe, Chinua, **1**: 88

Adorno, Theodor W., **1**: 310

Agee, James, **1**: 169

Agee, Philip, **1**: 119

al-Daif, Rashid, **3**: 356

Alexie, Sherman, **2**: 32

al-Khamissi, Khaled, **2**: 66

Ambedkar, Bhimrao Ramji, **3**: 149

Anouilh, Jean, **3**: 193

Aristophanes, **2**: 108

Aristotle, **1**: 359

Arthur, T. S., **1**: 84

Asimov, Isaac, **3**: 105

Assange, Julian, **1**: 144

Atwood, Margaret, **3**: 93

Auden, W. H., **2**: 285

B

Babel, Isaac, **3**: 346

Baker, Ray Stannard, **1**: 109

Baldwin, James, **3**: 282

Baldwin, William, **2**: 243

Bale, John, **3**: 225

Barbauld, Anna Laetitia, **3**: 278

Barthes, Roland, **1**: 327

Baudrillard, Jean, **1**: 317

Baum, Lyman Frank, **3**: 179

Beard, Charles Austin, **1**: 213

Beinhart, Larry, **3**: 3

Bellamy, Edward, **3**: 115

Benedict, Ruth, **2**: 155

Bernays, Edward, **1**: 344

Biko, Steve, **2**: 105

Blake, William, **3**: 153

Boisrond-Tonnerre, Louis Félix, **1**: 30

Bolívar, Simón, **2**: 152

Bourke-White, Margaret, **1**: 165

Bradbury, Ray, **3**: 329

Bray, Thomas, **1**: 314

Brecht, Bertolt, **2**: 346

Brooke, Rupert, **3**: 228

Brown, Dee, **1**: 207

Browning, Elizabeth Barrett, **3**: 156

Buckley, Christopher, **3**: 49

Bunyan, John, **1**: 77

Burdekin, Katharine, **3**: 130

Burke, Edmund, **2**: 273

Butler, Samuel, **3**: 83

C

Cabezas, Omar., **2**: 98

Cabral, Amílcar, **1**: 249

Caesar, Gaius Julius, **1**: 221

Callenbach, Ernest, **3**: 76

Capote, Truman, **2**: 263

Card, Orson Scott, **3**: 79

Carson, Rachel, **1**: 137

Castro, Fidel, **1**: 232

Çetin, Fethiye, **1**: 245

Chang, Eileen, **2**: 277

Charles, Hugh, **3**: 5701

Chomsky, Noam, **1**: 323

Churchill, Winston, **1**: 26

Coetzee, J. M., **3**: 203

Collins, Suzanne, **3**: 101

Condon, Richard, **3**: 28

Conrad, Joseph, **1**: 297

Cooper, Thomas, **2**: 361

Cortés, Hernán, **2**: 188

Cowper, William, **1**: 37

Cromwell, Oliver, **1**: 34

Cruikshank, George, **1**: 189

D

Davis, Rebecca Harding, **2**: 335

Dee, Jonathan, **3**: 25

Delany, Martin, **2**: 92

DeLillo, Don, **2**: 257

Dessalines, Jean-Jacques, **1**: 30

Dewey, John, **1**: 351

Dick, Philip K., **3**: 73

Dickens, Charles, **3**: 145

Dixon, Thomas, Jr., **2**: 250

Dos Passos, John, **1**: 197

Dow, Unity, **3**: 11

Du Bois, W. E. B., **1**: 307

Dunlap, William, **3**: 189

E

Echeverría, Esteban, **2**: 253

Ellsberg, Daniel, **1**: 134

Ellul, Jacques, **1**: 347

TITLE INDEX

The title index includes works that are represented in *The Literature of Propaganda*. Numbers in **Bold** indicate volume, with page numbers following after colons.